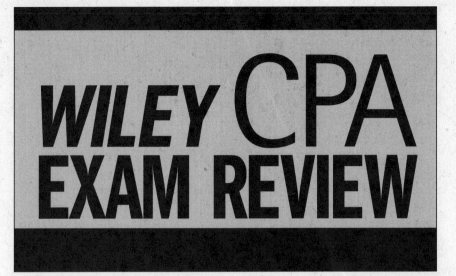

WILEY CPA
EXAM REVIEW

WILEY CPA EXAM REVIEW 2009

Business Environment and Concepts

O. Ray Whittington, CPA, PhD

Patrick R. Delaney, CPA, PhD

WILEY

JOHN WILEY & SONS, INC.

CONTENTS

[1] *As explained in Chapter 1, this book is organized into 8 modules (manageable study units). The numbering of the modules commences with number 38 to correspond with the numbering system used in our two-volume set.*

PREFACE

Passing the CPA exam upon your first attempt is possible! The *Wiley CPA Examination Review* preparation materials provide you with the necessary materials (visit our Web site at www.wiley.com/cpa for more information). It's up to you to add the hard work and commitment. Together we can beat the pass rate on each section of about 40%. All Wiley CPA products are continuously updated to provide you with the most comprehensive and complete knowledge base. Choose your products from the Wiley preparation materials and you can proceed confidently. You can select support materials that are exam-based and user-friendly. You can select products that will help you pass!

Remaining current is one of the keys to examination success. Here is a list of what's new in this edition of the *Wiley CPA Examination Review Business Environment and Concepts* **text.**

- The AICPA Content Specification Outlines on Business Environment and Concepts for the Computerized CPA Examination
- AICPA questions released in 2008

The objective of this work is to provide you with the knowledge to pass the Accounting and Reporting portion of the Uniform Certified Public Accounting (CPA) Exam. The text is divided up into eight areas of study called modules. Each module contains written text with discussion, examples, and demonstrations of the key exam concepts. Following each text area, actual American Institute of Certified Public Accountants (AICPA) unofficial questions and answers are presented to test your knowledge. We are indebted to the AICPA for permission to reproduce and adapt examination materials from past examinations. Author constructed questions are provided for new areas or areas that require updating. All author constructed questions are modeled after AICPA question formats. The multiple-choice questions are grouped into topical areas, giving candidates a chance to assess their areas of strength and weakness. Selection and inclusion of topical content is based upon current AICPA Content Specification Outlines. Only testable topics are presented. If the CPA exam does not test it, this text does not present it.

The CPA exam is one of the toughest exams you will ever take. It will not be easy. But if you follow our guidelines and focus on your goal, you will be thrilled with what you can accomplish.

Ray Whittington
November 2008

**Don't forget to visit our Web site at www.wiley.com/cpa
for supplements and updates.**

ABOUT THE AUTHORS

Ray Whittington, PhD, CPA, CMA, CIA, is the dean of the College of Commerce at DePaul University. Prior to joining the faculty at DePaul, Professor Whittington was the Director of Accountancy at San Diego State University. From 1989 through 1991, he was the Director of Auditing Research for the American Institute of Certified Public Accountants (AICPA), and he previously was on the audit staff of KPMG. He previously served as a member of the Auditing Standards Board of the AICPA and as a member of the Accounting and Review Services Committee and the Board of Regents of the Institute of Internal Auditors. Professor Whittington has published numerous textbooks, articles, monographs, and continuing education courses.

Patrick R. Delaney, deceased, was the dedicated author and editor of the *Wiley CPA Exam Review* books for twenty years. He was the Arthur Andersen LLP Alumni Professor of Accountancy and Department Chair at Northern Illinois University. He received his PhD in Accountancy from the University of Illinois. He had public accounting experience with Arthur Andersen LLP and was coauthor of *GAAP: Interpretation and Application*, also published by John Wiley & Sons, Inc. He served as Vice President and a member of the Illinois CPA Society's Board of Directors, and was Chairman of its Accounting Principles Committee; was a past president of the Rockford Chapter, Institute of Management Accountants; and had served on numerous other professional committees. He was a member of the American Accounting Association, American Institute of Certified Public Accountants, and Institute of Management Accountants. Professor Delaney was published in *The Accounting Review* and was a recipient of the Illinois CPA Society's Outstanding Educator Award, NIU's Excellence in Teaching Award, and Lewis University's Distinguished Alumnus Award. He was involved in NIU's CPA Review Course as director and instructor.

ABOUT THE CONTRIBUTORS

Mark L. Frigo, PhD, CPA, CMA, is Director of The Center for Strategy, Execution and Valuation in Kellstadt Graduate School of Business and Ledger & Quill Distinguished Professor of Strategy and Leadership in the School of Accountancy at DePaul University. Professor Frigo authored the Performance Measures module for the Business Environment and Concepts section of this manual.

Duane R. Lambert, JD, MBA, CPA, is a Professor of Business Administration at California State University, Hayward, where he teaches courses in Business Law and Accounting. He also has been a Visiting Lecturer and Visiting Professor at the University of California, Berkeley. Professor Lambert has "Big Six" experience and teaches in CPA review courses. He wrote and revised modules to reflect current treatment in Chapter 6, Business Law and Professional Responsibilities.

Patricia L. McQueen, MBA, CPA, is an instructor in the School of Accountancy at DePaul University. She has a background in auditing and financial accounting. She has audit experience with KPMG. She contributed to the auditing modules.

Kurt Pany, PhD, CPA, is a Professor of Accounting at Arizona State University. Prior to entering academe, he worked as a staff auditor for Deloitte and Touche LLP. He is a former member of the AICPA's Auditing Standards Board and has taught in the Arizona State University CPA Review Course.

1 BEGINNING YOUR CPA REVIEW PROGRAM

To maximize the efficiency of your review program, begin by studying (not merely reading) this chapter and the next three chapters of this volume. They have been carefully organized and written to provide you with important information to assist you in successfully completing the Business Environment & Concepts (BEC) section of the CPA exam. Beyond providing a comprehensive outline to help you organize the material tested on the BEC section, Chapter 1 will assist you in organizing a study program to prepare for the BEC exam. Self-discipline throughout your study program is essential.

GENERAL COMMENTS ON THE EXAMINATION

The Uniform CPA Examination is delivered using computer-based testing (CBT). Computer-based testing has several advantages. You may take the exam one section at a time. As a result, your studies can be focused on that one section, improving your chances for success. In addition, the exam is no longer offered twice a year. During eight months of ever year, you may take the exam on your schedule, six days a week and in the morning or in the afternoon.

Successful completion of the BEC section of the CPA Examination is an attainable goal. Keep this point foremost in your mind as you study the first four chapters in this volume and develop your study plan.

Purpose of the Examination[1]

The Uniform CPA Examination is designed to test the entry-level knowledge and skills necessary to protect the public interest. These knowledge and skills were identified through a Practice Analysis performed in 2000, which served as a basis for the development of the content specifications for the new exam. The skills identified as necessary for the protection of the public interest include

- Analysis—the ability to organize, process, and interpret data to develop options for decision making.
- Judgment—the ability to evaluate options for decision-making and provide an appropriate conclusion.
- Communication—the ability to effectively elicit and/or express information through written or oral means.
- Research—the ability to locate and extract relevant information from available resource materials.
- Understanding—the ability to recognize and comprehend the meaning and application of a particular matter.

[1] More information may be obtained from the AICPA's **Uniform CPA Examination Candidate Bulletin,** which you can find on the AICPA's Web site at www.cpa-exam.org.

For the BEC section the Board of Examiners has provided the following matrix to illustrate the interaction of content and skills.

Content Specification Outline Areas	Skill Categories					Content Weights
	Communication	Research	Analysis	Judgment	Understanding	
I. Business structure						17-23%
II. Economic concepts						8-12%
III. Financial management						17-23%
IV. Information technology						22-28%
V. Planning and measurement						22-28%
Skills Weights	0-13%	0-13%	8-18%	6-16%	55-65%	

You should keep these skills foremost in your mind as your prepare and sit for the BEC Section.

The CPA examination is one of many screening devices to assure the competence of those licensed to perform the attest function and to render professional accounting services. Other screening devices include educational requirements, ethics examinations, and work experience.

The examination appears to test the material covered in accounting programs of the better business schools. It also appears to be based upon the body of knowledge essential for the practice of public accounting and the audit of a medium-sized client. Since the examination is primarily a textbook or academic examination, you should plan on taking it as soon as possible after completing your required accounting education.

Examination Content

The BEC section of the CPA exam is designed to test

- Knowledge of the general business environment and business concepts that candidates need to know in order to understand the underlying business reasons for and accounting implications of business transactions, and
- The skills to apply that knowledge in performing financial statement audit and attestation engagements and other functions normally performed by CPAs that affect the public interest.

Specific guidance concerning topical content of the new computer-based exam in BEC can be found in two documents prepared by the Board of Examiners of the AICPA: (1) *Uniform CPA Examination—Examination Content Specifications,* and (2) *Business Environment and Concepts: Additional Detail Corresponding to Content Specifications Outline dated June 14, 2002.* We have included the detailed content outline for BEC at the beginning of Chapter 5. The outline should be used as an indication of the topics' relative emphasis on the exam.

The Board's objective in preparing this detailed listing of topics tested on the exam is to help "in assuring the continuing validity and reliability of the Uniform CPA Examination." These outlines are an excellent source of guidance concerning the areas and the emphasis to be given each area on future exams. They are provided to each candidate in *CPA Candidate Bulletin* along with the examination application, or may be downloaded at the AICPA's exam Web site, www.cpa-exam.org.

New accounting, auditing, and ethics pronouncements, including those in the governmental and not-for-profit areas, are tested in the testing window starting six months after the pronouncement's *effective* date. If early application is permitted, a pronouncement is tested six months after the *issuance* date; candidates are responsible for the old pronouncement also until it is superseded. For the BEC section, federal laws are tested six months following their *effective* date and for uniform acts one year after their adoption by a simple majority of jurisdictions. If there is no federal or uniform law on a topic, the questions are intended to test knowledge of the law of the majority of jurisdictions. The AICPA posts content changes regularly on its Internet site. The address is www.cpa-exam.org.

Nondisclosure and Computerization of Examination

Beginning May 1996, the Uniform CPA Examination became nondisclosed. For each exam section, candidates are required to agree to a *Statement of Confidentiality,* which states that they will not divulge the nature and content of any exam question. In April of 2004, the CPA exam became computer-based. Candidates take the exam at Prometric sites in the 54 jurisdictions in which the CPA exam is offered. From April 5, 2004, going forward the CPA exam is offered continually during the testing windows shown below.

Testing Window (Exam Available)	January through February	April through May	July through August	October through November
AICPA Review & Update (Exam Unavailable)	March	June	September	December

One or more exam sections may be taken during any exam window, and the sections may be taken in any desired order. **However, no candidate will be allowed to sit for the same section more than once during any given testing window.** In addition, a candidate must pass all four sections of the CPA exam within a "rolling" eighteen-month period, which begins on the date he or she passes a section. In other words, you must pass the other three sections of the exam within eighteen months of when you pass the first section. If you do not pass all sections within the eighteen-month period, credit for any section(s) passed outside the eighteen-month period will expire and the section(s) must be retaken.

The following table compares the sections of the prior pencil-and-paper exam with the new computer-based exam.

Pencil-and-Paper Examination up to November 2003 (15.5 hours in 2 days)	*Computer-Based Examination commencing April 5, 2004 (14 hours over flexible period of time)*
Auditing (4.5 hours)	Auditing & Attestation (4.5 hours)
Financial Accounting & Reporting (4.5 hours)	Financial Accounting & Reporting (4 hours)
Accounting & Reporting (3.5 hours)	Regulation (3 hours)
Business Law & Professional Responsibilities (3 hours)	Business Environment & Concepts (2.5 hours)

Types of Questions

The computer-based Uniform CPA Examination consists of two basic question formats.

1. Multiple-Choice—questions requiring the selection of one of four responses to a short scenario.
2. Simulations—case studies that are used to assess knowledge and skills in a context approximating that found on the job, through the use of realistic scenarios and tasks, and access to normally available and familiar resources.

The multiple-choice questions are much like the ones that have constituted a majority of the CPA examination for years. **And the good news is that these types of questions constitute 100% of the BEC section. The BEC section has no simulations at this time.**

Process for Sitting for the Examination

While there are some variations in the process from state to state, the basic process for sitting for the CPA examination may be described as follows:

1. Apply to take the examination (request, complete, and submit an application)
2. Receive your Notice to Schedule (NTS)
3. Schedule your examination(s)
4. Take your examination(s)
5. Receive you score report(s)

Applying to Take the Examination

The right to practice public accounting as a CPA is governed by individual state statutes. While some rules regarding the practice of public accounting vary from state to state, all State Boards of Accountancy use the Uniform CPA Examination and AICPA advisory grading service as one of the requirements to practice public accounting. Every candidate should contact the applicable State Board of Accountancy to determine the requirements to sit for the exam (e.g., education requirements). For comparisons of requirements for various state boards and those policies that are uniform across jurisdictions you should refer to the Web site of the National Association of State Boards of Accountancy (NASBA) at www.nasba.org.

A frequent problem candidates encounter is failure to apply by the deadline. **Apply to sit for the examination early. Also, you should use extreme care in filling out the application and mailing required materials to your State Board of Accountancy.** If possible, have a friend review your completed application before mailing with check and other documentation. Candidates may miss a particular CPA examination window simply because of minor technical details that were overlooked (check not signed, items not enclosed, question not answered on application, etc.). **Because of the very high volume of applications received in the more populous states, the administrative staff does not have time to call or write to correct minor details and will simply reject your application.**

The various state boards, their Web sites, and telephone numbers are listed on the following page. Be sure to inquire of your state board for specific and current requirements.

It is possible for candidates to sit for the examination at a Prometric site in any state or territory. Candidates desiring to do so should contact the State Board of Accountancy in their home state.

Exam Scheduling

Once you have been cleared to take the exam by the applicable state board, you will receive by mail a Notice to Schedule (NTS) and may then schedule to sit for one or more sections of the exam. **Make sure that your name is exactly correct on the NTS.**

You have the following three options for scheduling your examination:

1. **Visit www.prometric.com/cpa on the Internet**

    This is the easiest and quickest way to schedule an examination appointment (or cancel and reschedule an appointment, if necessary). Simply go to the Web site, select SCHEDULE APPOINTMENT, and follow the directions. It is advised that you print and keep for your records the confirmation number for your appointment.

2. **Call 800-580-9648 (Candidate Services Call Center)**

    Before you call, you must have your NTS in front of you, and have in mind several times, dates, and locations that would work for you. You will not receive written confirmation of your appointment. Be sure to write down the date, time, location, and confirmation number for each of your appointments.

3. **Call your local test center**

    While this method is not recommended, you may call your local test center and schedule appointments. Again, be sure to have your NTS in front of you and write down the date, time, location, and confirmation number for each of your appointments.

You should also be aware that if you have to cancel or reschedule your appointment, you may be subject to a cancellation/rescheduling fee. The AICPA's *Uniform CPA Examination Candidate Bulletin* lists the rescheduling and cancellation fees.

To assure that you get your desired location and time period it is imperative that you schedule early. To get your first choice of dates, you are advised to schedule at least 45 days in advance. You will not be scheduled for an exam fewer than 5 days before testing.

ATTRIBUTES OF EXAMINATION SUCCESS

Your primary objective in preparing for the BEC section is to pass. Other objectives such as learning new and reviewing old material should be considered secondary. The six attributes of examination success discussed below are **essential**. You should study the attributes and work toward achieving/developing each of them **before** taking the examination.

1. **Knowledge of Material**

    Two points are relevant to "knowledge of material" as an attribute of examination success. **First,** there is a distinct difference between being familiar with material and knowing the material. Frequently candidates confuse familiarity with knowledge. Can you remember when you just could not answer an examination question or did poorly on an examination, but maintained to yourself or your instructor that you knew the material? You probably were only familiar with the material. On the CPA examination, familiarity is insufficient; you must know the material. Remember, the exam will test your ability to analyze data, make judgments, and demonstrate understanding of the material. For example, you may be familiar with the concepts of strategic performance measurement, but you may have difficulty linking measures to particular strategies in a balanced scorecard framework. Once again, a major concern must be to know the material rather than just being familiar with it. **Second,** the BEC exam tests a literally overwhelming amount of material at a rigorous level. From an undergraduate point of view, the CPA examination in BEC includes material from the following courses:

    Economics
    Finance
    Business Law
    Management Information systems
    Managerial/Cost Accounting

	STATE BOARD WEB ADDRESS	TELEPHONE #
AK	www.commerce.state.ak.us/occ/pcpa.htm	(907) 465-3811
AL	www.asbpa.alabama.gov	(334) 242-5700
AR	www.state.ar.us/asbpa	(501) 682-1520
AZ	www.azaccountancy.gov	(602) 364-0804
CA	www.dca.ca.gov/cba	(916) 263-3680
CO	www.dora.state.co.us/accountants	(303) 894-7800
CT	www.ct.gov/sboa	(860) 509-6179
DC	dcra.dc.gov/dcra	(202) 442-4320
DE	www.dpr.delaware.gov	(302) 744-4500
FL	www.myflorida.com	(850) 487-1395
GA	www.sos.state.ga.us/plb/accountancy/	(478) 207-1400
GU	www.guamboa.org	(671) 647-0813
HI	www.hawaii.gov/dcca/areas/pvl/boards/accountancy	(808) 586-2696
IA	www.state.ia.us/iacc	(515) 281-5910
ID	www.isba.idaho.gov	(208) 334-2490
IL	www.ilboa.org	(217) 531-0950
IN	www.in.gov/pla/bandc/accountancy/	(317) 234-3040
KS	www.ksboa.org	(785) 296-2162
KY	cpa.ky.gov	(502) 595-3037
LA	www.cpaboard.state.la.us	(504) 566-1244
MA	www.mass.gov/reg/boards/pa	(617) 727-1806
MD	www.dllr.state.md.us/license/occprof/account.html	(410) 230-6322
ME	www.maineprofessionalreg.org	(207) 624-8603
MI	www.michigan.gov/accountancy	(517) 241-9249
MN	www.boa.state.mn.us	(651) 296-7938
MO	pr.mo.gov/accountancy.asp	(573) 751-0012
MS	www.msbpa.state.ms.us	(601) 354-7320
MT	www.publicaccountant.mt.gov	(406) 841-2389
NC	www.nccpaboard.gov	(919) 733-4222
ND	www.state.nd.us/ndsba	(800) 532-5904
NE	www.nol.org/home/BPA	(402) 471-3595
NH	www.nh.gov/accountancy	(603) 271-3286
NJ	www.state.nj.us/lps/ca/nonmed.htm	(973) 504-6380
NM	www.rld.state.nm.us/b&c/accountancy/index.htm	(505) 841-9108
NV	www.nvaccountancy.com/	(775) 786-0231
NY	www.op.nysed.gov/cpa.htm	(518) 474-3817
OH	www.acc.ohio.gov/	(614) 466-4135
OK	www.oab.state.ok.us	(405) 521-2397
OR	egov.oregon.gov/BOA/	(503) 378-4181
PA	www.dos.state.pa.us/account	(717) 783-1404
PR	www.estado.gobierno.pr/contador.htm	(787) 722-4816
RI	www.dbr.state.ri.us	(401) 222-3185
SC	www.llr.state.sc.us/POL/Accountancy	(803) 896-4770
SD	www.state.sd.us/dcr/acountancy	(605) 367-5770
TN	www.state.tn.us/commerce/boards/tnsba/index.html	(615) 741-2550
TX	www.tsbpa.state.tx.us	(512) 305-7800
UT	www.dopl.utah.gov	(801) 530-6396
VA	www.boa.virginia.gov	(804) 367-8505
VI	www.dlca.gov.vi	(340) 773-4305
VT	vtprofessionals.org/opr1/accountants	(802) 828-2837
WA	www.cpaboard.wa.gov	(360) 753-2585
WI	www.drl.wi.gov/index.htm	(608) 266-5511
WV	www.wvboacc.org	(304) 558-3557
WY	cpaboard.state.wy.us	(307) 777-7551

NOTE: The publisher does not assume responsibility for errors in the above information. You should request information concerning requirements in your state at least six months in advance of the exam dates.

2. **Commitment to Exam Preparation**

    Your preparation for the CPA exam should begin at least two months prior to the date you plan to schedule your seating for an exam section. If you plan to take more than one section, you should start earlier. Over the course of your preparation, you will experience many peaks and valleys. There will be days when you feel completely prepared and there will also be days when you feel totally overwhelmed. This is not unusual and, in fact, should be expected.

    The CPA exam is a very difficult and challenging exam. How many times in your college career did you study months for an exam? Probably not too many. Therefore, candidates need to remain focused on the objective—succeeding on the CPA exam.

    Develop a personal study plan so that you are reviewing material daily. Of course, you should schedule an occasional study break to help you relax, but don't schedule too many breaks. Candidates who dedicate themselves to studying have a much greater chance of going through this process only one time. On the other hand, a lack of focus and piecemeal preparation will only extend the process over a number of exam sittings.

3. **Solutions Approach**

    The solutions approach is a systematic approach to solving the multiple-choice questions found on the CPA examination. Many candidates know the material fairly well when they sit for the CPA exam, but they do not know how to take the examination. Candidates generally neither work nor answer questions efficiently in terms of time or grades. The solutions approach permits you to avoid drawing "blanks" on CPA exam questions; using the solutions approach coupled with grading insights (see below) allows you to pick up a sizable number of points on test material with which you are not familiar. Chapter 3 outlines the solutions approach for multiple-choice questions.

4. **Grading Insights**

    The multiple-choice questions within each section are organized into three groups which are referred to as testlets. Each multiple-choice testlet is comprised of approximately 30 multiple-choice questions. The multiple-choice testlets vary in overall difficulty. A testlet is labeled either "medium difficult" or "difficult" based on its makeup. A "difficult" testlet has a higher percentage of hard questions than a "medium difficult" testlet. Every candidate's first multiple-choice testlet in each section will be a "medium difficult" testlet. If a candidate scores well on the first testlet, he or she will receive a "difficult" second testlet. Candidates that do not perform well on the first testlet receive a second "medium difficult" testlet. Because the scoring procedure takes the difficulty of the testlet into account, candidates are scored fairly regardless of the type of testlets they receive.

    The AICPA includes sample examinations on its Web site that allow you to get experience with the use of the actual computer tools used on the CPA exam. Also, more experience with computer testing can be obtained by using Wiley CPA Review Practice software.

5. **Examination Strategy**

    Prior to sitting for the examination, it is important to develop an examination strategy (i.e., an approach to working efficiently throughout the exam). Your ability to cope successfully with 2 ½ hours of examination can be improved by

    a. Recognizing the importance and usefulness of an examination strategy
    b. Using Chapter 4, Taking the Examination, and previous examination experience to develop a "personal strategy" for the exam
    c. Testing your "personal strategy" on example examinations under conditions similar to those at the testing centers

6. **Examination Confidence**

    You need confidence to endure the physical and mental demands of 2 ½ hours of test-taking under tremendous pressure. Examination confidence results from proper preparation for the exam which includes mastering the first four attributes of examination success. Examination confidence is necessary to enable you to overcome the initial frustration with questions for which you may not be specifically prepared.

    This study manual, when properly used, contributes to your examination confidence. Build confidence by completing the questions contained herein.

Common Candidate Mistakes

The CPA Exam is a formidable hurdle in your accounting career. With a pass rate of about 40% on each section, the level of difficulty is obvious. The good news, though, is that about 75% of all candidates (first-time and re-exam) sitting for each examination eventually pass. The authors believe that the first-time pass rate could be higher if candidates would be more careful. Eight common mistakes that many candidates make are

1. Failure to understand the exam question requirements
2. Misunderstanding the supporting text of the question
3. Lack of knowledge of material tested, especially recently issued pronouncements
4. Failure to develop proficiency with computer-based testing and practice tools such as electronic research databases and spreadsheets
5. Inability to apply the solutions approach
6. Lack of an exam strategy (e.g., allocation of time)
7. Sloppiness and computational errors
8. Failure to proofread and edit

These mistakes are not mutually exclusive. Candidates may commit one or more of the above items. Remind yourself that when you decrease the number of common mistakes, you increase your chances of successfully becoming a CPA. Take the time to read carefully the exam question requirements. Do not jump into a quick start, only to later find out that you didn't understand what information the examiners were asking for. Read slowly and carefully. Take time to recall your knowledge. Respond to the question asked. Apply an exam strategy such as allocating your time among all testlets. Answer questions quickly but precisely, avoid common mistakes, and increase your score.

PURPOSE AND ORGANIZATION OF THIS REVIEW TEXTBOOK

This book is designed to help you prepare adequately for the BEC Examination. There is no easy way to prepare for the successful completion of the CPA Examination; however, through the use of this manual, your approach will be systematic and logical.

The objective of this book is to provide study materials supportive to CPA candidates. While no guarantees are made concerning the success of those using this text, this book promotes efficient preparation by

1. Explaining how to **maximize your score** through analysis of examination grading and illustration of the solutions approach.
2. **Defining areas tested** through the use of the content specification outlines. Note that predictions of future exams are not made. You should prepare yourself for all possible topics rather than gambling on the appearance of certain questions.
3. **Organizing your study program** by comprehensively outlining all of the subject matter tested on the examination in 8 easy-to-use study modules. Each study module is a manageable task which facilitates your exam preparation. Turn to Chapter 5 and peruse the contents to get a feel for the organization of this book.
4. **Providing CPA candidates with previous examination questions** organized by topic (e.g., cost measurement, planning, control and analysis, etc.) Since about 70% of this examination content is material not previously tested, questions have been developed for new areas. Some have been adapted from other professional exams, (i.e., the Certified Management Accountants and Certified Internal Auditors exams).
5. **Explaining the AICPA unofficial answers** to the examination questions included in this text. The AICPA publishes unofficial answers for all questions from exams administered prior to 1996 and for any released questions from exams administered on or after May 1996. However, no explanation is made of the approach that should have been applied to the examination questions to obtain these unofficial answers. Relatedly, the AICPA unofficial answers to multiple-choice questions provide no justification and/or explanation.

As you read the next few paragraphs which describe the contents of this book, flip through the chapters to gain a general familiarity with the book's organization and contents. Chapters 2, 3, and 4 are to help you "maximize your score."

Chapter 2　Examination Grading and Grader Orientation
Chapter 3　The Solutions Approach
Chapter 4　Taking the Examination

Chapters 2, 3, and 4 contain material that should be kept in mind throughout your study program. Refer back to them frequently. Reread them for a final time just before you sit for the exam.

Chapter 5 (BEC Modules) contains

1. AICPA Content Specification Outlines of material tested on the BEC Examination
2. Multiple-choice questions
3. Author's explanations for the multiple-choice questions

Also included at the end of this text is a complete Sample BEC Examination. The sample exam is included to enable candidates to gain experience in taking a "realistic" exam. While studying the modules, the candidate can become accustomed to concentrating on fairly narrow topics. By working through the sample examination near the end of their study programs, candidates will be better prepared for taking the actual examination.

Other Textbooks

This text is a comprehensive compilation of study guides and outlines; it should not be necessary to supplement them with accounting textbooks and other materials for most topics. You probably already have economics, cost accounting, finance, and information systems textbooks. In such a case, you must make the decision whether to replace them and trade familiarity (including notes therein, etc.), with the cost and inconvenience of obtaining the newer texts containing a more updated presentation.

Before spending time and money acquiring a new book, begin your study program with *CPA EXAMINATION REVIEW: BUSINESS ENVIRONMENT & CONCEPTS* to determine your need for a supplemental text.

Ordering Other Textual Materials

If you want to order AICPA materials, locate an AICPA educator member to order your materials, since educator members are entitled to a 30% discount and may place Web site or telephone orders.

AICPA (CPA2Biz)　　　　　　　　　　Address:　Order Department
　　　　　　　　　　　　　　　　　　　　　　　CPA2Biz
　Telephone:　888-777-7077　　　　　　　　　P.O. Box 2209
　Web site:　www.CPA2Biz.com　　　　　　　Jersey City, NJ 07303-2209

A variety of supplemental CPA products are available from John Wiley & Sons, Inc. By using a variety of learning techniques, such as software, computer-based learning, and audio CDs, the candidate is more likely to remain focused during the study process and to retain information for a longer period of time. Visit our Web site at **www.wiley.com/cpa** for other products, supplements, and updates.

Working CPA Questions

The AICPA content outlines, study outlines, etc., will be used to acquire and assimilate the knowledge tested on the examination. This, however, should be only **one-half** of your preparation program. The other half should be spent practicing how to work questions. Some candidates probably spend over 90% of their time reviewing material tested on the CPA exam. Much more time should be allocated to working examination questions **under exam conditions**. Working examination questions serves two functions. First, it helps you develop a solutions approach that will maximize your score. Second, it provides the best test of your knowledge of the material.

The multiple-choice questions and answer explanations can be used in many ways. First, they may be used as a diagnostic evaluation of your knowledge. For example, before beginning to review financial management you may wish to answer 10 to 15 multiple-choice questions to determine your ability to answer CPA examination questions on financial management. The apparent difficulty of the questions and the correctness of your answers will allow you to determine the necessary breadth and depth of your review. Additionally, exposure to examination questions prior to review and study of the material should provide motivation. You will develop a feel for your level of proficiency and an understanding of the scope and difficulty of past examination questions. Moreover, your review materials will explain concepts encountered in the diagnostic multiple-choice questions.

Second, the multiple-choice questions can be used as a poststudy or postreview evaluation. You should attempt to understand all concepts mentioned (even in incorrect answers) as you answer the questions. Refer to the explanation of the answer for discussion of the alternatives even though you selected the correct response. Thus, you should read the explanation of the answer unless you completely understand the question and all of the alternative answers.

Third, you may wish to use the multiple-choice questions as a primary study vehicle. This is probably the quickest but least thorough approach in preparing for the exam. Make a sincere effort to understand the question and to select the correct response before referring to the answer and explanation. In many cases, the explanations will appear inadequate because of your lack of familiarity with the topic. Always refer back to an appropriate study source, such as the outlines and text in this volume, your economics, information systems, finance and cost accounting textbooks, etc.

After you have reviewed for the BEC section of the exam, work the complete BEC Sample Exam provided in Appendix A.

SELF-STUDY PROGRAM

CPA candidates generally find it difficult to organize and complete their own self-study programs. A major problem is determining **what** and **how** to study. Another major problem is developing the self-discipline to stick to a study program. Relatedly, it is often difficult for CPA candidates to determine how much to study (i.e., determining when they are sufficiently prepared.) The following suggestions will assist you in developing a **systematic**, **comprehensive**, and **successful** self-study program to help you complete the BEC exam.

Remember that these are only suggestions. You should modify them to suit your personality, available study time, and other constraints. Some of the suggestions may appear trivial, but CPA candidates generally need all the assistance they can get to systemize their study programs.

Study Facilities and Available Time

Locate study facilities that will be conducive to concentrated study. Factors that you should consider include

1. Noise distraction
2. Interruptions
3. Lighting
4. Availability (e.g., a local library is not available at 5:00 A.M.)
5. Accessibility (e.g., your kitchen table vs. your local library)
6. Desk or table space

You will probably find different study facilities optimal for different times (e.g., your kitchen table during early morning hours and local libraries during early evening hours).

Next review your personal and professional commitments from now until the exam to determine regularly available study time. Formalize a schedule to which you can reasonably commit yourself. At the end of this chapter, you will find a detailed approach to managing your time available for the exam preparation program.

Self-Evaluation

The *CPA EXAMINATION REVIEW: BUSINESS ENVIRONMENT & CONCEPTS* self-study program is partitioned into 8 topics or modules. Since each module is clearly defined and should be studied separately, you have the task of preparing for the CPA BEC exam by tackling 8 manageable tasks. Partitioning the overall project into 8 modules makes preparation psychologically easier, since you sense yourself completing one small step at a time rather than seemingly never completing one or a few large steps.

By completing the following "Preliminary Estimate of Your Present Knowledge of Subject" inventory below, organized by the 8 modules in this program, you will tabulate your strong and weak areas at the beginning of your study program. This will help you budget your limited study time. Note that you should begin studying the material in each module by answering up to 1/4 of the total multiple-choice questions covering that module's topics (see instruction 4.A. in the next section). This "mini-exam" should constitute a diagnostic evaluation as to the amount of review and study you need.

PRELIMINARY ESTIMATE OF YOUR PRESENT KNOWLEDGE OF SUBJECT*

No.	Module	Proficient	Fairly Proficient	Generally Familiar	Not Familiar
38	Business Structure				
39	Information Technology				
40	Economics & Strategy				
41	Financial Management				
42	Risk Management & Capital Budgeting				
43	Performance Measures				
44	Cost Measurement				
45	Planning, Control & Analysis				

* *NOTE: The numbering of modules in this text commences with number 38 to correspond with the numbering system used in our two-volume set.*

Time Allocation

The study program below entails an average of 50 hours (Step 5. below) of study time. The breakdown of total hours is indicated in the left margin.

[1 hr.]   1.   Study Chapters 2-4 in this volume. These chapters are essential to your efficient preparation program. (Time estimate includes candidate's review of the examples of the solutions approach in Chapters 2 and 3.)

[1 hr.]   2.   Begin by studying the introductory material at the beginning of Chapter 5.

         3.   Study one module at a time. The modules are listed above in the self-evaluation section.

         4.   For each module

[5 hrs.]   A.   Work 1/4 of the multiple-choice questions (e.g., if there are 40 multiple-choice questions in a module, you should work every 4th question, 10 total questions). Score yourself.
             This diagnostic routine will provide you with an index of your proficiency and familiarity with the type and difficulty of questions.
             Time estimate: 3 minutes each, not to exceed 1 hour total.

[27 hrs.]   B.   Study the outlines and illustrations. Where necessary, refer to your economics, information systems, finance, and cost accounting textbooks. (This will occur more frequently for topics in which you have a weak background.)
             Time estimate: 2 hour minimum per module with more time devoted to topics less familiar to you.

[12 hrs.]   C.   Work the remaining multiple-choice questions. Study the explanations of the multiple-choice questions you missed or had trouble answering.
             Time estimate: 3 minutes to answer each question and 2 minutes to study the answer explanation of each question missed.

[4 hrs.]   D.   Work through the sample CPA examination presented as Appendix A.
             Take the examination under simulated exam conditions (i.e., in a strange place with other people present [your local municipal library or a computer lab]). Apply your solutions approach to each question and your exam strategy to the overall exam.
             You should limit yourself to the time you will have when taking the actual CPA exam section (2 ½ hours for the BEC section). Spend time afterwards grading your work and reviewing your effort.
             Time estimate: To take the exam and review it later, approximately 4 hours.

         5.   The total suggested time of 50 hours is only an average. Allocation of time will vary candidate by candidate. Time requirements vary due to the diverse backgrounds and abilities of CPA candidates. Allocate your time so you gain the most proficiency in the least time. Remember that while 50 hours will be required, you should break the overall project down into 8 more manageable tasks. Do not study more than one module during each study session.

Using Notecards

Below are one candidate's notecards on BEC topics which illustrate how key definitions, lists, etc., can be summarized on index cards for quick review. Since candidates can take these anywhere they go, they are a very efficient review tool.

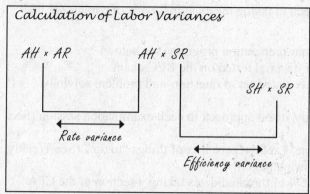

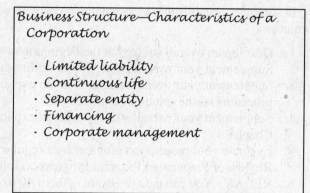

Level of Proficiency Required

What level of proficiency must you develop with respect to each of the topics to pass the exam? You should work toward a minimum correct rate on the multiple-choice questions of 80%. Working toward a correct rate of 80% or higher will give you a margin.

Multiple-Choice Feedback

One of the benefits of working through exam questions is that it helps you to identify your weak areas. Once you have graded your answers, your strong areas and weak areas should be clearly evident. Yet, the important point here is that you should not stop at a simple percentage evaluation. The percentage only provides general feedback about your knowledge of the material contained within that particular module. The percentage **does not** give you any specific feedback regarding the concepts which were tested. In order to get this feedback, you should look at the questions missed on an individual basis because this will help you gain a better understanding of **why** you missed the question.

This feedback process has been facilitated by the fact that within each module where the multiple-choice answer key appears, two blank lines have been inserted next to the multiple-choice answers. As you grade the multiple-choice questions, mark those questions which you have missed. However, instead of just marking the questions right and wrong, you should now focus on marking the questions in a manner which identifies **why** you missed the question. As an example, a candidate could mark the questions in the following manner: ✓ for math mistakes, x for conceptual mistakes, and ? for areas which the candidate was unfamiliar with. The candidate should then correct these mistakes by reworking through the marked questions.

The objective of this marking technique is to help you identify your weak areas and thus, the concepts which you should be focusing on. While it is still important for you to get between 75% and 80% correct when working multiple-choice questions, it is more important for you to understand the concepts. This understanding applies to both the questions answered correctly and those answered incorrectly. Remember, questions on the CPA exam will be different from the questions in the book; however, the concepts will be the same. Therefore, your preparation should focus on understanding concepts, not just getting the correct answer.

Conditional Candidates

If you have received conditional status on the examination, you must concentrate on the remaining section(s). Unfortunately, many candidates do not study after conditioning the exam, relying on luck to get them through the remaining section(s). Conditional candidates will find that material contained in Chapters 1- 4 and the information contained in the appropriate modules will benefit them in preparing for the remaining section(s) of the examination.

PLANNING FOR THE EXAMINATION

Overall Strategy

An overriding concern should be an orderly, systematic approach toward both your preparation program and your examination strategy. A major objective should be to avoid any surprises or anything else that would rattle you during the examination. In other words, you want to be in complete control as much as possible. Control is of paramount importance from both positive and negative viewpoints. The presence of control on your part will add to your confidence and your ability to prepare for and take the exam. Moreover, the presence of control will make your preparation program more enjoyable (or at least less distasteful). On the other hand, a lack of organization will result in inefficiency in preparing for and taking the examination, with a highly predictable outcome. Likewise, distractions during the examination (e.g., inadequate lodging, long drive) are generally disastrous.

In summary, establishing a systematic, orderly approach to taking the examination is of paramount importance.

1. Develop an overall strategy at the beginning of your preparation program (see below)
2. Supplement your overall strategy with outlines of material tested on the BEC exam
3. Supplement your overall strategy with an explicitly stated set of question-and problem solving-procedures—the solutions approach
4. Supplement your overall strategy with an explicitly stated approach to each examination session (See Chapter 4)
5. Evaluate your preparation progress on a regular basis and prepare lists of things "to do." (See Weekly Review of Preparation Program Progress on following page.)
6. RELAX: You can pass the exam. About 40 to 45% of the candidates taking a section of the CPA examination pass. But if you take out the individuals that did not adequately prepare, these percentages increase substantially. You will be one of those who pass if you complete an efficient preparation program and execute well (i.e., solutions approach and exam strategy) while taking the exam.

The following outline is designed to provide you with a general framework of the tasks before you. You should tailor the outline to your needs by adding specific items and comments.

A. Preparation Program (refer to Self-Study Program discussed previously)

1. Obtain and organize study materials
2. Locate facilities conducive for studying and block out study time
3. Develop your solutions approach
4. Prepare an examination strategy
5. Study the material tested recently and prepare answers to actual exam questions on these topics under examination conditions
6. Periodically evaluate your progress

B. Physical Arrangements

1. Apply to and obtain acceptance from your state board
2. Schedule your test location and time

C. Taking the Examination (covered in detail in Chapter 4)

1. Become familiar with location of the test center and procedures
2. Implement examination strategies and the solutions approach

Weekly Review of Preparation Program Progress

The following pages contain a hypothetical weekly review of program progress. You should prepare a similar progress chart. This procedure, taking only 5 minutes per week, will help you proceed through a more efficient, complete preparation program.

Make notes of materials and topics

1. That you have studied
2. That you have completed
3. That need additional study

Weeks to go	*Comments on progress, "to do" items, etc.*
11	1) Read Business Structure Module 2) Made notecards 3) Worked MC questions 4) Need to use solutions approach

10	1)	Read Economics & Strategy Module
	2)	Made notecards
	3)	Worked the MC questions
	4)	Need to work more questions on types of markets

9	1)	Read Financial Management Module
	2)	Made notecards
	3)	Worked some MC questions
	4)	Need to work more capital asset pricing questions

8	1)	Read Risk Management and Capital Budgeting Module
	2)	Made notecards
	3)	Worked some MC questions
	4)	Need to work more on probability analysis

7	1)	Read Information Technology Module
	2)	Made notecards
	3)	Worked some MC questions
	4)	Need to finish Economics, Risk Measurement and Financial Management MC

6	1)	Read Performance Measures Module
	2)	Made notecards
	3)	Worked the MC questions
	4)	Need to study the balanced scorecard

5	1)	Reviewed Cost Measurement Module
	2)	Completed MC for prior Modules
	3)	Made notecards
	4)	Worked some MC questions

4	1)	Read Planning, Control, and Analysis Module
	2)	Made notecards
	3)	Worked the MC questions
	4)	Need to review standard costing

| 3 | 1) | Reviewed all Modules |
| | 2) | Completed all MC questions |

2	1)	Took BEC Sample Exam
	2)	Wrote down topics I still do not feel confident in
	3)	Worked variance analysis, working capital management, and balanced scorecard questions— Am now finally confident in these areas

| 1 | 1) | Reviewed the Economics & Strategy and Financial Management Modules and worked all the MC again |
| | 2) | Reviewed all notecards |

| 0 | 1) | Tried to relax and review topics |

Time Management of Your Preparation

As you begin your CPA exam preparation, you obviously realize that there is a large amount of material to cover over the course of the next two to three months. Therefore, it is very important for you to organize your calendar, and maybe even your daily routine, so that you can allocate sufficient time to studying. An organized approach to your preparation is much more effective than a last week cram session. An organized approach also builds up the confidence necessary to succeed on the CPA exam.

An approach which we have already suggested is to develop weekly "to do" lists. This technique helps you to establish intermediate objectives and goals as you progress through your study plan. You can then focus your efforts on small tasks and not feel overwhelmed by the entire process. And as you accomplish these tasks you will see yourself moving one step closer to realizing the overall goal, succeeding on the CPA exam.

Note, however, that the underlying assumption of this approach is that you have found the time during the week to study and thus accomplish the different tasks. Although this is an obvious step, it is still a very important step. Your exam preparation should be of a continuous nature and not one that jumps around the calendar. Therefore, you should strive to find available study time within your daily schedule, which can be utilized on a consistent basis. For example, everyone has certain hours of the day which are already committed for activities such as jobs, classes, and, of course, sleep. There is also going to be the time you spend relaxing because CPA candidates should try to maintain some balance in their lives. Sometimes too much studying can be counterproductive. But there will be some time available to you for studying and working through the questions. Block off this available time and use it only for exam prep. Use the time to accomplish your weekly tasks and to keep yourself committed to the process. After awhile your preparation will develop into a habit and the preparation will not seem as overwhelming as it once did.

**NOW IS THE TIME
TO MAKE YOUR COMMITMENT**

2 EXAMINATION GRADING

All State Boards of Accountancy use the AICPA advisory grading service. As your grade is to be determined by this process, it is very important that you understand the AICPA grading process and its **implications for your preparation program and for the solution techniques you will use during the examination.**

The AICPA has a full-time staff of CPA examination personnel under the supervision of the AICPA Board of Examiners, which has responsibility for the CPA examination.

This chapter contains a description of the AICPA grading process including a determination of the passing standard.

Setting the Passing Standard of the Uniform CPA Examination

As a part of the development of any licensing process, the passing score on the licensing examination must be established. This passing score must be set to distinguish candidates who are qualified to practice from those who are not. After conducting a number of studies of methods to determine passing scores, the Board of Examiners decided to use candidate-centered methods to set passing scores for the computer-based Uniform CPA Examination. In candidate-centered methods, the focus is on looking at actual candidate answers and making judgments about which sets of answers represent the answers of qualified entry-level CPAs. To make these determinations, the AICPA convened panels of CPAs during 2003 to examine candidate responses and set the passing scores for multiple-choice questions and simulations. The data from these panels provide the basis for the development of question and problem points (relative weightings). **As with the previous pencil-and-paper exam, a passing score on the computer-based examination is 75%.**

Grading the Examination

Only multiple-choice questions appear on the Business Environment and Concepts section. Multiple-choice questions are graded electronically and, therefore, only the candidates' responses are graded. No consideration is given to any comments or explanations. **The AICPA pretests multiple-choice questions on the exam; 5 of the questions in each testlet of the exam are pretest questions that are not included in the candidate's grade.** Different versions of each exam testlet contain different pretest questions, and you cannot determine which questions are being pretested.

Multiple-Choice Grading

Business Environment and Concepts exams contain three multiple-choice testlets of 30 questions each. The possible score on a question and on a testlet will vary based on the difficulty of the questions. You will receive more raw points for hard and medium questions than for easy questions.

3 THE SOLUTIONS APPROACH

The solutions approach is a systematic problem-solving methodology. The purpose is to assure efficient, complete solutions to CPA exam questions, some of which are complex and confusing relative to most undergraduate accounting problems. This is especially true with regard to the new simulation type problems. Unfortunately, there appears to be a widespread lack of emphasis on problem-solving techniques in accounting courses. Most accounting books and courses merely provide solutions to specific types of problems. Memorization of these solutions for examinations and preparation of homework problems from examples is "cookbooking." "Cookbooking" is perhaps a necessary step in the learning process, but it is certainly not sufficient training for the complexities of the business world. Professional accountants need to be adaptive to a rapidly changing complex environment. For example, CPAs have been called on to interpret and issue reports on new concepts such as price controls, energy allocations, and new taxes. These CPAs rely on their problem-solving expertise to understand these problems and to formulate solutions to them.

The steps outlined below are only one of many possible series of solution steps. Admittedly, the procedures suggested are **very** structured; thus, you should adapt the suggestions to your needs. You may find that some steps are occasionally unnecessary, or that certain additional procedures increase your own problem-solving efficiency. Whatever the case, substantial time should be allocated to developing an efficient solutions approach before taking the examination. You should develop your solutions approach by working questions.

As discussed in Chapter 1, The Business Environment and Concepts section of the exam includes only multiple-choice questions. The steps below relate to these types of questions; overall examination or section strategies are discussed in Chapter 4.

Multiple-Choice Screen Layout

The following is a computer screenshot that illustrates the manner in which multiple-choice questions will be presented:

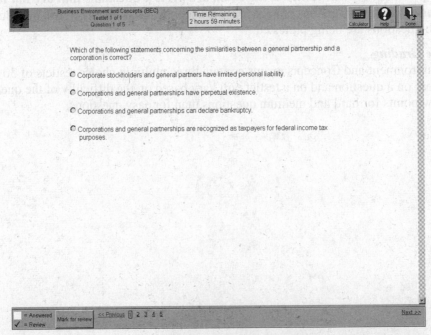

Characteristics of the computerized testlets of multiple-choice questions include the following:

1. You may move freely within a particular testlet from one question to the next or back to previous questions until you click the "Done" button. Once you have indicated that you have finished the testlet by clicking on the "Done" button, you can never return to that set of questions.
2. A button on the screen will allow you to mark a question for review if you wish to come back to it later.
3. A four-function computer calculator is available as a tool.
4. The time remaining for the entire exam section is shown on the screen.
5. The number of the questions out of the total in the testlet is shown on the screen.
6. The "Help" button will provide you with help in navigating and completing the testlet.

The screenshot above was obtained from the AICPA's tutorial at www.cpa-exam.org. Candidates are urged to complete the tutorial and other example questions on the AICPA's Web site to obtain additional experience with the computer-based testing.

Multiple-Choice Question Solutions Approach Algorithm

1. **Work individual questions in order.**

   a. If a question appears lengthy or difficult, skip it until you can determine that extra time is available. **Mark it for review** to remind you to return to a question that you have skipped or need to review.

2. **Read the stem of the question without looking at the answers.**

   a. The answers are sometimes misleading and may cause you to misread or misinterpret the question.

3. **Read each question *carefully* to determine the topical area.**

   a. Study the requirements **first** so you know which data are important.
   b. Note keywords and important data.
   c. Identify pertinent information with notations in the margin of the exam.
   d. Be especially careful to note when the requirement is an **exception** (e.g., "Which of the following is **not** included in gross income?").
   e. If a set of data is the basis for two or more questions, read the requirements of each of the questions first before beginning to work the first question (sometimes it is more efficient to work the questions out of order or simultaneously).
   f. Be alert to read questions as they are, not as you would like them to be. You may encounter a familiar looking item; do not jump to the conclusion that you know what the answer is without reading the question completely.
   g. For comprehensive questions, prepare intermediary solutions as you read the question.

4. **Anticipate the answer before looking at the alternative answers.**

   a. Recall the applicable principle (e.g., job order costing) and the applicable model (e.g., net present value), or the applicable law section (e.g., Chapter 7 of the US Bankruptcy Law).
   b. If a question deals with a complex area like standard costing, set up full-blown diagrams on the scratch paper provided, if necessary, using abbreviations that enable you to follow your work.

5. **Read the answers and select the *best* alternative.**

   a. If the answer you have computed is not among the choices, quickly check the logic of your solution. If you do not arrive at one of the given answers in the time you have allotted for that particular problem, make an educated guess or mark it for review.

6. **Click on the correct answer (or your educated guess).**
7. **After completing all of the questions including the ones marked for review click on the "Done" button to close out the testlet. Remember once you have closed out the testlet you can never return to it.**

Multiple-Choice Question Solutions Approach Example
A good example of the multiple-choice solutions approach is provided, using an actual multiple-choice question from a previous CPA examination.

Step 3:

Topical area? Job order costing

Step 4a:

Production costs include direct materials used, direct labor, and manufacturing overhead applied. Since there is no ending WIP inventory, all production costs are for jobs completed.

Under Pick Co.'s job order costing system manufacturing overhead is applied to work in process using a predetermined annual overhead rate. During January 2003, Pick's transactions included the following:

Direct materials issued to production	$90,000
Indirect materials issued to production	8,000
Manufacturing overhead incurred	125,000
Manufacturing overhead applied	113,000
Direct labor costs	107,000

Pick had <u>neither beginning nor ending work in process</u> inventory. What was the cost of jobs completed in January 2003?

a. $302,000
b. $310,000
c. $322,000
d. $330,000

WIP

90
107 | 310
113
0

Currently, all multiple-choice questions are scored based on the number correct, weighted by a difficulty rating (i.e., there is no penalty for guessing). The rationale is that a "good guess" indicates knowledge. Thus, you should answer all multiple-choice questions.

Time Requirements for the Solutions Approach

Many candidates bypass the solutions approach, because they feel it is too time-consuming. Actually, the solutions approach is a time-saver and, more importantly, it helps you prepare better solutions to all questions.

Without committing yourself to using the solutions approach, try it step-by-step on several multiple-choice questions. After you conscientiously go through the step-by-step routine a few times, you will begin to adopt and modify aspects of the technique which will benefit you. Subsequent usage will become subconscious and painless. The important point is that you must try the solutions approach several times to accrue any benefits.

Efficiency of the Solutions Approach

The mark of an inefficient solution is one wherein the candidate immediately selects an answer. Remember, the final solution is one of the last steps in the solutions approach. You should have the solution under complete control before you decide on your final answer.

While the large amount of intermediary work in the solutions approach may appear burdensome and time-consuming, this technique results in better answers in less time than do haphazard approaches. Moreover, the solutions approach really allows you to work out problems that you feel unfamiliar with at first reading. The solutions approach, however, must be mastered prior to sitting for the CPA examination. In other words, the candidate must be willing to invest a reasonable amount of time into perfecting the solutions approach.

In summary, the solutions approach may appear foreign and somewhat cumbersome. At the same time, if you have worked through the material in this chapter, you should have some appreciation for it. Develop the solutions approach by writing down the steps in the solutions approach algorithm at the beginning of this chapter, and keep them before you as you work CPA exam questions. Remember that even though the suggested procedures appear **very structured** and **time-consuming,** integration of these procedures into your own style of problem solving will help improve **your** solutions approach. The next chapter discusses strategies for the overall examination.

NOW IS THE TIME
TO MAKE YOUR COMMITMENT

4 TAKING THE EXAMINATION

This chapter is concerned with developing an examination strategy (e.g., how to cope with the environment at the examination site, the way in which to work problems, etc.).

EXAMINATION STRATEGIES

Your performance during a particular examination is final and not subject to revision. While you may sit for the examination again if you are unsuccessful, the majority of your preparation will have to be repeated, requiring substantial, additional amounts of time. Thus, examination strategies (discussed in this chapter) that maximize your exam-taking efficiency are very important.

Getting "Psyched Up"

The CPA exam is quite challenging and worthy of your best effort. Explicitly develop your own psychological strategy to get yourself "up" for the exam. Pace your study program such that you will be able to operate at peak performance when you are actually taking the exam. A good aspect of the new computerized exam is that if you have scheduled early in a testing window and do not feel well, you can reschedule your sitting. However, once you start the exam, you cannot retake it in the same testing window, so do not leave the exam early. Do the best you can.

Lodging, Meals, Exercise

If you must travel to the test center, make advance reservations for comfortable lodging convenient to the test center. Do not stay with friends, relatives, etc. Both uninterrupted sleep and total concentration on the exam are a must. Consider the following in making your lodging plans:

1. Proximity to the test center
2. Availability of meals and snacks
3. Recreational facilities

Plan your meal schedule to provide maximum energy and alertness during the day and maximum rest at night. Do not experiment with new foods, drinks, etc., around your scheduled date. Within reasonable limits, observe your normal eating and drinking habits. Recognize that overconsumption of coffee during the exam could lead to a hyperactive state and disaster. Likewise, overindulgence in alcohol to overcome nervousness and to induce sleep the night before might contribute to other difficulties the following morning.

Tenseness should be expected before and during the examination. Rely on a regular exercise program to unwind at the end of the day. As you select your lodging for the examination, try to accommodate your exercise pleasure (e.g., running, swimming etc.). Continue to indulge in your exercise program on the days of the examination.

To relieve tension or stress while studying, try breathing or stretching exercises. Use these exercises before and during the examination to start and to keep your adrenaline flowing. Remain determined not to go through another sitting for the Business Environment and Concepts section to obtain your certificate.

In summary, the examination is likely to be both rigorous and fatiguing especially if you sit for more than one part over a few days. Expect it and prepare for it by getting in shape, planning methods of relaxation during the exam and the evening before, and finally, building the confidence and competence to complete the exam (successfully).

Test Center and Procedures

If possible, visit the test center before the examination to assure knowledge of the location. Remember: no surprises. Having a general familiarity with the facilities will lessen anxiety prior to the examination.

Talking to a recent veteran of the examination will give you background for the general examination procedures. **You must arrive at the testing center 30 minutes before your scheduled time.**

Upon completion of check-in at the test location, the candidate

- Is seated at a designated workstation
- Begins the exam after the proctor launches the session
- Is monitored by a Test Center Administrator
- Is videotaped

Upon completion of the examination, the candidate

- Signs out
- Collects his/her belongings
- Turns in scratch paper
- Is given a Post Exam Information sheet

If you have any remaining questions regarding examination procedure, call or write your state board or go to Prometric's Web site at www.prometric.com/cpa.

Allocation of Time

Budget your time. Time should be carefully allocated in an attempt to maximize points per minute. While you must develop your own strategy with respect to time allocation, some suggestions may be useful. Allocate 5 minutes to reading the instructions. When you begin the exam you will be given an inventory of the total number of testlets and suggested times. Budget your time based on this inventory. Plan on spending 1 1/2 to 2 minutes per individual multiple-choice question.

Techniques for Time Management

The Business Environment & Concepts (BEC) exam will have three testlets of multiple-choice questions with 24 questions each. Referring to the above guidelines, note that the maximum time you should take to complete a testlet of 24 questions is about 36 to 48 minutes. As you complete each testlet keep track of how you performed in relation to this standard.

Examination Rules

1. Prior to the start of the examination, you will be required to sign a *Statement of Confidentiality*.
2. You will not be allowed to take any materials with you. Lockers will be provided for your personal effects. Any reference during the examination to books or other materials or the exchange of information with other persons shall be considered misconduct sufficient to bar you from further participation in the examination.
3. Penalties will be imposed on any candidate who is caught cheating before, during, or after the examination. These penalties may include expulsion from the examination, denial of applications for future examinations, and civil or criminal penalties.
4. You may not leave the examination room with any notes about the examination.

Refer to the brochure *CPA Candidate Bulletin* for other rules.

CPA EXAM CHECKLIST

One week before you are scheduled to sit

___ 1. Review outlines (your own or those in this volume) underlining buzzwords.

___ 2. If time permits, work through a few questions in your weakest areas so that techniques/concepts are fresh in your mind.

___ 3. Assemble notecards and key outlines of major topical areas into a manageable "last review" notebook to be taken with you to the exam.

What to bring

___ 1. *Notice to Schedule (NTS)*—You must bring the proper NTS with you.

___ 2. *Identification*—Bring two valid forms of ID. One must be government issued. The name on the ID must match exactly the name on the NTS. The *CPA Candidate Bulletin* lists valid primary and secondary IDs.

___ 3. *Hotel confirmation*—(if you must travel).

___ 4. *Cash*—Payment for anything by personal check is rarely accepted.

___ 5. *Major credit card*—American Express, Master Card, Visa, etc.

___ 6. *Alarm clock*—This is too important an event to trust to a hotel wake-up call that might be overlooked.

___ 7. *Clothing*—Should be comfortable and layered to suit the possible temperature range in the testing room.

___ 8. *Earplugs*—Even though examinations are being given, there may be constant activity in the testing room (e.g., people walking around, rustling of paper, clicking of keyboards, people coughing, etc.). The use of earplugs may block out some of this distraction and help you concentrate better.

___ 9. *Other*—Any "Last review" materials.

Evenings before exams

1. Reviewing the evening before the exam could earn you the extra points needed to pass a section. Just keep this last-minute effort in perspective and do **not** panic yourself into staying up all night trying to cover every possible point. This could lead to disaster by sapping your body of the endurance needed to attack questions creatively during the next day.

2. Reread key outlines or notecards, reviewing important topics in which you feel deficient.

3. Go over mnemonics and acronyms you have developed as study aids. Test yourself by writing out the letters on paper while verbally giving a brief explanation of what the letters stand for.

4. **Set your alarm and get a good night's rest!** Being well rested will permit you to meet each day's challenge with a fresh burst of creative energy. **You should arrive 30 minutes before your scheduled time.**

Exam-taking strategy

1. Do not spend an excess amount of time on the introductory screens. If you take longer than 10 minutes on these screens, the test session will automatically terminate. If the exam session terminates, it will not be possible to restart the examination and you will have to reapply to take the section.

2. Report equipment/software issues to the test center staff immediately. Do not attempt to correct the problem yourself and do not use examination time thinking about it before reporting it. Remind the test center staff to file a report describing the problem. The test center staff should be able to handle any equipment or software problems. However, if you believe the problem was not handled appropriately, contact NASBA at candidatecare@nasba.org.

3. Report any concerns about test questions to test center staff after you have completed the session. The members of the test center staff know nothing about the CPA Examination content. The test center staff can report the issues to the AICPA. You should also report concerns about the questions in writing to the AICPA (FAX to [609] 671-2922). If possible, the question and testlet numbers should be included in the FAX.

4. In the event of a power outage or incident requiring a restart, the computer clock will stop and you will not lose examination time. Your responses up to the time of the restart will not be lost as responses are saved at frequent intervals throughout the examination.

5. If you have questions about the examination software functions, you should read the instructions and "Help" tab information. The test center staff is not familiar with the functioning of the examination software and, therefore, will not be able to help you.

6. The crucial technique to use for multiple-choice questions is to read through each question stem **carefully,** nothing keywords such as "oral," "without disclosing," "qualified pension plan," etc. Then **read each choice** carefully before you start eliminating inappropriate answers. Often the first or second answer may **sound** correct, but a later answer may be **more correct.** Be discriminating! Reread the question and choose the best answer.

7. If you are struggling with questions beyond a minute or two, use the strategy of dividing multiple-choice questions into two categories.

   a. Questions for which you **know** you lack knowledge to answer: Drawing from any responses you have, narrow answers down to as few as possible, then make an **educated guess.**

   b. Questions for which you feel you should be getting the correct answer: Mark the question for review. Your mental block may clear, or you may spot a simple error in logic that will be corrected when you rereview the question.

8. Remember: **Never** change a first impulse answer later unless you are absolutely certain you are right. It is a proven fact that your subconscious often guides you to the correct answer.

9. Constantly compare your progress with the time remaining. **Never** spend excessive amounts of time on one testlet.

10. The cardinal rule is **never,** but **never,** leave an answer blank.

After taking the examination

1. Retain the Confirmation of Attendance form issued after the examination because it provides valuable contact information.

2. Report any examination incidents/concerns in writing, even if the issues were already reported to test center staff.

3. If you feel that the circumstances surrounding your test administration prevented you from performing at a level consistent with your knowledge and skills, immediately contact NASBA at candidatecare@nasba.org.

HAVE YOU MADE YOUR
COMMITMENT?

5 BUSINESS ENVIRONMENT AND CONCEPTS

BUSINESS ENVIRONMENT AND CONCEPTS EXAM CONTENT

The content of the Business Environment and Concepts (BEC) examination includes a number of general business and accounting topics. The areas are covered as shown below.

Topic	*Percentage*
Business Structure	17-23
Economic Concepts	8-12
Financial Management	17-23
Information Technology	22-28
Planning and Measurement	22-28

The BEC section of the exam only tests using multiple-choice questions. **No simulations currently appear on this section of the exam.**

Despite the fact that there are no simulations, the basic concepts for preparation remain the same. Thus, the candidate still needs to have the skills and knowledge necessary to solve both **how** (number crunching) and **why** (conceptual) type questions.

First, become acquainted with the nature of the BEC exam itself. With the computerization of the exam, the AICPA has issued a set of content specifications. These content specifications are printed below.

Relatedly, you should evaluate your competence by working 10 to 20 multiple-choice questions from each of the modules (38-45). This diagnostic routine will acquaint you with the specific nature of the questions tested on each topic as well as indicate the amount of study required per topic. However, do not get discouraged. Remember, more difficult questions are more heavily weighted in determining your score. See discussion of self-study programs (Chapter 1) and examination grading (Chapter 2).

Second, study the content of modules 38-45, emphasizing the mechanics of each topic such as economic concepts, strategic performance measurement, working capital management, etc. Use simple examples, journal entries, and diagrams to get a handle on the basic concepts underlying each topic. You may have to refer to your textbooks, etc., for topics to which you have had no previous exposure.

Third, work as many multiple-choice questions as time allows and take the sample examination at the end of Volume 2.

AICPA Content Specification Outline

The AICPA Content Specification Outline of the coverage of Business Environment and Concepts appears below. This outline was issued by the AICPA, effective for 2005.

AICPA CONTENT SPECIFICATION OUTLINE: BUSINESS ENVIRONMENT AND CONCEPTS

I.   Business Structure (**17%-23%**)

   A. Advantages, Implications, and Constraints of Legal Structures for Business

      1. Sole Proprietorships and General and Limited Partnerships

      2. Limited Liability Companies (LLC), Limited Liability Partnerships (LLP), and Joint Ventures

      3. Subchapter C and Subchapter S Corporations

   B. Formation, Operation, and Termination of Businesses

   C. Financial Structure, Capitalization, Profit and Loss Allocation, and Distributions

   D. Rights, Duties, Legal Obligations, and Authority of Owners and Management (Directors, Officers, Stockholders, Partners, and Other Owners)

II. Economic Concepts Essential to Obtaining an Understanding of an Entity's Business and Industry (**8%-12%**)

   A. Business Cycles and Reasons for Business Fluctuations

   B. Economic Measures and Reasons for Changes in the Economy, Such as Inflation, Deflation, and Interest Rate Changes

   C. Market Influences on Business Strategies, Including Selling, Supply Chain, and Customer Management Strategies

   D. Implications to Business of Dealings in Foreign Currencies, Hedging, and Exchange Rate Fluctuations

III. Financial Management (**17%-23%**)

   A. Financial Modeling, Including Factors Such as Financial Indexes, Taxes and Opportunity Costs, and Models Such as Economic Value Added, Cash Flow, Net Present Value, Discounted Payback, and Internal Rate of Return

      1. Objectives

      2. Techniques

      3. Limitations

   B. Strategies for Short- and Long-Term Financing Options, Including Cost of Capital and Derivatives

   C. Financial Statement and Business Implications of Liquid Asset Management

1. Management of Cash and Cash Equivalents, Accounts Receivable, Accounts Payable, and Inventories
2. Characteristics and Financial Statement and Business Implications of Loan Rates (Fixed vs. Variable) and Loan Covenants

IV. Information Technology (IT) Implications in the Business Environment **(22%-28%)**

A. Role of Business Information Systems

1. Reporting Concepts and Systems
2. Transaction Processing Systems
3. Management Reporting Systems
4. Risks

B. Roles and Responsibilities within the IT Function

1. Roles and Responsibilities of Database/ Network/Web Administrators, Computer Operators, Librarians, Systems Programmers, and Applications Programmers
2. Appropriate Segregation of Duties

C. IT Fundamentals

1. Hardware and Software, Networks, and Data Structure, Analysis, and Application, Including Operating Systems, Security, File Organization, Types of Data Files, and Database Management Systems
2. Systems Operation, Including Transaction Processing Modes, such as Batch, Online Real-Time, and Distributed Processing, and Application Processing Phases, such as Data Capture; Edit Routines; Master File Maintenance; Reporting, Accounting, Control, and Management; Query, Audit Trail, and Ad Hoc Reports; and Transaction Flow

D. Disaster Recovery and Business Continuity, Including Data Backup and Data Recovery Procedures, Alternate Processing Facilities (Hot Sites), and Threats and Risk Management

E. Financial Statement and Business Implications of Electronic Commerce, Including Electronic Fund Transfers, Point-of-Sale Transactions, Internet-Based Transactions and Electronic Data Interchange

V. Planning and Measurement **(22%-28%)**

A. Planning and Budgeting

1. Planning Techniques, Including Strategic and Operational Planning
2. Forecasting and Projection Techniques
3. Budgeting and Budget Variance Analysis

B. Performance Measures

1. Organizational Performance Measures, Including Financial and Nonfinancial Scorecards
2. Benchmarking, Including Quality Control Principles, Best Practices, and Benchmarking Techniques

C. Cost Measurement

1. Cost Measurement Concepts (Standard, Joint Product, and By-Product Costing)
2. Accumulating and Assigning Costs (Job Order, Process, and Activity-Based Costing)
3. Factors Affecting Production Costs

References—Business Environment and Concepts

Current Textbooks on

- Business Law
- Managerial Accounting
- Management
- Finance
- Economics
- Accounting Information Systems
- Management Information Systems
- Budgeting and Measurement

AICPA Audit Risk Alerts

Business Periodicals Provide Background

BUSINESS STRUCTURE

Overview

A sole proprietorship has only one owner, which creates both advantages and disadvantages. A partnership is an association of two or more persons to carry on a business as co-owners for profit. The major areas tested on partnerships are the characteristics of a partnership, comparisons with other structures, rights and liabilities of the partnership itself, the rights, duties, and liabilities of the partners among themselves and to third parties, the allocation of profits and losses, and the rights of various parties, including creditors, upon dissolution.

The law of joint ventures is similar to that of partnerships with some exceptions. Note that the joint venture is more limited in scope than the partnership form of business. The former is typically organized to carry out one single business undertaking or a series of related undertakings; whereas, the latter is formed to conduct ongoing business.

Subchapter S corporations are those corporations that elect to be taxed similar to partnerships under Subchapter S. Corporations that do not make this election are called Subchapter C corporations. In both cases, a corporation is an artificial person that is created by or under law and which operates under a common name through its elected management. It is a legal entity, separate and distinct from its shareholders. The corporation has the authority vested in it by statute and its corporate charter. The candidate should understand the characteristics and advantages of the corporate form over other forms of business organization.

Basic to preparation for questions on corporation law is an understanding of the following: the liabilities of a promoter who organizes a new corporation; the liability of shareholders; the liability of the corporation with respect to the preincorporation contracts made by the promoter; the fiduciary relationship of the promoter to the stockholders and to the corporation; the various circumstances under which a stockholder may be liable for the debts of the corporation; the rights of shareholders particularly concerning payment of dividends; the rights and duties of officers, directors, and other agents or employees of the corporation to the corporation, to stockholders, and to third persons; subscriptions; and the procedures necessary to merge, consolidate, or otherwise change the corporate structure.

State laws are now widely based on the Revised Business Corporation Act upon which changes to this module are based.

A. Nature of Sole Proprietorships

1. There is only one owner of business

   a. Business is not a separate legal entity apart from owner
   b. Owner does not share power or decision making with other owners

2. Advantages over other business structures

   a. Sole proprietorship is simplest type of business structure

      (1) Easy to form and to operate

         (a) Federal or state governments do not require formal filing or approval to begin operation

            1] If business is operating under name other than that of sole proprietor, most states require that it file fictitious name statement with government

   b. Business can be sold without need to obtain approval from others such as shareholders or partners
   c. Owner has right to make all business decisions such as direction company should go, who to hire or fire, etc.
   d. If business generates profit, sole owner need not share it with other owners or investors
   e. The profits of the business are taxed on the personal tax return of the owner—profits are taxed only once

3. Disadvantages over other business structures

   a. If company has loss, sole proprietor suffers all of it
   b. Sole proprietorship cannot obtain capital from partners, shareholders, etc.

      (1) Capital is limited by funds the owner has or can borrow

   c. Sole proprietor has unlimited personal liability

B. Nature of Partnerships

1. A partnership is an association of two or more persons to carry on a business as co-owners for profit

   a. The phrase "to carry on a business" includes almost every trade, occupation, or profession

    (1) It does not include passive co-ownership of property (e.g., joint tenants of a piece of land)

    (2) Partnerships do not include nonprofit unincorporated associations (e.g., labor unions, charitable organizations, clubs)

  b. Co-ownership of the "business" (and not merely of assets used in a business) is an important element in determining whether a partnership exists

    (1) The most important and necessary element of co-ownership (and thereby partnership) is profit sharing

      (a) Need not be equal

      (b) Receipt of a share of profits is *prima facie evidence* (raises a presumption) of a partnership

        1] Presumption rebutted by establishing that profit sharing was only for payment of debt, interest on loan, services performed, rent, etc.

    (2) Another important element of co-ownership is joint control

      (a) Each partner has an equal right to participate in management. Right to manage may be contracted away to a managing partner

    (3) Under Revised Uniform Partnership Act, now adopted by majority of states, partner is no longer co-owner of partnership property

2. Partnership relationship creates a fiduciary relationship between partners

  a. Fiduciary relationship arises because each partner is an agent for partnership and for each other in partnership business

3. Partnership relationship is based on contract but arrangements may be quite informal

  a. Agreement can be inferred from conduct (e.g., allowing someone to share in management and profits may result in partnership even though actual intent to become partner is missing)

4. Draws heavily on agency law because each partner is an agent as well as a principal of partnership

  a. Most rules can be changed in individual cases by agreement between parties affected (e.g., rights and duties between partners)

    EXAMPLE: A, B, and C form a partnership in which all three partners agree that A is liable for all of the product liability cases against the partnership. This agreement is enforceable between A, B, and C but not against other parties that never agreed to this. Therefore, as long as A is solvent, B and C can collect from A even though a third party recovers from all of them on a product liability problem.

5. Generally, any person (entity) who has the capacity to contract may become a partner

  a. Corporations

  b. Minors—but contract of partnership is voidable

  c. Partnerships can become partners

6. Common characteristics of partnerships

  a. Limited duration

  b. Transfer of ownership requires agreement

  c. May sue and be sued as separate legal entities

  d. Unlimited liability of partners for partnership debts

  e. Ease of formation, can be very informal

  f. Partnership does not pay federal income tax; partners must include their share of partnership operations on their tax returns

C. Types of Partnerships and Partners

1. Limited partnership is a special statutory relationship consisting of one or more general partners and one or more limited partners

  a. Limited partners only contribute capital and are usually only liable to that extent (analogous to shareholder)

    b.   Limited partners do not take part in management of partnership

  2. General partners are ones who share in management of business and have unlimited liability to creditors of partnership

    a.   Silent partner does not help manage partnership but still has unlimited liability

D. Formation of Partnership

  1. By agreement, express or implied

    a.   Agreement to share profits is *prima facie evidence* that partnership exists

      (1) Need not agree to share losses because agreement to share profits assumes sharing of losses
      (2) Sharing of gross receipts does not establish partnership

    b.   Partnership not implied if profits received for some other purpose such as for payment of debt, wages, or lease

  2. Creation of a partnership may be very informal, either oral or written

    a.   Written partnership agreement not required unless within Statute of Frauds (e.g., partnership that cannot be completed within one year)

> EXAMPLE: *A, B, and C form a partnership that, although they expect it to last for several years, has no time period specified. This partnership agreement may be oral.*

> EXAMPLE: *X, Y, and Z organize XYZ partnership which by agreement will last at least five years. This partnership agreement must be in writing.*

      (1) Usually wise to have in writing

    b.   Filing not required

  3. Articles of copartnership (partnership agreement)—not legally necessary, but a good idea to have
  4. Fictitious name statutes require partners to register fictitious or assumed names

    a.   Failure to comply does not invalidate partnership but may result in fine
    b.   The purpose is to allow third parties to know who is in partnership

E. Partner's Rights

  1. Partnership agreement, whether oral or written, would be controlling

    a.   The following rules are used unless partnership agreement states otherwise

  2. Partnership interest

    a.   Refers to partner's right to share in profits and return of contribution on dissolution
    b.   Is considered personal property

      (1) Even if partnership property is real estate

    c.   Does not include specific partnership property, merely right to use it for partnership purposes
    d.   Freely assignable without other partner's consent

      (1) Assignee is not substituted as a partner without consent of all other partners
      (2) Assignee does **not** receive right to manage partnership, to have an accounting, to inspect books, to possess or own any individual partnership property—merely receives rights in the assigning partner's share of profits and return of partner's capital contribution (unless partners agree otherwise)

        (a) Typically, assignments are made to secure a loan

> EXAMPLE: *C, a CPA, wishes to obtain a large loan. He is a member of a CPA firm and assigns rights in his partnership to the bank to secure the loan.*

      (3) Assignor remains liable as a partner
      (4) Does not cause dissolution unless assignor also withdraws

3. Partnership property

    a. Includes

        (1) Property acquired with partnership funds unless different intent is shown
        (2) Property not acquired in partnership name is, however, partnership property if

            (a) Partner acquires title to it in his/her capacity as a partner, or
            (b) Property acquired with partnership funds

    b. Not assignable or subject to attachment individually, only by a claim on partnership

        (1) Property may be assigned by agreement of all partners
        (2) Any partner can assign or sell property if for the apparent purpose of carrying on the business of the partnership in the usual way

    c. Upon partner's death, his/her estate is entitled to deceased partner's share of profits and capital, but not to any specific partnership property

        (1) Remaining partners have duty to account to the heirs of the deceased for value of interest
        (2) Heirs not automatically partners

4. Participate in management

    a. Right to participate equally in management

        (1) Ordinary business decisions by a majority vote
        (2) Unanimous consent needed to make fundamental changes

    b. Power to act as an agent for partnership in partnership business
    c. Also has right to inspect books and have full knowledge of partnership affairs
    d. Silent partner is one who does not help manage

        (1) Still has personal, unlimited liability

5. Share in profits and losses

    a. Profits and losses are shared equally unless agreement specifies otherwise

        (1) Even if contributed capital is not equal
        (2) For example, agreement may specify one partner to receive greater share of profits for doing more work, etc., while losses still shared equally

    b. If partners agree on unequal profit sharing but are silent on loss sharing, losses are shared per the profit-sharing proportions

        (1) May choose to share losses in a different proportion from profits

            EXAMPLE: A, B, and C form a partnership with capital contributions as follows: A, $100,000; B, $20,000; and C, $20,000. Their agreement is silent on how to split profits or losses. Therefore, profits and losses will be split equally.

            EXAMPLE: Same as above except that they agree to give A 50% of the profits and B and C each get 25%. Profits as well as losses will be split based on these stated percentages.

            EXAMPLE: Assume that A, B, and C agree to a 50%, 25%, 25% split if there is a profit but to a 20%, 40%, 40% split, respectively, for any annual losses. If there is a $100,000 annual loss, A will suffer $20,000 and B and C each will suffer $40,000 of the loss.

6. Other rights

    a. Indemnification for expenses incurred on behalf of the partnership
    b. General partners may be creditors, secured or unsecured, of the partnership

        (1) May receive interest on loans
        (2) No interest on capital contributions unless stated in partnership agreement

    c. No right to salary for work performed because this is a duty unless they agree otherwise

        (1) It is common for partners to agree to pay salaries, especially if only one or two do most of the work

    d. May obtain formal accounting of partnership affairs

        (1) Each partner has the right if used reasonably

  7. Every partner owes a fiduciary duty to every other partner (this is important)

    a. Each must act in best interest of others

        (1) May pursue own self-interest as long as it is not competition and does not interfere with partner's duty to partnership

        (2) Any wrongly derived profits must be held by partner for others

        (3) Must abide by partnership agreement

        (4) Liable to others partners for liability caused by going beyond actual authority

  8. Incoming partners new to partnership have same rights as previous partners

    a. Requires consent of all partners to admit new partner

    b. Profit sharing, loss sharing, and capital contributions are by agreement between all partners

    c. A partnership may also be partner of separate partnership if all partners agree

F. Relationship to Third Parties

  1. Partners are agents of the partnership

    a. Can bind partnership to contracts with third parties

        (1) Even where no actual authority, can bind partnership where there is apparent (ostensible) authority, authority by estoppel, or implied authority

            (a) Apparent (ostensible) or purported partnership is created when parties misrepresent to others that they are partners

                1] Similar in concept to apparent (ostensible) agency

                2] Partnership may make public recording of limitation on partner authority or statement of partnership authority to limit possible liability

                3] Individuals are called apparent (ostensible) partners and are liable to third parties as if they were actual partners

                    a] Usually liable even if this allows others to misrepresent him/her as partner

            (b) Partnership by estoppel created when parties misrepresent to others that they are partners and others are hurt as they rely on this

                1] Many courts treat partnership by estoppel and apparent partnership as essentially the same

                2] Not actual partners but liable as if were actual partners

                3] Individuals are called partners by estoppel

            EXAMPLE: A, B, and C form a partnership to sell widgets. Contrary to the wishes of B and C, A decides to buy in the partnership name some "super-widgets" from T. Even though A did not have actual authority to buy these, T can enforce the contract based on apparent authority. A, of course, breached his fiduciary duty to B and C.

    b. Partners normally have implied authority to buy and sell goods, receive money, and pay debts for partnership

        (1) Each partner is agent of partnership to carry out typical business of firm or business of the kind carried on by partnership

        (2) Third parties can rely on implied authority even though secret limitations may exist which were unknown to those third parties

            EXAMPLE: A and B have a partnership to sell furniture in a retail outlet. A and B agreed that neither would buy more than $10,000 of furniture from suppliers without the consent of the other. A, however, buys $20,000 of furniture from a regular supplier who was unaware of this limitation. When the supplier attempts to deliver, B refuses the furniture. Since A had implied authority, the supplier can enforce the contract for the full $20,000.

   c. Partnership is not liable for acts of partners outside of express, implied, or apparent authority

> EXAMPLE: *A partner of a hardware store attempts to buy some real estate in the name of the partnership. Here apparent authority does not exist.*

   d. Partnership is liable for partner's torts committed in course and scope of business and for partner's breach of trust (i.e., misapplication of third party's funds)

> EXAMPLE: *A partner takes a third party's money on behalf of the partnership to invest in government bonds. Instead he uses it himself to build an addition onto his home.*

> EXAMPLE: *A partner, while driving on partnership business, injures a third party. If the partner is negligent, the partnership is also liable.*

2. Unanimous consent of partners is needed (so no implied authority) for

   a. Admission of a new partner
   b. Amending the partnership agreement
   c. Assignment of partnership property
   d. Making partnership a surety or guarantor
   e. Admitting to a claim against partnership in court
   f. Submitting partnership claim to arbitrator
   g. Any action outside the scope of the partnership business

3. Partner's liability is personal, that is, extends to all his/her personal assets (not just investment in partnership) to cover all debts and liabilities of partnership

   a. Partners are jointly and severally liable for all debts

      (1) The Revised Uniform Partnership Act (RUPA) requires creditors to first attempt collection from partnership before partners unless partnership is bankrupt

   b. Partners may split losses or liability between themselves according to any proportion agreed upon; however, third parties can still hold each partner personally liable despite agreement

      (1) If any partner pays more than his/her agreed share, s/he can get reimbursed from other partners

> EXAMPLE: *X, Y, and Z as partners agreed to split losses 10%, 20%, and 70% respectively. A third party recovers $100,000 from X only based on a partnership tort. X can get $20,000 from Y and $70,000 from Z so that she ends up paying only her 10%.*

> EXAMPLE: *Same as before except that Y is insolvent. X can recover the proportionate share from Z or $87,500 ($100,000 × 70%/80%).*

> EXAMPLE: *A, B, and C are partners who agree to split losses 10%, 10%, and 80%, respectively. Y sues the partners for a tort based on the partnership business. C takes out bankruptcy. Y can recover from A and B and is not bound by the agreement between A, B, and C.*

   c. New partners coming into a partnership are liable for existing debts only to the extent of their capital contributions

      (1) Unless new partners assume personal liability for old debts

   d. Partners withdrawing are liable for existing liabilities
   e. Partners withdrawing are liable for subsequent liabilities unless notice of withdrawal or death is given to third parties

      (1) Actual notice to creditors who previously dealt with partnership
      (2) Constructive (e.g., published) notice is sufficient for others who merely knew of partnership's existence

   f. Estates of deceased partners are liable for partners' debts
   g. Liability of withdrawing partner may be limited by agreement between partners but agreement is not binding on third parties (unless they join in on agreement)
   h. Partners are not criminally liable unless they personally participate in some way or unless statute prescribes liability to all members of management (e.g., environment regulation or sale of alcohol to a minor)

G. Termination of a Partnership

1. Termination happens when

    a. First, dissolution occurs (i.e., partners stop carrying on business together)
    b. Second, winding up takes place

        (1) Collecting partnership assets and paying partnership debts

2. Dissolution can occur by

    a. Prior agreement (e.g., partnership agreement)
    b. Present agreement of partners
    c. By decree of court in such cases as

        (1) Partner continually or seriously breaches partnership agreement
        (2) Partner guilty of conduct that harms business

    d. Assignment, selling, or pledging of partnership interest does **not** cause dissolution even if there is no consent of other partners
    e. Under RUPA, unlike previous law, partner's withdrawal, death, or bankruptcy does **not** automatically cause dissolution of partnership

        (1) Partners that own majority of partnership may choose to continue general partnership within ninety days of partners' withdrawal, death, or bankruptcy
        (2) Any partner has power to dissociate from partnership even if had agreed not to, but is liable for breach of such a contract; dissociation can result from

            (a) Notice to the partnership by the partner
            (b) An event set forth in the agreement
            (c) Expulsion of the partner under the terms of the agreement
            (d) Expulsion of the partner by unanimous vote of the other partners because of issues with the partner (e.g., business cannot be legally conducted with the partner involved)
            (e) Court order
            (f) Incapacity
            (g) Death
            (h) Insolvency
            (i) Distribution of the entire interest by a trust or estate

3. Winding up

    a. Remaining partners may elect to wind up and terminate partnership or not wind up and continue business

4. Order of distribution upon termination of general partnership

    a. To creditors including partners as creditors
    b. Capital contributions and profits or losses are calculated together

        (1) Partners may receive money or even need to pay money at this stage

5. Partners are personally liable to partnership for any deficits in their capital accounts and to creditors for insufficiency of partnership assets

    a. Priority between partnership creditors and partner's personal creditors

        (1) Partnership creditors have first priority to partnership assets; any excess goes to personal creditors
        (2) Usually, personal creditors have first priority to personal assets; any excess goes to partnership creditors

6. Partners can bind other partners and the partnership on contracts until third parties who have known of the partnership are given notice of dissolution

a. Actual notice must be given to third parties who have dealt with the partnership prior to dissolution

b. Constructive notice (e.g., notice in newspaper) is adequate for third parties who have only known of the partnership

7. Dissolution of a general partnership does not require the filing of a dissolution document with the state

H. Limited Partnerships

1. Revised Uniform Limited Partnership Act (RULPA) is designed to modernize law because today many limited partnerships are very large with many limited partners.

   a. RULPA has been adopted by majority of states

2. Creation of limited partnership

   a. Unlike general partnership that requires no formal procedures to create it, limited partnership requires compliance with state statute to create it

   b. Must file certificate of limited partnership with Secretary of State; if the partnership does not, it will be treated as a general partnership

      (1) Must be signed by all general partners and include names of all general partners

         (a) Name and address of the limited partnership
         (b) Name and address of its agent
         (c) Latest date the partnership is to dissolve
         (d) Names of limited partners not required
         (e) Must amend certificate of partnership to show any additions or deletions of general partners

            1] Must also amend certificate if any general partner becomes aware of false information in certificate

   c. Requires at least one general partner and at least one limited partner

      (1) Sole general partner may be a corporation
      (2) Liability of limited partner(s) is limited to amount of capital contributions (with some exceptions below)

   d. General or limited partners' capital contributions may not only be in cash, services performed, or property, but may also now be in promise to perform services, to give cash, or property in future

   e. Name of limited partner may not be used in name of limited partnership unless name is also name of a general partner.

      (1) If a limited partner **knowingly or negligently** allows his/her name to be part of limited partnership name, then the partner is liable to creditors who extend credit to business (unless creditors knew that limited partner was not a general partner)

   f. "Limited partnership" words must be in firm's name

   g. Partnership interests may be purchased with cash, property, services rendered, promissory note

   h. Defective formation of limited partnership causes limited partners to be liable as general partners

      (1) Under RULPA, partner who believes s/he is limited partner may avoid liability of general partner if upon learning of defective formation either

         (a) Withdraws from partnership and renounces all future profits, or
         (b) Files amendment or new certificate that cures defect

      (2) However, limited partner is liable for past transactions before withdrawal or amendment to any third party transacting business while believing partner was general partner

   i. Foreign limited partnership is one doing business in given state but was formed in another state

      (1) Foreign limited partnership must register with Secretary of State before doing business in state

3. Rights of partners in limited partnership

    a. General partners manage partnership

    b. Limited partners invest

        (1) Limited partner who substantially manages partnership like general partner obtains liability like general partner to third parties who believed s/he was general partner

        (2) Limited partner allowed to do following without risking loss of limited liability

            (a) Acting as an agent or employee of limited partnership or a general partner

            (b) Consulting with and advising general partner or limited partnership about partnership business

            (c) Approving or disapproving amendments to limited partnership agreement

            (d) Voting on dissolution or winding up of limited partnership

            (e) Voting on loans of limited partnership

            (f) Voting on change in nature of business

            (g) Voting on removal of a general partner

            (h) Bringing derivative lawsuit on behalf of limited partnership

            (i) Being surety for limited partnership

    c. Profit or loss sharing

        (1) Profits or losses are shared as agreed upon in certificate agreement

            (a) Losses and any liability are limited to capital contributions for limited partners

            (b) If no agreement on profit and losses exists, then shared based on percentages of capital contributions

                1] Note how this differs from a general partnership in which losses and profits are shared equally unless agreed otherwise

    d. Admission of new limited partner requires written agreement of all partners unless partnership agreement provides otherwise

        (1) Admission of new general partner requires approval of only general partners

    e. Limited partnership interests may be assigned in part or in whole

        (1) If all interest assigned, then ceases to be partner unless otherwise agreed

        (2) Assignee becomes actual limited partner if all other partners consent or if assignor gives assignee that status pursuant to authority (if given in certificate of partnership)

            (a) In such case, former limited partner is generally not released from liability to limited partnership

        (3) Assignment does not cause dissolution of partnership

    f. Limited partners have right to inspect partnership books and tax return information

    g. Can be a limited and general partner at same time

        (1) Has rights, powers, and liability of a general partner

        (2) Has rights against other partners with respect to contribution as a limited partner and also as a general partner

    h. Limited partners may own competing interests

    i. Limited partner may be a secured or unsecured creditor of partnership

    j. Limited partner may not withdraw capital contribution if it impairs creditors

4. Duties of partners

    a. General partners owe fiduciary duties to general and limited partners—limited partners in general do not owe fiduciary duties

5. Dissolution of limited partnership takes place upon following events

    a. Completion of time period specified in certificate

    b. Upon event specified in partnership agreement

    c. Unanimous written consent of all partners

    d. Dissolution of court decree when not practical to continue partnership

    e. Event that causes partnership business to be illegal

    f. Withdrawal of general partner by retirement, removal, bankruptcy (but not mere insolvency), fraud against other partners, insanity, death

      (1) Unless all partners agree in writing to continue business

      (2) Unless partnership agreement allows partners to continue business

      (3) Withdrawal of limited partner does not cause dissolution

      (4) Death of limited partner does not cause dissolution

  6. If partnership not continued, winding up takes place with the following distribution of assets of partnership in order of priority

    a. To creditors including partners who are creditors

    b. To partners and ex-partners to pay off unpaid distributions

    c. To partners to return capital contributions

    d. To partners for partnership interests in proportions they share in distributions

    e. Note that in these priorities general and limited partners share equally

    f. Also, note that partners can vary their rights by agreement of all parties affected

  7. Upon dissolution, remaining partners typically complete winding-up process

  8. Dissolution of a limited partnership requires the filing of a dissolution document with the state.

I. Joint Ventures

  1. Joint venture—An association of two or more persons (or entities) organized to carry out a single business undertaking (or series of related undertakings) for profit

    a. Generally, corporations may engage in joint ventures

      EXAMPLE: X Corporation, O Corporation, and N Corporation decide to form a joint venture to bring oil from the north to the south of Alaska.

  2. Law of joint ventures is similar to that of partnerships with some exceptions

    a. Each joint venturer is not necessarily an agent of other joint venturers—limited power to bind others

    b. Death of joint venturer does not automatically dissolve joint venture

    c. Joint venture is interpreted as special form of partnership

      (1) Fiduciary duties of partners in partnership law apply

      (2) Each member has right to participate in management

      (3) Liability is unlimited and each joint venturer is personally liable for debts of joint venture

  3. Generally a joint venture is not required to file a document or certificate with the state

J. Limited Liability Companies (LLC)

  1. Laws for this relatively new form of business have been developing in the majority of states and have come to be fairly uniform

    a. This material will cover the laws passed by what is now a majority of states (and therefore testable on CPA exam)

    b. All states have passed some version (often with minor changes) of an LLC statute

  2. LLC is not considered a corporation but a majority of states provide

    a. All owners (often called members) have limited liability and therefore no personal liability

      (1) Liability of owners limited to their capital contributions plus any equity in LLC

        (a) Typically, limited liability is retained even if members fail to follow usual formalities in conducting business

        *EXAMPLE: Members of LLC fail to keep minutes of the LLC's meetings. This failure does **not** expose them to personal liability for the debts of the LLC.*

          1] Note that if a **corporation** does not follow the corporate formalities such as corporate meetings with relevant minutes, the corporate veil can be pierced, thus the corporate entity is disregarded and then shareholders of company obtain personal liability for corporation's debts

             a] This is another important advantage of LLC

    (2) Compare with limited partnership in which only limited partners can have limited liability

    (3) Some states allow sole proprietorship to be formed into LLC to obtain its advantages

  b. LLC must be formed according to limited liability company statute of the state in which it is formed

    (1) Some general partnerships or limited partnerships convert over to an LLC in which case partners retain liability they had in former partnership; they obtain benefits as new members of LLC only for transactions that take place after conversion date to LLC

    (2) LLC is foreign LLC in other states in which it does business, and laws of state where it was formed typically govern LLC in those other states

  c. LLC is separate legal entity so can sue or be sued in own name

    (1) Foreign LLC must register with Secretary of State before doing business in another state or cannot sue in state courts

  d. Most states require that name of LLC include either phrase of limited liability company or initials LLC to give notice to public

    (1) Many states allow phrase of limited company or just two initials of LC

  e. To form LLC, members must file Articles of Organization with Secretary of State

    (1) May be amended by filing articles of amendment with Secretary of State

3. Member of LLC has no interest in any specific property in LLC but has interest (personal property interest) in LLC in general

  a. Member has right to distributions according to profit and loss sharing agreed upon in operating agreement

    (1) Under Uniform Limited Liability Company Act, in absence of agreement otherwise, members divide profits and losses equally

      (a) They may instead decide to share profits in proportion to their capital contributions

      (b) They may agree to divide profits differently than losses based on different formulas

> *EXAMPLE: The members agree that the various members each receive profits and losses on bases that are different for each member. Member Q, for example, receives 15% if there is a profit in a given year, but suffers a loss of 20% if the LLC were to suffer a loss. Member R, however, is allocated 12% whether there is a profit or a loss. This is enforceable since the members agree to this.*

  b. Member has management interest

    (1) Includes rights to manage affairs of firm, vote within firm, and get information about LLC

    (2) Unless agreed otherwise, each member has equal voice in management

  c. Member may assign financial interest in LLC unless operating agreement specifies otherwise

    (1) Assignee does not become member, only receives assignor's share of profits assigned unless other members agree otherwise

    (2) Member's interest not freely transferable

4. Authority and duties in LLCs

  a. When LLC designated as member-managed LLC, all members have authority to bind LLC under agency law to contracts on behalf of LLC

  b. When LLC designated as manager-managed LLC, only managers have authority to bind LLC to contracts for LLC

(1) LLC is bound only to contracts that

   (a) Either LLC has authorized under agency law, or
   (b) Are made in the ordinary course of business

c.   In either case

   (1) Authority of both members and managers to bind LLC to contracts can be restricted in articles of organization or in operating agreement
   (2) Apparent authority of either members or managers to make contracts with third parties not affected for those who have proper notice of restrictions on contract-making authority

      (a) Restrictions in articles of organization are deemed proper notice to third parties if they are filed with Secretary of State
      (b) Restrictions in operating agreement are deemed to be proper notice to those third parties who actually receive direct notification of those restrictions

5. Other compensation

   a.   Member who is not manager has no right to compensation for services performed

      (1) Exception is for services performed in winding up LLC

   b.   Managers of LLCs receive compensation according to agreed contract
   c.   LLC must reimburse members and managers for payments they made in name of LLC
   d.   LLC is required to indemnify managers and/or members

6. Fiduciary duties owed by members and managers to LLC

   a.   Managers of manager-managed LLC and members of member-managed LLC owe LLC fiduciary duties

      (1) Both owe duty of due care to LLC but is very limited

         (a) Duty includes

            1]   To not be grossly negligent so that LLC is injured

               a]   Note that this duty of due care does not include ordinary negligence

            2]   To not intentionally, recklessly, or by breaking laws injure LLC

      (2) Both owe duty of due care to not cause injury to third parties while acting within course and scope of LLC business

         (a) This includes all duties listed above to not commit gross negligence and to not intentionally or recklessly or by breaking law injure third parties

            1]   Note that unlike duties owed to LLCs directly, this duty also makes LLCs liable for ordinary negligence of managers and members for conduct causing injury to third parties within course and scope of LLC business

      (3) Both mangers and members owe duty of loyalty to their LLC

         (a) This includes duty to act honestly, to not usurp LLC's business opportunities for self, to not secretly compete with their LLC, to not make secret deals, to not receive kickbacks or to not take position that harms their LLC

> EXAMPLE: Push, a member of a member-manager LLC, discovers a good deal on property that his LLC would want. Push wants this good deal for himself. Push must disclose the facts of the deal and let the LLC have the deal if the LLC chooses it.

7. Dissolution of LLC

   a.   Most state LLC statutes cause LLC to dissolve when

      (1) All members agree in writing to dissolution
      (2) Time period passes or event happens as specified in operating agreement
      (3) Member withdraws, is voted out, dies, goes bankrupt, or becomes incompetent

(a) Most states allow remainder of members to continue LLC if agreed upon unanimously

(4) Court order dissolves it

8. Distribution of assets upon dissolution are made in following priorities:

   a. To creditors including managers and members except for their shares in the distribution of profits
   b. To members and past members for unpaid distributions unless agreed otherwise
   c. To members to receive back capital contributions, unless agreed otherwise
   d. To members for their distributions as agreed in operating agreement, or if not agreed upon, in proportion to contributions they had made

9. Dissolution of a LLC requires the filing of a dissolution document with the state.

K. Limited Liability Partnerships (LLP)

1. Majority of states now allow LLP
2. Formation of LLP

   a. Must file articles of LLP with Secretary of State
   b. Statutes of all jurisdictions require firm's name to include phrase of limited liability partnership or registered limited liability partnership or initials LLP or RLLP to notify public
   c. Majority of states require only majority, not unanimous, approval of partners to become LLP
   d. Generally, laws of state in which the LLP is formed govern affairs of the LLP in all other states
   e. The LLP often works well for professionals who want to do business as professionals in a partnership but still pass through tax benefits while limiting personal liability of the partners
   f. Most states allow an easy transition from conventional partnership into limited liability partnership
   g. Most common law and statutory law from partnership law applies to LLP

3. Liability provisions of partners in LLP

   a. Under traditional general partnerships and limited partnerships, big disadvantage is that general partners in both firms have unlimited personal liability for partnership obligations

      (1) Most states allow LLP to be formed so there is no general partner who has unlimited personal liability

         (a) In essence, each partner is limited partner with some exceptions

            1] Regulations require specified amounts of liability malpractice insurance to, in theory, take the place of former unlimited liability of general partners
            2] In general, partners in LLP under modern trend retain full unlimited liability for their own negligence and for wrongful acts of those in LLP they supervise or have control over
            3] LLP statutes on partners' limits on liability vary somewhat by state but typically state statutes provide limits to partners' liability in important ways

               a] Some states limit liability for all debts of LLP
               b] When more than one partner is liable for negligence, liability is often proportioned

   b. Under LLP, partners avoid some personal liability for mistakes or malpractice of other partners

      (1) Popular for professionals such as accounting firms and law firms

L. Subchapter C Corporations

1. Under Federal Subchapter S Revision Act, all corporations are divided into two categories

   a. Subchapter S corporations are discussed later in this module
   b. Subchapter C corporations are all corporations that are not Subchapter S corporations

      (1) Majority of this module covers "regular corporation" also referred to as Subchapter C corporation

(a) In general most provisions for Subchapter C corporations and Subchapter S corporations are similar such as limited liability of shareholders and structure of corporate management

    1] Main distinction is tax treatment

M. Characteristics and Advantages of Corporate Form

1. Limited liability

    a. Generally a shareholder in a corporation risks only his/her investment

2. Transferability of interest

    a. Shares in corporations are represented by stocks and can be freely bought, sold, or assigned unless shareholders have agreed to restrictions

3. Continuous life

    a. Unlike a partnership, a corporation is not terminated by death of a shareholder, or his/her incapacity

       (1) Regarded as perpetual, and continues to exist until dissolved, merged, or otherwise terminated

4. Separate entity

    a. A corporation is a legal entity in itself and is treated separately from its stockholders

       (1) Can take, hold, and convey property
       (2) Can contract in own name with shareholders or third parties
       (3) Can sue and be sued

5. Financing

    a. Often easier to raise large amounts of capital than in other business organizations by issuance of stock or other securities (e.g., bonds)
    b. More flexible because can issue different classes of stock and/or bonds to suit its needs and market demands

6. Corporate management

    a. Persons who manage corporations are not necessarily shareholders and therefore may be more qualified
    b. Management of a corporation is usually vested in board of directors elected by shareholders
    c. Directors could be removed from office before their elected term is finished only for cause under common law

       (1) Increasingly states have been passing laws that allow directors to be removed at any time with shareholders' consent

N. Disadvantages of Corporate Business Structure

1. Tax treatment

    a. Tax burdens may be more than on other business structures because of double taxation

       (1) This often happens when income is taxed at corporate level and then dividends paid from after-tax income are taxed again at shareholder level

          (a) Tax breaks may partially or completely avoid double taxation

> EXAMPLE: *Single, who owns an incorporated sole proprietorship, has no taxable income at the corporate level because, in part, he pays himself a high salary rather than reporting taxable income at the corporate level and then paying himself dividends. His salary, although high, "passes muster" and he thus avoids double taxation. He pays taxes once on his salary.*

Corporation may alleviate double taxation as Subchapter S corporation by being taxed similar to partnership

    1] It may still retain advantages such as limited liability of shareholders

   2. Costs of incorporating, because must meet formal creation requirements

   3. Formal operating requirements must be met

   4. If the corporation goes public

      (1) There substantial costs of compliance with federal securities laws

      (2) May be subject to hostile takeover

O. Types of Corporations

   1. Domestic corporation is one that operates and does business within the state in which it was incorporated

   2. Foreign corporation is one doing business in any state except one in which it was incorporated

     a. Foreign corporations, if "doing business" in a given state, are not exempt from many requirements and details that domestic corporations must meet

       (1) Doing business in state is typically defined as maintaining an office or selling personal property in state

         (a) These are not considered doing business in state

            1] Defending against a lawsuit

            2] Holding bank account

            3] Using mail to solicit orders

            4] Collecting debts

            5] Using independent contactors to make sales

       (2) Foreign corporations can be required to qualify to do business in state; accomplished by obtaining certificate of authority from state

         (a) Must appoint agent to receive service of process for suits against corporation

         (b) Must pay specified fees

         (c) Must file information with Secretary of State

     b. If foreign corporation does not qualify to do business in a state

       (1) May be denied access to courts to sue

       (2) Is liable to the state for any fees, taxes, interest, and penalties as if it had qualified to do business

       (3) Is subject to fines

   3. Professional corporations are ones under state laws that allow professionals to incorporate (e.g., doctors, accountants, attorneys)

     a. All states allow professional corporations

     b. Typically, shares may be owned only by licensed professionals

     c. Retain personal liability for their professional acts

     d. Obtain other corporation benefits (e.g., limited liability for corporate debts, some tax benefits)

   4. Model Statutory Close Corporation Supplement was passed to allow corporations to choose to be close corporations.

     a. Often helps corporations made up of entrepreneurial individuals

     b. Close corporations can also be called closely held corporations or closed corporations

     c. Only corporations having 50 or fewer shareholders may choose status of statutory close corporations

       (1) To choose such status, two-thirds of shares of each class of shares of corporation must approve it

       (2) Articles of corporation must contain a statement it is a statutory close corporation

       (3) All share certificates must clearly state they are issued by statutory close corporation

     d. Close corporations may function without some of formalities of operating corporations

       (1) If all shareholders approve, close corporation may function without board of directors

(a) It is then managed by shareholders

(2) Close corporation need not hold shareholders' meetings unless at least one shareholder demands in writing that meetings be held

(3) Basically, shareholders may treat close corporation as a partnership for purposes of governing

(a) Very importantly, statutory close corporation status allows shareholders to have limited liability

5. **De facto** corporation has been formed in fact but has not been formed properly under the law

   a. Usually defective because of some small error

   b. Now, filing by Secretary of State of Articles of Incorporation is deemed conclusive proof that incorporators did all that was necessary to incorporate

     (1) Third parties cannot now challenge that corporation exists

     (2) Only state can challenge existence and dissolve or cancel corporation

6. **De jure** corporation has been formed correctly in compliance with the incorporation statute

P. Formation of Corporation

1. Promoters are persons who form corporations and arrange capitalization to begin corporations

   a. Promoter handles issuing of the prospectus, promoting stock subscriptions, and drawing up charter

   b. Promoter has a fiduciary relationship with corporation, and is not permitted to act against interests of corporation

     (1) Does not prevent personal profit if fully disclosed

   c. Promoter is not an agent of the corporation, because the corporation is still not in existence

     (1) Any agreements (preincorporation contracts) made by promoter are not binding on the future corporation until adopted after corporation comes into existence

       (a) Requires actual resolution of board of directors

       (b) Normally promoter is personally liable on contract. Adoption by corporation does not relieve promoter; **novation is required to relieve promoter**. The other party must agree to substituting the corporation

         1] Promoter has liability even if promoter's name does not appear on contract

         2] However, promoter is not liable if third party clearly states that s/he would look only to corporation for performance

       (c) Corporation is not liable to promoter for his/her services unless adopted by corporation

2. Formed only under state incorporation statutes ("Creature of statute")

3. Incorporation

   a. Articles of Incorporation (charter) are filed with the state and contain

     (1) Proposed name of corporation and initial address

     (2) Purpose of corporation

     (3) Powers of corporation

     (4) Name of registered agent of corporation

     (5) Name and address of each incorporator

       (a) Incorporators may be promoters

     (6) Number of authorized shares of stock and types of stock

   b. First shareholders' meeting

     (1) Stock certificates issued to shareholders

     (2) Resignation of temporary directors and election of new

   c. At same meeting or subsequent meeting, directors

      (1) Elect officers
      (2) Adopt or reject preincorporation contracts
      (3) Begin business of corporation
      (4) Adopt initial bylaws

         (a) These need not be filed with any government agency
         (b) Provide specific rules for management

   4. Articles of Incorporation may be subsequently amended

      a. Approval of any adversely affected shareholders of amendment needed

         (1) Often majority vote or sometimes two-thirds vote required

            (a) Dissenting minority shareholders may assert right of appraisal and therefore receive fair value for shares

               1] Fair value is value just before vote

Q. Corporate Financial Structure

   1. Definitions

      a. Uncertificated securities—securities not represented by written documents
      b. Authorized stock—amount permitted to be issued in Articles of Incorporation (e.g., amount and types)
      c. Issued stock—authorized and delivered to shareholders
      d. Unissued stock—authorized but not yet issued
      e. Outstanding stock—issued and not repurchased by the corporation (i.e., it is still owned by shareholders)
      f. Treasury stock—issued but not outstanding (i.e., corporation repurchased it)

         (1) Are not votable and do not receive dividends
         (2) Corporation does not recognize gain or loss on transactions with its own stock
         (3) Must be purchased out of unreserved or unrestricted earned surplus as defined below and as permitted by state law

            (a) If Articles of Incorporation so permit or if majority of voting shareholders permit, unrestricted capital surplus (see below) may also be used

         (4) May be distributed as part of stock dividend
         (5) May be resold without regard to par value
         (6) Can be resold without regard to preemptive rights
         (7) No purchase of treasury stock may be made if it renders corporation insolvent

      g. Canceled stock—stock purchased or received by corporation that is canceled

         (1) No longer issued or outstanding
         (2) Makes room for more stock to be issued

      h. Par-value stock

         (1) Par value is amount set in Articles of Incorporation
         (2) Stock should be issued for this amount or more
         (3) May subsequently be traded for any amount
         (4) Creditors may hold purchaser liable if stock originally purchased at below par

            (a) Contingently liable for difference between amount paid and par value
            (b) Subsequent purchaser also liable unless purchased in good faith without notice that sale was below par

      i. No-par stock—stock issued without a set par value

         (1) May have a stated value

      j. Stated capital (legal capital)—number of shares issued times par value (or stated value)

(1) If no par or stated value, then includes total consideration received by corporation

    (a) Under limited circumstances, portion may be allocated by board of directors to capital surplus as permitted by law

(2) Dividends normally may not be declared or paid out of it

(3) Following also increase stated capital by number of shares increased times par value (or stated value)

    (a) Exercise of stock option
    (b) Small common stock dividend

(4) Following do not change stated capital

    (a) Acquisition or reissuance of treasury stock under cost method
    (b) Stock splits

        1] Increase number of shares issued and decrease par or stated value (e.g., 2-for-1 stock split doubles the number of shares issued and cuts in half the par or stated value)
        2] Do not distribute assets or capital

    (c) Payment of organization costs

k. Earned surplus (retained earnings)—cumulative amount of income (net of dividends) retained by the corporation during its existence or since a deficit was properly eliminated

    (1) Note that under modern terminology, this is correctly referred to as retained earnings as indicated above; since laws written using old terms, CPA candidates should be familiar with old as well as new terms as learned in accounting

l. Net assets—excess of total assets over total debts

m. Surplus—excess of net assets over stated capital

n. Capital surplus—entire surplus of corporation less earned surplus

    (1) Note that paid-in capital is considered capital surplus

o. Contributed capital—total consideration received by corporation upon issuance of stock

2. Classes of stock

a. Common stock usually gives each shareholder one vote per share and is entitled to dividends if declared by the directors

    (1) Has no priority over other stock for dividends
    (2) Shareholders entitled to share in final distribution of assets
    (3) Votes may be apportioned to shares in other ways (e.g., one vote per ten shares)
    (4) Corporation may issue more than one class of common stock with varying terms (e.g., class may have no voting rights or different par value, etc.)

b. Preferred stock is given preferred status as to liquidations and dividends, but dividends are still discretionary

    (1) Usually nonvoting stock
    (2) Dividend rate is generally a fixed rate
    (3) Cumulative preferred means that if a periodic dividend is not paid at the scheduled time, it accumulates and must be satisfied before common stock may receive a dividend

        (a) These arrearages are not liabilities of corporation until declared by board of directors

            1] Disclosed in footnotes to financial statements

        (b) Noncumulative preferred means that if the dividend is passed, it will never be paid
        (c) Held to be implicitly cumulative unless different intent shown

    (4) Participating preferred stock participates further in corporate earnings remaining after a fixed amount is paid to preferred shares

(a) Participation with common shares is generally on a fixed percentage basis

   c. Callable (or redeemable) stock may be redeemed at a fixed price by the corporation

      (1) Call price is fixed in Articles of Incorporation or may be subject to agreement among shareholders themselves

   d. Convertible preferred gives shareholder option to convert preferred stock to common stock at a fixed exchange rate

  3. Marketing of stock

   a. Stock subscriptions are contracts to purchase a given number of shares in an existing corporation or one to be organized

      (1) Subscription to stock is a written offer to buy and is not binding until accepted by the corporation
      (2) Under the Model Business Corporation Act, stock subscriptions are irrevocable for six months
      (3) Once accepted, the subscriber becomes liable

         (a) For the purchase, and
         (b) As a corporate shareholder

      (4) An agreement to subscribe in the future is not a subscription

   b. Watered stock

      (1) Stock is said to be watered when the cash or property exchanged is less than par value or stated value
      (2) Stock must be issued for consideration equal to or greater than the par or stated value under most state laws

         (a) No-par stock may be issued for consideration that the directors determine to be reasonable

      (3) Creditors of the corporation may recover from the stockholders the amount of water in their shares; that is, the amount the stockholders would have paid to the corporation had they paid the full amount required (i.e., par value less amount paid)

         (a) If the corporation becomes insolvent
         (b) Subsequent purchaser of watered stock is not liable unless s/he had knowledge thereof

   c. Valid consideration or value for shares can be any benefit to corporation

      (1) Including cash, property, services performed, intangible property, promissory notes, other securities, or services contracted to be performed in future

         (a) Directors have duty to set value on property received

            1] Directors' value set is conclusive unless fraud shown

  4. Debt securities (holders are not owners but creditors)

   a. Debenture is instrument for long-term unsecured debt
   b. Bond is instrument for long-term secured debt

R. Powers and Liabilities of Corporation

  1. Corporations generally have following powers

   a. To acquire their own shares (treasury stock) or retire their own shares

      (1) Typically limited to amount of surplus

   b. To make charitable contributions
   c. To guarantee obligations of others only if in reasonable furtherance of corporation's business
   d. Loans to directors require shareholder approval
   e. Loans to employees (even employees who are also directors) do not need shareholder approval and are appropriate if they benefit corporation

      f.   Generally, a corporation may also be a partner of a partnership

  2. Crimes

      a.   Corporations are liable for crimes they are capable of committing

      b.   Punishment generally consists of fines or forfeiture, although directors have been faced with prison sentences for crimes of the corporation

  3. Contracts

      a.   Rules under agency law apply in corporate dealings

  4. Torts

      a.   Corporations are liable for the damages resulting from torts committed by their officers, directors, agents, or employees within the course and scope of their corporate duties

           EXAMPLE: Fraudulent deceit against a customer.

           EXAMPLE: Employee assaults a complaining customer.

  5. **Ultra vires** acts

      a.   Illegal and **ultra vires** acts are not the same

         (1) Illegal acts are acts in violation of statute or public policy

             EXAMPLE: False advertising.

         (2) Whereas **ultra vires** acts are merely beyond the scope of the corporate powers (i.e., a legal act may be **ultra vires**)

             EXAMPLE: Although legal to become a surety, the Articles of Incorporation may not allow it.

      b.   The State's Attorney General may dissolve corporation for **ultra vires** act

      c.   Stockholders have right to object to ultra vires acts

      d.   Directors or officers may be sued by shareholders on behalf of the corporation or by the corporation itself if there are damages to the corporation for ultra vires acts

S. Directors and Officers of Corporations

  1. Directors are elected by shareholders
  2. Directors' duties and powers

      a.   A director as an individual has no power to bind the corporation—must act as a board member at a duly constituted meeting of the board

         (1) Majority vote of those present is needed for most business decisions if quorum is present
         (2) Action may be taken by board with no meeting

            (a) Unless prohibited by Articles of Incorporation or by corporate bylaws, and
            (b) There must be unanimous written consent by board members for action to be taken

      b.   Powers and duties in general

         (1) Declaration of dividends
         (2) Selection of officers
         (3) Must comply with Articles of Incorporation. The Articles of Incorporation can only be amended by voting shareholders.
         (4) Typically delegate some authority (e.g., day to day or routine matters to officers and agents)
         (5) Directors are not entitled to compensation unless so provided in articles, bylaws, or by a resolution of the board passed before the services are rendered

           (a) May be reimbursed for expenses incurred on behalf of corporation

3. Director's liability

   a. General rule is that directors must exercise ordinary care, due diligence in performing the duties entrusted to them by virtue of their positions as directors, and acts in a manner he or she believes to be in the best interests of the corporation

      (1) Directors are liable for own torts committed even if acting for corporation

         (a) Corporation is **also** liable if committed within the scope of corporate duties

      (2) Business judgment rule—as long as director is acting in good faith s/he will not be liable for errors of judgment unless s/he is negligent

      (3) Directors are chargeable with knowledge of the affairs of the corporation

         (a) If director does not prevent (intentionally or negligently) wrongs of other directors, may be held liable
         (b) Normally may rely on reports of accountants, officers, etc. if reasonable judgment used

      (4) If corporation does not actually exist, then director as well as others in business have personal liability

   b. Directors liable for negligence if their action was the cause of the corporation's loss

      (1) Corporation may indemnify directors (also officers, employees, agents) against suits based on their duties for the corporation if acted in good faith and in best interests of corporation

         (a) Also applies to criminal actions if s/he reasonably believed that actions were lawful

      (2) Corporation may purchase liability insurance for officers and directors

         (a) Corporation pays premiums
         (b) Policies usually cover litigation costs as well as judgment or settlement costs

   c. Directors owe a fiduciary duty to the corporation

      (1) Owe fiduciary duties of loyalty and due care to the corporation
      (2) Conflicts of interest

         (a) Transactions of a corporation with director(s) or other corporation in which director(s) has interest are valid as long as at least one of the following can be established

            1] Conflict of interest is disclosed or known to board and majority of disinterested members approve of transaction
            2] Conflict of interest is disclosed or known to shareholders and those entitled to vote approve it by a majority
            3] Transaction is fair and reasonable to corporation

            > EXAMPLE: *A plot of land already owned by a director is sold at the fair market value to the corporation. This contract is valid even without approval if the land is needed by the corporation.*

   d. Directors are personally liable for **ultra vires** acts of the corporation unless they specifically dissented on the record

      > EXAMPLE: *Loans made to stockholders by a corporation.*

   e. Directors are personally liable to corporation for approving and paying dividends that are illegal

      (1) Directors who act in good faith may use defense of business judgment rule

4. Officers

   a. Typically operate day-to-day business

      (1) Delegated from directors

   b. An officer of the corporation is an agent and can bind corporation by his/her individual acts if within the scope of his/her authority as set forth in the bylaws

      (1) Corporation is not bound by acts of an agent beyond the scope of authority

(2) President usually has authority for transactions that are part of usual and regular course of business

(a) No authority for extraordinary transactions

(3) Acts of officers may be ratified by board

c. Officers and directors may be the same persons
d. Officers are selected by the directors for a fixed term under the bylaws

(1) If a term is not definite, it is governed by the directors

e. Officers have a fiduciary duty to corporation
f. Courts recognize a fiduciary duty owed by majority shareholders to minority shareholders when the majority shareholders have de facto control over the corporation

5. Officers, like directors, are liable for own torts, even if committed while acting for corporation

a. Corporation is also liable if officer was acting within the scope of his/her authority

6. Requirements of the Sarbanes-Oxley Act of 2002

a. Requires all members of the audit committee of the board of directors to be independent and one must be a financial expert
b. The audit committee must appoint, compensate, and oversee the work of the firm's public accounting firm
c. The chief executive officer (CEO) and chief financial officer (CFO) must certify that the financial statements are fairly presented
d. Prohibits officer or director from exerting improper influence on the conduct of the audit
e. CEO and CFO must return compensation that was derived from misstated financial statements resulting from material noncompliance with the reporting requirements

T. Stockholder's Rights

1. Right to transfer stock by endorsement and delivery or by separate assignment

a. Stock certificates are negotiable instruments
b. Limitations on transfer may be imposed, but they must be reasonable

(1) UCC requires that any restrictions must be plainly printed on the certificate to be effective against third party
(2) These limitations are most often imposed in closely held corporations

EXAMPLE: *Existing shareholders of the corporation may have first option to buy.*

2. Stockholder has no right to manage corporation unless s/he is also officer or director

a. Retains limited liability unlike limited partner who participates in management

3. Right to vote for election of directors, decision to dissolve the corporation, and any other fundamental corporate changes

a. Governed by the charter and class of stock owned
b. Annual meetings are required as specified in the bylaws
c. Stockholders may have voting agreements that are enforceable which provide that they will vote a certain way on issues or vote for specified people for the board of directors
d. Cumulative voting may be required (i.e., a person gets as many votes as s/he has shares times the number of directors being elected)

EXAMPLE: *100 shares × 5 directors is 500 votes.*

(1) Gives minority shareholders an opportunity to get some representation by voting all shares for one or two directors

e. Can vote by proxy—an assignment of voting rights
f. Directors have the power to amend or repeal the bylaws unless reserved to the shareholders by the Articles of Incorporation

g. Amendment of the Articles of Incorporation and approval of fundamental corporate changes such as a merger, consolidation, or sale of all assets generally require majority approval by shareholders

4. Right to dividends

a. Shareholder generally has no right to dividends unless they are declared by the board of directors

    (1) Power to declare is discretionary based on the board's assessment of business needs
    (2) When there is a surplus together with available cash, the shareholders may be able to compel declaration of dividends if board's refusal to declare a dividend is in bad faith or its refusal is unreasonable, but this is difficult to establish

b. Dividends become a liability of corporation only when declared

    (1) True for all types of stock such as common stock or even cumulative preferred stock

        EXAMPLE: Knave Corporation declares dividends of $10,000 to the 10,000 $1 cumulative preferred stock-holders (there is no average on these shares) and $20,000 to the 500 common stockholders. The following year is so bad that Knave Corporation is liquidated. Furthermore, no dividends are declared and general creditors are owed more than the corporation has. None of the shareholders get any dividends in this following year.

c. Cash dividends may be paid out of unrestricted and unreserved earned surplus (retained earnings) unless corporation already is or will be insolvent because of dividend

    (1) Some states have other regulations, sometimes allowing reductions in other accounts, too
    (2) Under Model Business Corporation Act, dividends are prohibited that cause total liabilities to exceed total assets after effect of the distribution is considered

5. Right of stockholders to inspect books and records exists

a. These books and records include minute books, stock certificate books, stock ledgers, general account books
b. Demand must be made in good faith and for a proper purpose

    (1) May get list of shareholders to help wage a proxy fight to attempt to control corporation
    (2) May not get list of shareholders or customers to use for business mailing list

6. Preemptive right

a. This is the right to subscribe to new issues of stock (at FMV) so that a stockholder's ownership will not be diluted without the opportunity to maintain it

    EXAMPLE: A corporation has one class of common stock. Stockholder A owns 15%. A new issue of the same class of stock is to be made. Stockholder A has the right to buy 15% of it.

b. Usually only applies to common stock, not preferred
c. Not for treasury stock
d. There is no preemptive right to purchase stock unless Articles of Incorporation so provide

7. Stockholder's right to sue

a. Stockholder can sue in his/her own behalf where his/her interests have been directly injured, for example

    (1) Denial of right to inspect records
    (2) Denial of preemptive right if provided for

b. Stockholders can sue on behalf of the corporation (i.e., a derivative suit)

    (1) In cases where a duty to the corporation is violated and corporation does not enforce, for example

        (a) Director violates his/her fiduciary duty to corporation
        (b) Illegal declaration of dividends (e.g., rendering corporation insolvent)
        (c) Fraud by officer on corporation

    (2) Unless demand would be futile, must first demand that directors sue in name of corporation and then may proceed if they refuse

(a) Suit may be barred if directors make good faith business judgment that the suit is not in corporation's best interests

(3) Damages go to corporation

8. Right to a pro rata share of distribution of assets on dissolution after creditors have been paid

U. Stockholder's Liability

1. Generally stockholder's liability is limited to his/her price paid for stock
2. May be liable to creditors for

   a. Original issue stock sold at below par value

   (1) Contingently liable for the difference between par value and original issuance price

   b. Unpaid balance on no-par stock
   c. Dividends paid which impair capital if the corporation is insolvent

3. Piercing the corporate veil—courts disregard corporate entity and hold stockholders personally liable

   a. Rarely happens but may occur if

   (1) Corporation used to perpetrate fraud (e.g., forming an undercapitalized corporation)
   (2) Owners/officers do not treat corporation as separate entity
   (3) Shareholders commingle assets, bank accounts, financial records with those of corporation
   (4) Corporate formalities not adhered to

4. Majority shareholders owe fiduciary duty to minority shareholders and to corporation

   a. Even shareholder who controls corporation (majority ownership not now needed) has fiduciary duty

V. Substantial Change in Corporate Structure

1. Merger

   a. Union of two corporations where one is absorbed by other

   (1) Surviving corporation issues its own shares (common and/or preferred) to shareholders of original corporations

2. Consolidation

   a. Joining of two (or more) corporations into a single new corporation
   b. All assets and liabilities are acquired by the new company
   c. New corporation is liable for debts of old corporations

3. Requirements to accomplish a merger or consolidation

   a. Boards of both corporations must prepare and submit plan to shareholders of both corporations
   b. Approval of board of directors of both companies
   c. Shareholders of both corporations must be given copy or summary of merger plan
   d. Majority vote of shareholders of each corporation
   e. Surviving corporation gets all assets and liabilities of merging corporations
   f. Dissatisfied shareholders of subsidiary may dissent and assert appraisal rights, thereby receiving the FMV of their stock

4. Dissolution

   a. Once corporation is dissolved, it may do business only to wind up and liquidate business

   (1) Liquidation is the winding up of affairs and distribution of assets

   (a) Liquidation occurs in the following order

   1] Expenses of liquidation and creditors
   2] Preferred shareholders
   3] Common shareholders

           (2) Termination occurs when winding up and liquidation are completed

      b. May be done by voluntary dissolution or involuntary dissolution by state for cause

           (1) Voluntary dissolution occurs when board of directors passes resolution to dissolve

               (a) Resolution must be ratified by majority of stockholders entitled to vote

      c. Shareholder may petition for judicial dissolution if directors or shareholders are deadlocked

  5. Dissolution of a corporation requires the filing of a dissolution document with the state.

W. Subchapter S Corporation

  1. Herein are some basics
  2. When corporation elects to be Subchapter S corporation it can avoid double taxation by not paying tax at the corporate level

      a. Instead, the corporation income flows through to the income tax returns of the individual shareholders
      b. Shareholders report the income or loss even when income not distributed to them
      c. This flow-through may nevertheless be an advantage under some situations

  3. Rules involving the criteria needed to be met to be taxed as a Subchapter S corporation can change to one's detriment, creating another potential disadvantage of needing to stay abreast of rule changes

      a. Some of the rules to watch out for involve

           (1) Corporation must be incorporated in the US and have only one class of stock
           (2) Number of shareholders Subchapter S corporation can have is limited to 75
           (3) Shareholders are limited to individuals, estates, qualified trusts, and similar entities
           (4) Nonresident aliens cannot own shares
           (5) The corporation cannot have excessive amounts of passive income

MULTIPLE-CHOICE QUESTIONS (1-97)

1. Which of the following statements is not true of a sole proprietorship?
   a. Federal and state governments typically require a formal filing with the appropriate government officials whether or not the sole proprietorship uses a fictitious name.
   b. The sole proprietorship is not a separate legal entity apart from its owner.
   c. The capital to start the business is generally limited to the funds the sole proprietor either has or can borrow.
   d. It is generally considered to be the simplest type of business structure.

2. A general partnership must
   a. Pay federal income tax.
   b. Have two or more partners.
   c. Have written articles of partnership.
   d. Provide for apportionment of liability for partnership debts.

3. Which of the following can be a partnership?
   a. Karen and Sharon form a charitable organization in which they received donations to give to their favorite charities.
   b. Frank and Pablo are members of a union at work that has 150 members.
   c. Janice and Stanley form a club to encourage business contacts for computer programmers.
   d. None of the above.

4. A silent partner in a general partnership
   a. Helps manage the partnership without letting those outside the partnership know this.
   b. Retains unlimited liability for the debts of the partnership.
   c. Both of the above are correct.
   d. None of the above is correct.

5. Which of the following statements is correct with respect to a limited partnership?
   a. A limited partner may not be an unsecured creditor of the limited partnership.
   b. A general partner may not also be a limited partner at the same time.
   c. A general partner may be a secured creditor of the limited partnership.
   d. A limited partnership can be formed with limited liability for all partners.

6. A partnership agreement must be in writing if
   a. Any partner contributes more than $500 in capital.
   b. The partners reside in different states.
   c. The partnership intends to own real estate.
   d. The partnership's purpose **cannot** be completed within one year of formation.

7. Sydney, Bailey, and Calle form a partnership under the Revised Uniform Partnership Act. During the first year of operation the partners have fundamental questions regarding the rights and obligations of the partnership as well as the individual partners. Which of the following questions can correctly be answered in the affirmative?

   I. Is the partnership allowed legally to own property in the partnership's name?

   II. Do the partners have joint and several liability for breaches of contract of the partnership?
   III. Do the partners have joint and several liability for tort actions against the partnership?

   a. I only.
   b. I and II only.
   c. II and III only.
   d. I, II, and III.

8. Which of the following is not true of a general partnership?
   a. Ownership by the partners may be unequal.
   b. It is a separate legal entity.
   c. An important characteristic is that the partners share in the profits equally.
   d. Each partner has an equal right to participate in management.

9. The partnership agreement for Owen Associates, a general partnership, provided that profits be paid to the partners in the ratio of their financial contribution to the partnership. Moore contributed $10,000, Noon contributed $30,000, and Kale contributed $50,000. For the year ended December 31, 2008, Owen had losses of $180,000. What amount of the losses should be allocated to Kale?
   a. $ 40,000
   b. $ 60,000
   c. $ 90,000
   d. $100,000

10. Lark, a partner in DSJ, a general partnership, wishes to withdraw from the partnership and sell Lark's interest to Ward. All of the other partners in DSJ have agreed to admit Ward as a partner and to hold Lark harmless for the past, present, and future liabilities of DSJ. As a result of Lark's withdrawal and Ward's admission to the partnership, Ward
   a. Acquired only the right to receive Ward's share of DSJ profits.
   b. Has the right to participate in DSJ's management.
   c. Is personally liable for partnership liabilities arising before and after being admitted as a partner.
   d. Must contribute cash or property to DSJ to be admitted with the same rights as the other partners.

11. Cobb, Inc., a partner in TLC Partnership, assigns its partnership interest to Bean, who is not made a partner. After the assignment, Bean asserts the rights to

   I. Participate in the management of TLC.
   II. Cobb's share of TLC's partnership profits.

   Bean is correct as to which of these rights?
   a. I only.
   b. II only.
   c. I and II.
   d. Neither I nor II.

12. The apparent authority of a partner to bind the partnership in dealing with third parties
   a. Will be effectively limited by a formal resolution of the partners of which third parties are aware.
   b. Will be effectively limited by a formal resolution of the partners of which third parties are unaware.
   c. Would permit a partner to submit a claim against the partnership to arbitration.
   d. Must be derived from the express powers and purposes contained in the partnership agreement.

13. In a general partnership, which of the following acts must be approved by all the partners?
  a.   Dissolution of the partnership.
  b.   Admission of a partner.
  c.   Authorization of a partnership capital expenditure.
  d.   Conveyance of real property owned by the partner-ship.

14. Under the Revised Uniform Partnership Act, partners have joint and several liability for
  a.   Breaches of contract.
  b.   Torts committed by one of the partners within the scope of the partnership.
  c.   Both of the above.
  d.   None of the above.

15. Which of the following actions require(s) unanimous consent of the partners under partnership law?

  I. Making partnership a surety.
 II. Admission of a new partner.

  a.   I only.
  b.   II only.
  c.   Both I and II.
  d.   Neither I nor II.

16. Which of the following statements best describes the effect of the assignment of an interest in a general partnership?
  a.   The assignee becomes a partner.
  b.   The assignee is responsible for a proportionate share of past and future partnership debts.
  c.   The assignment automatically dissolves the partnership.
  d.   The assignment transfers the assignor's interest in partnership profits and surplus.

17. Under the Revised Uniform Partnership Act, in which of the following cases will property be deemed to be partnership property?

  I.   A partner acquires property in the partnership name.
 II.   A partner acquires title to it in his/her own name using partnership funds.
III.   Property owned previously by a partner is used in the partnership business

  a.   I only.
  b.   I and II only.
  c.   II only.
  d.   I, II, and III.

18. Wind, who has been a partner in the PLW general partnership for four years, decides to withdraw from the partnership despite a written partnership agreement that states, "no partner may withdraw for a period of five years." Under the Uniform Partnership Act, what is the result of Wind's withdrawal?
  a.   Wind's withdrawal causes a dissolution of the partnership by operation of law.
  b.   Wind's withdrawal has **no** bearing on the continued operation of the partnership by the remaining partners.
  c.   Wind's withdrawal is **not** effective until Wind obtains a court-ordered decree of dissolution.
  d.   Wind's withdrawal causes a dissolution of the partnership despite being in violation of the partnership agreement.

19. Dowd, Elgar, Frost, and Grant formed a general partnership. Their written partnership agreement provided that the profits would be divided so that Dowd would receive 40%; Elgar, 30%; Frost, 20%; and Grant, 10%. There was no provision for allocating losses. At the end of its first year, the partnership had losses of $200,000. Before allocating losses, the partners' capital account balances were: Dowd, $120,000; Elgar, $100,000; Frost, $75,000; and Grant, $11,000. Grant refuses to make any further contributions to the partnership. Ignore the effects of federal partnership tax law.

After losses were allocated to the partners' capital accounts and all liabilities were paid, the partnership's sole asset was $106,000 in cash. How much would Elgar receive on dissolution of the partnership?
  a. $37,000
  b. $40,000
  c. $47,500
  d. $50,000

20. Sharif, Hirsch, and Wolff formed a partnership with Sharif and Hirsch as general partners. Wolff was the limited partner. They failed to agree upon a profit-sharing plan but put in capital contributions of $120,000, $140,000, and $150,000, respectively. At the end of the first year how should they divide the profits?
  a.   Sharif and Hirsch each receives half and Wolff receives none.
  b.   Each of the three partners receives one-third.
  c.   The profits are shared in proportion to their capital contribution.
  d.   None of the above.

21. Which of the following is(are) true of a limited partnership?

  I. Limited partnerships must have at least one general partner.
 II. The death of a limited partner terminates the partnership.

  a.   I only.
  b.   II only.
  c.   Neither I nor II.
  d.   Both I and II.

22. Alchorn, Black, and Chan formed a limited partnership with Chan becoming the only limited partner. Capital contributions from these partners were $20,000, $40,000, and $50,000, respectively. Chan, however, helped in the management of the partnership and Ham, who had several contracts with the partnership, thought Chan was a general partner. Ham won several breach of contract actions against the partnership and the partnership does not have sufficient funds to pay these claims. What is the potential liability for Alchorn, Black, and Chan?
  a.   Unlimited liability for all three partners.
  b.   Unlimited liability for Alchorn and Black; $50,000 for Chan.
  c.   Up to each partner's capital contribution.
  d.   None of the above.

23. To create a limited partnership, a certificate of limited partnership must be filed with the Secretary of State. Which of the following must be included in this certificate under the Revised Uniform Limited Partnership Act?

  I. Names of all of the general partners.
 II. Names of the majority of the general partners.

III. Names of all of the limited partners.
IV. Names of the majority of the limited partners.

    a. I only.
    b. II only.
    c. I and III only.
    d. I and IV only.

24. Mandy is a limited partner in a limited partnership in which Strasburg and Hua are the general partners. Which of the following may Mandy do without losing limited liability protection?

  I. Mandy acts as an agent of the limited partnership.
  II. Mandy votes to remove Strasburg as a general partner.

    a. I only.
    b. II only.
    c. Both I and II.
    d. Neither I nor II.

25. In a limited partnership, the limited partners' capital contribution may be in which of the following forms?
    a. A promise to perform services in the future for the partnership.
    b. An agreement to pay cash.
    c. A promise to give property.
    d. All of the above.

26. Hart and Grant formed Hart Limited Partnership. Hart put in a capital contribution of $20,000 and became a general partner. Grant put in a capital contribution of $10,000 and became a limited partner. During the second year of operation, a third party filed a tort action against the partnership and both partners. What is the potential liability of Hart and Grant respectively?
    a. $20,000 and $0.
    b. $20,000 and $10,000.
    c. Unlimited liability and $0.
    d. Unlimited liability and $10,000.

27. The admission of a new general partner to a limited partnership requires approval by

  I. A majority of the general partners.
  II. All of the general partners.
III. A majority of the limited partners.
IV. All of the limited partners.

    a. I only.
    b. II only.
    c. I and III only.
    d. II and IV only.

28. The admission of a new limited partner to a limited partnership requires approval by

  I. A majority of the general partners.
  II. All of the general partners.
III. A majority of the limited partners.
IV. All of the limited partners.

    a. I only.
    b. II only.
    c. I and III only.
    d. II and IV only.

29. Riewerts, Morgar and Stonk form a limited partnership. Riewerts is the one general partner. Which of the following events will cause this limited partnership to be dissolved?

  I. Riewerts dies and is survived by the other two partners.
  II. Morgan dies leaving Riewerts and Stonk.

III. Riewerts takes out personal bankruptcy.
IV. Stonk takes out personal bankruptcy.

    a. I only.
    b. I and II only.
    c. I and III only.
    d. III and IV only.

30. Which of the following is **not** true of a joint venture?
    a. Each joint venturer is personally liable for the debts of a joint venture.
    b. Each joint venturer has the right to participate in the management of the joint venture.
    c. The joint venturers owe each other fiduciary duties.
    d. Death of a joint venturer dissolves the joint venture.

31. Which form(s) of a business organization can have characteristics common to both the corporation and the general partnership?

	Limited liability company	Subchapter S corporation
a.	Yes	Yes
b.	Yes	No
c.	No	Yes
d.	No	No

32. Which of the following is true of a limited liability company under the laws of the majority of states?
    a. At least one of the owners must have personal liability.
    b. The limited liability company is a separate legal entity apart from its owners.
    c. Limited liability of the owners is lost if they fail to follow the usual formalities in conducting the business.
    d. All of the above are true.

33. Which of the following is **not** characteristic of the typical limited liability company?
    a. Death of a member (owner) causes it to dissolve unless the remaining members decide to continue the business.
    b. All members (owners) are allowed by law to participate in the management of the firm.
    c. The company has, legally, a perpetual existence.
    d. All members (owners) have limited liability.

34. Owners and managers of a limited liability company (LLC) owe
    a. A duty of due care.
    b. A duty of loyalty.
    c. Both a duty of due care and a duty of loyalty.
    d. None of the above.

35. Which of the following is true of the typical limited liability company?
    a. It provides for limited liability for some of its members (owners), that is, those identified as limited members (owners).
    b. The members' (owners') interests are not freely transferable.
    c. Voting members (owners) but not all members can help choose the managers of the company.
    d. No formalities are required for its formation.

36. In which of the following respects do general partnerships and limited liability partnerships **differ**?

  I. In the level of liability of the partners for torts they themselves commit.
 II. In the level of liability of the partners for torts committed by other partners in the same firm.
III. In the amount of liability of the partners for contracts signed by other partners on behalf of the partnership.
IV. In the amount of liability of the partners for contracts they themselves signed on behalf of the firm.

 a. I only.
 b. II only.
 c. I and IV only.
 d. II and III only.

37. Under the federal Subchapter S Revision Act, all corporations are designated as
 a. Subchapter S corporations only.
 b. Either a Subchapter S corporation or a Subchapter C corporation.
 c. One of seven different types of corporations.
 d. Both a Subchapter S corporation and a Subchapter C corporation at the same time.

38. Under the federal Subchapter S Revision Act all corporations are
 a. Now treated as Subchapter S corporations.
 b. Divided into either a Subchapter C corporation or a Subchapter S corporation.
 c. Divided into either a Subchapter C corporation, a Subchapter E corporation, or a Subchapter S corporation.
 d. None of the above.

39. Which of the following statements is(are) true?
 a. Both Subchapter C corporations and Subchapter S corporations have limited liability for their shareholders.
 b. Both Subchapter C corporations and Subchapter S corporations are similar in their corporate management structure.
 c. All of the above are true.
 d. None of the above are true.

40. The main difference between Subchapter S corporations and Subchapter C corporations is
 a. Their tax treatment.
 b. That the federal Subchapter S Revision Act covers Subchapter S corporations but does not cover Subchapter C corporations.
 c. Their limited liability of their shareholders.
 d. Their structure of their corporate management.

41. Which of the following statements best describes an advantage of the corporate form of doing business?
 a. Day-to-day management is strictly the responsibility of the directors.
 b. Ownership is contractually restricted and is **not** transferable.
 c. The operation of the business may continue indefinitely.
 d. The business is free from state regulation.

42. Which of the following is not considered to be an advantage of the corporate form of doing business over the partnership form?

 a. A potential perpetual and continuous life.
 b. The interests in the corporation are typically easily transferable.
 c. The managers in the corporation and shareholders have limited liability.
 d. Persons who manage the corporation are not necessarily shareholders.

43. Which of the following is **not** a characteristic of a corporation?
 a. It has a continuous life.
 b. Shares in the corporation can normally be freely transferred.
 c. A corporation is treated as a legal entity separate from its shareholders.
 d. A corporation is automatically terminated upon the death of a majority of its shareholders.

44. A corporation as a separate legal entity can do which of the following?
 a. Contract in its own name with its own shareholders.
 b. Contract in its own name with its own shareholders only if a majority of its shareholders agree that such a contract can be made.
 c. Contract in its own name with third parties.
 d. Both a. and c. are correct.

45. Which of the following are characteristics of the corporate form of doing business?
 a. Persons who manage corporations need not be shareholders.
 b. The corporation may convey or hold property in its own name.
 c. The corporation can sue or be sued in its own name.
 d. All of the above are true.

46. Which of the following is a disadvantage of a Subchapter C corporation?
 a. It may face higher tax burdens than a Subchapter S corporation.
 b. The shareholders lose their limited liability when they switch from a general partnership to a corporation.
 c. A Subchapter C corporation is not well defined under the law.
 d. A Subchapter C corporation does not protect its shareholders from liability as well as a Subchapter S corporation does.

47. Bond Company is incorporated in Florida but not in Georgia. Bond has branch offices in both states. Which of the following is correct?

  I. Bond is a domestic corporation in Georgia.
 II. Bond is a domestic corporation in Florida.
III. Bond needs to incorporate also in Georgia.

 a. I and II only.
 b. II only.
 c. II and III only.
 d. I, II, and III.

48. Colby formed a professional corporation along with two other attorneys. They took out loans in the name of the corporation. During the first year, Colby failed to file some papers on time for a client causing the client to lose a very

good case. For which does Colby have the corporate protection of limited liability?

I. The negligence for failure to file the papers on time.
II. The corporate loans.

a. I only.
b. II only.
c. Both I and II.
d. Neither I nor II.

49. Macro Corporation was incorporated and doing business in Illinois. It is doing business in various other states including Nevada. Which of the following statements is(are) true?

a. Macro must incorporate in Nevada.
b. Macro is a domestic corporation in Nevada.
c. Macro is a domestic corporation in Illinois.
d. All of the above are true.

50. Cleanit Corporation was incorporated in Colorado. Cleanit wishes to perform some transactions in other states but does not want to incorporate or obtain a certificate of authority to qualify to do business in those other states. Which of the following normally would require Cleanit to obtain a certificate of authority in other states?

a. Using the US mail to solicit orders in those states.
b. Holding bank accounts in those states.
c. Collecting debts in those states.
d. None of the above.

51. Which of the following statements is true of professional corporations under the various state laws?

I. The professionals in the corporation have personal liability for their professional acts.
II. Normally under state laws, only licensed professionals are permitted to own shares in professional corporations.

a. I only is true.
b. II only is true.
c. Both I and II are true.
d. Neither I nor II is true.

52. Which of the following statements is correct with respect to the differences and similarities between a corporation and a limited partnership?

a. Stockholders may be entitled to vote on corporate matters but limited partners are prohibited from voting on any partnership matters.
b. Stock of a corporation may be subject to the registration requirements of the federal securities laws but limited partnership interests are automatically exempt from those requirements.
c. Directors owe fiduciary duties to the corporation and limited partners owe such duties to the partnership.
d. A corporation and a limited partnership may be created only under a state statute and each must file a copy of its organizational document with the proper governmental body.

53. Under the Revised Model Business Corporation Act, which of the following must be contained in a corporation's articles of incorporation?

a. Quorum voting requirements.
b. Names of stockholders.
c. Provisions for issuance of par and nonpar shares.

d. The number of shares the corporation is authorized to issue.

54. Which of the following facts is(are) generally included in a corporation's articles of incorporation?

	Name of registered agent	Number of authorized shares
a.	Yes	Yes
b.	Yes	No
c.	No	Yes
d.	No	No

55. Absent a specific provision in its Articles of Incorporation, a corporation's board of directors has the power to do all of the following, **except**

a. Repeal the bylaws.
b. Declare dividends.
c. Fix compensation of directors.
d. Amend the Articles of Incorporation.

56. Which of the following statements is correct concerning the similarities between a limited partnership and a corporation?

a. Each is created under a statute and must file a copy of its certificate with the proper state authorities.
b. All corporate stockholders and all partners in a limited partnership have limited liability.
c. Both are recognized for federal income tax purposes as taxable entities.
d. Both are allowed statutorily to have perpetual existence.

57. Promoters of a corporation which is not yet in existence

a. Are persons that form the corporation and arrange for capitalization to help begin the corporation.
b. Are agents of the corporation.
c. Can bind the future corporation to presently made contracts they make for the future corporation.
d. Are shielded from personal liability on contracts they make with third parties on behalf of the future corporation.

58. Johns owns 400 shares of Abco Corp. cumulative preferred stock. In the absence of any specific contrary provisions in Abco's Articles of Incorporation, which of the following statements is correct?

a. Johns is entitled to convert the 400 shares of preferred stock to a like number of shares of common stock.
b. If Abco declares a cash dividend on its preferred stock, Johns becomes an unsecured creditor of Abco.
c. If Abco declares a dividend on its common stock, Johns will be entitled to participate with the common stock shareholders in any dividend distribution made after preferred dividends are paid.
d. Johns will be entitled to vote if dividend payments are in arrears.

59. Gallagher Corporation issued 100,000 shares of $40 par value stock for $50 per share to various investors. Subsequently, Gallagher purchased back 10,000 of those shares for $30 per share and held them as treasury stock. When the price of the stock recovered somewhat, Gallagher sold this treasury stock to Thomas for $35 per share. Which of the following statements is correct?

I. Gallagher's purchase of the stock at below par value is illegal.

II. Gallagher's purchase of the stock at below par value is void as an ultra vires act.

III. Gallagher's resale of the treasury stock at below par value is valid.

   a.   I only.
   b.   II only.
   c.   III only.
   d.   I and II only.

60. An owner of common stock will **not** have any liability beyond actual investment if the owner

   a.   Paid less than par value for stock purchased in connection with an original issue of shares.
   b.   Agreed to perform future services for the corporation in exchange for original issue par value shares.
   c.   Purchased treasury shares for less than par value.
   d.   Failed to pay the full amount owed on a subscription contract for no-par shares.

61. Which of the following securities are corporate debt securities?

	Convertible bonds	Debenture bonds	Warrants
a.	Yes	Yes	Yes
b.	Yes	No	Yes
c.	Yes	Yes	No
d.	No	Yes	Yes

62. All of the following distributions to stockholders are considered asset or capital distributions, **except**

   a.   Liquidating dividends.
   b.   Stock splits.
   c.   Property distributions.
   d.   Cash dividends.

63. Which of the following constitute(s) valid consideration or value to purchase shares of stock?

   a.   Services performed.
   b.   Intangible property.
   c.   Services contracted to be performed in the future.
   d.   All of the above.

64. Brawn subscribed to 1,000 shares of $1 par value stock of Caldo Corporation at the agreed amount of $20 per share. She paid $5,000 on April 1 and then paid $9,000 on August 1. Caldo Corporation filed for bankruptcy on December 1 and the creditors of the corporation sought to hold Brawn liable under her subscription agreement. Which of the following is true?

   a.   Brawn has no liability to the creditors because subscription contract was with the corporation, not the creditors.
   b.   Brawn has no liability to the creditors because she has paid more than $1,000 to the corporation which is the par value of the 1,000 shares.
   c.   Brawn is liable for $6,000 to the creditors for the amount unpaid on the subscription price.
   d.   Brawn is liable for $6,000 to the creditors based on the doctrine of ultra vires.

65. Pearl Corporation has some treasury stock on hand. Which of the following is(are) true?

   a.   Pearl may not vote these shares of treasury stock.
   b.   Pearl's treasury stock does not receive any dividends.

   c.   Both of the above statements are true.
   d.   None of the above statements are true.

66. Treasury stock of a corporation is stock that

   a.   Has been issued by that corporation but is not outstanding.
   b.   Was purchased from another corporation and is retained for a specified purpose.
   c.   Has been cancelled.
   d.   None of the above is true.

67. By law, a corporation

   a.   Must issue both common stock and preferred stock.
   b.   May issue more than one class of common stock as well as more than one class of preferred stock.
   c.   Must issue dividends if it has earned a profit.
   d.   Must issue at least some cumulative preferred stock.

68. Mesa Corporation is planning on issuing some debt securities. Which of the following statements is true?

   a.   The holders of debt securities are owners of the corporation.
   b.   A bond is an instrument for long-term secured debt.
   c.   A debenture is an instrument for long-term secured debt.
   d.   None of the above is true.

69. Stock of a corporation is called watered stock when the cash or property exchanged to acquire the stock is

   a.   Less than the market value of the stock.
   b.   More than the market value of the stock.
   c.   Less than the par value or stated value of the stock.
   d.   More than the par value or stated value of the stock.

70. Corporations generally have which of the following powers without shareholder approval?

I. Power to acquire their own shares.
II. Power to make charitable contributions.
III. Power to make loans to directors.

   a.   I only.
   b.   I and II only.
   c.   II and III only.
   d.   I, II, and III.

71. Murphy is an employee of Landtry Corporation. Which of the following acts would make the corporation liable for Murphy's actions?

I. Murphy deceived a customer to convince him to purchase one of Landtry's products.
II. Murphy hit a customer with his fist breaking his jaw. The management had warned Murphy that he and not the corporation would be responsible for any aggression against customers.

   a.   I only.
   b.   II only.
   c.   Both I and II.
   d.   Neither I nor II.

72. Which of the following statements is(are) true?

I. Corporations can be found liable for crimes.
II. Directors can face prison sentences for crimes committed by their corporations.

III. Employees can be found guilty of crimes they commit while working for their corporation.

    a. I only.
    b. I and II only.
    c. III only.
    d. I, II, and III.

73. Norwood was a promoter of Parker Corporation. On March 15, Norwood purchased some real estate from Burrows in Parker's name and signed the contract "Norwood, as agent of Parker Corporation." Parker Corporation, however, did not legally come into existence until June 10. Norwood never informed Burrows on or before March 15 that Parker Corporation was not yet formed. After the corporation was formed, the board of directors refused to adopt the preincorporation contract made by Norwood concerning the real estate deal with Burrows. Burrows sued Parker, Norwood, and the board of directors. Which of the following is correct?

    a. None of these parties can be held liable.
    b. Norwood only is liable.
    c. Norwood and Parker are liable but not the board of directors.
    d. Norwood, Parker, and the board of directors are all liable.

74. Under the Revised Model Business Corporation Act, which of the following statements is correct regarding corporate officers of a public corporation?

    a. An officer may **not** simultaneously serve as a director.
    b. A corporation may be authorized to indemnify its officers for liability incurred in a suit by stockholders.
    c. Stockholders always have the right to elect a corporation's officers.
    d. An officer of a corporation is required to own at least one share of the corporation's stock.

75. The officers of West Corporation wish to buy some used equipment for West Corporation. The used equipment is actually owned by Parks, a director of West Corporation. For this transaction to **not** be a conflict of interest for Parks, which of the following is (are) required to be true?

I. Parks sells the used equipment to West Corporation in a contract that is fair and reasonable to the corporation.
II. Parks' ownership of the used equipment is disclosed to the shareholders of West who approve it by majority vote.
III. Parks' ownership of the used equipment is disclosed to the board of directors, who approve it by a majority vote of the disinterested directors.

    a. Any one of I, II, or III.
    b. I and II are both required.
    c. I and III are both required.
    d. All three of I, II, and III are required.

76. The following are two statements concerning a fiduciary duty in a corporation.

I. Officers and directors of a corporation owe a fiduciary duty to that corporation.
II. Majority shareholders of a corporation can owe a fiduciary duty to the minority shareholders.

Which of the statements is(are) correct?

    a. I only.
    b. II only.

    c. Both I and II.
    d. Neither I nor II.

77. Hogan is a director of a large corporation. Hogan owns a piece of land that the corporation wishes to purchase and Hogan desires to sell this land at the fair market price. If he sells the land to the corporation, has he breached any fiduciary duty?

    a. No, a director does not owe a fiduciary duty to his corporation.
    b. No, since Hogan is selling the land to his corporation in a fair and reasonable contract.
    c. Yes, unless he discloses his conflict of interest to the shareholders who must then approve the sale of by a simple majority.
    d. Yes, unless he discloses his conflict of interest to the shareholders who must then approve the sale by a two-thirds vote.

78. Which of the following is **not** a power of the board of directors?

    a. May select the officers of the corporation.
    b. May declare the dividends to be paid to the shareholders.
    c. May amend the Articles of Incorporation.
    d. All of the above are powers of the board of directors.

79. Which of the following statements is(are) true under the law affecting corporations?

I. A corporation may indemnify directors against lawsuits based on their good-faith actions for the corporation.
II. A corporation may indemnify officers against lawsuits based on their good-faith actions for the corporation.
III. A corporation is allowed to purchase liability insurance for its directors.

    a. I only.
    b. I and II only.
    c. I and III only.
    d. I, II, and III.

80. Which of the following is(are) true concerning corporations?

    a. Directors owe a fiduciary duty to the corporation.
    b. Officers owe a fiduciary duty to the corporation.
    c. Both of the above are true.
    d. None of the above are true.

81. McGarry is an officer of Norton Corporation. McGarry has committed a tort while acting for Norton Corporation within the scope of her authority. Which of the following is(are) true?

    a. McGarry is liable for the tort committed.
    b. Norton Corporation is liable for the tort committed.
    c. Both McGarry and Norton are liable for the tort committed.
    d. Neither McGarry nor Norton are liable for the tort committed.

82. Acorn Corp. wants to acquire the entire business of Trend Corp. Which of the following methods of business combination will best satisfy Acorn's objectives without requiring the approval of the shareholders of either corporation?

    a. A merger of Trend into Acorn, whereby Trend shareholders receive cash or Acorn shares.

b.   A sale of all the assets of Trend, outside the regular course of business, to Acorn for cash.

c.   An acquisition of all the shares of Trend through a compulsory share exchange for Acorn shares.

d.   A cash tender offer, whereby Acorn acquires at least 90% of Trend's shares, followed by a short-form merger of Trend into Acorn.

83. Price owns 2,000 shares of Universal Corp.'s $10 cumulative preferred stock. During its first year of operations, cash dividends of $5 per share were declared on the preferred stock but were never paid. In the second year, dividends on the preferred stock were neither declared nor paid. If Universal is dissolved, which of the following statements is correct?

a.   Universal will be liable to Price as an unsecured creditor for $10,000.

b.   Universal will be liable to Price as a secured creditor for $20,000.

c.   Price will have priority over the claims of Universal's bond owners.

d.   Price will have priority over the claims of Universal's unsecured judgment creditors.

84. Under the Revised Model Business Corporation Act, when a corporation's bylaws grant stockholders preemptive rights, which of the following rights is(are) included in that grant?

	The right to purchase a proportionate share of a newly issued stock	The right to a proportionate share of corporate assets remaining on corporate dissolution
a.	Yes	Yes
b.	Yes	No
c.	No	Yes
d.	No	No

85. Under the Revised Model Business Corporation Act, which of the following actions by a corporation would entitle a stockholder to dissent from the action and obtain payment of the fair value of his/her shares?

I.   An amendment to the articles of incorporation that materially and adversely affects rights in respect of a dissenter's shares because it alters or abolishes a preferential right of the shares.

II. Consummation of a plan of share exchange to which the corporation is a party as the corporation whose shares will be acquired, if the stockholder is entitled to vote on the plan.

a.   I only.

b.   II only.

c.   Both I and II.

d.   Neither I nor II.

86. To which of the following rights is a stockholder of a public corporation entitled?

a.   The right to have annual dividends declared and paid.

b.   The right to vote for the election of officers.

c.   The right to a reasonable inspection of corporate records.

d.   The right to have the corporation issue a new class of stock.

87. Which of the following is correct pertaining to the rights of stockholders in a corporation?

a.   Stockholders have no right to manage their corporation unless they are also directors or officers.

b.   Stockholders have a right to receive dividends.

c.   Stockholders have no right to inspect the books and records of their corporation.

d.   Stockholders have a right to get a list of their corporation's customers to use for a business mailing list.

88. The limited liability of a stockholder in a closely held corporation may be challenged successfully if the stockholder

a.   Undercapitalized the corporation when it was formed.

b.   Formed the corporation solely to have limited personal liability.

c.   Sold property to the corporation.

d.   Was a corporate officer, director, or employee.

89. The corporate veil is most likely to be pierced and the shareholders held personally liable if

a.   The corporation has elected S corporation status under the Internal Revenue Code.

b.   The shareholders have commingled their personal funds with those of the corporation.

c.   An ultra vires act has been committed.

d.   A partnership incorporates its business solely to limit the liability of its partners.

90. Which of the following is correct about the law of corporations?

a.   Each shareholder owes a fiduciary duty to his or her corporation.

b.   Majority shareholders owe a fiduciary duty to their corporation.

c.   Majority shareholders do not owe a fiduciary duty to minority shareholders.

d.   All of the above are correct.

91. A parent corporation owned more than 90% of each class of the outstanding stock issued by a subsidiary corporation and decided to merge that subsidiary into itself. Under the Revised Model Business Corporation Act, which of the following actions must be taken?

a.   The subsidiary corporation's board of directors must pass a merger resolution.

b.   The subsidiary corporation's dissenting stockholders must be given an appraisal remedy.

c.   The parent corporation's stockholders must approve the merger.

d.   The parent corporation's dissenting stockholders must be given an appraisal remedy.

92. Under the Revised Model Business Corporation Act, a merger of two public corporations usually requires all of the following **except**

a.   A formal plan of merger.

b.   An affirmative vote by the holders of a majority of each corporation's voting shares.

c.   Receipt of voting stock by all stockholders of the original corporations.

d.   Approval by the board of directors of each corporation.

93. Which of the following statements is a general requirement for the merger of two corporations?

    a.   The merger plan must be approved unanimously by the stockholders of both corporations.

    b.   The merger plan must be approved unanimously by the boards of both corporations.

    c.   The absorbed corporation must amend its articles of incorporation.

    d.   The stockholders of both corporations must be given due notice of a special meeting, including a copy or summary of the merger plan.

94. Which of the following must take place for a corporation to be voluntarily dissolved?

    a.   Passage by the board of directors of a resolution to dissolve.

    b.   Approval by the officers of a resolution to dissolve.

    c.   Amendment of the certificate of incorporation.

    d.   Unanimous vote of the stockholders.

95. A corporate stockholder is entitled to which of the following rights?

    a.   Elect officers.

    b.   Receive annual dividends.

    c.   Approve dissolution.

    d.   Prevent corporate borrowing.

96. When a consolidation takes place under the law of corporations, which of the following is true?

    a.   Two or more corporations are joined into one new corporation.

    b.   All assets are acquired by the new corporation.

    c.   The new corporation is liable for the debts of each of the old corporations.

    d.   All of the above are true.

97. When a corporation elects to be a Subchapter S corporation, which of the following statements is(are) true regarding the federal tax treatment of the corporation's income or loss?

  I. The corporation's income is taxed at the corporate level and not the shareholders' level.

  II. The shareholders report the corporation's income on their tax returns when the income is distributed to them.

 III. The shareholders report the corporation's income on their tax returns even if the income is not distributed to them.

 IV. The shareholders generally report the corporation's loss on their tax returns.

    a.   I only is true.

    b.   II only is true.

    c.   III only is true.

    d.   III and IV only are true.

MULTIPLE-CHOICE ANSWERS*

1. a __ __	21. a __ __	41. c __ __	61. c __ __	81. c __ __
2. b __ __	22. a __ __	42. c __ __	62. b __ __	82. d __ __
3. d __ __	23. a __ __	43. d __ __	63. d __ __	83. a __ __
4. b __ __	24. c __ __	44. d __ __	64. c __ __	84. b __ __
5. c __ __	25. d __ __	45. d __ __	65. c __ __	85. c __ __
6. d __ __	26. d __ __	46. a __ __	66. a __ __	86. c __ __
7. d __ __	27. b __ __	47. b __ __	67. b __ __	87. a __ __
8. c __ __	28. d __ __	48. b __ __	68. b __ __	88. a __ __
9. d __ __	29. c __ __	49. c __ __	69. c __ __	89. b __ __
10. b __ __	30. d __ __	50. d __ __	70. b __ __	90. b __ __
11. b __ __	31. a __ __	51. c __ __	71. c __ __	91. b __ __
12. a __ __	32. b __ __	52. d __ __	72. d __ __	92. c __ __
13. b __ __	33. c __ __	53. d __ __	73. b __ __	93. d __ __
14. c __ __	34. c __ __	54. a __ __	74. b __ __	94. a __ __
15. c __ __	35. b __ __	55. d __ __	75. a __ __	95. c __ __
16. d __ __	36. b __ __	56. a __ __	76. c __ __	96. d __ __
17. b __ __	37. b __ __	57. a __ __	77. b __ __	97. d __ __
18. d __ __	38. b __ __	58. b __ __	78. c __ __	
19. a __ __	39. c __ __	59. c __ __	79. d __ __	1st: __/97 = __%
20. c __ __	40. a __ __	60. c __ __	80. c __ __	2nd: __/97 = __%

MULTIPLE-CHOICE ANSWER EXPLANATIONS

A. Nature of Sole Proprietorships

1.   (a)   Federal or state governments do not typically require any formal filing. If the business operates under a name different from that of the sole proprietor, most states require that a fictitious name statement be filed. Answer (b) is incorrect because the sole proprietorship and the sole proprietor are not separate legal entities. Answer (c) is incorrect because a sole proprietor does not have partners or shareholders from whom to obtain capital. Answer (d) is incorrect because the simplicity of this business structure is one of its advantages in its formation and operation.

B. Nature of Partnerships

2.   (b)   A general partnership is an association of two or more persons to carry on a business as co-owners for profit. There must be at least two partners involved in order for a partnership to exist. Answer (a) is incorrect because a general partnership is normally not recognized as a taxable entity under federal income tax laws. Answer (c) is incorrect because execution of written articles of partnership is not required to create a general partnership. A partnership agreement may be oral or in writing. Answer (d) is incorrect because a partnership does not have to provide for apportionment of liability for partnership debt. Note that even if the partners agreed to split partnership liability in a specified proportion, third parties can still hold each partner personally liable despite the agreement.

3.   (d)   A partnership involves two or more persons to carry on a business as co-owners for a profit. Partnerships do not include nonprofit associations such as charitable organizations, labor unions or clubs.

4.   (b)   A silent partner does not help manage the partnership but still has unlimited liability.

C. Types of Partnerships and Partners

5.   (c)   A general partner has a voice in management and has unlimited personal liability. Anyone, including a secured creditor of the limited partnership, may be a general partner if he/she takes on these responsibilities. Answer (a) is incorrect because an unsecured creditor of the limited partnership may also be a limited partner. A limited partner is defined as having no voice in management and his/her liability is limited to the extent of his/her capital contribution. Answer (b) is incorrect because a general partner may also be a limited partner at the same time. This partner would have the rights, powers, and liability of a general partner, and the rights against other partners with respect to his/her contribution as both a limited and a general partner. Answer (d) is incorrect because every limited partnership must have at least one general partner who will be liable for the partnership obligations.

D. Formation of Partnership

6.   (d)   A partnership agreement may be expressed or implied based upon the activities and conduct of the partners. The expressed agreement may be oral or in writing with, in general, one exception. A partnership agreement that cannot be completed within one year from the date on which it is entered into must be in writing. Answer (b) is incorrect because the partners may reside in different states without having to put the partnership agreement in writing. Answer (a) is incorrect because the $500 amount applies to the sale of goods which must be in writing, not partnerships. Answer (c) is incorrect because the purpose of the partnership is irrelevant. Agreements to buy and sell real estate must be in writing, while an agreement to form a partnership whose principal activity will involve the buying and selling of real estate normally need not be in writing unless the stated duration exceeds one year.

7.   (d)   Under RUPA, the partnership is a legal entity that can own property in its own name. The partners also

---

have joint and several liability for all debts whether they are based in contract or tort.

8. **(c)** The partners may agree to share profits as well as losses unequally. Answer (a) is incorrect because the partners may agree that ownership in the partnership is unequal. Answer (b) is incorrect because under RUPA, the partnership is a separate legal entity. Answer (d) is incorrect because the partners may agree to unequal management rights.

E. Partner's Rights

9. **(d)** Profits and losses in a general partnership are shared equally unless otherwise specified in the partnership agreement. If partners agree on unequal profit sharing but are silent on loss sharing, then losses are shared per the profit sharing proportions. The partnership agreement for Owen Associates provided that profits be paid to the partners in the ratio of their financial contribution to the partnership. The ratios are as follows:

Total contributed $10,000 + 30,000 + 50,000 = $90,000

Moore	$10,000 ÷ 90,000 = 1/9
Noon	$30,000 ÷ 90,000 = 1/3
Kale	$50,000 ÷ 90,000 = 5/9

For the year ended December 31, 2008, Owen had losses of $180,000. Therefore, Kale would be allocated $100,000 of the losses ($180,000 × 5/9).

10. **(b)** An incoming partner has the same rights as all of the existing partners. Thus, an incoming partner has the right to participate in the management of the partnership. Answer (c) is incorrect since a person admitted as a partner into an existing partnership is only liable for existing debts of the partnership to the extent of the incoming partner's capital contribution. Answer (d) is incorrect because a partner need not make a capital contribution to be admitted with the same rights as the other partners.

11. **(b)** A partner is free to assign his interest in any partnership to a third party. However, the assignee does not become a partner by virtue of this assignment, but merely succeeds to the assignor's rights as to profits and return of partner's capital contribution. The assignee does not receive the right to manage, to have an accounting, to inspect the books, or to possess or use any individual partnership property. Since Bean was not made a partner, he is entitled to Cobb's share of TLC's profits, but does not have the right to participate in the management of TLC.

F. Relationship to Third Parties

12. **(a)** A partner's apparent authority is derived from the reasonable perceptions of third parties due to the manifestations or representations of the partnership concerning the authority each partner possesses to bind the partnership. However, if third parties are aware of a formal resolution which limits the partner's actual authority to bind the partnership, then that partner's apparent authority will also be limited. Answer (b) is incorrect because if third parties are unaware of such a resolution which limits the partner's actual authority, then the partner retains apparent authority to bind the partnership. Answer (c) is incorrect because third parties should be aware that in order for a partner to submit a claim against the partnership to arbitration, unanimous consent of the partners is needed. Therefore, a partner has no apparent authority to take such an action. Answer (d) is

incorrect because as stated above, the apparent authority of a partner to bind the partnership is not derived from the express powers and purposes contained in the partnership agreement.

13. **(b)** In a general partnership, unanimous consent is required of all of the partners to admit a new partner. Answer (a) is incorrect because any one partner can cause a dissolution by actions such as withdrawing. Answer (c) is incorrect because each partner is an agent of the general partnership and thus may purchase items for the business of the firm. Answer (d) is incorrect; an individual partner may sell real property on behalf of the partnership because s/he is an agent of the partnership.

14. **(c)** Under the Revised Uniform Partnership Act, partners have joint and several liability for not only torts but also breaches of contract. This is a change from previous law.

15. **(c)** Although individual partners normally have implied authority to buy and sell goods for the partnership, they do not have implied authority to do such things as making the partnership a surety or admitting a new partner. These require the consent of all partners.

16. **(d)** A partner's interest in a partnership is freely assignable without the other partners' consent. A partner's interest refers to the partners' right to share in profits and return of contribution. Answer (a) is incorrect because the assignee does not become a partner without the consent of all the other partners. Answer (b) is incorrect because the assignor remains liable as a partner. The assignee has only received the partner's right to share in profits and capital return. Answer (c) is incorrect because assignment of a partner's interest does not cause dissolution unless the assignor also withdraws.

G. Termination of a Partnership

17. **(b)** Under RUPA, partnership property not only includes property purchased in the partnership name but also includes property purchased by a partner, who is an agent of the partnership, with partnership funds. Note that a partner may use property in the partnership business without it becoming partnership property.

18. **(d)** Even if a partner has agreed not to withdraw before a certain period of time, s/he has the power to do so anyway. That partner's withdrawal is a break of contract and causes a dissolution of the partnership. Answer (a) is incorrect because this dissolution is caused by an act of a partner rather than by operation of law. Answer (b) is incorrect because Wind's withdrawal does have an effect on the remaining partners because they must decide on what new terms they will operate or else wind up and terminate the partnership. Answer (c) is incorrect because the dissolution is effective once Wind does withdraw from the partnership. A court decree is not necessary.

19. **(a)** The best approach to answer this question is to make a chart as follows:

	Dowd 40%	Elgar 30%	Frost 20%	Grant 10%
Capital Balance	$120,000	$100,000	$75,000	$11,000
Allocation of Loss $200,000	(80,000)	(60,000)	(40,000)	(20,000)
Remaining bal- ance	40,000	40,000	35,000	(9,000)
Distribution of deficit of insol- vent Partner:				9,000
40/90 × 9,000	(4,000)			
30/90 × 9,000		(3,000)		
20/90 × 9,000			(2,000)	
Balance	36,000	37,000	33,000	0
Cash distribution $106,000	(36,000)	(37,000)	(33,000)	0
	0	0	0	0

A capital deficit may be corrected by the partner investing more cash or assets to eliminate the deficit or by distributing the deficit to the other partners in their resulting profit and loss sharing ratio. The latter was done in this case, as the facts in the question indicated that Grant refuses to make any further contributions to the partnership. The remaining cash is then used to pay the three partners' capital balances.

H. Limited Partnerships

20. **(c)** Under the Revised Uniform Limited Partnership Act, when the partners do not agree how to split profits, the split is made in proportion to their capital contributions. Note that this is different for general partners under the Revised Uniform Partnership Act.

21. **(a)** Limited partnerships must have at least one general partner who has the unlimited personal liability of the firm. Unlike a general partner, the death of a limited partner does not cause a dissolution or termination of a partner.

22. **(a)** Since Chan acted like a general partner and Ham thought he was a general partner, Chan has the liability of a general partner to Ham. Answers (b), (c), and (d) are incorrect because Ham believed Chan was a general partner based on Chan's actions. Therefore, Chan had the liability of a general partner, that is, unlimited liability.

23. **(a)** Under the Revised Uniform Limited Partnership Act, none of the names of the limited partners need to be listed in the certificate of limited partnership that is filed with the Secretary of State. However, all of the general partners must be listed.

24. **(c)** A limited partner is allowed, without losing the protection of limited liability, to act as an agent of the limited partnership. The limited partner may also vote on the removal of a general partner.

25. **(d)** Partners' capital may not only be in cash, property, or services already performed, but also may be in the form of promises to give or perform these at a future date.

26. **(d)** If the liability is more than the partnership can pay, each partner loses its capital contribution and then the general partner has personal, unlimited liability for the debt.

27. **(b)** The admission of a new general partner to a limited partnership under the Revised Uniform Limited Partnership Act requires the approval of all the general partners. Approval of the limited partners is not needed.

28. **(d)** Unlike the admission of a new general partner, the admission of a new limited partner requires the written approval of not only all of the general partners but also all of the limited partners.

29. **(c)** Death or bankruptcy of a general partner in a limited partnership will cause dissolution of the limited partnership. However, this is not true if a limited partner dies or goes bankrupt.

I. Joint Ventures

30. **(d)** The law of joint ventures is similar to the law of partnerships with some exceptions. One of these exceptions is that the death of a joint venturer does not automatically dissolve the joint venture. Answers (a), (b), and (c) are all incorrect because these are all examples in which joint venture law and partnership law are similar, involving liability, right to participate in management, and fiduciary duties.

J. Limited Liability Companies (LLC)

31. **(a)** A limited liability company provides for limited liability of its members, similar to the limited liability of the shareholders of a corporation. However, it typically has a limited duration of existence, similar to that of a partnership in which the death or withdrawal of a member or partner causes the business to dissolve unless the remaining members or partners choose to continue the business. The limited liability company can also be taxed similar to a partnership if formed to do so. The Subchapter S corporation has the limited liability of the corporation but is taxed similar to a partnership.

32. **(b)** The limited liability company statutes provide that it is a separate legal entity apart from its owners. Thus it may sue or be sued in its own name. Answer (a) is incorrect because all owners have limited rather than personal liability. Answer (c) is incorrect because limited liability is normally retained even if the owners fail to follow the formalities usual in conducting the business. Answer (d) is incorrect because (b) is correct.

33. **(c)** Limited liability companies typically have a limited life. Provisions often provide that they exist for thirty years at most and dissolve if a member dies. Therefore (a) is an incorrect response. Answer (b) is also not chosen because members (owners) are permitted to participate in the management of the LLC or can choose the management. Answer (d) is an incorrect response because one of the main benefits of an LLC is the limited liability of its members (owners).

34. **(c)** Owners and managers of an LLC owe a duty of due care to not be grossly negligent. They also owe a duty to be loyal to their LLC.

35. **(b)** In the typical limited liability company (LLC), unlike the common corporation, the interests of the members are not freely transferable. The other members have to agree to admit new members. Answer (a) is incorrect because it provides for limited liability of all of its members. Answer (c) is incorrect because all members have a voice in the management of the LLC. Answer (d) is incorrect because a limited liability company must be formed pursuant to the filing requirements of the relevant state statute.

K.   Limited Liability Partnerships (LLP)

36.   (b)   In a limited liability partnership (LLP), where permitted by state statute, the basic difference between it and a general partnership is limited liability in some cases. In the LLP, partners have limited liability for the torts of the other partners. This is not true of a general partnership. Answer (a) is wrong because both in the LLP and the general partnership, the partners have unlimited liability for their own torts. Answers (c) and (d) are wrong because any contracts signed on behalf of the firm make all of the partners jointly liable in both the LLP and the general partnership.

L.   Subchapter C Corporations

37.   (b)   The federal Subchapter S Revision Act specifies that all corporations that do not meet the criteria of a Subchapter S corporation are categorized as a Subchapter C corporation. Answers (a), (c), and (d) are incorrect because the Act provides that a corporation is either a Subchapter S or Subchapter C corporation but not both at the same time.

38.   (b)   All corporations are divided under the federal Subchapter S Revision Act as being either a Subchapter C corporation or a Subchapter S corporation. Answer (a) is incorrect because the federal Subchapter S Revision Act provides that there are two categories of corporations: Subchapter C and Subchapter S corporations. Answer (c) is incorrect because this federal law provides for only two categories of corporations. A Subchapter E corporation is not one of these. Answer (d) is incorrect because answer (c) is correct.

39.   (c)   Both Subchapter C corporations and Subchapter S corporations are similar in their provisions for the limited liability of their shareholders and also in their corporate management structures. Answer (a) is incorrect because it does not include the similarity of the corporate management structures. Answer (b) is incorrect because it does not mention the similarity of the shareholders' limited liability. Answer (d) is incorrect for the reason that answer (c) is correct.

40.   (a)   Tax treatment is the main reason why Subchapter S corporations are formed instead of Subchapter C corporations. Answer (b) is incorrect because this federal Act covers both types of corporations. Answers (c) and (d) are incorrect because the provisions on the limited liability of shareholders and the provisions for the structure of corporate management are some of the ways that Subchapter C and Subchapter S corporations are generally similar.

M.   Characteristics and Advantages of Corporate Form

41.   (c)   One advantage of the corporate form of business is that it has a continuous life and is not terminated by the death of a shareholder or manager. Answer (a) is incorrect because although the power to manage the corporation is vested in the board of directors, they usually delegate the day-to-day management responsibilities to various managers. Answer (b) is incorrect because in most corporations, ownership is not contractually restricted. In fact, free transferability of the shares of stock is a major advantage of the corporate form of business. Answer (d) is incorrect because corporations are not free from state regulation.

42.   (c)   A major advantage is that shareholders have limited liability, that is, typically limited to what they paid for the stock. However, managers do not have limited liability for their actions as managers. If a manager is also a shareholder, that person has limited liability for the ownership in the stock but can still be sued for misdeeds as a manager. Answers (a), (b), and (d) are all considered to be advantages of a corporation. Note that since a person can manage a corporation without necessarily being an owner, this can encourage professional managers to get involved.

43.   (d)   The death of one or more of a corporation's shareholders does not automatically terminate it. Answer (a) is incorrect because a corporation continues to exist until it is dissolved, merged or otherwise terminated. Answer (b) is incorrect because shares in a corporation, represented by stocks, can be freely bought, sold, or assigned unless the shareholders have agreed to restrict this. Answer (c) is incorrect because a corporation is legally a separate entity apart from its shareholders.

44.   (d)   A corporation may make contracts in its own name with both its shareholders and third parties. Answer (a) is incorrect because it may also make contracts with third parties. Answer (b) is incorrect because corporations do not generally need the consent of other shareholders to contract with one shareholder. Answer (c) is incorrect because it may also contract with its shareholders.

45.   (d)   Persons who manage a corporation may be, but need not be, shareholders of that corporation. Also, a corporation as a separate legal entity may convey or hold property. It may also sue or be sued in its own name. Answers (a), (b), and (c) are not comprehensive enough.

N.   Disadvantages of Corporate Business Structure

46.   (a)   A Subchapter S corporation is often formed to help avoid the double taxation that a Subchapter C corporation may face. Answer (b) is incorrect because partners in a general partnership have unlimited personal liability. Shareholders of a corporation have limited liability with few exceptions. Answer (c) is incorrect because a Subchapter C corporation is any corporation that is not a Subchapter S corporation. Answer (d) is incorrect because both Subchapter C and Subchapter S corporations provide their shareholders with limited liability with few exceptions.

O.   Types of Corporations

47.   (b)   Bond is a domestic corporation in Florida since it incorporated there. It is a foreign corporation in Georgia since it did not incorporate there. Bond does not need to incorporate in Georgia but must qualify to do business there because it has branch offices in Georgia. This qualifying normally entails filing required documents with the state.

48.   (b)   In a professional corporation, the professional has most of the benefits of a corporation such as limited liability for corporate debts. However, the professional has personal liability for professional acts. Colby cannot avoid liability for the damage caused the client due to negligence in a professional act.

49.   (c)   A domestic corporation is one that operates and does business in the state in which it was incorporated. Answer (a) is incorrect because Macro, instead of incorporating in Nevada, may qualify to do business by obtaining a certificate of authority from Nevada. Answer (b) is incorrect because Macro is a foreign corporation in Nevada because it did not incorporate there. Answer (d) is incorrect because the statement in (c) is the only one that is true.

50. (d)   None of the listed items are normally considered doing business in the other states such that Cleanit would be required to qualify to do business and thus have to obtain certificates of authority from those states. Therefore, answers (a), (b), and (c) are incorrect.

51. (c)   Normally, under state laws, only licensed professionals may own shares in professional corporations. Furthermore, the licensed professionals retain personal liability for their professional acts in the professional corporation. Therefore (a), (b), and (d) are incorrect.

P.   Formation of Corporation

52. (d)   Corporations and limited partnerships may only be created pursuant to state statutes. Normally, both the Articles of Incorporation and a Certificate of Limited Partnership must be filed with the Secretary of State. Answer (c) is incorrect since limited partners do not owe fiduciary duties to the partnership. Answer (a) is incorrect since limited partners have the right to vote on partnership matters such as the dissolution or winding up of the partnership, loans of the partnership, a change in the nature of the business of a partnership, and the removal of a general partner without jeopardizing their limited partner status. Answer (b) is incorrect since sale of limited partnership interests is not automatically exempted from the general securities laws' registration requirements.

53. (d)   Under the Revised Model Business Corporation Act, a corporation's Articles of Incorporation generally must include the name of the corporation, the purpose of the corporation, the powers of the corporation, the name of the incorporators, the name of the registered agent of the corporation and the number of shares of stock the corporation is authorized to issue.

54. (a)   The Articles of Incorporation are filed with the state and contain the names of the corporation, registered agent, and incorporators. This document also contains the purpose and powers of the corporation as well as a description of the types of stock and number of authorized shares.

55. (d)   Normally, the board of directors of a corporation has the power to adopt, amend, and repeal the bylaws. It also has the power to declare dividends and fix the compensation of the directors. However, it does not have the power to amend the Articles of Incorporation.

56. (a)   Corporations and limited partnerships may only be created pursuant to state statutes. Normally, both the Articles of Incorporation and a Certificate of Limited Partnership must be filed with the Secretary of State. Answer (b) is incorrect because a limited partnership requires at least one general partner who retains unlimited personal liability. Answer (c) is incorrect because a limited partnership is treated the same as a general partnership for tax purposes in that it is not recognized as a separate taxable entity. Answer (d) is incorrect because a limited partnership is not statutorily allowed perpetual existence.

57. (a)   The basic concept of a promoter is one who forms a corporation with the goal of the corporation eventually coming into existence. Answer (b) is incorrect because for there to be an agent, there must be a principal. There is

no principal yet because the corporation is not yet formed. Answer (c) is incorrect because the promoters are not agents who can bind the future corporations to contracts. Answer (d) is incorrect because the promoters are not agents and thus cannot use agency law to protect them.

Q.   Corporate Financial Structure

58. (b)   The Articles of Incorporation must include, among other things, the amount of capital stock authorized and the types of stock to be issued. Specific provisions applicable to stock must also be stated. Examples of stock provisions which must be authorized by the Articles of Incorporation include number of authorized shares, whether the stock is to be par value or no-par value, and classes of stock, including voting rights and dividend provisions. Preferred stock is given preferred status as to liquidations and dividends. This is part of the definition of preferred stock and need not be specifically included in the Articles of Incorporation in order to be enforceable. Therefore, Johns becomes an unsecured creditor upon Abco's declaration of preferred stock dividend. In order for Johns to be entitled to convert his/her preferred shares to common shares, to participate with common shareholders in any dividend distribution made after preferred dividends are paid, or to be entitled to vote if dividend payments are in arrears, it must be stated in the Articles of Incorporation.

59. (c)   Gallagher originally sold the stock at above par value. It may buy back and resell the shares without regard to par value.

60. (c)   A corporation may resell treasury shares without regard to par value. Therefore, an owner of common stock who purchased treasury shares for less than par value will not have any liability beyond actual investment. Answer (a) is incorrect because an owner of common stock who paid less than par value for stock purchased in connection with an original issue of shares is contingently liable in many states to creditors for the difference between the amount paid and par value. Answer (b) is incorrect because a promise to perform future services in exchange for original issue par value shares is an executory promise which is not considered valid consideration for shares. An owner of common stock who agreed to perform future services for the corporation in exchange for original issue par value shares is liable to creditors for the difference between any valid consideration (i.e., cash, property, or services performed) given and par value. Answer (d) is incorrect because once the corporation accepts an offer to buy stock subscriptions, the subscriber becomes liable for the purchase. Therefore, an owner of common stock who failed to pay the full amount owed on a subscription contract for no-par shares is liable for the difference between any amounts already paid and the full amount owed according to the contract.

61. (c)   Corporate debt securities include the following: (1) registered bonds, (2) bearer bonds, (3) debenture bonds, (4) mortgage bonds, (5) redeemable bonds, and (6) convertible bonds. A warrant is not a corporate debt security, but rather is written evidence of a stock option which grants its owner the option to purchase a specified amount of shares of stock at a stated price within a specified period of time.

62. (b)   A stock split increases the number of shares outstanding and proportionately decreases the par value per share. However, the total outstanding par value does not change and therefore no charge is made to retained earnings or capital. Liquidating dividends represent a return of the stockholders' capital and are considered a capital distribution. Both cash and property distributions are considered asset distributions. Property distributions are recorded at the fair market value of the asset at the date of transfer.

63.   (d)   Valid consideration or value to purchase shares of stock can be any benefit to the corporation including any services contracted for that are yet to be performed in the future.

64.   (c)   Since Brawn had a contract to purchase 1,000 shares at $20 per share, this is binding. Therefore, the creditors can recover in bankruptcy the remainder of the price not paid. Answer (a) is incorrect because the creditors have the right to see that the bankruptcy estate includes this amount owed the corporation. Answer (b) is incorrect because the contract required that the full $20,000 be paid, not just the par value. Answer (d) is incorrect because ultra vires acts are acts that are beyond the scope of the powers of the corporation. These do not apply to this fact pattern.

65.   (c)   Treasury stock are not votable nor do they receive dividends. Therefore, answers (a), (b), and (d) are incorrect.

66.   (a)   Treasury stock is stock that a corporation issued previously but is no longer outstanding because the corporation repurchased it back. Answer (b) is incorrect because treasury stock is a corporation's own stock that it has repurchased. Answer (c) is incorrect because canceled stock is no longer issued or outstanding. Answer (d) is incorrect because (a) is correct.

67.   (b)   A corporation by law may issue one or more classes of common stock. This is also true for preferred stock. Answer (a) is incorrect because a corporation is not required to issue preferred stock. Answer (c) is incorrect because it is at the discretion of the board of directors to declare a dividend. They may wish to keep the earnings in the corporation for expansion purposes, etc. Answer (d) is incorrect because if it issues preferred stock, it may be either cumulative preferred stock or noncumulative preferred stock.

68.   (b)   A bond represents long-term secured debt. Answer (a) is incorrect because holders of debt securities are creditors rather than owners of the corporation. Answer (c) is incorrect because a debenture represents long-term unsecured debt not long-term secured debt. Answer (d) is incorrect because there was one correct answer.

69.   (c)   The definition of watered stock refers to when the stock is acquired by exchanging cash or property worth less than the par or stated value of the stock.

R.   Powers and Liabilities of Corporation

70.   (b)   Corporations generally have the power to acquire or retire their own shares without shareholder approval. They can also make charitable contributions without such approval. Loans to directors require shareholder approval.

71.   (c)   A business is liable for the torts of its employees committed within the course and scope of employment. This is true even if management has warned the employee that he and not the corporation will be liable. The injured third party can hold both the employee and the corporation liable in either case.

72.   (d)   All three statements are true in the interest of punishing all parties who commit crimes.

S.   Directors and Officers of Corporations

73.   (b)   Since the corporation never adopted the contract by words or actions, it is not liable. The board of directors is not personally liable either because they never agreed to the contract. However, Norwood is personally liable on the contract because he signed the contract and agency law will not protect him. This is true because he was not an agent, even though he claimed to be, because there was no principal to authorize him when the contract was made on March 15.

74.   (b)   Under the Revised Model Business Corporation Act, a corporation is authorized to indemnify its officers for expenses, attorney fees, judgments, fines and amounts paid in settlement incurred in a suit by stockholders when the liability is a result of the officer's good faith, nonnegligent actions on behalf of the best interest of the corporation. Answer (a) is incorrect because a corporate officer may also serve as a director. Answer (c) is incorrect because officers are appointed by the directors of a corporation who are in turn elected by the shareholders. Answer (d) is incorrect because there is no requirement that an officer must own any shares of the corporation's stock.

75.   (a)   The transaction the director wishes to have with the corporation is not a conflict of interest if any one of the following is true. (1) The transaction is fair and reasonable for the corporation. (2) The shareholders are given the relevant facts and they approve it by a majority vote. (3) The board of directors are given the relevant facts and they approve it by a majority vote of the disinterested members of the board of directors.

76.   (c)   Officers and directors are in important positions in a corporation. As such, they owe a fiduciary duty to the corporation to act in the best interests of the corporation. Courts have also recognized that because majority shareholders can exercise a lot of power in a corporation from their stockholdings and voting rights, they owe a fiduciary duty to the minority shareholders when these majority shareholders have de facto control over the corporation by virtue of their concentrated ownership.

77.   (b)   A contract between a director and his/her corporation is valid if it is reasonable to the corporation. Hogan has not breached his fiduciary duty with the corporation since he is selling the land at fair market value. Answer (a) is incorrect because a director does owe a fiduciary duty to his/her corporation to act in its best interests. Answers (c) and (d) are incorrect because since the transaction is fair and reasonable to the corporation, the shareholders need not approve it.

78.   (c)   The Articles of Incorporation may be amended by the shareholders' vote, not by the board of directors. Answer (a) is incorrect because one of the important powers of the directors is to select the officers of the corporation. Answer (b) is incorrect because it is up to the board of directors to declare any dividends to the shareholders. Answer (d) is incorrect because answer (c) is correct.

79. (d)   A corporation may indemnify both its directors as well as its officers against suits based on their duties for the corporation if they acted in good faith and in the best interests of the corporation. A corporation may also purchase insurance to cover the liability for lawsuits lost based on actions of its directors and also its officers.

80. (c)   Both directors as well as officers owe a fiduciary duty to their corporation.

81. (c)   McGarry is liable for the tort she committed. Because she was acting within the scope of her authority in the corporation, Norton corporation is also liable. Note that McGarry is not relieved of liability even though Norton Corporation is also liable because McGarry is the one who committed the tort. Therefore, answers (a), (b), and (d) are incorrect.

T.   Stockholder's Rights

82. (d)   When Acorn pays cash and buys 90% or more of Trend's shares, it has control of the Trend stock. It can then accomplish a short-form merger of Trend Corp. into Acorn Corp. Answer (a) is incorrect because this can require the approval of Acorn shareholders. Answer (b) is incorrect because this is not a regular sale of Trend's assets and will require shareholder approval. Answer (c) is incorrect because the entire compulsory exchange for Acorn shares to accomplish the acquisition does require shareholder approval.

83. (a)   Upon declaration, a cash dividend on preferred stock becomes a legal debt of the corporation, and the preferred shareholders become unsecured creditors of the corporation. However, any dividends not paid in any year concerning cumulative preferred stock are not a liability of the corporation until they are declared. Therefore, Universal will be liable to Price as an unsecured creditor for $10,000, which is the amount of the declared dividends. Answers (c) and (d) are incorrect because Price has become a general unsecured creditor for the declared dividends and will have the same priority as the debenture (unsecured) bond owners and the unsecured judgment creditors. Answer (b) is incorrect because the undeclared dividends did not become a legal liability to Universal.

84. (b)   The preemptive right gives the shareholder the right to purchase newly issued stock so as to keep the same overall percentage of ownership of the corporation. The way this is done is by allowing him/her to purchase a proportionate share. Otherwise, his/her ownership of the overall corporation may become diluted.

85. (c)   When the rights of individual shareholders may be adversely affected, the shareholder is given the right to dissent and receive payment of the fair value of his/her shares. This is true even if the dissenting shareholder has voting rights when s/he is being outvoted. In I., the shareholder has this right because his/her preference rights are being abolished. In II., the dissenting shareholder has this right because his/her shares being acquired by another corporation may affect the value and rights of the shares of stock.

86. (c)   Shareholders have the right to inspect the corporate records if done in good faith for a proper purpose. Answer (a) is incorrect because shareholders do not have a right to dividends. It is the decision of the board of directors

whether or not to declare dividends. Answer (b) is incorrect because although at least one class of stock must have voting rights to elect the **board of directors,** the **officers** may be selected by the board of directors. Answer (d) is incorrect because the shareholders cannot force an issuance of a new class of stock.

87. (a)   Stockholders do not have the right to manage their corporation. However, stockholders who are also directors or officers do have the right to manage as part of their rights as directors and officers. Answer (b) is incorrect because stockholders generally have no right to receive dividends unless the board of directors declares such dividends. Answer (c) is incorrect because stockholders are given the right to inspect the books and records of their corporation. Answer (d) is incorrect because the stockholders may demand a list of shareholders for a proper purpose such as to help wage a proxy fight; however, they may not require the corporation to give them a list of its customers to use for a mailing list.

U.   Stockholder's Liability

88. (a)   Normally, the liability of shareholders of corporations is limited to their capital contribution. However, the court will "pierce the corporate veil" and hold the shareholders personally liable for the debts of the corporation if the corporate entity is being used to defraud people or to achieve other injustices. Thus, if the shareholders establish a corporation, knowing that it would have less capital than required for it to pay its debts, then the court will "pierce the corporate veil" and hold the shareholders personally liable. Answer (c) is incorrect because a shareholder may sell property to the corporation without becoming personally liable for the debts of the corporation. Answer (d) is incorrect because shareholders may also be corporate officers, directors or employees without jeopardizing their limited liability status. Answer (b) is incorrect because the formation of a corporation solely to limit personal liability is a valid purpose so long as it is done without intent to defraud.

89. (b)   The court will disregard the corporate entity and hold the shareholders individually liable when the corporate form is used to perpetrate a fraud or is found to be merely an agent or instrument of its owners. An example of when the corporate veil is likely to be pierced is if the corporation and its shareholders commingle assets and financial records. In such a situation, the shareholders lose their limited liability and will be held personally liable for the corporation's legal obligations. Answer (a) is incorrect because the election of S corporation status is allowable under the law and is not, in itself, grounds for piercing the corporate veil. Answer (d) is incorrect because the desire of shareholders to limit their personal liability is a valid reason to form a corporation. Limited personal liability is one advantage of the corporate entity. Answer (c) is incorrect since the court will hold personally liable only those corporate officers responsible for the commission of an **ultra vires** act. The court will not pierce the corporate veil and hold the shareholders personally liable for such an act.

90. (b)   Majority shareholders now owe a fiduciary duty to their corporation. Answer (a) is incorrect because minority shareholders do not owe a fiduciary duty to their corporation. Their main purpose normally is to be investors. Answer (c) is incorrect because majority shareholders now not only owe a fiduciary duty to their corporation but also to the minority shareholders. Answer (d) is incorrect because answer (b) is correct.

V. Substantial Change in Corporate Structure

91. (b) Under the Revised Model Business Corporation Act, a corporation that owns at least 90% of the outstanding shares of each class of stock of the subsidiary may merge the subsidiary into itself without approval by the shareholders of the parent or subsidiary. The approval of the shareholders or the subsidiary's board of directors is unnecessary since the parent owns 90% of the subsidiary. This ownership assures that the plan of the merger would be approved. The only requirement is a merger resolution by the board of directors of the parent corporation. Furthermore, the dissenting shareholders of the subsidiary must be given an appraisal remedy, that is the right to obtain payment from the parent for their shares. The shareholders of the parent do not have this appraisal remedy because the merger has not materially changed their rights.

92. (c) In order for a merger of two public corporations to be accomplished, it is required that a formal plan of merger be prepared and that the merger plan be approved by a majority of the board of directors and stockholders of both corporations.

93. (d) As one of the steps leading up to a merger of two corporations, the stockholders need to be given notice of the merger plan. This is true of the stockholders of both corporations, so a special meeting is called inviting both sets of stockholders. Answers (a) and (b) are incorrect because unanimous approval is not needed by either the stockholders or the boards of either corporation. Answer (c) is incorrect because the absorbed corporation will no longer exist after the merger plan is accomplished.

94. (a) A corporation voluntarily dissolves when its board of directors passes a resolution to dissolve and liquidate. Answer (d) is incorrect because this resolution must be ratified by a majority of stockholders who are entitled to vote. Following ratification, the corporation must file a certificate of dissolution with the proper state authority, cease business, wind up its affairs, and publish notice of its dissolution. Answers (b) and (c) are incorrect because they are not requirements of a voluntary dissolution.

95. (c) Shareholders have the right to vote on the dissolution of the corporation. Stockholders also have the right to elect the directors of the corporation, who in turn elect the officers. Answer (b) is incorrect as shareholders do not have the right to receive dividends unless they are declared by the board of directors. Answer (d) is incorrect as shareholders are not necessarily involved in the management of the corporation and cannot prevent corporate borrowing.

96. (d) Under corporate law when a consolidation takes place, one new corporation comes from the joining of two or more corporations. Also, the assets and liabilities of the old corporations are acquired by the new corporation and the new corporation is liable for the debts of the old corporations.

W. Subchapter S Corporation

97. (d) When a corporation elects to be a Subchapter S corporation, the corporate income and loss flow through to the income tax returns of the individual shareholders even when the income is not distributed to them. Answer (a) is incorrect because the corporation's income is not taxed at the corporate level when the Subchapter S election is made. Answer (b) is incorrect because the income flows through to the stockholders' tax returns regardless of when the distribution takes place. Answer (c) is incorrect because statement IV as well as statement III are both correct as discussed above.

INFORMATION TECHNOLOGY

Computers have become the primary means used to process financial accounting information and have resulted in a situation in which auditors must be able to use and understand current information technology. Accordingly, knowledge of information technology implications is included in the Business Environment & Concepts section of the CPA exam. In addition, auditing procedures relating to information technology (IT) are included in the Auditing & Attestation portion of the CPA exam.

Ideally, to effectively reply to technology-related questions, you should have previously studied or worked in computerized business environments. However, if you do not have this background, we believe that the information in this module should prepare you to perform reasonably well on a typical exam. Keep in mind that the review of these materials cannot make you an expert, and a module such as this cannot cover all possible topics related to information technology. However, this material should help you to understand the complexities introduced by computers in sufficient detail to answer most questions.

Study Program for IT Implications

This module is organized as follows:

A. Information Systems within a Business

 1. Definition
 2. Manual vs. Computer Systems
 3. General Types of Computer Systems

B. Characteristics of Computer Systems—General

 1. Types of Computers, Hardware and Software
 2. Methods of Processing
 3. Methods of Data Structure

C. Characteristics of Computer Systems—Specific

 1. Types of Networks
 2. Local Area Networks
 3. Microcomputers
 4. End-User Computing
 5. Electronic Commerce
 6. Telecommunications
 7. Computer Service Organizations (Bureaus, Centers)

D. Effect of IT on Internal Control

 1. Principles of a Reliable System and Examples of Overall Risks
 2. Control Environment
 3. Risk Assessment
 4. Information and Communication
 5. Monitoring
 6. Control Activities—Overall
 7. Computer General Control Activities
 8. Computer Application Control Activities—Programmed Control Activities
 9. Application Controls—Manual Follow-Up of Computer Exception Reports
 10. User Control Activities
 11. Disaster Recovery

E. Flowcharting

 1. Common Flowcharting Symbols
 2. Types and Definitions
 3. Other Documentation Charting Techniques

A.   Information Systems within a Business

1.   **Definition**—An information system processes data and transactions to provide users with the information they need to plan, control and operate an organization, including

   a.   Collecting transaction and other data
   b.   Entering it into the information system
   c.   Processing the data
   d.   Providing users with the information needed
   e.   Controlling the process

2.   **Manual vs. Computer Systems**

   a.   On an overall basis, manual accounting systems have in most circumstances been replaced by computerized accounting information systems of various types, although portions of many systems remain manual.
   b.   Computer processing tends to reduce or eliminate processing time

      (1)   Computational errors
      (2)   Errors in processing routine transactions (when fraud is not involved)

3.   **General Types of Computer Systems**

   a.   **Transaction processing systems**—Involve the daily processing of transactions (e.g., airplane reservation systems, payroll recording, cash receipts, cash disbursements)
   b.   **Management reporting systems**—Designed to help with the decision making process by providing access to computer data

      (1)   **Management information systems**—Systems designed to provide past, present and future information for planning, organizing and controlling the operations of the organization
      (2)   **Decision support systems**—Computer-based information systems that combine models and data to resolve nonstructured problems with extensive user involvement
      (3)   **Expert systems**—Computer systems that apply reasoning methods to data in a specific relatively structured area to render advice or recommendations, much like a human expert
      (4)   **Executive information systems**—Computerized systems that are specifically designed to support executive work

   NOTE: It is helpful to consider these two distinct roles for systems—that is, (a) recording transactions of various types versus (b) providing support for decision making. These topics are discussed in detail under topic B.2. (Methods of Processing).

B.   Characteristics of Computer Systems—General

1.   **Types of Computers, Hardware, and Software**

   a.   **Types of computers (in order of size and power)**

      (1)   **Supercomputers**—Extremely powerful, high-speed computers used for extremely high-volume and/or complex processing needs
      (2)   **Mainframe computers**—Large, powerful, high-speed computers. While less powerful than supercomputers, they are ordinarily more powerful than smaller computers.
      (3)   **Minicomputers**—While large and powerful, they are not as large or as powerful as mainframe computers.
      (4)   **Microcomputers (e.g., personal computers, laptop computers)**—Small computers, such as those in many homes and businesses
      (5)   **Personal digital assistants (PDA)**—Mobile, handheld computers

   b.   **Hardware—Physical equipment**

      (1)   **Central processing unit (CPU)**—The principal hardware components of a computer. It contains an arithmetic/logic unit, primary memory, and a control unit. The major function of the CPU is to fetch stored instructions and data, decode the instructions, and carry out the instructions.

         (a)   **Arithmetic/logic unit**—Performs mathematical operations and logical comparisons

(b) **Primary memory (storage)**—Active data and program steps that are being processed by the CPU. It may be divided into RAM (random-access memory) and ROM (read-only memory). Application programs and data are stored in the RAM at execution time.

(c) **Control unit**—Interprets program instructions and coordinates input, output, and storage devices.

(2) **Secondary storage**

(a) **Method of access**

1] **Random**—Accessed directly regardless of how it is physically stored. Disks are random-access devices, although they can also process data sequentially. Also referred to as direct access.

2] **Sequential**—Data must be processed in the order in which it is physically stored. Magnetic tape is a sequential storage device.

(b) **Storage devices**

1] **Magnetic tape (or cartridge)**—Cheapest type of storage available. A primary medium for backing up random-access disk files.

2] **Magnetic disks**

a] Those for mainframe computers appear as a stack of CDs, except the space between them includes a read/write head.

b] Those for microcomputers are referred to as "hard disks" or "hard drives."

3] **RAID (Redundant array of independent [previously, inexpensive] disks)**—A way of storing the same data redundantly on multiple magnetic disks

a] When originally recorded, data is written to multiple disks to decrease the likelihood of loss of data.

b] If a disk fails, at least one of the other disks has the information and continues operation.

4] **Compact disks**—Small, easily transportable, greater storage capacity than floppy disks

5] **Floppy disks**—Small, easily transportable

6] **Zip disks**—Similar to floppy diskettes, but with much greater storage capacity

7] **Optical disks**—Use laser technology to store and read data

(c) **Manner in which information is represented in a computer**

1] **Digital**—A computer that represents information by numerical (binary) digits; computers that process accounting information are ordinarily digital

2] **Analog**—A computer that represents information by variable quantities; used for research in design where many different shapes and speeds can be tried out quickly (e.g., an analog computer may be used to measure the effects of differing weights on automobile suspension)

(d) **Related computer terms**

1] **Online**—Equipment in direct communication with, and under the control of, the CPU

2] **Off-line**—Equipment not in direct communication with the CPU; the operator generally must intervene to connect off-line equipment or data to the CPU (e.g., mount a magnetic tape of archival data)

3] **Console**—A terminal used for communication between the operator and the computer (e.g., the operator of a mainframe computer)

4] **Peripheral equipment**—All non-CPU hardware that may be placed under the control of the central processor. Classified as online or off-line, this equipment consists of input, storage, output, and communication.

5] **Controllers**—Hardware units designed to operate specific input-output units

6] **Buffer**—A temporary storage unit used to hold data during computer operations

    7] **MIPS**—Millions of instructions per second; a unit for measuring the execution speed of computers

(3) Input devices

(a) Keying data

    1] **Key-to-tape** and **key-to-disk** in which data is entered on tapes and disks respectively, and then read into a computer

(b) Online entry

    1] **Visual display terminal**—Uses keyboard to directly enter data into computer

      a] **Input interface**—A program that controls the display for the user (usually on a computer monitor) and that allows the user to interact with the system

      b] **Graphical user interface (GUI)** uses icons, pictures, and menus instead of text for inputs (e.g., Windows).

      c] **Command line interface**—Uses text-type commands

    2] **Mouse, joystick, light pens**—Familiar devices that allow data entry

    3] **Touch-sensitive screen**—Allows users to enter data from a menu of items by touching the surface of the monitor

(c) Turnaround documents—Documents that are sent to the customer and returned as inputs (e.g., utility bills)

(d) Automated source data input devices

    1] **Magnetic tape reader**—A device capable of sensing information recorded as magnetic spots on magnetic tape

    2] **Magnetic ink character reader (MICR)**—Device that reads characters that have been encoded with a magnetic ink (e.g., bank check readers)

    3] **Scanner**—A device that reads characters on printed pages

    4] **Automatic teller machine (ATM)**—A machine used to execute and record transactions with financial institutions

    5] **Radio frequency data communication**—Using radio waves to directly input data

    6] **Point-of-sale (POS) recorders**—Devices that read price and product code data (e.g., recall purchasing groceries—items are frequently passed over a POS recorder). POS recorders ordinarily function as both a terminal and a cash register.

      a] POS processing allows one to record and track customer orders, process credit and debit cards, connect to other systems in a network, and manage inventory. Generally, a POS terminal has as its core a personal computer, which is provided with application-specific programs and input/output devices for the particular environment in which it will serve.

      b] POS terminals are used in most industries that have a point of sale such as a service desk, including restaurants, lodging, entertainment, and museums. For example, a POS system for a restaurant is likely to have all menu items stored in a database that can be queried for information in a number of ways.

      c] Increasingly, POS terminals are also Web-enabled, which makes remote training and operation possible, as well as inventory tracking across geographically dispersed locations.

    7] **Voice recognition**—A system that understands spoken words and transmits them into a computer

(e) Electronic commerce and electronic data interchange—Involves one company's computer communicating with another's computer. For example, a buyer electronically sending a purchase order to a supplier. Discussed in further detail in section C.5. of this module.

(4) Output devices

    (a) Many automated source data input devices and electronic commerce/electronic data interchange devices [(3)(d) and (e) above] are capable of outputting data ("writing" in addition to "reading") and therefore become output devices as well as input devices.

    (b) **Monitors**—Visually display output

    (c) **Printers**—Produce paper output

    (d) **Plotters**—Produce paper output of graphs

    (e) **Computer output to microfilm or microfiche (COM)**—Makes use of photographic process to store output

c.   **Software—Computer programs that control hardware**

    (1) **Systems software**

        (a) **Operating system**—Manages the input, output, processing and storage devices and operations of a computer (e.g., Windows, Linux, Unix)

            1] Performs scheduling, resource allocation, and data retrieval based on instructions provided in job control language

        (b) **Utility programs**—Handle common file, data manipulation and "housekeeping" tasks

        (c) **Communications software**—Controls and supports transmission between computers, computers and monitors, and accesses various databases

    (2) **Applications software**—Programs designed for specific uses, or "applications," such as

        (a) Word processing, graphics, spreadsheets, and database systems

        (b) Accounting software

            1] **Low-end**—All in one package, designed for small organizations

            2] **High-end**—Ordinarily in modules (e.g., general ledger, receivables)

            3] **Enterprise Resource Planning (ERP)**—Designed as relatively complete information system "suites" for large and medium size organizations (e.g., human resources, financial applications, manufacturing, distribution). Major vendors are well known—SAP, PeopleSoft, Oracle, BAAN, and J.D. Edwards.

               a] Advantages of ERP systems—Integration of various portions of the information system, direct electronic communication with suppliers and customers

               b] Disadvantages of ERP systems—Complexity, costs, integration with supplier and customer systems may be more difficult than anticipated

    (3) **Software terms**

        (a) **Compiler**—Produces a machine language object program from a source program language

        (b) **Multiprocessing**—Simultaneous execution of two or more tasks, usually by two or more CPUs that are part of the same system

        (c) **Multitasking**—The simultaneous processing of several jobs on a computer

        (d) **Object program**—The converted source program that was changed using a compiler to create a set of machine readable instructions that the CPU understands

        (e) **Source program**—A program written in a language from which statements are translated into machine language; computer programming has developed in "generations"

            1] Machine language (composed of combinations of 1's and 0's that are meaningful to the computer)

            2] Assembly language (e.g., Fortran)

            3] "High-level" programming languages (e.g., C++, Java)

               a] C++ and Java are considered object-oriented programs (OOP) in that they are based on the concept of an "object" which is a data structure that uses a set of routines, called "methods," which operate on the data. The "objects" are efficient in that they often are reusable in other programs.

b] Object-oriented programs keep together data structures and procedures (methods) through a procedure referred to as encapsulation. Basic to object-oriented programs are the concepts of a class (a set of objects with similar structures) and inheritance (the ability to create new classes from existing classes).

4] An "application specific" language usually built around database systems. These programs are ordinarily closer to human languages than the first three generations (e.g., an instruction might be *Extract all Customers where "Name" is Jones*).

5] A relatively new and developing form that includes visual or graphical interfaces used to create source language that is usually compiled with a 3rd or 4th language compiler

(f) **Virtual memory (storage)**—Online secondary memory that is used as an extension of primary memory, thus giving the appearance of larger, virtually unlimited internal memory

(g) **Protocol**—Rules determining the required format and methods for transmission of data

(4) **Programming terms**

(a) **Desk checking**—Review of a program by the programmer for errors before the program is run and debugged on the computer

(b) **Debug**—To find and eliminate errors in a computer program. Many compilers assist debugging by listing errors in the program such as invalid commands.

(c) **Edit**—To correct input data prior to processing

(d) **Loop**—A set of program instructions performed repetitively a predetermined number of times, or until all of a particular type of data has been processed

(e) **Memory dump**—A listing of the contents of storage

(f) **Patch**—A section of coding inserted into a program to correct a mistake or to alter a routine

(g) **Run**—A complete cycle of a program including input, processing and output

2. **Methods of Processing**

a. **Batch or online real-time**

(1) **Batch**

(a) Transactions flow through the system in groups of like transactions (batches). For example, all cash receipts on accounts receivable for a day may be aggregated and run as a batch.

(b) Ordinarily leaves a relatively easy-to-follow audit trail

(2) **Online real-time** (also referred to as **direct access processing**)

General: Transactions are processed in the order in which they occur, regardless of type. Data files and programs are stored online so that updating can take place as the edited data flows to the application. System security must be in place to restrict access to programs and data to authorized persons. Online systems are often categorized as being either online transaction processing systems or online analytical processing systems.

(a) **Online transaction processing (OLTP)**

1] Databases that support day-to-day operations

2] Examples: airline reservations systems, bank automatic teller systems, and Internet Web site sales systems

(b) **Online analytical processing (OLAP)**

1] A category of software technology that enables the user to query the system (retrieve data), and conduct an analysis, etc., ordinarily while the user is at a PC. The result is generated in seconds. OLAP systems are primarily used for analytical analysis.

EXAMPLE: An airline's management downloads its OLTP reservation information into another database to allow analysis of that reservation information. At a minimum, this will allow analysis without tying up the OLTP system that is used on a continuous basis; the restructuring of the data into another database is also likely to make a more detailed analysis possible.

2] Uses statistical and graphical tools that provide users with various (often multidimensional) views of their data, and allows them to analyze the data in detail

3] These techniques are used as **decision support systems** (computer-based information systems that combine models and data in an attempt to solve relatively unstructured problems with extensive user involvement).

4] One approach to OLAP is to periodically download and combine operational databases into a **data warehouse** (a subject-oriented, integrated collection of data used to support management decision-making processes) or a **data mart** (a data warehouse that is limited in scope).

     a] **Data mining**—Using sophisticated techniques from statistics, artificial intelligence and computer graphics to explain, confirm and explore relationships among data (which is often stored in a data warehouse or data mart)

5] **Artificial intelligence (AI)**—Computer software designed to help humans make decisions. AI may be viewed as an attempt to model aspects of human thought on computers. AI ordinarily deals with decisions that may be made using a relatively structured approach. It frequently involves using a computer to quickly solve a problem that a human could ultimately solve through extremely detailed analysis.

6] **Expert system**—One form of AI. A computerized information system that guides decision processes within a well-defined area and allows decisions comparable to those of an expert. Expert knowledge is modeled into a mathematical system.

     EXAMPLE: An expert system may be used by a credit card department to authorize credit card purchases so as to minimize fraud and credit losses.

b. **Centralized, Decentralized, or Distributed**

   (1) **Centralized**

     (a) Processing occurs at one location.
     (b) Historically, this is the model used in which a mainframe computer processes data submitted to it through terminals.
     (c) Today, centralized vs. decentralized processing is often a matter of degree—how much is processed by a centralized computer vs. how much by decentralized computers.

   (2) **Decentralized**

     (a) Processing (and data) are stored on computers at multiple locations.
     (b) Ordinarily the computers involved are not interconnected by a network, so users at various sites cannot share data.
     (c) May be viewed as a collection of independent databases, rather than a single database.
     (d) End-user computing (topic C.4. below) is relatively decentralized.

   (3) **Distributed**

     (a) Transactions for a single database are processed at various sites.

       EXAMPLE: Payroll is processed for Minneapolis employees in Minneapolis, and for Santa Fe employees in Santa Fe. Yet the overall payroll information is in one database.

     (b) Processing may be on either a batch or online real-time basis.
     (c) An overall single data base is ordinarily updated for these transactions and available at the various sites.

3. **Methods of Data Structure**

a. **Data organization for computer operations**

   (1) **Bit**—A binary digit (0 or 1) which is the smallest storage unit in a computer

(2) **Byte**—A group of adjacent bits (usually 8) that is treated as a single unit by the computer. Alphabetic, special and some numeric characters can be represented by a bit. A numeric character that is used in computations may use more than one byte.

(3) **Character**—A letter, number, or other symbols; a character is ordinarily printable as a symbol (e.g., the character "a" or ";")

(4) **Alphanumeric**—Alphabetic, numeric, and special characters (special characters are pluses, minuses, dollar signs, etc.)

(5) **Field**—A group of related characters (e.g., a social security number)

(6) **Record**—An ordered set of logically related fields. For example, all payroll data (including the social security number field and others) relating to a single employee.

(7) **Array**—In a programming language, an aggregate that consists of data objects with attributes, each of which may be uniquely referenced by an index (address). For example, an array may be used to request input of various payroll information for a new employee in one step. Thus an array could include employee name, social security number, withholdings, pay rate, etc.—for example (John Jones, 470-44-5044, 2, $18.32, …). Name would be indexed as 1 (or zero), with each succeeding attribute receiving the next higher number as an address. Also arrays may be multidimensional. They are often used with object-oriented programming such as C++ and Java.

(8) **File**—A group of related records (e.g., all the weekly pay records year-to-date) which is usually arranged in sequence

(9) **Master file**—A file containing relatively permanent information used as a source of reference and periodically updated with a detail (transaction) file (e.g., permanent payroll records)

(10) **Detail or transaction file**—A file containing current transaction information used to update the master file (e.g., hours worked by each employee during the current period used to update the payroll master file)

b. **Data file structure**

(1) **Traditional file processing systems**—These systems focus upon data processing needs of individual departments. Each application program or system is developed to meet the needs of the particular requesting department or user group. For accounting purposes these systems are often similar to traditional accounting systems, with files set up for operations such as purchasing, sales, cash receipts, cash disbursements, etc.

(a) **Advantages of traditional processing systems**

1] Currently operational for many existing (legacy) systems
2] Often cost effective for simple applications

(b) **Disadvantages of traditional processing systems**

1] Data files are dependent upon a particular application program.
2] In complex business situation there is much duplication of data between data files.
3] Each application must be developed individually.
4] Program maintenance is expensive.

(2) **Database systems**

(a) **Definitions**

1] **Database**—A collection of interrelated files, ordinarily most of which are stored online

a] **Normalization**—The process of separating the database into logical tables to avoid certain kinds of updating difficulties (referred to as "anomalies")

2] **Database system**—Computer hardware and software that enables the database(s) to be implemented

3] **Database management system**—Software that provides a facility for communications between various applications programs (e.g., a payroll preparation program) and

the database (e.g., a payroll master file containing the earnings records of the employees)

4] **Data independence**—Basic to database systems is this concept which separates the
data from the related application programs

5] **Data modeling**—Identifying and organizing a database's data, both logically and
physically. A data model determines what information is to be contained in a database, how the information will be used, and how the items in the database will be related to each other.

   a] **Entity-relationship modeling**—An approach to data modeling. The model divides the database in two logical parts—entities (e.g. "customer," "product") and
   relations ("buys," "pays for").

   b] **REA data model**—A data model designed for use in designing accounting information databases. REA is an acronym for the model's basic types of objects:
   Resources—Identifiable objects that have economic value, **E**vents—An organization's business activities, **A**gents—People or organizations about which data is
   collected.

6] **Data Dictionary** (also referred to as a **data repository** or **data directory** system)—A
data structure that stores meta-data

   a] **Meta-data**—Definitional data that provides information about or documentation
   of other data managed within an application or environment. For example, data
   about data elements, records and data structures (length, fields, columns, etc.).

7] **Structured query language (SQL)**—The most common language used for creating
and querying relational databases (see (b)3] below), its commands may be classified
into three types

   a] **Data definition language (DDL)**—Used to define a database, including creating,
   altering, and deleting tables and establishing various constraints

   b] **Data manipulation language (DML)**—Commands used to maintain and query a
   database, including updating, inserting in, modifying, and querying (asking for
   data). For example, a frequent query involves the joining of information from
   more than one table.

   c] **Data control language (DCL)**—Commands used to control a database, including
   controlling which users have various privileges (e.g., who is able to read from and
   write to various portions of the database)

(b) **Database structures**

1] **Hierarchical**—The data elements at one level "own" the data elements at the next
lower level (think of an organization chart in which one manager supervises several
assistants, who in turn each supervise several lower level employees).

2] **Networked**—Each data element can have several owners and can own several other
elements (think of a matrix-type structure in which various relationships can be sup-
ported.

3] **Relational**—A database with the logical structure of a group of related spreadsheets.
Each row represents a record, which is an accumulation of all the fields related to the
same identifier or key; each column represents a field common to all of the records.
Relational databases have in many situations largely replaced the earlier developed hierarchical and networked databases.

4] **Object-oriented**—Information (attributes and methods) are included in structures
called object classes. This is the newest database management system technology.

5] **Object-relational**—Includes both relational and object-oriented features

6] **Distributed**—A single database that is spread physically across computers in multiple
locations that are connected by a data communications link. (The structure of the database is most frequently relational, object-oriented, or object-relational.)

(c) **Database controls**

1] **User department**—Because users directly input data, strict controls over who is authorized to read and/or change the database are necessary.

2] **Access controls**—In addition to the usual controls over terminals and access to the system, database processing also maintains controls within the database itself. These controls limit the user to reading and/or changing (updating) only authorized portions of the database.

   a] **Restricting privileges**—This limits the access of users to the database, as well as operations a particular user may be able to perform. For example, certain employees and customers may have only read, and not write, privileges.

   b] **Logical views**—Users may be provided with authorized *views* of only the portions of the database for which they have a valid need.

3] **Backup and recovery**—A database is updated on a continuous basis during the day. Three methods of backup and recovery are

   a] **Backup of database and logs of transactions** (sometimes referred to as "systems logs"). The approach is to backup the entire database several times per week, generally to magnetic tape. A log of all transactions is also maintained. If there is extensive damage to a major portion of the database due to catastrophic failure, such as disk crash, the recovery method is to restore the most recent past copy of the database and to reconstruct it to a more current state by reapplying or redoing transactions from the log up to the point of failure.

   b] **Database replication.** To avoid catastrophic failure, another approach is to replicate the database at one or more locations. Thus, all data may be recorded to both sets of the database.

   c] **Backup facility.** Another approach is to maintain a backup facility with a vendor who will process data in case of an emergency.

   Further information on backup and recovery is included under Disaster Recovery—D.11 of this module.

4] **Database administrator (DBA)**—Individual responsible for maintaining the database and restricting access to the database to authorized personnel

5] **Audit software**—Usually used by auditors to test the database; see Auditing with Technology Module

(d) **Advantages of database systems**

1] **Data independence**—Data can be used relatively easily by differing applications.

2] **Minimal data redundancy**—The manner in which data is structured results in information being recorded in only one place, thus making updating much easier than is the case with traditional file systems.

3] **Data sharing**—The sharing of data between individuals and applications is relatively easy.

4] Reduced program maintenance

5] Commercial applications are available for modification to a company's needs.

(e) **Disadvantages of database systems**

1] Need for specialized personnel with database expertise

2] Installation of database costly

3] Conversion of traditional file systems (legacy systems) costly

4] Comprehensive backup and recovery procedures are necessary

C. Characteristics of Computer Systems—Specific

1. Types of Networks

a. Background

(1) A network is a group of interconnected computers and terminals.

(2) The development of **telecommunications**—The electronic transmission of information by radio, fiber optics, wire, microwave, laser, and other electromagnetic systems—has made possible the electronic transfer of information between networks of computers. This topic is discussed in detail later in this module.

b. **Classified by geographical scope**

(1) **Local area networks** (LAN)—Privately owned networks within a single building or campus of up to a few miles in size. Because this topic has been emphasized in AICPA materials, it is discussed further later in this module.

(2) **Metropolitan area network** (MAN)—A larger version of a LAN. For example, it might include a group of nearby offices within a city.

(3) **Wide area networks** (WAN)—Networks that span a large geographical area, often a country or continent. It is composed of a collection of computers and other hardware and software for running user programs.

c. **Classified by ownership**

(1) **Private**—One in which network resources are usually dedicated to a small number of applications or a restricted set of users, as in a corporation's network

(a) A typical approach is to lease telephone lines that are dedicated to the network's use.
(b) Also, traditional EDI systems (discussed below) use a private network.
(c) Advantages: Secure, flexible, performance often exceeds that of public
(d) Disadvantage: Costly

(2) **Public**—Resources are owned by third-party companies and leased to users on a usage basis (also referred to as public-switched networks [PSN]).

(a) Access is typically through dial-up circuits.
(b) Example: Applications using the Internet
(c) Advantages and disadvantage: In general, the opposite of those for private networks, but certainly a significant disadvantage is that they are less secure.

1] Improvements in Internet communications will decrease the disadvantages and will lead to a dramatic increase in the use of public networks (e.g., rapid increases in the use of Internet-based electronic commerce).

d. **Classified by use of Internet**
General: The following all use the Internet. They have in common that data communications are ordinarily through **Hypertext Markup Language (HTML)** and/or **Extensible Markup Language (XML)**—languages used to create and format documents, link documents to other Web pages, and communicate between Web browsers. XML is increasingly replacing HTML in Internet applications due to its superior ability to tag (i.e., label) and format documents that are communicated among trading partners.

Extensible Business Reporting Language (XBRL) is an XML-based language being developed specifically for the automation of business information requirements, such as the preparation, sharing, and analysis of financial reports, statements, and audit schedules. XBRL can be used in filings with the SEC that are made available on EDGAR, the SEC's Electronic Data Gathering and Retrieval database.

(1) **Internet**—An international collection of networks made up of independently owned computers that operate as a large computing network

(a) Primary applications of the Internet include

1] E-mail
2] News dissemination
3] Remote log-in of computers
4] File transfer among computers
5] Electronic commerce

(b) Terminology

1] **Hypertext Transfer Protocol (HTTP)**—A language used to transfer documents among different types of computers and networks

2] **Uniform Resource Locator (URL)**—A standard for finding a document by typing in an address (e.g., www.azdiamondbacks.com). URLs work in much the same way as addresses on mail processed by the postal department.

3] **World Wide Web (The Web or WWW)**—A framework for accessing linked documents spread out over the thousands of machines all over the Internet

4] **Web browser**—Software that provides the user with the ability to display Web site pages and locates those pages and sites on request (e.g., Internet Explorer, Netscape)

5] **Web servers**—Large computers on the Internet that are distributed around the world and contain various types of data

6] **Firewall**—A method for protecting an organization's computers and computer information from outsiders. A firewall consists of security algorithms and router communications protocols that prevent outsiders from tapping into corporate database and e-mail systems.

7] **Router**—A communications interface device that connects two networks and determines the best way for data packets to move forward to their destinations

8] **Bridge**—A device that divides a LAN into two segments, selectively forwarding traffic across the network boundary it defines; similar to a switch

9] **Switch**—A device that channels incoming data from any of multiple input ports to the specific output port that will take the data toward its intended destination

10] **Gateway**—A combination of hardware and software that links to different types of networks. For examples, gateways between e-mail systems allow users of differing e-mail systems to exchange messages.

11] **Proxy server**—A server that saves and serves copies of web pages to those who request them (e.g., potential customers). When a Web page is requested, the proxy server is able to access that page either through its cache (reserve of Web pages already sent or loaded) or by obtaining it through the original server. A proxy server can both increase efficiency of Internet operations and help assure data security.

12] **Bulletin board**—A computer system that functions as a centralized information source and message switching system for users with a particular interest. Users dial-up the bulletin board, review and leave messages for other users, as well as communicate to other users on the system at the same time.

13] **TCP/IP (Transmission Control Protocol/Internet Protocol)**—The basic communication language or protocol of the Internet. It has two layers. The higher layer assembles messages or files into smaller packets that are transmitted over the internet. The lower layer assigns IP addresses and insures that messages are delivered to the appropriate computer.

14] **IP address**—The number that identifies a machine as unique on the Internet

15] **ISP (Internet Service Provider)**—An entity that provides access to the Internet

(c) The nature of the Internet has resulted in the spread of a series of malicious programs (often through e-mail) that may adversely affect computer operations, including

1] **Virus**—A program (or piece of code) that requests the computer operating system to perform certain activities not authorized by the computer user. Viruses can be easily transmitted through use of files that contain macros that are sent as attachment to e-mail messages.

a] **Macro**—A single computer instruction that results in a series of instructions in machine language; macros are used to reduce the number of keystrokes needed in a variety of situations. Most macros serve valid purposes, but those associated with viruses cause problems.

b] Unexpected changes in, or losses of, data may be an indication of the existence of a virus on one's computer.

c] E-mail attachments and *public domain software* (generally downloadable from the Internet at no cost to users) are notorious sources of viruses.

2] **Trojan horse**—A malicious, security-breaking program that is disguised as something benign, such as a game, but actually is intended to cause IT damage

3] **Worm**—A program that propagates itself over a network, reproducing itself as it goes

Antivirus software—Is used to attempt to avoid the above types of problems. But the rapid development of new forms of viruses, Trojan horses, and worms results in a situation in which antivirus software developers are always behind the developers.

(2) **Intranet**—A local network, usually limited to an organization, that uses internet-based technology to communicate within the organization.

(3) **Extranet**—Similar to an intranet, but includes an organization's external customers and/or suppliers in the network.

e. **Database client-server architecture**

General: When considering networks, it is helpful to consider their architecture (design). Bear in mind that the architecture must divide the following responsibilities (1) input, (2) processing, and (3) storage. In general the client-server model may be viewed as one in which communications ordinarily take the form of a request message from the client to the server asking for some service to be performed. A "client" may be viewed as the computer or **workstation** of an individual user. The server is a high-capacity computer that contains the network software and may provide a variety of services ranging from simply "serving" files to a client to performing analyses.

(1) **Overall client-server systems**—A networked computing model (usually a LAN) in which database software on a server performs database commands sent to it from client computers

Illustration of Client/Server Architecture

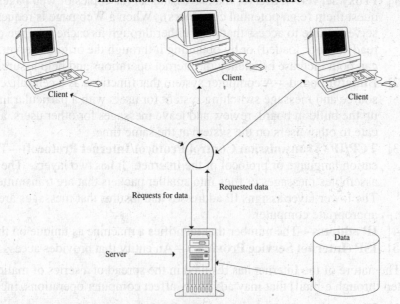

(2) **Subtypes of client/server architectures**

(a) **File servers**—The file server manages file operations and is shared by each of the client PCs (ordinarily attached to a LAN). The three responsibilities (input/output, processing, and storage) are divided in a manner in which most input/output, and processing occurs on client computers rather than on the server. The file server acts simply as a shared data storage device, with all data manipulations performed by client PCs.

(b) **Database servers**—Similar to file servers, but the server here contains the database management system and thus performs more of the processing.

NOTE: The above two architectures are referred to as "two-tier" architecture—client tier and server database tier.

(c) **Three-tier architectures**—A client/server configuration that includes three tiers. The change from the above systems is that this architecture includes another server layer in addition to the two tiers discussed above. For example, application programs (e.g., a transaction processing monitor that controls the input of transactions to the database) may reside on the additional server rather than on the individual clients. This system of adding additional servers may generalize to additional tiers and thus become **n-tier** architecture. Examples of other servers that may be added are as follows:

1] **Print server**—Make shared printers available to various clients
2] **Communications server**—May serve a variety of tasks, such as acting as a gateway (i.e., means of entrance) to the internet or to the corporate intranet
3] **Fax server**—Allow clients on the network to share the hardware for incoming and outgoing fax transmissions

(3) **Distributed systems**—These systems connect all company locations to form a distributed network in which each location has its own input/output, processing, and storage capabilities. These local computers also pass data among themselves and possibly to a server (often referred to as a "host" in this context) for further processing. An illustration of this type of system is presented in the database section of this outline.

2. **Local Area Networks (LANs)**—Privately owned networks within a single building or campus of up to a few miles in size.

a. **Software**

(1) Software allows devices to function cooperatively and share network resources such as printers and disk storage space.
(2) Common services

(a) Network server
(b) File server
(c) Print server
(d) Communications server

b. **Hardware components**

(1) **Workstations**—Ordinarily microcomputers
(2) **Peripherals**—For example, printers, magnetic tapes, disks, optical scanners, fax board, modems
(3) **Transmission media**—Physical path that connect components of LAN, ordinarily twisted-pair wire or coaxial cable
(4) **Network interface cards**—Connect workstation and transmission media

c. **Control implications**

(1) General controls are often weak (e.g., controls over development and modification of programs, access and computer operations).
(2) Controls often rely upon end users, who may not be control conscious.
(3) Often users may not be provided adequate resources for problem resolution, troubleshooting and recovery support.
(4) Controlling access and gaining accountability through logging of transactions enforces a segregation of duties.
(5) Good management controls are essential—for example, access codes, passwords.
(6) LAN software ordinarily does not provide security features available in larger scale environments.

NOTE: Tests of controls may address whether controls related to the above are effective.

d. LANs generally make possible the computer audit techniques that may be performed either by internal auditors or external auditors.

3. **Microcomputers**

a. The proliferation of microcomputers (e.g., personal computers [PC], laptop computers) has had a profound effect on information systems. A small-business client will probably use a PC to run a commercially purchased general ledger package (off-the-shelf software) Segregation of duties becomes especially difficult in such an environment because one individual may perform all recordkeeping (processing) as well as maintain other nonrecordkeeping responsibilities.

   b. A larger client may use a network of PCs that may or may not be linked to a large corporate mainframe computer. In all systems, management policies should be in place regarding the development and modification of programs and data files.

   c. Regardless of the system, the control objectives remain the same. When small computers are involved, the following points need to be considered:

     (1) **Security**—Security over small computers, while still important, may not be as critical as security over the data and any in-house developed software. Most companies can easily replace the hardware, but may suffer a severe setback if the data and/or in-house developed software is lost. Access to the software diskettes should be controlled and backup copies should be made. Access to the hard drive must be restricted since anyone turning on the power switch can read the data stored on those files. Also, a control problem may exist because the computer operator often understands the system and also has access to the diskettes. The management of the company may need to become more directly involved in supervision when a lack of segregation of duties exists in data processing.

     (2) **Verification of processing**—Periodically, an independent verification of the applications being processed on the small computer system should be made to prevent the system from being used for personal projects. Also, verification helps prevent errors in internally developed software from going undetected. Controls should be in operation to assure the accuracy of in-house created spreadsheets and databases.

     (3) **Personnel**—Centralized authorization to purchase hardware and software should be required to ensure that appropriate purchasing decisions are made, including decisions that minimize software and hardware compatibility difficulties. Software piracy and viruses may be controlled by prohibiting the loading of unauthorized software and data on company-owned computers.

       (a) Software is copyrighted, and violation of copyright laws may result in litigation against the company.

       (b) A company may control possible software piracy (the use of unlicensed software) by employees by procedures such as

         1] Establishing a corporate software policy
         2] Maintaining a log of all software purchase
         3] Auditing individual computers to identify installed software

 4. **End-User Computing (EUC)**—The end user is responsible for the development and execution of the computer application that generates the information used by that same end user.

   a. User substantially eliminates many of the services offered by an MIS department.

   b. Risks

     (1) End-user applications are not always adequately tested before implemented.
     (2) More client personnel need to understand control concepts.
     (3) Management often does not review the results of applications appropriately.
     (4) Old or existing applications may not be updated for current applicability and accuracy.

   c. Overall physical access controls become more difficult when companies leave a controlled MIS environment and become more dependent upon individual users for controls.

   d. Control implications

     (1) Require applications to be adequately tested before used
     (2) Require adequate documentation
     (3) Physical access controls, including

       (a) Clamps or chains to prevent removal of hard disks or internal boards
       (b) Diskless workstations that require download of files
       (c) Regular backup
       (d) Security software to limit access to those who know user ID and password
       (e) Control over access from outside

    (f) Commitment to security matters written into job descriptions, employee contracts, and personnel evaluation procedures

  (4) Control access to appropriate users

    (a) Passwords and user IDs

    (b) Menus for EUC access to database

    (c) Protect system by restricting user ability to load data

    (d) When end user uploads data, require appropriate validation, authorization, and reporting control

    (e) Independent review of transactions

    (f) Record access to company databases by EUC applications

  (5) Control use of incorrect versions of data files

    (a) Use control totals for batch processing of uploaded data

  (6) Require backup of files

  (7) Provide applications controls (e.g., edit checks, range tests, reasonableness checks)

  (8) Support programmed or user reconciliations to provide assurance that processing is correct

> *NOTE: Since end-user computing relies upon microcomputers, the controls here required for microcomputers and EUC are similar. Also, tests of controls may address whether controls related to the above are effective.*

5. **Electronic Commerce**

  a. **General:** Electronic commerce involves individuals and organizations engaging in a variety of electronic transactions with computers and telecommunication networks. The networks involved may be publicly available (e.g., the Internet) or private to the individuals and organizations involved (e.g., through telephone lines privately leased by the parties involved). Recent wide acceptance of the Internet (more specifically, that portion of the Internet referred to as the World Wide Web, or the Web) is currently leading to a great expansion in electronic commerce.

  b. Five areas of risk associated with electronic commerce IT systems (as well as to varying degrees with other IT systems) are (1) security, (2) availability, (3) processing integrity, (4) online privacy, and (5) confidentiality. See section D.1 of this module for a discussion.

  c. Use of the Web is growing rapidly as both the number and types of electronic transactions increase. However, many believe that risks such as those listed above are currently impairing its growth.

    (1) As discussed further in the Reporting Module (Section C.2.), the AICPA and the Canadian Institute of Chartered Accountants have developed a form of assurance referred to as the "WebTrust Seal of Assurance" that tells potential customers that the firm has evaluated a Web site's business practices and controls to determine whether they are in conformity with Web-Trust principles.

    (2) Digital certificates, also referred to as digital IDs, are a means of assuring data integrity.

      (a) A digital certificate (signature) allows an individual to digitally sign a message so the recipient knows that it actually came from that individual and was not modified in any manner.

      (b) Ordinarily the message is encrypted and the recipient decrypts it and is able to read the contents.

    (3) **Encryption**—The conversion of data into a form called a cipher text, that cannot be easily understood by unauthorized people. **Decryption** is the process of converting encrypted data back into its original form so it can be understood. The conversion is performed using an algorithm and key which only the users control.

      (a) **Algorithm**—A detailed sequence of actions to perform to accomplish some task (in this case to encrypt and/or decode data)

      (b) **Key**—In the content of encryption, a value that must be fed into the algorithm used to decode an encrypted message in order to reproduce the original plain text

      (c) **Private key system**—An encryption system in which both the sender and receiver have access to the electronic key, but do not allow others access. The primary disadvantage is that both parties must have the key.

(d) Encryption is important in a variety of contexts, including any time two or more computers are used to communicate with one another, and even to keep private information on one computer.

(e) The machine instructions necessary to encrypt and decrypt data constitute **system overhead;** that is, they slow down the rate of processing.

d. **Electronic funds transfer (EFT)**—Making cash payments between two or more organizations or individuals electronically rather than by using checks (or cash)

(1) Banks first became heavily involved with EFT; it is now a major part of most types of electronic commerce.

(2) EFT systems are vulnerable to the risk of unauthorized access to proprietary data and to the risk of fraudulent fund transfers; controls include

  (a) Control of physical access to network facilities

  (b) Electronic identification should be required for all network terminals authorized to use EFT.

  (c) Access should be controlled through passwords.

  (d) Encryption should be used to secure stored data and data being transmitted. See section C.5.c.(3) for more information on encryption.

e. **Electronic data interchange (EDI)**—The electronic exchange of business transactions, in a standard format, from one entity's computer to another entity's computer through an electronic communications network

(1) Traditionally, the definition of electronic commerce has focused on EDI. Currently, Web-based commerce is replacing a portion of these EDI systems.

(2) Risks related to EDI

  (a) EDI is commonly used for sales and purchasing, and related accounts. The speed at which transactions occur often reduces amounts receivable (payables) due to electronic processing of receipts (payments). Another effect is to make preventive controls particularly desirable, since detective controls may be too late.

  (b) In these systems, documents such as purchase orders, invoices, shipping forms, bills of lading, and checks are replaced by electronic transactions.

    1] For example, in electronic funds transfer systems, a form of EDI, electronic transactions replace checks as a means of payment. As discussed below, EDI is often conducted on private networks.

    2] To determine that transactions are properly processed, effective audit trails for both internal auditors and external auditors include activity logs, including processed and failed transactions, network and sender/recipient acknowledgment of receipt of transactions, and proper time sequence of processing.

    3] In some EDI applications, portions of the documentation of transactions are retained for only short period of time; this may require auditors to pay particular attention to controls over the transactions and to test controls on a timely basis when records remain available.

(3) Methods of communication between trading partners

  (a) **Point-to-point**—A direct computer-to-computer private network link

    1] Automakers and governments have traditionally used this method.

    2] Advantages

      a] No reliance on third parties for computer processing

      b] Organization controls who has access to the network.

      c] Organization can enforce proprietary (its own) software standard in dealings with all trading partners.

      d] Timeliness of delivery may be improved since no third party is involved.

3] Disadvantages

    a] Must establish connection with each trading partner
    b] High initial cost
    c] Computer scheduling issues
    d] Need for common protocols between partners
    e] Need for hardware and software compatibility

(b) **Value-added network (VAN)**

1] A VAN

    a] Is a privately owned network that routes the EDI transactions between trading partners, and in many cases provides translation, storage, and other processing
    b] Is designed and maintained by an independent company that offers specialized support to improve the transmission effectiveness of a network
    c] Alleviates problems related to interorganizational communication that results from the use of differing hardware and software

2] A VAN receives data from sender, determines intended recipient, and places data in the recipient's electronic mailbox.

3] Advantages

    a] Reduces communication and data protocol problems since VANs can deal with differing protocols (eliminating need for trading partners to agree on them)
    b] Partners do not have to establish the numerous point-to-point connections.
    c] Reduces scheduling problems since receiver can request delivery of transactions when it wishes
    d] In some cases, VAN translates application to a standard format the partner does not have to reformat.
    e] VAN can provide increased security.

4] Disadvantages

    a] Cost of VAN
    b] Dependence upon VAN's systems and controls
    c] Possible loss of data confidentiality

(c) **Public networks**—For example, the Internet-based commerce solutions described earlier

1] Advantages

    a] Avoids cost of proprietary lines
    b] Avoids cost of VAN
    c] Directly communicates transactions to trading partners
    d] Software is being developed which allows communication between differing systems.

2] Disadvantages

    a] Possible loss of data confidentiality on the Internet
    b] Computer or transmission disruption
    c] Hackers and viruses
    d] Attempted electronic frauds

(d) **Proprietary networks**—In some circumstances (e.g., health care, banking) organizations have developed their own network for their own transactions. These systems are costly to develop and operate (because of proprietary lines), although they are often extremely reliable.

(4) Controls required for other network systems are required for EDI systems. In addition, disappearance of "paper transactions" and the direct interrelationship with another organization's

computer makes various authentication and encryption controls particularly important for these transactions.

(a) **Authentication**—Controls must exist over the origin, proper submission, and proper delivery of EDI communications. Receiver of the message must have proof of the origin of the message, as well as its proper submission and delivery.

(b) **Packets**—A block of data that is transmitted from one computer to another. It contains data and authentication information.

(c) **Encryption**—The conversion of plain text data into cipher text data used by an algorithm and key which only the users control. See section C.5.c.(3) for more information on encryption.

(5) The AICPA Auditing Procedures Study, *Audit Implications of EDI*, lists the following benefits and exposures of EDI:

(a) Benefits

1] Quick response and access to information
2] Cost efficiency
3] Reduced paperwork
4] Accuracy and reduced errors and error-correction costs
5] Better communications and customer service
6] Necessary to remain competitive

(b) Exposures

1] Total dependence upon computer system for operation
2] Possible loss of confidentiality of sensitive information
3] Increased opportunity for unauthorized transactions and fraud
4] Concentration of control among a few people involved in EDI
5] Reliance on third parties (trading partners, VAN)
6] Data processing, application and communications errors
7] Potential legal liability due to errors
8] Potential loss of audit trails and information needed by management due to limited retention policies
9] Reliance on trading partner's system

6. **Telecommunications**—The electronic transmission of information by radio, wire, fiber optic, coaxial cable, microwave, laser, or other electromagnetic system

a. Transmitted information—Voice, data, video, fax, other
b. Hardware involved

(1) Computers for communications control and switching
(2) Transmission facilities such as copper wire, fiber optic cables, microwave stations and communications satellites
(3) Modems may be used to provide compatibility of format speed, etc.

c. Software controls and monitors the hardware, formats information, adds appropriate control information, performs switching operations, provides security, and supports the management of communications.

d. While telecommunications is **not** an end of itself, it enables technologies such as the following:

(1) Electronic data interchange
(2) Electronic funds transfer
(3) Point of sale systems
(4) Commercial databases
(5) Airline reservation systems

e. Controls needed

(1) System integrity at remote sites

(2) Data entry

(3) Central computer security

(4) Dial-in security

(5) Transmission accuracy and completeness

(6) Physical security over telecommunications facilities

NOTE: Tests of controls may address whether controls related to the above are effective.

7. **Computer Service Organizations (Bureaus, Centers)**—Computer service organizations record and process data for companies. These organizations allow companies (users) to do away with part of the data processing function. While many computer service organizations simply record and process relatively routine transactions for a client (e.g., prepare payroll journals and payroll checks), a VAN is a service organization that takes a broader role of providing network, storing, and forwarding (mailbox) services for the companies involved in an EDI system. Information on service organizations is presented in the Internal Control Module (Section D.4.) and in the outline of AU 324.

D. Effect of a Computer on Internal Control

*NOTE: We have already discussed the effect of a computer on internal control of several systems under C. (microcomputers, end-user computing, and electronic commerce). In this section we discuss the effect in general terms as presented in the AICPA Audit Guide, **Consideration of Internal Control in a Financial Statement Audit**. This section presents information on controls a company may have. Information on how auditors test those controls and on audit procedures that use IT is presented in Module 6 of Auditing. We begin by discussing overall principles of a reliable system and overall risks. We then consider the effect of a computer on internal control using the five components of internal control—control environment, risk assessment, information and communication, monitoring, and control activities.*

1. **Principles of a Reliable System and Examples of Overall Risks**

    a. A reliable system is one that is capable of operating without material error, fault, or failure during a specified period in a specified environment

    b. One framework for analyzing a reliable system is presented by the AICPA's Trust Services. Trust Services, which provide assurance on information systems, use a framework with five principles of a reliable system—(1) security, (2) availability, (3) processing integrity, (4) online privacy, and (5) confidentiality. Accordingly, when a principle is not met a risk exists.

Principle	*Examples of Risks*
1. *Security.* The system is protected against unauthorized access (both physical and logical)	Physical access—A lack of physical security allows damage or other loss (e.g., theft) to the system • Weather • Acts of war • Disgruntled employees or others Logical access—A lack of security over access to the system allows • Malicious (or accidental) alteration of, or damage to, files and/or the system • Computer based fraud • Unauthorized access to confidential data
2. *Availability.* The system is available for operation and use as committed or agreed. The system is available for operation and use in conformity with the entity's availability policies.	System failure results in • Interruption of business operations • Loss of data
3. *Processing Integrity.* System processing is complete, accurate, timely, and authorized.	Invalid, incomplete, or inaccurate • Input data • Data processing • Updating of master files • Creation of output
4. *Online Privacy.* Personal information obtained as a result of e-commerce is collected, used, disclosed, and retained as committed or agreed.	Disclosure of customer information (or that of others) such as • Social security numbers • Credit card numbers • Credit rating • Medical conditions

5.	***Confidentiality.*** Information designated as confidential is protected as committed or agreed.	Examples of confidential data that might be disclosed • Transaction details • Engineering details of products • Business plans • Banking information • Legal documents • Inventory or other account information • Customer lists • Confidential details of operations

NOTE: Make certain that you are familiar not only with the above principles, but are familiar with the nature of the various risks relating to computer processing.

2.   Control Environment

a.   Recall the seven factors of the control environment

   I - Integrity and ethical values
   C - Commitment to competence
   H - Human resource policies and practices
   A - Assignment of authority and responsibility
   M - Management's philosophy and operating style
   B - Board of directors or audit committee participation
   O - Organizational structure

b.   Although all seven factors may be affected by computer processing, the organizational structure is modified to include an information systems department (EDP department). It is helpful to keep in mind that the information systems department is involved with two distinct functions—systems development and data processing.

c.   Steps in the ***system development lifecycle***

   (1) Software concept—identify the need for the new system.
   (2) Requirements analysis—determine the needs of the users.
   (3) Architectural design—determining the hardware, software, people, etc. needed.
   (4) Coding and debugging—acquiring and testing the software.
   (5) System testing—testing and evaluating the functionality of the system.

d.   Organizational structure

   (1) **Segregation controls**

      (a) Segregate functions between information systems department and user departments

         1]   User departments are the other departments of the company that utilize the data prepared by the information systems department.

      (b) Do not allow the information systems department to initiate or authorize transactions.
      (c) At a minimum, segregate programming, operations, and the library function within the information systems department.
      (d) A more complete segregation of key functions within the information systems department may be possible; one way to separate key functions is as follows:

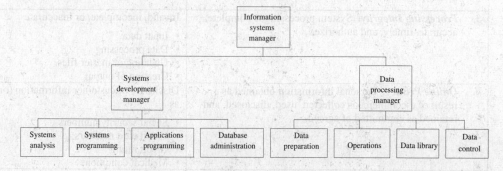

1] **Systems analysis**—The systems analyst analyzes the present user environment and requirements and may (1) recommend specific changes, (2) recommend the purchase of a new system, or (3) design a new information system. The analyst is in constant contact with user departments and programming staff to ensure the users' actual and ongoing needs are being met. A system flowchart is a tool used by the analyst to define the systems requirements.

2] **Systems programming**—The systems programmer is responsible for implementing, modifying, and debugging the software necessary for making the hardware work (such as the operating system, telecommunications monitor, and the database management system). For some companies the term "software engineer" is viewed as similar or identical to that of systems programmer. For others, the software engineer is involved with the creation of designs used by programmers.

3] **Applications programming**—The applications programmer is responsible for writing, testing, and debugging the application programs from the specifications (whether general or specific) provided by the systems analyst. A program flowchart is one tool used by the applications programmer to define the program logic.

4] **Database administration**—In a database environment, a database administrator (DBA) is responsible for maintaining the database and restricting access to the database to authorized personnel.

5] **Data preparation**—Data may be prepared by user departments and input by key to magnetic disk or magnetic tape.

6] **Operations**—The operator is responsible for the daily computer operations of both the hardware and the software. The operator mounts magnetic tapes on the tape drives, supervises operations on the operator's console, accepts any required input, and distributes any generated output. The operator should have adequate documentation available to run the program (a run manual), but should not have detailed program information.

   a] Help desks are usually a responsibility of operations because of the operational nature of their functions (for example, assisting users with systems problems and obtaining technical support/vendor assistance).

7] **Data library**—The librarian is responsible for custody of the removable media (i.e., magnetic tapes or disks) and for the maintenance of program and system documentation. In many systems, much of the library function is maintained and performed electronically by the computer.

8] **Data control**—The control group acts as liaison between users and the processing center. This group records input data in a control log, follows the progress of processing, distributes output, and ensures compliance with control totals.

Ideally, in a large system, all of the above key functions should be segregated; in a small computer environment, many of the key functions are concentrated in a small number of employees. For purposes of the CPA exam remember that, at a minimum, an attempt should be made to segregate *programming, operations,* and the *library* functions. Large organizations typically have a chief information officer (CIO) that oversees all information technology and activities.

(e) Electronic commerce has resulted in a number of new Web-related positions, including

1] **Web administrator (Web manager)**—Responsible for overseeing the development, planning, and the implementation of a Web site. Ordinarily a managerial position.

2] **Web master**—Responsible for providing expertise and leadership in the development of a Web site, including the design, analysis, security, maintenance, content development, and updates.

3] **Web designer**—Responsible for creating the visual content of the Web site

4] **Web coordinator**—Responsible for the daily operations of the Web site

5] **Internet developer**—Responsible for writing programs for commercial use. Similar to a software engineer or systems programmer.

6] **Intranet/Extranet developer**—Responsible for writing programs based on the needs of the company

3. **Risk Assessment**

a. Changes in computerized information systems and in operations may increase the risk of improper financial reporting.

4. **Information and Communication**

a. The computerized accounting system is affected by whether the company uses small computers and/or a complex mainframe system.

(1) For small computer systems, purchased commercial "off-the-shelf" software may be used.

(a) Controls within the software may be well known.
(b) Analysis of "exception reports" generated during processing is important to determine that exceptions are properly handled.

(2) For complex mainframe systems a significant portion of the software is ordinarily developed within the company by information systems personnel.

(a) Controls within the software are unknown to the auditor prior to testing.
(b) As with small computer systems, analysis of exception reports is important, but controls over the generation of such reports must ordinarily be tested to a greater extent.

5. **Monitoring**

a. Proper monitoring of a computerized system will require adequate computer skills to evaluate the propriety of processing of computerized applications.
b. A common method of monitoring for inappropriate access is review of system-access log.

6. **Control Activities—Overall**

a. Control activities in which a computer is involved may be divided into the following categories:

(1) Computer **general** control activities
(2) Computer **application** control activities

Programmed application control activities
Manual follow-up of computer exception reports

(3) **User** control activities to test the completeness and accuracy of computer processed controls

The following illustration, adapted from the AICPA Audit Guide, *Consideration of Internal Control in a Financial Statement Audit*, summarizes the relationships among the controls.

COMPUTER CONTROL ACTIVITIES

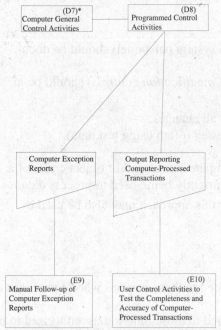

* *Section below in which control discussion is presented.*

EXPLANATION OF COMPUTER CONTROL ACTIVITIES

Computer General Control Activities control program development, program changes, computer operations, and access to programs and data. These control activities increase the assurance that programmed control activities operate effectively during the period.

Computer Application Control Activities

Programmed Control Activities relate to specific computer applications and are embedded in the computer program used in the financial reporting system. The concepts presented here related to programmed control activities may also apply to other activities within the computer accounting system.

Manual Follow-Up of Computer Exception Reports involves employee follow-up of items listed on computer exception reports. The effectiveness of application control activities that involve manual follow-up of computer reports depends on the effectiveness of both the programmed control activities that produce the exception report and the manual follow-up activities.

User Control Activities to Test the Completeness and Accuracy of Computer Processed Transactions represent manual checks of computer output against source document or other input, and thus provide assurance that programmed aspects of the accounting system and control activities have operated effectively.

7. **Computer General Control Activities**

> *NOTE: General control activities affect all computer applications. There are four types of general controls—(a) developing new programs and systems, (b) changing existing programs and systems, (c) controlling access to programs and data, and (d) controlling computer operations.*

a. **Developing new programs and systems**

(1) **Segregation controls**

(a) User departments participate in systems design.

(b) Both users and information systems personnel test new systems.

(c) Management, users, and information systems personnel approve new systems before they are placed into operation.

(d) All master and transaction file conversions should be controlled to prevent unauthorized changes and to verify the accuracy of the results.

(e) Programs and systems should be properly documented (see Section E. of outline).

(2) **Computer hardware is extremely reliable.** This is primarily due to the chip technology. However, it is also due to the controls built into the hardware and systems software to provide for a self-diagnostic mechanism to detect and prevent equipment failures. The following are examples of such controls:

(a) **Parity check**—A special bit is added to each character that can detect if the hardware loses a bit during the internal movement of a character.

(b) **Echo check**—Primarily used in telecommunications transmissions. During the sending and receiving of characters, the receiving hardware repeats back to the sending hardware what it received and the sending hardware automatically resends any characters that were received incorrectly.

(c) **Diagnostic routines**—Hardware or software supplied by the manufacturer to check the internal operations and devices within the computer system. These routines are often activated when the system is booted up.

(d) **Boundary protection**—Most CPUs have multiple jobs running simultaneously (multiprogramming environment). To ensure that these simultaneous jobs cannot destroy or change the allocated memory of another job, the systems software contains boundary protection controls.

(e) **Periodic maintenance**—The system should be examined periodically (often weekly) by a qualified service technician.

b. **Changing existing programs and systems**

(1) Suggestions for changes (from users and information system personnel) should be documented in a change request log.

(2) Proper *change control* procedures (also referred to as *modification controls*) should be in place.

    (a) The information systems manager should review all changes.

    (b) The modified program should be appropriately tested (often using test data).

    (c) Details of all changes should be documented.

    (d) A *code comparison program* may be used to compare source and/or object codes of a controlled copy of a program with the program currently being used to process data.

        1] This will identify any unauthorized changes (this approach may also be used by CPAs).

c. **Controlling access to programs and data**

(1) **Segregation controls**

    (a) Access to program documentation should be limited to those persons who require it in the performance of their duties.

    (b) Access to data files and programs should be limited to those individuals authorized to process data.

    (c) Access to computer hardware should be limited to authorized individuals such as computer operators and their supervisors.

(2) **Physical access to computer facility**

    (a) **Limited physical access**—The physical facility that houses the computer equipment, files, and documentation should have controls to limit access only to authorized individuals. Possible controls include using a guard, automated key cards, and manual key locks, as well as the new access devices that permit access through fingerprints or palm prints.

    (b) **Visitor entry logs**—Used to document those who have had access to the area

(3) **Hardware and software access controls**

    (a) **Access control software** (user identification)—The most used control is a combination of a unique *identification code* and a confidential *password*.

        1] Passwords should be made up of a combination of alphabetic, numeric, and symbol elements.

        2] Passwords should be changed periodically.

        3] Passwords should be disabled promptly when an employee leaves the company.

    (b) **Call back**—Call back is a specialized form of user identification in which the user dials the system, identifies him/herself, and is disconnected from the system. Then either (1) an individual manually finds the authorized telephone number or (2) the system automatically finds the authorized telephone number of the individual and calls back.

    (c) **Encryption**—Data is encoded when stored in computer files and/or before transmission to or from remote locations (e.g., through use of modems and telephone lines). This coding protects data, since to use the data unauthorized users must not only obtain access, but must also translate the coded form of the data. Encryption performed by physically secure hardware (often special-purpose computers) is ordinarily more secure, but more costly than that performed by software. See section C.5.c.(3) for more information on encryption.

d. **Controlling computer operations**

(1) **Segregation controls**

(a) Operators should have access to an ***operations manual*** that contains the instructions for processing programs and solving routine operational programs, but not with detailed program documentation.

(b) The control group should monitor the operator's activities and jobs should be scheduled.

(2) **Other controls**

(a) **Backup and recovery**—Discussed in Section D.11. in this module

(b) **Contingency processing**—Detailed contingency processing plans should be developed to prepare for system failures. The plans should detail the responsibilities of individuals, as well as the alternate processing sites that should be utilized. Backup facilities with a vendor may be used to provide contingent sites in case of an emergency. This topic is discussed further in Section D.11. of this module.

(c) **File protection ring**—A file protection ring is a processing control to ensure that an operator does not use a magnetic tape as a tape to write on when it actually has critical information on it. If the ring is on the tape, data cannot be written on the tape. A file protection ring on a magnetic tape serves the same purpose as the switch on a floppy diskette that makes it "read only."

(d) **Internal and external labels**—External labels are gummed-paper labels attached to a reel of tape or other storage medium which identify the file. Internal labels perform the same function through the use of machine readable identification in the first record of a file. The use of labels allows the computer operator to determine whether the correct file has been selected for processing. Trailer labels are often used on the end of a magnetic tape file to maintain information on the number of records processed.

8. **Computer Application Control Activities—Programmed Control Activities**

NOTE: Programmed application controls apply to a specific application rather than multiple applications. These controls operate to assure the proper input and processing of data. The input step converts human-readable data into computer-readable data. Ensuring the integrity of the data in the computer is critical during processing. The candidate should be prepared to identify the following common controls in a multiple-choice question.

a. **Input controls**

(1) **Overall controls**

(a) Inputs should be properly authorized and approved.

(b) The system should verify all significant data fields used to record information (editing the data).

(c) Conversion of data into machine-readable form should be controlled and verified for accuracy.

(2) **Input validation (edit) controls**

(a) **Preprinted form**—Information is preassigned a place and a format on the input form.

(b) **Check digit**—An extra digit added to an identification number to detect certain types of data transmission errors. For example, a bank may add a check digit to individuals' 7-digit account numbers. The computer will calculate the correct check digit based on performing predetermined mathematical operations on the 7-digit account number and will then compare it to the check digit.

(c) **Control, batch, or proof total**—A total of one numerical field for all the records of a batch that normally would be added, (e.g., total sales dollars)

(d) **Hash total**—A control total where the total is meaningless for financial purposes (e.g., a mathematical sum of employee social security numbers)

(e) **Record count**—A control total of the total records processed

(f) **Limit (reasonableness) test**—A test of the reasonableness of a field of data, given a predetermined upper and/or lower limit (e.g., for a field that indicates auditing exam scores, a limit check would test for scores over 100)

(g) **Menu driven input**—As input is entered, the operator responds to a menu prompting the proper response (e.g., What score did you get on the Auditing part of the CPA Exam [75-100]?).

(h) **Field check**—A control that limits the types of characters accepted into a specific data field (e.g., a pay rate should include only numerical data)

(i) **Validity check**—A control that allows only "valid" transactions or data to be entered into the system (e.g., a field indicating sex of an individual where 1=female and 2=male—if the field is coded in any other manner it would not be accepted)

(j) **Missing data check**—A control that searches for blanks inappropriately existing in input data (e.g., if an employee's division number were left blank an error message would result)

(k) **Field size check**—A control of an exact number of characters to be input (e.g., if part numbers all have 6 digits, an error message would result if more or less than 6 characters were input)

(l) **Logic check**—Ensures that illogical combinations of input are not accepted (e.g., if the Tuba City branch has no company officers, an error message would result if two fields for a specified employee indicated that the employee worked as an officer in Tuba City).

(m) **Redundant data check**—Uses two identifiers in each transaction record (e.g., customer account number and the first five letters of customer's name) to confirm that the correct master file record is being updated

(n) **Closed-loop verification**—A control that allows data entry personnel to check the accuracy of input data. For example, the system might retrieve an account name of a record that is being updated, and display it on the operator's terminal. This control may be used instead of a redundant data check.

(3) **Processing controls**

Overall: When the input has been accepted by the computer, it usually is processed through multiple steps. Processing controls are essential to ensure the integrity of data. Essentially all of the controls listed for input may also be incorporated during processing. For example, processed information should include limit tests, record counts, and control totals. In addition, external labels should be used on floppy disks and magnetic tape files, with internal header and trailer labels used to determine that all information on a file has been read.

NOTE: Previously, the professional standards divided application controls into three categories—input, processing, and output. The current categories of application controls (programmed and manual) and user controls have replaced that breakdown. As an aid to discussing controls we distinguish between input and processing above. User control activities include the essentials of the previous "output" controls.

9. **Application Controls—Manual Follow-Up of Computer Exception Reports**

a. These controls involve employee (operator and/or control group) follow-up of items listed on computer exception reports. Their effectiveness depends on the effectiveness of both the programmed control activities that produce the reports and the manual follow-up activities.

10. **User Control Activities to Test the Completeness and Accuracy of Computer-Processed Controls**

a. These manual controls, previously referred to as *output controls,* include

(1) Checks of computer output against source documents, control totals, or other input to provide assurance that programmed aspects of the financial reporting system and control activities have operated effectively

(2) Reviewing computer processing logs to determine that all of the correct computer jobs executed properly

(3) Maintaining proper procedures and communications specifying authorized recipients of output

b. These procedures are often performed by both the control group and users.

c. In some systems, user departments evaluate the reliability of output from the computer by extensive review and testing; in others, users merely test the overall reasonableness of the output.

11. **Disaster Recovery and Business Continuity**

a. A plan should allow the firm to

(1) Minimize the extent of disruption, damage, and loss
(2) Establish an alternate (temporary) method for processing information
(3) Resume normal operations as quickly as possible
(4) Train and familiarize personnel to perform emergency operations

b. A plan should include priorities, insurance, backup approaches, specific assignments, period testing and updating, and documentation, as described below.

(1) **Priorities**—Which applications are most critical?
(2) **Insurance to defer costs**
(3) **Backup approaches**

(a) Batch systems—The most common approach is the ***Grandfather-Father-Son*** method. A master file (e.g., accounts receivable) is updated with the day's transaction files (e.g., files of cash receipts and credit sales). After the update, the new file master file is the son. The file from which the father was developed with the transaction files of the appropriate day is the grandfather. The grandfather and son files are stored in different locations. If the son were destroyed, for example, it could be reconstructed by rerunning the father file and the related transaction files.

(b) Online databases and master files systems

1] **Checkpoint**—Similar to grandfather-father-son, but at certain points, "checkpoints," the system makes a copy of the database and this "checkpoint" file is stored on a separate disk or tape. If a problem occurs the system is restarted at the last checkpoint and updated with subsequent transactions.

2] **Rollback**—As a part of recovery, to undo changes made to a database to a point at which it was functioning properly

3] **Backup facilities**

a] **Reciprocal agreement**—An agreement between two or more organizations (with compatible computer facilities) to aid each other with their data processing needs in the event of a disaster. This is sometimes referred to as a mutual aid pact.

b] **Hot site**—A commercial disaster recovery service that allows a business to continue computer operations in the event of computer disaster. For example, if a company's data processing center becomes inoperable, that enterprise can move all processing to a hot site that has all the equipment needed to continue operation. This is also referred to as a recovery operations center (ROC) approach.

c] **Cold site**—Similar to a hot site, but the customer provides and installs the equipment needed to continue operations. A cold site is less expensive, but takes longer to get in full operation after a disaster. This is sometimes referred to as an "empty shell" in that the "shell" is available and ready to receive whatever hardware the temporary user needs

d] **Internal site**—Large organizations with multiple data processing centers sometimes rely upon their own sites for backup in the event of a disaster.

NOTE: Be aware that most approaches to control for catastrophic failures rely upon backup of the entire system in one form or another. Also, various combinations of the above approaches may be used.

(4) **Specific assignments, including having individuals involved with**

(a) Arranging for new facilities
(b) Computer operations
(c) Installing software
(d) Establishing data communications facilities
(e) Recovering vital records
(f) Arranging for forms and supplies

(5) **Periodic testing and updating of plan**
(6) **Documentation of plan**

E. Flowcharting

General: Flowcharts analytically describe some aspect of an information system. Flowcharting is a procedure to graphically show the sequential flow of data and/or operations. The data and operations portrayed include document preparation, authorization, storage, and decision making. The more common flowcharting symbols are illustrated below. Knowledge of them would help with occasional multiple-choice questions and with problems that present a detailed flowchart that must be analyzed.

1. Common Flowcharting Symbols

Symbol	Name	Description
	Document	This can be a manual form or a computer printout
	Computer Operation	Computer process which transforms input data into useful information
	Manual Operation	Manual (human) process to prepare documents, make entries, check output, etc.
	Decision	Determines which alternative path is followed (IF/THEN/ELSE Conditions)
	Input/Output	General input or output to a process. Often used to represent accounting journals and ledgers on document flowcharts
	Online Storage	Refers to direct access computer storage connected directly to the CPU. Data is available on a random access basis
	Disc Storage	Refers to data stored on a magnetic disk
	Off-Line Storage	Refers to a file or indicates the mailing of a document (i.e., invoices or statements to customers). A letter in the symbol below the line indicates the order in which the file is stored. (N-Numerical, C-Chronological, A-Alphabetical)
	Display	Visual display of data and/or output on a terminal screen
	Batch Total Tape	Manually computed total before processing (such as the number of records to be processed). This total is recomputed by the computer and compared after processing is completed
	Magnetic Tape	Used for reading, writing, or storage on sequential storage media
	Manual Data Entry	Refers to data entered through a terminal keyboard or key-to-tape or key-to-disk device
	Annotation	Provides additional description or information connected to symbol to which it annotates by a dotted line (not a flowline)
	Flowline	Shows direction of data flow, operations, and documents

	Communication Link	Telecommunication line linking computer system to remote locations
	Start/Termination	Used to begin or end a flowchart. (Not always used or shown in flowcharts on the CPA exam.) May be used to show connections to other procedures or receipt/ sending of documents to/from outsiders
	On Page Connector	Connects parts of flowchart on the same page
	Off Page Connector	Connects parts of flowchart on separate pages

2. **Types and Definitions**

   a. **System flowchart**—A graphic representation of a data processing application that depicts the interaction of all the computer programs for a given system, rather than the logic for an individual computer program

   b. **Program flowchart**—A graphic representation of the logic (processing steps) of a computer program

   c. **Internal control (audit) flowchart** or **document flowchart**—A graphic representation of the flow of documents from one department to another, showing the source flow and final disposition of the various copies of all documents. Most flowcharts on the CPA exam have been of this type.

3. **Other Documentation Charting Techniques**

   a. **Decision table**—Decision tables use a matrix format that lists sets of conditions, and the actions that result from various combinations of these conditions. See Module 2 on internal control for an example of a decision table.

   b. **Data flow diagram (DFD)**—Presents logical flows of data and functions in a system. For example, a data flow diagram for the delivery of goods to a customer would include a symbol for the warehouse from which the goods are shipped and a symbol representing the customer. It would not emphasize details such as computer processing and paper outputs.

MULTIPLE-CHOICE QUESTIONS (1-135)

1. A software package that is used with a large set of organized data that presents the computer as an expert on a particular topic is referred to as a(n)
    a. Data mining.
    b. Expert system.
    c. Artificial intelligence.
    d. Virtual reality.

2. Computer memory which is used to store programs that must be accessed immediately by the central processing unit is
    a. Primary storage.
    b. Secondary storage.
    c. Tertiary storage.
    d. Tape storage.

3. The most common output device is a(n)
    a. Mouse.
    b. Printer.
    c. Expert system.
    d. Keyboard.

4. The part of the computer that does most of the data processing is referred to as the
    a. Analyter.
    b. Compiler.
    c. CPU.
    d. Printer.

5. An "office suite" of software is least likely to include a(n)
    a. Databases.
    b. Operating system.
    c. Spreadsheet.
    d. Word processing.

6. Software that performs a variety of general technical computer-controlling operations is a(n)
    a. Integrated "suite."
    b. Shareware.
    c. Database.
    d. Operating system.

7. Which of the following is not a part of the central processing unit?
    a. Control unit.
    b. Arithmetic unit.
    c. Logic unit.
    d. Printer unit.

8. MIPS stands for
    a. Memory in protocol standards.
    b. Millions of instructions per second.
    c. Mitigating individualistic personnel standards.
    d. Multiple input physical savings.

9. Which of the following represents a type of applications software that a large client is most likely to use?
    a. Enterprise resource planning.
    b. Operating system.
    c. Central processing unit.
    d. Value-added network.

10. Which of the following characteristics distinguishes computer processing from manual processing?

    a. Computer processing virtually eliminates the occurrence of computational error normally associated with manual processing.
    b. Errors or fraud in computer processing will be detected soon after their occurrences.
    c. The potential for systematic error is ordinarily greater in manual processing than in computerized processing.
    d. Most computer systems are designed so that transaction trails useful for audit purposes do **not** exist.

11. Which computer application is most frequently used on mainframe computers?
    a. Databases.
    b. Graphics.
    c. Spreadsheets.
    d. Word processing.

12. Which computer application is most frequently used to analyze numbers and financial information?
    a. Computer graphics programs.
    b. WAN applications.
    c. Spreadsheets.
    d. Word processing programs.

13. Analysis of data in a database using tools which look for trends or anomalies without knowledge in advance of the meaning of the data is referred to as
    a. Artificial intelligence.
    b. Data mining.
    c. Virtual reality.
    d. Transitory analysis.

14. The most common type of primary storage in a computer is referred to as
    a. CMAN.
    b. RAM.
    c. ROM.
    d. Flash memory.

15. A set of step-by-step procedures used to accomplish a task is a(n)
    a. Algorithm.
    b. Compilation Master.
    c. Linux.
    d. Transitor.

16. Which of the following compiles a complete translation of a program in a high-level computer language before the program is run for the first time?
    a. Visual Basic.
    b. Java.
    c. Algorithm.
    d. Compiler.

17. GUI is the abbreviation for
    a. Grandfather, Uncle, Individual.
    b. Graphical User Interface.
    c. Graphics Utilization Institutes.
    d. Grand Union Internet.

18. Unix is a(n)
    a. Operating system.
    b. Singular disk drive.
    c. Central processing unit.
    d. Logic unit.

19. In a spreadsheet, each specific cell may be identified by a specific

    a. Address.
    b. Column.
    c. Row.
    d. Diagonal.

20. In a spreadsheet, which of the following is correct concerning rows and columns?

	Rows	_Columns_
a.	Numbered	Numbered
b.	Numbered	Lettered
c.	Lettered	Numbered
d.	Lettered	Lettered

21. Which of the following is **least** likely to be considered an advantage of a database?

    a. Easy to store large quantities of information.
    b. Easy to retrieve information quickly.
    c. Easy to organize and reorganize information.
    d. Easy to distribute information to every possible user.

22. Most current computers process data using which of the following formats?

    a. Analog.
    b. Digital.
    c. Memory enhanced.
    d. Organic.

23. A current day instruction to a computer such as "*Extract all Customers where 'Name' is Smith*" would most likely relate to a

    a. First generation programming language.
    b. Fourth generation programming language.
    c. Seventh generation programming language.
    d. Ninth generation programming language.

24. Several language interfaces exist in a database management system. These typically include a data definition language (DDL), a data control language (DCL), a data manipulation language (DML), and a database query language (DQL). What language interface would a database administrator use to establish the structure of database tables?

    a. DDL.
    b. DCL.
    c. DML.
    d. DQL.

25. Users making database queries often need to combine several tables to get the information they want. One approach to combining tables is known as

    a. Joining.
    b. Merging.
    c. Projecting.
    d. Pointing.

26. User acceptance testing is more important in an object-oriented development process than in a traditional environment because of the implications of the

    a. Absence of traditional design documents.
    b. Lack of a tracking system for changes.
    c. Potential for continuous monitoring.
    d. Inheritance of properties in hierarchies.

27. A company's management has expressed concern over the varied system architectures that the organization uses. Potential security and control concerns would include all of the following **except:**

    a. Users may have different user ID codes and passwords to remember for the several systems that they use.
    b. There are difficulties in developing uniform security standards for the various platforms.
    c. Backup file storage administration is often decentralized.
    d. Having data distributed across many computers throughout the organization increases the risk that a single disaster would destroy large portions of the organization's data.

28. All of the following are methods for distributing a relational database across multiple servers **except:**

    a. Snapshot (making a copy of the database for distribution).
    b. Replication (creating and maintaining replica copies at multiple locations).
    c. Normalization (separating the database into logical tables for easier user processing).
    d. Fragmentation (separating the database into parts and distributing where they are needed).

29. Client/server architecture may potentially involve a variety of hardware, systems software, and application software from many vendors. The best way to protect a client/server system from unauthorized access is through

    a. A combination of application and general access control techniques.
    b. Use of a commercially available authentication system.
    c. Encryption of all network traffic.
    d. Thorough testing and evaluation of remote procedure calls.

30. What technology is needed in order to convert a paper document into a computer file?

    a. Optical character recognition.
    b. Electronic data interchange.
    c. Bar-coding scanning.
    d. Joining and merging.

31. Unauthorized alteration of online records can be prevented by employing

    a. Key verification.
    b. Computer sequence checks.
    c. Computer matching.
    d. Database access controls.

32. A manufacturer of complex electronic equipment such as oscilloscopes and microscopes has been shipping its products with thick paper manuals but wants to reduce the cost of producing and shipping this documentation. Of the following, the best medium for the manufacturer to use to accomplish this is

    a. Write-once-read-many.
    b. Digital audio tape.
    c. Compact disc/read-only memory.
    d. Computer-output-to-microform.

33. Misstatements in a batch computer system caused by incorrect programs or data may **not** be detected immediately because

    a. Errors in some transactions may cause rejection of other transactions in the batch.

b. The identification of errors in input data typically is **not** part of the program.

c. There are time delays in processing transactions in a batch system.

d. The processing of transactions in a batch system is **not** uniform.

34. Which of the following is **not** a characteristic of a batch processed computer system?

a. The collection of like transactions which are sorted and processed sequentially against a master file.

b. Keypunching of transactions, followed by machine processing.

c. The production of numerous printouts.

d. The posting of a transaction, as it occurs, to several files, without intermediate printouts.

35. Able Co. uses an online sales order processing system to process its sales transactions. Able's sales data are electronically sorted and subjected to edit checks. A direct output of the edit checks most likely would be a

a. Report of all missing sales invoices.

b. File of all rejected sales transactions.

c. Printout of all user code numbers and passwords.

d. List of all voided shipping documents.

36. First Federal S & L has an online real-time system, with terminals installed in all of its branches. This system will not accept a customer's cash withdrawal instructions in excess of $1,000 without the use of a "terminal audit key." After the transaction is authorized by a supervisor, the bank teller then processes the transaction with the audit key. This control can be strengthened by

a. Online recording of the transaction on an audit override sheet.

b. Increasing the dollar amount to $1,500.

c. Requiring manual, rather than online, recording of all such transactions.

d. Using parallel simulation.

37. Mill Co. uses a batch processing method to process its sales transactions. Data on Mill's sales transaction tape are electronically sorted by customer number and are subjected to programmed edit checks in preparing its invoices, sales journals, and updated customer account balances. One of the direct outputs of the creation of this tape most likely would be a

a. Report showing exceptions and control totals.

b. Printout of the updated inventory records.

c. Report showing overdue accounts receivable.

d. Printout of the sales price master file.

38. Where disk files are used, the grandfather-father-son updating backup concept is relatively difficult to implement because the

a. Location of information points on disks is an extremely time-consuming task.

b. Magnetic fields and other environmental factors cause off-site storage to be impractical.

c. Information must be dumped in the form of hard copy if it is to be reviewed before used in updating.

d. Process of updating old records is destructive.

39. In a computerized system, procedure or problem-oriented language is converted to machine language through a(n)

a. Interpreter.

b. Verifier.

c. Compiler.

d. Converter.

40. What type of computer system is characterized by data that are assembled from more than one location and records that are updated immediately?

a. Microcomputer system.

b. Minicomputer system.

c. Batch processing system.

d. Online real-time system.

41. Which of the following characteristics distinguishes electronic data interchange (EDI) from other forms of electronic commerce?

a. EDI transactions are formatted using the standards that are uniform worldwide.

b. EDI transactions need **not** comply with generally accepted accounting principles.

c. EDI transactions ordinarily are processed without the Internet.

d. EDI transactions are usually recorded without security and privacy concerns.

42. LAN is the abbreviation for

a. Large Area Network.

b. Local Area Network.

c. Longitudinal Analogue Network.

d. Low Analytical Nets.

43. A computer that is designed to provide software and other applications to other computers is referred to as a

a. Microcomputer.

b. Network computer.

c. Server.

d. Supercomputer.

44. Which is **least** likely to be considered a component of a computer network?

a. Applications programs.

b. Computers.

c. Software.

d. Routers.

45. The network most frequently used for private operations designed to link computers within widely separated portions of an organization is referred to as a(n)

a. Bulletin board service.

b. Local area network.

c. Wide area network.

d. Zero base network.

46. A set of rules for exchanging data between two computers is a

a. Communicator.

b. Operating system.

c. Protocol.

d. Transmission speed.

47. A web page is most frequently created using

a. Java or C++.

b. Visual Basic.

c. SQL.

d. HTML or XML.

48. Laptop computers provide automation outside of the normal office location. Which of the following would pro-

vide the **least** security for sensitive data stored on a laptop computer?
- a. Encryption of data files on the laptop computer.
- b. Setting up a password for the screensaver program on the laptop computer.
- c. Using a laptop computer with a removable hard disk drive.
- d. Using a locking device that can secure the laptop computer to an immovable object.

49. When developing a new computer system that will handle customer orders and process customer payments, a high-level systems design phase would include determination of which of the following?
- a. How the new system will affect current inventory and general ledger systems.
- b. How the file layouts will be structured for the customer order records.
- c. Whether to purchase a turn-key system or modify an existing system.
- d. Whether formal approval by top management is needed for the new system.

50. A company using EDI made it a practice to track the functional acknowledgments from trading partners and to issue warning messages if acknowledgments did not occur within a reasonable length of time. What risk was the company attempting to address by this practice?
- a. Transactions that have not originated from a legitimate trading partner may be inserted into the EDI network.
- b. Transmission of EDI transactions to trading partners may sometimes fail.
- c. There may be disagreement between the parties as to whether the EDI transactions form a legal contract.
- d. EDI data may not be accurately and completely processed by the EDI software.

51. Management is concerned that data uploaded from a microcomputer to the company's mainframe system in batch processing may be erroneous. Which of the following controls would best address this issue?
- a. The mainframe computer should be backed up on a regular basis.
- b. Two persons should be present at the microcomputer when it is uploading data.
- c. The mainframe computer should subject the data to the same edits and validation routines that online data entry would require.
- d. The users should be required to review a random sample of processed data.

Items 52 and 53 are based on the following information:

One major category of computer viruses is programs that attach themselves to other programs, thus infecting the other programs. While many of these viruses are relatively harmless, some have the potential to cause significant damage.

52. Which of the following is an indication that a computer virus of this category is present?
- a. Frequent power surges that harm computer equipment.

- b. Unexplainable losses of or changes to data.
- c. Inadequate backup, recovery, and contingency plans.
- d. Numerous copyright violations due to unauthorized use of purchased software.

53. Which of the following operating procedures increases an organization's exposure to computer viruses?
- a. Encryption of data files.
- b. Frequent backup of files.
- c. Downloading public-domain software from electronic bulletin boards.
- d. Installing original copies of purchased software on hard disk drives.

54. Which of the following is a risk that is higher when an electronic funds transfer (EFT) system is used?
- a. Improper change control procedures.
- b. Unauthorized access and activity.
- c. Insufficient online edit checks.
- d. Inadequate backups and disaster recovery procedures.

55. The use of message encryption software
- a. Guarantees the secrecy of data.
- b. Requires manual distribution of keys.
- c. Increases system overhead.
- d. Reduces the need for periodic password changes.

**56. A company's management is concerned about computer data eavesdropping and wants to maintain the confidentiality of its information as it is transmitted. The company should utilize
- a. Data encryption.
- b. Dial-back systems.
- c. Message acknowledgement procedures.
- d. Password codes.

57. Which of the following is likely to be a benefit of electronic data interchange (EDI)?
- a. Increased transmission speed of actual documents.
- b. Improved business relationships with trading partners.
- c. Decreased liability related to protection of proprietary business data.
- d. Decreased requirements for backup and contingency planning.

58. The internal auditor is reviewing a new policy on electronic mail. Appropriate elements of such a policy would include all of the following **except:**
- a. Erasing all employee's electronic mail immediately upon employment termination.
- b. Encrypting electronic mail messages when transmitted over phone lines.
- c. Limiting the number of electronic mail packages adopted by the organization.
- d. Directing that personnel do not send highly sensitive or confidential messages using electronic mail.

59. Which of the following risks is more likely to be encountered in an end-user computing (EUC) environment as compared to a mainframe computer system?
- a. Inability to afford adequate uninterruptible power supply systems.
- b. User input screens without a graphical user interface (GUI).

   c.   Applications that are difficult to integrate with other information systems.
   d.   Lack of adequate utility programs.

60. Which of the following risks is **not** greater in an electronic funds transfer (EFT) environment than in a manual system using paper transactions?
   a.   Unauthorized access and activity.
   b.   Duplicate transaction processing.
   c.   Higher cost per transaction.
   d.   Inadequate backup and recovery capabilities.

61. Methods to minimize the installation of unlicensed microcomputer software include all of the following **except:**
   a.   Employee awareness programs.
   b.   Regular audits for unlicensed software.
   c.   Regular monitoring of network access and start-up scripts.
   d.   An organizational policy that includes software licensing requirements.

62. In traditional information systems, computer operators are generally responsible for backing up software and data files on a regular basis. In distributed or cooperative systems, ensuring that adequate backups are taken is the responsibility of
   a.   User management.
   b.   Systems programmers.
   c.   Data entry clerks.
   d.   Tape librarians.

63. An auditor is least likely to find that a client's data is input through
   a.   Magnetic tape reader.
   b.   Dynamic linking character reader.
   c.   Point-of-sale recorders.
   d.   Touch sensitive screens.

64. End-user computing is an example of which of the following?
   a.   Client/server processing.
   b.   A distributed system.
   c.   Data mining.
   d.   Decentralized processing.

65. End-user computing is most likely to occur on which of the following types of computers?
   a.   Mainframe.
   b.   Minicomputers.
   c.   Personal computers.
   d.   Personal reference assistants.

66. Which of the following statements is correct regarding the Internet as a commercially viable network?
   a.   Organizations must use firewalls if they wish to maintain security over internal data.
   b.   Companies must apply to the Internet to gain permission to create a homepage to engage in electronic commerce.
   c.   Companies that wish to engage in electronic commerce on the Internet must meet required security standards established by the coalition of Internet providers.
   d.   All of the above.

67. To reduce security exposure when transmitting proprietary data over communication lines, a company should use

   a.   Asynchronous modems.
   b.   Authentic techniques.
   c.   Call-back procedures.
   d.   Cryptographic devices.

68. Securing client/server systems is a complex task because of all of the following factors **except:**
   a.   The use of relational databases.
   b.   The number of access points.
   c.   Concurrent operation of multiple user sessions.
   d.   Widespread data access and update capabilities.

69. Which of the following would an auditor ordinarily consider the greatest risk regarding an entity's use of electronic data interchange (EDI)?
   a.   Authorization of EDI transactions.
   b.   Duplication of EDI transmissions.
   c.   Improper distribution of EDI transactions.
   d.   Elimination of paper documents.

70. Which of the following characteristics distinguish electronic data interchange (EDI) from other forms of electronic commerce?
   a.   The cost of sending EDI transactions using a value-added network (VAN) is less than the cost of using the Internet.
   b.   Software maintenance contracts are unnecessary because translation software for EDI transactions need not be updated.
   c.   EDI commerce is ordinarily conducted without establishing legally binding contracts between trading partners.
   d.   EDI transactions are formatted using strict standards that have been agreed to worldwide.

71. Which of the following is considered a component of a local area network?
   a.   Program flowchart.
   b.   Loop verification.
   c.   Transmission media.
   d.   Input routine.

72. Which of the following represents an additional cost of transmitting business transactions by means of electronic data interchange (EDI) rather than in a traditional paper environment?
   a.   Redundant data checks are needed to verify that individual EDI transactions are **not** recorded twice.
   b.   Internal audit work is needed because the potential for random data entry errors is increased.
   c.   Translation software is needed to convert transactions from the entity's internal format to a standard EDI format.
   d.   More supervisory personnel are needed because the amount of data entry is greater in an EDI system.

73. Many entities use the Internet as a network to transmit electronic data interchange (EDI) transactions. An advantage of using the Internet for electronic commerce rather than a traditional value-added network (VAN) is that the Internet
   a.   Permits EDI transactions to be sent to trading partners as transactions occur.
   b.   Automatically batches EDI transactions to multiple trading partners.

c.   Possesses superior characteristics regarding disaster recovery.

d.   Converts EDI transactions to a standard format without translation software.

74. Which of the following is not considered an exposure involved with electronic data interchange (EDI) systems as compared to other systems?

a.   Increased reliance upon computer systems.
b.   Delayed transaction processing time.
c.   Possible loss of confidentiality of information.
d.   Increased reliance upon third parties.

75. Which of the following statements is correct concerning internal control when a client is using an electronic data interchange system for its sales?

a.   Controls should be established over determining that all suppliers are included in the system.
b.   Encryption controls may help to assure that messages are unreadable to unauthorized persons.
c.   A value-added-network (VAN) must be used to assure proper control.
d.   Attention must be paid to both the electronic and "paper" versions of transactions.

76. Which of the following statements most likely represents a disadvantage for an entity that keeps microcomputer-prepared data files rather than manually prepared files?

a.   Random error associated with processing similar transactions in different ways is usually greater.
b.   It is usually more difficult to compare recorded accountability with physical count of assets.
c.   Attention is focused on the accuracy of the programming process rather than errors in individual transactions.
d.   It is usually easier for unauthorized persons to access and alter the files.

77. Which of the following is usually a benefit of transmitting transactions in an electronic data interchange (EDI) environment?

a.   A compressed business cycle with lower year-end receivables balances.
b.   A reduced need to test computer controls related to sales and collections transactions.
c.   An increased opportunity to apply statistical sampling techniques to account balances.
d.   No need to rely on third-party service providers to ensure security.

78. Which of the following is a network node that is used to improve network traffic and to set up as a boundary that prevents traffic from one segment to cross over to another?

a.   Router.
b.   Gateway.
c.   Firewall.
d.   Heuristic.

79. Which of the following is an example of how specific controls in a database environment may differ from controls in a nondatabase environment?

a.   Controls should exist to ensure that users have access to and can update only the data elements that they have been authorized to access.
b.   Controls over data sharing by diverse users within an entity should be the same for every user.

c.   The employee who manages the computer hardware should also develop and debug the computer programs.

d.   Controls can provide assurance that all processed transactions are authorized, but **cannot** verify that all authorized transactions are processed.

80. A retail entity uses electronic data interchange (EDI) in executing and recording most of its purchase transactions. The entity's auditor recognized that the documentation of the transactions will be retained for only a short period of time. To compensate for this limitation, the auditor most likely would

a.   Increase the sample of EDI transactions to be selected for cutoff tests.
b.   Perform tests several times during the year, rather than only at year-end.
c.   Plan to make a 100% count of the entity's inventory at or near the year-end.
d.   Decrease the assessed level of control risk for the existence or occurrence assertion.

81. Which of the following is an encryption feature that can be used to authenticate the originator of a document and ensure that the message is intact and has **not** been tampered with?

a.   Heuristic terminal.
b.   Perimeter switch.
c.   Default settings.
d.   Digital signatures.

82. In building an electronic data interchange (EDI) system, what process is used to determine which elements in the entity's computer system correspond to the standard data elements?

a.   Mapping.
b.   Translation.
c.   Encryption.
d.   Decoding.

83. Which of the following passwords would be most difficult to crack?

a.   OrCa!FlSi
b.   language
c.   12 HOUSE 24
d.   pass56word

84. Which of the following is a password security problem?

a.   Users are assigned passwords when accounts are created, but do **not** change them.
b.   Users have accounts on several systems with different passwords.
c.   Users copy their passwords on note paper, which is kept in their wallets.
d.   Users select passwords that are **not** listed in any online dictionary.

85. Which of the following procedures would an entity most likely include in its computer disaster recovery plan?

a.   Develop an auxiliary power supply to provide uninterrupted electricity.
b.   Store duplicate copies of critical files in a location away from the computer center.
c.   Maintain a listing of entity passwords with the network manager.

d. Translate data for storage purposes with a cryptographic secret code.

86. A company is concerned that a power outage or disaster could impair the computer hardware's ability to function as designed. The company desires off-site backup hardware facilities that are fully configured and ready to operate within several hours. The company most likely should consider a

    a. Cold site.
    b. Cool site.
    c. Warm site.
    d. Hot site.

87. Which of the following procedures would an entity most likely include in its disaster recovery plan?

    a. Convert all data from EDI format to an internal company format.
    b. Maintain a Trojan horse program to prevent illicit activity.
    c. Develop an auxiliary power supply to provide uninterrupted electricity.
    d. Store duplicate copies of files in a location away from the computer center.

88. Almost all commercially marketed software is

	Copyrighted	Copy protected
a.	Yes	Yes
b.	Yes	No
c.	No	Yes
d.	No	No

89. A widely used disaster recovery approach includes

    a. Encryption.
    b. Firewalls.
    c. Regular backups.
    d. Surge protectors.

90. A "hot site" is most frequently associated with

    a. Disaster recovery.
    b. Online relational database design.
    c. Source programs.
    d. Temperature control for computer.

91. Output controls ensure that the results of computer processing are accurate, complete, and properly distributed. Which of the following is **not** a typical output control?

    a. Reviewing the computer processing logs to determine that all of the correct computer jobs executed properly.
    b. Matching input data with information on master files and placing unmatched items in a suspense file.
    c. Periodically reconciling output reports to make sure that totals, formats, and critical details are correct and agree with input.
    d. Maintaining formal procedures and documentation specifying authorized recipients of output reports, checks, or other critical documents.

92. Minimizing the likelihood of unauthorized editing of production programs, job control language, and operating system software can best be accomplished by

    a. Database access reviews.
    b. Compliance reviews.
    c. Good change-control procedures.
    d. Effective network security software.

93. Some companies have replaced mainframe computers with microcomputers and networks because the smaller computers could do the same work at less cost. Assuming that management of a company decided to launch a downsizing project, what should be done with respect to mainframe applications such as the general ledger system?

    a. Plan for rapid conversion of all mainframe applications to run on a microcomputer network.
    b. Consider the general ledger system as an initial candidate for conversion.
    c. Defer any modification of the general ledger system until it is clearly inadequate.
    d. Integrate downsized applications with stable mainframe applications.

94. A corporation receives the majority of its revenue from top-secret military contracts with the government. Which of the following would be of greatest concern to an auditor reviewing a policy about selling the company's used microcomputers to outside parties?

    a. Whether deleted files on the hard disk drive have been completely erased.
    b. Whether the computer has viruses.
    c. Whether all software on the computer is properly licensed.
    d. Whether the computer has terminal emulation software on it.

95. A manufacturer is considering using bar-code identification for recording information on parts used by the manufacturer. A reason to use bar codes rather than other means of identification is to ensure that

    a. The movement of all parts is recorded.
    b. The movement of parts is easily and quickly recorded.
    c. Vendors use the same part numbers.
    d. Vendors use the same identification methods.

96. A company often revises its production processes. The changes may entail revisions to processing programs. Ensuring that changes have a minimal impact on processing and result in minimal risk to the system is a function of

    a. Security administration.
    b. Change control.
    c. Problem tracking.
    d. Problem-escalation procedures.

97. Pirated software obtained through the Internet may lead to civil lawsuits or criminal prosecution. Of the following, which would reduce an organization's risk in this area?

  I. Maintain a log of all software purchases.
  II. Audit individual computers to identify software on the computers.
III. Establish a corporate software policy.
IV. Provide original software diskettes to each user.

    a. I and IV only.
    b. I, II, and III only.
    c. II and IV only.
    d. II and III only.

98. Good planning will help an organization restore computer operations after a processing outage. Good recovery planning should ensure that

    a. Backup/restart procedures have been built into job streams and programs.

b. Change control procedures cannot be bypassed by operating personnel.

c. Planned changes in equipment capacities are compatible with projected workloads.

d. Service level agreements with owners of applications are documented.

99. In a large organization, the biggest risk in not having an adequately staffed information center help desk is

a. Increased difficulty in performing application audits.

b. Inadequate documentation for application systems.

c. Increased likelihood of use of unauthorized program code.

d. Persistent errors in user interaction with systems.

100. To properly control access to accounting database files, the database administrator should ensure that database system features are in place to permit

a. Read-only access to the database files.

b. Updating from privileged utilities.

c. Access only to authorized logical views.

d. User updates of their access profiles.

101. When evaluating internal control of an entity that processes sales transactions on the Internet, an auditor would be most concerned about the

a. Lack of sales invoice documents as an audit trail.

b. Potential for computer disruptions in recording sales.

c. Inability to establish an integrated test facility.

d. Frequency of archiving and data retention.

102. Which of the following statements is correct concerning internal control in an electronic data interchange (EDI) system?

a. Preventive controls generally are more important than detective controls in EDI systems.

b. Control objectives for EDI systems generally are different from the objectives for other information systems.

c. Internal controls in EDI systems rarely permit control risk to be assessed at below the maximum.

d. Internal controls related to the segregation of duties generally are the most important controls in EDI systems.

103. Which of the following statements is correct concerning the security of messages in an electronic data interchange (EDI) system?

a. When the confidentiality of data is the primary risk, message authentication is the preferred control rather than encryption.

b. Encryption performed by physically secure hardware devices is more secure than encryption performed by software.

c. Message authentication in EDI systems performs the same function as segregation of duties in other information systems.

d. Security at the transaction phase in EDI systems is **not** necessary because problems at that level will usually be identified by the service provider.

104. Which of the following is an essential element of the audit trail in an electronic data interchange (EDI) system?

a. Disaster recovery plans that ensure proper backup of files.

b. Encrypted hash totals that authenticate messages.

c. Activity logs that indicate failed transactions.

d. Hardware security modules that store sensitive data.

105. Which of the following are essential elements of the audit trail in an electronic data interchange (EDI) system?

a. Network and sender/recipient acknowledgments.

b. Message directories and header segments.

c. Contingency and disaster recovery plans.

d. Trading partner security and mailbox codes.

106. To avoid invalid data input, a bank added an extra number at the end of each account number and subjected the new number to an algorithm. This technique is known as

a. Optical character recognition.

b. A check digit.

c. A dependency check.

d. A format check.

107. Preventing someone with sufficient technical skill from circumventing security procedures and making changes to production programs is best accomplished by

a. Reviewing reports of jobs completed.

b. Comparing production programs with independently controlled copies.

c. Running test data periodically.

d. Providing suitable segregation of duties.

108. Computer program libraries can best be kept secure by

a. Installing a logging system for program access.

b. Monitoring physical access to program library media.

c. Restricting physical and logical access.

d. Denying access from remote terminals.

109. Which of the following security controls would best prevent unauthorized access to sensitive data through an unattended data terminal directly connected to a mainframe?

a. Use of a screen saver with a password.

b. Use of workstation scripts.

c. Encryption of data files.

d. Automatic log-off of inactive users.

110. An entity has the following invoices in a batch:

Invoice #	Product	Quantity	Unit price
201	F10	150	$ 5.00
202	G15	200	$10.00
203	H20	250	$25.00
204	K35	300	$30.00

Which of the following most likely represents a hash total?

a. FGHK80

b. 4

c. 204

d. 810

111. A customer intended to order 100 units of product Z96014, but incorrectly ordered nonexistent product Z96015. Which of the following controls most likely would detect this error?

a. Check digit verification.

b. Record count.

c. Hash total.

d. Redundant data check.

112. In entering the billing address for a new client in Emil Company's computerized database, a clerk erroneously entered a nonexistent zip code. As a result, the first month's bill mailed to the new client was returned to Emil Company. Which one of the following would **most likely have led to discovery of the error at the time of entry into Emil Company's computerized database?
a. Limit test.
b. Validity test.
c. Parity test.
d. Record count test.

113. Which of the following controls is a processing control designed to ensure the reliability and accuracy of data processing?

	Limit test	Validity check test
a.	Yes	Yes
b.	No	No
c.	No	Yes
d.	Yes	No

114. Which of the following activities would most likely be performed in the information systems department?
a. Initiation of changes to master records.
b. Conversion of information to machine-readable form.
c. Correction of transactional errors.
d. Initiation of changes to existing applications.

115. The use of a header label in conjunction with magnetic tape is **most** likely to prevent errors by the
a. Computer operator.
b. Keypunch operator.
c. Computer programmer.
d. Maintenance technician.

116. For the accounting system of Acme Company, the amounts of cash disbursements entered into a terminal are transmitted to the computer that immediately transmits the amounts back to the terminal for display on the terminal screen. This display enables the operator to
a. Establish the validity of the account number.
b. Verify the amount was entered accurately.
c. Verify the authorization of the disbursement.
d. Prevent the overpayment of the account.

117. When computer programs or files can be accessed from terminals, users should be required to enter a(n)
a. Parity check.
b. Personal identification code.
c. Self-diagnosis test.
d. Echo check.

118. The possibility of erasing a large amount of information stored on magnetic tape most likely would be reduced by the use of
a. File protection rings.
b. Check digits.
c. Completeness tests.
d. Conversion verification.

119. Which of the following controls most likely would assure that an entity can reconstruct its financial records?
a. Hardware controls are built into the computer by the computer manufacturer.

b. Backup diskettes or tapes of files are stored away from originals.
c. Personnel who are independent of data input perform parallel simulations.
d. System flowcharts provide accurate descriptions of input and output operations.

120. Which of the following input controls is a numeric value computed to provide assurance that the original value has **not** been altered in construction or transmission?
a. Hash total.
b. Parity check.
c. Encryption.
d. Check digit.

121. Which of the following is an example of a validity check?
a. The computer ensures that a numerical amount in a record does **not** exceed some predetermined amount.
b. As the computer corrects errors and data are successfully resubmitted to the system, the causes of the errors are printed out.
c. The computer flags any transmission for which the control field value did **not** match that of an existing file record.
d. After data for a transaction are entered, the computer sends certain data back to the terminal for comparison with data originally sent.

122. Which of the following is a computer test made to ascertain whether a given characteristic belongs to the group?
a. Parity check.
b. Validity check.
c. Echo check.
d. Limit check.

123. A control feature in an electronic data processing system requires the central processing unit (CPU) to send signals to the printer to activate the print mechanism for each character. The print mechanism, just prior to printing, sends a signal back to the CPU verifying that the proper print position has been activated. This type of hardware control is referred to as
a. Echo control.
b. Validity control.
c. Signal control.
d. Check digit control.

124. Which of the following is an example of a check digit?
a. An agreement of the total number of employees to the total number of checks printed by the computer.
b. An algebraically determined number produced by the other digits of the employee number.
c. A logic test that ensures all employee numbers are nine digits.
d. A limit check that an employee's hours do not exceed fifty hours per workweek.

125. Which of the following most likely represents a significant deficiency in internal control?
a. The systems analyst reviews applications of data processing and maintains systems documentation.
b. The systems programmer designs systems for computerized applications and maintains output controls.

c.   The control clerk establishes control over data received by the information systems department and reconciles control totals after processing.

d.   The accounts payable clerk prepares data for computer processing and enters the data into the computer.

126. Internal control is ineffective when computer department personnel

a.   Participate in computer software acquisition decisions.

b.   Design documentation for computerized systems.

c.   Originate changes in master files.

d.   Provide physical security for program files.

127. Which of the following activities most likely would detect whether payroll data were altered during processing?

a.   Monitor authorized distribution of data control sheets.

b.   Use test data to verify the performance of edit routines.

c.   Examine source documents for approval by supervisors.

d.   Segregate duties between approval of hardware and software specifications.

128. Which of the following tools would best give a graphical representation of a sequence of activities and decisions?

a.   Flowchart.

b.   Control chart.

c.   Histogram.

d.   Run chart.

Items 129 and 130 are based on the following flowchart of a client's revenue cycle:

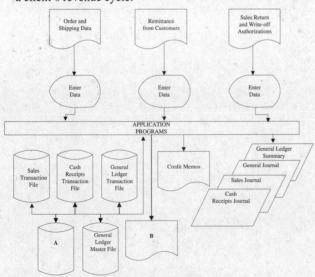

129. Symbol A most likely represents

a.   Remittance advice file.

b.   Receiving report file.

c.   Accounts receivable master file.

d.   Cash disbursements transaction file.

130. Symbol B most likely represents

a.   Customer orders.

b.   Receiving reports.

c.   Customer checks.

d.   Sales invoices.

131. An auditor's flowchart of a client's accounting system is a diagrammatic representation that depicts the auditor's

a.   Assessment of control risk.

b.   Identification of weaknesses in the system.

c.   Assessment of the control environment's effectiveness.

d.   Understanding of the system.

Item 132 is based on the following flowchart:

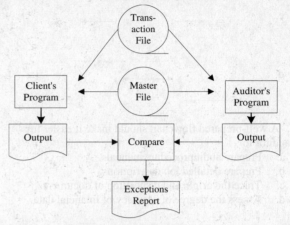

132. The above flowchart depicts

a.   Program code checking.

b.   Parallel simulation.

c.   Integrated test facility.

d.   Controlled reprocessing.

Item 133 is based on the following flowchart:

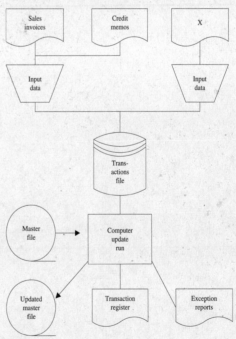

133. In a credit sales and cash receipts system flowchart, symbol X could represent

a.   Auditor's test data.

b.   Remittance advices.

c.   Error reports.

d.   Credit authorization forms.

134. Which of the following symbolic representations indicate that a file has been consulted?

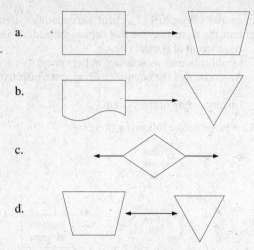

135. A well-prepared flowchart should make it easier for the auditor to

a. Prepare audit procedure manuals.
b. Prepare detailed job descriptions.
c. Trace the origin and disposition of documents.
d. Assess the degree of accuracy of financial data.

MULTIPLE-CHOICE ANSWERS

1. b __ __	29. a __ __	57. b __ __	85. b __ __	113. a __ __
2. a __ __	30. a __ __	58. a __ __	86. d __ __	114. b __ __
3. b __ __	31. d __ __	59. c __ __	87. d __ __	115. a __ __
4. c __ __	32. c __ __	60. c __ __	88. b __ __	116. b __ __
5. b __ __	33. c __ __	61. c __ __	89. c __ __	117. b __ __
6. d __ __	34. d __ __	62. a __ __	90. a __ __	118. a __ __
7. d __ __	35. b __ __	63. b __ __	91. b __ __	119. b __ __
8. b __ __	36. a __ __	64. d __ __	92. c __ __	120. d __ __
9. a __ __	37. a __ __	65. c __ __	93. d __ __	121. c __ __
10. a __ __	38. d __ __	66. a __ __	94. a __ __	122. b __ __
11. a __ __	39. c __ __	67. d __ __	95. b __ __	123. a __ __
12. c __ __	40. d __ __	68. a __ __	96. b __ __	124. b __ __
13. b __ __	41. a __ __	69. c __ __	97. b __ __	125. b __ __
14. b __ __	42. b __ __	70. d __ __	98. a __ __	126. c __ __
15. a __ __	43. c __ __	71. c __ __	99. d __ __	127. b __ __
16. d __ __	44. a __ __	72. c __ __	100. c __ __	128. a __ __
17. b __ __	45. c __ __	73. a __ __	101. b __ __	129. c __ __
18. a __ __	46. c __ __	74. b __ __	102. a __ __	130. d __ __
19. a __ __	47. d __ __	75. b __ __	103. b __ __	131. d __ __
20. b __ __	48. b __ __	76. d __ __	104. c __ __	132. b __ __
21. d __ __	49. c __ __	77. a __ __	105. a __ __	133. b __ __
22. b __ __	50. b __ __	78. c __ __	106. b __ __	134. d __ __
23. b __ __	51. c __ __	79. a __ __	107. d __ __	135. c __ __
24. a __ __	52. b __ __	80. b __ __	108. c __ __	
25. a __ __	53. c __ __	81. d __ __	109. d __ __	
26. d __ __	54. b __ __	82. a __ __	110. d __ __	
27. d __ __	55. c __ __	83. a __ __	111. a __ __	1st: __/135 __%
28. c __ __	56. a __ __	84. a __ __	112. b __ __	2nd: __/135 __%

MULTIPLE-CHOICE ANSWER EXPLANATIONS

A. Information Systems within a Business

1. **(b)** The requirement is to identify a type of software package that uses a large set of organized data that presents the computer as an expert on a particular topic. Answer (b) is correct because an expert system presents the computer as such an expert. Answer (a) is incorrect because data mining uses tools which look for trends or anomalies without advance knowledge of the meaning of the data. Answer (c) is incorrect because artificial intelligence is a branch of computer science that involves computer programs that can solve specific problems creatively. Answer (d) is incorrect because virtual reality involves computer creation of an artificial, three-dimension world that may be interacted with.

2. **(a)** The requirement is to identify the type of computer memory used to store programs that must be accessed immediately by the central processing unit. Answer (a) is correct because primary memory is quickly accessed and generally used to store programs that must be accessed immediately. Answer (b) is incorrect because secondary storage is accessed less quickly. Answer (c) is incorrect because the term tertiary storage has no meaning in information technology. Answer (d) is incorrect because tape storage requires relatively long access times.

3. **(b)** The requirement is to identify the most common output device. Answer (b) is correct because a printer is a common output device and because the other replies represent input, not output devices.

4. **(c)** The requirement is to identify the part of the computer that does most of the data processing. Answer (c) is correct because the CPU, the central processing unit, does the primary processing for a computer. Answer (a) is incorrect because the word "analyter" has no meaning in information technology. Answer (b) is incorrect because a compiler is used to compile a particular type of computer program. Answer (d) is incorrect because a printer is an output device.

5. **(b)** The requirement is to identify the software least likely to be included in an "office suite" of software. Answer (b), operating systems (e.g., Windows, Linux, Unix) is not ordinarily included in an office suite. Answers (a), (c) and (d) are all incorrect because databases, spreadsheets, and word processing software are often included.

6. **(d)** The requirement is to identify the software that performs a variety of technical operations. Answer (d) is correct because an operating system controls the execution of computer programs and may provide various services. Answer (a) is incorrect because an integrated "suite" (e.g., Microsoft Office) is a series of applications such as a word processor, database, and spreadsheet. Answer (b) is incorrect because shareware is generally considered to be software made available at a low, or no, cost to users. Answer (c) is incorrect because a database system deals with more specific technical processing.

7. **(d)** The requirement is to identify the part listed that is not considered a part of the central processing unit. Answer (d) is correct because the printer is a separate output device. Answers (a), (b), and (c) are all incorrect because a computer includes control, arithmetic, and logic units.

8. **(b)** The requirement is to identify the meaning of MIPS. Answer (b) is correct because MIPS is an abbreviation for millions of instructions per second, a unit for measuring the execution speed of computers. Answers (a), (c), and (d) all include combinations of words with no particular meaning in information technology.

9. **(a)** The requirement is to identify the type of applications software that a large client is most likely to use. Answer (a) is correct because enterprise resource planning (ERP) software is a form of applications software that provides relatively complete information systems for large and medium size organizations. Answer (b) is incorrect because a computer operating system is considered systems software, not applications software. Answer (c) is incorrect because the central processing unit is the principal hardware component of a computer, not software. Answer (d) is incorrect because a value-added network is a privately owned network whose services are sold to the public.

10. **(a)** The requirement is to identify a characteristic that distinguishes computer processing from manual processing. Answer (a) is correct because the high degree of accuracy of computer computation virtually eliminates the occurrence of computational errors. Answer (b) is incorrect because errors or fraud in computer processing may or may not be detected, depending upon the effectiveness of an entity's internal control. Answer (c) is incorrect because a programming error will result in a high level of systematic error in a computerized system and therefore, such errors may occur in either a manual or a computerized system. Answer (d) is incorrect because most computer systems are designed to include transaction trails.

B. Characteristics of Computer Systems—General

11. **(a)** The requirement is to identify the most frequently used mainframe computer application. Answer (a) is correct because mainframe computers (the largest and most powerful computers available at a particular point in time) are generally used to store and process extremely large computer databases. Answers (b), (c), and (d) are all incorrect because they are less frequent mainframe computer applications.

12. **(c)** The requirement is to identify the computer application most frequently used to analyze numbers and financial information. Answer (c) is correct because the purpose of a spreadsheet is generally to process numbers and financial information; for example, spreadsheets are often used to perform "what if" analysis which makes various assumptions with respect to a particular situation. Answer (a) is incorrect because while computer graphics programs may present numbers and financial information, they do not in general process them to the extent of spreadsheets. Answer (b) is incorrect because a WAN is a wide area network, and not an application used to analyze numbers and financial information. Answer (d) is incorrect because the emphasis of word processing programs is not ordinarily on processing numbers and financial information.

13. **(b)** The requirement is to identify the type of analysis that uses a database and tools to look for trends or anomalies, without knowledge in advance of the meaning of the data. Answer (b) is correct because data mining uses tools which look for trends or anomalies without such advance knowledge. Answer (a) is incorrect because artificial intelligence is a branch of computer science that involves computer programs that can solve specific problems crea-

tively. Answer (c) is incorrect because virtual reality involves computer creation of an artificial, three-dimension world that may be interacted with. Answer (d) is incorrect because the term transitory analysis has no meaning relating to information technology.

14. **(b)** The requirement is to identify the most common type of primary storage in a computer. Answer (b) is correct because RAM (Random Access Memory) is the most common computer memory which can be used by programs to perform necessary tasks; RAM allows information to be stored or accessed in any order and all storage locations are equally accessible. Answer (a) is incorrect because CMAN has no meaning in information technology. Answer (c) is incorrect because ROM (Read Only Memory) is memory whose contents can be accessed and read but cannot be changed. Answer (d) is incorrect because it is a nonvolatile storage that can be electrically erased and programmed anew that is less common than RAM.

15. **(a)** The requirement is to identify a set of step-by-step procedures that are used to accomplish a task. Answer (a) is correct because an algorithm uses a step-by-step approach to accomplish a task. Answer (b) is incorrect because the term "compilation master" has no meaning in information technology. Answer (c) is incorrect because Linux is a form of operating system. Answer (d) is incorrect because the term "transitor" has no meaning in information technology.

16. **(d)** The requirement is to identify the item that compiles a complex translation of a program in a high-level computer language before the program is run for the first time. Answer (d) is correct because a compiler decodes instructions written in a higher order language and produces an assembly language program. Answers (a) and (b) are incorrect because Visual Basic and JAVA are programming languages. Answer (c) is incorrect because an algorithm is a "step-by-step" approach used to accomplish a particular task.

17. **(b)** The requirement is to identify the meaning of the abbreviation GUI. Answer (b), graphical user interface, is correct. The other replies all represent combinations of words with no meaning in information technology.

18. **(a)** The requirement is to identify the nature of Unix. Answer (a) is correct because Unix is a powerful operating system, originally developed by AT&T Bell Labs, that is used by many users of high-end computing hardware. Answers (b), (c), and (d) are all incorrect because Unix is not a singular disk drive, a central processing unit, or a logic unit.

19. **(a)** The requirement is to identify how each specific cell within a spreadsheet is identified. Answer (a) is correct because each cell has an address, composed of a combination of its column and row in the spreadsheet. Answer (b) is incorrect because the column portion of the address is not specific to the cell. Answer (c) is incorrect because the row portion of the address is not specific to the cell. Answer (d) is incorrect because no diagonal is ordinarily used to identify a particular cell.

20. **(b)** The requirement is to identify whether rows and columns of a spreadsheet are numbered or lettered. Answer (b) is correct because rows are numbered and columns are lettered. The other replies are all incorrect because they include incorrect combinations of "numbered" and "lettered."

21.   (d)   The requirement is to identify what is **least** likely to be considered an advantage of a database. Answer (d) is correct because a database itself does not make it easy to distribute information to every possible user—information must still be distributed either electronically or physically. Answer (a) is incorrect because a database is used to store large quantities of information. Answer (b) is incorrect because information may ordinarily be required quickly from a database. Answer (c) is incorrect because specific normalization rules have been identified for organizing information within a database.

22.   (b)   The requirement is to identify the most frequent current format for computer processing of data. Answer (b) is correct because most current computers process data using a digital approach in that they represent information by numerical (binary) digits. Answer (a) is incorrect because analog computers, which represent information by variable quantities (e.g., positions or voltages), are less frequent in practice than digital computers. Answer (c) is incorrect because "memory enhanced" is not a format for processing information. Answer (d) is incorrect because "organic" is not a format for processing information.

23.   (b)   The requirement is to identify the generation of programming language most likely to include an instruction such as *"Extract all Customers where 'Name' is Smith."* Answer (b) is correct because fourth generation programs ordinarily include instructions relatively close to human languages—such as the instruction in this question. Answer (a) is incorrect because first generation instructions are in terms of "1's" and "0's." Answers (c) and (d) are incorrect because seventh and ninth generation programming languages have not yet been developed (a few fifth generation languages with extensive visual and graphic interfaces are currently in process).

24.   (a)   The requirement is to identify the language interface used to establish the structure of database tables. Answer (a) is correct because DDL is used to define (i.e., determine) the database. Answer (b) is incorrect because DCL is used to specify privileges and security rules. Answer (c) is incorrect because DML provides programmers with a facility to update the database. Answer (d) is incorrect because DQL is used for ad hoc queries.

25.   (a)   The requirement is to identify the function used in a database query to combine several tables. Answer (a) is correct because joining is the combining of one or more tables based on matching criteria. For example, if a supplier table contains information about suppliers and a parts table contains information about parts, the two tables could be joined on supplier number (assuming both tables contained this attribute) to give information about the supplier of particular parts. Answers (b), (c), and (d) are all incorrect.

26.   (d)   The requirement is to identify a reason that user acceptance testing is more important in an object-oriented development process than in a traditional environment. Answer (d) is correct because user acceptance testing is more important in object-oriented development because of the fact that all objects in a class inherit the properties of the hierarchy, which means that changes to one object may affect

other objects, which increases the importance of user acceptance testing to verify correct functioning of the whole system. Answer (a) is incorrect because instead of traditional design documents, items such as the business model, narratives of process functions, iterative development screens, computer processes and reports, and product descriptions guides are produced in object-oriented development, but the existence of specific documents does not affect the importance of user acceptance testing. Answer (b) is incorrect because in general, object-oriented development systems do include tracking systems for changes made to objects and hierarchies. Answer (c) is incorrect; because object-oriented systems are usually developed in client/server environments there is the potential for continuous monitoring of system use, but continuous monitoring typically occurs during system operation, not during development.

27.   (d)   The requirement is to identify the reply that does not represent a potential security and control concern. Answer (d) is correct because the distribution of data actually decreases this risk so this would not cause a control concern; it is a potential advantage to distributed systems of various architectures versus centralized data in a single mainframe computer. Answer (a) is incorrect because password proliferation is a considerable security concern because users will be tempted to write their passwords down or make them overly simplistic. Answer (b) is incorrect because consistent security across varied platforms is often challenging because of the different security features of the various systems and the decentralized nature of those controlling security administration. Answer (c) is incorrect because under centralized control, management can feel more confident that backup file storage is being uniformly controlled. Decentralization of this function may lead to lack of consistency and difficulty in monitoring compliance.

28.   (c)   The requirement is to determine which answer is not a method for distributing a relational database across multiple servers. Answer (c) is correct because normalization is a process of database design, not distribution. Answer (a) is incorrect because making a copy of the database for distribution is a viable method for the described distribution. Answer (b) is incorrect because creating and maintaining replica copies at multiple locations is a viable method for the described distribution. Answer (d) is incorrect because separating the database into parts and distributing where they are needed is a viable method for the described distribution.

29.   (a)   The requirement is to identify the best way to protect a client/server system from unauthorized access. Answer (a) is correct because since there is no perfect solution, this is the best way. Answer (b) is incorrect because authentication systems, such as Kerberos, are only a part of the solution. Answer (c) is incorrect because this only affects general access control techniques. Answer (d) is incorrect because testing and evaluation of remote procedure calls may be a small part of an overall security review.

30.   (a)   The requirement is to identify the technology needed to convert a paper document into a computer file. Answer (a) is correct because optical character recognition (OCR) software converts images of paper documents, as read by a scanning device, into text document computer files. Answer (b) is incorrect because electronic data interchange involves electronic transactions between trading partners. Answer (c) is incorrect because bar-code scanning reads price and item information, but does not convert a paper document into a computer file. Answer (d) is incorrect because joining and merging are processes applied to computer files.

31. (d) The requirement is to identify the best method for preventing unauthorized alteration of online records. Answer (d) is correct because users can gain access to databases from terminals only through established recognition and authorization procedures, thus unauthorized access is prevented. Answer (a) is incorrect because key verification ensures the accuracy of selected fields by requiring a second keying of them, ordinarily by another individual. Answer (b) is incorrect because sequence checks are used to ensure the completeness of input or update data by checking the use of preassigned document serial numbers. Answer (c) is incorrect because computer matching entails checking selected fields of input data with information held in a suspense master file.

32. (c) The requirement is to identify a way of eliminating thick paper manuals and reducing costs. Answer (c) is correct since a compact disc/read-only memory (CD-ROM) would be cheaper to produce and ship than the existing paper, yet would permit large volumes of text and images to be reproduced. Answer (a) is incorrect because write-once-read-many (WORM) is an optical storage technique often used as an archival medium. Answer (b) is incorrect because digital audio tape is primarily used as a backup medium in imaging systems and as a master for CD-ROM. Answer (d) is incorrect because computer-output-to-microform is used for frequent access to archived documents such as canceled checks in banking applications.

33. (c) The requirement is to identify a reason that misstatements in a batch computer system may **not** be detected immediately. Answer (c) is correct because batch programs are run periodically and thereby result in delays in processing; accordingly, detection of misstatements may be delayed. Answer (a) is incorrect because errors will be detected in the batch. Answer (b) is incorrect because the identification of errors in input data is typically included as a part of a batch program. Answer (d) is incorrect because a batch system will ordinarily process transactions in a uniform manner.

34. (d) The requirement is to determine which answer is **not** a characteristic of a batch processed computer system. Simultaneous posting to several files is most frequently related to an online real-time system, not a batch system. Answer (a) is incorrect since a batch system may process sequentially against a master file. Answer (b) is incorrect because keypunching is followed by machine processing in batch systems. Answer (c) is incorrect because the numerous batches ordinarily result in numerous printouts.

35. (b) The requirement is to identify the most likely direct output of an edit check included in an online sales order processing system. Edit checks are used to screen incoming data against established standards of validity, with data that pass all edit checks viewed as "valid" and then processed. Answer (b) is correct because an edit check will ordinarily create an output file of rejected transactions. Answer (a) is incorrect because sales invoices may not have

been prepared at the point of the sales order processing and because the answer is much less complete than answer (b). Answer (c) is incorrect because while periodic printouts of user code numbers and passwords should be prepared, this is not a primary purpose of an edit check. Answer (d) is incorrect because shipping documents will not ordinarily be prepared at this point and because the answer is much less complete than answer (b).

36. (a) The requirement is to determine a control which will strengthen an online real-time cash withdrawal system. Answer (a) is correct because documentation of all situations in which the "terminal audit key" has been used will improve the audit trail. Answer (b) is incorrect because increasing the dollar amount required for use of the key will simply reduce the number of times it is used (and allow larger withdrawals to be made without any required special authorization). Answer (c) is incorrect because there is no reason to believe that a manual system will be more effective than an online system. Answer (d) is incorrect because parallel simulation, running the data through alternate software, would seem to have no particular advantage for processing these large withdrawals.

37. (a) The requirement is to identify a direct output of a sorting, editing, and updating program. Answer (a) is correct because the program will output both exceptions and control totals to determine whether all transactions have been processed properly. Answers (b), (c), and (d) are all incorrect because while a program such as this may output such schedules, this will occur after exceptions are cleared and control totals are reconciled.

38. (d) The requirement is to determine why the grandfather-father-son updating backup concept is relatively difficult to implement for disk files. Answer (d) is correct because updating destroys the old records. Answer (a) is incorrect because the location of information points on disks is **not** an extremely time consuming task if the disks have been properly organized and maintained. Answer (b) is incorrect because off-site storage through disks is possible, though costly. Answer (c) is incorrect because information need not be dumped in the form of hard copy.

39. (c) The requirement is to determine the item which converts problem oriented language to machine language. A compiler produces a machine-language object program from a source-program (i.e., problem oriented) language. Answer (a) is incorrect because an interpreter is used to make punched cards easily readable to people. Answer (b) is incorrect because a verifier is used to test whether key punching errors exist on punched cards. Answer (d) is incorrect because a converter changes a program from one form of problem oriented language to another, related form (e.g., from one form of COBOL to another form of COBOL).

40. (d) The requirement is to determine the type of computer system characterized by more than one location and records that are updated immediately. Answer (d) is correct because online real-time systems typically allow access from multiple locations, and always have the immediate update of records. Answers (a) and (b) are incorrect because small computers often are limited to one location, and they may or may not allow immediate updating for particular applications. Answer (c) is incorrect because batch processing is a method which does not update records immediately (e.g., processing the "batch" of the firm's daily sales each evening, not at the moment they occur).

41. **(a)** The requirement is to identify a characteristic that distinguishes electronic data interchange (EDI) from other forms of electronic commerce. Answer (a) is correct because EDI transactions are ordinarily formatted using one of the available uniform worldwide sets of standards. Answer (b) is incorrect because, when financial statements are prepared, EDI transactions must follow generally accepted accounting principles. Answer (c) is incorrect because EDI transactions may or may not be processed using the Internet. Answer (d) is incorrect because security and privacy are considered when recording EDI transactions. See the Auditing Procedure Study *Audit Implications of EDI* for more information on electronic data interchange.

C. Characteristics of Computer Systems—Specific

42. **(b)** The requirement is to identify the meaning of the abbreviation LAN. Answer (b) is correct because LAN is the abbreviation for local area network. A local area network is a computer network for communication between computers. For example, a local area network may connect computers, word processors and other electronic office equipment to create a communication system within an office. Answers (a), (c) and (d) are all incorrect because they are combinations of words that have no specific meaning in information technology.

43. **(c)** The requirement is to identify the type of computer that is designed to provide software and other applications to other computers. Answer (c) is correct because a server provides other computers ("clients") with access to files and printers as shared resources to a computer network. Answer (a) is incorrect because a microcomputer is a small digital computer based on a microprocessor and designed to be used by one person at a time. Answer (b) is incorrect because a network computer is a low-cost personal computer for business networks that is configured with only essential equipment. Answer (d) is incorrect because a supercomputer is a mainframe computer that is one of the most powerful available at a given time.

44. **(a)** The requirement is to identify the item **least** likely to be considered a component of a computer network. Answer (a) is least likely because application program is a program that gives a computer instructions that provide the user with tools to accomplish a specific task (e.g., a word processing application) Answer (b) is incorrect because computers are an integral part of a computer network. Answer (c) is incorrect because software is required for operation of the network. Answer (d) is incorrect because routers are used to forward data within a computer network.

45. **(c)** The requirement is to identify the type of network used to link widely separated portions of an organization. Answer (c) is correct because a wide area network is used to span a wide geographical space to link together portions of an organization. Answer (a) is incorrect because a bulletin board is a computer that is running software that allows users to leave messages and access information of general interest. Answer (b) is incorrect because a local area network's coverage is restricted to a relatively small geographical area. Answer (d) is incorrect because the term "zero base network" has no meaning in information technology.

46. **(c)** The requirement is to identify a set of rules for exchanging data between two computers. Answer (c) is correct because a protocol is such a set of rules. Answer (a) is incorrect because the term "communicator" is very general and has no specific meaning in this context. Answer (b) is incorrect because while an operating system controls the execution of computer programs and may provide various services related to computers, it is not a set of rules for exchanging data. Answer (d) is incorrect because transmission speed is the speed at which computer processing occurs.

47. **(d)** The requirement is to identify the approach most frequently used to create a Web page. Answer (d) is correct because HTML (hypertext markup language) or XML (extensible markup language) are used to develop hypertext documents such as Web pages. Answers (a), (b), and (c) are all incorrect because while such tools may be used on Web page creation, they are not as fundamentally related as are HTML or XML.

48. **(b)** The requirement is to identify the reply that would provide the least security for sensitive data stored on a laptop computer. Answer (b) is correct because password protection for a screensaver program can be easily bypassed. Answer (a) is incorrect because data encryption provides adequate security for laptop computers. Answer (c) is incorrect because removable hard drives would provide adequate security. Answer (d) is incorrect because security is promoted by physically locking the laptop computer to an immovable object.

49. **(c)** The requirement is to identify the most likely procedure to be included in the high-level systems design phase of a computer system that will handle customer orders and process customer payments. Answer (c) is correct because the determination of what type of system to obtain is made during the high-level design phase. Answer (a) is incorrect because the effect of the new system would be part of the feasibility study. Answer (b) is incorrect because the file layouts are part of the detailed design phase. Answer (d) is incorrect because formal approval is made during the request for the systems design phase.

50. **(b)** The requirement is to identify the risk being controlled when a company using EDI makes it a practice to track the functional acknowledgments from trading partners. Answer (b) is correct because tracking of customers' functional acknowledgments, when required, will help to ensure successful transmission of EDI transactions. Answer (a) is incorrect because to address this issue, unauthorized access to the EDI system should be prevented, procedures should be in place to ensure the effective use of passwords, and data integrity and privacy should be maintained through the use of encryption and authentication measures. Answer (c) is incorrect because contractual agreements should exist between the company and the EDI trading partners. Answer (d) is incorrect because the risk that EDI data may not be completely and accurately processed is primarily controlled by the system.

51. **(c)** The requirement is to identify the best control to assure that data uploaded from a microcomputer to the company's mainframe system in batch processing is properly handled. Answer (c) is correct because this could help prevent data errors. Answer (a) is incorrect because while this practice is a wise control, it does not address the issue of upload-data integrity. Backups cannot prevent or detect data-upload problems, but can only help correct data errors that a poor upload caused. Answer (b) is incorrect because this control may be somewhat helpful in preventing fraud in data uploads, but it is of little use in preventing errors. Answer (d) is incorrect because this control is detective in nature, but the error could have already caused erroneous reports and management decisions. Having users try to find errors in uploaded data would be costly.

52.   (b)   The requirement is to identify the most likely indication that a computer virus is present. Answer (b) is correct because unexplainable losses of or changes to data files are symptomatic of a virus attack. Answer (a) is incorrect because power surges are symptomatic of hardware or environmental (power supply) problems. Answer (c) is incorrect because inadequate backup, recovery, and contingency plans are symptomatic of operating policy and/or compliance problems. Answer (d) is incorrect because copyright violations are symptomatic of operating policy and/or compliance problems.

53.   (c)   The requirement is to identify the operating procedure most likely to increase an organization's exposure to computer viruses. Answer (c) is correct because there is a risk that downloaded public-domain software may be contaminated with a virus. Answers (a) and (b) are incorrect because viruses are spread through the distribution of computer programs. Answer (d) is incorrect because original copies of purchased software should be virus-free and cannot legally be shared.

54.   (b)   The requirement is to identify the risk that increases when an EFT system is used. Answer (b) is correct because unauthorized access is a risk which is higher in an EFT environment. Answers (a), (c), and (d) are all incorrect because this is a risk which is common to each IT environment.

55.   (c)   The requirement is to identify the statement that is correct concerning message encryption software. Answer (c) is correct because the machine instructions necessary to encrypt and decrypt data constitute system overhead, which means that processing may be slowed down. Answer (a) is incorrect because no encryption approach absolutely guarantees the secrecy of data in transmission although encryption approaches are considered to be less amenable to being broken than others. Answer (b) is incorrect because keys may be distributed manually, but they may also be distributed electronically via secure key transporters. Answer (d) is incorrect because using encryption software does not reduce the need for periodic password changes because passwords are the typical means of validating users' access to unencrypted data.

56.   (a)   The requirement is to identify the method to prevent data eavesdropping. Answer (a) is correct because data encryption prevents eavesdropping by using codes to ensure that data transmissions are protected from unauthorized tampering or electronic eavesdropping. Answer (b) is incorrect because dial back systems ensure that data are received from a valid source. Answer (c) is incorrect because message acknowledgment procedures help ensure that data were received by the intended party. Answer (d) is incorrect because password codes are designed to prevent unauthorized access to terminals or systems.

57.   (b)   The requirement is to identify a likely benefit of EDI. Answer (b) is correct because improved business relationships with trading partners is a benefit of EDI. Answer (a) is incorrect because EDI transmits document data, not the actual document. Answer (c) is incorrect because liability issues related to protection of proprietary business data are a major legal implication of EDI. Answer (d) is incorrect because EDI backup and contingency planning requirements are not diminished.

58.   (a)   The requirement is to identify the **least** likely part of a company's policy on electronic mail. Answer (a) is correct because the company should have access to the business-related e-mail that is left behind. Access to e-mail can also be critical in business or possible criminal investigations. The privacy concerns of the individual case must be mitigated by compelling business interests: the need to follow up on business e-mail and to assist in investigations. Answer (b) is incorrect because encryption helps prevent eavesdropping by unauthorized persons trying to compromise e-mail messages. Answer (c) is incorrect because limiting the number of packages would decrease the number of administrators who might have access to all messages. Answer (d) is incorrect because controlling the transmission of confidential information by e-mail will help avoid theft of information through intrusion by outsiders.

59.   (c)   The requirement is to identify the most likely risk relating to end-user computing as compared to a mainframe computer system. Answer (c) is correct because this risk is considered unique to end-user computing (EUC) system development. Answer (a) is incorrect because this risk relates to both traditional information systems and end-user computing (EUC) environments. Answer (b) is incorrect because this risk relates to both traditional information systems and end-user computing (EUC) environments. Answer (d) is incorrect because this risk relates to all computing environments.

60.   (c)   The requirement is to identify the risk that is not greater in an EFT environment as compared to a manual system using paper transactions. Answer (c) is correct because per transaction costs are lower with electronic funds transfer. Answer (a) is incorrect because this is a major risk factor inherent to electronic funds transfer (EFT). Answer (b) is incorrect because this is another inherent risk factor. Answer (d) is incorrect because this is a critical risk factor.

61.   (c)   The requirement is to identify the reply that is not a method to minimize the risk of installation of unlicensed microcomputer software. Answer (c) is correct because this technique will not affect introduction of unlicensed software. Answer (a) is incorrect because this technique works. Answer (b) is incorrect because such audits are a must to test the other controls that should be in place. Answer (d) is incorrect because the basis for all good controls is a written policy.

62.   (a)   The requirement is to determine whose responsibility it is to back up software and data files in distributed or cooperative systems. Answer (a) is correct because in distributed or cooperative systems, the responsibility for ensuring that adequate backups are taken is the responsibility of user management because the systems are under the control of users. Answer (b) is incorrect because in distributed environments, there will be no systems programmers comparable to those at central sites for traditional systems. Answer (c) is incorrect because in distributed environments, there may be no data entry clerks because users are typically performing their own data entry. Answer (d) is incorrect because in distributed environments, there are no tape librarians.

63. (b)   The requirement is to identify the least likely way that a client's data will be input. Answer (b) is correct because the term "dynamic linking character reader" is a combination of terms that has no real meaning. The other three terms all represent methods of data input.

64. (d)   The requirement is to identify what end-user computing is an example of. Answer (d) is correct because end-user computing involves individual users performing the development and execution of computer applications in a decentralized manner. Answer (a) is incorrect because client/server processing involves a networked model, rather than end-user approach. Answer (b) is incorrect because a distributed system involves networked computers processing transactions for a single (or related) database. Answer (c) is incorrect because using sophisticated techniques from statistics, artificial intelligence and computer graphics to explain, confirm and explore relationships among data may be performed in many environments.

65. (c)   The requirement is to identify the type of computer that end-user computing is most likely to occur on. Answer (c) is correct because end-user computing involves individual users performing the development and execution of computer applications in a decentralized manner and these individuals are most likely to be using personal computers. Answers (a) and (b) are incorrect because they represent computers less frequently used by end users. Answer (d) is incorrect because "personal reference assistants" is a term not used in information technology.

66. (a)   The requirement is to identify the correct statement regarding the Internet as a commercially viable network. Answer (a) is correct because companies that wish to maintain adequate security must use firewalls to protect data from being accessed by unauthorized users. Answer (b) is incorrect because anyone can establish a homepage on the Internet without obtaining permission. Answer (c) is incorrect because there are no such security standards for connecting to the Internet.

67. (d)   The requirement is to identify a method of reducing security exposure when transmitting proprietary data over communication lines. Answer (d) is correct because cryptographic devices protect data in transmission over communication lines. Answer (a) is incorrect because asynchronous modems handle data streams from peripheral devices to a central processor. Answer (b) is incorrect because authentication techniques confirm that valid users have access to the system. Answer (c) is incorrect because callback procedures are used to ensure incoming calls are from authorized locations.

68. (a)   The requirement is to identify the reply which is **not** a reason that securing client/server systems is a complex task. Answer (a) is correct because client/server implementation does not necessarily use relational databases. Answers (b), (c), and (d) are all incorrect because the number of access points, concurrent operation by multiple users, and widespread data access and update capabilities make securing such systems complex.

69. (c)   The requirement is to identify what an auditor would ordinarily consider the greatest risk regarding an entity's use of electronic data interchange (EDI). Answer (c) is correct because an EDI system must include controls to make certain that EDI transactions are processed by the proper entity, using the proper accounts. Answers (a) and (b) are incorrect because authorization of EDI transactions and duplication of EDI transmissions ordinarily pose no greater risk than for other systems. Answer (d) is incorrect because the elimination of paper documents in and of itself does not propose a great risk.

70. (d)   The requirement is to identify the characteristic that distinguishes electronic data interchange (EDI) from other forms of electronic commerce. Answer (d) is correct because standards for EDI transactions, within any one group of trading partners, have been agreed upon so as to allow the system to function efficiently. Answer (a) is incorrect because the cost of EDI transaction using a VAN will often exceed the cost of using the Internet. Answer (b) is incorrect because software maintenance contracts are often necessary. Answer (c) is incorrect because EDI commerce involves legally binding contracts between trading partners.

71. (c)   The requirement is to identify a component of a local area network. Answer (c) is correct because a local area network requires that data be transmitted from one computer to another through some form of transmission media. Answers (a), (b), and (d) are all general replies that are not requirements of a local area network.

72. (c)   The requirement is to identify an additional cost of transmitting business transactions by means of electronic data interchange (EDI) rather than in a traditional paper environment. Answer (c) is correct because such transactions must be translated to allow transmission. Answer (a) is incorrect because no particular controls are required for redundant data checks under EDI as compared to a traditional paper environment. Answer (b) is incorrect because there need be no increase in random data entry errors under EDI. Answer (d) is incorrect because since computer controls are ordinarily heavily relied upon under EDI, often fewer supervisory personnel are needed.

73. (a)   The requirement is to identify an advantage of using the Internet for electronic commerce EDI transactions as compared to a value-added network (VAN). Answer (a) is correct because such simultaneous processing of transactions is more likely under an Internet system in which lines are often available at a fixed or nearly fixed rate. Answer (b) is incorrect because the Internet itself will not automatically prepare such batches. Answer (c) is incorrect because an Internet system will not ordinarily have superior characteristics regarding disaster recovery. Answer (d) is incorrect because translation software is needed both for Internet and VAN systems.

74. (b)   The requirement is to identify the statement which does not represent an exposure involved with electronic data interchange (EDI) systems. Answer (b) is correct because EDI ordinarily decreases transaction processing time; it does not delay transaction processing time. Answer (a) is incorrect because increased reliance upon both one's own computers and those of other parties are involved in EDI. Answer (c) is incorrect because involvement with other parties in EDI systems may result in the loss of confidentiality of information. Answer (d) is incorrect because EDI systems involve third parties such as customers, suppliers, and those involved with the computer network, and accordingly result in increased reliance upon their proper performance of their functions.

75. (b) The requirement is to identify the correct statement concerning internal control when a client uses an electronic data interchange system for processing its sales. Answer (b) is correct because encryption controls are designed to assure that messages are unreadable to unauthorized persons and to thereby control the transactions. Answer (a) is incorrect because suppliers are not ordinarily included in a company's sales controls and because even in a purchasing EDI system all suppliers need not be included. Answer (c) is incorrect because a value-added-network that provides network services may or may not be used in an EDI system. Answer (d) is incorrect because "paper" versions of transactions typically disappear in an EDI system.

76. (d) The requirement is to identify the statement that represents a disadvantage for an entity that keeps microcomputer-prepared data files rather than manually prepared files. Answer (d) is correct because persons with computer skills may be able to improperly access and alter microcomputer files. When a system is prepared manually such manipulations may be more obvious. Answer (a) is incorrect because random error is more closely associated with manual processing than with computer processing. Answer (b) is incorrect because comparing recorded accountability with the physical count of assets should not be affected by whether a manual or a microcomputer system is being used. Answer (c) is incorrect because the accuracy of the programming process is not generally tested when microcomputers are used.

77. (a) The requirement is to identify a benefit of transmitting transactions in an electronic data interchange (EDI) environment. Answer (a) is correct because the speed at which transactions can occur and be processed electronically results in lower year-end receivables since payments occur so quickly. Answer (b) is incorrect because an EDI environment requires many controls related to sales and collections. Answer (c) is incorrect because sampling may or may not be used in such circumstances. Answer (d) is incorrect because third-party service providers are often involved in such transactions—accordingly they are relied upon. See Auditing Procedure Study *Audit Implications of EDI* for information on electronic data interchange systems.

78. (c) The requirement is to identify the network node that is used to improve network traffic and to set up as a boundary that prevents traffic from one segment to cross over to another. Answer (c) is correct because a firewall is a computer that provides a defense between one network (inside the firewall) and another network (outside the firewall) that could pose a threat to the inside network. Answer (a) is incorrect because a router is a computer that determines the best way for data to move forward to their destination. Answer (b) is incorrect because a gateway is a communications interface device that allows a local area network to be con-

nected to external networks and to communicate with external computers and databases. Answer (d) is incorrect because a heuristic is a simplified rule to help an individual make decisions.

79. (a) The requirement is to identify the best example of how specific controls in a database environment may differ from controls in a nondatabase environment. Answer (a) is correct because a primary control within a database environment is to appropriately control access and updating by the many users; in most nondatabase environments there are ordinarily far fewer users who are able to directly access and update data. Answer (b) is incorrect because controls over data sharing differ among users for both database and nondatabase environments. Answer (c) is incorrect because under both database and nondatabase systems, the programmer should debug the program. Answer (d) is incorrect because controls can verify that authorized transactions are processed under either a database or nondatabase environment.

80. (b) The requirement is to identify an effective audit approach in an EDI environment in which documentation of transactions will be retained for only a short period of time. Answer (b) is correct because performing tests throughout the year will allow the auditor to examine transaction documentation before the transactions are destroyed. Answer (a) is incorrect because if documentation relating to the transactions is not maintained, it will be impossible to perform such cutoff tests. Answer (d) is incorrect because such a situation need not lead to a 100% count of inventory at or near year-end. Answer (d) is incorrect because an increase in the assessed level of control risk rather than a decrease is more likely.

81. (d) The requirement is to identify the encryption feature that can be used to authenticate the originator of a document and to ensure that the message is intact and has not been tampered with. Answer (d) is correct because digital signatures are used in electronic commerce to authenticate the originator and to ensure that the message has not been tampered with. Answers (a), (b), and (c) are all incorrect because they do not directly deal with such authentication.

82. (a) The requirement is to identify the process used in building an electronic data interchange (EDI) system to determine that elements in the entity's computer system correspond to the standard data elements. Answer (a) is correct because mapping, or "data mapping," is the processes of selecting the appropriate data fields from the various application databases and passing them to the EDI translation software. Answer (b) is incorrect because translation involves the actual modification of the data into a standard format that is used by the EDI system. Answer (c) is incorrect because encryption is a technique for protecting information within a computer system in which an algorithm transforms that data to render it unintelligible; the process can be reversed to regenerate the original data for further processing. Answer (d) is incorrect because decoding is the process of making data intelligible. See the Auditing Procedure Study *Audit Implications of EDI* for more information on electronic data interchange.

83. (a) The requirement is to identify the password that would be most difficult to crack. A password is a secret series of characters that enables a user to access a file, computer, or program; ideally, the password should be something nobody could guess. Answer (a) is correct because OrCA!FlSi does not seem like a password that one would guess or even recall if seen briefly. Answers (b), (c), and (d) are all incorrect because they represent passwords that would be easier to identify.

84.   (a)   The requirement is to determine which reply represents a password security problem. A password is a secret series of characters that enables a user to access a file, computer, or program; ideally the password should be something that nobody could guess. Answer (a) is correct because individuals have a tendency to not change passwords, and over time, others may be able to identify them. Answer (b) is incorrect because using different passwords for different accounts on several systems represents a control (assuming the user can remember them). Answer (c) is incorrect because copying of passwords to a secure location (e.g., a wallet) does not ordinarily represent a security problem. Answer (d) is incorrect because passwords should be kept secret and not listed in an online dictionary.

D.   Effect of IT on Internal Control

85.   (b)   The requirement is to identify the most likely procedure to be included in a computer disaster recovery plan. Answer (b) is correct because duplicate copies of critical files will allow an entity to reconstruct the data whose original files have been lost or damaged. Answer (a) is incorrect because an auxiliary power supply will provide uninterrupted electricity to avoid the need for a recovery since it may reduce the likelihood of such a disaster. Answer (c) is incorrect because simply maintaining passwords will not allow the entity to reconstruct data after a disaster has occurred. Answer (d) is incorrect because while cryptography will enhance the security of files from unintended uses, it is not a primary method to recover from a computer disaster.

86.   (d)   The requirement is to identify the type of backup site a company would most likely consider when there is concern about a power outage and desires for a fully configured and ready to operate system. Answer (d) is correct because a hot site is a site that is already configured to meet a user's requirements. Answer (a) is incorrect because a cold site is a facility that provides everything necessary to quickly install computer equipment but doesn't have the computers installed. Answers (b) and (c) are incorrect because they represent terms not frequently used in such circumstances.

87.   (d)   The requirement is to identify the procedure an entity would most likely include in its disaster recovery plan. Answer (d) is correct because storing duplicate copies of files in a different location will allow recovery of contaminated original files. Answer (a) is incorrect because converting all data from EDI format to an internal company format is ordinarily inefficient, and not a disaster recovery plan. Answer (b) is incorrect because a Trojan horse program (one which masquerades as a benign application but actually causes damage) ordinarily causes illicit activity, it does not prevent illicit activity. Answer (c) is incorrect because an auxiliary power supply is meant to prevent disaster, not recover from disaster.

88.   (b)   The requirement is to determine whether almost all commercially marketed software is copyrighted, copy protected, or both. Answer (b) is correct because while almost all such software is copyrighted, much of it is not copy protected. Answer (a) is incorrect because it suggests that almost all such software is copy protected. Answer (c) is incorrect both because it suggests that such software is not copyrighted and that it is copy protected. Answer (d) is incorrect because it suggests that such software is not copyrighted.

89.   (c)   The requirement is to identify a widely used disaster recovery approach. Answer (c) is correct because regular backups (copying) of data allows recovery when original records are damaged. Answer (a) is incorrect because encryption is used with a goal of making files impossible to read by those other than the intended users. Answer (b) is incorrect because firewalls are designed to control any possible inappropriate communication between computers within one system and those on the outside. Answer (d) is incorrect because surge protectors are electrical devices inserted in a power line to protect equipment from sudden fluctuations in current, and thereby prevent disasters, not recover from them.

90.   (a)   The requirement is to identify what a "hot site" is most frequently associated with. Answer (a) is correct because a hot site is a commercial disaster recovery service that allows a business to continue computer operations in the event of computer disaster. For example, if a company's data processing center become inoperable, that enterprise can move all processing to a hot site that has all the equipment needed to continue operation. Answer (b) is incorrect because a hot site is not frequently associated with online relational database design. Answer (c) is incorrect because source programs (programs written in a language from which statements are translated into machine language) are not directly related to a hot site. Answer (d) is incorrect because when used in information technology, the term hot site is not directly related to temperature control for computers.

91.   (b)   The requirement is to determine which reply is **not** a typical output control. Answer (b) is correct because matching the input data with information held on master or suspense files is a processing control, not an output control, to ensure that data are complete and accurate during updating. Answer (a) is incorrect because a review of the computer processing logs is an output control to ensure that data are accurate and complete. Answer (c) is incorrect because periodic reconciliation of output reports is an output control to ensure that data are accurate and complete. Answer (d) is incorrect because maintaining formal procedures and documentation specifying authorized recipients is an output control to ensure proper distribution.

92.   (c)   The requirement is to identify the best way to minimize the likelihood of unauthorized editing of production programs, job control language, and operating system software. Answer (c) is correct because program change control comprises: (1) maintaining records of change authorizations, code changes, and test results; (2) adhering to a systems development methodology (including documentation; (3) authorizing changeovers of subsidiary and headquarters' interfaces; and (4) restricting access to authorized source and executable codes. Answer (a) is incorrect because the purpose of database reviews is to determine if (1) users have gained access to database areas for which they have no authorization; and (2) authorized users can access the database using programs that provide them with unauthorized privileges to view and/or change information. Answer (b) is incorrect because the purpose of compliance reviews is to determine whether an organization has complied with applicable internal and external procedures and regulations. Answer (d) is incorrect because the purpose of network security software is to provide logical controls over the network.

93. (d)   The requirement is to determine the most likely actions relating to mainframe applications when a company decides to launch a downsizing project. Answer (d) is correct because mainframe applications represent a significant investment and may still provide adequate service. The fact that mainframes can provide a stable platform for enterprise applications may be an advantage while exploring other nonmainframe options. Answer (a) is incorrect because the costs of converting mainframe applications to a microcomputer network and retraining the personnel who would rewrite and maintain them preclude any rapid transition. Answer (b) is incorrect because general ledger programs that aggregate business data on a regular basis will be among the last to be converted. Answer (c) is incorrect because incremental modifications may have high paybacks.

94. (a)   The requirement is to identify the greatest concern relating to a client's setting of used microcomputers when that corporation receives the majority of its revenue from top-secret military contracts with the government. Answer (a) is correct because while most delete programs erase file pointers, they do not remove the underlying data. The company must use special utilities that fully erase the data; this is especially important because of the potential for top-secret data on the microcomputers. This risk is the largest because it could cause them to lose military contract business. Answer (b) is incorrect because while it could create a liability for the company if a virus destroyed the purchasing party's data or programs the purchasing party should use antiviral software to detect and eliminate any viruses. This concern, while important, is not as serious as the one in answer (a). Answer (c) is incorrect because the purchasing party has a responsibility to insure that all their software is properly licensed. If the company represented that all the software was properly licensed, this could create a liability. However, this liability is not as serious as the implication from answer (a). Answer (d) is incorrect because terminal emulation software is widely available.

95. (b)   The requirement is to identify a reason to use bar codes rather than other means of identifying information on parts. Answer (b) is correct because a reason to use bar codes rather than other means of identification is to record the movement of parts with minimal labor costs. Answer (a) is incorrect because the movement of parts can escape being recorded with any identification method. Answer (c) is incorrect because each vendor has its own part-numbering scheme, which is unlikely to correspond to the buyer's scheme. Answer (d) is incorrect because each vendor has its own identification method, although vendors in the same industry often cooperate to minimize the number of bar code systems they use.

96. (b)   The requirement is to identify the function that ensures that changes in processing programs have a minimal impact on processing and result in minimal risk to the system. Answer (b) is correct because change control is the process of authorizing, developing, testing, and installing coded changes so as to minimize the impact on processing and the risk to the system. Answer (a) is incorrect because security administration is not involved as directly applicable as is change control. Answer (c) is incorrect because problem tracking is the process of collecting operational data about processes so that they can be analyzed for corrective action. Answer (d) is incorrect because problem-escalation procedures are a means of categorizing problems or unusual circumstances so that the least skilled person can address them.

97. (b)   The requirement is to identify the approach(es) that may reduce an organization's risk of civil lawsuit due to the use of pirated software. Answer (b) is correct because: (I) Maintaining a log protects an organization since a log documents software purchases. (II) Auditing individual computers will discourage illegal software usage. (III) Establishing a corporate software policy will discourage illegal software usage. (IV) Allowing users to keep original diskettes increases both the likelihood of illegal copies being made and the loss of diskettes. Answers (a), (c), and (d) are all incorrect.

98. (a)   The requirement is to identify a benefit of good recovery planning. Answer (a) is correct because an essential component of a disaster recovery plan is that the need for backup/restart has been anticipated and provided for in the application systems. Answer (b) is incorrect because change control procedures should not be bypassed by operating personnel, but that is not generally a consideration in disaster recovery planning. Answer (c) is incorrect because planned changes in equipment capacities should be compatible with projected workloads, but that is not generally a consideration in disaster recovery planning. Answer (d) is incorrect because service level agreements with owners of critical applications should be adequate, but that is not generally a consideration in disaster recovery planning.

99. (d)   The requirement is to identify the biggest risk in not having an adequately staffed information center help desk. Answer (d) is correct because not having such a help desk may lead to a situation in which users will unknowingly persist in making errors in their interaction with the information systems. Answer (a) is incorrect because application audits should be about the same difficulty with or without an adequately staffed help desk. Answer (b) is incorrect because the preparation of documentation is a development function, not a help desk function. Answer (c) is incorrect because the likelihood of use of unauthorized program code is a function of change control, not of a help desk.

100. (c)   The requirement is to determine how a database administrator should ensure that the database system properly controls access to accounting database files. Answer (c) is correct because one security feature in database systems is their ability to let the database administrator restrict access on a logical view basis for each user. Answer (a) is incorrect because if the only access permitted is read-only, then there could no updating of database files Answer (b) is incorrect because permitting catalog updating from privileged software would be a breach of security, which might permit unauthorized access. Answer (d) is incorrect because updating of users' access profiles should be a function of a security officer, not the user.

101. (b) The requirement is to identify a major auditor concern when a client processes sales transactions on the Internet. Answer (b) is correct because computer disruptions may result in the incorrect recording of sales. Answer (a) is incorrect because electronic sales invoices may replace sales invoice documents in such an environment. Answer (c) is incorrect because there may or may not be a need to establish an integrated test facility in such circumstances. Answer (d) is incorrect because the frequency of archiving and data retention is not as important as is ensuring that such policies appropriately control system backup.

102. (a) The requirement is to identify the correct statement concerning internal control in an electronic data interchange (EDI) system. Answer (a) is correct because preventive controls are important and often cost-effective in an EDI environment so as to not allow the error to occur, and because detective controls may detect misstatements too late to allow proper correction. Answer (b) is incorrect because the control objectives under EDI systems generally remain the same as for other information systems. Answer (c) is incorrect because a well-controlled EDI system may allow control risk to be assessed below the maximum. Answer (d) is incorrect because the programmed nature of most EDI controls limits the possible segregation of duties within the system. See Auditing Procedure Study *Audit Implications of EDI* for information on electronic data interchange systems.

103. (b) The requirement is to identify the correct statement relating to the security of messages in an electronic data interchange (EDI) system. Answer (b) is correct because both the physical security of the hardware and the hardware itself create a situation in which the encryption is ordinarily more secure than encryption performed by software. Answer (a) is incorrect because message authentication deals with whether the message received is the same as that sent, and not as directly with confidentiality. Answer (c) is incorrect because message authentication deals most directly with whether changes have been made in the message sent, and not with the variety of other potential problems addressed by segregation of duties. Answer (d) is incorrect because security is necessary at the transaction phase in EDI systems. See Auditing Procedure Study *Audit Implications of EDI* for information on electronic data interchange systems.

104. (c) The requirement is to identify an essential element of the audit trail in an electronic data interchange (EDI) system. Answer (c) is correct because effective audit trails need to include activity logs, including processed and failed transactions, network and sender/recipient acknowledgments, and time sequence of processing. Answer (a) is incorrect because disaster recovery plans, while essential to the overall system, are not an essential element of the audit trail. Answer (b) is incorrect because encrypted hash totals deal less directly with the audit trail than do activity logs. Answer (d) is incorrect because hardware security modules that store sensitive data do not deal directly with the audit trail. See Auditing Procedure Study *Audit Implications of EDI* for information on electronic data interchange systems.

105. (a) The requirement is to identify an essential element of the audit trail in an electronic data interchange (EDI) system. Answer (a) is correct because effective audit trails need to include activity logs, including processed and failed transactions, network and sender/recipient acknowledgments, and time sequence of processing. Answer (b) is incorrect because neither message directories nor header segments directly affect the audit trial. Answer (c) is incorrect because contingency and disaster recovery plans, while important, are not as directly related to the audit trail as are the acknowledgments suggested in answer (a). Answer (d) is incorrect because while knowing trading partner security and mailbox codes is essential, it is more closely related to overall security than is answer (a). See Auditing Procedure Study *Audit Implications of EDI* for information on electronic data interchange systems.

106. (b) The requirement is to identify the type of control that involves adding an extra number at the end of an account number and subjecting the new number to an algorithm. Answer (b) is correct because a check digit is an extra reference number that follows an identification code and bears a mathematical relationship to the other digits. Answer (a) is incorrect because optical character recognition involves a computer being able to "read in" printed data. Answer (c) is incorrect because a dependency check involves some form of check between differing related pieces of data. Answer (d) is incorrect because a format check involves determining whether the proper type of data has been input or processed (e.g., numerical data input under account withdrawal amount).

107. (d) The requirement is to identify the best control for preventing someone with sufficient technical skill from circumventing security procedures and making changes to production programs. Answer (d) is correct because a suitable segregation of duties will make such alteration impossible since when duties are separated, users cannot obtain the detailed knowledge of programs and computer operators cannot gain unsupervised access to production programs. Answers (a), (b), and (c) are all incorrect because the reviews of jobs processed, comparing programs with copies, and running attest data will all potentially disclose such alteration, but will not prevent it.

108. (c) The requirement is to identify the best method of keeping computer program libraries secure. Answer (c) is correct because restricting physical and logical access secures program libraries from unauthorized use in person or remotely via terminals. Answers (a) and (b) are incorrect because installing a logging system for program access or monitoring physical access would permit detection of unauthorized access but would not prevent it. Answer (d) is incorrect because denying all remote access via terminals would likely be inefficient and would not secure program libraries against physical access.

109. (d) The requirement is to identify the security control that would best prevent unauthorized access to sensitive data through an unattended data terminal directly connected to a mainframe. Answer (d) is correct because automatic log-off of inactive users may prevent the viewing of sensitive data on an unattended data terminal. Answer (a) is incorrect because data terminals do not normally use screen-saver protection, and because a screen saver would not prevent access. Answer (b) is incorrect because scripting is the use of a program to automate a process such as startup. Answer (c) is incorrect because encryption of data files will not prevent viewing of data on an unattended data terminal.

110. (d)   The requirement is to identify the reply that most likely represents a hash total. A hash total is a control total where the total is meaningless for financial purposes, but has some meaning for processing purposes. Answer (d) is correct because 810 represents the sum of the invoice numbers. Answer (a) is incorrect because it appears to be an accumulation of all letters, plus a sum of the numbers. Answer (b) is more likely to be considered a record count. Answer (c) is incorrect because it is simply the invoice number of the last invoice in the batch.

111. (a)   The requirement is to determine the type of control that would detect a miscoding of a product number on an order from a customer. Answer (a) is correct because a check digit is an extra digit added to an identification number to verify that the number is authorized and to thereby detect such coding errors. Answer (b) is incorrect because a record count involves a count of the number of records processed which is not being considered here. Answer (c) is incorrect because the term "hash total" ordinarily relates to a total of items and is meaningless for financial purposes (e.g., the total of the invoice numbers for a particular day's sales), but has some meaning for processing purposes. Answer (d) is incorrect because a redundant data check uses two identifiers in each transaction record to confirm that the correct master file record has been updated (e.g., the client account number and first several letters of the customer's name can be used to retrieve the correct customer master record from the accounts receivable file).

112. (b)   The requirement is to identify the technique that would most likely detect a nonexistent zip code. Answer (b) is correct because a zip code that is nonexistent would not pass a validity test. It would not be a valid item. Answer (a) is incorrect because a limit test restricts the amount of a transaction that will be processed. Answer (c) is incorrect because a parity test prevents loss of digits in processing. Answer (d) is incorrect because a record count test helps prevent the loss of records.

113. (a)   The requirement is to determine whether limit tests and validity check tests are processing controls designed to ensure the reliability and accuracy of data processing. Answer (a) is correct because both a limit test and a validity check test may serve as a control over either inputs or processing in an accounting system. A limit test will establish an upper and/or lower limit as reasonable, with results outside of those limits indicated (e.g., after net pay is calculated, an "error message" is printed for any employee with a weekly salary in excess of a certain amount). A validity check test allows only "valid" transactions or data to be processed in the system (e.g., during the processing of payroll, a control determines whether a paycheck is improperly issued to an ex-employee).

114. (b)   The requirement is to identify the activity most likely to be performed in the information systems department. Answer (b) is correct because the conversion of information into machine-readable form is essential to the inputting of data; computer equipment is generally used to perform this function. Answer (a) is incorrect because under good internal control, the initiation of changes to master

records should be authorized by functions independent of those which process the records. Answer (c) is incorrect because a separate function should exist to correct transactional errors. Answer (d) is incorrect because changes to computer applications should be initiated by the appropriate user group.

115. (a)   The requirement is to determine the errors which a header label is likely to prevent. Since the header label is actually on the magnetic tape, it is the computer operator whose errors will be prevented. Answer (b) is incorrect because the keypunch operator deals with punch cards. Answer (c) is incorrect because the programmer will write the programs and not run them under good internal control. Answer (d) is incorrect because the maintenance technician will not run the magnetic tape.

116. (b)   The requirement is to determine the purpose of programming computer to immediately transmit back to the terminal for display information that has been input on cash disbursements. Answer (b) is correct because the entry of disbursement **amounts** and the subsequent display of the amounts on the terminal screen will allow the operator to visually verify that the data provided to be input was entered accurately. Answer (a) is incorrect because displaying on the screen the data entered does not ensure the validity of the data, only that the data was entered correctly. Answer (c) is incorrect because no evidence has been provided as to whether the disbursement was authorized. Answer (d) is incorrect because the display of the amount will not be compared to a "correct" amount—only to the amount that was to be input.

117. (b)   The requirement is to identify a useful control when computer programs or files can be accessed from terminals. Answer (b) is correct because use of personal identification codes (passwords) will limit access to the programs or files on the terminal to those who know the codes. Answers (a), (c), and (d) are all incorrect because while they list valid controls used in computer systems, none of them require entry of data by the user. A parity check control is a special bit added to each character stored in memory to help detect whether the hardware has lost a bit during the internal movement of that character. A self-diagnosis test is run on a computer to check the internal operations and devices within the computer system. An echo check is primarily used in telecommunications transmissions to determine whether the receiving hardware has received the information sent by the sending hardware.

118. (a)   The requirement is to identify the item which would reduce the possibility of erasing a large amount of information stored on magnetic tape. Answer (a) is correct because a file protection ring is a control that ensures that an operator does not erase important information on a magnetic tape. Answer (b) is incorrect because a check digit is a digit added to an identification number to detect entry errors. Answer (c) is incorrect because a completeness test would generally be used to test whether all data were processed. Answer (d) is incorrect because conversion verification would address whether the conversion of data from one form to another (e.g., disk to magnetic tape) was complete.

119. (b)   The requirement is to identify the controls most likely to assure that an entity can reconstruct its financial records. Answer (b) is correct because backup diskettes or tapes may be maintained that will provide the information needed to reconstruct financial records. Answer (a) is incorrect because while hardware controls are meant to assure the proper processing of data, when reconstruction is needed, hardware controls will not have the data necessary to reconstruct the financial records. Answer (c) is incorrect because parallel simulations will only occasionally be run and will not maintain adequate data to reconstruct records. Answer (d) is incorrect because while systems flowcharts will provide information on the design of the overall system, they will not assure the reconstruction of financial records.

120. (d) The requirement is to identify the type of input control that is a numeric value computed to provide assurance that the original value has not been altered in construction or transmission. Answer (d) is correct because a check digit is an extra digit added to an identification number to detect such errors. Answer (a) is incorrect because the term "hash total" ordinarily relates to a total of items and is meaningless for financial purposes (e.g., the total of the invoice numbers for a particular day's sales), but has some meaning for processing purposes. Answer (b) is incorrect because a parity check is a process in which a computer reads or receives a set of characters and simultaneously sums the number of 1 bits in each character to verify that it is an even (or alternatively, odd) number. Answer (c) is incorrect because encryption involves a coding of data, ordinarily for purposes of ensuring privacy and accuracy of transmission.

121. (c) The requirement is to identify the best example of a validity check. A validity test compares data (for example, employee, vendor, and other codes) against a master file for authenticity. Answer (c) is correct because the computer flagging of inappropriate transactions due to data in a control field that did not match that of an existing file record is such a test. Answer (a) is incorrect because a limit test ensures that a numerical amount in a record does not exceed some predetermined amount. Answer (b) is incorrect because the resubmission of data is not a validity check. Answer (d) is incorrect because the reading back of data to the terminal is an echo check.

122. (b) The requirement is to identify type of computer test made to ascertain whether a given characteristic belongs to a group. Answer (b) is correct because a validity check determines whether a character is legitimate per the given character set. Note the validity check determines whether a given character is within the desired group. Answer (a) is incorrect because a parity check is a summation check in which the binary digits of a character are added to determine whether the sum is odd or even. Another bit, the parity bit, is turned on or off so the total number of bits will be odd or even as required. Answer (c) is incorrect because an echo check is a hardware control wherein data is transmitted back to its source and compared to the original data to verify the transmission correctness. Answer (d) is incorrect because a limit or reasonableness check is a programmed control based on specified limits. For example, a calendar month cannot be numbered higher than twelve, or a week cannot have more than 168 hours.

123. (a) The requirement is to identify the type of hardware control that requires the CPU to send signals to the printer to activate the print mechanism for each character. Answer (a) is correct because an echo check or control consists of transmitting data back to the source unit for compari-

son with the original data that were transmitted. In this case, the print command is sent to the printer and then returned to the CPU to verify that the proper command was received. A validity check [answer (b)] consists of the examination of a bit pattern to determine that the combination is legitimate for the system character set (i.e., that the character represented by the bit combination is valid per the system). Answer (c), a signal control or signal check, appears to be a nonsense term. Answer (d), check digit control, is a programmed control wherein the last character or digit can be calculated from the previous digits.

124. (b) The requirement is to identify an example of a check digit. Answer (b) is correct because a check digit is an extra digit in an identification number, algebraically determined, that detects specified types of data input, transmission, or conversion errors. Answer (a) is incorrect because the agreement of the total number of employees to the checks printed is an example of a control total. Answer (c) is incorrect because ensuring that all employee numbers are nine digits could be considered a logic check, a field size check, or a missing data check. Answer (d) is incorrect because determining that no employee has more than fifty hours per workweek is a limit check.

125. (b) The requirement is to determine the most likely significant deficiency in internal control. Answer (b) is correct because the systems programmer should not maintain custody of output in a computerized system. At a minimum, the programming, operating, and library functions should be segregated in such computer systems.

126. (c) The requirement is to identify the weakness in internal control relating to a function performed by computer department personnel. Answer (c) is correct because individuals outside of the computer department should originate changes in master files; this separates the authorization of changes from the actual processing of records. Answer (a) is incorrect because participation of computer department personnel in making computer software acquisition decisions is often appropriate and desirable given their expertise in the area. Answer (b) is incorrect for similar reasons as (a). In addition, computer department personnel will often be able to effectively design the required documentation for computerized systems. Answer (d) is incorrect because the physical security for program files may appropriately be assigned to a library function within the computer department.

127. (b) The requirement is to identify the activity most likely to detect whether payroll data were altered during processing. Answer (b) is correct because test data may be used to provide evidence on whether edit routines (routines to check the validity and accuracy of input data) are operating and have not been altered. Answer (a) is incorrect because the distribution of any data control sheets will provide little information on altered data. Answer (c) is incorrect because the approval of source documents is not at issue—it is the alteration of payroll data. Answer (d) is incorrect because any segregation activities may eliminate future alterations, but would have little effect on prior alterations.

E. Flowcharting

128. (a) The requirement is to identify the tool that would best give a graphical representation of a sequence of activities and decisions. Answer (a) is correct because a flowchart is a graphical representation of a sequence of activities and decisions. Answer (b) is incorrect because a control chart is used to monitor actual versus desired quality measurements during repetition operation. Answer (c) is incorrect because a histogram is a bar chart showing conformance to a standard bell curve. Answer (d) is incorrect because a run chart tracks the frequency or amount of a given variable over time.

129. (c) The requirement is to determine what the symbol A represents in the flowchart of a client's revenue cycle. Answer (c) is correct because the accounts receivable master file will be accessed during the revenue cycle and does not appear elsewhere on the flowchart. Answers (a), (b), and (d) are all incorrect because remittance advices, receiving reports, and cash disbursements transaction files are not a primary transaction file accessed during the revenue cycle.

130. (d) The requirement is to determine what the symbol B represents in the flowchart of a client's revenue cycle. Answer (d) is correct because it represents the only major document of the revenue cycle that is not presented elsewhere on the flowchart and because one would expect generation of a sales invoice in the cycle. Answer (a) is incorrect because the customer order appears in the top left portion of the flowchart. Answer (b) is incorrect because no receiving report is being generated during the revenue cycle. Answer (c) is incorrect because the customer's check (remittance) is represented on the top portion of the flowchart.

131. (d) The requirement is to identify the correct statement concerning an auditor's flowchart of a client's accounting system. Answer (d) is correct because a flowchart is a diagrammatic representation that depicts the auditor's understanding of the system. See AU 319 for various procedures auditors use to document their understanding of internal control. Answer (a) is incorrect because the flowchart depicts the auditor's understanding of the system, not the assessment of control risk. Answer (b) is incorrect because while the flowchart may be used to identify weaknesses, it depicts the entire system—strengths as well as weaknesses. Answer (c) is incorrect because the flowchart is of the accounting system, not of the control environment.

132. (b) The requirement is to determine the approach illustrated in the flowchart. Answer (b) is correct because parallel simulation involves processing actual client data through an auditor's program. Answer (a) is incorrect because program code checking involves an analysis of the client's actual program. Answer (c) is incorrect because an integrated test facility approach introduces dummy transactions into a system in the midst of live transaction processing and is usually built into the system during the original design. Answer (d) is incorrect because controlled reprocessing often includes using the auditor's copy of a client program, rather than the auditor's program.

133. (b) The requirement is to identify the item represented by the "X" on the flowchart. Answer (b) is correct because the existence of a credit memo, in addition to a sales invoice, would indicate that this portion of the flowchart deals with cash receipts; therefore, the "X" would represent the remittance advices. Thus, the receipt transactions are credited to the accounts receivable master file, and an updated master file, a register of receipts, and exception reports are generated. Answer (a) is incorrect because an auditor's

test data will not result in an input into the transactions file. Answer (c) is incorrect because since no processing has occurred at the point in question—an error report is unlikely. Answer (d) is incorrect because credit authorization will generally occur prior to the preparation of credit memos.

134. (d) The requirement is to determine the symbolic representations that indicate that a file has been consulted. Answer (d) indicates that a manual operation (the trapezoid symbol) is accessing data from a file and returning the data to the file (i.e., "consulting" the file). Answer (a) is incorrect because it represents a processing step (the rectangle) being followed by a manual operation. Answer (b) is incorrect because it represents a document being filed. Answer (c) is incorrect because the diamond symbol represents a decision process.

135. (c) The requirement is to determine a benefit of a well-prepared flowchart. A flowchart may be used to document the auditor's understanding of the flow of transactions and documents. Answer (a) is incorrect because while an audit procedures manual may suggest the use of flowcharts, flowcharts will not in general be used to prepare such a manual. Answer (b) is less accurate than (c) because while it may be possible to obtain general information on various jobs, the flowchart will not allow one to obtain a **detailed** job description. Answer (d) is incorrect because a flowchart does not directly address actual accuracy of financial data within a system.

ECONOMICS AND STRATEGY

This module covers two interrelated topics: economics and business strategy. The module begins with a discussion of microeconomic and macroeconomic concepts, and concludes with a description of the effects of the economy on business strategies.

MICROECONOMICS

A. Microeconomics focuses on the behavior and purchasing decisions of individuals and firms. In a market economy goods and services are distributed through a system of prices. Goods and services are sold to those willing and able to pay the market price. The market price is determined based on demand and supply.

B. Demand

Demand is the quantity of a good or service that consumers are willing and able to purchase at a range of prices at a particular time. Therefore, market demand for a product is actually a schedule of the amount that would be purchased at various prices, with all other variables that affect demand being held constant. Graphically a demand curve shows an inverse relationship between the price and quantity demanded. That is, less products are demanded at higher prices. Illustrated below is the demand schedule and demand curve for Product X.

Market Demand for Product X

Price per unit	Quantity Demanded
$70	2,000
60	2,500
50	3,000
40	4,000
30	6,000
20	10,000

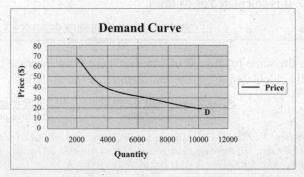

As illustrated, at a price of $50, 3,000 units of Product X will be bought. If the price of Product X changes, more or less will be bought.

1. **Demand curve shift.** A demand curve shifts when demand variables other than price change. For example, if the price of substitute products for Product X increase in price, the demand for Product X would shift upward and to the right. A demand curve shift is illustrated in the graph below.

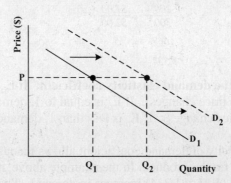

2. Variables that may cause a demand curve shift include changes in the price of other goods and services, consumer tastes, spendable income, wealth, and the size of the market. The table below summarizes the effects of these factors on the demand for a particular product.

Factors Affecting the Demand for a Product other than Its Price

Factor	*Effect*
Price of other goods and services (e.g. substitute goods)	**Direct relationship.** As goods that may be purchased instead go up in price the demand for the product goes up. As an example, if the price of pork increases the demand for beef may increase.
Price of complement products (i.e., products that must be used with the product or enhance its usefulness)	**Inverse relationship.** As the prices of complement goods go up, the demand for the product goes down. As an example, if the price of hamburger increases the demand for hamburger buns decreases.
Expectations of price increase	**Direct relationship.** If the price of the good is expected to increase in the future, there will be an increase in demand.
Consumer income and wealth	**Generally a direct relationship.** As consumer income (wealth) goes up the demand for many products (normal goods) goes up. However, there are certain **goods that are inferior** (e.g., bread, potatoes, etc.) and the demand for such goods actually goes up as consumer income (wealth) goes down. This is because consumers buy more inferior goods when they are short of money.
Consumer tastes	**Indeterminate relationship.** The effect depends on whether the shift is towards or away from the product.
Size of the market	**Direct relationship.** As the size of the market increases, the demand for the product will increase.
Group boycott	**Inverse relationship.** If a group of consumers boycott a product, demand will be decreased.

3. **Price elasticity of demand.** The elasticity of demand measures the sensitivity of demand to a change in price. It is calculated as follows:

$$E_D = \frac{\text{Percentage change in quantity demanded}}{\text{Percentage change in price}}$$

To make results the same regardless of whether there is an increase or decrease in price, the amount is usually calculated using the *arc method* as shown below.

$$E_D = \frac{\text{Change in quantity demanded}}{\text{Average quantity}} \div \frac{\text{Change in price}}{\text{Average price}}$$

EXAMPLE: Assume that you are operating a hot dog stand and sell hot dogs for $2.50. Your usual demand for hot dogs is 200 per day. To increase sales, you decide to run a $1.50 hot dog special and you sell 400 hot dogs for the day. The price elasticity of hot dogs is calculated as follows:

The change in quantity demanded = 200 (400 – 200)
The change in price = $1.00 ($2.50 – $1.50)
The average quantity = 300 [(200 + 400) ÷ 2]
The average price = $2.00 [($2.50 + $1.50) ÷ 2]

$$E_D = \frac{\text{Change in quantity demanded}}{\text{Average quantity}} \div \frac{\text{Change in price}}{\text{Average price}}$$

$$= \frac{200}{300} \div \frac{\$1.00}{\$2.00}$$

$$= .667 \div .5$$

$$= 1.334$$

Interpretation of the demand elasticity coefficient. If E_D is greater than 1, demand is said to be elastic (sensitive to price changes). If E_D is equal to 1, demand is said to be unitary (not sensitive or insensitive to price changes). If E_D is less than 1, demand is said to be inelastic (not sensitive to price changes).

The price elasticity of demand coefficient allows management to calculate the effect of a price change on demand for the product. In the example above, a 10% decrease in the price of a hot dog results in a 13.34% (10% × 1.334) increase in demand. The elasticity of demand is greater for a product when there are more substitutes for the good, a larger proportion of income is spent on the good, or a longer period of time is considered. For example, the demand for luxury goods tends to be more elastic than for necessities.

4. **Relationship between price elasticity and total revenue.** Total revenue from the sale of a good is equal to the price times the quantity. Price elasticity is an important concept because if demand is elastic an increase in sales price results in a decrease in total revenue for all producers. If demand is unitary total revenue remains the same if price changes, and total revenue increases if price is increased when demand is inelastic. These relationships are shown in the following table:

Effect of Price Changes on Various Types of Goods

Price Change	*Elastic Demand E > 1*	*Inelastic Demand E < 1*	*Unitary Demand E = 1*
Price increase	Total revenue decreases	Total revenue increases	Total revenue does not change
Price decrease	Total revenue increases	Total revenue decreases	Total revenue does not change

In the example of the hot dog stand above, we calculated price elasticity to be 1.334. Therefore, demand is elastic and, as expected, we find that the price decline resulted in an increase in total revenue, $600 ($1.50 × 400) versus $500 ($2.50 × 200).

Price elasticity is an important concept because it reveals whether the firm is likely to be able to pass on cost increases to its customers. Obviously, when demand is inelastic the firm can increase its price with less of a negative impact.

5. **Income elasticity of demand.** Income elasticity of demand measures the change in the quantity demanded of a product given a change in income. Income elasticity is calculated as follows:

$$E_I = \frac{\text{Percentage change in quantity demanded}}{\text{Percentage change in income}}$$

The income elasticity of demand can be used to describe the nature of the product. The demand for normal products increases as consumer income increases. For example, the demand for **normal goods,** such as beefsteaks increases as consumer income increases. Therefore, E_I for beefsteaks is positive. The demand for **inferior goods,** such as beans, decreases as income increases; E_I is negative. The demand for inferior goods increases as income declines, because when individuals have less money they substitute these less expensive goods for normal goods.

6. **Cross-elasticity of demand.** Cross-elasticity of demand measures the change in demand for a good when the price of a related or competing product is changed. For example, Coca Cola Company would be interested in knowing how an increase in the price of Pepsi would affect the sales of Coca Cola. The coefficient of cross-elasticity is calculated as follows:

$$E_{XY} = \frac{\text{Percentage change in the quantity demanded of Product X}}{\text{Percentage change in the price of Product Y}}$$

In our case Pepsi would be Product Y, the competing product with the price change, and Coca Cola would be Product X. The coefficient describes the relationship between the two products. If the coefficient is positive, the products are substitutes (like Pepsi and Coca Cola). If the coefficient is negative, the products are complements (like hamburger and hamburger buns) and if the coefficient is zero, the products are unrelated. The table below illustrates these relationships.

Cross-Elasticity of Demand

Coefficient	*Relationship between goods*
Coefficient of cross-elasticity positive ($E_{xy} > 0$)	Substitutes
Coefficient of cross-elasticity negative ($E_{xy} < 0$)	Complements
Coefficient of cross-elasticity zero ($E_{xy} = 0$)	Unrelated

EXAMPLE: *Assume that the cross-elasticity of demand for Product X in relation to Product Y is calculated to be 2.00. If the price of Product Y increases by 5%, then the demand for Product X would increase by 10% (5% × 2.00).*

7. **Consumer demand and utility.**

   a. As illustrated previously, the demand curve for a particular good is downward sloping. As the price of the good declines, consumers will purchase more because of substitution and income effects. The **substitution effect** refers to the fact that as the price of a good falls, consumers will use it to replace similar goods. As an example, as the price of pork falls, consumers will purchase more pork than other types of meat. The **income effect** refers to the fact that as the price of a good falls, consumers can purchase more with a given level of income.

b. An individual demands a particular good because of the utility (satisfaction) he or she receives from consuming it. The more goods an individual consumes the more total utility the individual receives. However, the marginal (additional) utility from consuming each additional unit decreases. This is referred to as the **law of diminishing marginal utility**.

c. A consumer maximizes utility from spending his or her income when the marginal utility of the last dollar spent on each commodity is the same. Utility maximization may be presented mathematically as shown below.

$$\frac{\text{Marginal Utility of A}}{\text{Price of A}} = \frac{\text{Marginal Utility of B}}{\text{Price of B}} = \frac{\text{Marginal Utility of Z}}{\text{Price of Z}}$$

d. To simplify this concept most economics books illustrate marginal utility with only two types of goods (e.g., chocolate bars and cans of soda). They construct a series of **indifference curves** which illustrate the combinations of chocolate bars and soda that provide equal utility. The optimal level of consumption of the two goods is then found where the individual's **budget constraint** line intersects the highest possible utility curve. At this point the individual receives the greatest amount of utility for the amount of money available. This relationship is illustrated below.

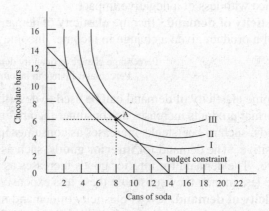

As illustrated, the individual gets the greatest satisfaction for the funds available at point A.

e. Consumption decisions depend on many factors but the main one is **personal disposable income**. This is the amount of income consumers have after receiving transfer payments from the government (e.g., welfare payments) and paying their taxes. When their personal disposable income goes up, consumers buy more. They buy less when it goes down.

f. The relationship between changes in personal disposable income and consumption is described by a **consumption function**. The function is typically described as follows:

$$C = c_0 + c_1 Y_D$$

Where

     C = Consumption for a period

     Y_D = Disposable income for the period

     c_0 = The constant

     c_1 = The slope of the consumption function

The important factor from the above function is the slope, c_1. It measures the consumer's **marginal propensity to consume (MPC)** describing how much of each additional dollar in personal disposable income that the consumer will spend. A consumption function is shown graphically below.

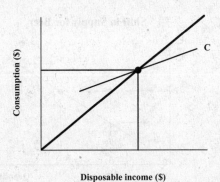

Disposable income ($)

g. The **marginal propensity to save (MPS)** is the percentage of additional income that is saved. Since a consumer can either spend or save money, the marginal propensity to consume plus the marginal propensity to save is equal to one as shown below.

$$MPC + MPS = 1$$

h. Certain nonincome factors may also affect consumption, including

    (1) Expectations about future prices of goods
    (2) Quantity of consumer liquid assets
    (3) Amount of consumer debt
    (4) Stock of consumer durable goods
    (5) Attitudes about saving money
    (6) Interest rates

C. Supply

A supply curve shows the amount of a product that would be supplied at various prices. Graphically a supply curve shows a direct relationship between price and quantity sold. The higher the price the more products that would be supplied. A supply schedule and supply curve for Product X are presented below.

Market Supply for Product X

Price per unit	Quantity supplied
$70	10,000
60	6,000
50	4,000
40	1,800
30	1,000
20	500

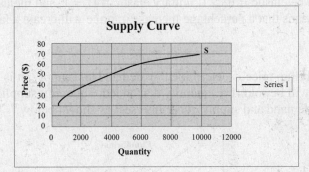

A change in the market price of the product results in a shift along the existing supply curve. For example, at $50, the market would supply 4,000 units but if the price changes to $60, the amount supplied will increase to 6,000.

1. **Supply curve shift.** A supply curve shift occurs when supply variables other than price change. As an example, if the costs to produce the product increase, the supply curve would shift upward and to the left. A shift in the supply curve is illustrated below.

Shift in Supply for Beer

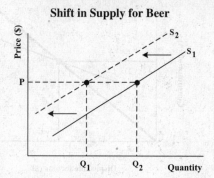

2. Variables that cause a supply curve shift include changes in the number or size of producers, changes in various production costs (wages, rents, raw materials), technological advances, and government actions. The effects of these variables are shown in the table below.

Factors Affecting the Supply of a Product other than Its Price

Factor	*Effect*
Number of producers	**Direct relationship.** Generally an increase in the number of producers will cause an increase in the amount of goods supplied at a given price.
Change in production costs or technological advances	**Inverse relationship.** As production costs go up fewer products will be supplied at a given price. If costs go down, more products will be produced.
Government subsidies	**Direct relationship.** Subsidies in effect reduce the production cost of goods and, therefore, increase the goods supplied at a given price.
Government price controls	Price controls would tend to limit the amount of goods supplied by holding the price artificially low.
Prices of other goods	**Inverse relationship.** If other products can be produced with greater returns, producers will produce those goods.
Price expectations	**Direct relationship.** If it is expected that prices will be higher for the good in the future, production of the good will increase.

3. **Elasticity of supply.** The elasticity of supply measures the percentage change in the quantity supplied of a product resulting from a change in the product price. The elasticity of supply is calculated as follows:

$$E_s = \frac{\text{Percentage change in quantity supplied}}{\text{Percentage change in price}}$$

- Supply is said to be elastic if $E_s > 1$, unitary elastic if $E_s = 1$, and inelastic if $E_s < 1$.
- Elastic supply means that a percentage increase in price will create a larger percentage increase in supply.

D. Market Equilibrium

A product's equilibrium price is determined by demand and supply; it is the price at which all the goods offered for sale will be sold (i.e., quantity demanded = quantity supplied). The equilibrium price is the price at which the demand and supply curve intersect as shown below.

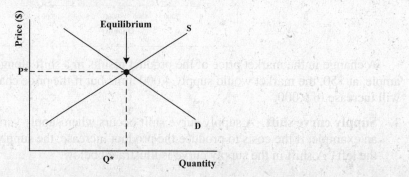

1. **Government intervention.** Government actions may change market equilibrium through taxes, subsidies, and rationing. For example, a subsidy paid to farmers will reduce the cost of producing a par-

ticular farm product and, therefore, cause the equilibrium price to be lower than it would be without the subsidy. Import taxes, on the other hand, would increase the cost of an imported product causing the equilibrium price to be higher.

    a. **Price ceiling.** A price ceiling is a specified maximum price that may be charged for a good. If the price ceiling is set for a good below the equilibrium price, it will cause good shortages because suppliers will devote their production facilities to producing other goods.

    b. **Price floor.** A price floor is a minimum specified price that may be charged for a good. If the price floor is set for a good above the equilibrium price, it will cause overproduction and surpluses will develop.

        Therefore, we see that government intervention in terms of taxes, subsidies, or price controls interfere with the free market and can result in an inefficient allocation of resources. Too many resources are devoted to certain sectors of the economy at the expense of other sectors.

2. **Externalities.** Another factor that causes inefficiencies in the pricing of goods in the market is the existence of externalities. **Externalities** is the term used to describe damage to common areas that is caused by the production of certain goods. A prominent example of an externality is pollution. Because these externalities are not included in the production costs of the goods, the supply is higher and the price is lower than is appropriate. Government laws and regulations (e.g., Environmental Protection Agency regulations) attempt to force firms to change their production methods to make externalities part of the cost of production. This causes the market price of these products to be a more accurate reflection of the cost of the goods to society.

3. **The effects of shifts in demand and supply.** The effects on equilibrium of shifts in demand and supply are shown in the following graphs.

Increase in Demand and New Equilibrium   **Increase in Supply and New Equilibrium**

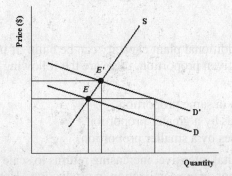
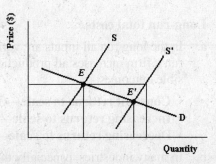

The effects of shifts in demand and supply can be complex especially when both shift simultaneously. The following table describes the effects of these changes:

Change in demand or supply	*Effect*
1. Increase (decrease) in demand, no change in supply	Equilibrium price will increase (decrease) and quantity purchased will increase (decrease)
2. Increase (decrease) in supply, no change in demand	Equilibrium price will decrease (increase) and quantity purchased will increase (decrease)
3. Both demand and supply increase (decrease)	Quantity purchased will increase (decrease) and the new equilibrium price is indeterminate
4. Demand increases and supply decreases	Equilibrium price will increase and quantity purchased is indeterminate.
5. Demand decreases and supply increases	Equilibrium price will decrease and quantity purchased is indeterminate

E. Costs of Production

1. **Short-run total costs.**

    a. In the short run, firms have both fixed and variable costs. Total fixed costs are those that are committed and will not change with different levels of production. An example of a fixed cost is the rent paid on a long-term lease for a factory. Variable costs are the costs of variable inputs, such as raw materials, variable labor costs, and variable overhead. These costs are directly related to the level of production for the period. In the short run, costs behave as follows:

- **Average fixed cost (AFC)**—Fixed cost per unit of production. It goes down consistently as more units are produced.
- **Average variable cost (AVC)**—Total variable costs divided by the number of units produced. It initially stays constant until the inefficiencies of producing in a fixed-size facility cause variable costs to begin to rise.
- **Marginal cost (MC)**—The added cost of producing one extra unit. It initially decreases but then begins to increase due to inefficiencies.
- **Average total cost (ATC)**—Total costs divided by the number of units produced. Its behavior depends on the makeup of fixed and variable costs.

b. The cause of the inefficiencies described above is referred to as the **law of diminishing returns**. This law states that as we try to produce more and more output with a fixed productive capacity, marginal productivity will decline. The graph below illustrates the relationships between various short-run costs.

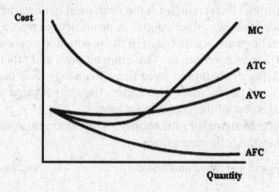

2. **Long-run total costs.**

a. In the long run all inputs are variable because additional plant capacity can be built. If in the long run a firm increases all production factors by a given proportion, there are the following three possible outcomes:

- **Constant returns to scale**—Output increases in same proportion.
- **Increasing returns to scale**—Output increases by a greater proportion.
- **Decreasing returns to scale**—Output increases by a smaller proportion.

b. In many industries, especially those that are capital intensive, increasing returns to scale occur up to a point, generally as a result of division of labor and specialization in production. However, beyond a certain size, management has problems controlling production and decreasing returns to scale arise. The following graph illustrates a long-run average total cost (ATC) curve which begins with increasing returns to scale (A), and proceeds to constant returns to scale (B), and eventually decreasing returns to scale (C) as the firm grows.

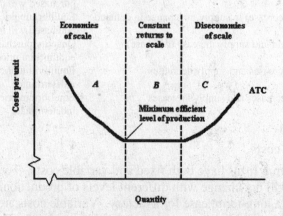

3. **Profits.** Economists refer to two different types of profit.

    a. **Normal profit**—The amount of profit necessary to compensate the owners for their capital and/or managerial skills. It is just enough profit to keep the firm in business in the long run.

    b. **Economic profit**—The amount of profit in excess of normal profit. In a perfectly competitive market, economic profit cannot be experienced in the long run.

F. Production

1. Management makes production decisions based on the relationship between marginal revenue and marginal cost. **Marginal revenue** is the additional revenue received from the sale of one additional unit of product. A good should be produced and sold as long as the marginal cost (MC) of producing the good is less than or equal to the marginal revenue (MR) from sale of that good. This relationship is shown in the following graph.

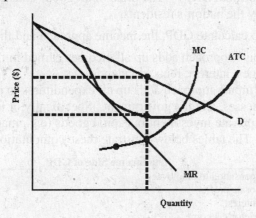

2. The price of input resources (e.g., labor, raw materials, etc.) is determined by demand and supply. If the price of an input increases, demand will decline. On the other hand, demand will increase if the price declines. In making decisions about the employment of resources, management considers the marginal product for each input resource. The **marginal product** is the additional output obtained from employing one additional unit of a resource. The change in total revenue from employing one additional unit of a resource is referred to as the **marginal revenue product**.

> *EXAMPLE: Thorp Corporation produces Product G and has developed the following chart illustrating relationships between number of workers producing the product, the number of units produced, and the revenue generated.*
>
> | Number of workers | Products produced | Revenue generated |
> |:-:|:-:|:-:|
> | 4 | 100 | $200,000 |
> | 5 | 120 | $240,000 |
> | 6 | 139 | $275,000 |
> | 7 | 157 | $300,000 |
>
> *The marginal product of employing the 6th worker is equal to 19 (139 – 120), and the marginal revenue product is equal to $35,000 ($275,000 – $240,000).*

3. The **marginal revenue per-unit** is calculated by dividing the marginal revenue product by the increase in products produced by employing one additional unit of resource. Using the above example of employing a 6th worker, the marginal revenue per-unit is equal to $1,842.11 [$35,000 (marginal revenue product) ÷ 19 (139 – 120) increase in products produced].

4. To be competitive management must produce the optimal output in the most efficient manner. The cost of production in the long run is minimized when the marginal product (MP) per dollar of every input (resource) is the same. Similar to utility maximization for a consumer, the least cost formula is

$$\frac{\text{MP of input A}}{\text{Price of input A}} = \frac{\text{MP of input B}}{\text{Price of input B}} = \frac{\text{MP of input C}}{\text{Price of input C}} = \frac{\text{MP of input Z}}{\text{Price of input Z}}$$

MACROECONOMICS

A. Macroeconomics looks at the economy as a whole. It focuses on measures of economic output, employment, inflation, and trade surpluses or deficits. It also examines the spending of the three major segments of the economy, consumers, business, and government. The levels of economic activity is measured using a number of benchmarks, including

- **Nominal Gross Domestic Product (GDP)**—The price of all goods and services produced by a domestic economy for a year at current market prices.
- **Real GDP**—The price of **all** goods and services produced by the economy at price level adjusted (constant) prices. Price level adjustment eliminates the effect of inflation on the measure.
- **Potential GDP**—The maximum amount of production that could take place in an economy without putting pressure on the general level of prices. The difference between **potential GDP** and **real GDP** is called the GDP gap. When it is positive it indicates that there are unemployed resources in the economy and we would expect unemployment. Alternatively, when it is negative, it indicates that the economy is running above normal capacity and prices should begin to rise.
- **Net Domestic Product (NDP)**—GDP minus depreciation.
- **Gross National Product (GNP)**—The price of all goods and services produced by labor and property supplied by the nation's residents.

1. There are two ways to calculate GDP, the income approach and the expenditure approach.

    a. The income (output) approach adds up all incomes earned in the production of final goods and services, such as wages, interest, rents, dividends, etc.

    b. The expenditure (input) approach adds up all expenditures to purchase final goods and services by households, businesses, and the government. Specifically, it includes personal consumption expenditures, gross private investment in capital goods (e.g., machinery). It also includes the country's net exports. The tables below illustrate these computations.

The Income Side of GDP

Compensation to employees	6,010
Corporate profits	767
Net interest	554
Proprietor's income	743
Rental income of persons	143
National income	8,217
Plus: indirect taxes	794
Minus: other, including statutory discrepancy	(160)
Net national product	8,851
Plus: consumption of fixed capital	1,351
Gross national product	10,202
Plus: payments of factor income to other countries	341
Minus: receipts of labor income from other countries	(335)
Gross domestic product	10,208

The Product Side of GDP

Personal consumption expenditures	7,065
Gross private domestic fixed investment	
Business	1,246
Residential	446
Government purchases	
Federal	616
State and local	1,223
Net exports	(330)
Changes in business inventories	(58)
Gross domestic product	10,208

B. Aggregate Demand and Supply

1. An aggregate demand curve depicts the demand of consumers, businesses, and government as well as foreign purchasers for the goods and services of the economy at different price levels. The aggregate demand curve looks like the demand curve for a single product (presented above); it is inversely related to price level. The price level affects aggregate demand for several reasons.

    a. **Interest rate effect**—As price levels increase (inflation increases) nominal interest rates increase causing a decrease in interest sensitive spending. Interest sensitive spending includes spending for items such as houses, automobiles, and appliances.

    b. **Wealth effect**—When price levels increase, the market value of certain financial assets decreases (e.g., fixed rate bonds) causing individuals to have less wealth and therefore they reduce their consumption.

c. **International purchasing power effect**—When domestic price levels increase relative to foreign currencies, foreign products become less expensive causing an increase in imported goods and a decrease in exported goods. This decreases the aggregate demand for domestic products.

2. An aggregate demand curve shifts when consumers, businesses, or governments are willing to spend more or less, or when there is an increase or decrease in the demand for domestic products abroad (i.e., an increase or decrease in net exports). Government can affect aggregate demand through its own spending levels, taxes, and monetary policy. For example, a reduction in individual or corporate taxes increases the spendable income of consumers or businesses. This would be expected to increase spending.

3. An aggregate supply (output) schedule presents the relationship between goods and services supplied and the price level, assuming that all other variables that affect supply are held constant. While there is not complete agreement on the shape of the aggregate supply curve, it is generally depicted as shown below.

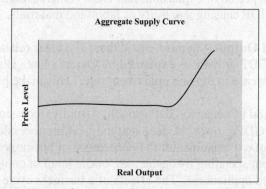

     As shown, prices remain relatively constant until the economy reaches near capacity, at which time prices begin to increase at a significant rate. Shifts in the aggregate supply curve may be caused by technology improvements, changes in resource availability, or changes in resource costs.

4. Equilibrium GDP occurs when the output level of the economy creates just enough spending to purchase the entire output.

5. **The multiplier.** The multiplier refers to the fact than an increase in spending by consumers, businesses, or the government has a multiplied effect on equilibrium GDP. The reason for this is that increased spending generates increases in income to businesses and consumers which in turn increases their spending, which again increases the income of other consumers and businesses, etc. Therefore, the increased spending ripples through the economy increasing GDP by much more than the original increase in spending. The effect of the multiplier can be estimated by examining an economy's **marginal propensity to consume (MPC)** and **marginal propensity to save (MPS)**. From our previous discussion we know that additional income is either spent or saved as shown below.

$$MPS + MPC = 1$$

The multiplier may be calculated from the following formula:

$$\frac{1}{MPS} \times \text{Change in spending}$$

EXAMPLE: If MPS is .25 (MPC = .75) and spending increases by $1,000,000, the increase in equilibrium GDP is calculated below.

$$\frac{1}{.25} \times \$1,000,000 = \$4,000,000$$

C. Business Cycles

1. A business cycle is a fluctuation in aggregate economic output that lasts for several years. Business cycles are recurring but vary in terms of both length and intensity. They are depicted as a series of peaks and troughs. A peak marks the end of a period of economic expansion and the beginning of a recession (contraction) while a trough marks the end of a recession and the beginning of an economic recovery (expansion). The chart below illustrates the nature of the business cycle.

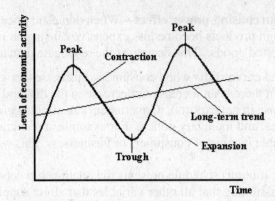

2. Economic contractions are characterized by a decrease in real gross domestic product (GDP) due to reduced spending. In a period of expansion, real GDP is increasing. At the peak real GDP generally surpasses potential GDP causing a scarcity of labor and materials. These shortages generally cause inflation.

3. **Unemployment and Output**—In most cases, there is a clear relationship between the change in unemployment and GDP growth, as explained by Okum's law. High output growth is generally associated with a decrease in the unemployment rate. This make perfect sense because when output increases less.

4. A **recession** is a period of negative GDP growth. Usually, recession refers to at least two consecutive quarters of negative GDP growth. A deep and long-lasting recession is referred to as a **depression**.

5. There are a number of explanations for the occurrence of business cycles but they generally relate to the level of investment spending by businesses, or the level of consumer spending for durable goods (e.g., automobiles and appliances). The effects of a business cycle vary by business sector. For obvious reasons, heavy manufacturing is one of the sectors that is most affected. Such businesses are referred to as **cyclical** businesses because they perform better in periods of expansion and worse in periods of recession. Some business sectors are called **defensive** because they are affected little by business cycles and some may actually perform better in periods of recession.

6. Economists attempt to predict business cycles using economic indicators. Some indicators lead future economic trends, others coincide with economic trends, and still others lag economic trends. The Conference Board, a private research group, has developed the following list of indicators:

    a. Leading indicators

    • Average weekly hours, manufacturing
    • Average weekly initial claims for unemployment insurance
    • Manufacturer's new orders, consumer goods and materials
    • Vendor performance, slower deliveries diffusion index
    • Manufacturer's new orders, nondefense capital goods
    • Building permits, new private housing units
    • Stock prices, 500 common stocks
    • Money supply, M2
    • Interest rate spread, 10-year Treasury bonds less federal funds
    • Index of consumer expectations

    b. Coincident indicators

    • Employees on nonagricultural payrolls
    • Personal income less transfer payments
    • Industrial production
    • Manufacturing and trade sales

    c. Lagging indicators

    • Average duration of unemployment
    • Inventories to sales ratio, manufacturing and trade
    • Labor cost per unit of output, manufacturing
    • Average prime rate

- Commercial and industrial loans
- Consumer installment credit to personal income ratio
- Consumer price index for services

7. **Investment.** Investment includes expenditures for residential construction, inventories, and plant and equipment. The most important determinant of business investment is expectations about profitability. Accordingly, the following factors affect investment spending:

    a. **The rate of technology growth.** In periods of high technology growth, firms tend to invest more because new products and innovations tend to be more profitable.

    b. **The real interest rate (nominal rate minus the inflation premium).** Lower real interest rates reduce the cost of investment.

    c. **The stock of capital goods.** If there are already enough capital goods in the economy to meet aggregate demand there is little incentive to invest.

    d. **Actions by the government.** Government fiscal policy can be used to stimulate investment spending (e.g., reductions in taxes, tax incentives, or increased government spending).

    e. **The acquisition and operating cost of capital goods.** As the purchase price or operating cost of plant and equipment decreases, firms will invest more.

Investment spending is the most volatile portion of GDP. **Autonomous investment** includes expenditures made by businesses based on expected profitability that are independent of the level of national income. That is, they are constant regardless of whether the economy is expanding or contracting. **Induced investment** is incremental spending based on an increased level of economic activity.

8. **Accelerator theory.** Accelerator theory states that as economic activity increases, capital investment must be made to meet the level of increased demand. The increased capital investment in turn creates additional economic demand which further feeds the economic expansion.

D. Economic Measures

Previously we described several important measures of economic activity: GDP, GNP, etc. In this section we will describe other economic measures, such as rates of unemployment, inflation, and personal disposable income.

1. **Unemployment**

The unemployment rate is the percent of the total labor force that is unemployed at a given time. Individuals may be unemployed because of frictional, structural, or cyclical causes.

    a. **Frictional unemployment** occurs because individuals are forced or voluntarily change jobs. At any point in time some individuals will be temporarily unemployed while they look for a job. New entrants into the workforce also fall into this category.

    b. **Structural unemployment** occurs due to changes in demand for products or services, or technological advances causing not as many individuals with a particular skill to be needed. Structural unemployment is reduced by retraining programs.

    c. **Cyclical unemployment** is caused by the condition in which real GDP is less than potential GDP. Therefore, such unemployment increases during recessions and decreases during expansions.

2. **Inflation**

    a. **Inflation** is the rate of increase in the price level of goods and services, usually measured on an annual basis.

    b. **Deflation** is a term used to describe a decrease in the price levels. While Japan has experienced deflation in prices recently, the US has not experienced an annual rate of decrease in price level since the 1930s. Deflation is very damaging because businesses do not want to borrow money and pay it back with money that has more purchasing power, and they do not want to invest in plant and equipment given that the cost of plant and equipment is declining.

    c. High rates of inflation are not good for the economy either. It generally causes economic activity to contract and redistributes income and wealth.

    d. A price index measures the prices of a basket of goods and/or services at a point in time in relation to the prices in a base period.

(1) **The consumer price index** (CPI) measures the price that urban consumers paid for a fixed basket of goods and services in relation to the price of the same goods and services purchased in some base period.

(2) **The producer price index** (PPI) measures the prices of finished goods and materials at the wholesale level.

(3) **The GDP deflator** measures the prices for net exports, investment, government expenditures, and consumer spending. It is the most comprehensive measure of price level.

3. **Causes of inflation.** There are generally two causes for inflation that are commonly referred to as demand-pull and cost-push.

    a. **Demand-pull** inflation occurs when aggregate spending exceeds the economy's normal full-employment output capacity. It generally occurs at the peak of a business cycle and is characterized by real GDP exceeding potential GDP. Because labor is short companies bid up the price and inflation occurs.

    b. **Cost-push** inflation occurs from an increase in the cost of producing goods and services. It is usually characterized by decreases in aggregate output and unemployment because consumers are not willing to pay the inflated prices.

There is an inverse relationship between inflation and unemployment. When the unemployment rate is low, inflation tends to increase. Inflation tends to decrease when the unemployment rate is high. This relationship is depicted by the **Phillips curve**.

4. **Personal disposable income** is the amount of income that individuals receive and have available to purchase goods and services. Personal disposable income has a significant effect on the economy because it is a large determinant of consumer demand. Personal disposable income is equal to **personal income** minus personal taxes.

5. **Interest rates.** Interest is the price paid for the use of money. Economists typically focus on the risk-free or pure rate of interest. In practice, interest rates are also affected by credit risk, maturity, and administrative costs. As with other commodities, interest rates are determined by demand and supply. The intersection of the demand and supply curves for money determines the equilibrium price or interest rate. On the demand side, firms borrow money to make investments in assets and will continue to borrow as long as investment return exceeds the interest rate at which the funds are borrowed. The supply of funds is affected by the past and current savings of individuals and firms, but it is also affected by the monetary policy of the government. Interest rates are often quoted as

    a. **Real interest rate**—Interest rate in terms of goods. These rates are adjusted for inflation.

    b. **Nominal interest rate**—Interest rate in terms of the nation's currency. These are the rates that are quoted by financial institutions and in the financial pages of newspapers. The difference between the real rate and the nominal rate is the inflation premium, which represents the expected inflation rate. The higher the expected inflation rate the larger the inflation premium. The interest rate charged to a particular business or individual will be higher than the nominal rate due to **credit risk,** which is the risk that the firm will not pay the interest or principal of the loan.

6. **Government budget surplus (deficit)**—The excess (deficit) of government taxes in relation to government transfer payments and purchases. To finance a deficit the government issues debt (e.g., Treasury bonds).

7. **Money.** Money in an economy serves three major purposes—a medium of exchange; a common denominator to measure prices, revenue, expenses, and income; and a store of value allowing individuals and firms to save. Economists use three basic measures of money, M_1, M_2, and M_3. M_1 includes only currency and demand deposits, M_2 is equal to M_1 plus savings accounts and small-time deposits (less $100,000), and M_3 is equal to M_2 plus other (larger) time deposits. In regulating the economy the Federal Reserve focuses on M_2.

E. Monetary Policy

Depository institutions (banks, savings and loans, and credit unions, etc.) borrow savers' money and lend the money to consumers, businesses, and governments. The Federal Reserve (the US central bank), through its open market controls the actions of depository institutions and can affect the supply of money in the following ways:

1. **Reserve requirements.** When a bank lends money, it gives the borrower a check drawn on the bank itself. The Federal Reserve controls a bank's ability to issue check-writing deposits by imposing a reserve requirement on checking deposits. The institution must hold in reserve (much of which is on deposit at a Federal Reserve Bank) a certain percentage of their total checking deposits. The Federal Reserve can influence interest rates by changing the reserve requirements and therefore increasing or decreasing the supply of money. However, making changes in reserve requirements is rarely done.

2. **Open-market operations.** A more common instrument of monetary policy is open-market operations (by the **Federal Open-Market Committee**), which involves the purchase or sale of government securities using the Federal Reserve Bank deposits. If the Federal Reserve purchases government securities, they are able to increase the monetary supply and, therefore, put downward pressure on interest rates. When a central bank is purchasing government securities and expanding the money supply, it is called an **expansionary open-market operation**. If a central bank is selling government securities it is said to be pursuing a **contractionary open-market operation,** because this reduces the money supply.

3. **The discount rate.** When a bank has a reserve deficiency it may borrow funds from a Federal Reserve Bank. By setting the discount rate for such borrowing, the Federal Reserve can influence interest rates in the economy.

4. **Economic analysis.** In making its monetary decisions, the Federal Open-Market Committee does extensive economic analysis. In speeches by the members and when providing the basis for its decisions insights are provided into the state of the economy. This information also may have an effect on economic factors such as interest rates, business spending, and the stock prices.

5. The Federal Reserve uses monetary policy to attempt to sustain economic growth while keeping inflation under control. Monetary policy works on the principle that a decrease in interest rates will stimulate the economy, and an increase in interest rates will slow the economy. Lower interest rates tend to encourage consumer and business spending because finance charges are lower. Higher interest rates tend to discourage spending because finance charges are higher. It also encourages saving because the return on savings is higher.

6. The effects of monetary policy depend on their effects on the expectations of investors, businesses, and consumers. If monetary expansion leads the financial markets to revise their expectations about inflation, interest rates and output, the effect on output will be dramatic. On the other hand, if expectations remain unchanged, the effects will be minimal.

7. **Rational expectations** assume that investors, firms, and consumers develop expectations about inflation, interest rates, and output based on a consideration of all available information. This is contrasted to adaptive expectations in which investors, firms and consumers adjust their expectations based on new information. As an example, if they find that inflation is higher than expected, they adjust their expectation upward.

F. Fiscal Policy

Fiscal policy is government actions, such as taxes, subsidies, and government spending, designed to achieve economic goals. As an example, a reduction of taxes increases personal disposable income, which will serve to stimulate economic activity. The economy may also be stimulated through increased government spending. An increase in deficit, either due to an increase in government spending or to a decrease in taxes, is called a **fiscal expansion**. On the other hand, increases in taxes to reduce a deficit is called **fiscal contraction**.

1. **Taxes.** Taxes are levied by a government based on two general principles: (1) the ability to pay (e.g., progressive income taxes), and (2) derived benefit (e.g., gasoline taxes used to pay for roads). The following are the major types of taxes:

    a. **Income tax.** Income taxes are levied on taxable income. In the US the rate structure is generally progressive. However, there are a number of social and economic incentives built into the system that dilute its progressive structure.

    b. **Property tax.** Property taxes are levied based on wealth. They generally are progressive based on the value of the property.

    c. **Sales tax.** Sales taxes are levied based on the amount of income spent. Sales taxes are viewed as regressive because low-income individuals pay the same percentage rate as high-income individuals.

d. **Wage taxes.** The most significant wage tax in the US is the social security tax. This tax is borne both directly (the employee's share) and indirectly (the employer's share) by employees because without the tax, wages would be higher.

e. **Value-added tax.** A tax commonly used in other industrial nations is the value-added tax (VAT). Value-added taxes are levied on the increase in value of each product as it proceeds through production and distribution processes. Ultimately, the tax is paid by the final consumer. The VAT is thought to encourage savings because it taxes consumption instead of earnings.

2. Both monetary and fiscal policy take time to have the desired effects for a number of reasons, including

   a. Consumers take time to adjust their consumption based on changes in personal disposal income
   b. Firms take time to adjust investment based on changes in sales
   c. Firms take time to adjust spending based on changes in interest rates
   d. Firms take time to adjust production based on changes in sales

3. Fiscal polices can have a large effect on the size of budget deficits. In the long and medium run, a budget deficit reduction is likely to be beneficial to the economy. Lower budget deficits usually mean more savings and investment, and therefore, more output. In the short run, a reduction in budget deficit leads to reductions in spending and therefore less output.

G. **Economic Theories**

1. **Classical economic theory**—This theory holds that market equilibrium will eventually result in full employment over the long run without government intervention. This theory does not support the use of fiscal policy to stimulate the economy.

2. **Keynesian theory**—This theory holds that the economy does not necessarily move towards full employment on its own. It focuses on the use of fiscal policy (e.g., reductions in taxes and government spending) to stimulate the economy.

3. **Monetarist theory**—This theory holds that fiscal policy is too crude a tool for control of the economy. It focuses on the use of monetary policy to control economic growth.

4. **Supply-side theory**—This theory holds that bolstering an economy's ability to supply more goods is the most effective way to stimulate growth. A decrease in taxes (especially for businesses and individuals with high income) increases employment, savings, and investments and is an effective way to stimulate the economy. The tax revenue lost from the reduction in taxes is more than offset by the increase in taxes from increased economic activity. However, this predicted effect only occurs when rates are too high. The **Laffer Curve** attempts to explain how consumers react to changes in rates of income tax. The curve illustrates that if taxes are already too low decreasing them will result in less tax revenue.

5. **Neo-Keynesian theory**—This theory combines Keynesian and monetarist theories. It focuses on using a combination of fiscal and monetary policy to stimulate the economy and control inflation.

H. **International Trade**

   International trade is very important to almost every business. The world truly is a global economy. If a country has an **absolute advantage** (e.g., low-cost labor, technology, etc.) in the production of a particular good, there is an incentive for that country to produce more than its citizens need to export the good to countries with higher production costs. This is especially true if it also has a comparative advantage to producing the good. A **comparative advantage** means that country has no alternate uses of its resources that would involve a higher return (i.e., the **opportunity costs** are less). In the long term, production of specific goods and services will migrate to countries that have a **comparative advantage**. By exploiting its comparative advantages and exporting goods and services, a nation can import the goods for which it has a comparative disadvantage. In this manner all nations will be better off.

1. **Obstacles to free trade.** Even though trade can be a source of major gains, many nations restrict free trade by imposing tariffs and quotas. An import **tariff** is a tax on an imported product. An import **quota** is a restriction on the amount of a good that may be imported during a period.

   Trade restrictions are advocated by labor unions and firms making products that are more inexpensively produced in other nations. Thus, trade restrictions generally impose a burden on society as a whole because they reduce the availability of goods and increase their prices. Arguments in favor of trade restrictions include

    a. To protect domestic labor against inexpensive foreign labor
    b. To reduce domestic unemployment
    c. To protect young or infant industries
    d. To protect industries important to the nation's defense

    Most of these arguments are not valid. Trade restrictions in the US are advocated by labor and firms in the US in industries that have lost their competitive advantage, such as producers of shoes, textiles, and steel. Some firms and industries in the US have been able to regain their competitive advantage through the introduction of new technology.

2. **North American Free Trade Agreement (NAFTA)**

    a. NAFTA is a free trade agreement between the countries of Canada, Mexico, and the US. It was adopted by the US Congress in 1993. NAFTA offers a number of advantages for US businesses including

        (1) The ability to take advantage of the lower labor costs in Mexico for such functions as manufacturing and assembly

        (2) The opening of new markets for goods of US industries that have a comparative advantage, such as technology.

    b. Disadvantages to US businesses and labor markets include

        (1) Some US industries, such as producers of shoes and apparel, are concerned that the firms will be hurt by the availability of less expensive products from Mexico.

        (2) Certain jobs in the US will be lost because of the availability of lower-cost labor in Mexico combined with more lax environmental laws and regulations.

3. **Balance of payments.** The balance of payments is an account summary of a nation's transactions with other nations. It has three major sections: the current account, the capital account, and the official reserve account.

    a. **Current account**—Shows the flow of goods and services and government grants for a period of time.

        (1) The **balance of trade** for a period is the difference between the total goods exported and the total goods imported.

        (2) The **balance on goods and services** is the difference between the total value of goods and services exported and the total value of goods and services imported.

        (3) When a nation exports more than it imports a **trade surplus** occurs.

        (4) When a nation imports more than it exports a **trade deficit** occurs.

    b. **Capital account**—Shows the flow of investments in fixed and financial assets for a period of time.

    c. The **balance of payments** surplus or deficit is the amount that nets the current and capital accounts. In other words, when the sum of the outflows exceeds the inflows a deficit in balance of payment occurs. The deficit is settled in currency of other nations, or by an increase in the holdings of the nation's currency by other nations. A deficit is an unfavorable balance of payments while a surplus is a favorable balance of payments.

    d. **Official reserve account**—Shows the changes in the nation's reserves (e.g., gold and foreign currency).

4. **The International Monetary Fund (IMF)** has a pool of currencies from which member countries can borrow to meet short-term deficits in balance of payments.

I. Foreign Exchange Rates

    Firms that do business internationally must be concerned with exchange rates, which are the relationships among the values of currencies. For example, a US firm selling products in Europe is very interested in the relationship of the euro to the US dollar.

1. **Factors influencing exchange rates.** As with any other market, the exchange rate between two currencies is determined by the supply of, and the demand for, those currencies. However, these rates are also subject to intervention by the central banks of countries. Therefore, exchange rates are often said to be determined by **managed float**. In general, the following factors will affect the exchange rate of a particular currency:

   a. **Inflation.** Inflation tends to deflate the value of a currency because holding the currency results in reduced purchasing power.

   b. **Interest rates.** If interest returns in a particular country are higher relative to other countries, individuals and companies will be enticed to invest in that country. As a result there will be increased demand for the country's currency.

   c. **Balance of payments.** Balance of payments is used to refer to a system of accounts that catalogs the flow of goods between the residents of two countries. If country X is a net exporter of goods and therefore has a surplus balance of trade, countries purchasing the goods must use country X's currency. This increases the demand for the currency and therefore its relative value.

   d. **Government intervention.** Through intervention (e.g., buying or selling the currency in the foreign exchange markets), the central bank of a country may support or depress the value of its currency.

   e. **Other factors.** Other factors that may affect exchange rates are political and economic stability, extended stock market rallies, or significant declines in the demand for major exports.

2. **Spot rates and forward rates.** The spot rate for a currency is the exchange rate of the currency for immediate delivery. On the other hand, the forward rate is the exchange rate for a currency for future delivery. For example, a forward contract might obligate a company to purchase or sell euros at a specific exchange rate three months hence. The difference between the spot rate and the forward rate is referred to as the discount or premium. If the forward rate is less (greater) than the spot rate, the market believes that the value of the currency is going to decline (increase).

   > *EXAMPLE: Assume that a multinational company sells products to a French company for a receivable payable in 60 days in the amount of 10,000 euros. If at the time of the sale the exchange rate is 1.25 US dollars to the euro, the sale is equal to $12,500 (1.25 × 10,000). If the euro depreciates by 2% against the US dollar in the 60-day period between the sale and collection, the firm has experienced a loss. The 2% depreciation would mean that the new exchange rate is 1.225 (1.25 × 98%) euros to the US dollar. Therefore, the firm has lost $12,500 − $12,250 (1.225 × 10,000) = $250.*

3. The foreign exchange risk for a multinational company is divided into two types: **translations (accounting) risk** and **transaction risk**. Translation risk is the exposure that a multinational company has because its financial statements must be converted to its functional currency. Statement of Financial Accounting Standards 52 describes the accounting for this conversion and includes procedures that reduce the impact of translation exposure.

4. Transaction risk relates to the possibility of gains and losses resulting from income transactions occurring during the year. The example above involving the sale of goods for a receivable in euros illustrates transaction risk. Transaction risk can cause volatility in reported earnings that motivates management to use strategies to minimize the company's exposure. These strategies include

   a. **Hedging in the forward exchange market.** Companies can use forward contracts to hedge foreign currency transactions. As an example, assume that Company X has agreed to deliver 20,000 units of product in six months to a Japanese company who will pay for the product in yen. To mitigate the risk of losses from devaluation of the yen, Company X could enter into a forward contract to sell the yen for delivery in six months. This contract in effect locks in the price for the sale in terms of US dollars.

   b. **Money market hedge.** A second way to eliminate the transaction risk described in a. is to borrow money in yen when the agreement is executed. This strategy immediately converts the yen to US dollars. Then, when the yen are collected from the sale, the loan can be repaid resulting in no foreign exchange loss or gain over the six-month period.

   c. **Currency futures market hedge.** Futures markets exist that allow a company to purchase or sell contracts to deliver foreign currency. These contracts can be used to hedge a foreign currency transaction much like a forward contract. However, because futures contracts are standard in nature and traded on organized exchanges, they can be readily bought and sold.

J. Foreign Investment

1. Foreign direct investments are usually quite large and many are exposed to **political risk**. Repatriation (transfer) of a foreign subsidiary's profits may be blocked. In the extreme case a foreign government may even expropriate (take) the firm's assets. Strategies to reduce risk include the use of joint ventures, financing with local-country capital, and the purchase of insurance.

2. **Transfer pricing.** Transfer pricing is the price at which services or products are bought and sold across international borders between related parties. As an example, if a US parent company purchases products from its French subsidiary, a transfer price must be established for the products. Because the transfer price affects the parent and subsidiary's net income, it affects the taxes that the firm pays in the US and France. Multinational companies can minimize their overall tax burden by using transfer prices to minimize net income in jurisdictions with higher income tax rates, and maximizing net income in jurisdictions with lower income tax rates. However, many governments have established tax regulations that are designed to help ensure that transfer prices estimate market prices.

THE EFFECTS OF THE ECONOMIC ENVIRONMENT ON STRATEGY

A firm's objectives are the overall plans for the firm as defined by management. Management attempts to achieve these objectives by developing strategies (operational actions). However, achieving management's objectives is always subject to business risks faced by the firm. **Business risks** are conditions that threaten management's ability to execute strategies and achieve the firm's objectives. A comprehensive understanding of the firm's internal and external environments is necessary for management to understand the firm's present condition and its business risks. This understanding includes comprehension of both the general and industry environments.

A. The **general environment** includes the following factors:

- Economic—Inflation rates, interest rates, budget deficits, personal saving rate, gross domestic product, etc.
- Demographic—Population size, workforce, ethnic mix, income distribution, geographic distribution, etc.
- Political and legal—Antitrust laws, tax laws, deregulation philosophies, etc.
- Sociocultural—Workforce diversity, environmental concerns, shifts in consumer preferences, etc.
- Technological segment—Societal innovations in technology and products, focus of the economy on research and development, etc.
- Global—Important global political events, developments in global markets, etc.

The general aspects of the environment are out of the control of management of the firm. Management must adapt to its general environment.

B. The industry environment is the set of factors that influence the firm's competitive actions. Michael Porter developed a model for industry analyses that focuses on five forces: (1) competitors, (2) potential entrants into the market, (3) equivalent products, (4) bargaining power of customers, and (5) bargaining power of input suppliers.[1]

---

[1] *M. Porter, **Competitive Strategy,** New York Free Press (1980).*

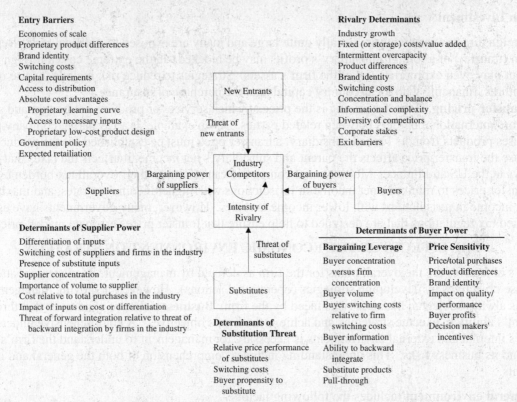

Entry Barriers

Economies of scale
Proprietary product differences
Brand identity
Switching costs
Capital requirements
Access to distribution
Absolute cost advantages
    Proprietary learning curve
    Access to necessary inputs
    Proprietary low-cost product design
Government policy
Expected retaliation

Rivalry Determinants

Industry growth
Fixed (or storage) costs/value added
Intermittent overcapacity
Product differences
Brand identity
Switching costs
Concentration and balance
Informational complexity
Diversity of competitors
Corporate stakes
Exit barriers

Determinants of Supplier Power

Differentiation of inputs
Switching cost of suppliers and firms in the industry
Presence of substitute inputs
Supplier concentration
Importance of volume to supplier
Cost relative to total purchases in the industry
Impact of inputs on cost or differentiation
Threat of forward integration relative to threat of
    backward integration by firms in the industry

Determinants of Substitution Threat

Relative price performance
    of substitutes
Switching costs
Buyer propensity to
    substitute

Determinants of Buyer Power

Bargaining Leverage	**Price Sensitivity**
Buyer concentration versus firm concentration	Price/total purchases
	Product differences
	Brand identity
Buyer volume	Impact on quality/ performance
Buyer switching costs relative to firm switching costs	Buyer profits
Buyer information	Decision makers' incentives
Ability to backward integrate	
Substitute products	
Pull-through	

1. The industry environment directly affects the firm and the types of strategies it must develop to compete. It is most relevant to the firm's profit potential. Management attempts to position the firm where it can influence the industry factors and successfully defend against their influence. **Remember, management has little or no control over the general environment factors but through its actions may have significant influence over industry factors.** Generally, the larger the firm's market share the more influence it can have on its industry environment.

2. Since firms must make strategic decisions that involve long-term commitments (e.g., investments in technology, plant, etc.), management must not only deal with the current environment, it must forecast the future. Effective management must analyze and forecast the general environment to identify opportunities and threats to the firm. In doing so, the following techniques are used:

    a. **Scanning**—A study of all segments in the general environment. The objective is to predict the effects of the general environment on the firm's industry. Management can use this information to modify its strategies and operating plans. Scanning of the general environment is critical to firms in volatile industries. Sources of information for scanning include trade publications, newspapers, business publications, public polls, government publications, etc.

    b. **Monitoring**—A study of environmental changes identified by scanning to spot important trends. As an example, the trend in aging of the population in this country would definitely be important to firms that provide services to retired individuals. Effective monitoring involves identifying the firm's major stakeholders (e.g., customers, investors, employees, etc.).

    c. **Forecasting**—Developing probable projections of what might happen and its timing. As an example, management might attempt to forecast changes in personal disposable income or the timing of introduction of a major technological development.

    d. **Assessing**—Determining changes in the firm's strategy that are necessary as a result of the information obtained from scanning, monitoring, and forecasting. It is the process of evaluating the implications of changes in the general environment on the firm.

C. Industry Analysis

1. An industry is a group of firms that produce products that are substitutes or close substitutes. Industries are often classified by their fundamental economics as perfect competition, pure monopoly, monopolistic competition, and oligopoly.

    a. **Perfect (Pure) competition**

(1) An industry is perfectly competitive if

   (a) It is composed of a large number of sellers, each of which are too small to affect the price of the product or service

   (b) The firms sell a virtually identical product

   (c) Firms can enter or leave the market easily (i.e., no barriers to entry)

   There are few perfectly competitive markets; common examples include the commodity markets, such as markets for wheat, soybeans, and corn.

(2) In this market, the **firm's demand curve** is perfectly elastic (horizontal). The firm can sell as many goods as it can produce at the equilibrium price but no goods at a higher price. The firm is a price taker. The **market demand curve** is downwards sloping. Therefore, demand will increase if all suppliers lower prices and will decrease if all suppliers raise their prices.

(3) In a perfectly competitive market a firm will continue to produce and sell products until the margin cost is greater than marginal revenue.

(4) Theoretically, no economic profits can be generated in the long run. The price will reflect the costs plus the normal profit of the most efficient producers.

(5) In a perfectly competitive market there is no product differentiation and the key to being successful is being the lowest cost producer in the marketplace. Innovation is restricted to attempting to make production, distribution, and sales processes more efficient.

b. **Pure monopoly**

(1) A pure monopoly is a market in which there is a single seller of a product or service for which there are no close substitutes. A monopoly may exist for one or more of the following reasons:

   (a) Increasing returns to scale

   (b) Control over the supply of raw materials

   (c) Patents (e.g., a drug manufacturer)

   (d) Government franchise (e.g., a public utility)

(2) Monopolies that exist when economic or technical conditions permit only one efficient supplier are called **natural monopolies.**

(3) The monopolist sets the price for the product (unless it is set by regulation). The demand curve for the firm is negatively sloping; the company must reduce price to sell more output. The firm will continue to produce and sell products as long as the marginal revenue is greater than average variable cost.

(4) Entry barriers make it possible for the firm to make economic profit in the long run.

(5) In pure monopoly, the company has little market incentive to innovate or control costs. The company has no market control on the price it charges. As a result pure monopolies are generally subject to government regulation. Price boards generally review the company's prices and costs. From a strategic standpoint monopolistic firms want to create a positive image with the public to forestall additional regulation. Therefore any advertising expenditures they incur tend to be for public relations. These firms also spend a lot of effort attempting to influence laws and regulations. They can increase total revenue if they can engage in price discrimination by market segment (e.g., charging business customers more than individual customers).

(6) The US government has passed legislation to discourage the development of monopolies because prices are higher and output less in such markets as compared to competitive markets. These laws include the Sherman Act of 1890, the Clayton Act of 1914, the Robinson-Patman Act of 1936, and the Celler-Kefauver Anti-Merger Act of 1950.

c. **Monopolistic competition**

(1) Monopolistic competition is characterized by many firms selling a differentiated product or service. The differentiation may be real or only created by advertising, and there is relatively easy entry to the market but not as easy as in a perfectly competitive market. This type of market is prevalent in retailing, including the markets for groceries, detergents, and breakfast cereals.

(2) The demand curve in a monopolistic competitive market is negatively sloped and firms tend to produce and sell products until the marginal revenue is less than average variable cost. There-

fore, goods tend to be priced somewhat higher than in a perfectly competitive market but less than in a monopoly. Also, there tends to be underproduction as compared to a perfectly competitive market.

(3) The strategies of firms in monopolistic competitive markets tend to focus on product or service innovation. Companies may spend heavily on product development. Customer relations and advertising necessarily are important to firm strategies.

d. **Oligopoly**

(1) Oligopoly is a form of market characterized by significant barriers to entry. As a result there are few (generally large) sellers of a product. Because there are few sellers the actions of one affect the others. An example of an oligopoly is the automobile industry. Other examples are found in the production of steel, aluminum, cigarettes, personal computers, and many electrical appliances.

(2) Oligopolists often attempt to engage in nonprice competition (e.g., by product differentiation or providing high levels of service). However, during economic downturns and periods of overcapacity, price competition in an oligopolistic market can turn fierce.

(3) The kinked-demand-curve model seeks to explain the price rigidity in oligopolistic markets. This model holds that the demand curve is kinked down at the market price because other oligopolists will not match price increases but will match price decreases. Generally, in the oligopolistic market there is a price leader that determines the pricing policy for the other producers.

(4) If left unregulated, ologopolists tend to establish **cartels** that engage in price fixing. Regulations in the US prohibit collusion by firms to set prices.

2. The competitive market of the firm determines the intensity of competition and threats to new entrants to the industry. However, the firm must also consider the threat of substitute products, bargaining power of suppliers, and bargaining power of its customers.

3. **Threat of substitute products.** Substitute products are goods or services from outside a given industry that perform similar functions. As an example, plastic containers constrain the price of glass containers.

4. **Bargaining power of suppliers.**

a. The power of suppliers affects a firm's ability to negotiate price or quality concessions. When suppliers have a good deal of power, they will be able to increase prices, and the firm purchasing those supplies may or may not be able to pass the cost on to its customers. Suppliers have power, for example, when the market is dominated by a few large companies, the industry firms are not significant customers for suppliers, or there are large costs to switching to another supplier.

b. The supplier market also includes the firm's labor market. The firm's ability to influence wage rate will depend on the other firms that are competing for the labor, and actions of the government and labor unions.

c. A **monopsony** is a market where only one buyer exists for all sellers. A monopsonist has monopoly power in the purchase of a resource. The marginal cost curve for a monopsonist is different from other firms' in that each time it purchases an additional unit of product or labor it increases the cost of all of the resource.

5. **Bargaining power of customers.** The power of customers determines the firm's ability to increase prices or lower quality of their products. When customers are powerful, the firm has difficulty passing cost increase on to them. Therefore the firm must concentrate on controlling costs. Customers are powerful, for example, when they purchase a large percentage of the industry output, they could switch to another product with little cost, the industry's products are standardized and the customers pose a threat to integrate backward into the firm's market.

6. **Techniques for industry analysis.** Firms use a variety of techniques to analyze their industries. In this section we will describe three of those techniques, competitor analysis, price elasticity analysis, and target market analysis.

a. **Competitor analysis.** In formulating strategy, management must consider the strategies of the firm's competitors. Competitor analysis is of vital importance to devising strategies in concentrated industries. Competitor analysis involves two major activities: (1) gathering information about competitors' capabilities, objectives, strategies, and assumptions (competitor intelligence), and (2) using the information to understand the competitors' behavior. Management uses a number of sources of information for competitor analysis including the competitor's

- Annual reports and SEC filings
- Interviews with analysts
- Press releases

However, management must also consider information derived from the actions of the competitor such as the following:

- Research and development projects
- Capital investments
- Promotional campaigns
- Strategic partnerships
- Mergers and acquisitions
- Hiring practices

In a competitor analysis, management seeks to understand

- What are the competitor's objectives?
- What can and is the competitor doing based on its current strategy?
- What does the competitor assume about the industry?
- What are the competitor's strengths and weaknesses?

Information from the analysis of the competitor's objectives, assumptions, strategy and capabilities can be developed into a **response profile** of possible actions that may be taken by the competitor under varying circumstances. This will allow management to anticipate or influence the competitor's actions to the firm's advantage.

b. **Price elasticity analysis.** Recall that the price elasticity of demand measures the effect of a change in price on the demand for the product. It is calculated with the following equation:

$$E_D = \frac{\text{Change in quantity demanded}}{\text{Average quantity}} \div \frac{\text{Change in price}}{\text{Average price}}$$

In order to develop a pricing strategy, management may perform price elasticity analysis of product or service. By observing the effects of price changes management can obtain a better understanding of the relationship. Regression analysis may be used to perform a more sophisticated analysis.

EXAMPLE: Assume that Carlton Corp. manufactures Product X, a commodity-type product. Management is attempting to understand the price elasticity of the product to assist in planning production levels. Management has collected the following historical data regarding the price and aggregate demand for Product X. The prices have been price-level adjusted to take out the effects of inflation.

Date	Price	Quantity Sold	Date	Price	Quantity Sold
1/1/X1	$5.00	10,000	3/31/X2	$4.00	14,500
3/31/X1	4.50	13,000	6/30/X2	4.25	13,000
6/30/X1	4.00	15,000	9/30/X2	5.00	10,500
9/30/X1	5.50	9,000	1/1/X3	5.50	9,000
1/1/X2	5.25	10,000	3/31/X3	6.00	7,500

Management decides to use regression analysis on a spreadsheet program to assist with estimating the relationship between price and quantity demanded. The results of the analysis are illustrated below.

	A	B	C	D	E	F	G
1	**SUMMARY OUTPUT**						
2							
3							
4	**Regression Statistics**						
5	Multiple R	0.986247					
6	R Square	0.972684					
7	Adjusted R						
8	Square	0.969269					
9	Standard Error	447.0297					
10	Observations	10					
11							
12	**ANOVA**						
13		df	SS	MS	F	Significance F	
14	Regression	1	56926316	56926316	284.8658	1.54E-07	
15	Residual	8	1598684	199835.5			
16	Total	9	58525000				
17							
18		Coefficients	Standard error	t Stat	P-value	Lower 95%	Upper 95%
19	Intercept	29030.7	1068.801	27.16194	3.64E-09	26566.04	31495.36
20	X variable 1	-3649.12	216.2063	-16.878	1.54E-07	-4147.7	-3150.55

As expected, the results indicate that there is a very significant relationship between price and aggregate demand for the product. The adjusted R Squared indicates that about 97% of the variance in quantity demanded is explained by price. The equation for simple regression is as follows:

$$y = a + bx$$

Where

y = the dependent variable—in this case demand volume
a = the y-axis intercept
b = the slope of the line
x = the independent variable—in this case price

Assuming that management wants to predict aggregate demand if the price was set at $5.75, we can use the equation that was developed from the analysis. Under the column Coefficients we see Intercept of 29030.7 and X variable 1 (price) of 3649.12. The equation to predict aggregate demand would be

Demand	=	a + (b)Price
	=	29030.7 + (-3649.12 × Price)
	=	29030.7 + (-3649.12 × 5.75)
	=	8,048

At a price of $5.75, the firm should expect aggregate demand to be about 8,048. Notice that the slope of the line (b) is negative indicating a negative relationship between demand and price, which is what we would expect. Regression analysis is explained in detail in Module 45.

c. **Target market analysis.**

(1) A firm's target market is the market in which the firm actually sells or plans to sell its product or services. A thorough understanding of the market is key to accurate sales forecasts. Just defining the market in geographic terms is not enough. Management should perform target market analysis to understand exactly who the firm's customers are. Management needs to understand why customers purchase the firm's product or service. For an individual customer the purpose might be to satisfy a basic need, to make things easier, or for entertainment. Target market analysis generally involves market segmentation, which involves breaking the market into groups that have different levels of demand for the firm's product or service. For example, a clothing store like the GAP, that sells clothing primarily for teens, is interested in the size of the segment of the market—the number of teens in the geographical area that the

store serves. Segmentation may be performed along any dimension that defines the firm's market, including

(a) Demographics (e.g., sex, education, income, etc.)
(b) Psychographics (e.g., lifestyle, social class, opinions, activities, attitudes, etc.)

(2) If the firm's customers are businesses, segmentation might be performed in terms of other relevant dimensions including

(a) Industry
(b) Size (in terms of sales, total employees, etc.)
(c) Location
(d) How they purchase (e.g., seasonality, volume, who makes the purchasing decision)

Unlike individuals, businesses purchase products to increase revenue, decrease costs, or maintain status quo.

(3) Target market analysis may be essential to the firm's success. The greater the understanding management has of the firm's market, the more effective it can be at making marketing decisions. Advertising, for example, can be tailored to particular market segments. The firm may even be able to use differential pricing in which they charge different prices to different market segments. As an example, airlines have long attempted to develop fare schedules and restrictions that segment the business traveler from the vacation traveler because the business traveler will generally pay more for a ticket.

D. Strategic Planning

Strategic planning involves identifying an organization's long-term goals and determining the best approaches to achieving those goals. To facilitate strategic planning an organization may establish a planning department, committee, or planning officer. Strategic planning should include involvement from decision makers at all company levels—the corporate, business, and functional levels. It is important to get as many stakeholders as possible involved in the process. Because strategic decisions have a huge impact on the company and require large commitments of financial resources, top management must approve and embrace the strategic plan.

In developing business strategies, management will often begin with a **SWOT** (strengths, weaknesses, opportunities and threats) analysis that evaluates the strengths and weaknesses of the firm as well as its opportunities and threats. This evaluation is then used to develop strategies to minimize risks and take advantage of major opportunities. This analysis is usually displayed in a SWOT matrix.

SWOT Matrix

	Strengths	*Weaknesses*
Opportunities For example, unfilled customer need, new technologies, etc.	*Strength-opportunity strategies* Strategies to pursue opportunities that are a good fit for the firm's strengths.	*Weakness-opportunity strategies* Strategies to overcome weaknesses to pursue opportunities.
Threats For example, shifts in consumer tastes away from the firm's product, new regulations, etc.	*Strength-threat strategies* Strategies to use strengths to overcome threats.	*Weakness-threat strategies* Defensive strategies to prevent the firm's weaknesses from making it highly vulnerable to threats.

Business strategies are generally classified as being product differentiation or cost leadership.

1. **Product differentiation.** Product differentiation involves modification of a product to make it more attractive to the target market or to differentiate it from competitors' products. Products may be differentiated in the following ways:

a. Physical characteristics (e.g., aesthetics, durability, reliability, performance, serviceability, features, etc.)
b. Perceived differences (e.g., advertising, brand name, etc.)
c. Support service differences (e.g., exchange policies, assistance, after-sale support, etc.)

By differentiating its products, the firm may be able to charge higher prices than its competitors or higher prices for the same products sold in different market segments.

2. **Cost leadership.** Striving for cost leadership fundamentally involves focusing on reducing the costs and time to produce, sell, and distribute a product or service. A number of techniques are used to at-

tempt to reduce costs and time, including process reengineering, lean manufacturing (production), supply chain management, strategic alliances, and outsourcing.

a. **Process reengineering** involves a critical evaluation and major redesign of existing processes to achieve breakthrough improvements in performance. Process reengineering differs from total quality management (TQM) in that TQM involves gradual improvement of processes, while reengineering often involves radical redesign and drastic improvement in processes. Many of the significant improvements in processes over the last few years have been facilitated with innovations in information technology.

b. **Lean manufacturing** is a management technique that involves the identification and elimination of all types of waste in the production function. Operations are reviewed for those components, processes, or products that add cost rather than value. A basic premise underlying lean manufacturing is by focusing on improving design, increasing flexibility, and reducing time, defects, and inventory, costs can be minimized.

c. **Supply chain management.**

(1) The term supply chain describes the flow of goods, services, and information from basic raw materials through the manufacturing and distribution process to delivery of the product to the consumer, regardless of whether those activities occur in one or many firms.

EXAMPLE: *A supply chain is illustrated below.*

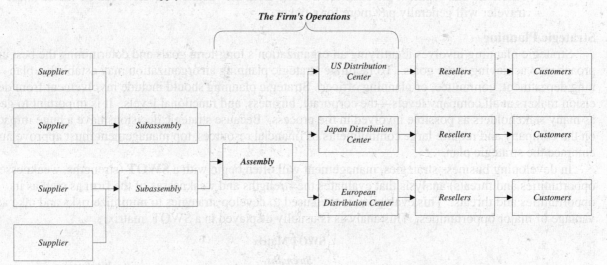

As shown, the firm's operations include only the assembly and distribution processes. Other firms supply raw materials, perform subassembly, and are the resellers of the final product. In viewing the supply chain, it is critical to go beyond the firm's immediate suppliers and customers to encompass the entire chain.

(2) To improve operations and manage the relationships with their suppliers many firms use a process known as **supply chain management**. A key aspect of supply chain management is the sharing of key information from the point of sale to the final consumer back to the manufacturer, the manufacturer's suppliers, and the suppliers' suppliers. As an example, if a manufacturer/distributor shares its sales forecasts with its suppliers and they in turn share their sales forecasts with their suppliers, the need for inventories for all firms is significantly decreased. The manufacturer/distributor, for example, needs far less raw materials inventory than normally would be the case because its suppliers are aware of the manufacture's projected needs and is prepared to have the materials available when needed. Specialized software facilitates this process of information sharing along the supply chain network.

(3) Supply chain management also focuses on improving processes to reduce time, defects, and costs all along the supply chain. By focusing on the entire supply chain, management may evaluate the full cost of inefficient processes, defective materials, and inaccurate forecasts of sales.

(4) However, supply chain management ecent presents the company with a number of problems and risks including those arising from

(a) Incompatible information systems

(b) Refusal of some companies to share information

(c) Failure of suppliers or customers to meet their obligations

d. **Strategic alliances** involve collaborative agreements between two or more firms. They may be organized as joint ventures, equity ventures, equity investments, or simple agreements (such as co-marketing or codevelopment agreements). Firms enter into strategic alliances for a number of reasons, including to

(1) Refocus the firm's efforts on its core competencies and value creation activities

(2) Speed innovation

(3) Compensate for limited resources

(4) Reduce risk

e. **Outsourcing** involves contracting for the performance of processes by other firms. Outsourcing provides a way for firms to focus on their core competencies and value creation activities. Any processes, such as information technology, human resources, product service, etc., for which the firm does not have a competitive advantage may be outsourced to other firms that can perform the process more effectively or efficiently. In doing so, the firm may be able to decrease its costs.

E.   Estimating the Effects of Economic Changes

1. Successful management involves being able to anticipate changes in economic conditions and competitor actions and devising strategies and plans to react to those changes. To begin with, management must thoroughly understand the effects of economic changes on the firm. "How will demand for the firm's products or services be affected?" and "How will the change affect the firm's costs?" are key questions. In order to estimate the effects, management will collect and analyze historical data. Quantitative techniques such as regression analysis may be used. Management will also examine the effects of any competitor analysis that has been performed. The following table illustrates the process.

Economic change	*Estimated effects*	*Response*
1. Management of an airline predicts an economic downturn that will cause a significant decline in business travel.	• Revenue from business travel will decline. • The firm is in an ologopolistic market, and competitors will react to the economic downturn by reducing fares.	• Execute a preemptive price decrease in the vacation travel segment of the business. • Disguise the price decrease by selling the fares with travel packages and through Priceline.
2. A financial institution predicts a significant increase in interest rates.	• The increase will increase the institution's cost of capital and therefore increase its interest expense. Based on historical data, the estimated effect is an increase in interest expense of 15%. • Because the institution has a significant amount of long-term loans at fixed rates, the increase cannot be passed on to a significant segment of its customers.	• Management decides to use interest rate swaps to minimize the effects of the projected interest rate increase.
3. Management of an appliance manufacturer expects an upturn in economic activity resulting in an increase in demand for the firm's products. The upturn is expected to increase the cost of raw materials.	• Revenue will increase due to increased sales and costs will increase.	• The increase in demand is built into the firm's forecasts to assure that products will be available. • Management decides to purchase futures contracts to hedge the cost of raw materials.

2. On the CPA exam you can expect questions that will require you to determine the effects of economic changes and competitor actions on the firm's financial results. If no data to predict the effect of the change are provided, the solution to the question will merely require you to predict the direction of the change. For example, if personal disposable income increases, how are sales for a chain of jewelry stores affected? Obviously, the effect will be an increase in sales. However, without historical data on the effect of changes in personal disposable income on jewelry sales there would be no way to determine the extent of the effect. Other questions may provide you with indications of the effects of economic changes allowing the determination of a more precise answer. For example, if you were pro-

vided with the price elasticity of demand for a product, say 1.5, and told that the price was to be increased by 10% you could estimate the effects of the price increase on demand using the formula for price elasticity as shown below.

$$E_D = \frac{\text{Percentage change in quantity demanded}}{\text{Percentage change in price}}$$

We know that the percentage change in quantity demanded can be calculated as follows:

$$
\begin{aligned}
\text{Percentage change in quantity demanded} &= E_D \times \text{Percentage change in price} \\
&= 1.5 \times 10\% \\
&= 15\%
\end{aligned}
$$

Still other questions might provide you with historical data on the effect of changes in economic variables on the firm's results, and ask you to estimate the impact of some anticipated change in economic conditions on the firm's future financial results.

MULTIPLE-CHOICE QUESTIONS (1-120)

**1. If both the supply and the demand for a good increase, the market price will

a. Rise only in the case of an inelastic supply function.

b. Fall only in the case of an inelastic supply function.

c. Not be predictable with only these facts.

d. Rise only in the case of an inelastic demand function.

**2. A supply curve illustrates the relationship between

a. Price and quantity supplied.

b. Price and consumer tastes.

c. Price and quantity demanded.

d. Supply and demand.

3. As a business owner you have determined that the demand for your product is inelastic. Based upon this assessment you understand that

a. Increasing the price of your product will increase total revenue.

b. Decreasing the price of your product will increase total revenue.

c. Increasing the price of your product will have no effect on total revenue.

d. Increasing the price of your product will increase competition.

Items 4 and 5 are based on the following information:

Assume that demand for a particular product changed as shown below from D1 to D2.

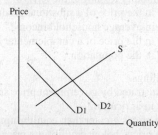

4. Which of the following could cause the change shown in the graph?

a. A decrease in the price of the product.

b. An increase in supply of the product.

c. A change in consumer tastes.

d. A decrease in the price of a substitute for the product.

5. What will be the result on the equilibrium price for the product?

a. Increase.

b. Decrease.

c. Remain the same.

d. Cannot be determined.

**6. Which one of the following has an inverse relationship with the demand for money?

a. Aggregate income.

b. Price levels.

c. Interest rates.

d. Flow of funds.

**7. An improvement in technology that in turn leads to improved worker productivity would most likely result in

a. A shift to the right in the supply curve and a lowering of the price of the output.

b. A shift to the left in the supply curve and a lowering of the price of the output.

c. An increase in the price of the output if demand is unchanged.

d. Wage increases.

8. Which of the following market features is likely to cause a surplus of a particular product?

a. A monopoly.

b. A price floor.

c. A price ceiling.

d. A perfect market.

**9. A decrease in the price of a complementary good will

a. Shift the demand curve of the joint commodity to the left.

b. Increase the price paid for a substitute good.

c. Shift the supply curve of the joint commodity to the left.

d. Shift the demand curve of the joint commodity to the right.

**10. Demand for a product tends to be price inelastic if

a. The product is considered a luxury item.

b. Few good complements for the product are available.

c. The population in the market area is large.

d. People spend a large share of their income on the product.

11. Which of the following has the highest price elasticity coefficient?

a. Milk.

b. Macaroni and cheese.

c. Bread.

d. Ski boats.

**12. The local video store's business increased by 12% after the movie theater raised its prices from $6.50 to $7.00. Thus, relative to movie theater admissions, videos are

a. Substitute goods.

b. Superior goods.

c. Complementary goods.

d. Public goods.

*13. An individual receives an income of $3,000 per month, and spends $2,500. An increase in income of $500 per month occurs, and the individual spends $2,800. The individual's marginal propensity to save is

a. 0.2

b. 0.4

c. 0.6

d. 0.8

**14. In any competitive market, an equal increase in both demand and supply can be expected to always

a. Increase both price and market-clearing quantity.

b. Decrease both price and market-clearing quantity.

c. Increase market-clearing quantity.

d. Increase price.

**15. Given the following data, what is the marginal propensity to consume?

Level of	
Disposable income	*Consumption*
$40,000	$38,000
48,000	44,000

a. 1.33
b. 1.16
c. 0.95
d. 0.75

*16. Which of the following will cause a shift in the supply curve of a product?
a. Changes in the price of the product.
b. Changes in production taxes.
c. Changes in consumer tastes.
d. Changes in the number of buyers in the market.

**17. When the federal government imposes health and safety regulations on certain products, one of the most likely results is
a. Greater consumption of the product.
b. Lower prices for the product.
c. Greater tax revenues for the federal government.
d. Higher prices for the product.

18. In which of the following situations would there be inelastic demand?
a. A 5% price increase results in 3% decrease in the quantity demanded.
b. A 4% price increase results in a 6% decrease in the quantity demanded.
c. A 4% price increase results in a 4% decrease in the quantity demanded.
d. A 3% price decrease results in 5% increase in the quantity demanded.

**19. In a competitive market for labor in which demand is stable, if workers try to increase their wage
a. Employment must fall.
b. Government must set a maximum wage below the equilibrium wage.
c. Firms in the industry must become smaller.
d. Product supply must decrease.

*20. A polluting manufacturing firm tends, from the societal viewpoint, to
a. Price its products too low.
b. Produce too little output.
c. Report too little profitability.
d. Employ too little equity financing.

**21. If the federal government regulates a product or service in a competitive market by setting a maximum price below the equilibrium price, what is the long-run effect?
a. A surplus.
b. A shortage.
c. A decrease in demand.
d. No effect on the market.

**22. A valid reason for the government to intervene in the wholesale electrical power market would include which one of the following?
a. A price increase that is more than expected.
b. Electricity is an essential resource and the wholesale market is not competitive.

c. The electricity distribution companies are losing money.
d. Foreign power generators have contracts with the local government at very high prices.

23. If the income elasticity of demand coefficient for a particular product is 3.00, the good is likely
a. A luxury good.
b. A complementary good.
c. An inferior good.
d. A necessity.

**24. Long Lake Golf Course has raised greens fees for a nine-hole game due to an increase in demand.

	Previous rate	*New rate*	*Average games played at previous rate*	*Average games played at new rate*
Regular weekday	$10	$11	80	70
Senior citizen	6	8	150	82
Weekend	15	20	221	223

Which one of the following is correct?
a. The regular weekday and weekend demand is inelastic.
b. The regular weekday and weekend demand is elastic.
c. The senior citizen demand is elastic, and weekend demand is inelastic.
d. The regular weekday demand is inelastic, and weekend demand is elastic.

**25. Which one of the following would cause the demand curve for a commodity to shift to the left?
a. A rise in the price of a substitute product.
b. A rise in average household income.
c. A rise in the price of a complementary commodity.
d. A rise in the population.

**26. Price ceilings
a. Are illustrated by government price support programs in agriculture.
b. Create prices greater than equilibrium prices.
c. Create prices below equilibrium prices.
d. Result in persistent surpluses.

*27. X and Y are substitute products. If the price of product Y increases, the immediate impact on product X is
a. Price will increase.
b. Quantity demanded will increase.
c. Quantity supplied will increase.
d. Price, quantity demanded, and supply will increase.

28. Wilson Corporation has a major competitor that produces a product that is a close substitute for Wilson's good. If the coefficient of cross-elasticity of demand for Wilson's product with respect to the competitor's product is 2.00 and the competitor decreases its price by 5%, what is the expected effect on demand for Wilson's product?
a. A 5% increase in demand.
b. A 5% decrease in demand.
c. A 10% increase in demand.
d. A 10% decrease in demand.

**29. As the price for a particular product changes, the quantity of the product demanded changes according to the following schedule:

_____

* CIA adapted
** CMA adapted

Total quantity demanded	Price per unit
100	$50
150	45
200	40
225	35
230	30
232	25

Using the arc method, the price elasticity of demand for this product when the price decreases from $50 to $45 is
- a. 0.20
- b. 10.00
- c. 0.10
- d. 3.80

**30. As the price for a particular product changes, the quantity of the product demanded changes according to the following schedule:

Total quantity demanded	Price per unit
100	$50
150	45
200	40
225	35
230	30
232	25

Using the arc method, the price elasticity of demand for this product when the price decreases from $40 to $35 is
- a. 0.20
- b. 0.88
- c. 10.00
- d. 5.00

**31. If a group of consumers decide to boycott a particular product, the expected result would be
- a. An increase in the product price to make up lost revenue.
- b. A decrease in the demand for the product.
- c. An increase in product supply because of increased availability.
- d. That demand for the product would become completely inelastic.

32. Which of the following is not likely to affect the supply of a particular good?
- a. Changes in government subsidies.
- b. Changes in technology.
- c. Changes in consumer income.
- d. Changes in production costs.

**33. If a product's demand is elastic and there is a decrease in price, the effect will be
- a. A decrease in total revenue.
- b. No change in total revenue.
- c. A decrease in total revenue and the demand curve shifts to the left.
- d. An increase in total revenue.

**34. All of the following are complementary goods except
- a. Margarine and butter.
- b. Cameras and rolls of film.
- c. VCRs and video cassettes.
- d. Razors and razor blades.

**35. The law of diminishing marginal utility states that
- a. Marginal utility will decline as a consumer acquires additional units of a specific product.

- b. Total utility will decline as a consumer acquires additional units of a specific product.
- c. Declining utilities causes the demand curve to slope upward.
- d. Consumers' wants will diminish with the passage of time.

36. In the pharmaceutical industry where a diabetic must have insulin no matter the cost and where there is no other substitute, the diabetic's demand curve is **best described as
- a. Perfectly elastic.
- b. Perfectly inelastic.
- c. Elastic.
- d. Inelastic.

**37. Because of the existence of economies of scale, business firms may find that
- a. Each additional unit of labor is less efficient than the previous unit.
- b. As more labor is added to a factory, increases in output will diminish in the short run.
- c. Increasing the size of a factory will result in lower average costs.
- d. Increasing the size of a factory will result in lower total costs.

**38. In the long run, a firm may experience increasing returns due to
- a. Law of diminishing returns.
- b. Opportunity costs.
- c. Comparative advantage.
- d. Economies of scale.

**39. The measurement of the benefit lost by using resources for a given purpose is
- a. Economic efficiency.
- b. Opportunity cost.
- c. Comparative advantage.
- d. Absolute advantage.

Items 40 and 41 are based on the following information:

Total units of product	Average fixed cost	Average variable cost	Average total cost
6	$15.00	$25.00	$40.00
7	12.86	24.00	36.86
8	11.25	23.50	34.75
9	10.00	23.75	33.75

**40. The total cost of producing seven units is
- a. $ 90.02
- b. $168.00
- c. $258.02
- d. $280.00

**41. The marginal cost of producing the ninth unit is
- a. $23.50
- b. $23.75
- c. $25.75
- d. $33.75

**42. Daily costs for Kelso Manufacturing include $1,000 of fixed costs and total variable costs are show below.

Unit output	10	11	12	13	14	15
Cost	$125	$250	$400	$525	$700	$825

The average total cost at an output level of 11 units is
- a. $113.64
- b. $125.00

** CMA adapted

c. $215.91
d. $250.00

Items 43 through 45 are based on the following information:

Number of workers	Total product units	Average selling price
10	20	$50.00
11	25	49.00
12	28	47.50

**43. The marginal physical product when one worker is added to a team of 10 workers is
  a. 1 unit.
  b. 8 units.
  c. 5 units.
  d. 25 units.

**44. The marginal revenue per unit when one worker is added to a team of 11 workers is
  a. $105.00
  b. $225.00
  c. $ 35.00
  d. $ 47.50

**45. The marginal revenue product when one worker is added to a team of 11 workers is
  a. $ 42.00
  b. $225.00
  c. $105.00
  d. $ 47.50

**46. Marginal revenue is
  a. Equal to price in monopolistic competition.
  b. The change in total revenue associated with increasing prices.
  c. Greater than price in pure competition.
  d. The change in total revenue associated with producing and selling one more unit.

**47. In microeconomics, the distinguishing characteristic of the long run on the supply side is that
  a. Only supply factors determine price and output.
  b. Only demand factors determine price and output.
  c. Firms are not allowed to enter or exit the industry.
  d. All inputs are variable.

48. What is the main factor that differentiates the short-run cost function from the long-run cost function?
  a. Nothing, the two functions are identical.
  b. The level of technology.
  c. Changes in government subsidies.
  d. The nature of the costs.

49. If consumer confidence falls, the impact upon the economy is
  a. A downturn.
  b. An upturn.
  c. No change.
  d. Consumer confidence does not have an impact upon the economy.

**50. If an increase in government purchases of goods and services of $20 billion causes equilibrium GDP to rise by $80 billion, and if total taxes and investment are constant, the marginal propensity to consume out of disposable income is

a. 0.75
b. 0.25
c. 1.25
d. 4.00

**51. During the recessionary phase of a business cycle
  a. The purchasing power of money is likely to decline rapidly.
  b. The natural rate of unemployment will increase dramatically.
  c. Potential national income will exceed actual national income.
  d. Actual national income will exceed potential national income.

*52. For a given level of tax collections, prices, and interest rates, a decrease in governmental purchases will result in a(n)
  a. Increase in aggregate demand.
  b. Increase in aggregate supply.
  c. Decrease in aggregate demand.
  d. Decrease in aggregate supply.

**53. In national income terms, aggregate demand is the
  a. Demand for money by the community in a period of full employment.
  b. Total expenditure on capital goods by entrepreneurs during a period of full employment.
  c. Demand that is needed if a country's economy is to operate at optimum level and the level of investment is to be raised.
  d. Total expenditures on consumer goods and investment, including government and foreign expenditures, during a given period.

*54. Which one of the following would not be included in the calculation of the gross domestic product (GDP)?
  a. Purchase of a new home.
  b. An automotive worker's wages.
  c. A doctor's fee.
  d. Purchase of common stock.

55. An upturn in economic activity is indicated by all of the following, except
  a. Increased housing starts.
  b. Reduction in the quantity of unemployment claims.
  c. Increase in personal travel.
  d. Reduction in the amount of luxury purchases.

56. Which of the following may provide a leading indicator of a future increase in gross domestic product?
  a. A reduction in the money supply.
  b. A decrease in the issuance of building permits.
  c. An increase in the timeliness of delivery by vendors.
  d. An increase in the average hours worked per week of production workers.

*57. Disposable income is calculated as
  a. Gross domestic product minus the capital cost allowance.
  b. Net domestic product minus indirect business taxes plus net income earned abroad.
  c. Personal income minus transfer payments.
  d. Personal income minus personal taxes.

* *CIA adapted*
** *CMA adapted*

*58. The primary reason for allowing legal immigration into industrial nations is the immigrants' potential for
   a. Reducing a trade deficit.
   b. Fulfilling a trade agreement.
   c. Contributing to economic growth.
   d. Fulfilling a political agreement.

*59. Some economic indicators lead the economy into a recovery or recession, and some lag it. An example of a lagging indicator is
   a. Chronic unemployment.
   b. Orders for consumer and producer goods.
   c. Housing starts.
   d. Consumer expectations.

**60. Government borrowing to finance large deficits increases the demand for lendable funds and
   a. Increases the supply of lendable funds.
   b. Exerts downward pressure on interest rates.
   c. Has no impact on interest rates.
   d. Puts upward pressure on interest rates.

**61. A period of rising inflation
   a. Increases the price level, which benefits those who are entitled to receive specific amounts of money.
   b. Enhances the positive relationship between the price level and the purchasing power of money.
   c. Will not be affected by contracts that include the indexing of payments.
   d. Increases the price level, which is negatively related to the purchasing power of money.

**62. The most effective fiscal policy program to help reduce demand-pull inflation would be to
   a. Decrease the rate of growth of the money supply.
   b. Increase both taxes and government spending.
   c. Decrease taxes and increase government spending.
   d. Increase taxes and decrease government spending.

*63. The money supply in a nation's economy will decrease following
   a. Open-market purchases by the nation's central bank.
   b. A decrease in the discount rate.
   c. An increase in the reserve ratio.
   d. A decrease in the margin requirement.

**64. The Federal Reserve Board most directly influences a corporation's decision of whether or not to issue debt or equity financing when it revises the
   a. Corporate income tax rate.
   b. Prime rate at which the Federal Reserve Bank lends money to member banks.
   c. Discount rate at which the Federal Reserve Bank lends money to member banks.
   d. Discount rate at which member banks lend money to their customers.

**65. According to fiscal policy principles, a tax increase will
   a. Increase spending and increase aggregate demand.
   b. Increase spending and reduce aggregate demand.
   c. Reduce spending and increase aggregate demand.
   d. Reduce spending and reduce aggregate demand.

**66. If the Federal Reserve Board wanted to implement an expansionary monetary policy, which one of the following actions would the Federal Reserve Board take?
   a. Raise the reserve requirement and the discount rate.
   b. Purchase additional US government securities and lower the discount rate.
   c. Reduce the reserve requirement and raise the discount rate.
   d. Raise the discount rate and sell US government securities.

**67. The Federal Reserve System's reserve ratio is
   a. The specified percentage of a commercial bank's deposit liabilities that must be deposited in the central bank.
   b. The rate that the central bank charges for loans granted to commercial banks.
   c. The ratio of excess reserves to legal reserves that are deposited in the central bank.
   d. The specified percentage of a commercial bank's demand deposits to total liabilities.

*68. Which of the following instruments of monetary policy is the most important means by which the money supply is controlled?
   a. Changing the reserve ratio.
   b. Open-market operations.
   c. Manipulation of government spending.
   d. Changing the discount rate.

*69. If a government were to use only fiscal policy to stimulate the economy from a recession, it would
   a. Raise consumer taxes and increase government spending.
   b. Lower business taxes and government spending.
   c. Increase the money supply and increase government spending.
   d. Lower consumer taxes and increase government spending.

**70. The federal budget deficit is the
   a. Total accumulation of the federal government's surpluses and deficits.
   b. Excess state, local, and federal spending over their revenues.
   c. Amount by which the federal government's expenditures exceed its revenues in a given year.
   d. Amount by which liabilities exceed assets on the federal government's balance sheet.

*71. Which of the following is a tool of monetary policy that a nation's central bank could use to stabilize the economy during an inflationary period?
   a. Selling government securities.
   b. Lowering bank reserve requirements.
   c. Lowering bank discount rates.
   d. Encouraging higher tax rates.

**72. Economists and economic policy makers are interested in the multiplier effect because the multiplier explains why
   a. A small change in investment can have a much larger impact on gross domestic product.
   b. Consumption is always a multiple of savings.

c.   The money supply increases when deposits in the banking system increase.

d.   The velocity of money is less than one.

73. Assume that the United States Congress passes a tax law that provides for a "rebate" to taxpayers. One of the goals of the rebate is

a.   Increase consumer disposable income and expand the economy.

b.   Increase consumer disposable income and contract the economy.

c.   Decrease consumer disposable income and expand the economy

d.   Increase consumer disposable income and contract the economy.

74. The rate of unemployment caused by changes in the composition of unemployment opportunities over time is referred to as the

a.   Frictional unemployment rate.

b.   Cyclical unemployment rate.

c.   Structural unemployment rate.

d.   Full-employment unemployment rate.

75. The producer price index measures

a.   The price of a basket of commodities at the point of the first commercial sale.

b.   Price changes for all products sold by domestic producers to foreigners.

c.   Price changes of goods purchased from other countries.

d.   The price of a fixed market basket of goods and services purchased by a typical urban consumer.

76. The formula for calculating a price index for the year 2009, using the year 2004 as a reference period is

a. $\dfrac{\text{Price of 2009 market basket in 2009}}{\text{Price of 2009 market basket in 2004}} \times 100$

b. $\dfrac{\text{Price of 2004 market basket in 2009}}{\text{Price of 2004 market basket in 2004}} \times 100$

c. $\dfrac{\text{Price of 2009 market basket in 2004}}{\text{Price of 2004 market basket in 2004}} \times 100$

d. $\dfrac{\text{Price of 2004 market basket in 2004}}{\text{Price of 2004 market basket in 2009}} \times 100$

**77. The discount rate set by the Federal Reserve System is the

a.   Required percentage of reserves deposited at the central bank.

b.   Rate that commercial banks charge for loans to each other.

c.   Rate that commercial banks charge for loans to the general public.

d.   Rate that the central bank charges for loans to commercial banks.

78. Which of the following is true about deflation?

a.   It motivates consumers to borrow money.

b.   It motivates businesses to make investments.

c.   It results in very low interest rates.

d.   It results in economic expansion.

79. Economies often experience inflation but seldom experience long period of deflation. Which of the following is true about a deflationary economy?

a.   Companies are hesitant to make investments.

b.   The lower prices encourage consumers to make major purchases.

c.   Interest rates tend to be high.

d.   Actual GDP is above potential GDP.

80. What factor explains the difference between real and nominal interest rates?

a.   Inflation risk.

b.   Credit risk.

c.   Default risk.

d.   Market risk.

81. All of the following are true about international trade **except that

a.   The gains from international trade depend on specialization with comparative advantage.

b.   Absolute advantage without comparative advantage does not result in gains from international trade.

c.   Absolute advantage is defined as the ability of one nation to produce a product at a relatively lower opportunity cost than another nation.

d.   Where there is reciprocal absolute advantage between two countries, specialization will make it possible to produce more of each product.

82. If the central bank of a country raises interest rates sharply, the country's currency will **most likely

a.   Increase in relative value.

b.   Remain unchanged in value.

c.   Decrease in relative value.

d.   Decrease sharply in value at first and then return to its initial value.

83. Which one of the following groups would be the **primary beneficiary of a tariff?

a.   Domestic producers of export goods.

b.   Domestic producers of goods protected by the tariff.

c.   Domestic consumers of goods protected by the tariff.

d.   Foreign producers of goods protected by the tariff.

84. In the law of comparative advantage, the country which should produce a specific product is determined by

a.   Opportunity costs.

b.   Profit margins.

c.   Economic order quantities.

d.   Tariffs.

**85. Assuming exchange rates are allowed to fluctuate freely, which one of the following factors would likely cause a nation's currency to appreciate on the foreign exchange market?

a.   A relatively rapid rate of growth in income that stimulates imports.

b.   A high rate of inflation relative to other countries.

c.   A slower rate of growth in income than in other countries, which causes imports to lag behind exports.

d.   Domestic real interest rates that are lower than real interest rates abroad.

**86. If the US dollar declines in value relative to the currencies of many of its trading partners, the likely result is that

    a. Foreign currencies will depreciate against the dollar.

    b. The US balance of payments deficit will become worse.

    c. US exports will tend to increase.

    d. US imports will tend to increase.

**87. Exchange rates are determined by

    a. Each industrial country's government.

    b. The International Monetary Fund.

    c. Supply and demand in the foreign currency market.

    d. Exporters and importers of manufactured goods.

**88. If the value of the US dollar in foreign currency markets changes from $1 = 6 marks to $1 = 4 marks

    a. The German mark has depreciated against the dollar.

    b. German imported products in the US will become more expensive.

    c. US tourists in Germany will find their dollars will buy more German products.

    d. US exports to Germany should decrease.

*89. Which of the following measures creates the most restrictive barrier to exporting to a country?

    a. Tariffs.

    b. Quotas.

    c. Embargoes.

    d. Exchange controls.

**90. When net exports are negative, there is a net flow of

    a. Goods from firms in foreign countries to the domestic country.

    b. Money from foreign countries to the firms of the domestic country.

    c. Goods from the firms of the domestic country to foreign countries.

    d. Goods and services which result in a trade surplus.

91. Which of the following factors is least likely to affect a country's currency foreign exchange rates?

    a. Interest rates in the country.

    b. Political stability in the country.

    c. Inflation in the country.

    d. The tax rate in the country.

92. Assume that the exchange rate of US dollars to euros is $1.80 to 1 euro. How much would a US company gain or lose if the company has a 10,000 euro receivable and the exchange rate went to $1.75 to 1 euro?

    a. $10,000 loss.

    b. $10,000 gain.

    c. $500 loss

    d. $500 gain.

93. Simon Corp., a US company, has made a large sale to a French company on a 120-day account payable in euros. If management of Simon wants to hedge the transaction risk related to a decline in the value of the euro, which of the following strategies would be appropriate?

    a. Lend euros to another company for payment in 120 days.

    b. Enter into a forward exchange contract to purchase euros for delivery in 120 days.

    c. Enter into a futures contract to sell euros for delivery in the future.

    d. Purchase euros on the spot market.

94. Which of the following is not a means by which a firm might hedge the political risk of an investment in another country?

    a. Insurance.

    b. Buy futures contracts for future delivery of the country's currency.

    c. Finance the operations with local-country capital.

    d. Enter into joint ventures with local-country firms.

Items 95 and 96 are based on the following information:

Karen Parker wants to establish an environmental testing company that would specialize in evaluating the quality of water found in rivers and streams. However, Parker has discovered that she needs either certification or approval from five separate local and state agencies before she can commence business. Also, the necessary equipment to begin would cost several million dollars. Nevertheless, Parker believes that if she is able to obtain capital resources, she can gain market share from the two major competitors.

**95. The large capital outlay necessary for the equipment is an example of a(n)

    a. Entry barrier.

    b. Minimum efficient scale.

    c. Created barrier.

    d. Production possibility boundary.

**96. The market structure Karen Parker is attempting to enter is best described as

    a. A natural monopoly.

    b. A cartel.

    c. An oligopoly.

    d. Monopolistic competition.

**97. Patents are granted in order to encourage firms to invest in the research and development of new products. Patents are an example of

    a. Vertical integration.

    b. Market concentration.

    c. Entry barriers.

    d. Collusion.

**98. The distinguishing characteristic of oligopolistic markets is

    a. A single seller of a homogeneous product with no close substitutes.

    b. A single seller of a heterogeneous product with no close substitutes.

    c. Lack of entry and exit barriers in the industry.

    d. Mutual interdependence of firm pricing and output decisions.

**99. Economic markets that are characterized by monopolistic competition have all of the following characteristics except

    a. One seller of the product.

    b. Economies or diseconomies of scale.

    c. Advertising.

    d. Heterogeneous products.

---

  * *CIA adapted*
  ** *CMA adapted*

100. Which type of economic market structure is characterized by a few large sellers of a product or service, engaging primarily in nonprice competition?
  a. Monopoly.
  b. Oligopoly.
  c. Perfect competition.
  d. Monopolistic competition.

101. Which type of economic market structure is composed of a large number of sellers, each producing an identical product, and with no significant barriers to entry and exit?
  a. Monopoly.
  b. Oligopoly.
  c. Perfect competition
  d. Monopolistic competition.

102. The market for product RK-25 is perfectly competitive. The current market price is $30, and the quantity demanded is 4 million. Due to changes in consumer tastes, a permanent increase in demand for RK-25 is expected in the near term. If nothing else changes in this market, which of the following would be the **most feasible levels of short-term and long-term prices?

	Short-term	Long-term
a.	$39	$35
b.	$35	$39
c.	$35	$30
d.	$30	$35

**103. A natural monopoly exists because
  a. The firm owns natural resources.
  b. The firms holds patents.
  c. Economic and technical conditions permit only one efficient supplier.
  d. The government is the only supplier.

104. A market with many independent firms, low barriers to entry, and product differentiation is **best classified as
  a. A monopoly.
  b. A natural monopoly.
  c. Monopolistic competition.
  d. An oligopoly.

105. Which of the following is **not a key assumption of perfect competition?
  a. Firms sell a homogeneous product.
  b. Customers are indifferent about which firm they buy from.
  c. The level of a firm's output is small relative to the industry's total output.
  d. Each firm can price its product above the industry price.

106. The ultimate purpose of competitor analysis is to
  a. Identify the competition.
  b. Determine the competition's strength and weaknesses.
  c. Identify the competition's major customers.
  d. Understand and predict the behavior of the competition.

107. Which of the following is not an important aspect of supply chain management?
  a. Information technology.

  b. Accurate forecasts.
  c. Customer relations.
  d. Communications.

108. Which of the following types of organizations would more likely engage in public relations type advertising?
  a. An airline.
  b. A hotel chain.
  c. A toy manufacturer.
  d. An electric utility company.

109. Target marketing analysis involves
  a. Analyzing the firm's input markets.
  b. Understanding and segmenting the firm's customer markets.
  c. Analyzing the firm's market structure.
  d. Deciding on whether to offer a new product line.

110. If a firm's customers are businesses, market segmentation might be performed along all of the following dimensions, except
  a. Industry.
  b. Location.
  c. Lifestyle.
  d. Size.

Items 111 through 112 are based on the following information:

Yeager Corporation has used regression analysis to perform price elasticity analysis. In doing so management regressed the quantity demanded (y variable) against price (x variable) with the following results:

Multiple R	.86798
Adjusted R squared	.72458
Standard error	542.33
Intercept	56400.50
Price coefficient	–4598.20

111. What percentage of the variation in quantity demanded is explained by price?
  a. 86.798%
  b. 72.458%
  c. 56.4%
  d. 54.233%

112. Calculate the predicted quantity demanded if price is set at $7.00.
  a. 24,213
  b. 88,588
  c. 31,234
  d. 18,454

113. Which of the following is not one of the five forces in Porter's model for industry analysis?
  a. Competitors.
  b. Bargaining power of customers.
  c. Bargaining power of suppliers.
  d. General economic conditions.

114. Which of the following is a defining characteristic of supply chain management?
  a. Focuses on the sharing of information with suppliers and customers.
  b. Focuses on redesigning processes.
  c. Focuses on improving quality.
  d. Focuses on strategic alliances.

** CMA adapted

115. Which of the following is not a likely strategy for a firm in a purely competitive market?

    a. Lean manufacturing.

    b. Supply chain management.

    c. Process reengineering.

    d. Development of a brand name.

116. What is the purpose of a response profile in competitor analysis?

    a. To develop an understanding of the firm's industry.

    b. To analyze the firm's strengths in relation to its competitors.

    c. To identify possible actions by competitors.

    d. To understand the nature of the firm's major markets.

**117. The process of dividing all potential consumers into smaller groups of buyers with distinct needs, characteristics, or behaviors, who might require a similar product or service mix, is called

    a. Strategic planning.

    b. Market segmentation.

    c. Product positioning.

    d. Objective setting.

118. Which of the following measures of unemployment would be of least importance to management when trying to predict the future state of the economy?

    a. Structural unemployment.

    b. Cyclical unemployment.

    c. Frictional unemployment.

    d. Overall unemployment.

119. Which of the following best describes the steps involved in performing competitor analysis?

    a. Gathering information about the competitor and using it to predict the competitor' behavior.

    b. Determining the type of market structure and the number of competitors.

    c. Assessing the general environment and determining how that affects competition.

    d. Assessing the market structure to predict when new competitors will enter the market.

**120. An oligopolist faces a "kinked" demand curve. This terminology indicates that

    a. When an oligopolist lowers its price, the other firms in the oligopoly will match the price reduction, but if the oligopolist raises its price, the other firms will ignore the price change.

    b. An oligopolist faces a nonlinear demand for its product, and price changes will have little effect on demand for that product.

    c. An oligopolist can sell its product at any price, but after the "saturation point" another oligopolist will lower its price and, therefore, shift the demand curve to the left.

    d. Consumers have no effect on the demand curve, and an oligopolist can shape the curve to optimize its own efficiency.

** CMA adapted

MULTIPLE-CHOICE ANSWERS

1. c	26. c	51. c	76. a	101. c
2. a	27. b	52. c	77. d	102. c
3. a	28. d	53. d	78. c	103. c
4. c	29. d	54. d	79. a	104. c
5. a	30. b	55. d	80. a	105. d
6. c	31. b	56. d	81. c	106. d
7. a	32. c	57. d	82. a	107. c
8. b	33. d	58. c	83. b	108. d
9. d	34. a	59. a	84. a	109. b
10. d	35. a	60. d	85. c	110. c
11. d	36. b	61. d	86. c	111. b
12. a	37. c	62. d	87. c	112. a
13. b	38. d	63. c	88. b	113. d
14. c	39. b	64. c	89. c	114. a
15. d	40. c	65. d	90. a	115. d
16. b	41. c	66. b	91. d	116. c
17. d	42. a	67. a	92. c	117. b
18. a	43. c	68. b	93. c	118. c
19. a	44. c	69. d	94. d	119. a
20. a	45. c	70. c	95. a	120. a
21. b	46. d	71. a	96. c	
22. b	47. d	72. a	97. c	
23. a	48. d	73. a	98. d	
24. c	49. a	74. c	99. a	1st: __/120 __%
25. c	50. a	75. a	100. b	2nd: __/120 __%

MULTIPLE-CHOICE ANSWER EXPLANATIONS

Demand, Supply, and Market Equilibrium

1. (c) The requirement is to predict the market price based on an increase in both supply and demand. The correct answer is (c) because without additional information about the extent of the change, the effect on price is not determinable. Answer (a), (b), and (d) are incorrect because the price elasticity of the demand or supply function does not provide enough information to determine the effect.

2. (a) The requirement is to describe the relationship shown by a supply curve. A supply curve illustrates the quantity supplied at varying prices at a point in time. Therefore, the correct answer is (a). Answers (b) and (c) are incorrect because they deal with demand. Answer (d) is incorrect because it deals with demand-supply equilibrium.

3. (a) The requirement is to apply the concept of price-elasticity of demand. If demand is inelastic an increase in price will increase total revenue. Answer (a) is correct because it accurately states this rule. Answer (b) is incorrect because if demand is inelastic the quantity demanded will not be affected significantly by a change in price. Answer (c) is incorrect because if the quantity demanded is not significantly affected by an increase in price, total revenue will increase. Answer (d) is incorrect because an increase in price may, or may not, increase competition.

4. (c) The requirement is to identify the reason for the shift in demand. The correct answer is (c) because a shift demand could result from a change in consumer tastes. Answer (a) is incorrect because this would result in movement along the existing demand curve. Answer (b) is incorrect because a change in supply would not affect the demand function. Answer (d) is incorrect because a decrease in price of a substitute would result in a shift of the curve to the left.

5. (a) The requirement is to determine the effect of the shift in the demand function on the price of the product. The correct answer is (a) because the shift (increase) in demand will increase the price of the product. Answer (b) is incorrect because a shift of the demand curve to the left would have to occur to decrease price. Answers (c) and (d) are incorrect because the effect on price will not be to remain the same and it can be determined.

6. (c) The requirement is to identify the item that has an inverse relationship with the demand for money. The correct answer is (c) because as interest rates increase the demand for money decreases. Answers (a), (b), and (d) are incorrect because they do not have an inverse relationship with the demand for money.

7. (a) The requirement is to describe the effect of an improvement in technology that leads to increased worker productivity. If the cost of producing a good declines more will be supplied at a given price. Therefore, the supply curve will shift to the right and answer (a) is correct. Answer (b) is incorrect because a shift to the left would result in decreased supplies. Answer (c) is incorrect because price would not increase, and answer (d) is incorrect because wages would not necessarily increase.

8. (b) The requirement is to identify the market feature that is likely to cause a surplus of a particular product. Answer (b) is correct because a price floor, if it is above the equilibrium price, will cause excess production and a surplus. Answer (a) is incorrect because a monopoly market is likely to be characterized by underproduction of the product. Answer (c) is incorrect because a price ceiling, if it is below the equilibrium price, will cause underproduction and shortages. Answer (d) is incorrect because in a perfect market with no intervention demand and supply will be equal.

9. (d) The requirement is to describe the effect on demand for a good if a complementary good decreases in price. If the price of a complementary good decreases, demand for the joint commodity will increase. This is due to the fact that the total cost of using the two products decreases. If demand for a product increases the demand curve will shift to the right. Therefore, answer (d) is correct. Answer (a) is incorrect because a shift in the demand curve to the left depicts a decrease in demand. Answers (b) and (c) deal with supply and are not relevant.

10. (d) The requirement is to identify a characteristic of a product with price inelastic demand. The correct answer is (d) because price inelasticity means that the quantity demanded does not change much with price changes. This would be a characteristic of a good with few substitutes. Answers (a), (b), and (c) are characteristics of goods that have price elastic demand.

11. (d) The requirement is to apply the concept of price elasticity of demand. If substitutes for a good are readily available then the demand for the good is more elastic. Answer (d) is correct because there are many substitutes for luxury goods. Answers (a), (b), and (c) are all considered to be necessities and demand for them is less elastic.

12. (a) The requirement is to identify the relationship between two products for which one has increased demand when the other's price increases. Answer (a) is correct. Substitute goods are selected by a consumer based on price. When the price of one goes up, demand for the other increases. Answer (b) is incorrect because superior goods are those whose demand is directly influenced by income. Answer (c) is incorrect because complementary goods are used together and when the price of one goes up, demand for the other goes down. Answer (d) is incorrect because a public good is one for which it is difficult to restrict use, such as a national park.

13. (b) The requirement is to calculate the marginal propensity to save. Answer (b) is correct because the marginal propensity to save is the change in savings divided by the change in income [($700 – $500)/($3,500 – $3,000) = .4]. Answer (a) is incorrect because the average propensity to save would be calculated by dividing the new savings by the new income ($700/$3,500 = .2). Answer (c) is incorrect because the marginal propensity to consume is the change in spending divided by the change in income [($2,800 – $2,500)/($3,500 – $3,000) = .6]. Answer (d) is incorrect because the average propensity to consume would be calculated by dividing the new consumption by the new income ($2,800/$3,500 = .8).

14. (c) The requirement is to describe market conditions in a competitive market when both demand and supply increase. In a competitive market, the market will always clear at the equilibrium price. If there is an equal increase in both demand and supply, the equilibrium price may increase, decrease, or remain the same. However, there will be more units sold and, therefore, answer (c) is correct. Answers (a), (b), and (d) are incorrect because the equilibrium price may increase, decrease, or remain the same.

15. (d) The requirement is to calculate the marginal propensity to consume. Answer (d) is correct because the marginal propensity to consume is calculated by dividing the change in consumption by the change in disposable income.

Therefore, the marginal propensity to consume would be .75 [($44,000 – $38,000)/($48,000 – $40,000)].

16. (b) The requirement is to determine the item that will cause a shift in the supply curve. A shift in the supply curve may result from (1) changes in production technology, (2) changes or expected changes in resource prices, (3) changes in the prices of other goods, (4) changes in taxes or subsidies, (5) changes in the number of sellers in the market, and (6) expectations about the future price of the product. Answer (b) is correct because it identifies changes in production taxes, which will alter the supply curve. Answer (a) is incorrect because a change in the price of the product involves movement along the existing supply curve, not a shift in the supply curve. Answers (c) and (d) are incorrect because they identify changes that result in a shift in the demand curve.

17. (d) The requirement is to identify the effects of government regulation on a product. Government regulation increases the cost of the product and therefore will most likely result in higher prices. Thus answer (d) is correct. Answer (a) is incorrect because the regulation has no relationship to consumption. Answer (b) is incorrect because an increase in cost is not likely to result in a decrease in price. Answer (c) is incorrect because tax revenue will likely decline due to the added production costs and reduced sales.

18. (a) The requirement is to identify which of the situations indicate inelastic demand. Elasticity of demand is measured by the percentage change in the quantity demanded divided by the percentage change in price. If the quotient is greater than one, demand for product is price elastic, and if it less than one, demand for the product is price inelastic. A quotient of exactly one indicates unitary elasticity. Answer (a) is correct because the price elasticity quotient is equal to 0.6 (3%/5%). Answer (b) is incorrect because the quotient is 1.5 (6%/4%). Answer (c) is incorrect because the quotient is 1 (4%/4%). Answer (d) is incorrect because the quotient is equal to 1.67 (5%/3%).

19. (a) The requirement is to describe the effect of an increase in wages on demand for labor. Answer (a) is correct because, like any other good or service, if price is increased for labor, the demand will fall and employment will fall. Answer (b) is incorrect because setting a maximum wage will not allow workers to increase wages. Answer (c) is incorrect because firms may or may not change in size. Answer (d) is incorrect because supply will only decrease if the price of the product decreases.

20. (a) The requirement is to identify the market effects of a polluting manufacturer's actions. Answer (a) is correct because a polluting firm calculates its profits without considering the costs of environmental damage and, as a result, prices its products too low. Answer (b) is incorrect because the polluting manufacturer is producing too much, not too little output. Answer (c) is incorrect because the manufacturer reports too much, not too little profitability. Answer (d) is incorrect because there is no direct relationship between the use of equity versus debt financing and the externalities involved in the production activities of the firm.

21. (b) The requirement is to describe the effects of a government-mandated maximum price. If the government mandates a maximum price below the equilibrium price, the product will be selling at an artificially low price resulting in shortages. Thus the correct answer is (b). Answer (a) is incorrect because price floors result in surpluses. Answer (c) is incorrect because price ceilings would probably result in more demand. Answer (d) is incorrect because the market would be affected.

22.   (b)   The requirement is to identify a valid reason for government intervention in a wholesale market. Answer (b) is correct because a valid reason for government intervention is the lack of a competitive market. Answers (a), (c), and (d) are incorrect because they provide no indication that the market is not competitive.

23.   (a)   The requirement is to identify the type of good that is likely to have income elasticity coefficient of 3.00. Answer (a) is correct because an income elasticity coefficient of 3.00 indicates that demand for the good is very sensitive to income levels. This is a characteristic of a luxury good. Answer (b) is incorrect because while the good may be complementary, it would have to be complementary to a luxury good. Answer (c) is incorrect because an inferior good's coefficient will be negative. Answer (d) is incorrect because demand for a necessity is not sensitive to income levels.

24.   (c)   The requirement is to calculate the price elasticity of demand for golf. The price elasticity of demand is calculated as the percentage change in quantity divided by the percentage change in price. If the result is greater than one, demand is elastic; if it is less than one, it is inelastic; and if it is equal to one, it is unitary elastic. The regular weekday demand is elastic as calculated below.

$$\frac{(80 - 70) \div [(80 + 70) \div 2]}{(\$11 - \$10) \div [(\$11 + \$10) \div 2]} = 1.4$$

The weekend demand is inelastic as calculated below.

$$\frac{(223 - 221) \div [(223 + 221) \div 2]}{(\$20 - \$15) \div [(\$20 + \$15) \div 2]} = .03$$

The senior citizen demand is elastic as calculated below.

$$\frac{(150 - 82) \div [(150 + 82) \div 2]}{(\$8 - \$6) \div [(\$8 + \$6) \div 2]} = 2.05$$

The only statement that correctly defines these relationships is answer (c).

25.   (c)   The requirement is to identify the factor that would cause the demand curve for a product to shift to the left. Answer (c) is correct because a shift in the demand curve to the left would be indicative of a decrease in demand for the product, and an increase in the price of a complementary commodity would cause such a shift. Answers (a), (b), and (d) are incorrect because they would all potentially cause an increase in demand, causing the demand curve to shift to the right.

26.   (c)   The requirement is to describe the effect of price ceilings. Price ceilings cause the price of a product to be artificially low resulting in decreased supply. The price is below the equilibrium price as indicated by answer (c). Answer (a) is incorrect because government price support is an example of a price floor. Answer (b) is incorrect because price ceilings create prices less than equilibrium prices. Answer (d) is incorrect because price ceilings create shortages, not surpluses.

27.   (b)   The requirement is to determine the immediate effect upon one product of an increase in the price of a sub-

stitute good. The demand and price of substitute products are directly related. If the price of a good increases, the demand for its substitute will also increase. Answer (b) is correct because it depicts this relationship. Answer (a) is incorrect because the price of a product will not increase due to an increase in a substitute product's price. Answer (c) is incorrect because the quantity supplied will not be impacted by an increase in price of a substitute product. Answer (d) is incorrect because even though the quantity demanded will increase with an increase in price of a substitute product, the price and supply will not be directly affected.

28.   (d)   The requirement is to calculate the effect a decrease in the price of a substitute good has on demand for a good. Answer (d) is correct because if the coefficient of cross-elasticity is 2.00, a 5% decrease in price will result in a 10% (5% × 2.00) decrease in the demand for Wilson's product. Answers (a), (b), and (c) are incorrect because they misstate the relationship.

29.   (d)   The requirement is to calculate the price elasticity of demand for a product. Price elasticity using the arc method is calculated by dividing the percentage change in quantity demanded by the percentage change in price, using the average changes. In this case, price elasticity is calculated below.

$$\frac{(150 - 100) \div [(150 + 100) \div 2]}{(\$50 - \$45) \div [(\$50 + \$45) \div 2]} = 3.8$$

Therefore answer (d) is correct.

30.   (b)   The requirement is to calculate the price elasticity of demand. Answer (b) is correct because the formula for price elasticity is equal to the percentage change in quantity demanded divided by the percentage change in price. In this case, the percentage change in price is 0.88 as calculated below.

$$\frac{(225 - 200) \div [(225 + 200) \div 2]}{(\$40 - \$35) \div [(\$40 + \$35) \div 2]} = .088$$

31.   (b)   The requirement is to identify the effect of a boycott on demand for a good. Answer (b) is correct because a boycott means less people are purchasing the good. Therefore, demand is decreased. Answer (a) would not occur because, if anything, a decrease in demand would lead to a decrease in price. Answer (c) is incorrect because demand does not affect supply. Answer (d) is incorrect because the elasticity of demand for a good is determined by its nature.

32.   (c)   The requirement is to identify the factor that is not likely to affect the supply of a good. Answer (c) is correct because changes in consumer income could affect the demand for the good, but not its supply. Answer (a) is incorrect because government subsidies reduce the cost of producing a good, and therefore, affect supply. Answer (b) is incorrect because changes in technology can alter production costs, and therefore, affect supply. Answer (d) is incorrect because changes in production costs affect the supply of a good.

33.   (d)   The requirement is to identify the effect on total revenue of a decrease in price of a price-elastic product. Answer (d) is correct because if a product's demand is price-elastic, a decrease in price will lead to an even larger percentage increase in quantity demanded. Therefore, total revenue will increase. Answers (a), (b), and (c) are incorrect because they do not describe the appropriate effect.

34. **(a)**   The requirement is to identify the goods that are not complementary goods. Complementary goods are those that are used together because they enhance each other's use. Margarine and butter are substitute goods, not complementary goods. Therefore, (a) is correct. Answers (b), (c), and (d) all are pairs of complementary goods.

35. **(a)**   The requirement is to describe the law of diminishing marginal utility. The law states that marginal utility declines as consumers acquire more of a good. Therefore, answer (a) is correct. Answer (b) is incorrect because total utility will not decline as more of a good is acquired. Answer (c) is incorrect because the demand curve slopes downward.

36. **(b)**   The requirement is to identify the price elasticity of an essential product with no substitutes. The correct answer is (b). Demand for the product is perfectly inelastic because the diabetic will purchase the product regardless of the price.

Costs of Production

37. **(c)**   The requirement is to define the implications of economies of scale. In the long run firms may experience increasing returns because they operate more efficiently. With growth comes specialization of labor and related production efficiencies related to the law of diminishing returns. This phenomenon is called economies of scale. Answer (c) is correct because it accurately describes this concept. Answers (a) and (b) are incorrect because they describe inefficiencies. Answer (d) is incorrect because total costs do not decline but average costs do.

38. **(d)**   The requirement is to identify the reason for increasing returns. In the long run firms may experience increasing returns because they operate more efficiently. With growth comes specialization of labor and related production efficiencies. This phenomenon is called economies of scale and, therefore, answer (d) is correct. Answer (a) is incorrect because the law of diminishing returns states that at some point firms get too large and diminishing returns occur. Answer (b) is incorrect because opportunity cost is the benefit foregone by the use of a particular resource. Answer (c) is incorrect because comparative advantage deals with the production choices of countries.

39. **(b)**   The requirement is to identify the term used to describe the benefit lost by using resources for a given purpose. The correct answer is (b) because opportunity cost is the benefit given up from not using the resource for another purpose. Answer (a) is incorrect because economic efficiency is a comparison among uses of resources. Answers (c) and (d) are incorrect because they involve comparisons across countries.

40. **(c)**   The requirement is to calculate the total cost of producing seven units. Total cost is equal to average total cost multiplied by the number of units produced. Therefore, the correct answer is (c) because 7 × $36.86 = $258.02.

41. **(c)**   The requirement is to calculate marginal cost. Marginal cost is the additional cost of producing one additional item. To calculate the marginal cost of producing the ninth unit we take the total cost of producing nine units and deduct the total cost of producing eight units. Thus, the correct answer is (c) because (9 × $33.75) − (8 × $34.75) = $25.75.

42. **(a)**   The requirement is to calculate the average total cost at an output level of 11 units. Answer (a) is correct because the average total cost is calculated by dividing total cost by the number of units: [($1,000 fixed cost + $250 variable cost)/11] = $113.64.

43. **(c)**   The requirement is to calculate the marginal physical product. The marginal physical product is the additional output obtained by adding one additional worker. When one worker is added to a team of 10, five (25 − 20) additional units are produced. Therefore, the correct answer is (c).

44. **(c)**   The requirement is to calculate the marginal revenue per unit. The total revenue of adding one additional worker to a team of 11 is equal to the difference between total revenue at 12 workers and total revenue at 11 workers, or $105 [(25 × $49) − (28 × $47.50)]. Answer (c) is correct because the marginal revenue per unit is $35 = $105/3. Answer (d) is incorrect because it is the average selling price for one unit.

45. **(c)**   The requirement is to calculate the marginal revenue product when one worker is added. The marginal revenue product is the increase in total revenue received by the addition of one worker. The total revenue from adding one additional worker to a team of 11 is equal to the difference between total revenue at 12 workers and total revenue at 11 workers, or $105 [(25 × $49) − (28 × $47.50)]. Therefore answer (c) is correct.

46. **(d)**   The requirement is to define marginal revenue. The correct answer is (d) because marginal revenue is the change in total revenue associated with the sale of one more unit of output. Answer (a) is incorrect because in a monopolistic competitive market, price is greater than marginal cost. Answer (b) is incorrect because marginal revenue is the increase in revenue associated with the sale of one additional product. Answer (c) is incorrect because in a purely competitive market, marginal revenue is equal to price.

47. **(d)**   The requirement is to identify the distinguishing characteristic of long-run supply. Answer (d) is correct because the distinguishing characteristic of the long-run production function is that all costs are variable. Answers (a) and (b) are incorrect because price and output are determined by demand and supply. Answer (c) is incorrect because firms can enter or exit the industry.

48. **(d)**   The requirement is to identify the main factor that differentiates the short-run cost function from the long-run cost function. Answer (d) is correct because in the short run firms have fixed and variable costs, whereas in the long run all costs are variable. Answer (a) is incorrect because all costs are variable in the long run. Answer (b) is incorrect because the level of technology will affect short-run and long-run cost functions in a similar manner. Answer (c) is incorrect because changes in government subsidies will not affect an industry's cost functions.

Aggregate Demand and Business Cycles

49. **(a)**   The requirement is to identify the impact of consumer confidence upon the economy. Answer (a) is correct because if consumer confidence falls then consumers will delay spending until the uncertainty is resolved. The end result is a downturn in the economy. Answers (b), (c), and

(d) are incorrect because they do not properly state the relationship between consumer confidence and the economy.

50.   (a)   The requirement is to determine the marginal propensity to consume given the multiplier. The multiplier refers to the fact that an increase in spending has a multiplied effect on GDP. The effect of the multiplier can be estimated using the economy's marginal propensity to consume, or vice versa. In this case, the multiplier is 4($80/20) and the marginal propensity to save is 25% (1.00/4). Therefore, answer (a) is correct because the marginal propensity to consume is one minus the marginal propensity to save, or 75% (100% – 25%).

51.   (c)   The requirement is to identify a characteristic of the trough of a business cycle. In the trough of a business cycle, actual output and income are below potential output and income. Therefore, the correct answer is (c). Answer (a) is incorrect because purchasing power is not directly related to business cycles. Answer (b) is incorrect because in a recession it is cyclical unemployment that is high, not natural unemployment. Answer (d) is incorrect because potential income will exceed actual income.

52.   (c)   The requirement is to describe the effect of a decrease in government spending on the economy. The government represents one segment of the economy that demands goods and services. If government spending decreases, aggregate demand decreases. Thus, answer (c) is correct. Answer (a) is incorrect because a decrease in government spending will result in a decrease in aggregate demand. Answers (b) and (d) are incorrect because a decrease in government spending will not immediately affect supply.

53.   (d)   The requirement is to define aggregate demand. The correct answer is (d) because aggregate demand is the total amount of expenditures for consumer goods and investment for a period of time. It includes purchases by consumers, businesses, government, and foreign entities.

54.   (d)   The requirement is to identify an item that would be included in GDP. Gross domestic product is the value of all final goods and services produced by the country by both domestic and foreign-owned sources. Answer (d) is correct because common stock is not a good or service; it is an ownership interest in a company. Answers (a), (b), and (c) are all incorrect because they all represent the value of goods or services produced.

55.   (d)   The requirement is to identify the indicator of an upturn in economic activity. Answer (d) is correct because a reduction in the amount of luxury purchases is an indicator of a downturn in economic activity. Answers (a), (b), and (c) are all indicators of positive economic changes.

56.   (d)   The requirement is to identify a leading indicator of economic expansion. Answer (d) is correct because an increase in weekly hours worked by production workers is a favorable leading indicator. Answer (a) is incorrect because a falling money supply is an indicator associated with falling GDP. Answer (b) is incorrect because a decline in the issuance of building permits signals lower expected building activity and a falling GDP. Answer (c) is incorrect because an increase in the timeliness of delivery by vendors indicates slacking business demand and potentially falling GDP.

57.   (d)   The requirement is to identify the definition of disposable income. Answer (d) is correct because disposable income equals personal income minus personal taxes. It is the portion of income that can be spent by the consumer. Answer (a) is incorrect because gross domestic product less the capital cost allowance is net domestic product. Answer (b) is incorrect because net domestic product minus indirect business taxes plus net income earned abroad is national income. Answer (c) is incorrect because disposable income is not measured by deducting transfer payments from personal income.

58.   (c)   The requirement is to identify the primary reason for allowing legal immigration into industrial nations. Answer (c) is correct because immigration will increase the supply of labor and lower its equilibrium price. This results in greater domestic and world output and increases income in the country to which workers migrate. Answer (a) is incorrect because the impact on trade deficit is less than that on growth. Answers (b) and (d) are incorrect because trade agreements and political agreements are not primary reasons.

59.   (a)   The requirement is to identify a lagging economic indicator. Lagging indicators include (1) average duration of unemployment in weeks, (2) the change in the index of labor cost per unit of output, (3) the average prime rate charged by banks, (4) the ratio of manufacturing and trade inventories to sales, (5) commercial and industrial loans outstanding, (6) the ratio of consumer installment credit outstanding to personal income, and (7) the change in the CPI for services. Answer (a) is correct because chronic unemployment is a lagging indicator. Answers (b), (c), and (d) are incorrect because they are all leading indicators.

Economic Measures and Policy

60.   (d)   The requirement is to identify the true statement about government borrowing to finance large deficits. The correct answer is (d) because increased borrowing by the government increases the demand for money, which puts upward pressure on interest rates. Answer (a) is incorrect because government borrowing reduces the amount of lendable funds; it does not increases them. Answer (b) is incorrect because government borrowing exerts upward pressure on interest rates not downward pressure. Answer (c) is incorrect because government borrowing puts upward pressure on interest rates.

61.   (d)   The requirement is to describe the effects of rising inflation. Answer (d) is correct because rising inflation increases the price level of goods, which means that individuals can purchase less. Answer (a) is incorrect because individuals that receive specific amounts of money lose purchasing power. Answer (b) is incorrect because there is an inverse relationship between price level and purchasing power. Answer (c) is incorrect because if the contracts have indexing provisions, the prices will increase.

62.   (d)   The requirement is to describe the most effective fiscal policy for reducing demand-pull inflation. Demand-pull inflation is caused by excess demand that bids up the cost of labor and other resources. The correct answer is (d) because the most effective government policy would involve reducing demand that could be done by taxation and reduced government spending. Answer (a) is incorrect because it involves monetary policy. Answers (b) and (c) are incorrect because increasing government spending would feed demand-pull inflation.

63. **(c)** The requirement is to identify an action that will cause a decrease in money supply. The correct answer is (c) because an increase in the reserve requirement will leave financial institutions with less money to lend and therefore decrease the money supply. Answers (a), (b), and (d) are incorrect because they would all result in an increase in the money supply.

64. **(c)** The requirement is to identify how the Federal Reserve Board most directly influences the decision of whether or not to issue debt or equity financing. Answer (c) is correct because the Board sets the discount rate at which the Federal Reserve Bank lends money to member banks, which directly influences the rates that commercial banks charge their customers. Answer (a) is incorrect because the Board does not affect the income tax rate. Answers (b) and (d) are incorrect because the Federal Reserve Bank charges member banks the discount rate.

65. **(d)** The requirement is to identify the effects of a tax increase. Answer (d) is correct because a tax increase reduces household income and, therefore, reduces spending and decreases aggregate demand.

66. **(b)** The requirement is to describe an expansionary monetary policy. The correct answer is (b) because purchasing US securities would increase the amount of money in the economy. Answer (a) is incorrect because raising the reserve requirement would decrease the amount of money in the economy. Answer (c) is incorrect because raising the discount rate would discourage borrowing by banks and therefore reduce the amount of money in the economy. Answer (d) is incorrect because both of the actions would tend to reduce the money supply.

67. **(a)** The requirement is to define the reserve ratio. The reserve ratio is the percentage of total checking deposits that a financial institution must hold on reserve in the central bank. Thus, the correct answer is (a). Answer is (b) is incorrect because it is the description of the discount rate.

68. **(b)** The requirement is to identify the most important way that the money supply is controlled. The correct answer is (b). The purchase and sale of government securities (open-market operations) is the most important way that the government controls the money supply. Answers (a) and (d) are incorrect because, while they are instruments of monetary policy, they are not the most important ways of controlling money supply. Answer (c) is incorrect because it describes an instrument of fiscal policy.

69. **(d)** The requirement is to define how the government uses fiscal policy to stimulate the economy. To stimulate the economy with fiscal policy, the government would lower taxes and/or increase spending. Therefore, the correct answer is (d). Answer (a) is incorrect because raising taxes does not stimulate the economy. Answer (b) is incorrect because decreasing government spending does not stimulate the economy. Answer (c) is incorrect because increasing the money supply involves monetary policy.

70. **(c)** The requirement is to define the federal budget deficit. The federal budget deficit is the amount by which the government's expenditures exceed its revenues in a given year. Thus, answer (c) is correct. Answer (a) is incorrect because it defines the government debt. Answer (b) is incorrect because state and local government amounts are not included in the federal budget deficit. Answer (d) is incorrect because the deficit does not deal with assets and liabilities of the government.

71. **(a)** The requirement is to identify the tool that would serve to control inflation. Answer (a) is correct because selling government securities serves to reduce capital available for other investments and, therefore, serves to contract the economy. Answer (b) is incorrect because lowering reserve requirements serves to increase the amount of funds available for investment. Answer (c) is incorrect because lowering the discount rate serves to decrease the cost of funds and increase investment. Answer (d) is incorrect because encouraging higher tax rates is a fiscal policy.

72. **(a)** The requirement is to determine the reason for the importance of the multiplier. The multiplier provides an indication of the impact of an increase in consumption or investment in GDP. An increase in spending ripples through the economy because individuals and business save only a portion of the increase in income. Therefore, the correct answer is (a).

73. **(a)** The requirement is to identify the purpose of a tax rebate. Answer (a) is correct because increasing the amount of funds available to the consumer increases disposable income that should stimulate economic activity. Consumers will spend the additional funds and correspondingly expand the economy. Answers (b), (c), and (d) are erroneous statements about the effects of the rebate.

74. **(c)** The requirement is to identify the definition of structural unemployment. Answer (c) is correct because structural unemployment exists when aggregate demand is sufficient to provide full employment, but the distribution of the demand does not correspond precisely to the composition of the labor force. This form of unemployment arises when the required job skills or the geographic distribution of jobs changes. Answer (a) is incorrect because frictional unemployment results from imperfections in the labor market. It occurs when both jobs and workers to fill them are available. Answer (b) is incorrect because cyclical unemployment is caused by contractions of the economy. Answer (d) is incorrect because the full-employment unemployment rate is the sum of frictional and structural unemployment.

75. **(a)** The requirement is to identify the nature of the producer price index. Answer (a) is correct because the price index measures the combined price of a selected group of goods and services for a specified period in comparison with the combined price of the same or similar goods for a base period. The US government's producer price index (PPI) is an example. It measures the price of a basket of 3,200 commodities at the point of their first sale by producers. Answer (b) is incorrect because the export price index measures price changes for all products sold by domestic producers to foreigners. Answer (c) is incorrect because the import price index measures price changes of goods purchased from other countries. Answer (d) is incorrect because the consumer price index measures the price of a fixed market basket of goods purchased by a typical urban consumer.

76. **(a)** The requirement is to identify the formula for calculating a price index. Answer (a) is correct because the 2009 price index using 2004 as a reference period is the price of the 2009 market basket in 2009 relative to the price of the same basket of goods in 2004. The correct formula is

$$\frac{\text{Price of market basket in a given year}}{\text{Price of same market basket in base year}} \times 100$$

Answer (b) is incorrect because the 2004 market basket is used. Answer (c) is incorrect because it uses two different market baskets. Answer (d) is incorrect because it uses the 2004 prices in the numerator and the denominator and different market baskets.

77. (d) The requirement is to describe the discount rate. The correct answer is (d) because the discount rate is the rate the central bank charges commercial banks for loans. Answer (a) is not correct because it describes the reserve requirement.

78. (c) The requirement is to identify which of the statements is true about deflation. Answer (c) is correct because deflation results in very low interest rates. They could even turn negative. Answer (a) is incorrect because consumers are not motivated to borrow money because they will be paying back the debt with money that has greater purchasing power. Answer (b) is incorrect because businesses are hesitant to make investments because prices for capital goods are declining. Answer (d) is incorrect because deflation typically stalls the economy.

79. (a) The requirement is to identify the characteristics of a deflationary economy. The correct answer is (a) because businesses are hesitant to make investments when the prices of assets are declining. Answer (b) is incorrect because consumers are hesitant to make major purchases when prices are declining. Answer (c) is incorrect because interest rates are very low in periods of deflation. Answer (d) is incorrect because when actual GDP exceeds potential GDP inflation will exist.

80. (a) The requirement is to identify the factor that explains the difference between real and nominal interest rates. Real interest rates are in terms of goods; they are adjusted for inflation. The difference between real and nominal rates is the inflation premium. Thus, answer (a) is correct. Answers (b) and (c) are incorrect because credit risk and default risk explain the difference between the nominal rate and the rate a particular borrower receives. Answer (d) is incorrect because market risk explains the difference between the nominal rate and the rate paid in a particular market.

International Economics

81. (c) The requirement is to identify the statement that is not true regarding international trade. Answer (c) is correct because absolute advantage is the ability to produce a product for less than other nations. Comparative advantage is the ability of one nation to produce at a relatively lower opportunity cost than another nation. Answers (a), (b), and (d) are all incorrect because they are true.

82. (a) The requirement is to describe the effect of an increase in the interest rate on a currency's value. The correct answer is (a) because if the interest rate is increased investors will be able to get a larger return on investment in the country. Therefore, demand for the currency will increase for investment purposes, and the relative value of the currency will increase.

83. (b) The requirement is to identify the group that would most benefit from a tariff. The correct answer is (b) because a tariff restricts the amount of imports of a specific good, and the group most benefiting would be the domestic producers of that good. Answers (a), (c), and (d) are incorrect because these groups would not benefit from the tariff.

84. (a) The requirement is to identify the description of comparative advantage. Answer (a) is correct because the respective opportunity costs determine which country will produce which product. Answer (b) is incorrect because profit margins do not enter into the decision. Answer (c) is incorrect because economic order quantity determines optimum inventory levels. Answer (d) is incorrect because tariffs would only come into play after each country produced its respective products.

85. (c) The requirement is to identify the scenario that would result in appreciation in the value of a country's currency. The correct answer is (c) because the lag in imports in relation to exports means that there will be more demand for the currency from other countries to pay for the country's exported goods. Answer (a) is incorrect because if the country is importing goods this will increase demand for other currencies and cause the country's currency to decline in relative value. Answer (b) is incorrect because a higher rate of inflation depresses a country's currency. Answer (d) is incorrect because lower interest rates means there will be less demand for the currency for investment.

86. (c) The requirement is to identify the effect of a decline in the US dollar. The correct answer is (c) because US goods will be cheaper in foreign countries and, therefore, US exports will increase. Answer (a) is incorrect because foreign currencies will appreciate if the dollar depreciates. Answer (b) is incorrect because the US balance of payments should improve due to the increase in exports. Answer (d) is incorrect because US imports will decline because of the increase in cost of foreign goods in dollars.

87. (c) The requirement is to describe how exchange rates are determined. The correct answer is (c) because exchange rates are determined in the same way price is determined for other goods, based on demand and supply. Answers (a), (b), and (d) are incorrect because while they can have a temporary influence on exchange rates, supply and demand is the major determining factor.

88. (b) The requirement is to determine the effect of changes in exchange rates. Answer (b) is correct because the dollar's value has declined against the mark and therefore German goods become more expensive. Answer (a) is incorrect because the German mark has appreciated against the dollar. Answer (c) is incorrect because the dollar will buy less in Germany. Answer (d) is incorrect because US exports to Germany should increase because they are less expensive in German marks.

89. (c) The requirement is to identify the most restrictive barrier to an exporting country. The correct answer is (c) because an embargo is a total ban on certain types of imports. Answer (a) is incorrect because a tariff is merely a tax on imports. Answer (b) is incorrect because quotas are merely restrictions on the amounts of imports. Answer (d) is incorrect because exchange controls are limits of the amount of foreign exchange that can be transacted or exchange rates.

90. **(a)** The requirement is to identify the effect of negative net exports. Answer (a) is correct because when a country has negative net exports, it imports more than it exports. Therefore, it results in a net flow of goods from firms in foreign countries to the domestic country.

91. **(d)** The requirement is to identify the factor that is least likely to affect a country's currency foreign exchange rate. Answer (d) is correct because the country's tax rate is least likely to affect the country's currency exchange rate. Answers (a), (b), and (c) are incorrect because they are all factors that affect the value of the country's currency.

92. **(c)** The requirement is to compute the foreign exchange loss or gain. The correct answer is (c) because before the decline in value, the receivable had a value of $18,000 (10,000 × $1.80), and after the decline in value, the receivable had a value of $17,500 (10,000 × $1.75). Therefore, the loss is equal to $500. Answers (a), (b), and (d) are incorrect because they inaccurately calculate the loss.

93. **(c)** The requirement is to identify the appropriate hedging strategy. The correct answer is (c) because by selling euros in the futures market, the firm has locked in the exchange rate today. Answer (a) is incorrect because lending euros puts the company at greater risk for changes in value of the euro. It would need to borrow euros to lock in the exchange rate. Answer (b) is incorrect because it involves the purchase of euros; the appropriate strategy would involve the sale of euros. Answer (d) is incorrect because the purchase of euros on the spot market would put the firm more at risk to losses from decline in the value of the euro.

94. **(d)** The requirement is to identify hedging strategies for political risk. Political risk is the risk related to actions by a foreign government, such as enacting legislation that prevents the repatriation of a foreign subsidiary's profits or seizing a firm's assets. Answer (d) is correct because by entering into joint ventures with local-country firms, the firm can reduce the risk of seizure of the investment by the government. Answer (a) is incorrect because a firm can purchase insurance to mitigate political risk. Answer (b) is incorrect because purchasing or selling futures contracts is designed to hedge transaction risks relating to foreign exchange rates. Answer (c) is incorrect because if the firm finances the investment with local-country capital, it may not be forced to repay the loans if assets are seized by the government.

Economics and Strategy

95. **(a)** The requirement is to describe how a large required capital outlay affects a market. The correct answer is (a) because a large capital outlay constitutes a barrier to entry into the market. Answer (b) is incorrect because minimum efficient scale indicates that a company must be of sufficient size to compete. This is not indicated by the scenario. Answer (c) is incorrect because a created barrier is one created by the competing firms. Answer (d) is incorrect because the production possibility boundary shows the maximum combination of outputs that can be achieved with a given number of inputs.

96. **(c)** The requirement is to identify the type of economic market. The correct answer is (c) because an oligopoly is characterized by a few firms in the industry. Answer (a) is incorrect because a natural monopoly has only one firm. Answer (b) is incorrect because a cartel is a group of firms that have joined together to fix prices. Answer (d) is incorrect because monopolistic competition is characterized by a large number of firms selling similar but differentiated products.

97. **(c)** The requirement is to describe how patents affect markets. The correct answer is (c) because a patent prevents another firm from coming into a market and selling the same or a very similar product. Therefore, it is a barrier to entry into the market. Answer (a) is incorrect because vertical integration refers to expansion into another phase of producing the same product. Answer (b) is incorrect because market concentration refers to how many firms compete in the market. Answer (d) is incorrect because collusion refers to firms acting collectively to control the market.

98. **(d)** The requirement is to identify the distinguishing characteristics of oligopolistic markets. The correct answer is (d) because of the small number of suppliers in an oligopolistic market, the actions of one affect the others; there is mutual interdependence with regard to pricing and output in an oligopolistic market. Answers (a) and (b) are incorrect because they describe monopolies. Answer (c) is incorrect because oligopolistic markets typically have barriers to entry.

99. **(a)** The requirement is to identify the characteristic that is not representative of monopolistic competition. The correct answer is (a) because monopolistic competition is a market that has numerous sellers of similar but differentiated products. Answers (b), (c), and (d) are incorrect because they are all characteristic of monopolistic competition.

100. **(b)** The requirement is to identify the market that is characterized by a few large sellers. Answer (b) is correct because it is the definition of an oligopoly. Answer (a) is incorrect because a monopoly has a single seller of a product or service for which there are no close substitutes. Answer (c) is incorrect because perfect competition is characterized by many firms selling an identical product or service. Answer (d) is incorrect because monopolistic competition is characterized by many firms selling a differentiated product or service.

101. **(c)** The requirement is to identify the different types of economic markets. Answer (c) is correct because it is the definition of perfect competition. Answer (a) is incorrect because a monopoly has a single seller of a product or service for which there are no close substitutes. Answer (b) is incorrect because an oligopoly is a form of market in which there are few large sellers of the product. Answer (d) is incorrect because monopolistic competition is characterized by many firms selling a differentiated product or service.

102. **(c)** The requirement is to estimate the short-term and long-term effects of an increase in demand in a perfectly competitive market. Answer (c) is correct because in the short term the price of the product will increase but in the long term it will return to the equilibrium price for the market. Answers (a), (b), and (d) are incorrect because the long-term price will not likely increase.

103. **(c)** The requirement is to identify the definition of a natural monopoly. The correct answer is (c) because a natural monopoly exists when, because of economic or technical conditions, only one firm can efficiently supply the product.

Answer (a) is incorrect because while owning natural resources may contribute to the establishment of a natural monopoly, the firm would still have to be the best possible producer of the product. Answer (b) is incorrect because a patent establishes a government-created monopoly. Answer (d) is incorrect because if the government is the only provider, the market is a government-created monopoly.

104. (c)   The requirement is to identify the market described as one with low barriers to entry and product differentiation. The correct answer is (c) because monopolistic competition is a market that is characterized by a large number of small producers of a differentiated product. Answer (a) is incorrect because a monopoly has only one producer. Answer (b) is incorrect because a natural monopoly is an industry in which there is only one producer based on the economics of the industry. Answer (d) is incorrect because an oligopoly is an industry that has a few large producers with barriers to entry.

105. (d)   The requirement is to identify the item that is not characteristic of perfect competition. In a perfectly competitive market there are a large number of small producers selling a standard product. Answer (d) is correct because all sellers must sell at the industry price. Answers (a), (b), and (c) are all characteristics of perfect competition.

106. (d)   The requirement is to identify the ultimate purpose of competitor analysis. Answer (d) is correct because the ultimate purpose of competitor analysis is to understand and predict the behavior of a major competitor. Answer (a) is not a part of competitor analysis. Answers (b) and (c) are part of competitor analysis but not the ultimate purpose.

107. (c)   The requirement is to identify the item that is not an important aspect of supply chain management. Supply chain management is primarily designed to manage the firm's relationships with suppliers by sharing key information all along the supply chain. The correct answer is (c) because the area of customer relations is not a primary focus of supply chain management. Answer (a) is incorrect because information technology is used extensively to share information electronically. Answer (b) is incorrect because accurate forecasts are essential to effective supply chain management. Answer (d) is incorrect because communication is the basis for supply chain management.

108. (d)   The requirement is to identify the type of organization that would most likely engage in public relations-type advertising. Firms that have monopolies are more likely to engage in public relations-type advertising to forestall additional regulation. Therefore, the correct answer is (d).

109. (b)   The requirement is to identify target market analysis. The correct answer is (b) because target market analysis involves obtaining a thorough understanding of the market in which the firm sells or plans to sell its product or services.

110. (c)   The requirement is to identify an unlikely market segmentation dimension for business customers. Answer (c) is correct because lifestyle is a possible individual customer market segmentation dimension for individuals, not businesses. Answers (a), (b), and (d) are incorrect because they all represent possible dimensions for business customer segmentation.

111. (b)   The requirement is to identify the percentage of variance in quantity demanded explained by price. Answer (b) is correct because the adjusted R squared (.72458) measures the percent of the variance in the dependent variable explained by the independent variable. Answer (a) is incorrect because it is the Multiple R that is the coefficient of correlation. Answer (c) is incorrect because it is the intercept that is used in the equation to predict quantity. Answer (d) is incorrect because it is the standard error that measures the standard deviation of the estimate of quantity.

112. (a)   The requirement is to calculate the predicted quantity demanded. The correct answer is (a) because the formula is Quantity demanded = a + bx = 56,400.50 + (7.00 × − 4,598.2) = 24,213.

113. (d)   The requirement is to identify the item that is not one of the forces in Porter's model for industry analysis. The correct answer is (d) because consideration of general economic conditions is not part of industry analysis. Answers (a), (b), and (c) are incorrect because the five forces include the threat of new entrants, the bargaining power of customers, the bargaining power of suppliers, the threat of substitute products or services, and the rivalry of the firms in the market.

114. (a)   The requirement is to identify the defining characteristic of supply chain management. The correct answer is (a) because a key aspect of supply chain management is the sharing of key information from the point of sale to the consumer back to the manufacturer, the manufacturer's suppliers, and the supplier's suppliers. Answer (b) is incorrect because it is the focus of process reengineering. Answer (c) is incorrect because it is the focus of total quality management. Answer (d) is incorrect because strategic alliances involve joint ventures and partnerships.

115. (d)   The requirement is to identify an unlikely strategy for a firm in a purely competitive market. The correct answer is (d) because in a purely competitive market firms compete based on price, and developing a brand name is a product differentiation strategy. Answers (a), (b), and (c) are all cost leadership strategies and appropriate for a firm in a purely competitive market.

116. (c)   The requirement is to identify the purpose of a response profile. The correct answer is (c) because a response profile is a description of possible actions that may be taken by a competitor in varying circumstances. Answers (a), (b), and (d) all involve aspects of industry analysis.

117. (b)   The requirement is to define the process of dividing all potential consumers into smaller groups of buyers with distinct needs, characteristics, or behaviors. Answer (b) is correct because this describes market segmentation. Answer (a) is incorrect because strategic planning involves deciding on the appropriate strategic initiatives for a period. Answer (c) is incorrect because product positioning involves deciding on a strategy for a particular product. Answer (d) is incorrect because objective setting involves establishing short-term goals.

118. (c)   The requirement is to identify the least important measure of unemployment in predicting the future state of the economy. Answer (c) is the correct answer because frictional unemployment measures the temporary unemployment that always exists as workers change jobs or new workers enter the workforce. Answer (a) is incorrect because structural unemployment measures the workforce that is unemployed due to a mismatch in job skills. Significant amounts of structural unemployment can drag down the economy. Answer (b) is incorrect because cyclical unemployment measures the workforce that is unemployed due to economic conditions. Answer (d) is incorrect because overall unemployment includes the workforce that is unemployed for all reasons.

119. (a) The requirement is to identify the steps involved in performing competitor analysis. Answer (a) is correct because competitor analysis is designed to predict the behavior of major competitors. Answers (b) and (c) are incorrect because they describe aspects of industry analysis. Answer (d) is incorrect because it describes aspects of general environment and industry analyses.

120. (a) The requirement is to describe the reason for the kinked demand curve in an oligopolist market. An oligopolist faces a kinked demand curve because competitors will often match price decreases but are hesitant to match price increases. Therefore, answer (a) is correct. Answer (b) is incorrect because an oligopolist does not face a nonlinear demand for its product. Answer (c) is incorrect because an oligopolist cannot sell its product for any price. Answer (d) is incorrect because consumer demand determines the demand curve in all markets.

FINANCIAL MANAGEMENT

A. Financial management includes the following five functions:

1. **Financing function**—Raising capital to support the firm's operations and investment programs.
2. **Capital budgeting function**—Selecting the best projects in which to invest firm resources, based on a consideration of risks and return.
3. **Financial management function**—Managing the firm's internal cash flows and its capital structure (mix of debt and equity financing) to minimize the financing costs and ensure that the firm can pay its obligations when due.
4. **Corporate governance function**—Developing an ownership and corporate governance system for the firm that will ensure that managers act ethically and in the best interest of stakeholders.
5. **Risk-management function**—Managing the firm's exposure to all types of risk.

B. The ultimate goal of management of a firm is the maximization of value for its owners, the stockholders. For a public company, this equates to maximization of the stock price of the firm. This is not easy because stock price maximization has a number of considerations and constraints.

1. Since stock prices are valued based on expected future cash flows of the firm it would seem that maximization of net income and cash flows would serve to maximize stockholder value. However, this is not necessarily the case.

   a. High-risk investments may increase net income but they also make the firm more risky. Stock price may actually decrease.
   b. Measurement of profit is not perfect. As an example, management may defer maintenance costs and increase profit but this is not in the best interest of the long-term profitability of the firm.
   c. Ethical and social responsibilities must also be considered. Socially desirable actions such as pollution control, equitable hiring practices, and fair pricing standards may at times be inconsistent with earning the highest possible profit.

2. As indicated above, financial managers are hired to maximize the wealth of the owners of the firm. Therefore, financial managers can be viewed as **agents** of the owners who hired them. However, managers have other personal goals, such as personal wealth, job security, prestige, and perquisites (e.g., country club memberships) that may cause their actions not to always be consistent with wealth maximization for stockholders. In **agency theory** such inconsistent behavior is referred to as agency costs. To control agency costs stockholders

   a. Rely on market forces to constrain management behavior. If management consistently behaves in its own interest, stock price will fall and eventually market forces will cause the removal of management.
   b. Incur monitoring costs to supervise management. As an example, the board of directors may force management to establish and maintain a large, competent, and independent internal audit department.
   c. Structure executive compensation packages, such as stock option plans, that align the interests of managers and stockholders.

C. Maximization of stockholder value is a complex process that involves making decisions that balance risk and return. Also, businesses and their economic environments are dynamic. The firm must be able to quickly adjust its strategies for production, investment, financing, and marketing.

D. Tax Considerations

Virtually every financial decision is influenced by tax considerations. Firms operating only in the US must be concerned with federal and state tax laws. Multinational firms are affected by these laws as well as the tax laws in all of the countries in which they do business. Some important things to remember about taxation include

1. The final returns to the firm and its stockholders are after-tax profits.
2. Interest is a tax-deductible expense to the firm. Dividends are not.
3. Alternative tax accounting methods are available that affect taxable income and the amount of taxes paid. For example, management may elect accelerated depreciation methods for certain assets.

4. Different tax rates apply to different types of income. As an example, individual taxpayers pay lower tax rates on capital gains.

5. Certain tax provisions are designed to stimulate the economy. For example, investment tax credits for investments in certain productive assets have been implemented over the years. The effect of the investment tax credit is a direct reduction in the cost of the productive assets.

WORKING CAPITAL MANAGEMENT

A. Working capital management involves managing and financing the current assets and current liabilities of the firm. The primary focus of working capital management is managing inventories and receivables.

1. **Managing the Firm's Cash Conversion Cycle**

   The cash conversion cycle of a firm is the length of time between when the firm makes payments and when it receives cash inflows. This cycle is illustrated below.

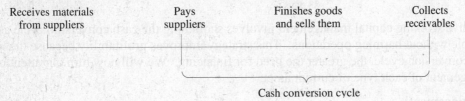

To enable more detailed analysis, the cash conversion cycle may be analyzed using the following three periods:

- Inventory conversion period
- Receivables collection period
- Payables deferral period

a. **Inventory conversion period**—The average time required to convert materials into finished goods and sell those goods.

$$\text{Inventory conversion period} = \frac{\text{Average inventory}}{\text{Sales per day}}$$

EXAMPLE: Assume that average inventory is $10,000,000 and annual sales are $40,000,000; the inventory conversion period is equal to 91 days, as calculated below.

$$\text{Inventory conversion period} = \frac{\$10,000,000}{\$40,000,000/365 \text{ days}}$$

$$= \quad 91 \text{ days}$$

b. **Receivables collection period (days sales outstanding)**—The average time required to collect accounts receivable.

$$\text{Receivables collection period} = \frac{\text{Average receivables}}{\text{Credit sales per day}}$$

EXAMPLE: Assume that the average receivables balance is $3,000,000 and credit sales are $40,000,000; the receivables collection period is equal to 27 days as calculated below.

$$\text{Receivables collection period} = \frac{\$3,000,000}{\$40,000,000/365 \text{ days}}$$

$$= \quad 27 \text{ days}$$

c. **Payables deferral period**—The average length of time between the purchase of materials and labor and the payment of cash for them.

$$\text{Payables deferral period} = \frac{\text{Average payables}}{\text{Purchases per day}}$$

$$= \frac{\text{Average payables}}{\text{Cost of goods sold}/365}$$

EXAMPLE: Assume that the average payables balance for labor and materials is $2,500,000 and cost of goods sold is $30,000,000; the payables deferral period is 30 days as calculated below.

$$\text{Payables deferral period} \quad = \quad \frac{\$2,500,000}{\$30,000,000/365 \text{ days}}$$

$$= \quad 30 \text{ days}$$

d. The cash conversion cycle nets the three periods described above and, therefore, measures the time period from the time the firm pays for its materials and labor to the time it collects its cash from sales of goods. The conversion period calculated from the above examples is shown below.

Cash conversion cycle	=	Inventory conversion period	+	Receivables conversion period	−	Payables deferral period
	=	91 days	+	27 days	−	30 days
	=	88 days				

e. Effective working capital management involves shortening the cash conversion cycle as much as possible without harming operations. This strategy improves profitability because the longer the cash conversion cycle, the greater the need for financing. We will now turn our attention to the management of each type of current asset.

2. **Cash Management**

A firm should attempt to minimize the amount of cash on hand while maintaining a sufficient amount to (1) take advantage of trade discounts, (2) maintain its credit rating, and (3) meet unexpected needs.

a. Firms hold cash for two basic purposes

- *Transactions.* Cash must be held to conduct business operations.
- *Compensation to financial institution.* Financial institutions require minimum balances (1) for certain levels of service or (2) as a requirement of loan agreements. Such minimums are referred to as **compensating balances**.

b. Firms prepare cash budgets to make sure that they have adequate cash balances to

- Take advantage of **trade discounts**. Suppliers often offer lucrative discounts for early payment of invoices.
- Assure that the firm maintains its credit rating.
- Take advantage of favorable business opportunities, such as opportunities for business acquisitions. These amounts are sometimes called **speculative balances**.
- Meet emergencies, such as funds for strikes, natural disasters, and cyclical downturns. These amounts are sometimes called **precautionary balances**.

c. A key technique for cash management is managing float. **Float** is the time that elapses relating to mailing, processing, and clearing checks. A float exists for both the firm's payments to suppliers and the firm's receipts from customers. **Effective cash management involves extending the float for disbursements and shortening the float for cash receipts.**

d. **Zero-balance accounts.** This cash management technique involves maintaining a regional bank account to which just enough funds are transferred daily to pay the checks presented. Regional banks typically receive the checks drawn on their customers' accounts in the morning from the Federal Reserve. The customer can then be notified as to the amount of cash needed to cover the checks and arrange to have that amount of cash transferred to the account. This arrangement has two advantages:

- Checks take longer to clear at a regional bank, providing more float for cash disbursements.
- Extra cash does not have to be deposited in the account for contingencies.

A zero-balance account is cost-effective if the amount the firm saves on interest costs from the longer float is adequate to cover any additional fees for account maintenance and cash transfers.

EXAMPLE. A firm has an opportunity to establish a zero-balance account system using three different regional banks. The total amount of the maintenance and transfer fees is estimated to be $5,000 per year. The firm believes *that it will increase the float on its operating disbursements by an average of three days, and its cost of short-term funds is 4%. Assuming that the firm estimates its average daily operating disbursements to be $50,000, should the firm establish the accounts?*

The solution to this problem is found by comparing the $5,000 cost in fees to the benefit in terms of reduced interest costs. If the float on the average is lengthened by three days, the firm gets the use of $150,000 of additional funds ($50,000 per day × 3 days). The annual value of the use of an extra $150,000 in funds is measured by the interest savings, or $6,000 ($150,000 × 4%). Therefore, the firm would save an estimated $1,000 ($6,000 – $5,000) by establishing the zero-balance accounts.

e. **Lockbox system**. In a lockbox system, customer payments are sent to a post office box that is maintained by a bank. Bank personnel retrieve the payments and deposit them into the firm's bank account. This technique has the following advantages:

- Increases the internal control over cash because firm personnel do not have access to cash receipts
- Provides for more timely deposit of receipts which reduces the need for cash for contingencies

If management is evaluating the feasibility of establishing a lockbox system solely based on the cash flow benefit, the system is cost effective if the interest costs saved due to obtaining more timely deposits is sufficient to cover the net increase in costs of cash receipt processing (bank fees less internal costs saved from having the bank process receipts). The computation would be similar to the one illustrated above for a zero-balance account.

> *EXAMPLE: Assume that a firm is evaluating whether to establish a lockbox system. The following information is available to make the decision:*
>
> - *The bank will charge $25,000 per year for the process and the firm will save approximately $8,000 in internal processing costs. Therefore, the estimated net additional cost of processing the receipts is $17,000 ($25,000 – $8,000).*
> - *The float for cash receipts will be reduced by an estimated two days. Therefore, the firm will receive use of the cash receipts on the average two days earlier.*
> - *Average daily cash receipts are equal to $300,000 and short-term interest costs are 4%.*
>
> *Should the firm establish the lockbox system?*
>
> *Based solely on cash flow considerations, the firm should establish the system if the interest savings is greater than the increased costs. In this case, the amount of interest savings is measured by multiplying the increase in average funds, $600,000 ($300,000 per day × 2 days), by the interest cost, 4%. The firm will save an estimated $24,000 ($600,000 × 4%) in annual interest costs. Therefore, the cost savings for the lockbox system is estimated to be $7,000, the savings in interest cost less the net increase in processing costs ($24,000 – $17,000). The real benefit may be even greater, because of the intangible value of the increase in internal control from having the bank process cash receipts. This reduces the firm's business risk.*

f. **Concentration banking.** Another way to speed up collection of payments on accounts is concentration banking. Using this technique, customers in an area make payments to a local branch office rather than firm headquarters. The local branch makes deposits in an account at a local bank. Then, surplus funds are periodically transferred to the firm's primary bank. Since these offices and banks are closer to customers, the firm gets the use of the funds more quickly. The float related to cash receipts is shortened. However, transferring funds between accounts can be costly. Wire transfers generally involve a significant fee. A slower but less expensive way of transferring funds is through the use of **official bank checks** (depository transfer checks) which are preprinted checks used to make transfers.

> *EXAMPLE: Assume that a firm is considering establishing a concentration banking system and has the following information to make the decision:*
>
> - *The concentration banking arrangement will allow access to the firm's average $100,000 daily cash receipts from customers two days faster.*
> - *Bank maintenance and transfer fees are estimated at $4,000 per year.*
> - *The firm's short-term borrowing cost is 3.5%.*
>
> *Should the firm establish the concentration banking system?*
>
> *Again, in evaluating the decision, management must compare the interest savings, $7,000 [($100,000 per day × 2 days) × 3.5%] to the additional costs, $4,000. Thus, management would save $3,000 ($7,000 – $4,000) by establishing the concentration banking system.*

g. **Electronic funds transfer.** Electronic funds transfer is a system in which funds are moved electronically between accounts without the use of a check. As an example, through a terminal at a supermarket a customer's payment is automatically charged with a "debit card" against the customer's bank account before he or she leaves the store.   Electronic funds transfer systems actually take the float out of both the receipts and disbursements processes.

h.   **International cash management.** Multinational firms can use various systems, including electronic systems, to manage the cash accounts they hold in various countries. Carefully managing international accounts may provide management with opportunities to increase earnings. As an example, management may be able to transfer funds to a country in which interest rates are higher, allowing increased returns on investments.

3.   **Marketable Securities Management**

In most instances firms hold marketable securities for the same reasons they hold cash. Such assets can generally be converted to cash very quickly, and marketable securities have an advantage over cash in that they provide an investment return. There are many securities to choose from for short-term investment. The factors that are considered in making the choice include

- **Minimum investment required**—Some investments, such as high-yield certificates of deposit, require larger investments.
- **Safety**—The risk to principal.
- **Marketability (liquidity)**—Relates to the speed with which the investment can be liquidated.
- **Maturity**—The length of time the funds are committed.
- **Yield**—Generally, the higher the yield the better. However, additional yield comes with higher risk or longer maturity.

Because short-term investments must be available to meet the current cash needs of the firm, the most important considerations with respect to these investments are liquidity and safety. Major types of short-term investments include

a.   **Treasury bills (T-bills)**—Short-term obligations of the federal government. Although treasury bills are initially offered with maturities of from 91 to 182 days, existing T-bills may be purchased on the market with virtually any maturity date up to 182 days. T-bills are popular short-term investments because the active market ensures liquidity.

b.   **Treasury notes**—Government obligations with maturities from one to ten years. These securities are appropriate for the investment of short- to intermediate-term funds.

c.   **Treasury Inflation Protected Securities (TIPS)**—Government obligations that pay interest that equates to a real rate of return specified by the US Treasury, plus principal at maturity that is adjusted for inflation. These are useful to a firm that wants to minimize interest rate risk.

d.   **Federal agency securities**—Offerings of government agencies, such as the Federal Home Loan Bank. These securities offer security, liquidity (active market), and pay slightly higher yields than treasury issues.

e.   **Certificates of deposit (CD)**—Savings deposits at financial institutions. There is actually a two-tier market for CDs—small CDs ($500 – $10,000) with lower interest rates and large ($100,000 or more) with higher interest rates. There is a secondary market for large CDs, providing some liquidity. Interest yields are higher on CDs than for government securities but CDs are not as liquid or as safe. CDs are normally insured up to $100,000 by the federal government.

f.   **Commercial paper**—Large unsecured short-term promissory notes issued to the public by large creditworthy corporations. Commercial paper has a two to nine month maturity period and is usually held to maturity by the investor because there is no active secondary market.

g.   **Banker's acceptance**—A draft drawn on a bank for payment when presented to the bank. Banker's acceptances generally arise from payments for goods by corporations in foreign countries. The corporation receiving the banker's acceptance may have to wait 30-90 days to present the acceptance for payment. As a result, a secondary market has developed for the sale of these instruments at a discount. Therefore, management may purchase banker's acceptances as short-term investments. Banker's acceptances involve slightly more risk than government securities but also offer slightly higher yields.

h.   **Eurodollar certificate of deposit**—Eurodollars are US dollars held on deposit by foreign banks and in turn lent by the banks to anyone seeking dollars. To obtain dollars, foreign banks offer Eurodollar certificates of deposit. As an investment, Eurodollar certificates of deposit pay higher yields than treasury bills or certificates of deposit at large US banks.

i.   **Money market funds**—Shares in a fund that purchases higher-yielding bank CDs, commercial paper, and other large-denomination, higher-yielding securities. Money market funds allow smaller investors to participate in these markets.

j.   **Money market accounts**—Similar to savings accounts, individual or business investors deposit idle funds in the accounts and the funds are used to invest in higher-yielding bank CDs, commercial paper, etc.

k.   **Equity and debt securities**—Management may also decide to invest in the publicly traded stocks and bonds of other corporations. Such investments have greater risk than other short-term investments, but they also offer higher average long-term returns. If management invests in such securities it should purchase a balanced portfolio to diversify away the **unsystematic risk** (e.g., default risk) of the individual investments.

4. **Inventory Management**

Effective inventory management starts with effective forecasting of sales and coordination of purchasing and production. The two goals of inventory management are

- To ensure adequate inventories to sustain operations, and
- To minimize inventory costs, including carrying costs, ordering and receiving costs, and cost of running out of stock.

a.   **Production pattern.** If the firm has seasonal demand for its products, management must decide whether to plan for level or seasonal production. Level production involves working at a consistent level of effort to manufacture the annual forecasted amount of inventory. Level production results in the most efficient use of labor and facilities throughout the year. However, it also results in inventory buildups during slow sales periods. This results in additional inventory holding costs. Seasonal production involves increasing production during periods of peak demand and reducing production during slow sales periods. Seasonal production often has additional operating costs for such things as overtime wages and maintenance.

> EXAMPLE: *A firm has projected the following data for the two alternatives of level production and seasonal production. The firm's short-term interest cost is 7%.*
>
> | | Level production | Seasonal production |
> |---|---|---|
> | *Average inventory* | *$200,000* | *$150,000* |
> | *Production costs* | *$1,000,000* | *$1,010,000* |
>
> *Which alternative is preferable?*
>
> Under the level production alternative, the firm would incur an additional $3,500 (($200,000 – $150,000) × 7%) in inventory holding costs, but it would also save $10,000 ($1,010,000 – $1,000,000) in production costs. Therefore, level production would be the best production alternative. It would save the firm $6,500 ($10,000 – $3,500).

b.   **Inventory and Inflation.** A firm's inventory policy also might be affected by inflation (deflation). As an example, if a firm uses silver as a raw material, the firm could experience significant gains or losses simply because of price fluctuations that occur in the silver market. Price instability occurs in a number of markets, such as copper, wheat, sugar, etc. The problem may be partially controlled by holding low levels of inventory. Another way would be to hedge the price movement with a futures contract to sell silver at a specified price in the future. In this manner, if the price of the silver falls, reducing the value of the inventory, the value of the future contract would rise to completely or partially offset the inventory loss.

c.   **Supply chain.** The term **supply chain** describes a good's production and distribution. It illustrates the flow of goods, services, and information from acquisition of basic raw materials through the manufacturing and distribution process to delivery of the product to the consumer, regardless of whether those activities occur in one or many firms. To manage inventories and their relationships with their suppliers many firms use a process known as **supply chain management.** A key aspect of supply chain management is the sharing of key information from the point of sale to the final consumer back to the manufacturer, to the manufacturer's suppliers, and to the suppliers' suppliers. As an example, if a manufacturer/distributor shares its sales forecasts with its suppliers and they in turn share their sales forecasts with their suppliers, the need for inventories for all firms is significantly decreased. The manufacturer/distributor, for example, needs far less raw materials inventory than normally would be the case because its suppliers are aware of the manufacturer's projected needs and are prepared to have the materials available when needed. Specialized software facilitates the process of information sharing along the supply chain network.

d. **Economic order quantity**

How much to order? The amount to be ordered is known as the **economic order quantity** (EOQ). The EOQ minimizes the sum of the ordering and carrying costs. The total inventory cost function includes **carrying costs** (which increase with order size) and **ordering costs** (which decrease with order size). The EOQ formula is derived by setting the annual carrying costs equal to annual ordering cost or by differentiating the cost function with respect to order size.

$$EOQ = \sqrt{\frac{2aD}{k}}$$

Where

a = cost of placing one order
D = annual demand in units
k = cost of carrying one unit of inventory for one year.

When to reorder? The objective is to order at a point in time so as to avoid **stockouts** but not so early that an excessive **safety stock** is maintained. Safety stocks may be used to guard against stockouts; they are maintained by increasing the lead time (the time that elapses from order placement until order arrival). Thus, safety stocks decrease stockout costs but increase carrying costs. Examples of these costs include

Carrying costs of safety stock *(and inventory in general)*	*Stockout costs*
1. Storage	1. Profit on lost sales
2. Interest	2. Customer ill will
3. Spoilage	3. Idle equipment
4. Insurance	4. Work stoppages
5. Property taxes	

The amount of safety stock held should minimize total stockout and carrying costs, as shown below.

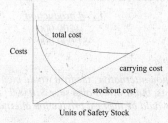

The most common approach to setting the optimum safety-stock level is to examine previous lead-time periods to determine the probabilities of running out of stock (a stockout) for different assessed levels of safety stock.

e. **Inventory Management and MRP.** Materials requirements planning (MRP) is a computerized system that manufactures finished goods based on demand forecasts. Demand forecasts are used to develop bills of materials that outline the materials, components, and subassemblies that go into the final products. Finally, a master production schedule is developed that specifies the quantity and timing of production of goods, taking into account the lead time required to purchase materials and to manufacture the various components of finished products. A key weakness of MRP is that it is a "push through" system. Once the master schedule is developed goods are pushed through the production process whether they are needed or not. Therefore, inventories may accumulate at various stages, especially if there are production slowdowns or unreliable demand forecasts. **MRP II** was developed as an extension of MRP and it features an automated closed loop system. That is, production planning drives the master schedule which drives the materials plans which is input to the capacity plan. It uses technology to integrate the functional areas of a manufacturing company.

f. **Just-in-Time (JIT) Purchasing.** Just-in-time (JIT) is a demand-pull inventory system which may be applied to purchasing so that raw material arrives just as it is needed for production. The primary benefit of JIT is **reduction of inventories, ideally to zero**. Because of its non-value-added nature, inventory is regarded as undesirable. In a JIT system, suppliers inspect their own goods and make frequent deliveries of materials, which are placed into production immediately upon receipt. This process eliminates the need for incoming inspection and the storeroom. Suppliers all along the supply chain are informed through specialized software (e.g., enterprise resource systems) about the forecasted demand for their products allowing them to plan to supply the items when needed.

Obviously, the most important aspect of a JIT purchasing system is selection of, and relationships with, suppliers. If suppliers do not make timely delivery of defect-free materials, stockouts and customer returns will occur and they will be more pronounced. In addition, if sales forecasts are not reliable, goods ordered will vary from what is expected, causing inventories to build up somewhere along the supply chain.

g. **Just-in-Time (JIT) Production.** JIT methodology can also be applied to production. JIT production is a "demand pull" system in which each component of a finished good is produced when needed by the next production stage. The production process is driven by the demand. It begins with an order by the customer triggering the need for a finished good and works its way back through each stage of production to the beginning of the process. A JIT system strives to produce high-quality products that meet the customer's needs on a timely basis and at the lowest possible cost. Obviously, JIT production reduces inventories to a minimal level. To accomplish JIT production, management must

- **Emphasize reducing production cycle time (manufacturing lead time) and setup time**. Cycle time is the time required to complete a product from the start of its production until it is finished. Setup time is the time required to get equipment and materials ready to start working on the product. The time for both is cut to a minimum in a JIT system.
- **Emphasize production flexibility.** Plant layout is organized around **manufacturing cells** that produce a product or type of product with the workers being able to operate a number of the different machines. Machinery is purchased that can be used for multiple functions.
- **Emphasize solving production problems immediately.** If it is discovered that parts are absent or defective, production is corrected on the spot. This practice contrasts with traditional systems, in which the production of defective products often continues because defective goods are sitting in inventory—awaiting sale and thus ultimate feedback from the customer. In a JIT system, each worker is responsible for the quality of his or her own work. Thus, JIT results in reductions in scrap and rework.
- **Focus on simplifying production activities.** The goal of JIT is to identify and eliminate non-value-added activities. Less factory space is used for inventory storage and production activities, and materials handling between workstations is streamlined.

JIT purchasing and production systems offer many advantages over traditional systems, including the following:

- Lower investments in inventories and in space to store inventory.
- Lower inventory carrying and handling costs.
- Reduced risk of defective and obsolete inventory.
- Reduced manufacturing costs.
- The luxury of dealing with a reduced number (when compared with traditional systems) of reliable, quality-oriented suppliers.
- JIT allows a simplified costing system called **backflush costing**. The lack of inventories in a JIT system makes choices about cost-flow (such as LIFO and FIFO) unimportant—all manufacturing costs are simply run through cost of goods sold.

On the other hand, JIT systems can break down with disastrous results if (1) suppliers do not provide timely delivery of quality materials, (2) employers are not well trained or supervised, or (3) technology and equipment are not reliable.

h. **Enterprise Resource Planning (ERP) Systems.** ERP systems are enterprise-wide computerized information systems that connect all functional areas within an organization. By sharing information from a common database, marketing, purchasing, production, distribution, and customer relations management can be effectively coordinated. ERP systems also facilitate supply chain management by connecting the firm electronically to its suppliers and customers.

5. **Receivables Management**

Effective receivables management involves systems for deciding whether or not to grant credit and for monitoring the receivables. Obviously, management should establish consistent credit evaluation procedures that balance the costs of lost sales with the costs of credit losses (uncollectible accounts). The firm's credit policy consists of the following four variables:

- Credit period—The length of time buyers are given to pay for their purchases.
- Discounts—Percentage provided and period allowed for discount for early payment.
- Credit criteria—Required financial strength of acceptable credit customers. Firms often use a statistical technique called **credit scoring** to evaluate a potential customer.
- Collection policy—Diligence used to collect slow-paying accounts.

a. The credit period and discount policies will be the major determinant of the eventual size of the receivables balance. If a firm has $10,000 in credit sales per day and allows 30 days for payment, the firm will carry an approximate balance of $300,000 ($10,000 × 30). If the firm extends the terms to 45 days, the receivables balance will swell to approximately $450,000 ($10,000 × 45).

b. In making an individual credit decision, management must determine the level of credit risk of the customer based on prior records of payment, financial stability, current financial position, and other factors. Credit information is available from sources such as **Dun & Bradstreet Information Services** to make such decisions. Dun & Bradstreet makes available its Business Information Report (BIR) and a number of credit scoring reports.

c. To provide overall monitoring of receivables, management will often use measures such as the days sales outstanding and aging schedules. The days sales outstanding provides an overall measure of the accumulation of receivables and is calculated as follows:

$$\text{Days sales outstanding} = \frac{\text{Receivables}}{\text{Sales per day}}$$

EXAMPLE: Assume that a firm's outstanding receivables balance is $2,000,000 and annual sales is $52,000,000; the days sales outstanding is calculated below.

$$\text{Days sales outstanding} = \frac{\$2,000,000}{\$52,000,000/365 \text{ days}} = 14 \text{ days}$$

An aging schedule breaks down receivables by age, as shown below.

Age of Account (Days)	Amount	Percentage
0-10	$1,355,000	67.7
11-30	505,000	25.3
31-45	90,000	4.5
46-60	43,000	2.2
Over 60	7,000	0.3
Total	$2,000,000	100.0

By monitoring days sales outstanding and the aging schedule, management can detect adverse trends and evaluate the performance of the credit department.

d. Management of accounts receivable also involves determining the appropriate credit terms and criteria to maximize profit from sales after considering the cost of holding accounts receivable and losses from uncollectible accounts.

EXAMPLE: Assume that management believes that if they relax the firm's credit standards, sales will increase by $240,000. The firm's average collection period for these new customers will be 60 days and the payment period for existing customers is not expected to change. Management expects 5% losses from uncollectible accounts for these new customers. If variable costs are 75% of sales, and the cost of financing accounts receivable is 10%, should management decide to relax credit standards? The answer to this question involves comparing incremental revenues to incremental costs as shown below.

Incremental revenue	*$240,000*
Variable costs ($240,000 × 75%)	*(180,000)*
Uncollectible account expense ($240,000 × 5%)	*(12,000)*
Interest cost on additional average receivables ($40,000 × 10%)	*(4,000)*
Incremental revenue	*$44,000*

The interest cost is calculated by recognizing that if collection takes approximately 60 days, there will be approximately 60 days sales outstanding during the year. Average outstanding receivables is calculated as

$$\begin{aligned}
\textit{Average outstanding receivables} \quad &= \quad \textit{(Sales/360 days)} \times \textit{60 days} \\
&= \quad \textit{($240,000/360)} \times 60 \\
&= \quad \textit{$40,000}
\end{aligned}$$

6. **Financing Current Assets**

   a. Because many firms have seasonal fluctuations in the demand for their products or services, current assets tend to vary in amount from month to month. Conventional wisdom would say that such assets should be financed with current liabilities—accounts payable, commercial bank loans, commercial paper, etc. However, a certain amount of current assets are required to operate the business in even the slowest periods of the year. This amount of current assets is called the amount of **permanent current assets**. Permanent current assets are more appropriately financed with long-term financing, such as stock or bonds. Additional current assets (inventory, accounts receivable, etc.) are accumulated during periods of higher production and sales. These current assets are called **temporary current assets,** and they may be appropriately financed with short-term financing.

   b. Various strategies are used to finance current assets. Since short-term debt is less expensive than long-term, firms generally attempt to finance current assets with short-term debt. However, use of extensive amounts of short-term debt is **aggressive** in that firms must pay off the debt or replace it as it comes due. A business recession may render the firm unable to meet these obligations. In addition, the amount of interest expense over time will be more volatile because the firm has not locked in an interest rate on a long-term basis. More **conservative** strategies involve financing some current assets with long-term debt which involves a more stable interest rate. However, as indicated above long-term debt tends to be more expensive, and the provisions or **covenants** of long-term debt agreements generally constrain the firm's future actions. Finally, prepayment penalties may make early repayment of long-term debt an expensive proposition.

   c. Illustrated in the graph below is a conservative short-term investment strategy in which permanent current assets are financed with long-term debt.

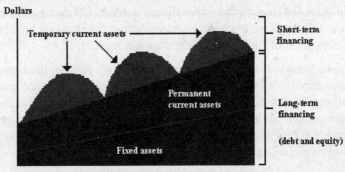

   d. The **maturity matching** or **self-liquidating approach** to financing assets involves matching asset and liability maturities. This strategy minimizes the risk that the firm will be unable to pay its maturing obligations.

   e. Generalizations about the cost, riskiness, and flexibility of short-term versus long-term debt depend on the type of short-term debt being used. We will now turn our attention to the different sources of short-term funds.

7. **Sources of Short-Term Funds**

   a. **Accounts payable (trade credit).** Firms generally purchase goods and services from other firms on credit. Trade credit, especially for small firms, is a very significant source of short-term funds. A major advantage of trade credit is that it arises in the normal course of conducting business and bears no interest cost, providing it is paid on time.

      Many firms have credit terms that allow a cash discount for early payment of the invoice. For example, a firm might sell on terms of 2/10, net 30, which means that payment is due in thirty days and a 2% discount is allowed for payment within 10 days. Generally, it is a good financial decision to take advantage of such discounts because the rate of interest realized for early payment is significant. The approximated cost of not taking the discount is calculated with the following formula:

$$\frac{\text{Discount percent}}{100\% - \text{Discount percent}} \times \frac{365 \text{ days}}{\text{Total pay period} - \text{Discount period}}$$

With our example of 2/10, net/30, the discount percentage is 2%, the total pay period is 30 days, and the discount period is 10 days. Therefore, the nominal annual cost is equal to 37.2% as calculated below.

$$\begin{aligned} \text{Nominal annual cost} \quad &= \frac{2\%}{100\% - 2\%} \times \frac{365 \text{ days}}{30 \text{ days} - 10 \text{ days}} \\ &= \quad 37.2\% \end{aligned}$$

The nominal rate does not consider the effects of compounding. Therefore, the effective annual rate is significantly higher than the 37.2%.

b. **Short-term bank loans.** Notes payable to commercial banks represents the second most important source of short-term funds. We will now turn our attention to key features of bank loans.

Maturity—While banks do make long-term loans, the majority of their lending has a maturity date of one year or less. Business loans typically mature every 90 days requiring the firm to pay or renew the loan on a regular basis.

Promissory note—Notes are executed using a signed promissory note. The note specifies the terms of the agreement.

Interest—The rate for short-term bank loans fluctuates with changes in short-term interest rates as measured by such indexes as

- *Prime rate*—The rate a bank charges its most creditworthy customers. The rate increases for customers with more credit risk. As an example, a customer might have a rate of prime plus one basis point, which would be equal to the prime rate plus one percent.
- *London Interbank Offered Rate (LIBOR)*—This rate is important because of the availability of dollars for loan on the international market. US companies can decide to borrow money in the US financial markets, London, or any other major money market center. LIBOR reflects price of funds in the international market.

Compensating balances—Loan agreements may require the borrower to maintain an average demand deposit balance equal to some percentage of the face amount of the loan. Such requirements increase the effective interest rate of the loan, because the firm does not get use of the full amount of the loan principal. As an example, if a firm gets a $100,000, 90-day loan at 6% with a 10% compensating balance arrangement, the effective interest rate on the loan would be calculated as follows:

Principal available	=	$100,000 − (10% × $100,000)
Interest for 90 days	=	$100,000 × 6% × (90 days/360 days)
	=	$1,500
Effective interest rate	=	Interest paid/Principal available × (360 days/90 days)
	=	$1,500/$90,000 × (360 days/90 days)
	=	6.67%

Informal line of credit—An informal specification of the maximum amount that the bank will lend the borrower.

Revolving credit agreements—A line of credit in which the bank is formally committed to lend the firm a specified maximum amount. The bank typically receives a commitment fee as a part of the agreement. Revolving credit arrangements are often used for intermediate-term financing.

Letter of credit—An instrument that facilitates international trade. A letter of credit, issued by the importer's bank, promises that the bank will pay for the imported merchandise when it is delivered. It is designed to reduce the risk of nonpayment by the importer.

c. **Commercial paper.** Commercial paper is a form of unsecured promissory note issued by large, creditworthy firms. It is sold primarily to other firms, insurance companies, pension funds, banks, and mutual funds. Commercial paper typically has maturity dates that vary from one day to nine months. This form of financing is very favorable for corporations with the financial strength to issue it. The rate is often 2 to 3% less than the prime rate and there are no compensating balance requirements. However, the market is less predictable than bank financing.

d. **Accounts receivable financing.**

(1) **Pledging of receivables.** Pledging accounts receivable involves committing the receivables as collateral for a loan from a financial institution. The financial institution will evaluate the receivables to see if they are of sufficient quality to serve as collateral. The interest rate will depend on the financial strength of the firm and the quality of the receivables. Typically, the financial institution will lend 60 to 80% of the value of the receivables and the outstanding balance of the loan will fluctuate with the amount of the receivables outstanding. Interest is computed based on the outstanding loan balance and tends to be quite high. However, for small or troubled companies the interest rate will be less than for unsecured loans.

(2) **Factoring.** When accounts receivable are factored, they are sold outright to a finance company. In such situations, the finance company is often directly involved in the credit decisions, and will submit the funds to the firm upon acceptance of the account. For taking the risk, the finance company is generally paid a fee of from 1 to 3% of the invoices accepted. In addition, the finance company receives the interest rate for advancing the funds.

> *EXAMPLE: Assume that a finance company charges a 2% fee and a 12% annual interest rate for factoring the firm's receivables which are payable in 30 days. The effective annual rate of interest on this arrangement would be calculated as follows:*
>
> *2% Fee*
> *1% Interest for 1 month (12% annual/12)*
> *3% Monthly × 12 = 36% annual rate*
>
> *Obviously, with the high rates associated with factoring, it is only considered by firms that have few other options.*

(3) **Asset-backed public offerings.** Large firms recently have begun floating public offerings of debt (e.g. bonds) collateralized by the firm's accounts receivable. Because they are collateralized, such securities generally carry a high credit rating, even though the issuing firm may have a lower credit rating. Therefore, this form of accounts receivable financing can be advantageous. The creation of asset-backed securities is also called **securitization of assets**.

e. **Inventory financing.** A firm may also borrow funds using its inventory as collateral. The extent of the feasibility of this strategy depends on the marketability of the inventory. Obviously, widely traded raw materials such as lumber, metals, and grains are easily used as collateral. The methods used by lenders to control the pledged inventories include

- **Blanket Inventory Lien**—This is simply a legal document that establishes the inventory as collateral for the loan. No physical control over inventory is involved.
- **Trust Receipt**—An instrument that acknowledges that the borrower holds the inventory and that proceeds from sale will be put in trust for the lender. Each item is tagged and controlled by serial number. When the inventory is sold, the funds are transferred to the lender and the trust receipt is cancelled. This form of financing is also referred to as *floor planning* and is widely used for automobile and industrial equipment dealers.
- **Warehousing**—This is the most secure form of inventory financing. The inventory is stored in a **public warehouse** or under the control of public warehouse personnel. The goods can only be removed with the lender's permission.

f. **Hedging to reduce interest rate risk.** Firms that must borrow significant amounts of short-term variable rate funds are exposed to high levels of interest rate risk. If interest rates go up suddenly, the firm could experience a significant increase in interest costs. To mitigate this interest rate risk, management may decide to hedge the risk with derivatives purchased or sold in the **financial futures market**. Derivatives and hedging strategies are described in the next module.

CAPITAL STRUCTURE

This section focuses on determining the appropriate **capital structure** of the firm which involves a combination of debt and equity.

A. Long-Term Debt

The characteristics of the various forms of financing available to the firm help determine the funding sources that are most appropriate.

1. **Public and Private Debt**

    Debt is increasingly a source of funds for US corporations. In issuing debt, management must first decide whether to issue the debt privately or publicly.

    a. **Private debt** is of two principal types. The first type is loans from financial institutions (either an individual institution or a syndicated loan from multiple institutions). Such loans almost universally have a floating interest rate that is tied to a base rate, usually **LIBOR** (the London Interbank Offered Rate) or the US bank prime interest rate. The second type of private debt involves the **private placement** of unregistered bonds sold directly to accredited investors (often pension funds or insurance companies). Such debt is typically less expensive to issue than public debt.

    b. In the United States, **public long-term debt** offerings involve selling SEC registered bonds directly to investors. The bond agreement specifies the par value, the coupon rate, and the maturity date of the debt. The par value is the face amount of the bond and most corporate bonds have a $1,000 face amount. The coupon rate is the interest rate paid on the face amount of the bond. Since most bonds pay a fixed rate of interest, the market value of the bond fluctuates with changes in the market interest rate. The maturity date is the final date on which repayment of the bond principal is due.

        > *EXAMPLE: Baker Corporation issued $500,000 in 6% bonds, maturing in 20 years. Assuming that the bonds were issued at face value and interest is paid semiannually, the coupon rate of 6% is paid in installments of $30 (3% × $1,000) every six month for each $1,000 bond. Total annual interest for the firm every year is $30,000 ($500,000 × 6%). If the market rate of interest increases to 7% after the bonds are issued, the market value of the bonds will decline to an amount that will allow a new purchaser to realize a 7% yield to maturity. On the other hand, if the market rate of interest decreases to 5%, the market price of the bond will increase to an amount that will allow the new purchaser to earn only a 5% yield to maturity. This example illustrates the **interest rate risk** that investors assume when they purchase long-term fixed-rate bonds.*

    c. A debt market with increasing importance is the market for **Eurobonds**. A Eurobond is a bond payable in the borrower's currency but sold outside the borrower's country. As an example, the bond of a US firm, payable in US dollars, might be sold in Germany, London, and Japan through an international syndicate of investment bankers. The registration and disclosure requirements for Eurobonds are less stringent than those of the SEC for US issued bonds. Therefore, the cost of issuance is less.

2. **Debt Covenants and Provisions**

    a. **Debt covenants.** Both private and public debt agreements contain restrictions, known as **debt covenants**. Such covenants allow investors (lenders) to monitor and control the activities of the firm. Otherwise, management could make decisions that would be detrimental to the interests of the debtholders. Negative covenants specify actions the borrower cannot take, such as restrictions on

        (1) The sale of certain assets.
        (2) The incurrence of additional debt.
        (3) The payment of dividends.
        (4) The compensation of top management.

        Positive covenants specify what the borrower must do and include such requirements as

        (1) Provide audited financial statements each year.
        (2) Maintain certain minimum financial ratios.
        (3) Maintain life insurance on key employees.

These covenants restrict the action of management and are an important consideration in determining the type of financing to obtain. In addition, major covenants must be disclosed in the footnotes to the firm's financial statements. Now, let's turn our attention to some typical provisions of debt agreements.

b. **Security provisions.** Debt may be secured or unsecured. Secured debt is one in which specific assets of the firm are pledged to the bondholders in the event of default. Based on their security provisions debt may be classified as follows:

(1) **Mortgage bond**—A bond secured with the pledge of specific property. The securing property is typically property or plant assets.

(2) **Collateral trust bond**—A bond secured by financial assets of the firm.

(3) **Debenture**—A bond that is not secured by the pledge of specific property. It is a general obligation of the firm. Because of the **default risk,** such bonds can only be issued by firms with the highest credit rating. Debentures typically have a higher yield than mortgage bonds and other secured debt.

(4) **Subordinated debenture**—A bond with claims subordinated to other general creditors in the event of bankruptcy of the firm. That is, the bondholders receive distributions only after general creditors and **senior** debt holders have been paid. As you would expect, subordinated debentures have higher yields than senior unsecured debt.

(5) **Income bond**—A bond with interest payments that are contingent on the firm's earnings. Obviously, these bonds also have a high degree of risk and carry even higher yields. These types of bonds are often associated with firms undergoing restructuring.

c. **Methods of payment.** Bonds may be paid as a single sum at maturity, or through

(1) **Serial payments**—**Serial bonds** are paid off in installments over the life of the issue. Serial bonds may be desirable to bondholders because they can choose their maturity date.

(2) **Sinking fund provisions**—The firm makes payments into a sinking fund which is used to retire bonds by purchase.

(3) **Conversion**—The bonds may be convertible into common stock and this may provide the method of payment.

(4) **Redeemable**—A bondholder may have the right to redeem the bonds for cash under certain circumstances (e.g., if the firm is acquired by another firm).

(5) **A call feature**—The bonds may have a call provision allowing the firm to force the bondholders to redeem the bonds before maturity. Call provisions typically call for payment of a 5 to 10% premium over par value to redeem the bonds. Investors generally do not like call features because they may be used to force them to liquidate their investment.

3. **Bond Yields**

a. There are three different yields that are relevant to bonds: the **coupon rate,** the **current yield,** and **yield to maturity**.

> EXAMPLE: *Assume that a bond has a par value of $1,000 and pays 12% interest, $120 ($1,000 × 12%) per year for the remaining term of 10 years. The bond is currently selling for $900.*
>
> • *The coupon rate (nominal yield) is equal to the 12% stated rate.*
> • *The current yield is the stated interest payment divided by the current price of the bond.*

$$\frac{\$120}{\$900} \;=\; 13.33\%$$

> • *The yield to maturity is the interest rate that will equate future interest payments and the maturity payment to the current market price. The future interest payments are $120 per year and the principal payment is $1,000 received at the end of 10 years. The current price of the bond is $900, and the yield to maturity can be estimated with the following formula:*

$$YM = \frac{\text{Annual interest payment} + \dfrac{\text{Principal payment} - \text{Bond price}}{\text{Number of years to maturity}}}{0.6\,(\text{Price of bond}) + 0.4\,(\text{Principal payment})}$$

$$= \frac{\$120 + \dfrac{\$1,000 - \$900}{10}}{0.6\,(\$900) + 0.4\,(\$1,000)}$$

$$= 13.83\%$$

b. The price of a bond is dependent on the current **risk-free interest rate** and the **credit risk** of the particular bond. Bond rating agencies have rating systems for bonds to capture credit risk. For example, Moody's Investor Service provides the following nine categories of ranking:

Aaa	Aa	A	Baa	Ba	B	Caa	Ca	C

Lowest risk   Highest risk

     For additional discussion of the valuation of bonds, review the section on present value in the next module.

4. **Other Types of Bonds**

a. **Zero-coupon rate bonds**—These types of bonds do not pay interest. Instead they sell at a deep discount from the face or maturity value. The return to the investor is the difference between the cost and the bond's maturity value. The advantage of these bonds is that there are no interest payment requirements until the bonds mature. In addition, the amortization of interest is tax-deductible even though the firm is not making any interest payments.

b. **Floating rate bonds**—The rate of interest paid on this type of bond floats with changes in the market rate (usually monthly or quarterly). Therefore the market price of the bond does not fluctuate as widely. **Reverse floaters** are floating rate bonds that pay a higher rate of interest when other interest rates fall and a lower rate when other rates rise. Reverse floaters are riskier than normal bonds.

c. **Registered bonds**—These bonds are registered in the name of the bondholder. Interest payments are sent directly to the registered owners.

d. **Junk bonds**—These bonds carry very high-risk premiums. Junk bonds often have resulted from **leveraged buyouts** or are issued by large firms that are in troubled circumstances. They may appeal to investors who feel they can diversify the risk by purchasing a portfolio of the bonds in different industries.

e. **Foreign bonds**—These bonds are international bonds that are denominated in the currency of the nation in which they are sold. Foreign bonds might serve as an effective hedge for a firm that is heavily invested in assets in the foreign country.

f. **Eurobonds**—As described above, these bonds are international bonds that are denominated in US dollars.

5. **Advantages and Disadvantages of Debt Financing**

     In deciding whether debt should be used as a form of financing, management must keep in mind the following advantages and disadvantages. The advantages of debt financing include

- Interest is tax-deductible.
- The obligation is generally fixed in terms of interest and principal payments.
- In periods of inflation, debt is paid back with dollars that are worth less than the ones borrowed.
- The owners (common stockholders) do not give up control of the firm.
- Debtors do not participate in excess earnings of the firm.
- Debt is less costly than equity. Therefore, the use of debt, up to some limit, will lower the firm's cost of capital. Cost of capital is discussed later in this module.

Disadvantages of debt financing include

- Interest and principal obligations must be paid regardless of the economic position of the firm.
- Interest payments are fixed in amount regardless of how poorly the firm performs.
- Debt agreements contain covenants that place restrictions of the flexibility of the firm.
- Excessive debt increases the risk of equity holders and therefore depresses share prices.

6. **Leasing as a Form of Financing**

a. Another potential source of intermediate or long-term financing involves leasing assets. From a financial statement standpoint, leases may be capital leases or operating leases. **Capital leases** are those that meet any one of the following four conditions as set forth in SFAS 13:

(1) The arrangement transfers ownership of the property to the lessee by the end of the lease.

(2) The lease contains a bargain purchase option at the end of the lease. The option price must be sufficiently low so exercise of the option appears reasonably certain.

(3) The lease term is equal to 75% or more of the estimated life of the leased property.

(4) The present value of the minimum lease payments equals 90% or more of the fair value of the leased property at the inception of the lease.

If a lease meets one of these conditions, the firm must record the leased asset and related liability on its balance sheet, and account for the asset much like it would a purchased asset. The asset is recorded at the present value of the future lease payments and amortized (depreciated). A liability is recorded at the same amount and each lease payment involves payment of interest and principal on the obligation.

b. An **operating lease** is one that does not meet the criteria to be treated as a capital lease. Operating leases are treated as rental agreements; the asset and obligation are not recorded on the firm's balance sheet. The lease payments are expensed as rent as they are incurred.

c. A **sale-leaseback** is a transaction in which the owner of the property sells the property to another and simultaneously leases it back. Such arrangements often provide financing and tax advantages.

d. Leases have a number of advantages over purchasing the asset and financing through other means, including

- A firm may be able to lease an asset when it does not have the funds or credit capacity to purchase the asset.
- The provisions of a lease agreement may be less stringent than a bond indenture.
- There may be no down payment requirement.
- Creditor claims on certain types of leases, such as real estate, are restricted in bankruptcy.
- The cost of a lease to the lessee may be reduced because the lease may be structured such that the lessor retains the tax benefits.
- Operating leases do not require recognition of a liability on the financial statement of the lessor.

e. On the other hand, the dollar cost of leasing an asset is often higher than the cost of purchasing the asset.

B. Equity

This section describes the use of various forms of equity used for long-term financing.

1. **Common Stock**

   The ultimate owners of the firm are the common shareholders. They generally have control of the business and are entitled to a residual claim to income of the firm after the creditors and preferred shareholders are paid. Common stock ownership involves a high degree of risk. The investor is the last in line to receive earnings and distributions upon liquidation of the firm. On the other hand, common stockholders have the potential opportunity to receive very high returns. The return of the common stockholder includes dividends and appreciation in the value of the stock.

   a. **Classes of common stock.** Most firms issue only one class of common stock. However, a firm may issue a second class of stock that differs with respect to the stockholders' right to vote or receive dividends. As an example, if the current stockholders do not wish to give up control of the firm, a class B stock might be issued that has limited voting rights. Obviously, the class B stock would sell for less than the class A stock as a result of the restriction.

   b. **Stock warrants.** Stock warrants are sometimes issued with bonds to increase their marketability. A stock warrant is an option to buy common stock at a fixed price for some period of time. Once the bond is sold, the stock warrants often may be sold separately and are traded on the market.

   c. **Advantages of issuing common stock**

   - The firm has no firm obligation, which increases financial flexibility.
   - Increased equity reduces the risk to borrowers and, therefore, will reduce the firm's cost of borrowing.
   - Common stock is more attractive to many investors because of the future profit potential.

   d. **Disadvantages of common stock**

   - Issuance costs are greater than for debt.

- Ownership and control is given up with respect to the issuance of common stock.
- Dividends are not tax-deductible by the corporation whereas interest is tax-deductible.
- Shareholders demand a higher rate of return than lenders.
- Issuance of too much common stock may increase the firm's cost of capital.

2. **Preferred stock** is a hybrid security. Preferred shareholders are entitled to receive a stipulated dividend and, generally, must receive the stipulated amount before the payment of dividends to common shareholders. In addition preferred stockholders have a priority over common stockholders in the event of liquidation of the firm. Common features of preferred stock include

- **Cumulative dividends**—Most issues are cumulative preferred stock and have a cumulative claim to dividends. That is, if dividends are not declared in a particular year, the amount becomes in arrears and the amount must be paid in addition to current dividends before common shareholders can receive a dividend.
- **Redeemability**—Some preferred stock is redeemable at a specified date. This makes the stock very similar to debt. On the firm's balance sheet such stock is often presented between debt and equity (the so-called mezzanine).
- **Conversion**—Preferred stock may be convertible into common stock.
- **Call feature**—Preferred stock, like debt, may have a call feature.
- **Participation**—A small percentage of preferred shares are participating, which means they may share with common shareholders in dividends above the stated amount.
- **Floating rate**—A small percentage of preferred shares have a floating rather than fixed dividend rate.

a. **Advantages of issuing preferred stock**

- The firm still has no obligation to pay dividends until they are declared, which increases financial flexibility.
- Increased equity reduces the risk to borrowers and, therefore, will reduce the firm's cost of borrowing.
- Common stockholders do not give up control of the firm.
- Preferred stockholders do not generally participate in superior earnings of the firm.

b. **Disadvantages of preferred stock**

- Issuance costs are greater than for debt.
- Dividends are not tax-deductible by the corporation whereas interest is tax-deductible.
- Dividends in arrears accumulated over a number of years may create financial problems for the firm.

3. **Convertible Securities**

A convertible security is a bond or share of preferred stock that can be converted, at the option of the holder, into common stock. When the security is initially issued it has a **conversion ratio** that indicates the number of shares that the security may be converted into.

The advantage of convertible securities is the fact that investors require a lower yield because of the prospects that conversion may result in a significant gain.

The major disadvantage is that conversion dilutes the ownership of other common stockholders.

4. **Spin-Offs**

A spin-off occurs when a public diversified firm separates one of its subsidiaries, distributing the shares on a pro rata basis to the existing stockholders. Spin-offs are often part of management's strategy to turn its focus to its core businesses.

5. **Tracking Stocks**

A tracking stock is a specialized equity offering that is based on the operations and cash flows of a wholly owned subsidiary of a diversified firm. They are hybrid securities, because the subsidiary is not separated from the parent, legally or operationally. The stock simply is entitled to the cash flows of the subsidiary and, therefore, the trading stock trades at a valuation based on the subsidiary's expected future cash flows. Managers that issue trading stock believe that stockholder wealth will be maximized by separate valuation of two or more parts of the consolidated group.

6.   **Venture Capital**

Venture capital is a pool of funds that is used to make actively managed direct equity investments in rapidly growing private companies. Such funds may be institutionally managed or involve ad hoc investments by wealthy individuals. In addition to capital, professional venture capitalists provide managerial oversight and business advice to the companies. Venture capitalists generally plan to exit the investment within three to seven years by selling the stock to another firm or by initiating a public offering of the stock. Venture capital provides a good source of capital for promising private companies, but it is expensive and management gives up significant control.

7.   **Going Public**

As a private firm grows, one decision that must be made is whether and when to go public. Going public involves registering the firm's shares with the SEC. From that point on, the firm must comply with the reporting and other requirements of the SEC and the exchange on which the stock trades.

   a.   **Advantages of going public**

   • An initial public offering provides the firm with access to a larger pool of equity capital.
   • Publicly traded stock may be used for acquisitions of other firms. If a private company decides to acquire another company it generally must do so with cash.
   • The firm can offer stock options and other stock-based compensation to attract and retain qualified managers.
   • Going public provides the owners of the private company liquidity for their investments. These individuals can more easily sell portions of their stock in the firm and diversify their portfolio with other investments.

   b.   **Disadvantages of going public**

   • Significant costs and management effort must be put into an initial public offering.
   • There are significant costs of being public related to compliance with the securities laws and SEC and stock exchange regulations. These costs have been significantly increased by the provisions of the Sarbanes-Oxley Act of 2002.
   • Being public necessarily causes management to be focused on maximizing stock price. This may or may not be in the best long-term interest of the firm.
   • Management must provide a great deal of information about the firm to investors.

8.   **Employee Stock Ownership Plans (ESOPs)**

Firms often reward management and key employees with stock or stock options as part of their compensation. These plans are designed to motivate management to focus on shareholder value. ESOPs are sometimes used as a vehicle for a **leveraged buyout**. ESOPs have certain tax advantages to the employees, and compensation expense may or may not have to be recognized by the firm.

9.   **Going Private**

Some public corporations have decided (often to concentrate control) to go private. These transformations are sometimes executed through a **leveraged buyout** (LBO). In an LBO large amounts of debt are used to buy all or a voting majority of the shares of stock outstanding. Obviously, the firm, after the LBO, is heavily leveraged with much greater risk.

C.   **Evaluating the Best Source of Financing**

To understand completely the considerations involved in making financing decisions, one must understand the concepts of leverage and cost of capital.

1.   **Leverage**

The finance literature generally discusses two types of leverage: operating leverage and financial leverage.

   a.   **Operating leverage.** Operating leverage measures the degree to which a firm builds fixed costs into its operations. If fixed costs are high a significant decrease in sales can be devastating. Therefore, all other things being equal, the greater a firm's fixed costs the greater its **business risk**. On the other hand, if sales increase for a firm with a high degree of operating leverage, there will be a larger increase in return on equity. The degree of operating leverage (DOL) may be computed using the following formula:

$$\text{DOL} \quad = \quad \frac{\text{Percent change in operating income}}{\text{Percent change in unit volume}}$$

Highly leveraged firms, such as Ford Motor Company, enjoy substantial increases in income when sales volume increases. Less leveraged firms enjoy only modest increases in income as sales volume increases.

b. **Financial leverage.** Financial leverage measures the extent to which the firm uses debt financing. While the use of debt can produce high returns to stockholders, it also increases their risk. Since debt generally is a less costly form of financing, a firm will generally attempt to use as much debt for financing as possible. However, as more and more debt is issued, the firm becomes more leveraged and the risk of its debt increases, causing the interest rate on additional debt to rise. Therefore, the optimal capital structure for a firm involves a mixture of debt and equity. The degree of financial leverage (DFL) for a firm may be computed using the following formula:

$$\text{DFL} \quad = \quad \frac{\text{Percent change in EPS}}{\text{Percent change in EBIT}}$$

Where

EPS = Earnings per share
EBIT = Earnings before interest and taxes

EXAMPLE: Let's examine two different leverage strategies. Under Plan 1 (the leveraged plan) management borrows $400,000 and sells 20,000 shares of common stock at $10 per share. Under Plan 2 (the conservative plan) the firm borrows $100,000 and issues 50,000 shares of stock at $10 per share. The debt bears interest at 10% and the firm has a 40% tax rate. These alternatives are illustrated below.

	Plan 1	Plan 2
Debt (10 % interest)	$400,000	$100,000
Common stock	200,000	500,000
Total financing	$600,000	$600,000
Common stock	20,000 shares	50,000 shares

Now let's examine two sets of financial results. First, assume that the firm loses $200,000 before interest and taxes (EBIT). The financial results under the two different financing scenarios is shown below.

	Plan 1	Plan 2
EBIT	$(200,000)	$(200,000)
Interest (10% × principal)	(40,000)	(10,000)
Earnings before taxes	$(240,000)	$(210,000)
Tax benefit (40% × EBT)	96,000	84,000
Net loss	$(144,000)	$(126,000)
Loss per share	($7.20)	($2.52)

Next, assume that the firm earns $200,000 before interest and taxes. Again, the financial results under the two different financing scenarios is shown below.

	Plan 1	Plan 2
EBIT	$200,000	$200,000
Interest (10% × principal)	(40,000)	(10,000)
Earnings before taxes	$160,000	$190,000
Tax expense (40% × EBT)	(64,000)	(76,000)
Net earnings	$96,000	$114,000
Earnings per share	$4.80	$2.28

As you can see from the tables, the more leveraged strategy results in much higher earnings for common stockholders when the firm performs well. However, it results in much larger loss per share when the firm performs poorly. These examples clearly illustrate the major advantages and disadvantages of financial leverage.

2. **Cost of Capital**

A firm's cost of capital is an important concept in discussing financing decisions, especially those involving financing capital projects (long-term financing). If a firm can earn a return on an investment that is greater than its cost of capital, it will increase the value of the firm. The cost of capital for a firm is the weighted-average cost of its debt and equity financing components. The cost of the various components are determined as described below.

a. The **cost of debt** is equal to the interest rate of the loan adjusted for the fact that interest is deductible. Specifically, the cost is calculated as the interest rate times one minus the marginal tax rate. As an example, if a firm's interest rate on a long-term debt is 6% and its marginal tax rate is 30%, the cost of the debt is 4.2% (0.06 × (1.00 - .30)). Remember in considering the cost of new debt, costs of issuing the debt (floatation costs) must be considered. For example, assume the firm issues at face value $20,000,000 of 6% coupon bonds and floatation costs are equal to $1,000,000. The maturity date of the bonds is in 10 years and interest is payable semiannually. To compute the cost of the debt, management should determine the interest rate (internal rate of return) that equates the future interest and principal payments with the present value of the debt. This is equivalent to the bond issue's yield to maturity. To get an accurate yield one would need to use a computer or programmable calculator. However, the following formula may be used to approximate the yield on bonds.

$$YM = \frac{\text{Annual interest payment} + \dfrac{\text{Principal payment} - \text{Bond price}}{\text{Number of years to maturity}}}{0.6 \,(\text{Price of bond}) + 0.4 \,(\text{Principal payment})}$$

$$= \frac{\$1,200,000 + \dfrac{\$20,000,000 - \$19,000,000}{10}}{0.6\,(\$19,000,000) + 0.4\,(\$20,000,000)}$$

$$= 6.70\%$$

b. The **cost of preferred equity** is determined by dividing the preferred dividend amount by the issue price of the stock. For example, if 1,000 shares of $8.00 preferred stock is issued for $102,500, the cost of preferred stock is equal to 7.8% ($8,000/$102,500).

c. The **cost of common equity** is greater than that of debt or preferred equity because common shareholders assume more risk. Thus, they demand a higher return for their investment. Common equity is raised in two ways: (1) by retaining earnings, and (2) by issuing new common stock. Equity raised by issuing stock has a somewhat higher cost due to the flotation costs involved with new stock issues.

3. **The Cost of Existing Common Equity**

    Firms use a number of techniques to estimate the cost of existing common equity including the Capital Asset Pricing Model, the Arbitrage Pricing Model, the Bond-Yield-Plus approach, and the Dividend-Yield-Plus-Growth-Rate approach.

    a. **The Capital Asset Pricing Model (CAPM) Method.** One method of estimating the cost of common equity is by using the Capital Asset Pricing Model (CAPM). The steps involved in estimating CAPM are

    (1) Estimate the risk-free rate of interest, k_{RF}. Generally, firms use the either the US Treasury bond rate or the short-term Treasury bill rate.

    (2) Estimate the stock's beta coefficient, b_i for use as an index of the stock's risk. The beta coefficient measures the correlation between the price volatility of the stock market and the price volatility of an individual firm's stock. If the stock price consistently rises and falls to the same extent as the overall market, the stock's beta would be equal to 1.00. Higher betas indicate more volatility and more risk. Betas are computed and reported by financial reporting services.

    (3) Estimate the expected rate of return on the market, k_M. This is the expected rate of return on stock investments with similar risk. This factor is designed to capture systematic risk of the stock investment.

    (4) Use the following equation to calculate the CAPM which can be used as an estimate of the cost of equity capital.

$$k_S \,(\text{CAPM}) = k_{RF} + (k_M - k_{RF})b_i$$

EXAMPLE: Assume the risk-free interest rate (k_{RF}) is equal to 5%, the expected market rate of interest (k_M) is equal to 10%, and the stock's beta coefficient (b_i) is equal to 0.9 for a given stock; CAPM is calculated as follows:

$$\begin{aligned} k_S \quad &= \quad 5\% + (10\% - 5\%)(0.9) \\ &= \quad 5\% + (5\%)(0.9) \\ &= \quad 5\% + 4.5\% \\ &= \quad 9.5\% \end{aligned}$$

Thus, an estimate of the cost of existing common equity is 9.5%

b. **Arbitrage pricing model.** As indicated previously, investors face two different types of risk for an investment.

- Systematic risk—Market risk that cannot be diversified away.
- Unsystematic risk—The risk of the specific investment that can be eliminated through diversification.

CAPM uses only one variable to capture systematic risk, the market rate of return or k_m. The arbitrage pricing model uses a series of systematic risk factors to develop a value that reflects the multiple dimensions of systematic risk. For example, systematic risk may be affected by future oil prices, exchange rates, interest rates, economic growth, etc. The formulation of the arbitrage pricing model is as follows:

$$r_p = b_1(k_1 - k_{RF}) + b_2(k_2 - k_{RF}) + b_3(k_3 - k_{RF}) \ldots$$

Where

r_p	=	The risk premium on the particular investment. This is the amount that should be added to the risk-free rate to get an estimate of the cost of capital.
k_{rf}	=	The risk-free interest rate.
$b_{1,2,3\ldots}$	=	The betas for the individual risk factors (e.g., exchange rate risk, oil price risk, interest rate risk, etc.).
$k_{1,2,3\ldots}$	=	The market interest rate associated with each of the risk factors.

As you can see, the amounts in the parentheses are equal to the risk premium associated with each of the factors, (i.e., the market rate for each factor minus the risk-free rate).

c. **Bond-yield-plus approach.** The bond-yield-plus approach simply involves adding a risk premium of 3 to 5% to the interest rate on the firm's long-term debt.

d. **Dividend-yield-plus-growth-rate approach.** The dividend-yield-plus-growth-rate (dividend valuation) approach estimates the cost of common equity by considering the investors' expected yield on their investment. Specifically, the following formula is used:

$$k_s = \frac{D_1}{P_0} + \text{Expected } g$$

Where

D_1	=	Next expected dividend
P_0	=	Current stock price
g	=	Growth rate in earnings

EXAMPLE: Assume that a firm's stock sells for $25, its next annual dividend is estimated to be $1 and its expected growth rate is 6%. The cost of existing common equity would be calculated as follows:

$$k_s = \frac{D_1}{P_0} + \text{Expected } g$$

$$k_s = \frac{\$1}{\$25} + 6\%$$

$$= 4\% + 6\%$$

$$= 10\%$$

4. **The Cost of New Common Stock**

If a firm is issuing new common stock, a slightly higher return must be earned. This higher return is necessary to cover the cost of distribution of the new securities (floatation or selling costs). As an example, assume that the cost of capital for existing stockholders is 10% and the current share price of the stock is $25. Also, assume that the cost of floating the new stock issue is $2 per share, the next expected dividend is $1, and the expected growth rate in earnings for the firm is 6%. Using the dividend-yield-plus-growth-rate approach the cost of issuing new stock would be calculated using the following formula:

$$k_s = \frac{D_1}{P_0 - F} + \text{Expected } G$$

Where

D_1	=	Next expected dividend
P_0	=	Current stock price
G	=	Growth rate in earnings
F	=	Flotation cost per share

$$k_s = \frac{D_1}{P_0 - F} + \text{Expected G}$$

$$k_s = \frac{\$1}{\$25 - \$2} + 6\%$$

$$= 10.35\%$$

5. **Evaluating the Cost of Capital—An Example**

Assume that Café Roma operates a chain of coffee shops located in the Northwest. Management has decided to undertake an aggressive expansion program into California and is considering the following three financing options to obtain the $38,000,000 needed.

a. Issuance of $40,000,000 bonds with an 8% coupon rate. After floatation costs the firm would receive approximately $39,000,000, and the effective yield would equal 8.5%.

b. Issuance of $40,000,000 in 6% preferred stock that would yield approximately $38,000,000 after floatation costs.

c. Issuance of 2,000,000 shares of common stock at $20 per share that would yield approximately $38,000,000 after floatation costs.

The current market value of Café Roma's common stock is $20 per share, and the common stock dividend for the year is expected to be $1 per share. Investors are expecting a growth rate in earnings and dividends for the firm of 5%. The firm is subject to an effective tax rate of 40%.

To determine which of the alternatives is least expensive in terms of cost of capital, the cost of each alternative would be calculated as shown below.

Cost of bond issue	=	Interest rate × (1.00 – The effective rate)
	=	8.5% (1.00 – .40)
	=	5.1%

Cost of preferred stock	=	Total dividend amount/Total issuance price
	=	The annual dividend amount/Issue price
	=	(6% × $40,000,000)/$38,000,000
	=	$2,400,000/$38,000,000
	=	6.3%

$$\text{Cost of common stock} = \frac{D_1}{P_0 - F} + \text{Expected G}$$

$$= \frac{\$1}{\$20 - \$1} + 5\%$$

$$= 10.3\%$$

Because total floatation costs are $2,000,000 [(2,000,000 × $20) – $38,000,000], floatation costs per share are $1 ($2,000,000/2,000,000).

6. **Optimal Capital Structure**

a. The optimal capital structure defines the mix of debt, preferred, and common equity that causes the firm's stock price to be maximized. The optimal or target capital structure involves a trade-off between risk and return. Incurring more debt generally leads to higher returns on equity but it also increases the risk borne by the stockholders of the firm. From a theoretical standpoint a firm's optimal capital structure is the one that minimizes the weighted-average cost of capital as shown in the graph below.

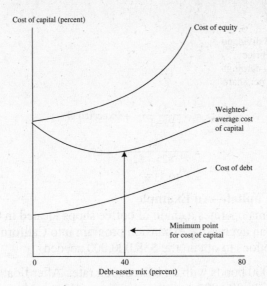

In practice, the following factors generally affect a firm's capital structure strategies:

(1) *Business risk.* The greater the inherent risk of the business the lower the optimal debt to equity ratio.

(2) *Tax position.* A major advantage of debt is the tax deductibility of interest payments. If the firm has a low marginal tax rate, debt becomes less advantageous as a form of financing.

(3) *Financial flexibility.* Financial flexibility is the ability of the firm to raise capital on reasonable terms under adverse conditions. Less debt should be assumed by firms with less financial flexibility.

(4) *Management conservatism or aggressiveness.* A firm's target capital structure will be affected by the risk tolerance of management. More aggressive management may take on more debt.

b. **Weighted-average cost of capital.** In determining the optimum capital structure, management often calculates the firm's weighted-average cost of capital (WACC). This process involves taking the cost of the various types of financing (debt, preferred equity, common equity, etc.) and weighting each by the actual or proposed percentage of total capital. A computation of weighted-average cost of capital is presented below.

Weighted-Average Cost of Capital

	Cost (after tax)	Weight	Weighted Cost
Debt	4.2%	40%	1.68%
Preferred stock	7.8%	10%	0.78%
Common stock	10.0%	50%	5.00%
Weighted-average			7.46%

As illustrated, the weighed-average cost of capital for the firm is 7.46%. Management can now use this model to evaluate various forms of proposed financing options in terms of their effects on the firm's average cost of capital.

> EXAMPLE: Assume that management, with the capital structure described in the table above, is considering calling the preferred stock and issuing 7% debentures. Assume that the costs to call the preferred shares are negligible and the firm's effective tax rate is 30%. What would be the effect on the firm's weighted-average cost of capital?

> The cost of the new debentures is calculated below.

> Cost of new debt   =   7% (1.00 – The effective tax rate)
> =   4.9%

> The following table recalculates the weighted-average cost of capital for the firm.

> **Weighted-Average Cost of Capital**

> | | Cost (after tax) | Weight | Weighted Cost |
> |---|---|---|---|
> | Existing debt | 4.2% | 40% | 1.68% |
> | New debt | 4.9% | 10% | 0.49% |
> | Common stock | 10.0% | 50% | 5.00% |
> | Weighted-average | | | 7.17% |

> By replacing the preferred stock with debt, the firm has reduced its cost of capital to 7.17%

D. Dividend Policy

1. The dividend policy of a firm relates to management's propensity to distribute earnings to stockholders. While it is unclear as to whether the distribution of dividends changes the value of the firm's stock, one of the major influences on dividend policy is where the firm is in its life cycle. The life cycle of a firm has the following four stages:

   a. Development stage
   b. Growth stage
   c. Expansion stage
   d. Maturity stage

   In its first two stages the firm needs to retain its profits to finance development and growth. If any dividends are issued, they tend to be stock dividends. When the firm hits the expansion stage, its need for investment declines and management may decide to issue small cash dividends. Finally, if the firm is successful in its maturity stage, it will tend to begin issuing regular and growing cash dividends.

2. Most people argue that the relevance of dividends is in their *information content*. Dividends **signal** to investors that management believes that the firm had a good year. Increases in dividends tend to increase share prices, while reductions tend to depress share prices. As a result, management is hesitant to decrease dividends.

3. Other factors that affect management's dividend policy include

   • *Legal requirements*—Most states forbid firms to pay dividends that would impair the initial capital contributions to the firm.
   • *Cash position*—Cash must be available to pay the dividends.
   • *Access to capital markets*—If the firm has limited access to capital markets, management is more likely to retain the earnings of the firm.
   • *Desire for control*—Retaining earnings results in less need for management to seek other forms of financing which might come with restrictions on management's actions.
   • *Tax position of shareholders*—Stockholders must pay taxes on dividends and wealthier individuals pay higher taxes.
   • *Clientele effect*—Some firms may have a strategy of attracting investors that require a dividend, such as retired individuals.
   • *Investment opportunities*—Retained earnings should be reinvested in the firm if the firm can earn a return that exceeds what the investor can earn on another investment with similar risk.

4. **Other Types of Dividends**

   a. **Stock dividends** are payments to existing stockholders of a dividend in the form of the firm's own stock. As an example, a 10% stock dividend would involve the issuance of 10% more shares to each stockholder. Such dividends are designed to signal to investors that the firm is performing well, but it does not require the firm to distribute cash.

   b. **Stock splits** are similar to stock dividends but they are generally designed to reduce the stock's price to a target level that will attract more investors. As an example, a 2-for-1 stock split doubles the number of shares outstanding and it would be expected that the price of the stock would drop approximately in half.

E. Share Repurchases

Firms will often repurchase some of their shares to have them available for executive stock options or acquisitions of other firms. However, management of some firms have undertaken other repurchase programs based on the following rationales:

• It sends a positive signal to investors that management believes the stock is undervalued.
• It reduces the number of shares outstanding and thereby increasing earnings per share.
• It provides a temporary floor for the stock.

Many analysts question the validity of these rationales. As an example, the impact on earnings per share is uncertain because investing the cash in operations instead of spending it to repurchase stock might actually increase earnings per share to a greater extent.

F. Financial Markets

Financial markets are markets in which financial assets are traded. Such markets facilitate borrowing and lending, sale of previously issued securities, and sale of newly issued securities. **Primary markets** are markets in which newly issued securities are sold, and **secondary markets** are markets in which previously issued securities are sold. Examples of markets for stocks and debt include the New York Stock Exchange, the US government bond market, and NASDAQ. Futures and option contracts are traded on exchanges such as the Chicago Board of Trade and the Chicago Mercantile Exchange. A rising market is referred to as a **bull market,** and a declining or lethargic market is referred to as a **bear market.** The major players in markets include

1. **Brokers**—Commissioned agents of buyers or sellers.
2. **Dealers**—Similar to brokers in that they match buyers and sellers. However, dealers can and do take positions in the assets and buy and sell their own inventory.
3. **Investment banks**—Assist in the initial sale of newly issued securities by providing advice, underwriting, and sales assistance.
4. **Financial intermediaries**—Financial institutions that borrow one form of financial asset (e.g., a savings deposit) and distribute the asset in another form (e.g., a commercial loan).

MERGERS

A. Business mergers involve many of the considerations involved in the acquisition of any asset or group of assets. However, there are additional considerations.

1. Firms often acquire other firms due to **synergies**; the two firms can perform more effectively together than separately. Synergies arise from operating or financial economies, as well as managerial efficiency.
2. Management may also acquire a firm for diversification or tax considerations, or to take advantage of a bargain purchase.

B. Types of Mergers

1. **Horizontal merger**—When a firm combines with another in the same line of business.
2. **Vertical merger**—When a firm combines with another firm in the same supply chain (e.g., a combination of a manufacturer with one of its suppliers.
3. **Congeneric merger**—When the merging firms are somewhat related but not enough to make it a vertical or horizontal merger.
4. **Conglomerate merger**—When the firms are completely unrelated. These types of mergers provide the greatest degree of diversification.

C. Several methodologies are used to value **target firms,** including

1. **Discounted cash flow analysis**—Application of capital budgeting techniques to an entire firm rather than a single investment.

   a. Two key items are needed for this valuation method

      (1) A set of pro forma financial statements are developed that project the incremental cash flows that are expected to result from the merger.
      (2) A discount rate, or cost of capital, to apply to the projected cash flows. The appropriate discount rate is the cost of equity rather than an overall cost of capital. The discount rate used must reflect the underlying riskiness of the target firm's operations (future cash flows).

   b. A risk analysis should be performed with the cash flows (e.g., sensitivity analysis, scenario analysis, etc.).

2. **Market multiple method**—Applies a market-determined multiple to some measure of earnings such as net income or earnings per share.

D. An acquisition may be accomplished through a purchase of the assets of the firm or a purchase of a controlling interest in the firm's stock. The acquisition may be for cash or the acquiring firms stock.

E. Goodwill is recognized as the difference between the fair market value of the identifiable assets and the total purchase price of the firm. Goodwill remains on the financial statements of the combined firms unless it becomes impaired.

MULTIPLE-CHOICE QUESTIONS (1-137)

1. Which of the following is not a function of financial management?
   a. Financing.
   b. Risk-management.
   c. Internal control.
   d. Capital budgeting.

2. The inventory conversion period is calculated as follows:

   a. $\dfrac{\text{Average inventory}}{\text{Sales per day}}$

   b. $\dfrac{\text{Year-end inventory}}{\text{Sales per day}}$

   c. $\dfrac{\text{Average inventory}}{\text{Accounts receivable}}$

   d. $\dfrac{\text{Year-end inventory}}{\text{Cost of sales}}$

3. The payables deferral period is calculated as follows:

   a. $\dfrac{\text{Average payables}}{\text{Sales per day}}$

   b. $\dfrac{\text{Beginning payables}}{\text{Sales per day}}$

   c. $\dfrac{\text{Average payables}}{\text{Purchases per day}}$

   d. $\dfrac{\text{Average payables}}{\text{Cost of goods sold}}$

4. All of the following statements in regard to working capital are correct **except:
   a. Current liabilities are an important source of financing for many small firms.
   b. Profitability varies inversely with liquidity.
   c. The hedging approach to financing involves matching maturities of debt with specific financing needs.
   d. Financing permanent inventory buildup with long-term debt is an example of an aggressive working capital policy.

**5. Determining the appropriate level of working capital for a firm requires
   a. Evaluating the risks associated with various levels of fixed assets and the types of debt used to finance these assets.
   b. Changing the capital structure and dividend policy of the firm.
   c. Maintaining short-term debt at the lowest possible level because it is generally more expensive than long-term debt.
   d. Offsetting the benefit of current assets and current liabilities against the probability of technical insolvency.

6. Which of the following actions is likely to reduce the length of a firm's cash conversion cycle?
   a. Adopting a new inventory system that reduces the inventory conversion period.
   b. Adopting a new inventory system that increases the inventory conversion period.
   c. Increasing the average days sales outstanding on its accounts receivable.
   d. Reducing the amount of time the firm takes to pay its suppliers.

7. Eagle Sporting Goods has $5 million in inventory and $2 million in accounts receivable. Its average daily sales are $100,000. The firm's payables deferral period is 30 days. What is the length of the firm's cash conversion period?
   a. 100 days.
   b. 60 days.
   c. 50 days.
   d. 40 days.

8. Jones Company has $5,000,000 of average inventory and sales of $30,000,000. Using a 365-day year, calculate the firm's inventory conversion period.
   a. 30.25 days.
   b. 60.83 days.
   c. 45.00 days.
   d. 72.44 days.

9. The length of time between the acquisition of inventory and payment for it is called the
   a. Operating cycle.
   b. Inventory conversion period.
   c. Accounts receivable period.
   d. Accounts payable deferral period.

10. If everything else remains constant and a firm increases its cash conversion cycle, its profitability will likely
   a. Increase.
   b. Increase if earnings are positive.
   c. Decrease.
   d. Not be affected.

*11. An organization offers its customers credit terms of 5/10 net 20. One-third of the customers take the cash discount and the remaining customers pay on day 20. On average, 20 units are sold per day, priced at $10,000 each. The rate of sales is uniform throughout the year. Using a 360-day year, the organization has days' sales outstanding in accounts receivable, to the nearest full day, of
   a. 13 days.
   b. 15 days.
   c. 17 days.
   d. 20 days.

**12. Troy Toys is a retailer operating in several cities. The individual store managers deposit daily collections at a local bank in a noninterest-bearing checking account. Twice per week, the local bank issues a depository transfer check (DTC) to the central bank at headquarters. The controller of the company is considering using a wire transfer instead. The additional cost of each transfer would be $25; collections would be accelerated by two days; and the annual interest rate paid by the central bank is 7.2% (0.02% per day). At what amount of dollars transferred would it be economically feasible to use a wire transfer instead of the DTC? Assume a 360-day year.
   a. It would never be economically feasible.
   b. $125,000 or above.
   c. Any amount greater than $173.
   d. Any amount greater than $62,500.

---

* *CIA adapted*
** *CMA adapted*

13. Which of the following is true about electronic funds transfer from a cash flow standpoint?
    a. It is always beneficial from a cash flow standpoint.
    b. It is never beneficial from a cash flow standpoint.
    c. It is beneficial from a cash receipts standpoint but not from a cash disbursements standpoint.
    d. It is beneficial from a cash disbursements standpoint but not from a cash receipts standpoint.

14. Management of Radker Corp. is considering a lockbox system. The bank will charge $10,000 annually for the service, which will save the firm approximately $5,000 in processing costs. The lockbox system will reduce the float for cash receipts by three days. Assuming that the average daily receipts are equal to $100,000, and short-term interest costs are 5%, calculate the benefit or loss from adopting the lockbox system.
    a. $5,000 loss.
    b. $10,000 loss.
    c. $10,000 benefit.
    d. $5,000 benefit.

15. Which of the following is true about a firm's float?
    a. A firm strives to minimize the float for both cash receipts and cash disbursements.
    b. A firm strives to maximize the float for both cash receipts and cash disbursements.
    c. A firm strives to maximize the float for cash receipts and minimize the float for cash disbursements.
    d. A firm strives to maximize the float for cash disbursements and minimize the float for cash receipts.

16. A firm is evaluating whether to establish a concentration banking system. The bank will charge $5,000 per year for maintenance and transfer fees. The firm estimates that the float will be reduced by two days if the concentration banking is put into place. Assuming that average daily receipts are $115,000 and short-term interest rates are 4%, what decision should the firm make regarding the concentration banking system?
    a. Do not establish the concentration banking system because the net cost is $5,000.
    b. Do not establish the concentration banking system because the net cost is $21,000.
    c. Establish the concentration banking system because the net benefit is $115,000.
    d. Establish the concentration banking system because the net benefit is $4,200.

17. A firm is evaluating whether to establish a lockbox system. The bank will charge $30,000 per year for the lockbox and the firm will save approximately $8,000 in internal processing costs. The firm estimates that the float will be reduced by three days if the lockbox system is put into place. Assuming that average daily cash receipts are $350,000 and short-term interest rates are 4%, what decision should the firm make regarding the lockbox system?
    a. Do not establish the lockbox system because the net cost is $30,000.
    b. Do not establish the lockbox system because the net cost is $22,000.

    c. Establish the lockbox system because the net benefit is $12,000.
    d. Establish the lockbox system because the net benefit is $20,000.

18. An organization has an opportunity to establish a zero balance account system using four different regional banks. The total amount of the maintenance and transfer fees is estimated to be $6,000 per annum. The organization believes that it will increase the float on its operating disbursements by an average of four days, and its cost of short-term funds is 4.5%. Assuming the organization estimates its average daily operating disbursements to be $40,000 what decision should the organization make regarding this opportunity?
    a. Do not establish the zero balance account system because it results in estimated additional net costs of $6,000.
    b. Do not establish the zero balance account system because it results in estimated additional net costs of $1,200.
    c. Establish the zero balance account system because it results in estimated net savings of $1,200.
    d. Establish the zero balance account system because it results in estimated net savings of $7,200.

**19. A working capital technique that increases the payable float and therefore delays the outflow of cash is
    a. Concentration banking.
    b. A draft.
    c. Electronic Data Interchange (EDI).
    d. A lockbox system.

**20. Newman Products has received proposals from several banks to establish a lockbox system to speed up receipts. Newman receives an average of 700 checks per day averaging $1,800 each, and its cost of short-term funds is 7% per year. Assuming that all proposals will produce equivalent processing results and using a 360-day year, which one of the following proposals is optimal for Newman?
    a. A $0.50 fee per check.
    b. A flat fee of $125,000 per year.
    c. A fee of 0.03% of the amount collected.
    d. A compensating balance of $1,750,000.

**21. A firm has daily cash receipts of $100,000. A bank has offered to reduce the collection time on the firm's deposits by two days for a monthly fee of $500. If money market rates are expected to average 6% during the year, the net annual benefit (loss) from having this service is
    a. $ 3,000
    b. $12,000
    c. $0
    d. $ 6,000

*22. A minimum checking account balance that a firm must maintain with a commercial bank is a
    a. Transaction balance.
    b. Compensating balance.
    c. Precautionary balance.
    d. Speculative balance.

**23. A firm has daily receipts of $100,000. A bank has offered to reduce the collection time on the firm's deposits by two days for a monthly fee of $500. If money market rates are expected to average 6% during the year, the net annual benefit from having this service is

a. $0
b. $ 3,000
c. $ 6,000
d. $12,000

**24. Cleveland Masks and Costumes Inc. (CMC) has a majority of its customers located in the states of California and Nevada. Keystone National Bank, a major west coast bank, has agreed to provide a lockbox system to CMC at a fixed fee of $50,000 per year and a variable fee of $.50 for each payment processed by the bank. On average, CMC receives 50 payments per day, each averaging $20,000. With the lockbox system, the company's collection float will decrease by 2 days. The annual interest rate on money market securities is 6%. If CMC makes use of the lockbox system, what would be the net benefit to the company? Use 365 days per year.

a. $ 51,750
b. $ 60,875
c. $111,750
d. $120,875

25. The most important considerations with respect to short-term investments are

a. Return and value.
b. Risk and liquidity.
c. Return and risk.
d. Growth and value.

**26. All of the following are alternative marketable securities suitable for investment except:

a. US treasury bills.
b. Eurodollars.
c. Commercial paper.
d. Convertible bonds.

27. Which of the following investments generally pay the highest return?

a. Money market accounts.
b. Treasury bills.
c. Treasury notes.
d. Commercial paper.

**28. Which one of the following is not a characteristic of a negotiable certificate of deposit? Negotiable certificates of deposit

a. Have a secondary market for investors.
b. Are regulated by the Federal Reserve System.
c. Are usually sold in denominations of a minimum of $100,000.
d. Have yields considerably greater that bankers' acceptances and commercial paper.

29. Which changes in costs are most conducive to switching from a traditional inventory ordering system to a just-in-time ordering system?

	Cost per purchase order	Inventory unit carrying costs
a.	Increasing	Increasing
b.	Decreasing	Increasing
c.	Decreasing	Decreasing
d.	Increasing	Decreasing

30. To determine the inventory reorder point, calculations normally include the

a. Ordering cost.
b. Carrying cost.
c. Average daily usage.
d. Economic order quantity.

31. Which of the following is **not a correct comparison of a just-in-time system with a traditional system?

	Traditional	Just-in-time
a.	Longer lead times	Shorter lead times
b.	Inventory is an asset	Inventory is a liability
c.	Some scrap tolerated	Zero defects desired
d.	Lot size based on immediate need	Lot size based on formulas

32. The benefits of a just-in-time system for raw materials usually include

a. Elimination of non-value-added operations.
b. Increase in the number of suppliers, thereby ensuring competitive bidding.
c. Maximization of the standard delivery quantity, thereby lessening the paperwork for each delivery.
d. Decrease in the number of deliveries required to maintain production.

33. Bell Co. changed from a traditional manufacturing philosophy to a just-in-time philosophy. What are the expected effects of this change on Bell's inventory turnover and inventory as a percentage of total assets reported on Bell's balance sheet?

	Inventory turnover	Inventory percentage
a.	Decrease	Decrease
b.	Decrease	Increase
c.	Increase	Decrease
d.	Increase	Increase

34. As a consequence of finding a more dependable supplier, Dee Co. reduced its safety stock of raw materials by 80%. What is the effect of this safety stock reduction on Dee's economic order quantity?

a. 80% decrease.
b. 64% decrease.
c. 20% increase.
d. No effect.

35. The economic order quantity formula assumes that

a. Periodic demand for the good is known.
b. Carrying costs per unit vary with quantity ordered.
c. Costs of placing an order vary with quantity ordered.
d. Purchase costs per unit differ due to quantity discounts.

36. Ral Co. sells 20,000 radios evenly throughout the year. The cost of carrying one unit in inventory for one year is $8, and the purchase order cost per order is $32. What is the economic order quantity?

a. 625
b. 400
c. 283
d. 200

37. The following information pertains to material X that is used by Sage Co.:

---

* *CIA adapted*
** *CMA adapted*

Annual usage in units	20,000
Working days per year	250
Safety stock in units	800
Normal lead time in working days	30

Units of material X will be required evenly throughout the year. The order point is

- a. 800
- b. 1,600
- c. 2,400
- d. 3,200

38. Firms that maintain very low or no inventory levels
- a. Have higher ordering costs.
- b. Have higher carrying costs.
- c. Have higher ordering and carrying costs.
- d. Have lower ordering and carrying costs.

**39. An example of a carrying cost is
- a. Disruption of production schedules.
- b. Quantity discounts lost.
- c. Handling costs.
- d. Obsolescence.

*40. Which of the following is a characteristic of just-in-time (JIT) inventory management systems?
- a. JIT users determine the optimal level of safety stocks.
- b. JIT is applicable only to large companies.
- c. JIT does not really increase overall economic efficiency because it merely shifts inventory levels further up the supply chain.
- d. JIT relies heavily on good quality materials.

*41. To evaluate the efficiency of purchase transactions, management decides to calculate the economic order quantity for a sample of the company's products. To calculate the economic order quantity, management would need data for all of the following **except:**
- a. The volume of product sales.
- b. The purchase prices of the products.
- c. The fixed cost of ordering products.
- d. The volume of products in inventory.

Items 42 and 43 are based on the following information:

Ethan, Inc. has seasonal demand for its products and management is considering whether level production or seasonal production should be implemented. The firms' short-term interest cost is 8%, and management has developed the following information to make the decision:

	Alternative 1 Level production	Alternative 2 Seasonal production
Average inventory	$2,000,000	$1,500,000
Production costs	$6,000,000	$6,050,000

42. Which alternative should be accepted and how much is saved over the other alternative?
- a. Alternative 1 with $500,000 in savings.
- b. Alternative 2 with $50,000 in savings.
- c. Alternative 2 with $10,000 in savings.
- d. Alternative 1 with $10,000 in savings.

43. At what rate of short-term interest rate would the two alternatives have the same cost?
- a. 6%
- b. 9%

- c. 10%
- d. 12%

**44. The amount of inventory that a company would tend to hold in stock would increase as the
- a. Sales level falls to a permanently lower level.
- b. Cost of carrying inventory decreases.
- c. Variability of sales decreases.
- d. Cost of running out of stock decreases.

*45. An appropriate technique for planning and controlling manufacturing inventories, such as raw materials, components, and subassemblies, whose demand depends on the level of production, is
- a. Materials requirements planning.
- b. Regression analysis.
- c. Capital budgeting.
- d. Linear programming.

46. The procedures followed by the firm for ensuring payment of its accounts receivables are called its
- a. Discount policy.
- b. Credit policy.
- c. Collection policy.
- d. Payables policy.

Items 47 and 48 are based on the following information:

Effective September 1, a company initiates seasonal dating as a component of its credit policy, allowing wholesale customers to make purchases early but not requiring payment until the retail selling season begins. Sales occur as follows:

Date of sale	Quantity sold
September 1	300 units
October 1	100 units
November 1	100 units
December 1	150 units
January 1	50 units

- Each unit has a selling price of $10, regardless of the date of sale.
- The terms of sale are 2/10 net 30, January 1 dating.
- All sales are on credit.
- All customers take the discount and abide by the terms of the discount policy.
- All customers take advantage of the new seasonal dating policy.
- The peak selling season for all customers is mid-November to late December.

47. For the selling firm, which of the following is **not** an expected advantage to initiating seasonal dating?
- a. Reduced storage costs.
- b. Reduced credit costs.
- c. Attractive credit terms for customers.
- d. Reduced uncertainty about sales volume.

48. For sales after the initiation of the seasonal dating policy on September 1, total collections on or before January 11 will be
- a. $0
- b. $6,370
- c. $6,860
- d. $7,000

49. Which of the following describes the appropriate formula for days' sales outstanding?

---

*   *CIA adapted*
**   *CMA adapted*

a. $\dfrac{\text{Average receivables}}{\text{Sales per day}}$

b. $\dfrac{\text{Receivables balance}}{\text{Sales per day}}$

c. $\dfrac{\text{Sales}}{\text{Average receivables}}$

d. $\dfrac{\text{Receivables balance}}{\text{Total sales}}$

50. Which of the following describes a firm's credit criteria?

    a. The length of time a buyer is given to pay for his/her purchases.

    b. The percentage of discount allowed for early payment.

    c. The diligence to collect slow-paying accounts.

    d. The required financial strength of acceptable customers.

Items 51 and 52 are based on the following information:

A company plans to tighten its credit policy. The new policy will decrease the average number of days in collection from 75 to 50 days and reduce the ratio of credit sales to total revenue from 70 to 60%. The company estimates that projected sales would be 5% less if the proposed new credit policy were implemented. The firm's short-term interest cost is 10%.

**51. Projected sales for the coming year are $50 million. Calculate the dollar impact on accounts receivable of this proposed change in credit policy. Assume a 360-day year.

    a. $ 3,819,445 decrease.

    b. $ 6,500,000 decrease.

    c. $ 3,333,334 decrease.

    d. $18,749,778 increase.

**52. What effect would the implementation of this new credit policy have on income before taxes?

    a. $2,500,000 decrease.

    b. $2,166,667 decrease.

    c. $ 83,334 increase.

    d. $ 33,334 increase.

**53. The sales manager at Ryan Company feels confident that if the credit policy at Ryan's were changed, sales would increase ancd consequently, the company would utilize excess capacity. The two credit proposals being considered are as follows:

	Proposal A	Proposal B
Increase in sales	$500,000	$600,000
Contribution margin	20%	20%
Bad debt percentage	5%	5%
Increase in operating profits	$ 75,000	$ 90,000
Desired return on sales	15%	15%

Currently, payment terms are net 30. The proposed payment terms for Proposal A and Proposal B are net 45 and net 90, respectively. An analysis to compare these two proposals for the change in credit policy would include all of the following factors except the

    a. Cost of funds for Ryan.

    b. Current bad debt experience.

    c. Impact on the current customer base of extending terms to only certain customers.

    d. Bank loan covenants on days' sales outstanding.

**54. A company enters into an agreement with a firm who will factor the company's accounts receivable. The factor agrees to buy the company's receivables, which average $100,000 per month and have an average collection period of 30 days. The factor will advance up to 80% of the face value of receivables at an annual rate of 10% and charge a fee of 2% on all receivables purchased. The controller of the company estimates that the company would save $18,000 in collection expenses over the year. Fees and interest are not deducted in advance. Assuming a 360-day year, what is the annual cost of financing?

    a. 10.0%

    b. 14.0%

    c. 16.0%

    d. 17.5%

**55. A company with $4.8 million in credit sales per year plans to relax its credit standards, projecting that this will increase credit sales by $720,000. The company's average collection period for new customers is expected to be 75 days, and the payment behavior of the existing customers is not expected to change. Variable costs are 80% of sales. The firm's opportunity cost is 20% before taxes. Assuming a 360-day year, what is the company's benefit (loss) from the planned change in credit terms?

    a. $0

    b. $ 28,800

    c. $144,000

    d. $120,000

56. Gild Company has been offered credit terms of 3/10, net 30. Using a 365-day year, what is the nominal cost of not taking advantage of the discount if the firm pays on the 35th day after the purchase?

    a. 14.2%

    b. 32.2%

    c. 37.6%

    d. 45.2%

57. Newton Corporation is offered trade credit terms of 3/15, net 45. The firm does not take advantage of the discount, and it pays the account after 67 days. Using a 365-day year, what is the nominal annual cost of not taking the discount?

    a. 18.2%

    b. 21.71%

    c. 23.48%

    d. 26.45%

58. Assume that Williams Corp is financed with a heavy reliance on short-term debt and short-term rates have increased. How do these facts impact the interest expense, net income, and financial risk for Williams Corp?

	Interest expense	Net income	Financial risk
a.	Decreases	Decreases	Decreases
b.	Increases	Decreases	Increase
c.	Decrease	Increases	Increases
d.	Increases	Decreases	Decreases

59. If a firm is offered credit terms of 2/10, net 30 on its purchases. Sound cash management practices would mean that the firm would pay the account on which of the following days?

    a. Day 2 and 30.

---

  * CIA adapted

** CMA adapted

b.   Day 2 and 10.
c.   Day 10.
d.   Day 30.

60. The following forms of short-term borrowings are available to a firm:

- Floating lien
- Factoring
- Revolving credit
- Chattel mortgages
- Bankers' acceptances
- Lines of credit
- Commercial paper

The forms of short-term borrowing that are unsecured credit are

a.   Floating lien, revolving credit, chattel mortgage, and commercial paper.
b.   Factoring, chattel mortgage, bankers' acceptances, and line of credit.
c.   Floating lien, chattel mortgage, bankers' acceptances, and line of credit.
d.   Revolving credit, bankers' acceptances, line of credit, and commercial paper.

*61.** A company obtaining short-term financing with trade credit will pay a higher percentage financing cost, everything else being equal, when

a.   The discount percentage is lower.
b.   The items purchased have a higher price.
c.   The items purchased have a lower price.
d.   The supplier offers a longer discount period.

62. If a firm borrows $500,000 at 10% and is required to maintain $50,000 as a minimum compensating balance at the bank, what is the effective interest rate on the loan?

a.   10.0%
b.   11.1%
c.   9.1%
d.   12.2%

63. If a retailer's terms of trade are 3/10, net 45 with a particular supplier, what is the cost on an annual basis of not taking the discount? Assume a 360-day year.

a.   24.00%
b.   37.11%
c.   36.00%
d.   31.81%

64. Which of the following is not related to loans involving inventory?

a.   Factoring.
b.   Blanket liens.
c.   Trust receipts.
d.   Warehousing.

65. The London Interbank Offered Rate (LIBOR) represents an example of a

a.   Risk-free rate.
b.   Nominal rate.
c.   Credit risk adjusted rate.
d.   Long-term rate

66. An advantage of the use of long-term debt as opposed to short-term debt to finance current assets is

a.   It decreases the risk of the firm.
b.   It generally is less costly than short-term debt.
c.   It generally places fewer restrictions on the firm.
d.   It is easy to repay.

67. The chief financial officer of Smith Glass Inc. follows the policy of matching the maturity of assets with the maturity of financing. The implications of this policy include all of the following **except** that

a.   The seasonal expansion of cash, receivables, and inventory should be financed by short-term debt such as vendor payables and bank debt.
b.   The minimum level of cash, receivables, and inventory required to stay in business can be considered permanent, and financed with long-term debt or equity.
c.   Cash, receivables, and inventory should be financed with long-term debt or equity.
d.   Long-term assets, like plant and equipment, should be financed with long-term debt or equity.

68. Which form of asset financing involves the public offering of debt collateralized by a firm's accounts receivables?

a.   Trust receipts.
b.   Warehousing.
c.   Blanket inventory liens.
d.   Securitization of assets.

69. Hagar Company's bank requires a compensating balance of 20% on a $100,000 loan. If the stated interest on the loan is 7%, what is the effective cost of the loan?

a.   5.83%
b.   7.00%
c.   8.40%
d.   8.75%

Items 70 and 71 are based on the following information:

CyberAge Outlet, a relatively new store, is a café that offers customers the opportunity to browse the Internet or play computer games at their tables while they drink coffee. The customer pays a fee based on the amount of time spent signed on to the computer. The store also sells books, tee shirts, and computer accessories. CyberAge has been paying all of its bills on the last day of the payment period, thus forfeiting all supplier discounts. Shown below are data on CyberAge's two major vendors, including average monthly purchases and credit terms.

Vendor	Average monthly purchases	Credit terms
Web Master	$25,000	2/10, net 30
Softidee	50,000	5/10, net 90

70. Assuming a 360-day year and that CyberAge continues paying on the last day of the credit period, the company's weighted-average annual interest rate for trade credit (ignoring the effects of compounding) for these two vendors is

a.   27.0%
b.   25.2%
c.   28.0%
d.   30.2%

71. Should CyberAge use trade credit and continue paying at the end of the credit period?

---

a. Yes, if the cost of alternative short-term financing is less.

b. Yes, if the firm's weighted-average cost of capital is equal to its weighted-average cost of trade credit.

c. No, if the cost of alternative long-term financing is greater.

d. Yes, if the cost of alternative short-term financing is greater.

72. With respect to the use of commercial paper by an industrial firm, which one of the following statements is **most** likely to be true?

a. The commercial paper is issued through a bank.

b. The commercial paper has a maturity of 60-270 days.

c. The commercial paper is secured by the issuer's assets.

d. The commercial paper issuer is a small company.

73. A company obtained a short-term bank loan of $250,000 at an annual interest rate of 6%. As a condition of the loan, the company is required to maintain a compensating balance of $50,000 in its checking account. The company's checking account earns interest at an annual rate of 2%. Ordinarily, the company maintains a balance of $25,000 in its checking account for transaction purposes. What is the effective interest rate of the loan?

a. 6.44%

b. 7.11%

c. 5.80%

d. 6.66%

*74. A manufacturing firm wants to obtain a short-term loan and has approached several lending institutions. All of the potential lenders are offering the same nominal interest rate, but the terms of the loans vary. Which of the following combinations of loan terms will be most attractive for the borrowing firm?

a. Simple interest, no compensating balance.

b. Discount interest, no compensating balance.

c. Simple interest, 20% compensating balance required.

d. Discount interest, 20% compensating balance required.

75. Elan Corporation is considering borrowing $100,000 from a bank for one year at a stated interest rate of 9%. What is the effective interest rate to Elan if this borrowing is in the form of a discount note?

a. 8.10%

b. 9.00%

c. 9.81%

d. 9.89%

76. The Red Company has a revolving line of credit of $300,000 with a one-year maturity. The terms call for a 6% interest rate and a 1/2% commitment fee on the unused portion of the line of credit. The average loan balance during the year was $100,000. The annual cost of this financing arrangement is

a. $6,000

b. $6,500

c. $7,000

d. $7,500

77. Which of the following financial instruments generally provides the largest source of short-term credit for small firms?

a. Installment loans.

b. Commercial paper.

c. Trade credit.

d. Mortgage bonds.

78. The prime rate is the

a. Size of the commitment fee on a commercial bank loan.

b. Effective cost of a commercial bank loan.

c. Rate charged on business loans to borrowers with high credit ratings.

d. Rate at which a bank borrows from the Federal Reserve central bank.

79. A compensating balance

a. Compensates a financial institution for services rendered by providing it with deposits of funds.

b. Is used to compensate for possible losses on a marketable securities portfolio.

c. Is a level of inventory held to compensate for variations in usage rate and lead time.

d. Is an amount paid by financial institutions to compensate large depositors.

80. On January 1, Scott Corporation received a $300,000 line of credit at an interest rate of 12% from Main Street Bank and drew down the entire amount on February 1. The line of credit agreement requires that an amount equal to 15% of the loan be deposited into a compensating balance account. What is the effective annual cost of credit for this loan arrangement?

a. 11.00%

b. 12.00%

c. 12.94%

d. 14.12%

81. Which of the following statements is correct when comparing bond-financing alternatives?

a. A bond with a call provision typically has a lower yield to maturity than a similar bond without a call provision.

b. A convertible bond must be converted to common stock prior to its maturity.

c. A call provision is generally considered detrimental to the investor.

d. A call premium requires the investor to pay an amount greater than par at the time of purchase.

82. Which of the following are characteristics of Eurobonds?

a. Are always denominated in Eurodollars.

b. Are always sold in some country other than the one in whose currency the bond is denominated.

c. Are sold outside the country of the borrower but are denominated in the currency of the county in which the issue is sold.

d. Are generally issued as registered bonds.

83. At the inception of an operating lease how should the leased asset be accounted for on the lessee financial statements?

a. The present value of the future lease payments is recorded as an asset on the balance sheet.
b. The total amount of the lease payments is recorded as an asset on the balance sheet.
c. An asset is not recorded. The lease payments are expensed as rent as they are incurred.
d. The future value of the lease payments is recorded as an asset on the balance sheet.

84. Capital and operating leases differ in that the lessee
   a. Obtains use of the asset only under a capital lease.
   b. Is using the lease as a source of financing only under an operating lease.
   c. Receives title to the asset in a capital lease.
   d. Capitalizes the net investment in the lease.

85. Which of the following is an advantage of debt financing?
   a. Interest and principal obligations must be paid regardless of the economic position of the firm.
   b. Debt agreements contain covenants.
   c. The obligation is generally fixed in terms of interest and principal payments.
   d. Excessive debt increases the risk of equity holders and therefore depresses share prices.

86. All of the following are advantages of debt financing except
   a. Interest is tax deductible.
   b. The use of debt will assist in lowering the firm's cost of capital.
   c. In periods of inflation, debt is paid back with dollars that are worth less than the ones borrowed.
   d. The acquisition of debt decreases stockholders' risk.

87. If an investor is concerned about interest rate risk, the investor should consider investing in
   a. Serial bonds.
   b. Sinking fund bonds.
   c. Convertible bonds.
   d. Floating rate bonds.

88. Bonds in which the principal amount is paid as a series of installments over the life of the bond issue are called
   a. Serial bonds.
   b. Sinking fund bonds.
   c. Convertible bonds.
   d. Callable bonds.

89. Wilson Corporation issued bonds two years ago. If the _____ interest rate _____, the market value of the bond will decrease.
   a. Coupon; increases.
   b. Coupon; decreases.
   c. Market; increases.
   d. Market; decreases.

**90. DQZ Telecom is considering a project for the coming year that will cost $50 million. DQZ plans to use the following combination of debt and equity to finance the investment:

- Issue $15 million of 20-year bonds at a price of 101, with a coupon rate of 8%, and flotation costs of 2% of par.
- Use $35 million of funds generated from earnings.

The equity market is expected to earn 12%. US Treasury bonds are currently yielding 5%. The beta coefficient for DQZ is estimated to be .60. DQZ is subject to an effective corporate income tax rate of 40%.

The before-tax cost of DQZ's planned debt financing, net of flotation costs, in the first year is
   a. 11.80%
   b. 8.08%
   c. 10.00%
   d. 7.92%

**91. The best reason corporations issue Eurobonds rather than domestic bonds is that
   a. These bonds are denominated in the currency of the country in which they are issued.
   b. These bonds are normally a less expensive form of financing because of the absence of government regulation.
   c. Foreign buyers more readily accept the issues of both large and small US corporations than do domestic investors.
   d. Eurobonds carry no foreign exchange risk.

92. Which of the following provisions is generally considered detrimental to the investor?
   a. Conversion.
   b. Redeemable.
   c. Callable.
   d. Serial maturity.

93. Which of the following is not an advantage of leasing as a form of financing?
   a. Up front costs may be less.
   b. The provisions of the agreement may be less stringent than for other debt agreements.
   c. The dollar cost.
   d. The firm may be able to lease the asset when it does not have the credit capacity to purchase the asset.

94. Nerco has a bond issue that matures in fifteen years. Recently, the company's bond rating has gone from B to Baa. How would this affect the market price of the bonds?
   a. Increase.
   b. Decrease.
   c. Remain the same.
   d. The effect cannot be predicted.

Items 95 through 97 are based on the following information:

Watco, Inc. issued $1,000,000 in 8% bonds, maturing in ten years and paying interest semiannually. The bonds were issued at face value.

95. What can you assume about the interest rates at the time the bonds were issued?
   a. The market rate for this bond was about 8%.
   b. The nominal rate of interest was about 8%.
   c. The coupon rate on the bond includes no premium for credit risk.
   d. The risk-free interest rate is about 6%.

96. If the market rate of interest for this type of bond increases to 9%, which of the following is true?
   a.   The market value of Watco's bond will increase.
   b.   The market value of Watco's bond will decrease.
   c.   The effect will depend on the change in the LIBOR rate.
   d.   The effect cannot be predicted.

97. Assume that one of Watco's bonds with $1,000 face is currently selling for $950. What is the current yield on the bond?
   a.   8.00%
   b.   9.00%
   c.   7.56%
   d.   8.42%

98. The market for outstanding, listed common stock is called the
   a.   Primary market.
   b.   New issue market.
   c.   Over-the-counter market.
   d.   Secondary market.

99. In capital markets, the primary market is concerned with
   a.   New issues of bonds and stock securities.
   b.   Exchanges of existing bond and stock securities.
   c.   The sale of forward or future commodities contracts.
   d.   New issues of bond and stock securities and exchanges of existing bond and stock securities.

*100. Which of the following is usually **not** a feature of cumulative preferred stock?
   a.   Has priority over common stock with regard to earnings.
   b.   Has priority over common stock with regard to assets.
   c.   Has voting rights.
   d.   Has the right to receive dividends in arrears before common stock dividends can be paid.

101. Which of the following is not an advantage of going public?
   a.   Access to capital.
   b.   Compliance.
   c.   Use of stock options.
   d.   Liquidity for owners' investments.

Items 102 and 103 are based on the following information:

The following information is available for Rothenberg, Inc.:

Balance sheet

Current assets	$ 500,000
Property, plant, and equipment	4,000,000
Total assets	$4,500,000
Current liabilities	$ 30,000
Long-term debt	2,500,000
Common stock	200,000
Retained earnings	1,770,000
Total liabilities and stockholders' equity	$4,500,000

Budget income information	*100,000 units*	*105,000 units*
Sales	$3,000,000	$3,150,000
Expenses	(2,800,000)	(2,850,000)
Operating income (EBIT)	$ 200,000	$ 300,000
Earnings per share (EPS)	$0.20	$1.20

102. What is Rothenberg's degree of operating leverage?
   a.   1/5
   b.   10
   c.   5
   d.   2/3

103. What is the degree of financial leverage for Rothenberg, Inc.?
   a.   10
   b.   5
   c.   1/6
   d.   1/10

104. Which of the following is an advantage of equity financing in comparison to debt financing?
   a.   Issuance costs are greater than for debt.
   b.   Ownership is given up with respect to the issuance of common stock.
   c.   Dividends are not tax deductible by the corporation whereas interest is tax deductible.
   d.   The company has no firm obligation to pay dividends to common shareholders.

105. Assume that Company A and Company B are alike in all respects except that Company A utilizes more debt financing and less equity financing than does Company B. Which of the following statements is true?
   a.   Company A has more net earnings variability than Company B.
   b.   Company A has more operating earnings variability than Company B.
   c.   Company A has less operating earnings variability than Company B.
   d.   Company A has less financial leverage than Company B.

106. Which of the following is not a source of capital used to finance long-term projects?
   a.   Common stock.
   b.   Long-term debt.
   c.   Preferred stock.
   d.   Line of credit.

107. Which of the following factors generally does not impact management's capital structure strategy?
   a.   Business risk.
   b.   Tax position.
   c.   Management aggressiveness.
   d.   Expected return on assets.

**108. A firm with a higher degree of operating leverage when compared to the industry average implies that the
   a.   Firm has higher variable costs.
   b.   Firm's profits are more sensitive to changes in sales volume.
   c.   Firm is more profitable.
   d.   Firm is less risky.

*109. When a company increases its degree of financial leverage
   a.   The equity beta of the company falls.
   b.   The systematic risk of the company falls.

---

* *CIA adapted*
** *CMA adapted*

c. The unsystematic risk of the company falls.
d. The standard deviation of returns on the equity of the company rises.

*110. A company has made the decision to finance next year's capital projects through debt rather than additional equity. The benchmark cost of capital for these projects should be
a. The before-tax cost of new-debt financing.
b. The after-tax cost of debt financing.
c. The cost of equity financing.
d. The weighted-average cost of capital.

Items 111 and 112 are based on the following information:

Management of Russell Corporation is considering the following two potential capital structures for a newly acquired business.

Alternative 1
Long-term debt, 6% interest $3,000,000
Common equity $3,000,000
Cost of common equity, 10%
Marginal tax rate, 15%

Alternative 2
Long-term debt, 7% interest $5,000,000
Common equity $1,000,000
Cost of common equity, 12%
Marginal tax rate, 15%

111. Which of the following statements is not true if management decides to accept Alternative 1?
a. Alternative 1 is the more conservative capital structure.
b. Alternative 1 provides the greatest amount of financial leverage.
c. Net income will be less variable under Alternative 1.
d. Total interest expense will be less under Alternative 1.

112. Which of the alternatives has the lowest weighted-average cost of capital and how much is the differential?
a. Alternative 1 by 1.5%
b. Alternative 2 by 0.59%
c. Alternative 1 by 0.167%
d. The alternatives have equal weighted-average cost of capital.

113. Management of Kelly, Inc. uses CAPM to calculate the estimated cost of common equity. Which of the following would reduce the firm's estimated cost of common equity?
a. A reduction in the risk-free rate.
b. An increase in the firm's beta.
c. An increase in expected inflation.
d. An increase in the risk-free interest rate.

**114. In general, it is more expensive for a company to finance with equity than with debt because
a. Long-term bonds have a maturity date and must, therefore, be repaid in the future.
b. Investors are exposed to greater risk with equity capital.
c. The interest on debt is a legal obligation.

d. Equity capital is in greater demand than debt capital.

115. Which of the following is not a characteristic of the capital asset pricing model for estimating the cost of equity?
a. The model is simple to understand and implement.
b. The model can be applied to all firms.
c. The model does not rely on any dividend assumptions or growth of dividends.
d. It is based upon the stock's actual market price.

116. Management of Terra Corp. is attempting to estimate the firm's cost of equity capital. Assuming that the firm has a constant growth rate of 5%, a forecasted dividend of $2.11, and a stock price of $23.12, what is the estimated cost of common equity using the dividend-yield-plus-growth approach?
a. 9.1%
b. 14.1%
c. 15.6%
d. 12.3%

117. If nominal interest rates increase substantially but expected future earnings and dividend growth for a firm over the long run are not expected to change, the firm's stock price will
a. Increase.
b. Decrease.
c. Stay constant.
d. Change, but in no determinable direction.

118. Assume that two companies, Company X and Company Y, are alike in all respects, except the market value of the outstanding common shares of Company X is greater than the market value of Company Y shares. This may indicate that
a. Company X's investors expect higher dividend growth than Company Y's investors.
b. Company X's investors expect lower dividend growth than Company Y's investors.
c. Company X's investors have longer expected holding periods than Company Y's investors.
d. Company X's investors have shorter expected holding periods than Company Y's investors.

119. Which of the following methods explicitly recognizes a firm's risk when determining the estimated cost of equity?
a. Capital asset pricing model.
b. Dividend-yield-plus-growth model.
c. Bond-yield-plus model.
d. Return on equity.

120. Assume a firm is expected to pay a dividend of $5.00 per share this year. The firm along with the dividend is expected to grow at a rate of 6%. If the current market price of the stock is $60 per share, what is the estimated cost of equity?
a. 8.3%
b. 6.0%
c. 14.3%
d. 12.0%

121. The bond-yield-plus approach to estimating the cost of common equity involves adding a risk premium of 3% to 5% to the firm's
a. Cost of short-term debt.
b. Cost of long-term debt.

---

*   *CIA adapted*
** *CMA adapted*

c. Return on assets.
d. Return on equity.

**122. In practice, dividends
    a. Usually exhibit greater stability than earnings.
    b. Fluctuate more widely than earnings.
    c. Tend to be a lower percentage of earnings for mature firms.
    d. Are usually changed every year to reflect earnings changes.

Items 123 and 124 are based on the following information:

Martin Corporation
STATEMENT OF FINANCIAL POSITION
December 31, 2009
(Dollars in millions)

Assets	
Current assets	$ 75
Plant and equipment	250
Total assets	$325
Liabilities and shareholders' equity	
Current liabilities	$ 46
Long-term debt (12%)	64
Common equity:	
Common stock, $1 par	10
Additional paid in capital	100
Retained earnings	105
Total liabilities and shareholders' equity	$325

Additional data

- The long-term debt was originally issued at par ($1,000/bond) and is currently trading at $1,250 per bond.
- Martin Corporation can now issue debt at 150 basis points over US Treasury bonds.
- The current risk-free rate (US Treasury bonds) is 7%.
- Martin's common stock is currently selling at $32 per share.
- The expected market return is currently 15%.
- The beta value for Martin is 1.25.
- Martin's effective corporate income tax rate is 40%

**123. Martin Corporation's current net cost of debt is
    a. 5.5%
    b. 7.0%
    c. 5.1%
    d. 8.5%

**124. Using the Capital Asset Pricing Model (CAPM), Martin Corporation's current cost of common equity is
    a. 8.75%
    b. 10.00%
    c. 15.00%
    d. 17.00%

Items 125 and 126 are based on the following information:

DQZ Telecom is considering a project for the coming year that will cost $50 million. DQZ plans to use the following combination of debt and equity to finance the investment.

- Issue $15 million of 20-year bonds at a price of 101, with a coupon rate of 8%, and flotation costs of 2% of par.
- Use $35 million of funds generated from earnings.

The equity market is expected to earn 12%. US Treasury bonds are currently yielding 5%. The beta coefficient for DQZ is estimated to be .60. DQZ is subject to an effective corporate income tax rate of 40%.

**125. Assume that the after-tax costs of debt is 7% and the cost of equity is 12%. Determine the weighted-average cost of capital.
    a. 10.50%
    b. 8.50%
    c. 9.50%
    d. 6.30%

**126. The Capital Asset Pricing Model (CAPM) computes the expected return on a security by adding the risk-free rate of return to the incremental yield of the expected market return that is adjusted by the company's beta. Compute DQZ's expected rate of return.
    a. 9.20%
    b. 12.20%
    c. 7.20%
    d. 12.00%

*127. When calculating the cost of capital, the cost assigned to retained earnings should be
    a. Zero.
    b. Lower than the cost of external common equity.
    c. Equal to the cost of external common equity.
    d. Higher than the cost of external common equity.

128. According to the Capital Asset Pricing Model (CAPM), the relevant risk of a security is its
    a. Company-specific risk.
    b. Diversifiable risk.
    c. Systematic risk.
    d. Total risk.

**129. Hi-Tech Inc. has determined that it can minimize its weighted-average cost of capital (WACC) by using a debt/equity ratio of 2/3. If the firm's cost of debt is 9% before taxes, the cost of equity is estimated to be 12% before taxes, and the tax rate is 40%, what is the firm's WACC?
    a. 6.48%
    b. 7.92%
    c. 9.36%
    d. 10.80%

Items 130 through 131 are based on the following information:

A new company requires $1 million of financing and is considering two arrangements as shown in the table below.

Arrangement	Amount of equity raised	Amount of debt financing	Before-tax cost of debt
#1	$700,000	$300,000	8% per annum
#2	$300,000	$700,000	10% per annum

In the first year of operations, the company is expected to have sales revenues of $500,000, cost of sales of $200,000, and general and administrative expenses of $100,000. The tax rate is 30%, and there are no other items on the income statement. All earnings are paid out as dividends at year-end.

130. If the cost of equity were 12%, then the weighted-average cost of capital under Arrangement #1, to the nearest full percentage point, would be
    a. 8%
    b. 10%

---

* CIA adapted
** CMA adapted

    c.   11%
    d.   12%

131. Which of the following statements comparing the two financing arrangements is true?
    a.   The company will have a higher expected gross margin under Arrangement #1.
    b.   The company will have a higher degree of operating leverage under Arrangement #2.
    c.   The company will have higher interest expense under Arrangement #1.
    d.   The company will have higher expected tax expense under Arrangement #1.

132. The return on equity will be <List A> and the debt ratio will be <List B> under Arrangement #2, as compared with Arrangement #1.

	List A	List B
a.	Higher	Higher
b.	Higher	Lower
c.	Lower	Higher
d.	Lower	Lower

*133. A parent company sold a subsidiary to a group of managers of the subsidiary. The purchasing group invested $1 million and borrowed $49 million against the assets of the subsidiary. This is an example of a
    a.   Spin-off.
    b.   Leveraged buyout.
    c.   Joint venture.
    d.   Liquidation.

**134. The acquisition of a retail shoe store by a shoe manufacturer is an example of
    a.   Vertical integration.
    b.   A conglomerate.
    c.   Market extension.
    d.   Horizontal integration.

**135. A horizontal merger is a merger between
    a.   Two or more firms from different and unrelated markets.
    b.   Two or more firms at different stages of the production process.
    c.   A producer and its supplier.
    d.   Two or more firms in the same market.

136. A soft drink producer acquiring a bottle manufacturer is an example of a
    a.   Horizontal merger.
    b.   Vertical merger.
    c.   Congeneric merger.
    d.   Conglomerate merger.

137. A shoe manufacturing firm acquiring a brokerage house is an example of a
    a.   Horizontal merger.
    b.   Vertical merger.
    c.   Congeneric merger.
    d.   Conglomerate merger.

---

*   CIA adapted
** CMA adapted

MULTIPLE-CHOICE ANSWERS

1. c	__ __	30. c	__ __	59. c	__ __	88. a	__ __	117. b	__ __
2. a	__ __	31. d	__ __	60. d	__ __	89. c	__ __	118. a	__ __
3. c	__ __	32. a	__ __	61. d	__ __	90. b	__ __	119. a	__ __
4. d	__ __	33. c	__ __	62. b	__ __	91. b	__ __	120. c	__ __
5. d	__ __	34. d	__ __	63. d	__ __	92. c	__ __	121. b	__ __
6. a	__ __	35. a	__ __	64. a	__ __	93. c	__ __	122. a	__ __
7. d	__ __	36. b	__ __	65. b	__ __	94. a	__ __	123. c	__ __
8. b	__ __	37. d	__ __	66. a	__ __	95. a	__ __	124. d	__ __
9. d	__ __	38. a	__ __	67. c	__ __	96. b	__ __	125. a	__ __
10. c	__ __	39. d	__ __	68. d	__ __	97. d	__ __	126. a	__ __
11. c	__ __	40. d	__ __	69. d	__ __	98. d	__ __	127. b	__ __
12. d	__ __	41. d	__ __	70. b	__ __	99. a	__ __	128. c	__ __
13. c	__ __	42. d	__ __	71. d	__ __	100. c	__ __	129. c	__ __
14. c	__ __	43. c	__ __	72. b	__ __	101. b	__ __	130. b	__ __
15. d	__ __	44. b	__ __	73. a	__ __	102. b	__ __	131. d	__ __
16. d	__ __	45. a	__ __	74. a	__ __	103. a	__ __	132. a	__ __
17. c	__ __	46. c	__ __	75. d	__ __	104. d	__ __	133. b	__ __
18. c	__ __	47. b	__ __	76. c	__ __	105. a	__ __	134. a	__ __
19. b	__ __	48. c	__ __	77. c	__ __	106. d	__ __	135. d	__ __
20. d	__ __	49. b	__ __	78. c	__ __	107. d	__ __	136. b	__ __
21. d	__ __	50. d	__ __	79. a	__ __	108. b	__ __	137. d	__ __
22. b	__ __	51. c	__ __	80. d	__ __	109. d	__ __		
23. c	__ __	52. b	__ __	81. c	__ __	110. d	__ __		
24. b	__ __	53. b	__ __	82. b	__ __	111. b	__ __		
25. b	__ __	54. d	__ __	83. c	__ __	112. b	__ __		
26. d	__ __	55. d	__ __	84. d	__ __	113. a	__ __		
27. d	__ __	56. d	__ __	85. c	__ __	114. b	__ __		
28. d	__ __	57. b	__ __	86. d	__ __	115. d	__ __	1st: __/137 = __%
29. b	__ __	58. b	__ __	87. d	__ __	116. b	__ __	2nd: __/137 = __%

MULTIPLE-CHOICE ANSWER EXPLANATIONS

Working Capital Management

1.   (c)   The requirement is to identify the function that is not related to financial management. The correct answer is (c) because internal control is a function of the controller's office. Answers (a), (b), and (d) are incorrect because the functions of financial management include: financing, capital, budgeting, financial management, corporate governance, and risk management.

2.   (a)   The requirement is to identify the formula for the inventory conversion period. Answer (a) is correct because the inventory conversion period describes the average time required to convert materials into finished goods and sell those goods. Answers (b), (c), and (d) are all incorrect versions of the formula.

3.   (c)   The requirement is to identify the formula for the calculation of the payables deferral period. Answer (c) is correct because the payables deferral period is equal to the average length of time between the purchase of materials and the payment of cash for them. Answers (a), (b), and (d) are all incorrect because they illustrate inaccurate versions of the formula.

4.   (d)   The requirement is to determine the false statement regarding working capital management. Answer (d) is correct because financing permanent inventory buildup with long-term debt is an example of a conservative working capital policy. Answers (a), (b), and (c) are all accurate statements about working capital management.

5.   (d)   The requirement is to identify the factor considered in determining the appropriate level of working capital. Answer (d) is correct because the main reason to retain working capital is to meet the firm's financial obligations. Therefore, the amount is determined by offsetting the benefit of current assets and current liabilities against the probability of technical insolvency. Answer (a) is incorrect because it is a consideration regarding long-term financing. Answer (b) is incorrect because it is a consideration regarding capital structure. Answer (c) is incorrect because short-term debt is generally less expensive than long-term debt.

6.   (a)   The requirement is to identify the impact of decisions on the cash conversion cycle. The cash conversion cycle is equal to the Inventory conversion period + Receivables collection period – Payables deferral period. Answer (a) is correct because the impact of a decreased inventory conversion period is a reduction in the cash conversion cycle. Answers (b), (c), and (d) are incorrect because these actions would increase the length of a firm's cash conversion cycle.

7.   (d)   The requirement is to calculate the cash conversion cycle. The cash conversion period is calculated as the Inventory conversion period + Receivables collection period – Payables deferral period. Answer (d) is correct because the inventory conversion period is $5,000,000/$100,000 = 50 days, and the receivable conversion period is $2,000,000/$100,000 = 20 days. Therefore, the cash conversion cycle is equal to 50 days + 20 days – 30 days = 40 days. Answer (a) is incorrect because is erroneously adds the payable deferral period.

8.   (b)   The requirement is to calculate the inventory conversion period. The inventory conversion period is calculated as average inventory/(sales per day). Answer (b) is correct because $5,000,000/($30,000,000/365) = 60.83 days.

9.   (d)   The requirement is to identify the definition of the payables deferral period. Answer (d) is correct because the payables deferral period is the average length of time between the purchase of materials and the payment of cash for them. Answer (a) is incorrect because the operating cycle is the period of time elapsing between the acquisition of goods and services involved in the manufacturing process and the final collection of cash from sale of the products. Answer (b) is incorrect because the inventory cycle is the average time required to convert materials into finished goods and sell those goods. Answer (c) is incorrect because the accounts receivable period is the length of time required to collect accounts receivable.

10.   (c)   The requirement is to identify the impact of the length of the cash conversion cycle on a firm's profitability. Answer (c) is correct because the longer the cash conversion cycle the greater the amount of time from when a firm pays its suppliers to the time it ultimately collects receivables. The greater the time frame the more likely the firm will have to borrow funds and incur interest expense which reduces profitability. Answers (a), (b), and (d) are incorrect because the incurrence of interest will reduce profitability.

11.   (c)   The requirement is to calculate the number of days' sales outstanding. Answer (c) is correct. One-third of the customers take advantage of the 5% cash discount and pay on day ten. The remaining two-thirds of the customers pay on day 20. Average days' sales outstanding is calculated as

Days' sales outstanding = (1/3) (10 days) + (2/3) (20 days) = 17 days

Answer (a) is incorrect because this inappropriately weights the two different types of customers. Answer (b) is incorrect because this uses a simple average of days rather than a weighted-average. Answer (d) is incorrect because this solution uses the 20-day collection period for customers not taking the cash discount as the days' sales outstanding, rather than the average days for payment by all customers.

Cash Management

12.   (d)   The requirement is to determine the effect of changing from using a depository transfer check to using a wire transfer. The change is feasible if the interest savings offsets the increased costs. For a fee of $25, the firm gets two extra days' interest on the average transfer amount. By dividing the $25 fee by the interest rate for two days, .04% (2 days × .02%), we get $62,500. Therefore, management should make the change if the average transfer is expected to be greater than $62,500. Answer (a) is incorrect because it is a calculating assuming there is only a one-day decrease in float.

13.   (c)   The requirement is to consider the cash flow implications of electronic funds transfer. Answer (c) is correct because electronic funds transfer takes the float out of both the cash receipts and disbursements processes. It is beneficial to take the float out of the cash receipts process but not the cash disbursements process.

14.   (c)   The requirement is to determine the benefit or loss from establishing the lockbox system. The firm saves money if the interest savings is greater than the increased cost of processing cash receipts. The increased cost of processing cash receipts is equal to $5,000 ($10,000 bank charge – $5,000 cost savings). The interest savings is measured by multiplying the increase in average funds by the short-term interest rate. The firm will have use of an additional $300,000 ($100,000 × 3 days) in average funds. Therefore, the interest savings is equal to $15,000 ($300,000 × 5%), and the overall benefit is equal to $10,000 ($15,000 – $5,000). Answer (a) is incorrect because it ignores the interest savings. Answer (b) is incorrect because it only considers the bank charge.

15.   (d)   The requirement is to describe how firms attempt to manage float. Float is the time that elapses relating to mailing, processing, and clearing checks. A firm strives to minimize its cash receipts float to get use of the receipts as soon as possible, and to maximize its cash disbursement float to get use of the funds for as long as possible. Therefore, the correct answer is (d).

16.   (d)   The requirement is to calculate the financial cost/benefit of establishing a concentration banking arrangement. The cost savings in interest from establishing the arrangement is equal to $9,200 [($115,000 × 2 days) × 4%]. Therefore, answer (d) is correct because implementing the concentration banking arrangement would result in a net savings of $4,200 ($9,200 – $5,000). Answer (a) is incorrect because it only considers the $5,000 cost. Answer (c) is incorrect because it considers the $115,000 in daily cash receipts the benefit.

17.   (d)   The requirement is to calculate the financial cost/benefit of establishing a lockbox system. Answer (d) is correct because the solution is found by comparing the cost in fees to the benefits in terms of reduced interest costs. Since the float is reduced by three days the firm gets the use of $1,050,000 ($350,000 × 3 days) in additional funds that results in interest savings of $42,000 ($1,050,000 × 4%). Therefore, the net benefit is equal to $20,000 ($42,000 – $22,000). Answer (a) is incorrect because it only considers the bank fee. Answer (b) is incorrect because it only considers the net change in processing costs.

18.   (c)   The requirement is to calculate the financial costs/benefit of establishing a zero balance account system. Answer (c) is correct because the solution is found by comparing the cost in fees to the benefit in terms of reduced interest costs. Since the float is reduced by four days then the firm gets the use of $160,000 ($40,000 × 4 days) additional funds which results in interest savings of $7,200 ($160,000 × 4.5%). The $1,200 savings is the excess of the interest savings of $7,200 over the costs of $6,000. Answer (a) is incorrect because it only considerers the cost without considering the interest savings. Answer (b) is incorrect because it is calculated by considering the $7,200 interest savings as a cost and the $6,000 in maintenance and transfer fees as a benefit. Answer (d) is incorrect because it only considers the interest savings.

19.   (b)   The requirement is to identify the working capital technique that increases the payable float. Answer (b) is the correct answer because payment by draft (e.g., a check) is slower than other methods of payment such as electronic cash transfers. Answers (a) and (d) are incorrect because they are techniques designed to speed the processing of cash receipts. Answer (c) is incorrect because EDI involves processing transactions electronically. This would speed up the payment of payables.

20.   (d)   The requirement is to determine the optimal agreement for a lockbox system. The number of checks issued during the year is determined by multiplying 700 times 360 days, which results in a total of 252,000 checks. The total amount of collections is equal to $453,600,000 (252,000 checks × $1,800 per check). Answer (d) is correct because it results in the lowest cost of $122,500 ($1,750,000 × 7%), which is the cost of maintaining the compensating balance. Answer (a) is incorrect because it results in a cost of $126,000 ($.50 × 252,000 checks). Answer (b) is incorrect because it results in a cost of $125,000. Answer (c) is incorrect because it results in a fee of $136,080 (3% × $453,600,000).

21.   (d)   The requirement is to calculate the annual benefit from accepting the bank's proposal. Answer (d) is correct because the net benefit from the reduction of the cash receipts float is $12,000 [($100,000 × 2) × 6%] minus the annual service fee, $6,000 ($500 × 12 months), which is equal to $6,000. Answer (b) is incorrect because it ignores the bank service charge. Answer (c) is incorrect because it assumes only a one-day reduction in float.

22.   (b)   The requirement is to identify the term used to describe a required minimum checking account balance. Answer (b) is correct because a compensating balance is a minimum balance required by the bank to compensate the bank for services. Answer (a) is incorrect because transactions balance is the amount of funds the firm needs on deposit to conduct day-to-day transactions. Answer (c) is incorrect because this precautionary balance represents the balance available for emergencies. Answer (d) is incorrect because this speculative balance represents the balance available for bargain purchases.

23.   (c)   The requirement is to calculate the net benefit from accepting the bank's proposal. The correct answer is (c) because the annual benefit is $6,000 which is equal to the interest income $12,000 ($100,000 × 2 days × 6%) – $6,000 ($500 × 12) cost.

24.   (b)   The requirement is to calculate the net benefit of using the lockbox system. Answer (b) is correct because the net benefit is equal to $60,875, which is equal to the interest savings of $120,000 ($20,000 average payment × 50 payments × 2 days × 6%) minus the cost of the service of $59,125 [$50,000 + (50 payments per day × 365 days × $0.50)].

Marketable Securities Management

25.   (b)   The requirement is to identify the most important consideration with respect to short-tem investments. Answer (b) is correct because short-term investments must be available to convert to cash when needed. Therefore, risk and liquidity are the most important considerations. Answers (a), (c), and (d) are incorrect because they are important considerations with respect to long-term investments.

26.   (d)   The requirement is to identify the security that is not suitable as a marketable investment. Answer (d) is correct because convertible bonds are long-term investments

that have more risk than securities that are typically used for short-term investment. The primary considerations regarding short-term investments are liquidity and safety. Answers (a), (b), and (c) are all appropriate as marketable investments. They are liquid and have a low degree of risk.

27.   (d)   The requirement is to identify the instrument with the highest return. Answer (d) is correct because commercial paper is issued by a corporation and, therefore, has more risk than Treasury notes, Treasury bonds, or money market accounts.

28.   (d)   The requirement is to identify the item that is not a characteristic of a negotiable certificate of deposit. The correct answer is (d) because negotiable certificates of deposit have lower yields than banker's acceptances and commercial paper—they have less risk. Answer (a) is incorrect because negotiable certificates of deposit do have a secondary market. Answer (b) is incorrect because negotiable certificates of deposit are regulated by the Federal Reserve System. Answer (c) is incorrect because they are usually sold in denominations of a minimum of $100,000.

Inventory Management

29.   (b)   In a just-in-time (JIT) purchasing system, orders are placed such that delivery of raw materials occurs just as they are needed for production. This system requires the placement of more frequent, smaller orders and ideally eliminates inventories. Conversely, in a traditional system large orders are placed less frequently and extra inventory is carried to avoid stockouts and the resulting production delays during order lead time. Certain cost changes would encourage managers to switch to a JIT system. One is **decreased** cost per purchase order, which would increase the attractiveness of placing the many more orders required. Another is **increased** inventory unit carrying costs, which would make the elimination of inventories desirable.

30.   (c)   Calculation of the reorder point includes consideration of the average daily usage, average delivery time, and stock-out costs. Answer (a) is incorrect because ordering costs are included in determining the economic order quantity but not the reorder point. Answer (b) is incorrect because carrying cost is considered in determining the economic order quantity but not the reorder point. Answer (d) is incorrect because the economic order quantity is not considered in determining the reorder point.

31.   (d)   The requirement is to identify the item that involves an incorrect comparison of a just-in-time system and a traditional system. Answer (d) is correct because in a just-in-time system the lot size is based on immediate need; a traditional system bases lot size on formulas. Answers (a), (b), and (c) are all incorrect because they express correct comparisons of just-in-time and traditional systems.

32.   (a)   The goal of a just-in-time system is to identify and eliminate all non-value-added activities. One of the major features of a just-in-time system is a decrease in the number of suppliers to build strong relations and ensure quality goods. In a just-in-time system raw material is purchased only as it is needed for production, thereby eliminating the need for costly storage. In a just-in-time system, vendors make more frequent deliveries of small quantities of materials that are placed into production immediately upon receipt.

32. **(c)** The purpose of a "just-in-time" production system is to decrease the size of production runs while increasing the number of lots processed during the year. This production philosophy requires that inventory be delivered as it is needed, rather than held in large quantities. Inventory turnover is computed as

$$\frac{\text{Cost of goods sold}}{\text{Average inventory}}$$

As average inventory decreases, inventory turnover increases. As average inventory levels decrease, inventory as a percentage of total assets will also decrease.

34. **(d)** The requirement is to determine the effect of a decrease in safety stock on Dee Co.'s economic order quantity (EOQ). The EOQ represents the optimal quantity of inventory to be ordered based on demand and various inventory costs. The formula for computing EOQ is

$$EOQ = \sqrt{\frac{2aD}{k}}, \text{ where}$$

D = Demand (in units) for a specified time period
a = Ordering costs per purchase order
k = Cost of carrying one unit in inventory for the specified time period

Safety stock is a buffer of excess inventory held to guard against stockouts. Safety stock is usually a multiple of demand and has no effect on a company's EOQ.

35. **(a)** The economic order quantity (EOQ) formula was developed on the basis of the following assumptions:

1. Demand occurs at a constant rate throughout the year and is known with certainty.
2. Lead-time on the receipt of orders is constant.
3. The entire quantity ordered is received at one time.
4. The unit costs of the items ordered are constant; thus, there can be no quantity discounts.
5. There are no limitations on the size of the inventory.

Answer (a) is correct because it is assumption 1. Answer (b) is incorrect because it contradicts assumption 5. Answers (c) and (d) are incorrect because they are the opposite of assumption 4.

36. **(b)** The requirement is to calculate the economic order quantity (EOQ). The EOQ formula is

$$EOQ = \sqrt{\frac{2aD}{k}}$$

In the above equation, a = cost of placing one order, D = annual demand in units, and k = cost of carrying one unit in inventory for one year. Substituting the given information, the equation becomes

$$EOQ = \sqrt{\frac{(2)(32)(20,000)}{8}} = \sqrt{160,000} = 400 \text{ units}$$

37. **(d)** The requirement is to determine the order point for material X. When safety stock is maintained, the order point is computed as follows:

$$\frac{\text{Daily}}{\text{Demand}} \times \frac{\text{Lead time}}{\text{in days}} + \frac{\text{Safety}}{\text{stock}}$$

Daily demand is eighty units (20,000 units ÷ 250 days). Therefore, the order point is 3,200 units [(80 × 30) + 800].

38. **(a)** The requirement is to identify the impact of inventory levels on costs. Maintaining a low level of inventory requires that many smaller orders of inventory be made in order to satisfy customer demand. Answer (a) is correct because each order incurs ordering cost and as the quantity of orders increases the ordering costs will also increase. Answer (b) is incorrect because carrying costs are higher with a higher level of inventory. Answer (c) is incorrect because although the ordering costs are higher the carrying costs are lower. Answer (d) is incorrect because the ordering costs would be higher.

39. **(d)** The requirement is to identify an inventory carrying cost. The correct answer is (d). Part of the cost of holding inventory is the cost of obsolescence. Answer (a) is an example of a stockout cost. Answer (a) is a stock-out cost. Answer (b) and (c) are examples of ordering costs.

40. **(d)** The requirement is to identify the characteristic of JIT inventory systems. Answer (d) is correct because JIT systems rely on quality materials; otherwise production shutdowns will occur because no extra materials are available. Answer (a) is incorrect because there are no safety stocks in JIT systems. Answer (b) is incorrect because JIT is applicable to all size corporations. Answer (c) is incorrect because JIT generally is applied all along the supply chain.

41. **(d)** The requirement is to identify the factor not used in the economic order quantity formula. Answer (d) is correct because the volume of products in inventory is not a component of the economic order quantity formula. Answers (a), (b), and (c) are incorrect because they are all components of the EOQ formula.

42. **(d)** The requirement is to determine the cost savings from selecting one of the production alternatives. Under the level production alternative, the firm would incur an additional $40,000 [($1,500,000 − $2,000,000) × 8%] in inventory holding costs but it would save $50,000 in production costs. Therefore, answer (d) is the correct answer. Alternative 1 results in $10,000 ($50,000 − $40,000) in savings over Alternative 2.

43. **(c)** The requirement is to calculate the short-term interest rate that would cause the two alternatives to have equal costs. The cost of implementing Alternative 2 is the $50,000 in additional production costs. When the inventory holding costs related to Alternative 1 equals that amount the costs are equal. By dividing the $50,000 by the $500,000 in additional average inventory, we get 10% ($50,000 ÷ $500,000). Therefore, the correct answer is (c) because at a 10% interest rate the cost of holding the additional inventory under Alternative 1 is equal to the additional production costs under Alternative 2.

44. **(b)** The requirement is to determine the factor that would increase inventory levels. In answering this question, you should consider the components of the EOQ formula. The correct answer is (b) because if the cost of holding inventory decreases it would enable the firm to carry more inventory. Answer (a) is incorrect because a decrease in sales would result in a decrease in the required level of inventory. Answer (c) is incorrect because a decrease in sales variability decreases the required level of inventory. Answer (d) is incorrect because a decrease in the cost of running out of stock decreases the required level of inventory.

45. (a) The requirement is to identify the technique used to plan and control manufacturing inventories. Answer (a) is correct because materials requirements planning is an inventory planning technique. Answer (b) is incorrect because regression analysis is a technique used to estimate the relationship between variables. Answer (c) is incorrect because capital budgeting is a technique used to evaluate investments in capital assets. Answer (d) is incorrect because linear programming is a technique used to determine the optimal decision when resources are constrained.

Receivables Management

46. (c) The requirement is to identify the definition of collection policy. Answer (c) is correct because a firm's collection policy is the diligence used to collect slow paying accounts. Answer (a) is incorrect because the discount policy is the policy regarding the percentage discount given for early payment. Answer (b) is incorrect because the credit policy is a firm's requirements for customers in order to grant them credit. Answer (d) is incorrect because the payables policy is unrelated to accounts receivable.

47. (b) The requirement is to identify which item is not an advantage of initiating seasonal dating. Seasonal dating is a procedure for inducing customers to buy early by not requiring payment until the customers' selling season, regardless of when the merchandise is shipped. Under seasonal dating the selling firm incurs higher credit costs, as customers take longer to pay. Therefore, answer (b) is correct because this is not an advantage of seasonal dating. Answer (a) is incorrect because under seasonal dating, customers buy earlier and the selling firm incurs lower storage costs. This is an advantage of seasonal dating. Answer (c) is incorrect because providing attractive credit terms for customers is an advantage of a seasonal dating policy. Answer (d) is incorrect because reduced uncertainty about sales volume is an advantage of a seasonal dating policy.

48. (c) The requirement is to calculate the total collections on or before January 11. Answer (c) is correct because if all customers take advantage of seasonal dating and all customers take the discount, then collections on or before January 11 will be

= (Number of units sold) (Unit selling price) (1 – Discount percentage)
= (700 units) × $10 (1 – .02) × .98 = $6,860

Answer (a) is incorrect because all customers take the discount and abide by the terms of the discount policy, so they will pay on or before January 11. Answer (b) is incorrect because this solution omits the collection of the January 1 sales revenue. Answer (d) is incorrect because this solution does not take the discount into account.

49. (b) The requirement is to identify the formula for days' sales in accounts receivable. Answer (b) is correct because days' sales in receivables provides an overall measure of the accumulation of receivables. It is calculated by dividing the balance of receivables by sales per day. Answers (a), (c), and (d) are incorrect because they do not accurately illustrate the formula.

50. (d) The requirement is to describe a firm's credit criteria. Answer (d) is correct because the credit criteria are the policies used to decide whether a customer should be extended credit. Answer (a) is incorrect because it describes the credit period. Answer (b) is incorrect because it de-

scribes a portion of the discount policy. Answer (c) is incorrect because it describes the collection policy.

51. (c) The requirement is to calculate impact of this change in policy on accounts receivable. Under the existing policy, sales are equal to $50,000,000, 70% of which are on credit. Therefore, the average accounts receivable balance is equal to $7,291,667 [($35,000,000 credit sales ÷ 360 days) × 75 days]. Under the new policy credit sales are estimated to be $28,500,000 [($50,000,000 × 95%) × 60%]. Accordingly, the average accounts receivable balance under the new policy is estimated to be $3,958,333 [($28,500,000 credit sales ÷ 360) × 50 days]. Answer (c) is correct because the change in accounts receivable balance is estimated to be a decrease of $3,333,334 ($7,291,667 – $3,958,333).

52. (b) The requirement is to calculate the effect of the new policy on net income before taxes. Answer (b) is correct because the decrease in operating income is equal to $2,166,667 [$2,500,000 loss in sales – ($3,333,334 × 10%) interest savings]. Answer (a) is incorrect because it only considers the loss in sales. Answer (c) is incorrect because it treats the entire $3,333,334 change in average receivables as a benefit.

53. (b) The requirement is to determine the factor that is not considered in determining whether to change credit policy. Answer (b) is correct because the current bad debt experience is irrelevant to the decision. Management should consider only those factors that change based upon the alternative selected. Answer (a) is incorrect because the cost of funds is relevant to the decision. Answer (c) is incorrect because if there is any impact on the current customer base, this factor should be considered. Answer (d) is incorrect because the impact on bank loan covenants is obviously relevant.

54. (d) The requirement is to calculate the annual cost of the financing. Answer (d) is correct because the total amount paid to the factor would be ($100,000 × 80%) × 10% + ($100,000 × 12) × 2% = $32,000. The net cost is equal to $14,000 ($32,000 – $18,000 cost savings). Therefore, the annual interest cost is equal to $14,000/$80,000 = 17.5%.

55. (d) The requirement is to calculate the benefit or loss from changing credit policy. Answer (d) is correct because the benefit is equal to the contribution margin received from the additional sales minus the cost of having incremental funds tied up in accounts receivable. The benefit from an increase in sales is equal to $144,000 ($720,000 sales × 20% contribution margin). The interest opportunity cost is equal to 75 days' interest on the variable portion of sales, or ($720,000 × 80%)/360 × 75 × 20% interest = $24,000. Therefore, the net benefit is equal to $120,000 ($144,000 – $24,000).

Financing Current Assets

56. (d) The requirement is to calculate the cost of not taking a trade discount. The cost is calculated with the following formula:

$$\frac{\text{Discount percent}}{100\% - \text{Discount percent}} \times \frac{365 \text{ days}}{\text{Total pay period} - \text{Discount period}}$$

Answer (d) is correct because the discount percentage is 3%, the total pay period is 35 days, and the discount period is 15 days. Therefore, the nominal cost is calculated as follows:

$$\frac{3\%}{100\% - 3\%} \times \frac{365 \text{ days}}{35 \text{ days} - 10 \text{ days}} = 45.2\%$$

57. (b) The requirement is to calculate the cost of not taking a trade discount. The cost is calculated with the following formula:

$$\frac{\text{Discount percent}}{100\% - \text{Discount percent}} \times \frac{365 \text{ days}}{\text{Total pay period} - \text{Discount period}}$$

Answer (b) is correct because the discount percentage is 3%, the total pay period is 67 days, and the discount period is 15 days. Therefore, the nominal cost is calculated as follows:

$$\frac{3\%}{100\% - 3\%} \times \frac{365 \text{ days}}{67 \text{ days} - 15 \text{ days}} = 21.71\%$$

58. (b) The requirement is to analyze the impact upon a firm of rising short-term interest rates. A heavy reliance on short-term debt means that interest expense and the related net income will be variable and this increases the financial risk of the firm. Answer (b) is correct because if short-term interest rates increase then interest expense will increase which will cause a related decrease in net income.

59. (c) The requirement is to evaluate credit terms to made sound cash management decisions. Answer (c) is correct because a firm should take advantage of the cash discount and pay on the last day of the discount period, which is day 10. Answers (a) and (b) are incorrect because "2" is the amount of the percentage discount; not the discount period. Answer (d) is incorrect because if a firm pays bills on the final due date, it will not have taken advantage of cash discounts which are very lucrative.

60. (d) The requirement is to identify the forms of borrowing that are unsecured. Answer (d) is correct because revolving credit agreements, bankers' acceptances, lines of credit, and commercial paper all represent unsecured obligations. Answer (a) is incorrect because floating liens and chattel mortgages are secured. Answer (b) is incorrect because factoring agreements and chattel mortgages are secured. Answer (c) is incorrect because floating liens and chattel mortgages are secured.

61. (d) The requirement is to evaluate the cost of trade credit. Answer (d) is correct because if the discount period is longer, the days of extra credit obtained by foregoing the discount are fewer. This makes the trade credit more costly. Answer (a) is incorrect because the lower the discount percentage, the lower the opportunity cost of foregoing the discount and using the trade credit financing. Answers (b) and (c) are incorrect because percentage financing cost is unaffected by the purchase price of the items.

62. (b) The requirement is to calculate the effective interest rate on a loan with a compensating balance requirement. The interest rate is calculated with the following formula:

$$\frac{\text{Interest cost}}{\text{Funds available}} = \frac{10\% \times \$500,000}{\$500,000 - \$50,000} = 11.1\%$$

Therefore, answer (b) is correct.

63. (d) The requirement is to calculate the cost of not taking a trade discount. The formula for computing the interest is

$$\frac{\text{Discount percent}}{100\% - \text{Discount percent}} \times \frac{360 \text{ days}}{\text{Total pay period} - \text{Discount period}}$$

$$\frac{3\%}{100\% - 3\%} \times \frac{360 \text{ days}}{45 \text{ days} - 10 \text{ days}} = 31.81\%$$

Therefore, answer (d) is correct.

64. (a) The requirement is to identify the term that is not related to loans involving inventory. Answer (a) is correct because factoring involves the sale of accounts receivable. Answer (b) is incorrect because a blanket inventory lien involves a legal document that establishes inventory as collateral for a loan. Answer (c) is incorrect because a trust receipt is an instrument that acknowledges that the borrower holds the inventory and the proceeds from sale will be put in trust for the lender. Answer (d) is incorrect because warehousing involves storing inventory in a public warehouse under the control of the lender.

65. (b) The requirement is to identify the nature of LIBOR. Answer (b) is correct because LIBOR, like the prime rate, is an example of a nominal rate. It is adjusted for inflation risk, but not credit risk. Answer (a) is incorrect because the risk-free rate is a theoretical rate that is not quoted. Answer (c) is incorrect because LIBOR is not credit risk adjusted. Answer (d) is incorrect because LIBOR is a short-term rate.

66. (a) The requirement is to identify the advantage of using long-term debt as a source of financing current assets. Answer (a) is correct because financing with long-term as opposed to short-term debt reduces the risk of the firm. Long-term debt does not have to be repaid as soon as short-term debt. Answer (b) is incorrect because long-term debt is generally more costly than short-term debt. Answer (c) is incorrect because the debt covenants are usually more restrictive in long-term debt agreements. Answer (d) is incorrect because early payment of long-term debt can result in prepayment penalties.

67. (c) The requirement is to identify the item that is not an implication of the policy of matching maturity assets with the maturity of financing. Answer (c) is correct because under this policy current assets are financed with current liabilities. Answers (a), (b), and (d) are incorrect because they are all appropriate implications of the policy.

68. (d) The requirement is to identify the term used to describe asset-backed public offerings. Answer (d) is correct because securitization of assets is the offering of debt collateralized by a firm's accounts receivable. Answer (a) is incorrect because a trust receipt is an instrument that acknowledges that the borrower holds a collateralized inventory and that proceeds from the sale will be put in trust for the lender. Answer (b) is incorrect because warehousing is the storage of inventory in a public warehouse that can only be removed with the lender's permission. Answer (c) is incorrect because a blanket inventory lien is a document that establishes the inventory as collateral for the loan.

69. (d) The requirement is to calculate the effective cost of a loan with a compensating balance requirement. Answer (d) is correct because the effective interest rate is equal to the interest paid, $7,000 ($100,000 × 7%) divided by the funds that are available, $80,000 (80% × $100,000). Therefore, the effective interest rate is equal to 8.75% ($7,000 ÷ $80,000). Answer (a) is not reasonable because the amount is less than the stated interest rate. Answer (b) is incorrect because it is the stated rate. Answer (c) is incorrect because it is computed by adding 20% of the stated rate to the stated rate.

70.   (b)   The requirement is to calculate the weighted-average annual interest rate for trade credit. If the company pays Web Master within the discount period, it will incur interest costs of $500 ($25,000 × 2%). This results in an annualized interest rate of 36.7347% [($500 ÷ $24,500) × 360 days ÷ (30 – 10 days)]. If the company does not pay the Softidee account during the discount period, it will incur interest cost of $2,500 ($50,000 × 5%). This results in an annualized interest rate of 23.6842% [($2,500 ÷ $47,500) × 360 days ÷ (90 – 10 days)]. To determine the weighted-average interest rate, we must first determine the average amount borrowed. For Web Master, this is equal to $24,500 × (20 days ÷ 360 days) = $1,361.11, and for Softidee, it is equal to $47,500 × (80 days ÷ 360 days) = $10,555.56. Therefore, the weighted-average interest rate is equal to 25.2% {[(36.7347% × $1,361.11) + (23.6842% × $10,555.56)] ÷ ($1,361.11 + $10,555.56)}. Answer (a) is incorrect because it uses weights of $25,000 and $50,000. Answer (c) is incorrect because it is based on weights of $24,500 and $47,500. Answer (d) is incorrect because it is the unweighted-average of the two rates.

71.   (d)   The requirement is to identify the statement that determines whether CyberAge should continue to use the trade credit. Answer (d) is correct because the company should continue to use the trade credit as long as the alternative cost of other forms of financing is higher. Answer (a) is incorrect because if alternative sources are less, the alternative should be used. Answer (b) is incorrect because in considering short-term financing alternatives, it is the marginal cost of capital that is important, not the weighted-average cost of capital. Answer (c) is incorrect because if the cost of long-term financing is greater, the trade credit should be used.

72.   (b)   The requirement is to identify the statement that is most likely true about commercial paper. Answer (b) is correct because commercial paper is normally issued with a short maturity period, usually 2 to 9 months. Answer (a) is incorrect because commercial paper is issued by the corporation. Answer (c) is incorrect because commercial paper is unsecured. Answer (d) is incorrect because commercial paper is typically issued by large corporations.

73.   (a)   The requirement is to calculate the effective interest on the loan. Answer (a) is correct because the effective interest is 6.44%. The effective interest rate is determined by calculating the net interest expense, which is $15,000 ($250,000 × 6%) minus the interest income from the compensating balance $500 ($25,000 × 2%) equals $14,500. Then, this amount is divided by the amount of money that the firm has available, $250,000 – $25,000 compensating balance. Thus, the effective interest rate is 6.44% ($14,500/$225,000).

74.   (a)   The requirement is to identify the loan with the most favorable terms. Answer (a) is correct because simple interest with no compensating balance is the most favorable terms from an effective interest basis. Answers (b), (c), and (d) are incorrect because discount interest and/or a compensating balance increase the effective interest rate on the loan.

75.   (d)   The requirement is to calculate the effective interest rate when a loan is in the form of a discounted note. When a note is on a discounted basis, the interest is withheld from the proceeds. Answer (d) is correct because the effective interest rate is calculated by dividing the total amount of interest by the amount of funds available. In this case, the interest is equal to $9,000 ($100,000 × 9%) and the funds available are $91,000 ($100,000 – $9,000). Thus the interest rate is 9.89% ($9,000/$91,000). Answer (b) is incorrect because it represents the stated rate, not the effective rate.

76.   (c)   The requirement is to calculate the annual cost of the financing arrangement. Answer (c) is correct because the annual cost of the arrangement is calculated as $7,000 (6% × $100,000) + [($300,000 – $100,000) × 1/2%)]. Answers (a), (b), and (d) are incorrect because they represent inaccurate computations of the cost of the financing.

77.   (c)   The requirement is to identify the largest source of short-term financing. Answer (c) is correct because trade credit is the largest source of short-term financing for most small firms. It occurs automatically with the purchase of goods and services. Answers (a) and (b) are incorrect because they are not the largest source of short-term financing for most small firms. Answer (d) is incorrect because mortgage bonds are a source of long-term financing.

78.   (c)   The requirement is to define the prime rate of interest. Answer (c) is correct because the prime rate of interest is the rate financial institutions charge their customers with the highest credit rating. Answer (a) is incorrect because a commitment fee is not related to the rate of interest. Answer (b) is incorrect because the effective rate on the bank loans of most firms is greater than the prime rate. Answer (d) is incorrect because the rate at which a bank borrows from the Federal Reserve central bank is the discount rate.

79.   (a)   The requirement is to describe the purpose of a compensating balance. Answer (a) is correct because a compensating balance provides a form of additional compensation to financial institutions. Answers (b), (c), and (d) are incorrect because they do not describe the purpose of a compensating balance.

80.   (d)   The requirement is to calculate the effective annual interest rate of the credit arrangement. Answer (d) is correct because the effective interest rate is equal to the interest cost divided by the available funds. The interest cost is $36,000 ($300,000 × 12%), and the available funds is equal to $255,000 [$300,000 – (15% × $300,00)]. Therefore, the effective interest rate is 14.12% ($36,000/$255,000).

Long-Term Debt

81.   (c)   The requirement is to identify the correct statement about bond financing alternatives. Answer (c) is correct because a call provision is detrimental to the investor because he or she may be forced to redeem the bond. Answer (a) is incorrect because a bond with a call provision typically has a higher yield than a similar bond without a call provision. Answer (b) is incorrect because a convertible bond is convertible at the option of the holder. Answer (d) is incorrect because the relationship of the stated rate on the bond to the market rate determines whether or not the bond will sell for more than par value.

82. (b) The requirement is to identify the definition of Eurobonds. Answer (b) is correct because Eurobonds are always sold in some country other than the one in whose currency the bond issue is denominated. The advantage of Eurobonds is that they are less regulated than other bonds and the transaction costs are lower. Answer (a) is incorrect because Eurobonds are not always denominated in Eurodollars, which are US dollars deposited outside the US. Answer (c) is incorrect because foreign bonds are denominated in the currency of the country in which they are sold. Answer (d) is incorrect because Eurobonds are usually issued not as registered bonds, but as bearer bonds.

83. (c) The requirement is to identify the proper accounting for an operating lease. Answer (c) is correct because an operating lease is one that does not meet the criteria to be a capital lease. Operating leases are treated as rental agreements and the payments are expensed as rent as incurred. Answer (a) is incorrect because it describes the proper accounting for a capital lease. Answers (b) and (d) are incorrect because they describe accounting that is not proper for either type of lease.

84. (d) The requirement is to identify the difference between a capital and an operating lease. Answer (d) is correct because in a capital lease, the risks and rewards of ownership are transferred to the lessee. If the risks/rewards are not transferred, the lease is a rental arrangement and is called an operating lease. In accounting for a capital lease, the lessee capitalizes the net investment in the lease. Answer (a) is incorrect because the lessee obtains use of the asset in all lease agreements. Answer (b) is incorrect because the lessee uses the lease as a source of financing under a capital lease. Answer (c) is incorrect because the lessee does not receive title to the asset in all cases.

85. (c) The requirement is to identify the advantages/disadvantages of debt versus equity financing. Answer (c) is correct because the fixed obligation of interest and principal is an advantage to debt financing. Answers (a), (b), and (d) are incorrect because they are all disadvantages of debt financing.

86. (d) The requirement is to identify the advantages/disadvantages of debt versus equity financing. Answer (d) is correct because debt actually increases stockholders' risk because the financial leverage of the firm is higher. Answers (a), (b), and (c) are incorrect because they are all advantages of debt financing.

87. (d) The requirement is to identify what type of bond has less interest rate risk. Answer (d) is correct because a floating rate bond has a rate of interest that floats with changes in the market interest rate. Therefore, the market price of the bond does not fluctuate as widely. Answer (a) is incorrect because serial bonds are those that are paid off in installments over the life of the issue. Answer (b) is incorrect because sinking fund bonds are those for which the firm makes payments into a sinking fund to be used to retire the bonds by purchase. Answer (c) is incorrect because convertible bonds are those that may be converted into common stock.

88. (a) The requirement is to identify the defining characteristic of serial bonds. Answer (a) is correct because serial bonds are those that are paid off in installments over the life of the issue. Answer (b) is incorrect because sinking fund bonds are those for which the firm makes payments into a sinking fund to be used to retire the bonds by purchase. Answer (c) is incorrect because convertible bonds are those that may be converted into common stock. Answer (d) is incorrect because callable bonds are those that have a call provision that allows the firm to force the bondholders to redeem the bonds before maturity.

89. (c) The requirement is to identify the impact of changes in the market rate of interest on bond valuation. Answer (c) is correct because if the market rate of interest increases, the bond value will decrease (an inverse effect). Answers (a) and (b) are incorrect because the coupon rate does not change after issuance and determines the amount of the periodic interest payments, not changes in the bond valuation. Answer (d) is incorrect because if the market rate decreases, the value of the bond will increase.

90. (b) The requirement is to calculate the first-year, before-tax cost of the planned debt financing, net of floatation costs. The first year cost would be calculated by dividing the interest rate by the amount of funds received after floatation costs. Therefore, the interest cost before tax is equal to 8% ÷ (101% issue price – 2% floatation costs) = 8.08%. Therefore, the correct answer is (b).

91. (b) The requirement is to identify the reason for issuing Eurobonds rather than domestic bonds. Answer (b) is correct because Eurobonds are not subject to extensive regulation like US issued domestic bonds; therefore, they are less expensive to issue. Answer (a) is incorrect because Eurobonds are not denominated in the currency of the country in which they are issued. Answer (c) is incorrect because foreign buyers are not more readily accepting of the issues. Answer (d) is incorrect because Eurobonds do carry foreign exchange risk for the investor; they have losses if the US dollar declines relative to the country's currency.

92. (c) The requirement is to identify the bond provision that is generally considered to be detrimental to the investor. Answer (c) is correct because a callable bond is one that can be redeemed at the option of the issuer. The investor has no choice but to redeem the bond. Answer (a) is incorrect because a conversion feature means the bond can be converted to common stock at the option of the investor. This is a favorable provision for the investor. Answer (b) is incorrect because redeemable bonds are redeemable at the option of the investor. Answer (d) is incorrect because bonds with serial maturity allow the investor to select the desired maturity date.

93. (c) The requirement is to identify the statement that is not an advantage of leasing as a form of financing. Answer (c) is correct because the dollar cost to lease an asset is generally greater than the cost to purchase and finance though other means. Answer (a) is incorrect because leases often do not require down payments. Answer (b) is incorrect because the provisions of lease agreements are usually less stringent than for other forms of debt. Answer (d) is incorrect because firms may be able to lease when they do not have the credit capacity to buy an asset.

94. (a) The requirement is to identify the effect of an increase in bond rating. Answer (a) is correct because going from a B rating to a Baa rating is an increase in the bond rating indicative of lower risk. Therefore, the market value of the bonds should increase. Answers (b), (c), and (d) are incorrect because the bond value should increase.

95. (a) The requirement is to identify the statement that can be assumed from the case scenario. Answer (a) is correct because if the bond sold at face value, then the coupon rate of 8% must have approximated the market rate for this bond. Answer (b) is incorrect because the nominal rate does not include credit risk. Answer (c) is incorrect because the coupon rate, if it was about equal to the market rate, includes a credit risk premium. Answer (d) is incorrect because the risk-free interest rate is always about 1 to 2%.

96. (b) The requirement is to identify the correct statement regarding the effect of a change in the market rate. Answer (b) is correct because an increase in the market rate will cause the bond to reduce in value until it sells at a price that will result in a yield to maturity equal to the current market rate. Answer (a) is incorrect because the market rate would have to decline for the bond to increase in value. Answer (c) is incorrect because LIBOR is only indirectly related to the long-term bond rate. Answer (d) is incorrect because the change in value can be predicted.

97. (d) The requirement is to calculate the current yield on a bond. The current yield is equal to the annual interest paid divided by the bond market price. Watco's $1,000 bond pays $80 per year in interest, the $1,000 face value × the 8% coupon rate. Answer (d) is correct because the current yield is equal to 8.42% ($80 ÷ $950). Answer (a) is incorrect because 8% is the coupon rate.

Equity

98. (d) The requirement is to identify the purpose of the secondary market. Answer (d) is correct because outstanding stocks of publicly owned companies are traded among investors in the secondary market. The original issuer receives no additional capital as a result of such trades. Answers (a) and (b) are incorrect because firms raise capital by issuing new securities in the primary market, and the initial public offering market is a frequently used term for the market in which previously privately owned firms issue new securities to the public. Answer (c) is incorrect because the over-the-counter market is the network of dealers that provides for trading in unlisted securities.

99. (a) The requirement is to identify the purpose of the primary market. Answer (a) is correct because the primary market is the market for new stocks and bonds. Answer (b) is incorrect because existing securities are traded on a secondary market. Answer (c) is incorrect because the futures market is where commodities contracts are sold, not the capital market. Answer (d) is incorrect because exchanges of existing securities do not occur in the primary market.

100. (c) The requirement is to identify the characteristic that is not usually a feature of cumulative preferred stock. Answer (c) is correct because preferred stock usually does not have voting rights. Preferred shareholders are generally given the right to vote for directors of the company only if the company has not paid the preferred dividend for a specified period of time, such as ten quarters. Answer (a) is incorrect because preferred stock does have priority over common stock with regard to earnings, so dividends must be paid on preferred stock before they can be paid on common stock. Answer (b) is incorrect because preferred stock does

have priority over common stock with regard to assets, so in the event of bankruptcy, the claims of preferred shareholders must be satisfied in full before the common shareholders receive anything. Answer (d) is incorrect because cumulative preferred stock does have the right to receive any dividends in arrears before common stock dividends are paid.

101. (b) The requirement is to identify the statement that describes an advantage of going public. Answer (b) is correct because the compliance cost of going public and complying with SEC regulations is substantial. Answer (a) is incorrect because going public does provide access to more capital. Answer (c) is incorrect because public companies can issue stock options to attract and retain management. Answer (d) is incorrect because owners obtain immediate liquidity for their investments when the firm goes public.

Optimal Capital Structure

102. (b) The requirement is to calculate the degree of operating leverage of the company. The formula for degree of operating leverage is

$$DOL = \frac{\text{Percent change in operating income}}{\text{Percent change in unit volume}}$$

In this case, the percent change in operating income is equal to 50% [($300,000 – $200,000) ÷ $200,000], and the percent change in unit volume is equal to 5% [(105,000 – 100,000 units) ÷ 100,000 units]. Therefore, the correct answer is (b) because DOL is equal to 10 (50% ÷ 5%).

103. (a) The requirement is to calculate the degree of financial leverage for the company. The formula for degree of financial leverage is

$$DFL = \frac{\text{Percent change in EPS}}{\text{Percent change in EBIT}}$$

In this case, the percent change in EPS is equal to 500% [($1.20 – $0.20) ÷ $0.20], and the percent change in EBIT is equal to 50% [($300,000 – $200,000) ÷ $200,000]. Therefore, the DFL is equal to 10 (500% ÷ 50%), and answer (a) is correct.

104. (d) The requirement is to identify the advantages/disadvantages of equity financing. Answer (d) is correct because the lack of a firm obligation to pay dividends to common shareholders is an advantage of equity financing. Answers (a), (b), and (c) are incorrect because they are all disadvantages of equity financing.

105. (a) The requirement is to identify the impact of debt versus equity financing. Answer (a) is correct because Company A is more highly leveraged. It has greater fixed charges in the form of interest. Therefore, Company A will have more volatile net earnings than Company B. Answers (b) and (c) are incorrect because the level of fixed financing charges does not affect operating earnings variability. Operating income is computed before interest expense. Answer (d) is incorrect because Company A has greater, not less, financial leverage than Company B.

106. (d) The requirement is to identify the item that is not a potential long-term source of funding for a firm. Answer (d) is correct because a line of credit is a short-term financing source. Answers (a), (b), and (c) are incorrect because they are possible sources of financing for long-term projects.

107. (d) The requirement is to identify the factor that does not affect management's judgment about the firm's capital structure. Answer (d) is correct because the expected return on assets is not a factor that affects management's judgment about the firm's capital structure. Answer (a) is incorrect because the greater the inherent risk of a business, the lower the optimal debt to equity ratio. Answer (b) is incorrect because a major advantage of debt is the tax deductibility of interest payments. Answer (c) is incorrect because a firm's target capital structure will be affected by the risk tolerance of management. More aggressive management may take on more debt.

108. (b) The requirement is to identify a characteristic of higher operating leverage. Higher operating leverage involves more fixed costs, which results in more operating variability and more risk. Answer (b) is correct because a firm's profits are more sensitive to changes in sales volume when the firm is more leveraged. Answer (a) is incorrect because higher leveraged firms have less variable costs. Answer (c) is incorrect because the firm may or may not be more profitable. Answer (d) is incorrect because a highly leveraged firm is more risky.

109. (d) The requirement is to identify the consequences of an increase in financial leverage. Answer (d) is correct because when the degree of financial leverage rises, fixed interest charges rise. This causes the standard deviation of returns to equity holders to increase. Answers (a) and (b) are incorrect because an increase in the degree of financial leverage is associated with an increase in equity beta and an increase in the systematic risk of the company. Equity beta is a measure of systematic risk of the company. Answer (c) is incorrect because unsystematic risk of the company does not fall.

110. (d) Answer (d) is correct because a weighted-average of the costs of all financing sources should be used, with the weights determined by the usual financing proportions. Answer (a) is incorrect because the cost of funds for a particular project does not represent the cost of capital for the firm. The cost of capital should also be calculated on an after-tax basis. Answer (b) is incorrect because the cost of capital is a composite, or weighted-average, of all financing sources in their usual proportions. Answer (c) is incorrect because the cost of capital is a composite, or weighted-average, of all financing sources in their usual proportions. It includes both the after-tax cost of debt and the cost of equity financing.

111. (b) The requirement is to identify the statement that is not true regarding the acceptance of Alternative 1. Answer (b) is correct because Alternative 1 involves much less financial leverage than Alternative 2. Answer (a) is incorrect because Alternative 1 is the more conservative capital structure because it involves less debt. Answer (c) is incorrect because net income will be less variable under Alternative 1. Answer (d) is incorrect because total interest expense will be less under Alternative 1.

112. (b) The requirement is to compare the weighted-average cost of capital for the two alternatives. Answer (b) is correct because the cost of debt after tax for is 5.1% [6% × (100% – 15% tax rate)] for Alternative 1 and 5.95% [7% × (100% – 15% tax rate)] for Alternative 2. The weighted-average cost of capital for Alternative 1 is 7.55% [(5.1% ×

$3,000,000 ÷ $6,000,000) + (10% × $3,000,000 ÷ $6,000,000)], and the weighted-average cost of capital for Alternative 2 is 6.96% [(5.95% × $5,000,000 ÷ $6,000,000) + (12% × $1,000,000 ÷ $6,000,000)]. Therefore, the differential is 0.59% (7.55% – 6.96%). Answer (a) is incorrect because it results from an unweighted computation. Answer (c) is incorrect because it is the before-tax computation.

Cost of Capital

113. (a) The requirement is to identify the factor that affects the calculation of the cost of equity using CAPM. Answer (a) is correct because a reduction in the risk-free rate would reduce the required return demanded by stockholders. Answers (b), (c), and (d) are incorrect because an increase in these items would cause the estimated cost of common equity to increase.

114. (b) The requirement is to identify the reason why it is more expensive to finance with equity than with debt. Answer (b) is correct because equity holders are subject to more risk than debt holders. Therefore, they require a higher rate of return.

115. (d) The requirement is to identify the item that does not describe a characteristic of the capital asset pricing model. Answer (d) is correct because CAPM does not include the stock's market price in its computation. Answers (a), (b), and (c) are incorrect because they are all characteristics of CAPM model.

116. (b) The requirement is to apply the dividend-yield-plus-growth approach to calculate the cost of common equity. The formula for estimated cost of common equity is equal to the expected dividend divided by the stock price plus the growth rate. Therefore, the correct answer is (b) because the estimated cost of equity is 14.1% [(2.11/23.13) + 5%].

117. (b) The requirement is to identify the impact of an increase in nominal interest rates on a company's share price. Answer (b) is correct because an increase in the nominal interest rate would mean that investors would expect a higher return on all investments. If the stock earnings and dividend growth is unchanged, the stock price will decrease.

118. (a) The requirement is to identify the impact of investor expectations on stock price. Answer (a) is correct because if investors expect a higher dividend growth rate, the market value of the common shares will be greater. Answer (b) is incorrect because if investors expect a lower dividend growth rate, the market value of common shares will be lower. Answers (c) and (d) are incorrect because holding periods are not related to the market value of common shares.

119. (a) The requirement is to identify the technique that explicitly considers risk in calculating the firm's estimated cost of equity. Answer (a) is correct because CAPM is the only technique that explicitly considers risk in the form of the firm's beta. Beta measures the relationship between the price volatility of the market as a whole and the price volatility of the individual stock. Answers (b) and (c) are incorrect because they do not directly incorporate the firm's risk in the calculation of the estimated cost of equity. Answer (d) is incorrect because it is not utilized to determine the estimated cost of equity.

120. (c)   The requirement is to use the dividend-yield-plus-growth-rate approach to calculate the estimated cost of equity. The estimated cost of equity is equal to the dividend divided by the price of the stock + the growth rate. Accordingly, answer (c) is correct because the estimated cost of equity is equal to 14.3% [($5 ÷ $60) + 6%].

121. (b)   The requirement is to identify how the bond-yield-plus approach to estimating the cost of equity is applied. Answer (b) is correct because the bond-yield-plus approach involves adding a risk premium of 3% to 5% to the interest rate of the firm's long-term debt. Answers (a), (c), and (d) are incorrect because they involve items that are not components of the formula.

122. (a)   The requirement is to identify the characteristic of typical dividend policies. Answer (a) is correct because management is hesitant to decrease dividends. Therefore, they are more stable than earnings. Answer (b) is incorrect because they do not fluctuate more widely than earnings. Answer (c) is incorrect because dividends tend to be higher for mature firms. Answer (d) is incorrect because dividends are usually not changed every year.

123. (c)   The requirement is to calculate the current net cost of debt. The current cost of debt before tax is 8.5% (7% Treasury bond rate + 1.5%), and the cost of debt after tax is 5.1% [8.5% × (1 − 40% tax rate)]. Therefore, the correct answer is (c).

124. (d)   The requirement is to calculate the cost of capital using CAPM. The CAPM formula is Cost of capital = Risk-free rate + (Market rate − Risk-free rate) × Beta. In this case, the estimated cost of equity is equal to 17% [7% + (15% − 7%) × 1.25]. Thus, the answer is (d).

125. (a)   The requirement is to calculate the weighted-average cost of capital. The weighted-average cost of capital is determined by summing the cost of each funding source weighted by its percentage of the total. In this case, the funds received from the debt are equal to 99% (101% − 2%) × $15,000,000, or $14,850,000, and the funds from equity is $35 million, the amount of retained earnings. Therefore, total funding is $49,850,000. The weighted-average cost of capital is equal to ($14,850,000/$49,850,000) × 7% + ($35,000,000/$49,850,000) × 12% = 10.50%. Thus, the answer is (a).

126. (a)   The requirement is to use the capital asset pricing model to compute the cost of equity (expected return of equity holders). The CAPM formula is: Cost of equity = Risk-free interest rate + (Market rate − Risk-free interest rate) × Beta. Therefore, the expected return = 9.2% [5% + (12% − 5%) × .60], or answer (a).

127. (b)   The requirement is to specify the cost of capital assigned to retained earnings. Answer (b) is correct because newly issued or "external" common equity is more costly than retained earnings because the company incurs issuance costs when raising new funds. Answer (a) is incorrect because the cost of retained earnings is the rate of return stockholders require on retained equity capital. The opportunity cost of retained funds will be positive. Answer (c) is incorrect because retained earnings will always be less costly than external equity financing because earnings retention does not involve the payment of issuance costs. An-

swer (d) is incorrect because the cost is lower as described above.

128. (c)   The requirement is to identify the relevant risk of a security according to CAPM. Answer (c) is correct because systematic risk is the component of the total risk of a security that cannot be eliminated through diversification and is relevant to valuation. Answer (a) is incorrect because "company-specific" risk can be eliminated through portfolio diversification and is not relevant to the valuation of the security. Answer (b) is incorrect because "diversifiable" risk can be eliminated through portfolio diversification and is not relevant to the valuation of the security. Answer (d) is incorrect because only the systematic component of total risk is relevant to security valuation.

129. (c)   The requirement is to calculate the weighted-average cost of capital (WACC). Answer (c) is correct because the WACC is calculated as 9.36% {2/5 × [9% × (1 − 40%)]} + (3/5 × 12%). Answers (a), (b), and (d) are incorrect because they represent inaccurate computations of the cost of the financing.

130. (b)   Answer (b) is correct because the weighted-average cost of capital is calculated as follows:

= (Weight of equity) × (Cost of equity) + (Weight of debt) ×
    (Before-tax cost of debt) × (1 − Tax rate)
= (.7) × (.12) + (.3) × (.08) × (1 − .3) = .084 + .0168 = 10%

Answer (a) is incorrect because 8% is the cost of equity before tax. Answer (c) is incorrect because this solution uses the before-tax cost of debt rather than the after-tax cost of debt. Answer (d) is incorrect because 12% is the cost of equity.

131. (d)   The requirement is to identify the true statement about the financing alternatives. Answer (d) is correct because taxes payable will be higher under Arrangement #1 because with lower interest expense, taxable income will be higher. Answer (a) is incorrect because expected gross margin is unaffected by the choice of financing arrangement. Answer (b) is incorrect because the degree of operating leverage is not affected by the method of financing. Answer (c) is incorrect because interest expense will be higher under Arrangement #2. Under Arrangement #1, interest expense will be $300,000 (.08) = $24,000, while under Arrangement #2, interest expense will be $700,000 (.10) = $70,000 per annum.

132. (a)   The requirement is to calculate the return on equity and the debt ratio. Answer (a) is correct because return on equity is calculated as net income divided by the amount of equity invested. The debt ratio is the amount of debt financing divided by total assets. Calculations of the two ratios for both financing arrangements are as follows:

	#1	#2
Sales revenue	$500,000	$500,000
Cost of sales	200,000	200,000
General & admin. expense	100,000	100,000
Interest expense	24,000	70,000
Taxable income	$176,000	$130,000
Tax payable (30%)	52,800	39,000
Net income	$123,200	$91,000
Equity invested	700,000	300,000
Return on equity	$\dfrac{123,200}{700,000}$	$\dfrac{91,000}{300,000}$
	17.6%	30.3%
Debt ratio	$\dfrac{300,000}{1,000,000}$	$\dfrac{700,000}{1,000,000}$
	.3	.7

Mergers

133. (b) The requirement is to identify the type of transaction described. Answer (b) is correct because a leveraged buyout is one that is financed primarily with debt using very little equity capital. Answer (a) is incorrect because a spin-off is a divestiture in which stock of a subsidiary are issued to existing shareholders of the parent. Answer (c) is incorrect because a joint venture is a project conducted jointly by two or more independent parties. Answer (d) is incorrect because liquidation involves the piecemeal sale of the assets of a firm.

134. (a) The requirement is to identify the type of merger described. Answer (a) is correct because vertical integration is a merger involving companies in the same industry, but at different levels of the supply chain. Answer (b) is incorrect because a conglomerate merger is one involving firms from different industries. Answer (c) is incorrect because market extension involves moving into new market areas. Answer (d) is incorrect because a horizontal merger involves firms that are competitors in the same market.

135. (d) The requirement is to identify a horizontal merger. Answer (d) is correct because a horizontal merger is one between competitors in the same market. Answer (a) is incorrect because it describes a conglomerate merger. Answers (b) and (c) are incorrect because they describe vertical mergers.

136. (b) The requirement is to identify the type of merger. Answer (b) is correct because a vertical merger is a merger between a firm and one of its suppliers or customers. A bottle manufacturer can supply bottles to be used by a soft drink producer. Answer (a) is incorrect because a horizontal merger is a combination of two firms producing the same type of good or service. Answer (c) is incorrect because a congeneric merger is a merger of firms in the same industry, but the two firms do not have a customer or supplier relationship (as in vertical merger). Answer (d) is incorrect because a conglomerate merger is a merger of companies in totally different industries.

137. (d) The requirement is to identify the type of merger. Answer (d) is correct because a conglomerate merger is a merger of companies in totally different industries. A shoe manufacturer and brokerage house are in totally different industries. Answer (a) is incorrect because a horizontal merger is a combination of two firms producing the same type of good or service. Answer (b) is incorrect because a vertical merger is a merger between a firm and

one of its suppliers or customers. Answer (c) is incorrect because a congeneric merger is a merger of firms in the same industry, but the two firms do not have a customer or supplier relationship (as in vertical merger).

RISK MANAGEMENT AND CAPITAL BUDGETING

This module describes the relationship between risk and return and the use of hedging to manage risk. It also describes the function of capital budgeting.

A. Risk and Return

There is a trade-off between risk and returns when considering investments—to achieve higher returns an investor must assume greater risk. This relationship is illustrated by the following chart that presents the means and standard deviations of real returns from stocks, bonds, and Treasury bills over a ten-year period. The results are as would be expected: stocks earned significantly higher returns but also with significantly higher risk (variance). The chart can be used to compute the **equity risk premium**. The equity risk premium is equal to the 8.7% real return on stocks minus the risk-free real return as measured by the return on Treasury bills, 1%, or 7.7% (8.7% – 1.0%). The average risk premium on common stock versus bonds over the ten-year period is about 6.6% (8.7% – 2.1%).

Real Returns of US Investments 1900 – 2000

Assets	Mean return (%)	Standard deviation (%)	Highest year (%)	Lowest Year (%)
Stocks	8.7	20.2	56.8	–38.0
Bonds	2.1	10.0	35.1	–19.3
Bills	1.0	4.7	20.0	–15.1
Inflation	3.3	5.0	20.4	–10.8

SOURCE: Dimson and Marsh, **Triumph of the Optimists,** (Princeton, NJ: Princeton University Press: 2002)

To understand why riskier investments offer a premium, it is necessary to make some assumptions about preferences of investors. Most financial models assume that investors are **risk averse**. Risk aversion does not mean investors will not take risks; it means that they must be compensated for taking risk. Most investors, and the market as a whole, are considered by most analysts to be risk averse. However, certain investors may exhibit different behavior.

1. **Risk-neutral investors**—Investors that prefer investments with higher returns whether or not they have risk. These investors disregard risk.
2. **Risk-seeking investors**—Investors that prefer to take risks and would invest in a higher-risk investment despite the fact that a lower-risk investment might have the same return.

B. Return on a Single Asset

1. Investment return is the total gain or loss on an investment for a period of time. It consists of the change in the asset's value (either gain or loss) plus any cash distributions (e.g., cash flow, interest, or dividends). The return is illustrated by the following equation:

$$R_{t+1} = \frac{P_{t+1} - P_t + CF_{t+1}}{P_t}$$

Where

R_{t+1}	=	The investment return from time t to $t + 1$
P_{t+1}	=	The asset's price (market value) at $t+1$
P_t	=	The asset's price (market value) at t
CF_{t+1}	=	Cash flow received from the asset from t to $t + 1$

This formula measures return on an *ex post* basis (after the fact) and, therefore, does not consider risk. Managers have to evaluate investments on an *ex ante* basis and, therefore, must use **expected returns** and **estimates of risk**.

2. **Estimating Expected Returns**

A common way to estimate expected returns is based on prior history. One could simply calculate the average historical returns on a similar investment to get the expected return. When making this computation two approaches are often used.

a. **Arithmetic average return**—Computed by simply adding the historical returns for a number of periods and dividing by the number of periods.

b. **Geometric average return**—This computation depicts the compound annual return earned by an investor who bought the asset and held it for the number of historical periods examined. If returns vary through time, the geometric average will always fall below the arithmetic average.

c. It is generally recommended that the arithmetic average return be used for assets with short hold-ing periods and the geometric average return be used for assets with longer holding periods.

3. **Estimating Risk**

a. Measures of risk also are often developed from historical returns. Many financial analysts assume that the pattern of historical returns of large numbers of similar investments approximates a **nor-mal distribution** (bell shaped curve) with the mean being the expected return and the variance, or standard deviation, measuring the dispersion around the expected return. Therefore, the most com-mon estimates of risk come from the variance or standard deviation of historical returns. Remem-ber, if you assume that the distribution is normal, about 95% of the returns will fall within the range created by expected return ± two standard deviations.

b. For many investments, management does not have significant historical data on returns to calcu-late the mean and variance. In these cases management must resort to **subjective** estimates of risk.

> EXAMPLE: *Assume that a defense contractor has the possibility of getting a lucrative government contract. The government intends to announce the winner of the contract today. An investor estimates that the probability of the firm getting the contract is 60%, in which case the stock price will increase 20%. If the contractor does not get the contract, the stock price is estimated to decline by 10%. Today's expected return on the stock investment would be computed as follows:*

$$Expected\ return\ =\ 0.60(20\%) + 0.40(-10\%)\ =\ 8.0\%$$

> *The variance of the return is measured by the following formula:*

$$Variance\ =\ E\{[R-E(R)]^2\}$$

> *Where*

> R = *A random possible return*
> $E(R)$ = *The expected value of the return*

> *Therefore to get the variance, we simply sum the squared deviations of the possible returns from the expected re-turn weighted by their probability, as shown below.*

$$Variance\ =\ 0.60(20\% - 8\%)^2 + 0.40(-10\% - 8\%)^2$$

$$Variance\ =\ 216\%$$

> *The standard deviation, which is equal to the square root of the variance, is calculated below.*

$$Standard\ deviation\ =\ \sqrt{216\%}\ =\ 14.70\%$$

> *Therefore, the investor can make a decision about whether to invest in the stock knowing that the expected return is 8.0% with a standard deviation of 14.70%.*

C. Portfolio Returns and Risk

1. **Expected Returns of a Portfolio**

When an investor invests in a portfolio of assets, the expected returns are simply the weighted-average of the expected returns of the assets making up the portfolio. The expected return may be calculated with the following formula:

$$E(R_p)\ =\ w_1E(R_1) + w_2E(R_2) + w_3E(R_3)\ldots$$

Where

$E(R_p)$ = The expected return on the portfolio

$w_{1,2,3\ldots}$ = The weight of each of the assets (1,2,3, etc.) in the portfolio

$E(R_{1,2,3\ldots})$ = The expected return of each of the assets (1, 2,3, etc.) in the portfolio

> EXAMPLE: *Assume that an investor has two assets (or types of assets) in his or her portfolio. Asset 1 is 60% of the portfolio, and it has an expected return of 10%. Asset 2 is 40% of the portfolio, and it has an expected return of 5%. The expected return of the portfolio is calculated below.*

$$E(R_p)\ =\ 0.60(10\%) + 0.40(5\%) = 8\%$$

2. **The Variance of Portfolio Returns**

a. The variance of portfolio returns depends on three factors

(1) The percentage of the portfolio invested in each asset (the weight)
(2) The variance of the returns of each individual asset

(3) The covariance among the returns of assets in the portfolio. The covariance captures the degree to which the asset returns move together over time. If returns on the individual assets move together, there is little benefit to holding the portfolio. On the other hand, if returns on some assets in the portfolio go up when returns on other assets in the portfolio go down, holding the portfolio reduces overall risk.

b. Portfolios allow investors to diversify away unsystematic risk. **Unsystematic risk** is the risk that exists for one particular investment or a group of like investments (e.g., technology stock). By having a balanced portfolio, investors can theoretically eliminate this risk. **Systematic risk** relates to market factors that cannot be diversified away. All investments are to some degree affected by them. Examples of systematic risk factors include fluctuations in GDP, inflation, interest rates, etc.

3. **Measuring the Systematic Risk of an Individual Investment**

The variance of an individual investment captures the total risk of the investment, both systematic an unsystematic. However, since unsystematic risk can be eliminated by diversification, the variance of a specific investment is not a particularly useful measure when considering a portfolio of investments. A standardized measure that has been developed to estimate an investment's systematic risk is **beta**.

$$\text{Beta} = b_i = \frac{\sigma_{im}}{\sigma^2_m}$$

The beta of a particular investment equals the covariance of the investment's returns with the returns of the overall portfolio divided by the portfolio's variance. It measures how the value of the investment moves with changes in the value of the total portfolio. Therefore, it can be used to evaluate the effect of an individual investment's risk on the risk of the entire portfolio.

4. An individual investor has a **risk preference function** which describes the investor's trade-off between risk and return. A portfolio that falls on the line described by this function is an **efficient portfolio**.

D. **Interest Rates**

Interest represents the cost of borrowing funds. Therefore, consideration of interest rates is a critical aspect of financing decisions. In this section, we will review aspects of interest rates that are significant to financing decisions.

1. **Interest Rates and Risk**

As discussed above, risk and return are directly related. Investors and creditors must be paid a premium for assuming higher degrees of risk. In determining the appropriate interest rate to accept, investors and creditors consider the **business risks** of the loan or investment. The following business risks are relevant:

• **Credit or default risk**—The risk that the firm will default on payment of interest or principal of the loan or bond. This may be divided into two parts: the individual firm's creditworthiness (or risk of default) and **sector risk** (the risk related to economic conditions in the firm's economic sector).
• **Interest rate risk**—The risk that the value of the loan or bond will decline due to an increase in interest rates.
• **Market risk**—The risk that the value of the loan or bond will decline due to a decline in the aggregate value of all the assets in the economy.

Credit risk is an example of an unsystematic (unique) risk. It is unique to the particular loan or investment. Credit risk can be eliminated by diversification (e.g., by investing in a portfolio of loans or bonds). Market and interest rate risks are part of systematic risk that must be accepted by the investor.

2. **Stated Versus Effective Annual Interest Rates**

Management must make objective comparisons of loan costs or investment returns over different compounding periods. In order to put interest rates on a common basis for comparison, management must distinguish between the **stated interest rate** and the **effective annual interest rate**. While the stated rate is the contractual rate charged by the lender, the effective annual rate is the true annual return to the lender. The simple annual rate may vary from the effective annual rate because interest is often compounded more often than annually. The formula for calculating the effective annual rate from the stated rate is presented below.

$$EAR = \left(1+\frac{r}{m}\right)^{m} - 1$$

Where

r = The stated interest rate
m = Compounding frequency

EXAMPLE: Assume that management is evaluating a loan that has a stated interest rate of 8% with compounding of interest quarterly. Since compounding is quarterly, m is equal to 4 because interest is compounded 4 times each year. Using the following equation, the effective annual rate may be computed as follows:

$$EAR = \left(1+\frac{.08}{4}\right)^{4} - 1$$

$$EAR = .0824 = 8.24\%$$

Management may now compare this 8.24% rate to other options on an effective interest basis.

3. **The Term Structure of Interest Rates**

The term structure of interest rates describes the relationship between long-and short-term rates. These relationships are important in determining whether to use long-term fixed or variable rate financing. A yield curve is used to illustrate the relative level of short-term and long-term interest rates at a point in time. At any point in time a yield curve may take any one of the following three forms:

a. **Normal yield curve**—An upward sloping curve in which short-term rates are less than intermediate-term rates which are less than long-term rates.
b. **Inverted (abnormal) yield curve**—A downward-sloping curve in which short-term rates are greater than intermediate-term rates which are greater than long-term rates.
c. **Flat yield curve**—A curve in which short-term, intermediate-term and long-term rates are all about the same.
d. **Humped yield curve**—A curve in which intermediate-term rates are higher than both short-term and long-term rates.

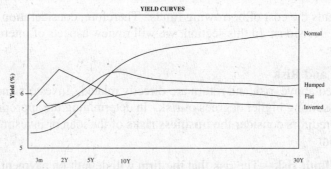

Long-term rates are usually higher (as described by the normal yield curve) because they involve more interest rate risk. Therefore, lenders require higher **maturity risk premiums** for long-term lending. However, market rates are also affected by expectations about the future levels of inflation, defaults, and liquidity, which can vary with the maturity date. These factors cause the relationships depicted by the inverted or humped yield curves.

There are a few theories that attempt to explain the shape of the yield curve, including

(1) **Liquidity preference (premium) theory.** This theory states that long-term rates should be higher than short-term rates, because investors have to be offered a premium to entice them to hold less liquid and more price-sensitive securities. Remember if interest rates increase and an investor holds a fixed-rate long-term security, the value of the security will decline.
(2) **Market segmentation theory.** This theory states that Treasury securities are divided into market segments by the various financial institutions investing in the market. Commercial banks prefer short-term securities to match their short-term lending strategies. Savings and loans prefer intermediate-term securities. Finally, life insurance companies prefer long-term securities because of the nature of their commitments to policyholders. The demand for vari-

ous term securities is therefore dependent on the demands of these segmented groups of investors.

(3) **Expectations theory.** This theory explains yields on long-term securities as a function of short-term rates. Specifically, it states that long-term rates reflect the average of short-term expected rates over the time period that the long-term security will be outstanding. Under this theory long-term rates tell us about market expectations of short-term rates. When long-term rates are lower than short-term rates, the market is expecting short-term rates to fall. Since interest rates are directly tied to inflation rates, long-term rates also tell us about the market's expectations about inflation. If long-term rates are lower than short-term rates, the market is indicating a belief that inflation will decline.

All of the theories and factors described above make it very difficult to predict interest rates, in general, and much less for varying maturities. Therefore, sound financial policy calls for using a combination of long- and short-term debt, and equity, to enable the firm to survive in any interest rate environment.

The mix of long- and short-term debt also affects the firm's financial statements. A heavy reliance on short-term or variable-rate debt means that interest expense and, therefore, net income will be more variable. This increases the financial risk of the firm and will cause creditors and investors to demand higher rates to compensate for the increased risk.

DERIVATIVES AND HEDGING

A. **The Nature of Derivatives**

1. A derivative is a financial instrument or contract whose value is derived from some other financial measure (underlyings, such as commodity prices, stock prices, interest rates, etc.) and includes payment provisions.

2. Common examples of derivatives include the following:

a. **Options**—Allow, but do not require, the holder to buy (call) or sell (put) a specific or standard commodity or financial instrument, at a specified price during a specified period of time (American option) or at a specified date (European option).

b. **Forwards**—Negotiated contracts to purchase and sell a specific quantity of a financial instrument, foreign currency, or commodity at a price specified at origination of the contract, with delivery and payment at a specified future date.

c. **Futures**—Forward-based standardized contracts to take delivery of a specified financial instrument, foreign currency, or commodity at a specified future date or during a specified period generally at the then market price.

d. **Currency swaps**—Forward-based contracts in which two parties agree to exchange an obligation to pay cash flows in one currency for an obligation to pay in another currency.

e. **Interest rate swaps**—Forward-based contracts in which two parties agree to swap streams of payments over a specified period of time. An example would be an interest-rate swap in which one party agrees to make payments based on a fixed rate of interest and the other party agrees to make payments based on a variable rate of interest.

f. **Swaption**—An option of a swap that provides the holder with the right to enter into a swap at a specified future date with specified terms, or to extend or terminate the life of an existing swap. These derivatives have characteristics of an option and an interest rate swap.

3. Forward contracts and swaps are often created and exchanged by **financial intermediaries,** such as

a. Commercial banks
b. Insurance companies
c. Pension funds
d. Savings and loan associations
e. Mutual funds
f. Finance companies
g. Investment bankers
h. Money market funds
i. Credit unions

The other party to the contract or agreement is referred to as the **counterparty**.

B. Risks in Using Derivatives

1. **Credit risk**—The risk of loss as a result of the counterparty to a derivative agreement failing to meet its obligation.

2. **Market risk**—The risk of loss from adverse changes in market factors that affect the fair value of a derivative, such as interest rates, foreign exchange rates, and market indexes for equity securities.

3. **Basis risk**—The risk of loss from ineffective hedging activities. Basis risk is the difference between the fair value (or cash flows) of the hedged item and the fair value (or cash flows) of the hedging derivative. The entity is subject to the risk that fair values (or cash flows) will change so that the hedge will no longer be effective.

4. **Legal risk**—The risk of loss from a legal or regulatory action that invalidates or otherwise precludes performance by one or both parties to the derivative agreement.

C. Uses of Derivatives

1. **Speculation**—As an investment to speculate on price changes in various markets.

2. **Hedging**—To mitigate a business risk that is faced by the firm. Hedging is an activity that protects the entity against the risk of adverse changes in the fair values or cash flows of assets, liabilities, or future transactions. A hedge is a defensive strategy.

D. Financial Statement Effects of Derivative Transactions

The financial statement effects of derivative transactions is governed primarily by Statement of Financial Accounting Standards 133 (SFAS 133), *Accounting for Derivative Instruments and Hedging Activities*. In this section we will briefly review the requirements of that standard.

1. SFAS 133 provides guidance on three types of hedging activities.

   a. **Fair value hedge**—A hedge of the changes in the fair value of a recognized asset or liability, or of an unrecognized firm commitment, that are attributable to a particular risk.

   b. **Cash flow hedge**—A hedge of the variability in the cash flows of a recognized asset or liability, or of a forecasted transaction, that is attributable to a particular risk.

   c. **Foreign currency hedges**

   (1) A fair value hedge of an unrecognized firm commitment or a recognized asset or liability valued in a foreign currency (a foreign currency fair value hedge).

   (2) A cash flow hedge of a forecasted transaction, an unrecognized firm commitment, the forecasted functional-currency-equivalent cash flows associated with a recognized asset or liability, or a forecasted intercompany transaction (a foreign currency cash flow hedge).

   (3) A hedge of a net investment in a foreign operation.

2. In general, SFAS 133 requires an entity to report all derivatives as assets and liabilities in the statement of financial position, measured at fair value. Unrealized gains and losses attributed to changes in a derivative's fair value are accounted for differently, depending on whether the derivative is designated and qualifies as a hedge.

   a. **Accounting for a fair value hedge**—The change in the fair value of a derivative designated and qualifying as a fair value hedge is recognized in earnings and is offset by the portion of the change in the fair value of the hedged asset or liability that is attributable to the risk being hedged. Accordingly, the carrying amount of the hedged asset or liability is adjusted for changes in fair value. If the hedge is completely effective, the change in the derivative's fair value will equal the change in the hedged item's fair value. Therefore, there will be no effect on earnings. However, if the hedge is not completely effective, earnings will be increased or decreased for the difference between the changes in the fair values of the derivative and the hedged item.

   b. **Accounting for a cash flow hedge**—The effective portion of the change in the fair value of a derivative designated and qualifying as a cash flow hedge is reported in other comprehensive income, and the ineffective portion is reported in earnings.

   c. **Accounting for foreign hedges**—The accounting for foreign exchange hedges is very similar to the accounting for fair value and cash flow hedges as describe above.

3. **Valuing Derivatives**

As indicated above, derivatives are valued on financial statements at fair values, which is the current market price of the derivative. Quoted market prices in active markets are the best source of fair value and may be used for many derivatives. If a quoted market price is not available, valuation techniques are used to estimate the fair value, such as option-pricing models, matrix pricing, option-adjusted spread models, and fundamental analysis. We will briefly describe two commonly used methods.

a. The **Black-Scholes option-pricing model** is a mathematical model for estimating the price of stock options, using the following five variables:

- Time to expiration of the option
- Exercise or strike price
- Risk-free interest rate
- Price of the underlying stock
- Volatility of the price of the underlying stock

Other methods that are used to value options include Monte-Carlo simulation and binomial trees.

b. The **zero-coupon method** is used to determine the fair value of interest rate swaps. The zero-coupon method is a present value model in which the net settlements from the swap are estimated and discounted back to their current value. The key variables in the model include

- Estimated net settlement cash flows (explained in the example below)
- Timing of the cash flows as specified by the contract
- Discount rate

> *EXAMPLE: Assume that management enters into an agreement to swap payments on a fixed-rate liability for a variable rate. If interest rates decline, the firm will receive a net positive cash flow from the swap because the amount received on the fixed rate will be greater than the amount due on the variable rate. The opposite is true if rates increase. The zero-coupon method estimates future cash flows by calculating the net settlement that would be required if future interest rates are equal to the rates implied by the current yield curve. That amount is discounted back to determine the current fair value of the swap for financial reporting purposes.*

E. Hedging Examples

*EXAMPLE: On January 1, 20X1, a firm forecasts that it will need $10,000,000 in financing December 31, 20X1. Management decides that the appropriate form of financing is a bond issue of 10 years with a fixed interest rate. The market rate at which the firm can issue the debt is based on the Treasury rate, which is the yield on US Treasury bonds. On January 1, 20X1, the Treasury rate is 4%. Since the Treasury rate is the risk-free rate, the firm's actual rate would be higher to compensate the investor for risk of default on the bonds. Assume that based on the firm's credit rating and economic conditions, the credit spread is two basis points. Therefore, the firm's interest rate at January 1, 20X1, is equal to 6% (4% risk free rate + 2% credit spread). Management would like to lock in the risk-free component of interest today to hedge against an increase in rates. The firm hedges the transaction by entering into futures contracts to sell $10,000,000 in 5-year Treasury bonds at the forward rate of 4%. A position such as this, in which the firm is committed to sell something it does not own, is referred to as a **short position**. Around December 31, 20X1, management intends to purchase the contracts to close out its short position. Assume that the interest rate for Treasury bonds increases by one basis point from January 1, 20X1, to December 31, 20X1. If the interest rate on Treasury bonds increases by 1% from the 4% rate at the beginning of the year, the price of the bonds will decrease to allow an investor to earn 5% on the Treasury bonds. Therefore, management can buy futures contracts at much less than the price they were sold at and realize a gain. If the futures contracts for the Treasury bonds can be purchased at $9,400,000 the gain would be $600,000 ($10,000,000 – $9,400,000). Since this is a hedge, the gain would be reported in other comprehensive income rather than ordinary income. Assume that the bond financing that was issued by the firm on December 31, 20X1, was at 7 ½ %, the 5% risk-free rate plus a 2 ½ % credit spread. Hedge accounting would in effect reduce the interest rate on the debt by the 1% increase in the risk-free rate. From an accounting standpoint the gain on the Treasury bond futures contracts would be amortized to reduce interest expense by 1% over the life of the bond. Notice that the credit spread increased from January 1, 20X1, to December 31, 20X1, by ½%. Credit risk cannot be hedged, and therefore, the effective rate (after amortization of the hedging gain) on the bond issue actually increased from the forecasted 6% (4% + 2%) at the beginning of the year to 6 ½% (4% + 2 ½%).*

EXAMPLE: Several years ago a firm entered into a $20,000,000, ten-year noncallable debt agreement. The agreement calls for variable interest payments tied to the London Interbank Offered Rate (LIBOR). LIBOR is currently 4.5% but management is concerned about the volatility of current rates and wants to lock in a fixed rate for this debt. The firm enters into an interest rate swap to pay 7% fixed interest for the remaining term of the loan instead of the variable rate. In this way it is able to hedge its interest rate risk. Instead of having a variable interest expense over the life of the loan, the firm will have a fixed rate of 7%. The financial statement effects of this transaction would be recognition of a 7% fixed rate of interest over the life of the loan as opposed to the variable rate.

*EXAMPLE: Assume that a firm carries approximately $200,000 in short-term financing at variable interest rates and management is concerned about the current instability of short-term interest rates. To lock in the current rate for a year, management decides to sell on the futures market $200,000 in Treasury notes to be delivered one year from today. Again, this sale gives the firm a **short position**. The futures contracts will sell at approximately the current yield on the short-term*

Treasury securities. If interest rates rise, the firm will pay more interest on its short-term debt but it will also experience a gain on the futures contract because the price of Treasury notes will decline. Near the end of the year, the firm will purchase Treasury note contracts to close its short position. If the Treasury note contracts can be purchased for $180,000 at the end of the year, the firm's gain on the contract would be calculated as shown below.

Sales price Treasury note contracts (beginning of year)	$200,000
Purchase price of Treasury note contracts (end of year)	180,000
Gain on the contracts	$ 20,000

If the hedge was completely effective, the $20,000 gain on the futures contracts will offset the increase in interest expense experienced by the firm due to the increase in short-term interest rates. From an accounting standpoint, the gain on the contracts would be used to reduce interest expense in operating income.

PRESENT VALUE

This section reviews the basic concepts related to time value of money.

A. The Time Value of Money

The concepts of time value of money are essential for successful completion of the BEC exam. You must understand the mechanics as well as the concepts. Note that the following abbreviations are used in the text that follows.

i = interest rate
n = number of periods or rents

On the CPA exam, you do not have to know the complex formulas that are used to compute time value of money factors (TVMF). The factors will be given to you or enough information will be given to you so that you can easily compute them or use a spreadsheet tool to compute them. Your main focus of attention should be centered on understanding which TVMF should be used in a given situation.

1. **Future Value (FV) of an Amount** (future value of $1)

     The future value of an amount is the amount that will be available at some point in the future if an amount is deposited today and earns compound interest for "n" periods. The most common application is savings deposits. For example, if you deposited $100 today at 10%, you would have $110 [$100 + ($100 × 10%)] at the end of the first year, $121[$100 + ($110 × 10%)] at the end of the second year, etc. The compounding feature allows you to earn interest on interest. In the second year of the example you earn $11 interest: $10 on the original $100 and $1 on the first year's interest of $10.

2. **Present Value (PV) of a Future Amount** (present value of $1)

     The present value of a future amount is the amount you would pay now for an amount to be received "n" periods in the future given an interest rate of "i." A common application would be the money you would lend today for a noninterest-bearing note receivable in the future. For example, if you were lending money at 10%, you would lend $100 for a $110 note due in one year or for a $121 note due in two years.

     The present value of $1 is the inverse of the future value of $1. Thus, given a future value of $1 table, you have a present value of $1 by dividing each value into 1.00. Look at the present value of $1 and future value of $1 tables on the next page. The future value of $1 at 10% in five years is 1.611. Thus, the present value of $1 in five years would be 1.00 ÷ 1.611 which is .621 (check the table). Conversely, the future value of $1 is found by dividing the present value of $1 into 1.00, that is, 1.00 ÷ .621 = 1.611.

3. **Compounding**

     When interest is compounded more than once a year, two extra steps are needed. First, **multiply** "n" by the number of times interest is compounded annually. This will give you the total number of interest periods. Second, **divide** "i" by the number of times interest is compounded annually. This will give you the appropriate interest rate for each interest period. For example, if the 10% was compounded semiannually, the amount of $100 at the end of one year would be $110.25 [$(1.05)^2$] instead of $110.00. The extra $.25 is 5% of the $5.00 interest earned in the first half of the year.

4. **Future Value of an Ordinary Annuity**

     The future value of an ordinary annuity is the amount available "n" periods in the future as a result of the deposit of an amount (A) at the end of every period 1 through "n." Compound interest is earned at the rate of "i" on the deposits. A common application is a bond sinking fund. A deposit is made at the end of the first period and earns compound interest for n-1 periods (not during the first period, because the deposit is made at the end of the first period). The next to the last payment earns one period's interest, that is, $n - (n-1) = 1$. The last payment earns no interest, because it is deposited at the end of the last (nth) period. Remember that in the FUTURE AMOUNT OF AN ORDINARY ANNU-ITY TABLE, all of the factors for any "n" row are based on one less interest period than the number of payments.

TIME VALUE OF MONEY FACTOR (TVMF) TABLES

Future Value (Amount) of $1

n	*6%*	*8%*	*10%*	*12%*	*15%*
1	1.060	1.080	1.100	1.120	1.150
2	1.124	1.166	1.210	1.254	1.323
3	1.191	1.260	1.331	1.405	1.521
4	1.262	1.360	1.464	1.574	1.749
5	1.338	1.469	1.611	1.762	2.011

Present Value of $1

n	*6%*	*8%*	*10%*	*12%*	*15%*
1	.943	.926	.909	.893	.870
2	.890	.857	.826	.797	.756
3	.840	.794	.751	.712	.658
4	.792	.735	.683	.636	.572
5	.747	.681	.621	.567	.497

Future Value (Amount) of an Ordinary Annuity of $1

n	*6%*	*8%*	*10%*	*12%*	*15%*
1	1.000	1.000	1.000	1.000	1.000
2	2.060	2.080	2.100	2.120	2.150
3	3.184	3.246	3.310	3.374	3.473
4	4.375	4.506	4.506	4.641	4.993
5	5.637	5.867	6.105	6.353	6.742

Present Value of an Ordinary Annuity of $1

n	*6%*	*8%*	*10%*	*12%*	*15%*
1	.943	.926	.909	.893	.870
2	1.833	1.783	1.736	1.690	1.626
3	2.673	2.577	2.487	2.402	2.283
4	3.465	3.312	3.170	3.037	2.855
5	4.212	3.993	3.791	3.605	3.352

5. Present Value of an Ordinary Annuity

The present value of an ordinary annuity is the value today, given a discount rate, of a series of future payments. A common application is the capitalization of lease payments by either lessors or lessees. Payments "1" through "n" are assumed to be made at the end of years "1" through "n," and are discounted back to the present.

EXAMPLE: Assume a five-year lease of equipment requiring payments of $1,000 at the end of each of the five years, which is to be capitalized. If the discount rate is 10%, the present value is $3,791 ($1,000 × 3.791). The behavior of the present value of the lease payment stream over the five-year period is shown below. Note that the liability (principal amount) grows by interest in the amount of 10% during each period and decreases by $1,000 at the end of each period.

<u>0</u>	<u>1</u>	2	3	4	5

$3,791 + 380 Int. = $4,171
                    − 1,000 Pay
                      $3,171 + 320 Int. = $3,491
                                        − 1,000 Pay
                                          $2,491 + 250 Int. = $2,741
                                                            − 1,000
                                                              $1,741 + 170 Int. = $1,911
                                                                                − 1,000
                                                                                  $ 911 + 91 Int. = $1,002
                                                                                                  − 1,000
                                                                                                      2*

* *Due to rounding*

6. **Distinguishing a Future Value of an Annuity from a Present Value of an Annuity**

    Sometimes confusion arises in distinguishing between the future value (amount) of an annuity and the present value of an annuity. These two may be distinguished by determining whether the total dollar amount in the problem comes at the beginning (e.g., cost of equipment acquired for leasing) or at the end (e.g., the amount needed to retire bonds) of the series of payments as illustrated below.

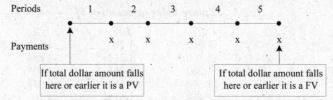

    Remember: if the total amount comes at the end of the series of payments, it is a **future value** of annuity situation. If the total amount comes at the beginning of the series of payments, it is a **present value** of annuity situation. The total dollar amount may be given in the problem or you may have to compute it; either way, it makes no difference in determining whether a problem involves a present value or future value situation.

    Some students feel the need to "convert" all time value of money problems into either present value or future value problems, depending on which they're most comfortable with. This process involves more work and more chance for errors, because an additional TVMF equation must be solved in the conversion. This is inefficient, and unnecessary, if you are able to correctly identify between the two initially. Become proficient at determining present value and future value situations, so that you may efficiently select the correct TVMF from the corresponding table.

7. **Annuities Due**

    In some cases, the payments or annuities may not conform to the assumptions inherent in the annuity tables. For example, the payments might be made at the beginning of each of the five years instead of at the end of each year. This is an annuity due (annuity in advance) in contrast to an ordinary annuity (annuity in arrears). Both annuity due and ordinary annuity payments are represented by the "x's" in the illustration below.

    If the payments in the 5-period lease example above were made at the beginning of the period, the present value of the first payment which is made today is $1,000 (i.e., the TVMF is 1.00). The remaining 4 payments comprise an ordinary annuity for 4 periods as you can see on the above diagram. Always use time diagrams to analyze application of annuities.

    To convert either a future value of an ordinary annuity or the present value of an ordinary annuity factor to an annuity due factor, multiply the ordinary annuity factor times (1 + i). For the above lease example, you would find the present value of an ordinary annuity factor for n = 5 which is 3.993. Then multiply 3.993 by 1.08 to arrive at the annuity due factor, 4.312. The present value of the payments would be $4,312 (4.312 × $1,000). Notice that the present value of the annuity due in the above example is $319 greater than the present value of the ordinary annuity because the payments are moved closer to the present.

8. **TVMF Applications**

    The basic formula to use is

$$\text{FV or PV} = \text{TVMF} \times \text{Amount}$$

If an annuity is involved, the amount is the periodic payment or deposit; if not, it is a single sum. Note that FV or PV is determined by three variables: time, interest rate, and payment. TVMF represents two variables: time and interest rate. The tables usually have the interest rate on the horizontal axis and time on the vertical axis. The above formula may also be stated as

$$\text{Amount} = \frac{\text{FV or PV}}{\text{TVMF}}$$

For example, if we need to accumulate $12,210 in five years to repay a loan, we could determine the required annual deposit with the above formula. If the savings rate were 10%, we would divide the FV ($12,210) by the TVMF of the future value of annuity, n=5, i=.10 (6.105) and get $2,000. Thus, $2,000 deposited at the end of each of five years earning 10% will result in $12,210. This formula may also be used to find future values of an amount, present values of amounts, and annuities in the same manner.

Another variation of the formula is

$$\text{TVMF} = \frac{\text{FV or PV}}{\text{Amount}}$$

For example, we may be offered a choice between paying $3,312 in cash or $1,000 a year at the end of each of the next four years. We determine the interest rate by dividing the annual payment into the present value of the annuity to obtain the TVMF (3.312) for n=4. We then find the interest rate which has the same or similar TVMF (in this case 8%).

Alternatively, using the above formula, we may know the interest rate but not know the number of payments. Given the TVMF, we can determine "n" by looking in the TVMF table under the known interest rate. Remember the TVMF reflects two variables: time and interest rate.

B. Valuation of Bonds

Bonds generally provide for periodic fixed interest payments at a coupon (contract) rate of interest. At issuance, or thereafter, the market rate of interest for the particular type of bond may be above, the same, or below the coupon rate. If the market rate exceeds the coupon rate, the book value will be less than the maturity value. The difference (discount) will make up for the coupon rate being below the market rate.

Conversely, when the coupon rate exceeds the market rate, the bond will sell for more than maturity value to bring the effective rate to the market rate. This difference (premium) will make up for the coupon rate being above the market rate. When the coupon rate equals the market rate, the bond will sell for the maturity value.

The market value of a bond is equal to the maturity value and interest payments discounted to the present. You may have to refer to the discussion of time value of money concepts in the previous section before working with the subsequent material. Finally, when solving bond problems, candidates must be careful when determining the number of months to use in the calculation of interest and discount/premium amortization. For example, candidates frequently look at a bond issue with an interest date of September 1 and count three months to December 31. This error is easy to make because candidates focus only on the fact that September is the ninth month instead of also noting whether the date is at the beginning or end of the month.

1. **Bond Valuation Example**

    $10,000 in bonds, semiannual interest at 6% coupon rate, maturing in six years, and market rate of 5%.

    a. Find present value of maturity value. Use present value of $1 factor. Discount $10,000 back 12 periods at 2 1/2% interest (Factor = .7436). (Semiannual compounding is going to be required to discount the semiannual payments so it is also assumed here.)

    $$\$10,000 \quad \times \quad .7436 \quad = \quad \$7,436$$

    b. Find the present value of the annuity of twelve $300 interest payments. Use present value of an ordinary annuity of $1 factor for twelve periods at 2 1/2% interest (Factor = 10.26).

    $$\$300 \quad \times \quad 10.26 \quad = \quad \$3,078$$

    c. Today's value is $10,514 (7,436 + 3,078)

CAPITAL BUDGETING

A. Capital budgeting is a technique to evaluate and control long-term investments. There are six stages to capital budgeting.

1. **Identification stage.** Management determines the type of capital projects that are necessary to achieve management's objectives and strategies.

2. **Search stage.** Management attempts to identify alternative capital investments that will achieve management's objectives.

3. **Information-acquisition stage.** Management attempts to revaluate the various investments in terms of their costs and benefits.
4. **Selection stage.** Management chooses the projects that best meet the criteria established.
5. **Financing stage.** Management decides on the best source of funding for the project. This process is described in Module 44.
6. **Implementation and control stage.** Management undertakes the project and monitors the performance of the investment.

This section will focus primarily on the techniques management uses to evaluate various projects. However, these techniques may also be used to monitor their performance. Capital budgeting alternatives are typically evaluated using discounted cash flow techniques. Such techniques involve evaluation of an investment today in terms of the present value of future cash returns from the investment. The objective is to identify the most profitable or best investment alternative. The cash returns can take two forms depending on the nature of the project. If the project will produce revenue, the return is the difference between the cash revenues (inflows) and cash expenses (outflows). Other projects generate cost savings (e.g., cash outflows for labor that are not made because a new machine is more efficient). The latter are, in effect, reductions in outflows, which for simplicity, can be treated as cash inflows. Conceptually, the results of both type of projects are the same. The entity ends up with more cash by making the initial capital investment.

The following terminology is useful to the understanding of capital budgeting analysis:

a. **Sunk, past, or unavoidable costs** are committed costs that are not avoidable and are therefore irrelevant to the decision process.
b. **Avoidable costs** are costs that will **not** continue to be incurred if a department or product is terminated.
c. **Committed costs** arise from a company's basic commitment to open its doors and engage in business (depreciation, property taxes, management salaries).
d. **Discretionary costs** are fixed costs whose level is set by current management decisions (e.g., advertising, research and development).
e. **Relevant costs** are future costs that will change as a result of a specific decision.
f. **Differential (incremental) cost** is the difference in cost between two alternatives.
g. **Opportunity cost** is the maximum income or savings (benefit) foregone by rejecting an alternative.
h. **Outlay (out-of-pocket) cost** is the cash disbursement associated with a specific project.

The choice among alternative investing decisions can be made on the basis of several capital budgeting models: (1) Payback or discounted payback; (2) Accounting rate of return; (3) Net present value, (4) Excess present value index, and (5) Internal (time-adjusted) rate of return.

B. Payback and Discounted Payback

The **payback** method evaluates investments on the length of time until recapture (return) of the investment. For example, if a $10,000 investment were to return a cash flow of $2,500 a year for eight years, the payback period would be four years. If the payback period is to be computed after income taxes, it is necessary to calculate cash flow as shown below, remembering that depreciation itself does not consume cash. Assuming an eight-year life with no salvage value and a 40% income tax rate, the after-tax payback period would be computed as follows:

Cash flow: $2,500 \times (1 - 40\%) = \$1,500$
Tax savings from depreciation: $1,250 \times 40\% = \$500$
Cash flow after tax: $1,500 + \$500 = \$2,000$
$10,000 \div \$2,000 = 5$ years

The payback method has a number of limitations. First, it ignores total project profitability and therefore has little or no connection to maximization of shareholder value. Second, the method is not really effective in taking into account the time value of money.

The **discounted payback** method is essentially the same as the payback method except that in calculating the payback period, cash flows are first discounted to their present value. This is only a minor improvement over the conventional payback method. It still ignores any cash flows after the cutoff period and therefore does not consider total project profitability.

Using the above example, assume that the cost of capital for the firm is 8%. The discounted payback would be calculated as shown below.

Discounted payback

Cash flow after taxes = $2,000

Year	Cash flow	Present value factor	Present value of cash flow	Cumulative present value
1	$2,000	.926	$1,852	$1,852
2	2,000	.857	1,714	3,566
3	2,000	.794	1,588	5,154
4	2,000	.735	1,470	6,624
5	2,000	.681	1,362	7,986
6	2,000	.630	1,260	9,246
7	2,000	.583	1,166	10,412
8	2,000	.540	1,080	11,492

From the table we see that the discounted payback occurs in year 7. Specifically, it occurs when $754 ($10,000 – $9,246) of cash flow is received in that year. By dividing the $754 needed cash flow by the total $1,166 cash flows in year 7, that we need .65 of year 7 cash flows. Therefore, the discounted payback period is 6.65 years.

C. Accounting Rate of Return

The **accounting rate of return** (ARR) method computes an approximate rate of return which ignores the time value of money. It is computed as follows:

$$ARR = Annual\ net\ income \div Average\ (or\ initial)\ investment$$

Using the same example and assuming the annual cash flows approximate annual net income before depreciation and taxes for the project, the ARR before taxes is

$$(\$2,500 - \$1,250) \div (\$10,000 \div 2) = 25\%$$

The ARR after taxes is

$$[(\$2,500 - \$1,250) \times 60\%] \div (\$10,000 \div 2) = 15\%$$

Note that the numerator is the increase in **net income,** not **cash flows,** so depreciation is subtracted. The average investment is one-half the initial investment because the initial investment is depreciated down to 0 by the end of the project. If a problem asked for ARR based on **initial** investment, you would not divide the investment by 2.

The advantage of the accounting rate of return method is that it is simple and intuitive. It also is often the measure that is used to evaluate management. However, it has a number of limitations including

- The results are affected by the depreciation method used
- ARR makes no adjustment for project risk
- ARR makes no adjustment for the time value of money

D. Net Present Value

The **net present value** (NPV) method is a discounted cash flow method which calculates the present value of the future cash flows of a project and compares this with the investment outlay required to implement the project. The net present value of a project is defined as

$$NPV = (Present\ value\ of\ future\ cash\ flows) - (Required\ investment)$$

The calculation of the present value of the future cash flows requires the selection of a discount rate (also referred to as the target or hurdle rate). The rate used should be the minimum rate of return that management is willing to accept on capital investment projects. The rate used should be no less than the cost of capital—the rate management currently must pay to obtain funds. A project which earns exactly the desired rate of return will have a net present value of 0. A positive net present value identifies projects which will earn in excess of the minimum rate. For example, if a company desires a minimum return of 6% on an investment of $10,000 that has an expected return of $2,500 for five years, the present value of the cash flows is $10,530 ($2,500 × 4.212: 4.212 is the TVMF for the present value of an annuity, n = 5, i = 6%; see the previous section on Present Value Concepts). The net present value of $5,300 ($105,300 – $100,000) indicates that the project will earn a return in excess of the 6% minimum desired. If the requirement were for a net-of-tax return of 6%, and the net-of-tax cash flow were $23,000, that amount would be multiplied by 4.212. This would result in a present value of $96,876 for the cash inflows, which is less than the $100,000 initial outlay. Therefore, this investment should not be made.

The NPV method is based on cash flows and would ignore depreciation if taxes were not considered. As shown earlier, however, depreciation results in a tax savings (tax shield) that must be factored into the evaluation. For example, assume that a company is considering the purchase of equipment costing $20,000 for use in a new project. MACRS is used to depreciate equipment for tax purposes, under which the machine has a useful life of seven years. The required rate of return of the company is 8%. The present value of the tax savings from depreciation would be as follows:

Year	Income tax deduction for depreciation	Income tax savings at 30% tax rate	8% Discount factor	Present value at 8%*
1	$2,858	$ 857	.926	$ 794
2	4,898	1,469	.857	1,259
3	3,498	1,049	.794	833
4	2,498	749	.735	551
5	1,786	536	.681	365
6	1,784	535	.630	337
7	1,786	536	.583	312
8	892	268	.540	145
				$4,596

* *Tax savings × Discount factor*

Therefore, $4,596 would be included in the NPV computation as a cash inflow from the equipment.

The **excess present value (profitability) index** computes the ratio of the present value of the cash inflows to the initial cost of a project. It is used to implement the net present value method when there is a limit on funds available for capital investments. Assuming other factors are equal, this is accomplished by allocating funds to those projects with the highest excess present value indexes.

First, the net present value of each alternative is calculated using the minimum required rate of return. Then the excess present value index is computed

$$\frac{\text{Present value of future net cash inflows}}{\text{Initial investment}} \times 100 = \text{Excess present value index}$$

If the index is equal to or greater than 100%, the project will generate a return equal to or greater than the required rate of return.

Net present value methods are the most widely accepted methods of evaluating a capital expenditure. Their advantages include

- Presents results in dollars which are easily understood
- Adjusts for the time value of money
- Considers the total profitability of the project
- Provides a straightforward method of controlling for the risk of competing projects—higher-risk cash flows can be discounted at a higher interest rate
- Provides a direct estimate of the change in shareholder wealth resulting from undertaking a project

The limitations of net present value methods include

- May not be considered as simple or intuitive as some other methods
- Does not take into account the management flexibility with respect to a project—management may be able to adjust the amount invested after the first year or two depending on the actual returns

E. Internal Rate of Return

The **internal (time-adjusted) rate of return** (IRR) method is another discounted cash flow method. It determines the rate of discount at which the present value of the future cash flows will exactly equal the investment outlay (i.e., the rate that results in a NPV of zero). This rate is compared with the minimum desired rate of return to determine if the investment should be made. The internal rate of return is determined by setting the investment today equal to the discounted value of future cash flows. The discounting factor (rate of return) is the unknown. The TVMF for the previous example is

PV (investment today) = TVMF × Cash flows
$100,000 = TVMF × $25,000
TVMF = 4.00

The interest rate of a TVMF of 4.00 where n = 5 is approximately 8%. The after-tax rate of return is determined using the $23,000 after-tax cash inflow amount as follows:

$$\begin{aligned} \$100,000 &= \text{TVMF} \times \$23,000 \\ \text{TVMF} &= 4.35 \end{aligned}$$

The interest rate of a TVMF of 4.35 where n = 5 is approximately 5%. The answers are worded "less than 5%, but greater than 0%," "less than 7%, but greater than 5%," etc.

The relationship between the NPV method and the IRR method can be summarized as follows:

NPV	*IRR*
NPV > 0	IRR > Discount rate
NPV = 0	IRR = Discount rate
NPV < 0	IRR < Discount rate

If the firm has sufficient funds to undertake all projects, the calculated internal rate of return on a project is compared to a prespecified **hurdle rate** which is the firm's minimum acceptable rate of return for the project. The hurdle rate is determined based on the market rate of return for projects with similar levels of risk.

1. The advantages of the internal rate of return method include

    a. Adjusts for the time value of money
    b. The hurdle rate is based on market interest rates for similar investments
    c. The results tend to be a little more intuitive than the results of the net present value method

2. Limitations of the internal rate of return method include

    a. Depending on the cash flow pattern there may be no unique internal rate of return for a particular project—there may be multiple returns depending on the assumptions used
    b. Occasionally, there may be no real discount rate that equates the project's NPV to zero
    c. The technique also has limitations when evaluating mutually exclusive investments as described in the next section

F. Mutually Exclusive Projects

1. Until now, we have assumed that management can invest in any project that meets the particular criteria being used. However, at times management must decide on one of several projects that are all acceptable. In other words, management must decide on the best project. This situation is often described as **capital rationing**.
2. To decide on the best investment, management must examine the characteristics of each. One way of summarizing the characteristics of an investment is through the use of the **net present value profile**. The profile allows us to portray the net present value of projects at different discounts rates.

> EXAMPLE: *Management is considering investment in one of two projects, both of which involve an initial investment of $20,000. Future cash flows from the two projects are shown below.*
>
> | Year | Investment A | Investment B |
> |---|---|---|
> | 1 | $3,000 | $18,000 |
> | 2 | 4,000 | 6,000 |
> | 3 | 5,000 | 2,400 |
> | 4 | 10,000 | |
> | 5 | 10,000 | |
>
> *The following graph shows the net present value for the two investments.*

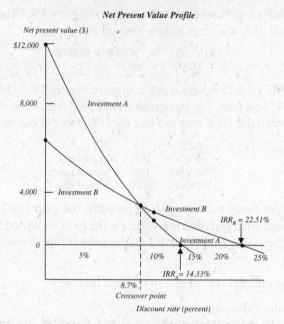

Net Present Value Profile

3. Comparing the two investments, we see that at low discount rates Investment A has a higher present value. Investment B has a higher net present value at higher discount rates. This is because most of the return from Investment B is loaded toward the early years of the investment. The crossover point is at 8.7%, at lower discount rates Investment A should be selected, and at higher rates Investment B should be accepted.

4. Net present value works better than the internal rate of return in a situation in which a choice must be made among a group of investments. The internal rate of return method is based upon an important assumption when comparing investments of different lives and different cash flow patterns. The method implicitly assumes that the cash inflows from an investment can be reinvested at the same internal rate of return. For example, assume a company must choose between two projects, C and D. The IRR on project C is 15% with a life of five years, while the IRR of project D is 13% with a life of ten years. Project C would be the one selected under the IRR criteria. However, the internal rate of return method assumes that the cash inflows from the project can be reinvested at 15%. If the cash inflows can only be reinvested at 9%, then project B may be the better alternative. **Therefore, we see that traditional IRR criteria may not arrive at the best solution in all cases.** As a result, many firms rely on net present value criteria when evaluating competing proposals.

G. Determining Future Cash Flows

1. In evaluating investment alternatives, one of the first challenges is determining the future cash flows that are relevant to the decision. Simply stated, relevant cash flows are those that are expected to differ among the alternatives. Examples of relevant cash flows include

a. The initial investment in long-term tangible or intangible assets for each investment alternative
b. Any initial investment in working capital for each investment alternative (e.g., inventories, accounts receivable, etc.)
c. Cash flow from the sale of any assets being replaced
d. Differences in cash flows from operations under the alternatives (e.g., cash inflows from sales and/or cash outflows for operating costs)

- Remember to focus on cash flows not accounting income
- Payments for incremental income taxes should be included
- Depreciation expense does not affect cash flows but the firm receives a tax savings (shield) from depreciation expense. It reduces taxable income and therefore reduces tax payments. Remember it is tax depreciation that generates the tax shield, and book depreciation may differ from tax depreciation.

e. Cash flows at the end of the expected life of the project.

- Terminal disposal price of any long-term tangible or intangible assets. If the tax basis (Initial cost – Tax depreciation taken) is expected to be different from the disposal price, the tax gain or loss will generate a tax inflow or outflow.
- Recovery of any working capital investment—This investment will be recovered at the end of the project by liquidation of inventories, accounts receivable, etc. There are generally no tax implications of this recovery because it is assumed that the cash received will be equal to the book value (tax basis) of the working capital items.

*EXAMPLE: Watson Corporation is considering replacing an existing machine with a more efficient model. The existing machine can operate for another five years and will have a terminal value (salvage value) of $0 at the end of five years. The book value and tax basis of the old machine is $30,000, and if it continues in operation, tax and book depreciation will equal $6,000 per year for the next five years. The new machine will not increase revenues but it will reduce operating costs. The required net initial investment for the new machine is $200,000, which consists of $210,000 cost of the new machine plus an additional cash investment in working capital (supplies for the machine) of $10,000, less cash of $20,000 from the disposal of the existing machine ($210,000 + $10,000 – $20,000 = $200,000). The new machine is expected to have a five-year useful life and a terminal value (salvage value) of $20,000. Tax and book depreciation per year on the new machine on a straight-line basis will be $38,000 [($210,000 cost – $20,000 salvage value)/ 5 years]. Management expects a cash flow savings in operating costs of $70,000 for the first three years and $60,000 for years four and five. **To simplify computations, operating cash flows are assumed to occur at the end of each year.** The working capital investment of $10,000 is expected to be recovered in full at the end of year five. Watson Corporation's tax rate is 40%. The relevant cash flows are presented below.*

Net initial investment

Purchase price of new machine		$(210,000)
Additional investment in working capital		(10,000)
Cash from disposal of old machine		20,000
Total effect of disposal of old machine:		
Cash from disposal	$20,000	
Less: Tax basis	(30,000)	
Loss on sale of old machine	(10,000)	
Tax rate	40%	
Tax benefit from sale of old machine		4,000
Net initial investment		$(196,000)

Operating cash flow for years 1 through 3

Cost savings before income taxes		$ 70,000
Less income taxes (40% × $70,000)		(28,000)
Cost savings after taxes		42,000
Tax savings from depreciation:		
Depreciation on new machine	$38,000	
Less depreciation on old machine	6,000	
Depreciation differential	$32,000	
Tax rate	40%	
Tax savings from incremental depreciation		12,800
Cash flow after taxes for years 1 through 3		$ 54,800

Operating cash flow for years 4 and 5

Cost savings before income taxes		$ 60,000
Less income taxes (40% × $60,000)		(24,000)
Cost savings after taxes		36,000
Total savings from depreciation:		
Depreciation on new machine	$38,000	
Less depreciation on old machine	6,000	
Depreciation differential	$32,000	
Tax rate	40%	
Tax savings from incremental depreciation		12,800
Cash flow after taxes for years 4 and 5		$ 48,800

Cash flow at end of year 5

Terminal price of new machine	$ 20,000
Recovery of working capital investment	10,000
Cash flow at end of year 5	$ 30,000

The pattern of relevant cash flows from investment in the new machine is summarized below.

	0	1	2	3	4	5
			Relevant Cash Flows			
Initial investment	$(196,000)					
Operating cash flow (after tax)		$54,800	$54,800	$54,800	$48,800	$48,800
Terminal price of new machine						20,000
Recovery of working capital						10,000
Total relevant cash flows	$(196,000)	$54,800	$54,800	$54,800	$48,800	$78,800

Assuming that Watson Corporation's cost of capital is 10%, the net present value of purchasing the new machine is calculated below.

Year	Cash flow	Present value factor (10%	Present value
0	$(196,000)	1.000	$(196,000)
1	54,800	.909	49,813
2	54,800	.826	45,265
3	54,800	.751	41,155
4	48,800	.683	33,330
5	78,800	.621	48,935
Net present value			$22,498

The results indicate that when using the net present value criteria, management should purchase the new machine.

EXAMPLE: *Taylor Corporation is considering investing in one of the following two projects. Taylor's marginal tax rate is 25% and its cost of capital is 10%*

Investment A

Initial investment	$150,000
Operating effects for 5-year useful life:	
Cash basis revenues	$200,000
Cash basis expenses	(160,000)
Net cash flow from operations (before taxes)	$ 40,000
Tax depreciation on the investment each year	$ 25,000
Terminal value of investment at end of 5 years	$ 25,000

Investment B

Initial investment	$210,000
Operating effects for 6-year useful life:	
Cash basis revenues	$250,000
Cash basis expenses	(200,000)
Net cash flow from operations (before taxes)	$ 50,000
Tax depreciation on the investment each year	$ 35,000
Terminal value of investment at end of 6 years	$ 0

The cash flows from the two projects may be scheduled out as follows:

Investment A

	0	1	2	3	4	5
			Relevant Cash Flows			
Initial investment	$(150,000)					
Operating cash flow (before taxes)		$40,000	$40,000	$40,000	$40,000	$40,000
Taxes on operating cash flows (25%)		(10,000)	(10,000)	(10,000)	(10,000)	(10,000)
Tax savings from added depreciation (25% × $25,000)		6,250	6,250	6,250	6,250	6,250
Terminal price of investment						25,000
Total relevant cash flows	$(150,000)	$36,250	$36,250	$36,250	$36,250	$61,250

Investment B

			Relevant Cash Flows				
	0	*1*	*2*	*3*	*4*	*5*	*6*
Initial investment	$(210,000)						
Operating cash flow (before taxes)		$50,000	$50,000	$50,000	50,000	$50,000	$50,000
Taxes on operating cash flows (25%)		(12,500)	(12,500)	(12,500)	(12,500)	(12,500)	(12,500)
Tax savings from added depreciation (25% × $35,000)		8,750	8,750	8,750	8,750	8,750	8,750
Terminal value of investment							0
Total relevant cash flows	$(210,000)	$46,250	$46,250	$46,250	$46,250	$46,250	$46,250

		Investment A		Investment B	
Year	Present value factor (10%)	Cash flow	Present value	Cash flow	Present value
0	1.000	$(150,000)	$(150,000)	$(210,000)	$(210,000)
1	.909	36,250	32,951	46,250	42,041
2	.826	36,250	29,943	46,250	38,203
3	.751	36,250	27,224	46,250	34,734
4	.683	36,250	24,759	46,250	31,589
5	.621	61,250	38,036	46,250	28,721
6	.564			46,250	26,085
			$(2,913)		$(8,627)

The results indicate that when using the net present value criteria, Investment A should be accepted and Investment B rejected.

H. Considering Risk in Capital Budgeting

Risk as applied to capital budgeting is defined in terms of variability of the possible outcomes from a given investment. **Projected cash flows are not known with certainty.** Like individual investors, it is assumed that management is **risk averse**—that is, given the same rate of return they would prefer an investment with less uncertainty. A number of statistical techniques have been developed to measure the extent of risk inherent in a particular situation.

1. Probability Analysis

One way to include risk in the capital budgeting analysis is to assign probabilities to possible outcomes. The probabilities provide a mathematical way of expressing uncertainty about the outcomes. They may be based on past experience, industry ratios and trends, economic forecasts, interviews with executives, or sophisticated simulation techniques.

a. The set of all possible outcomes from an investment with a probability assigned to each outcome is referred to as a **probability distribution**. Probability distributions may be discrete or continuous. A **discrete distribution** identifies a **limited number of potential outcomes** and assigns probabilities to each of the outcomes. **A continuous distribution** theoretically defines an infinite number of possible outcomes. A commonly used continuous distribution is the **normal distribution** (bell-shaped curve). The normal distribution is useful because it approximates many real-world situations and it can be completely described with only two statistics, its mean and its standard deviation. Normal distributions have the following fixed relationships between distance from the mean and area under the curve:

Distance in standard deviations from the mean	Area under the curve
1.00	68.3%
1.64	90.0%
1.96	95.0%
2.00	95.4%
2.57	99.0%

Therefore, by knowing the mean (expected value) and the standard deviation, management can construct a confidence interval for a particular outcome. As an example, 95% of the outcomes will fall within the mean (expected value) plus or minus 1.96 standard deviations. The following chart illustrates this point in graphic form:

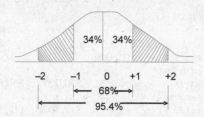

b. Once outcomes are determined and probabilities assigned, management can compute two important statistical measures—the expected value and the standard deviation. The following formula can be used to calculate the expected return:

$$\hat{k} = \sum_{i=1}^{n} k_i p_i$$

Where

$\hat{k}$ = the expected value of the returns
k = the returns from the various possible outcomes
p = the probabilities assigned to the possible outcomes

The standard deviation can be calculated using the following formula:

$$\sigma = \sum_{i}^{n} (k_i - \hat{k})^2 p_i$$

EXAMPLE: Assume a firm is considering investing in a project with the following possible outcomes and related probabilities.

Outcome (present value of future cash flows)	Probability of outcome	Assumption
$100,000	.2	Pessimistic
$150,000	.6	Most likely
$200,000	.2	Optimistic

The expected return would be $150,000 as calculated below.

k		p		
$100,000	×	.2	=	$20,000
$150,000	×	.6	=	90,000
$200,000	×	.2	=	40,000
$\hat{k}$			=	$150,000

The standard deviation of the expected return would be $31,623 as calculated below.

$$\sigma = \sum_{i}^{n} (k_i - \hat{k})^2 p_i$$

$k_i - \hat{k}$	$= (k_i - \hat{k})$	$(k_i - \hat{k})^2$	$p_i \times (k_i - \hat{k})^2$	$\sqrt{Square\ root}$
100,000 – 150,000 =	-50,000	2,500,000,000	500,000,000	$\sqrt{1,000,000,000}$
150,000 – 150,000 =	0	0	0	
200,000 – 150,000 =	50,000	2,500,000,000	$\dfrac{500,000,000}{1,000,000,000}$	= $31,623

c. The standard deviation provides a rough estimate of how far each outcome falls away from the mean. Generally, the larger the standard deviation, the greater the risk. However, the standard deviation as a measure of risk has a significant limitation. Its size depends on the size of the investment. The $31,623 may seem reasonable in relation to these possible outcomes, but what if the expected value of the investment was only $60,000. The standard deviation would be quite large. Therefore, it is difficult to use the standard deviation in comparing risk for investments of different sizes.

d. To eliminate the size difficulty analysts have developed a preferred measure, the **coefficient of variation,** which is simply the standard deviation divided by the expected value of the investment, as shown below.

$$\text{Coefficient of variation} = \frac{\sigma}{\hat{k}}$$

For the investment described above, the coefficient of variation would equal .2108 as calculated below.

$$\text{Coefficient of variation} = \frac{\$31,623}{\$150,000} = .2108$$

The coefficient of variation provides a measure of risk that is normalized for the size of the investment. Therefore, it allows comparisons across investments of varying size.

2. **Risk-Adjusted Discounted Rate**

a. A popular approach to adjust for risk involves using different discount rates for proposals with different levels of risk. Using this technique, management is applying **risk-adjusted discount rates**. A project with a normal level of risk is discounted at the firm's cost of capital and projects with greater levels of risk are discounted at higher rates.

b. Using the coefficient of variation as a risk measure, management could set different categories of risk with different risk premiums as shown in the following table:

(Risk coefficient of variation)	*Discount rate*
0.40 or less	10.0%
0.41 to 0.70	13.0%
0.71 to 1.00	16.0%
1.01 to 1.30	20.0%

Alternatively, management might simply establish qualitative measures of risk as shown below.

Risk (example)	*Discount rate*
Low risk (replace old equipment)	7.0%
Normal risk (add plant capacity	10.0%
Moderately above normal risk (new market)	15.0%
High risk (new product in foreign market)	20.0%

EXAMPLE: Assume that management is evaluating two alternative projects, Investment A and Investment B. Investment A has a normal level of risk and should be discounted at the firm's cost of capital, 10%. Investment B, on the other hand, has a significantly higher level of risk and management believes that 15% is the appropriate discount rate. Assume that Investment A would require an investment of $30,000, and Investment B would require an investment of $28,000. The table below presents the discounted cash flow for the two projects.

Investment A (10% discount rate)			*Investment B (15% discount rate)*		
Year			*Year*		
1	*$10,000 × 0.909 =*	*$ 9,090*	*1*	*$5,000 × 0.870 =*	*$4,350*
2	*20,000 × 0.826 =*	*16,520*	*2*	*7,000 × 0.756 =*	*5,292*
3	*10,000 × 0.751 =*	*7,510*	*3*	*10,000 × 0.658 =*	*6,580*
		$33,120	*4*	*10,000 × 0.572 =*	*5,720*
	Investment	*30,000*	*5*	*10,000 × 0.497 =*	*4,970*
	Net present value	*$ 3,120*			*$26,912*
				Investment	*28,000*
				Net present value	*$(1,088)*

As can be seen from the table, Investment A would be acceptable because it has a positive net present value. Project B would be rejected because its net present value is negative.

3. **Time-Adjusted Discount Rates**

Management's ability to accurately forecast cash flows diminishes as they are forecast further out in time. Therefore, cash flows projected in later years of a project's life are much more uncertain than those forecasted in the early years. Economic conditions, interest rates, inflation rates, etc., may fluctuate very significantly over a number of years in the future. This would imply that the cash flows later in a project's life should be discounted at higher rates than those in the first years. The table below illustrates how this might be done.

Time period	*Discount rate*
Years 1 through 4	10.0%
Years 5 through 8	13.0%
Years 9 through 12	16.0%

4. **Sensitivity Analysis**

   Most capital budgeting problems require management to make many assumptions before arriving at the investment's net present value. For example, forecasting projected cash flows may require assumptions about demand, costs of production, selling price, etc. When using sensitivity analysis, managers explore the importance of these assumptions. First, managers compute the expected (most likely) results. Then, management allows one variable to change while holding the others constant, and the net present value is recomputed. By repeating the process with all the important variables, management can determine how sensitive the net present value is to changes in each major assumption. Therefore, sensitivity analysis involves exploring "what if" situations to determine the variables to which the outcomes are particularly sensitive. Management can then challenge its assumptions about these sensitive variables.

5. **Scenario Analysis**

   Scenario analysis is a more complex variation of sensitivity analysis. Instead of exploring the effects of a change in one variable, management develops a scenario that might happen if a number of related variables change. As an example, if demand is lower than expected, sales price might have to be reduced, and unit production costs might be higher. Normally, management develops a most likely scenario and one or more pessimistic and optimistic ones. This is useful in illustrating the range of the possible net present values, and therefore the risk of the investment.

6. **Simulation Models**

   Computer simulation software makes it possible to model the effects of even more economic conditions on the results of an investment project. Monte Carlo simulation uses random variables for inputs distributed around the expected means of the economic variables. As an example, management may expect short-term interest rates to be about 4% over the life of the project with a standard deviation of 1.5%. This data would be input and the program would generate simulated results using random interest rates from a probability distribution with a mean of 4% and a standard deviation of 1.5%. Therefore, instead of just developing several possible outcomes for a project, management can generate a range of outcomes with a standard deviation. Some simulation models generate probability acceptance curves for capital budgeting decisions. These curves inform management of the probabilities of having a positive net present value for the project.

7. **Decision Trees**

   Most investment decisions are more complex than simply determining the net present value of future cash flows for a period of time and deciding to invest if the project has a positive net present value. Management often faces a series of decisions that may affect the value of the investment. Let's assume that management is deciding whether to introduce a new product. Management is evaluating whether to make an investment in the new product and test market it in a small geographical area. If the product sells well, management will expand the test market to a larger area. Finally, if the product does well in the larger area, management will introduce the product nationally, and there are several possible net present values from the product depending on how well it sells on a national basis. The project may be abandoned based on the results of either marketing test. A decision tree provides a visual representation of these decision points and potential decisions. The value of a decision tree is that it forces management to think through a series of "if then" scenarios that describe how the firm might react based on future events.

   EXAMPLE: Assume that a firm is considering a $1,250,000 investment in a new product. Management intends to test-market the product in a small market and if the product hits at least a moderate level of demand, management will expand the test market area. Otherwise, management will abandon the project with no value. Management believes that the probability of meeting a moderate level of sales in the initial test market is 50%. If the product sells at least a moderate level in the expanded test area, management will launch the product nationally. Otherwise, management will abandon the project with no value. Management believes that the probability of the product performing well in the expanded market area is 75%. If the product is launched nationally, management believes the following three outcomes are possible:

Possible outcome	*Probability*	*Net present value of future cash flows*
Pessimistic sales	*25%*	*$2,000,000*
Most likely sales	*50%*	*$4,000,000*
Optimistic sales	*25%*	*$6,000,000*

   The decision tree below depicts this investment opportunity.

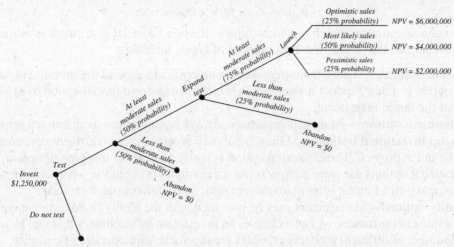

The appropriate way to calculate the expected net present value for the investment using a decision tree is to begin at the end and work backward to the initial decision from one decision point to another.

Expected net present value of future cash flows if the product is launched

Net present value of outcomes	Probability	Expected net present value
$2,000,000	25%	$ 500,000
$4,000,000	50%	2,000,000
$6,000,000	25%	1,500,000
		$4,000,000

The $4,000,000 in expected net present value in the previous step is used to calculate the expected net present value of future cash flows at the point of deciding whether to expand the market test.

Outcome	Net present value of outcomes	Probability	Expected net present value
Moderate sales (launch)	$4,000,000	75%	$3,000,000
Less than moderate sales (abandon)	0	25%	0
			$3,000,000

The $3,000,000 in expected net present value from the previous step is used to calculate the expected net present value of future cash flows at inception.

Outcome	Net present value of outcomes	Probability	Expected net present value
Moderate sales (expand test)	$3,000,000	50%	$1,500,000
Less than moderate sales (abandon)	0	50%	0
			$1,500,000

The final expected net present value after considering the initial investment is calculated below.

Expected net present value of cash flows	$1,500,000
Initial investment	1,250,000
Expected net present value of the investment	$ 250,000

Since the expected net present value is positive, the results indicate that the project should be accepted.

8. **Real Options**

Another technique that takes into account the dynamic nature of an investment decision is one that views an investment as a real option. This technique assumes that once management makes an initial investment, it has an option to take a number of future actions that will change the value of the investment. Therefore, the initial decision can be viewed as purchasing an option. Since net present value ignores the option value of an investment it sometimes does not provide the correct answer.

EXAMPLE: Assume that management is considering bidding on the rights to extract oil from a proven site over the next five years. The extraction costs are expected to be $22 per barrel. Oil is currently selling for $21 per barrel and management does not know whether the price will go up or down over the next five years. Using net present value with an expected price for the oil of $21, management would clearly decide not to make the investment. The expected value of the production costs, $22 per barrel, is greater than the expected sales price of the oil, $21 per barrel.

We get a different answer using the real option approach. Remember, the firm is not obligated to extract the oil, it only has an option to do so. Management knows that oil prices are very volatile and at least some time over the five-year period oil will sell for more than $22 per barrel. Therefore, the investment has value and management may reasonably bid on the rights. The net present value method understates or overstates a project's value depending on whether the investment creates or eliminates options for the firm. To correct this deficiency, the real options approach adds or subtracts an option value for the investment to get a more realistic value for the project.

$$\text{Project value} = \text{NPV} \pm \text{Option value}$$

The option value is estimated much like the option value of a financial instrument is estimated. For a particular investment, the option may be a number of types, including

a. **Expansion options**—Management may receive an option to expand the investment. An example of this option is a new product investment in which management has an option to expand production after the initial investment.

b. **Abandonment options**—Management almost always has an option to abandon a project.

c. **Follow-up investment options**—Management may receive other investment opportunities when investing in the project. The expansion option is really a subset of this type of option, but follow-up investment options are more complex. As an example, investing in a particular research and development project might offer management options for other related projects.

d. **Flexibility options**—Management may be provided with the ability to take advantages of changes in economic circumstances. As an example, an investment in machinery that can be used to produce a number of different products provides management with operating flexibility.

9. **Portfolio Risk**

a. Theoretically, management should evaluate all possible combinations of investment projects to determine which set will provide the best trade-off between risk and return. This process is very similar to an investor's process of putting together a portfolio of financial investments. Conceptually, the sets of portfolios that meet management's trade-off between risk and return can be visualized as falling on an indifference curve or **risk preference function**. A risk preference function, as presented in the graph below, illustrates the **efficient frontier** for portfolio investments. Any portfolio of investments that falls on the line is an efficient portfolio (e.g., A, B, and C); it meets management's objectives with respect to the trade-off between risk and return. Any portfolio that falls to the right is not efficient.

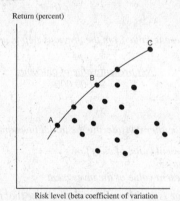

b. When considering a new investment to be added to an existing portfolio, management must consider the effect of the investment on the overall risk of the portfolio. Whether or not an individual investment will change the overall risk of the firm depends on its relationship to other investments in the portfolio. If a casualty insurance company purchases the casualty insurance division of another firm, there is little risk reduction. Highly correlated investments do nothing to diversify away risk. Investments that are negatively correlated do reduce overall risk. Investments that are negatively correlated are those with performance that moves in opposite directions with changing economic conditions. Simply illustrated, if you match an investment that performs poorly during recessions with one that performs well during recessions, the risk of the two investments combined is much less than the risk of them individually.

c. A measure that is used to express the extent of the correlation between a set of investments is the **coefficient of correlation** from multiple regression analysis. (Multiple regression is illustrated in Module 45.) This measure takes a value of from +1 to –1. The table below illustrates the relationship between the coefficient of correlation and the extent of risk reduction for the portfolio.

Significant risk reduction		Some risk reduction		Little risk reduction	
-1	-.5	0	+.5		+1

MULTIPLE-CHOICE QUESTIONS (1-85)

1. If an investment is expected to be held for a long period of time the preferred method of calculating the expected return is

    a. Arithmetic average.
    b. Median.
    c. Geometric average.
    d. Subjective estimate.

2. Which of the following expresses the relationship between risk and return?

    a. Inverse relationship.
    b. Direct relationship.
    c. Negative relationship.
    d. No relationship.

3. The expected return of a portfolio is measured by the

    a. Variance.
    b. Weighted average.
    c. Standard deviation.
    d. Beta.

4. Russell Inc. is evaluating four independent investment proposals. The expected returns and standard deviations for each of these proposals are presented below.

Investment proposal	Expected returns	Standard deviation
I	16%	10%
II	14%	10%
III	20%	11%
IV	22%	15%

Which one of the investment proposals has the **least** relative level of risk?

    a. Investment I.
    b. Investment II.
    c. Investment III.
    d. Investment IV.

Items 5 and 6 are based on the following:

Natco has the following investment portfolio.

	Expected return	Investment	Beta
Investment A	15%	$100,000	1.2
Investment B	10%	$300,000	-0.5
Investment C	8%	$200,000	1.5
Investment D	8%	$100,000	-1.0

5. What is the expected return of the portfolio?

    a. 10.25%
    b. 9.86%
    c. 12.5%
    d. 11.35%

6. If management decided to sell one of the investments, which one should be selected?

    a. Investment A.
    b. Investment B.
    c. Investment C.
    d. Investment D.

7. A market analyst has estimated the equity beta of Modern Homes Inc. to be 1.4. This beta implies that the company's

    a. Systematic risk is lower than that of the market portfolio.

    b. Systematic risk is higher than that of the market portfolio.
    c. Unsystematic risk is higher than that of the market portfolio.
    d. Total risk is higher than that of the market portfolio.

*8. A measure that describes the risk of an investment project relative to other investments in general is the

    a. Coefficient of variation.
    b. Beta coefficient.
    c. Standard deviation.
    d. Expected return.

**9. The expected rate of return for the stock of Cornhusker Enterprises is 20%, with a standard deviation of 15%. The expected rate of return for the stock of Mustang Associates is 10%, with a standard deviation of 9%. The riskier stock is

    a. Cornhusker because its return is higher.
    b. Cornhusker because its standard deviation is higher.
    c. Mustang because its standard deviation is higher.
    d. Mustang because its coefficient of variation is higher.

**10. A US company currently has domestic operations only. It is considering an equal-size investment in either Canada or Britain. The data on expected rate of return and the risk associated with each of these proposed investments are given below.

Proposed investment	Mean return	Standard deviation
British Investment	22%	10%
Canadian Investment	28%	15%

The mean return on the company's current, domestic only, business is 20% with a standard deviation of 15%. Using the above data and the correlation coefficients, the company calculated the following portfolio risk and return (based on a ratio of 50% US domestic operations and 50% international operations).

Proposed investment	Mean return	Standard deviation
US and Britain	21%	3%
US and Canada	24%	15%

The company plans to select the optimal combination of countries based on risk and return for the domestic and international investments taken together. Because the company is new to the international business environment, it is relatively risk averse. Based on the above data, which one of the following alternatives provides the best risk-adjusted return to the firm?

    a. Undertake the British investment.
    b. Undertake the Canadian investment.
    c. Do not undertake either investment.
    d. Unable to determine based on data given.

11. According to market segmentation theory long-term interest rates are determined primarily by

    a. Commercial banks.
    b. Savings institutions.
    c. Life insurance companies.
    d. Individual investors.

12. Questo borrowed $100,000 from a bank on a one-year 8% term loan, with interest compounded quarterly. What is the effective annual interest on the loan?

---

  * CIA adapted
  ** CMA adapted

a. 8%
b. 8.24%
c. 2%
d. 9.12%

13. The yield curve shown below implies that the

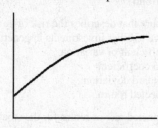

Interest
rate %

Years to maturity

a. Credit risk premium of corporate bonds has increased.
b. Credit risk premium of municipal bonds has increased.
c. Long-term interest rates have a higher annualized yield than short-term rates.
d. Short-term interest rates have a higher annualized yield than long-term rates.

14. Short-term interest rates are
a. Usually lower than long-term rates.
b. Usually higher than long-term rates.
c. Lower than long-term rates during periods of high inflation only.
d. Not significantly related to long-term rates.

*15. According to the expectations theory, if the yield curve on the New York money market is upward sloping while that on the Tokyo money market is downward sloping, then inflation in
a. The United States is expected to decrease.
b. The United States is expected to remain constant.
c. Japan is expected to decrease.
d. Japan is expected to remain constant.

*16. According to the expectations theory of the term structure of interest rates, if inflation is expected to increase, the yield curve is
a. Humped, with an upward slope that peaks and then turns downward.
b. Downward sloping.
c. Upward sloping.
d. Flat.

*17. A curve on a graph with the rate of return on the vertical axis and time on the horizontal axis depicts
a. The internal rate of return on an investment.
b. A yield curve showing the term structure of interest rates.
c. The present value of future returns, discounted at the marginal cost of capital, minus the present value of the cost.
d. A series of payments of a fixed amount for a specified number of years.

**18. The return paid for the use of borrowed capital is referred to as

a. Cash dividends.
b. Stock dividends.
c. Interest.
d. Principal payment.

19. Strobel Company has a large amount of variable rate financing due in one year. Management is concerned about the possibility of increases in short-term rates. Which of the following would be an effective way of hedging this risk?
a. Buy Treasury notes in the futures market.
b. Sell Treasury notes in the futures market.
c. Buy an option to purchase Treasury bonds.
d. Sell an option to purchase Treasury bonds.

20. In valuing interest rate swaps, the zero-coupon method uses all of the following variables except
a. Discount rate.
b. Timing of cash flows as specified by the contract.
c. Estimated net settlement cash flows.
d. Underlying assets.

21. Which of the following techniques is used to value stock options?
a. Black-Scholes method.
b. Zero-coupon method.
c. Weighted-average method.
d. Expected earnings method.

22. Which of the following risks relates to the possibility that a derivative might not be effective at hedging a particular asset?
a. Credit risk.
b. Legal risk.
c. Market risk.
d. Basis risk.

**23. An American importer of English clothing has contracted to pay an amount fixed in British pounds three months from now. If the importer worries that the US dollar may depreciate sharply against the British pound in the interim, it would be well advised to
a. Buy pounds in the forward exchange market.
b. Sell pounds in the forward exchange market.
c. Buy dollars in the futures market.
d. Sell dollars in the futures market.

**24. When a firm finances each asset with a financial instrument of the same approximate maturity as the life of the asset, it is applying
a. Working capital management.
b. Return maximization.
c. Financial leverage.
d. A hedging approach.

25. Banner Electronics has subsidiaries in several international locations and is concerned about its exposure to foreign exchange risk. In countries where currency values are likely to fall, Banner should encourage all of the following **except
a. Granting trade credit wherever possible.
b. Investing excess cash in inventory or other real assets.
c. Purchasing materials and supplies on a trade credit basis.
d. Borrowing local currency funds if an appropriate interest rate can be obtained.

---

 * CIA adapted
** CMA adapted

*26. A company has recently purchased some stock of a competitor as part of a long-term plan to acquire the competitor. However, it is somewhat concerned that the market price of this stock could decrease over the short run. The company could hedge against the possible decline in the stock's market price by

    a. Purchasing a call option on that stock.
    b. Purchasing a put option on that stock.
    c. Selling a put option on that stock.
    d. Obtaining a warrant option on that stock.

*27. The risk of loss because of fluctuations in the relative value of foreign currencies is called

    a. Expropriation risk.
    b. Sovereign risk.
    c. Multinational beta.
    d. Exchange rate risk.

**28. If a $1,000 bond sells for $1,125, which of the following statements are correct?

  I. The market rate of interest is greater than the coupon rate on the bond.
  II. The coupon rate on the bond is greater than the market rate of interest.
  III. The coupon rate and the market rate are equal.
  IV. The bond sells at a premium.
  V. The bond sells at a discount.

    a. I and IV.
    b. I and V.
    c. II and IV.
    d. II and V.

29. Para Co. is reviewing the following data relating to an energy saving investment proposal:

Cost	$50,000
Residual value at the end of 5 years	10,000
Present value of an annuity of 1 at 12% for 5 years	3.60
Present value of 1 due in 5 years at 12%	0.57

What would be the annual savings needed to make the investment realize a 12% yield?

    a. $ 8,189
    b. $11,111
    c. $12,306
    d. $13,889

30. On December 31, 2009, Jet Co. received a $10,000 note receivable from Maxx, Inc. in exchange for services rendered. Interest is calculated on the outstanding balance at the interest rate of 3% compounded annually and payable at maturity. The note from Maxx, Inc. is due in five years. The market interest rate for similar notes on December 31, 2009, was 8%. The compound interest factors are as follows:

Future value of $1 due in nine months at 3%	1.0225
Future value of $1 due in five years at 3%	1.1593
Present value of $1 due in nine months at 8%	.944
Present value of $1 due in five years at 8%	.680

At what amounts should this note receivable be reported in Jet's December 31, 2009 balance sheet?

    a. $6,800
    b. $7,820
    c. $6,200
    d. $7,883

31. The market price of a bond issued at a discount is the present value of its principal amount at the market (effective) rate of interest

    a. Less the present value of all future interest payments at the market (effective) rate of interest.
    b. Less the present value of all future interest payments at the rate of interest stated on the bond.
    c. Plus the present value of all future interest payments at the market (effective) rate of interest.
    d. Plus the present value of all future interest payments at the rate of interest stated on the bond.

32. At what stage of the capital budgeting process would management most likely apply present value techniques?

    a. Identification stage.
    b. Search stage.
    c. Selection stage.
    d. Financing stage.

33. How is the discounted payback method an improvement over the payback method in evaluating investment projects?

    a. It involves better estimates of cash flows.
    b. It considers the overall profitability of the investment.
    c. It considers the time value of money.
    d. It considers the variability of the return.

34. The capital budgeting technique known as payback period uses

	Depreciation expense	Time value of money
a.	Yes	Yes
b.	Yes	No
c.	No	No
d.	No	Yes

35. Which of the following is a strength of the payback method?

    a. It considers cash flows for all years of the project.
    b. It distinguishes the source of cash inflows.
    c. It considers the time value of money.
    d. It is easy to understand.

36. Tam Co. is negotiating for the purchase of equipment that would cost $100,000, with the expectation that $20,000 per year could be saved in after-tax cash costs if the equipment were acquired. The equipment's estimated useful life is ten years, with no residual value, and would be depreciated by the straight-line method. The payback period is

    a. 4.0 years.
    b. 4.4 years.
    c. 4.5 years.
    d. 5.0 years.

37. All of the following capital budgeting analysis techniques use cash flows as the primary basis for the calculation **except for the

    a. Net present value.
    b. Payback period.
    c. Discounted payback period.
    d. Accounting rate of return.

38. Which of the following is an advantage of the accounting rate of return method of evaluating investment returns?

    a. The technique considers depreciation.
    b. The technique corresponds to the measure that is often used to evaluate performance.

---

* CIA adapted
** CMA adapted

c.   The technique considers the time value of money.
d.   The technique considers the risk of the investment.

39. Tam Co. is negotiating for the purchase of equipment
that would cost $100,000, with the expectation that $20,000
per year could be saved in after-tax cash costs if the equipment were acquired. The equipment's estimated useful life
is ten years, with no residual value, and it would be depreciated by the straight-line method. Tam's predetermined
minimum desired rate of return is 12%. The present value of
an annuity of 1 at 12% for ten periods is 5.65. The present
value of 1 due in ten periods at 12% is .322. Accrual accounting rate of return based on the initial investment is
  a.   30%
  b.   20%
  c.   12%
  d.   10%

40. Lin Co. is buying machinery it expects will increase
average annual operating income by $40,000. The initial
increase in the required investment is $60,000, and the aver-
age increase in required investment is $30,000. To compute
the accrual accounting rate of return, what amount should be
used as the numerator in the ratio?
  a. $20,000
  b. $30,000
  c. $40,000
  d. $60,000

41. The capital budgeting technique known as accounting
rate of return uses

	Revenue over life of project	Depreciation expense
a.	No	Yes
b.	No	No
c.	Yes	No
d.	Yes	Yes

**42. If an investment project has a profitability index of
1.15, then the
  a.   Project's internal rate of return is 15%.
  b.   Project's cost of capital is greater than its internal
        rate of return.
  c.   Project's internal rate of return exceeds its net
        present value.
  d.   Net present value of the project is positive.

**43. The net present value (NPV) method of investment
project analysis assumes that the project's cash flows are
reinvested at the
  a.   Computed internal rate of return.
  b.   Risk-free interest rate.
  c.   Discount rate used in the NPV calculation.
  d.   Firm's accounting rate of return.

44. Kern Co. is planning to invest in a two-year project that
is expected to yield cash flows from operations, net of income taxes, of $50,000 in the first year and $80,000 in the
second year. Kern requires an internal rate of return of 15%.
The present value of $1 for one period at 15% is 0.870 and
for two periods at 15% is 0.756. The future value of $1 for
one period at 15% is 1.150 and for two periods at 15% is
1.323. The maximum that Kern should invest immediately
is

  a. $ 81,670
  b. $103,980
  c. $130,000
  d. $163,340

45. Pole Co. is investing in a machine with a three-year life.
The machine is expected to reduce annual cash operating
costs by $30,000 in each of the first two years and by
$20,000 in year three. Present values of an annuity of $1 at
14% are

Period 1	0.88
2	1.65
3	2.32

Using a 14% cost of capital, what is the present value of
these future savings?
  a. $59,600
  b. $60,800
  c. $62,900
  d. $69,500

46. For the next two years, a lease is estimated to have an
operating net cash inflow of $7,500 per annum, before ad-
justing for $5,000 per annum tax basis lease amortization,
and a 40% tax rate. The present value of an ordinary annuity of $1 per year at 10% for two years is 1.74. What is the
lease's after-tax present value using a 10% discount factor?
  a. $ 2,610
  b. $ 4,350
  c. $ 9,570
  d. $11,310

47. A project's net present value, ignoring income tax considerations, is normally affected by the
  a.   Proceeds from the sale of the asset to be replaced.
  b.   Carrying amount of the asset to be replaced by the
        project.
  c.   Amount of annual depreciation on the asset to be
        replaced.
  d.   Amount of annual depreciation on fixed assets
        used directly on the project.

48. The discount rate (hurdle rate of return) must be determined in advance for the
  a.   Payback period method.
  b.   Time-adjusted rate of return method.
  c.   Net present value method.
  d.   Internal rate of return method.

**49. The internal rate of return is the
  a.   Rate of interest that equates the present value of
        cash outflows and the present value of cash in-
        flows.
  b.   Minimum acceptable rate of return for a proposed
        investment.
  c.   Risk-adjusted rate of return.
  d.   Required rate of return.

**50. As used in capital budgeting analysis, the internal
rate of return uses which of the following items in its computation?

	Net incremental investment	Incremental average operating income	Net annual cash flows
a.	Yes	No	Yes
b.	Yes	Yes	No
c.	No	No	Yes
d.	No	Yes	Yes

** *CMA adapted*

**51. An organization is using capital budgeting techniques to compare two independent projects. It could accept one, both, or neither of the projects. Which of the following statements is true about the use of net present value (NPV) and internal rate of return (IRR) methods for evaluating these two projects?

    a. NPV and IRR criteria will always lead to the same accept or reject decision for two independent projects.

    b. If the first project's IRR is higher than the organization's cost or capital, the first project will be accepted but the second project will not.

    c. If the NPV criterion leads to accepting or rejecting the first project, one cannot predict whether the IRR criterion will lead to accepting or rejecting the first project.

    d. If the NPV criterion leads to accepting the first project, the IRR criterion will never lead to accepting the first project.

Items 52 and 53 are based on the following information:

A firm, with an 18% cost of capital, is considering the following projects (on January 1, 2009):

	Jan. 1, 2009, Cash outflow (000's omitted)	Dec. 31, 2013, Cash inflow (000's omitted)	Project internal rate of return
Project A	$3,500	$7,400	15%
Project B	4,000	9,950	?

Present Value of $1 Due at End of "N" Periods

N	12%	14%	15%	16%	18%	20%	22%
4	.6355	.5921	.5718	.5523	.5158	.4823	.4230
5	.5674	.5194	.4972	.4761	.4371	.4019	.3411
6	.5066	.4556	.4323	.4104	.3704	.3349	.2751

52. Using the net present value method, Project A's net present value is

    a. $ 316,920

    b. $0

    c. $(265,460)

    d. $(316,920)

53. Project B's internal rate of return is closest to

    a. 15%

    b. 18%

    c. 20%

    d. 22%

Items 54 thru 57 are based on the following information:

An organization has four investment proposals with the following costs and expected cash inflows:

Expected Cash Inflows

Project	Cost	End of year 1	End of year 2	End of year 3
A	Unknown	$10,000	$10,000	$10,000
B	$20,000	5,000	10,000	15,000
C	25,000	15,000	10,000	5,000
D	30,000	20,000	Unknown	20,000

Additional information

		Present value of $1 due at the end of n periods	Present value of an annuity of $1 per period for n periods
Discount rate	Number of periods	[PVIF]	[PVIFA]
5%	1	0.9524	0.9524
5%	2	0.9070	1.8594
5%	3	0.8638	2.7232
10%	1	0.9091	0.9091
10%	2	0.8264	1.7355
10%	3	0.7513	2.4869
15%	1	0.8696	0.8696
15%	2	0.7561	1.6257
15%	3	0.6575	2.2832

54. If Project A has an internal rate of return (IRR) of 15%, then it has a cost of

    a. $ 8,696

    b. $22,832

    c. $24,869

    d. $27,232

55. If the discount rate is 10%, the net present value (NPV) of Project B is

    a. $ 4,079

    b. $ 6,789

    c. $ 9,869

    d. $39,204

56. The payback period of Project C is

    a. 0 years.

    b. 1 year.

    c. 2 years.

    d. 3 years.

57. If the discount rate is 5% and the discounted payback period of Project D is exactly two years, then the year two cash inflow for Project D is

    a. $ 5,890

    b. $10,000

    c. $12,075

    d. $14,301

58. Tam Co. is negotiating for the purchase of equipment that would cost $100,000, with the expectation that $20,000 per year could be saved in after-tax cash costs if the equipment were acquired. The equipment's estimated useful life is ten years, with no residual value, and would be depreciated by the straight-line method. Tam's predetermined minimum desired rate of return is 12%. Present value of an annuity of 1 at 12% for ten periods is 5.65. Present value of 1 due in ten periods at 12% is .322. In estimating the internal rate of return, the factors in the table of present values of an annuity should be taken from the columns closest to

    a. 0.65

    b. 1.30

    c. 5.00

    d. 5.65

59. How are the following used in the calculation of the internal rate of return of a proposed project? Ignore income tax considerations.

	Residual sales value of project	Depreciation expense
a.	Exclude	Include
b.	Include	Include
c.	Exclude	Exclude
d.	Include	Exclude

** CMA adapted

60. Neu Co. is considering the purchase of an investment that has a positive net present value based on Neu's 12% hurdle rate. The internal rate of return would be

a.   0
b.   12%
c.   > 12%
d.   < 12%

61. Bennet Inc. uses the net present value method to evaluate capital projects. Bennet's required rate of return is 10%. Bennet is considering two mutually exclusive projects for its manufacturing business. Both projects require an initial outlay of $120,000 and are expected to have a useful life of four years. The projected after-tax cash flows associated with these projects are as follows:

Year	Project X	Project Y
1	$40,000	$10,000
2	40,000	20,000
3	40,000	60,000
4	40,000	80,000
Total	$160,000	$170,000

Assuming adequate funds are available, which of the following project options would you recommend that Bennet's management undertake?

a.   Project X only.
b.   Project Y only.
c.   Projects X and Y.
d.   Neither project.

Items 62 thru 64 are based on the following information:

Capital Invest Inc. uses a 12% hurdle rate for all capital expenditures and has done the following analysis for four projects for the upcoming year.

	Project 1	Project 2	Project 3	Project 4
Initial capital outlay	$200,000	$298,000	$248,000	$272,000
Annual net cash inflows				
Year 1	$ 65,000	$100,000	$80,000	$ 95,000
Year 2	70,000	135,000	95,000	125,000
Year 3	80,000	90,000	90,000	90,000
Year 4	40,000	65,000	80,000	60,000
Net present value	(3,798)	4,276	14,064	14,662
Profitability index	98%	101%	106%	105%
Internal rate of return	11%	13%	14%	15%

**62. Which project(s) should Capital Invest Inc. undertake during the upcoming year assuming it has no budget restrictions?

a.   All of the projects.
b.   Projects 1, 2, and 3.
c.   Projects 2, 3, and 4.
d.   Projects 1, 3, and 4.

**63. Which project(s) should Capital Invest Inc. undertake during the upcoming year if it has only $600,000 of funds available?

a.   Projects 1 and 3.
b.   Projects 2, 3, and 4.
c.   Projects 2 and 3.
d.   Projects 3 and 4.

**64. Which project(s) should Capital Invest Inc. undertake during the upcoming year if it has only $300,000 of capital funds available?

a.   Project 1.

b.   Projects 2, 3, and 4.
c.   Projects 3 and 4.
d.   Project 3.

**65. A depreciation tax shield is
a.   An after-tax cash outflow.
b.   A reduction in income taxes.
c.   The cash provided by recording depreciation.
d.   The expense caused by depreciation.

**66. Andrew Corporation is evaluating a capital investment that would result in a $30,000 higher contribution margin benefit and increased annual personnel costs of $20,000. The effects of income taxes on the net present value computation on these benefits and costs for the project are to
a.   Decrease both benefits and costs.
b.   Have no net effect on either benefits or costs.
c.   Decrease benefits but increase costs.
d.   Increase benefits but decrease costs.

67. Buff Co. is considering replacing an old machine with a new machine. Which of the following items is economically relevant to Buff's decision? (Ignore income tax considerations.)

	Carrying amount of old machine	Disposal value of new machine
a.	Yes	No
b.	No	Yes
c.	No	No
d.	Yes	Yes

Items 68 and 69 are based on the following information:

Assume that Straper Industries is considering investing in a project with the following characteristics:

Initial investment	$500,000
Additional investment in working capital	10,000
Cash flows before income taxes for years 1 through 5	140,000
Yearly tax depreciation	90,000
Terminal value of investment	50,000
Cost of capital	10%
Present value of $1 received after 5 years discounted at 10%	.621
Present value of an ordinary annuity of $1 for 5 years at 10%	3.791
Marginal tax rate	30%
Investment life	5 years

Assume that all cash flows come at the end of the year.

68. What is the amount of the after-tax cash flows in year 2?
a. $140,000
b. $125,000
c. $ 98,000
d. $ 70,000

69. What is the net present value of the investment?
a. $175,000
b. $ 58,000
c. $ 1,135
d. $ (12,340)

**70. The Madison Company has decided to introduce a new product. The company estimates that there is a 30% probability that the product will contribute $700,000 to profits, a 30% probability that it will contribute $200,000, and a 40% probability that the contribution will be a nega-

---

* CIA adapted
** CMA adapted

tive $400,000. The expected contribution of the new product is
- a. $500,000
- b. $110,000
- c. $166,667
- d. $380,000

**71. Philip Enterprises, distributor of compact disks (CDs) is developing its budgeted cost of goods sold for 2010. Philip has developed the following range of sales estimates and associated probabilities for the year.

Sales Estimate	Probability
$ 60,000	25%
85,000	40%
100,000	35%

Philip's cost of goods sold averages 80% of sales. What is the expected value of Philip's 2010 budgeted cost of goods sold?
- a. $85,000
- b. $84,000
- c. $68,000
- d. $67,200

72. Which of the following capital budgeting techniques would allow management to justify investing in a project that could not be justified currently by using techniques that focus on expected cash flows?
- a. Real options.
- b. Net present value.
- c. Accounting rate of return.
- d. Internal rate of return.

Items 73 and 74 are based on the following information:

Assume that Reston Corp. is considering investing in a project. To evaluate the project, management has developed the following cash flow projections and related probabilities.

Present value of future cash flows	Probability of occurrence
$200,000	.4
$500,000	.3
$800,000	.3

73. What is the expected return for the project?
- a. $750,000
- b. $500,000
- c. $470,000
- d. $400,000

74. Assume that the standard deviation of the returns for the project is $150,000. What is the coefficient of variation for the project?
- a. .2345
- b. .3191
- c. .4256
- d. 1.10

75. Which of the following techniques recognizes that management often faces a series of decisions that may affect the value of an investment?
- a. Probability analysis.
- b. Risk-adjusted discount rate.
- c. Decision tree.
- d. Sensitivity analysis.

76. Which of the following is not a technique for considering the risk of an investment?
- a. Probability analysis.
- b. Risk-adjusted discount rate.
- c. Simulation techniques.
- d. Internal rate of return.

*77. The level of risk that concerns investors who supply capital to a diversified company is
- a. Project risk (beta).
- b. Pure play risk (beta).
- c. The standard deviation of project risk (betas).
- d. The weighted-average of project risk (betas).

*78. A company uses portfolio theory to develop its investment portfolio. If the company wishes to obtain optimal risk reduction through the portfolio effect, it should make its next investment in
- a. An investment that correlates negatively to the current portfolio holdings.
- b. An investment that is uncorrelated to the current portfolio holdings.
- c. An investment that is highly correlated to the current portfolio holdings.
- d. An investment that is perfectly correlated to the current portfolio holdings.

79. During 2008, Deet Corp. experienced the following power outages:

Number of outages per month	Number of months
0	3
1	2
2	4
3	3
	12

Each power outage results in out-of-pocket costs of $400. For $500 per month, Deet can lease an auxiliary generator to provide power during outages. If Deet leases an auxiliary generator in 2009 the estimated savings (or additional expenditures) for 2009 would be
- a. $(3,600)
- b. $(1,200)
- c. $ 1,600
- d. $ 1,900

80. Polo Co. requires higher rates of return for projects with a life span greater than five years. Projects extending beyond five years must earn a higher specified rate of return. Which of the following capital budgeting techniques can readily accommodate this requirement?

	Internal rate of return	Net present value
a.	Yes	No
b.	No	Yes
c.	No	No
d.	Yes	Yes

81. Under frost-free conditions, Cal Cultivators expects its strawberry crop to have a $60,000 market value. An unprotected crop subject to frost has an expected market value of $40,000. If Cal protects the strawberries against frost, then the market value of the crop is still expected to be $60,000 under frost-free conditions and $90,000 if there is a frost. What must be the probability of a frost for Cal to be indifferent to spending $10,000 for frost protection?

---

* CIA adapted
** CMA adapted

    a.   .167
    b.   .200
    c.   .250
    d.   .333

82. Dough Distributors has decided to increase its daily muffin purchases by 100 boxes. A box of muffins costs $2 and sells for $3 through regular stores. Any boxes not sold through regular stores are sold through Dough's thrift store for $1. Dough assigns the following probabilities to selling additional boxes:

Additional sales	Probability
60	.6
100	.4

What is the expected value of Dough's decision to buy 100 additional boxes of muffins?
    a. $28
    b. $40
    c. $52
    d. $68

83. Which tool would most likely be used to determine the best course of action under conditions of uncertainty?
    a.   Cost-volume-profit analysis.
    b.   Expected value (EV).
    c.   Program evaluation and review technique (PERT).
    d.   Scattergraph method.

84. To assist in an investment decision, Gift Co. selected the most likely sales volume from several possible outcomes. Which of the following attributes would that selected sales volume reflect?
    a.   The midpoint of the range.
    b.   The median.
    c.   The greatest probability.
    d.   The expected value.

85. Probability (risk) analysis is
    a.   Used only for situations involving five or fewer possible outcomes.
    b.   Used only for situations in which the summation of probability weights is greater than one.
    c.   An extension of sensitivity analysis.
    d.   Incompatible with sensitivity analysis.

MULTIPLE-CHOICE ANSWERS

1. c __ __	19. b __ __	37. d __ __	55. a __ __	73. c __ __
2. b __ __	20. d __ __	38. b __ __	56. c __ __	74. b __ __
3. b __ __	21. a __ __	39. d __ __	57. c __ __	75. c __ __
4. c __ __	22. d __ __	40. c __ __	58. c __ __	76. d __ __
5. b __ __	23. a __ __	41. d __ __	59. d __ __	77. d __ __
6. c __ __	24. d __ __	42. d __ __	60. c __ __	78. a __ __
7. b __ __	25. a __ __	43. c __ __	61. a __ __	79. c __ __
8. b __ __	26. b __ __	44. b __ __	62. c __ __	80. d __ __
9. d __ __	27. d __ __	45. c __ __	63. d __ __	81. b __ __
10. a __ __	28. c __ __	46. d __ __	64. d __ __	82. c __ __
11. c __ __	29. c __ __	47. a __ __	65. b __ __	83. b __ __
12. b __ __	30. d __ __	48. c __ __	66. a __ __	84. c __ __
13. c __ __	31. c __ __	49. a __ __	67. b __ __	85. c __ __
14. a __ __	32. c __ __	50. a __ __	68. b __ __	
15. c __ __	33. c __ __	51. a __ __	69. c __ __	
16. c __ __	34. c __ __	52. c __ __	70. b __ __	
17. b __ __	35. d __ __	53. c __ __	71. d __ __	1st: __/85 = __%
18. c __ __	36. d __ __	54. b __ __	72. a __ __	2nd: __/85 = __%

MULTIPLE-CHOICE ANSWER EXPLANATIONS

Risk and Return

1. (c) The requirement is to identify the preferred method of calculating the expected return for an investment that is expected to be held for a long period of time. Answer (c) is correct because the geometric average depicts the compound annual return earned by the investor. This method is preferred for evaluating long-term investments. Answer (a) is incorrect because the arithmetic average does not provide as good a measure as the geometric average especially when the returns vary through time. Answer (b) is incorrect because the median is a poor measure of return. Answer (d) is incorrect because a subjective estimate is not as good as a mathematical average.

2. (b) The requirement is to identify the relationship between risk and return. Answer (b) is correct because there is a direct (positive) relationship between risk and return. Higher returns are associated with higher degrees of risk. Answers (a) and (c) are incorrect because an inverse (negative) relationship would imply that higher returns are associated with less risk. Answer (d) is incorrect because there is a direct relationship between risk and returns.

Portfolio Returns and Risk

3. (b) The requirement is to identify the measure of the expected return of a portfolio. Answer (b) is correct because the weighted-average of the expected returns of the assets in the portfolio is equal to the expected return of the portfolio. Answers (a), (c), and (d) are incorrect because they are all measures of variability.

4. (c) The requirement is to identify the proposal that has the least amount of relative risk. Relative risk is measured as the ratio of the standard deviation of the return to the expected return. Therefore, answer (c) is correct because this investment's relative risk is .550 (11%/20%). Answers (a), (b), and (d) are incorrect because they have higher measures of relative risk.

5. (b) The requirement is to calculate the expected return of the portfolio. Answer (b) is correct because the expected return of the portfolio is the weighted-average of the individual investments. The expected return is equal to 9.68% = [15% × ($100,000 ÷ 700,000)] + [10% × ($300,000 ÷ 700,000)] + (8% × $200,000 ÷ 700,000)] + [8% × ($100,000 ÷ 700,000)]. Answer (a) is incorrect because this is the unweighted return for the portfolio.

6. (c) The requirement is to select the investment that should be sold. Answer (c) is correct because Investment C has a low return and the highest positive beta. The positive beta indicates that its return is highly correlated with the return of the portfolio and, therefore, it increases the risk of the portfolio. Answer (a) is incorrect because Investment A has the highest return and its beta is not as high as Investment C. Answer (b) is incorrect because it has a higher return than Investment C and its beta is negative. Therefore, Investment B reduces the overall risk of the portfolio. Answer (d) is incorrect because Investment D has a large negative beta and therefore, it reduces the overall risk of the portfolio.

7. (b) The requirement is to interpret an equity beta of 1.4. Beta is a measure of systematic risk of the investment. Answer (b) is correct because a beta of greater than 1 means the investment's systematic risk is higher than that of the market portfolio. Answer (a) is incorrect because the beta would have to be less than 1 for this relationship to exist. Answers (c) and (d) are incorrect because beta focuses on systematic risk.

8. (b) The requirement is to identify the measure of the risk of an investment relative to other investments in general. Answer (b) is correct because the beta coefficient of an individual stock is the correlation between the stock's price and the price of the overall market. As an example, if the market goes up 5% and the individual stock's price, on average, goes up 10%, the stock's beta coefficient is 2.0. Answer (a) is incorrect because the coefficient of variation compares the risk of the stock to its expected return. Answer (c) is incorrect because the standard deviation measures the dispersion of the individual stock's returns. Answer (d) is incorrect because the expected return does not measure risk.

9. (d) The requirement is to identify the riskier stock. Answer (d) is correct because the coefficient of variation of Mustang is higher. The coefficient of variation provides a measure of the relative variability of investments. It is calculated by dividing the standard deviation of the investment by its expected return. The coefficient of variation for Cornhusker is .75 (.15 ÷ .20) and the coefficient of variation for Mustang is .9 (0.09 ÷ .10). Answer (a) is incorrect because a higher return does not always mean higher risk. Answer (b) is incorrect because the higher standard deviation must be viewed relative to the expected return. Answer (c) is incorrect because Mustang's coefficient of variation is higher than Cornhusker's coefficient of variation.

10.   (a)   The requirement is to identify the alternative that provides the best risk-adjusted rate of return. The correct answer is (a) because expanding the investment into Britain would increase the portfolio return from 20% to 21%, and, at the same time, reduce risk as measured by the standard deviation. Answer (b) is incorrect because undertaking the Canadian investment would increase the return from 20% to 24% without any reduction in the risk. Answer (c) is incorrect because the investment into Britain increases portfolio return while reducing risk. Answer (d) is incorrect because the answer can be determined.

Interest Rates

11.   (c)   The requirement is to identify the determinate of long-term interest rates under market segmentation theory. Market segmentation theory states that the Treasury securities market is divided into market segments by the various financial institutions investing in the market. Answer (c) is correct because life insurance companies prefer long-term securities because of the nature of their commitments to policyholders. Answer (a) is incorrect because commercial banks prefer securities with short maturities. Answer (b) is incorrect because savings institutions prefer intermediate-term maturities. Answer (d) is incorrect because individual investors do not significantly affect the market.

12.   (b)   The requirement is to calculate the effective annual interest rate. Answer (b) is correct because the effective interest rate (EAR) is calculated as follows:

$$EAR = \left(1 + \frac{r}{m}\right)^m - 1$$
$$= \left(1 + \frac{.08}{4}\right)^4 - 1$$
$$= \quad 8.24\%$$

Where

r = Stated interest rate
m = Compounding frequency

Answer (a) is incorrect because it is the stated interest rate. Answer (c) is incorrect because it is the interest rate for three months.

13.   (c)   The requirement is to interpret the yield curve. Answer (c) is correct because the term structure of interest rates is the relationship between yield to maturity and time to maturity. This relationship is depicted by a yield curve. The normal expectation is for long-term investments to pay higher rates because of their higher interest rate risk. Answers (a) and (b) are incorrect because the yield curve does not reflect the credit risk premium of bonds. Answer (d) is incorrect because long-term interest rates are normally higher than short-term rates.

14.   (a)   The requirement is to identify the true statement about short-term interest rates. Answer (a) is correct because there is less risk involved in the short run and investors are willing to accept lower rates on short-term investments because of their liquidity. Short-term rates have ordinarily been lower than long-term rates. Answer (b) is incorrect because short-term rates are typically lower than long-term rates. Answer (c) is incorrect because short-term rates are more likely to be greater than long-term rates if current levels of inflation are high. Answer (d) is incorrect because long-term rates may be viewed as short-term rates adjusted by a risk factor.

15.   (c)   The requirement is to predict the effect of inflation on the yield curve. The correct answer is (c) because a downward sloping yield curve indicates that long-term rates are lower than short-term rates. For this to be the case investors would have to be expecting a decline in the rate of inflation. Answers (a) and (b) are incorrect because an upward sloping yield curve would mean that investors are expecting an increase in inflation. Answer (d) is incorrect because a downward sloping yield curve would imply that investors are expecting inflation to decline.

16.   (c)   The requirement is to describe the effect on the yield curve of an expectation of an increase in inflation. Answer (c) is correct because if inflation is expected to increase, interest rates are expected to rise and therefore, intermediate-term and long-term rates will be higher than short-term rates. Answer (a) is incorrect because a humped yield curve is not consistent with expectations theory. Answer (b) is incorrect because a downward sloping curve would imply an expectation that inflation will decrease. Answer (d) is incorrect because a flat yield curve would imply inflation is expected to remain constant.

17.   (b)   The requirement is to identify a graph that depicts the rate of return on the vertical axis and time on the horizontal axis. Answer (b) is correct because such a graph presents a yield curve that shows the term structure of interest rates. The term structure of interest rates refers to how interest rates vary by time to maturity. Answer (a) is incorrect because internal rate of return is the interest rate that equates the present value of the future cash flows from an investment with its initial cost. Answer (c) is incorrect because it is the definition of net present value. Answer (d) is incorrect because it defines an annuity.

18.   (c)   The requirement is to identify the return paid for the use of borrowed capital. Answer (c) is correct because the return paid for the use of borrowed funds is called interest. Answers (a) and (b) are incorrect because dividends are paid to equity holders. Answer (d) is incorrect because the principal payment represents the return of capital.

Derivatives and Hedging

19.   (b)   The requirement is to identify the appropriate hedging strategy. Answer (b) is correct because by selling Treasury bonds for delivery in the future, the company can hedge increases in short-term interest rates. If interest rates increase, the value of the Treasury bonds will decline, resulting in a gain to the company. If the hedge is effective, the gain will offset the increase in the company's interest costs. Answer (a) is incorrect because buying Treasury notes would put the company at greater risk with respect to increases in interest rates. Answer (c) is incorrect because buying an option on Treasury bonds would hedge a decline in interest rates. Answer (d) is incorrect because an option allows the purchaser the option, but not the obligation, to purchase Treasury bonds. Therefore, selling options would not be effective at hedging increases in interest rates.

20. (d)   The requirement is to identify the variable that is not used in valuing an interest rate swap. Answer (d) is correct because the underlying assets are not relevant. An interest rate swap involves an exchange of cash flows, usually the exchange of fixed cash flows for variable cash flows. Answer (a), (b), and (c) are all incorrect because they are all variables that are used in the zero-coupon method.

21. (a)   The requirement is to identify the technique used to value stock options. Answer (a) is correct because the Black-Scholes option-pricing model is a commonly used option-pricing model. Answer (b) is incorrect because the zero-coupon method is used to value interest rate swaps. Answer (c) is incorrect because the weighted-average method is used to determine the expected return of a portfolio.

22. (d)   The requirement is to identify the risk that relates to the possibility that a derivative might not be effective at hedging a particular asset. Answer (d) is correct because basis risk is the risk of loss from ineffective hedging activities. Answer (a) is incorrect because credit risk is the risk of loss as a result of the counterparty to the derivative agreement failing to meet its obligation. Answer (b) is incorrect because market risk is the risk of loss from adverse changes in market factors. Answer (c) is incorrect because legal risk is the risk of loss from a legal or regulatory action that invalidates the derivative agreement.

23. (a)   The requirement is to identify how a company may hedge exchange risk. Answer (a) is the correct answer because by buying pounds today in the futures market, the firm protects itself against depreciation in the value of the dollar in relation to the pound. Answer (b) is incorrect because selling pounds would put the firm in greater risk with respect to appreciation of the pound. Answers (c) and (d) are incorrect because buying and selling dollars would do nothing to hedge the value of the pound.

24. (d)   The requirement is to identify the strategy of matching maturities. Answer (d) is correct because the strategy of matching asset and liability maturities is referred to as a hedging approach. The strategy helps ensure that funds are generated from the assets when the related liabilities are due. Answer (a) is incorrect because working capital management involves managing current assets and current liabilities. Answer (b) is incorrect because return maximization is a more aggressive strategy than maturity matching. Answer (c) is incorrect because financial leverage is the relationship between debt and equity financing.

25. (a)   The requirement is to identify the incorrect strategy when currency values are expected to fall. Answer (a) is correct because granting credit means that Banner will be paid back with currency that has less value. Answer (b) is incorrect because investing in assets will hedge a decrease in currency value. Answer (c) is incorrect because purchasing materials and supplies will hedge a decrease in currency value. Answer (d) is incorrect because if funds are borrowed they are paid back with currency with less value.

26. (b)   The requirement is to identify a means of hedging a decline in the price of stock. Answer (b) is correct because purchasing a put option on the stock allows the purchaser the option to sell the stock at the specified price in the future. Thus, if the price of the stock declines, the value of the put option will increase by an equivalent amount. Answer (a) is incorrect because purchasing a call option on the stock provides the company with an option to purchase stock at a specified price. Answer (c) is incorrect because selling a put option provides the purchaser with an option to sell stock at a specified price. Answer (d) is incorrect because a warrant provides the purchaser with the option of obtaining additional stock at a specified price.

27. (d)   The requirement is to identify the risk of loss because of fluctuations in the relative value of foreign currencies. Answer (d) is correct because the risk of fluctuations in the relative value of foreign currencies is referred to as exchange rate risk. Answers (a) and (b) are incorrect because expropriation and sovereign risks relate to the possibility that a country might seize a foreign investment. Answer (c) is incorrect because multinational beta would be risk of the individual investment relative to the multinational market as a whole.

Present Value

28. (c)   The requirement is to identify characteristics of bonds that sell at a premium. Item I is not correct because if the bond sells at a premium the market rate is less than the coupon rate. Item III is not correct because the coupon rate is higher than the market rate. Item V is incorrect because the bond sells at a premium not a discount. Therefore, answer (c) is the only answer with two correct characteristics, II and IV.

29. (c)   The requirement is to determine the annual savings needed for an investment to realize a 12% yield. The internal rate of return method of capital budgeting determines the rate of return at which the present value of the cash flows will exactly equal the investment outlay. In this problem, the desired IRR is given and the cash flows must be determined. The necessary annual savings can be computed as follows:

$$
\begin{aligned}
\text{TVMF} \times \text{Cash flows} &= \text{PV (investment today)} \\
3.60X + (.57 \times \$10,000) &= \$50,000 \\
3.60X &= \$50,000 - (.57 \times \$10,000) \\
3.60X &= \$44,300 \\
X &= \$12,306
\end{aligned}
$$

If the annual savings equals $12,306, the present value of the cash inflows will exactly equal the cash outflows.

30. (d)   APB 21 states that receivables bearing an unreasonably low stated interest rate should be recorded at their present value. The Maxx receivable would be recorded at its present value, since it matures in five years. The Maxx receivable will result in a lump-sum collection of $11,593 ($10,000 × 1.1593), so its present value is $7,883 ($11,593 × .680).

31. (c)   The market price of a bond issued at any amount (par, premium, or discount) is equal to the present value of all of its future cash flows, discounted at the current market (effective) interest rate. The market price of a bond issued at a discount is equal to the present value of both its principal and periodic future cash interest payments at the stated (cash) rate of interest, discounted at the current market (effective) rate.

Capital Budgeting

32. (c)   The requirement is to identify the stage that management is most likely to use present value techniques. Answer (c) is correct because present value techniques will most likely be used in the selection stage in which management evaluates various alternatives. Commonly used present value techniques include net present value and the internal rate of return. Answer (a) is incorrect because the identification stage involves determining the types of capital projects that are necessary to achieve management's strategies. Answer (b) is incorrect because in the search stage management attempts to identify capital investments that will achieve management's objectives. Answer (d) is incorrect because in the financing stage management decides on the best source of funding for projects.

Capital Budgeting: Payback and Discounted Payback

33. (c)   The requirement is to identify the difference between the payback method and the discounted payback method. Answer (c) is correct because the discounted payback method evaluates investments by discounting future cash flows and determining how many years it will take to recover the initial investment. Answer (a) is incorrect because the discounted payback method involves the same estimates of cash flows as the payback method. Answer (b) is incorrect because neither the payback method nor the discounted payback method considers the overall profitability of the investment. Answer (d) is incorrect because neither the payback method nor the discounted payback method considers variability of return.

34. (c)   The payback period is computed by dividing the initial investment by the annual net cash inflow. Depreciation expense is not subtracted from cash inflow; only the income taxes that are affected by the depreciation deduction are subtracted. One of the weaknesses of the payback period is that it ignores the time value of money.

35. (d)   The payback method is easy to understand but it is not very sophisticated. Answer (a) is incorrect because the payback method only considers cash flows until the cost is recovered. Answer (b) is incorrect because the payback method only considers net cash inflows from all sources. Answer (c) is incorrect because the payback method does not consider the time value of money.

36. (d)   The payback method evaluates investments on the length of time until total dollars invested are recouped in the form of cash inflows or cash outflows avoided. It is calculated as Initial investment ÷ Annual cash inflow of a project. The payback period of the equipment under consideration by Tam is

$$\$100,000 \div \$20,000 = 5 \text{ years}$$

Capital Budgeting: Accounting Rate of Return

37. (d)   The requirement is to identify the capital budgeting technique that does not use cash flows. Answer (d) is correct because the accounting rate of return uses accrual basis net income. Answers (a), (b), and (c) are incorrect because all of the other techniques use cash flows as the primary basis for the calculation.

38. (b)   The requirement is to identify the advantage of the accounting rate of return method. Answer (b) is correct because accounting return is often used as a performance evaluation measure. Therefore, if it is also used as an evaluation technique, the consistency may lead to better decisions. Answer (a) is incorrect because the fact that results are affected by the depreciation method used is a disadvantage. Answer (c) is incorrect because the accounting rate of return method does not consider the time value of money. Answer (d) is incorrect because the accounting rate of return method does not consider the risk of the investment.

39. (d)   The accounting rate of return (ARR) computes an approximate rate of return which ignores the time value of money. It is calculated as Expected increase in annual net income ÷ Initial (or Average) investment in a project. Tam's expected increase in annual income is as follows:

Annual savings in after-tax cash costs	$20,000
Annual depreciation on equipment	
($100,000 ÷ 10 years)	(10,000)
Increase in annual net income	$10,000

A $100,000 initial investment is required to purchase the equipment. Thus, the ARR of the equipment under consideration by Tam is

$$\$10,000 \div \$100,000 = 10\%$$

40. (c)   The **accounting rate of return** method (ARR) computes an approximate rate of return which ignores the time value of money. It is computed as follows:

ARR = Expected increase in annual net income ÷ Average investment

Therefore, $40,000 (as stated in problem) is the numerator, the expected increase in annual income.

41. (d)   The accounting rate of return (ARR) is based on financial statements prepared on the accrual basis. The formula to compute the ARR is

$$ARR = \frac{\text{Expected increase in annual net income}}{\text{Initial (or average) investment}}$$

Both the revenue over life of project and depreciation expense are used in the calculation of ARR. Depreciation expense over the project's life and other expenses directly associated with the project under consideration including income tax effects are subtracted from revenue over life of the project to determine net income over life of project. Net income over the project's life is then divided by the economic life to determine annual net income, the numerator of the ARR formula. This is a weakness of the ARR method because it does not consider actual cash flows or the time value of money.

Capital Budgeting: Net Present Value

42. (d)   The requirement is to identify the implications of a profitability index of 1.15. Answer (d) is correct because the profitability index is the net present value of future cash flows divided by the amount of the initial investment. If the index is greater than 1.00, the net present value of the investment is positive.

43. (c)   The requirement is to select the rate at which the NPV method assumes that the project's cash flows are reinvested. The correct answer is (c) because the NPV method assumes that cash flows can be reinvested at the discount rate used in the calculation. This is usually the cost of capital. Answer (a) is incorrect because the internal rate of re-turn method assumes that cash flows are reinvested at that rate. Answer (b) is incorrect because the risk-free rate is never used to evaluate a project. Answer (d) is incorrect because the accounting rate of return is not relevant to the NPV method.

44.   (b)   The maximum amount that Kern Co. should invest now to obtain a 15% internal rate of return is the present value of the project's total net cash flows as computed below.

Year	Net cash flows	×	Present value of an ord. annuity	=	Present value of net cash flows
1	$50,000	×	.870	=	$ 43,500
2	$80,000	×	.756	=	$ 60,480
	Total present value				$103,980

45.   (c)   The requirement is to determine the present value of the future cash savings resulting from purchase of the new machine. The present value of the $30,000 savings per year for the first two years is calculated using the present value of an annuity for two periods. Since the amount of the cash savings drops to $20,000 in year three, this amount must be calculated separately. The PV of an annuity for three periods minus the PV of an annuity for two periods, equals the PV of an amount to be received three years in the future. The total present value of the cash savings is calculated as follows:

PV of $30,000 for 2 periods = $30,000 × 1.65 = $49,500
PV of $20,000 in period 3 = $20,000 × (2.32 – 1.65) = 13,400
Total present value of cash savings $62,900

Alternatively, $20,000 could have been treated as an annuity for three years and an additional $10,000 for two years.

46.   (d)   The net present value of a project equals

NPV = (PV future cash flows) – (Investment)

Since this problem involves a lease requiring only annual payments there is no initial investment in this case. Lease amortization must be subtracted from cash inflows to determine income tax expense.

$7,500	Annual cash inflow
– 5,000	Tax basis lease amortization
$2,500	Taxable lease income
× 40%	
$1,000	Tax expense per year

However, lease amortization is **not** a cash outflow and is thus excluded from the calculation of NPV. The after-tax present value of the lease equals:

$ 7,500	Annual cash inflow
– 1,000	Cash outflow for taxes
$6,500	
× 1.74	PV factor for two years at 10%
$11,310	

47.   (a)   A project's net present value is determined by considering the project's cash inflows and cash outflows discounted to their present values using the required rate of return. The initial outlay for the replacement asset is considered to be the cash outflow reduced by any proceeds from the sale of the asset to be replaced.

48.   (c)   The requirement is to determine when the discount rate (hurdle rate) must be determined before a capital budgeting method can be used. The payback method measures the time it will take to recoup, in the form of cash in-flows from operations, the initial dollars invested in a project. The payback method does **not** consider the time value of money. The time-adjusted rate of return method is also called the internal rate of return method. This method computes the rate of interest at which the present value of expected cash inflows from a project equals the present value of expected cash outflows of the project. Here, the discount rate is not determined in advance but is the end result of the calculation. The net present value method is the correct answer because it calculates the expected net monetary gain or loss from a project by discounting all expected future cash inflows and outflows to the present using some predetermined minimum desired rate of return (hurdle rate).

Capital Budgeting: Internal Rate of Return

49.   (a)   The requirement is to identify a description of the application of the internal rate of return. Answer (a) is correct because the IRR is the interest rate that equates the present value of the future cash inflows with the present value of the future cash outflows.

50.   (a)   The requirement is to identify the items used in the computation of the internal rate of return. Answer (a) is correct because the IRR uses the net incremental investment and the net annual cash flows. However, it does not include the incremental average operating income.

51.   (a)   The requirement is to compare NPV and IRR. Answer (a) is correct because NPV and IRR criteria will always lead to the same accept or reject decision. Answer (b) is incorrect because if the second project's internal rate of return is higher than the first project's, the organization would accept the second project based on IRR.

52.   (c)   The requirement is to calculate the net present value of Project A. Answer (c) is correct. The December 31, 2013 cash inflow is five years from the present cash outflow, and the net present value method uses the firm's cost of capital of 18%. The present value factor for 18% for 5 years is .4371, and $7,400,000 times .4371 equals $3,234,540, which is $265,460 less than the present cash outflow of $3,500,000. Answer (a) is incorrect because this answer discounts the cash inflow at the correct discount rate (18%), but for four years instead of five. Answer (b) is incorrect because this answer discounts the cash inflow at 15% (the project's internal rate of return) instead of at 18% (the cost of capital), which the net present value method uses. Answer (d) is incorrect because this answer discounts the cash inflow at the correct discount rate (18%), but for four years instead of five, and also subtracts the cash outflow from the cash inflow, instead of vice versa.

53.   (c)   The requirement is to estimate Project B's internal rate of return. Answer (c) is correct because 20% is the rate of return that equates the cash inflows with the cash outflows. The present value of 20% for 5 years is .4019, which multiplied by $9,950,000 equals $3,998,905. Therefore, the net present value of the project approximates $0 using the 20% rate.

54.   (b)   The requirement is to calculate the cost of the project from its cash flow information. Answer (b) is correct. The internal rate of return is the discount rate that sets the net present value of the project to zero, so the present value of the costs equals the present value of the cash inflows. The cost of Project A can be calculated by determining the present value of the annual annuity of $10,000 cash flows discounted at 15%. Therefore, the cost of the investment is $22,832 ($10,000 × 2.2832). Answer (a) is incorrect because this solution uses the present value interest factor of 15%, one period rather than the present value interest factor for an annuity. Answer (c) is incorrect because this solution is obtained using a 10% rather than a 15% discount rate. Answer (d) is incorrect because this solution is obtained using a 5% rather than a 15% discount rate.

55.   **(a)**   The requirement is to calculate the net present value of Project B. Answer (a) is correct because the net present value is the present value of the cash inflows less the cost of the project. The net present value of the future inflows is $24,079 [($5,000 × .9091) + ($10,000 × .8264) + ($15,000 × .7513)]. Therefore, the net present value of the project is $4,079 ($24,079 – $20,000). Answer (b) is incorrect because this solution is obtained using a 5%, rather than a 10%, discount rate. Answer (c) is incorrect because this is the net present value of Project A at a 10% discount rate. Answer (d) is incorrect because this solution is obtained using the present value interest factor for annuities.

56.   **(c)**   The requirement is to calculate the payback period of Project C. Answer (c) is correct because after two years, the cumulative cash inflows for Project C are exactly equal to the initial investment outlay, $25,000 ($15,000 + 10,000). Answer (a) is incorrect because the payback period would be zero only if a project had no cost or provided immediate cash inflows in excess of the investment outlay. Project C does not provide an immediate payback of its investment cost. Answer (b) is incorrect because after one year, the cumulative cash inflows for Project C are only $15,000 versus an initial investment outlay of $25,000. The project has not yet recovered its costs. Answer (d) is incorrect because Project C pays back its initial investment outlay in only two years.

57.   **(c)**   The requirement is to calculate the year 2 cash inflow for Project D. Answer (c) is correct. The discounted payback period is the length of time required for discounted cash flows to recover the cost of the investment. The year two cash inflow for Project D that is consistent with a discounted payback period of 2 years can be calculated as follows:

> Investment cost = present value of year 1 and 2 cash inflows
> $30,000 = $20,000 × (.9524) + year 2 cash inflow × (0.9070)
> Year 2 cash inflow = [$30,000 – ($20,000 × .9524)] ÷ 0.9070
> = $12,075.

Answer (c) is incorrect because this solution is obtained using the present value interest factor for annuities. Answer (b) is incorrect because this solution is based on the regular payback period. Since the cash inflow in year 1 is $20,000, Project D pays back its $30,000 cost in two years if the cash inflow in year 2 is $10,000. Answer (d) is incorrect because this solution is obtained using a 10%, rather than a 5%, discount rate.

58.   **(c)**   The internal rate of return (IRR) determines the rate of discount at which the present value of the future cash flows will exactly equal the investment outlay. It is computed by setting up the following equation

> Initial investment = TVMF × Cash flows

and solving for the time value of money factor (TVMF). The IRR can then be found by locating the TVMF for (n)

periods in the present value of an ordinary annuity table and tracing to the top of that column to find the rate of return. The problem asks for the TVMF for the IRR of the equipment, which is calculated as follows:

$$\$100,000 = TVMF \times \$20,000$$
$$5.00 = TVMF$$

In estimating the IRR, the factors in the table of present values of an annuity should be taken from the columns closest to 5.00.

59.   **(d)**   The internal rate of return of a proposed project includes the residual sales value of a project but not the depreciation expense. This is true because the residual sales value represents a future cash flow whereas depreciation expense (ignoring income tax considerations) provides no cash inflow or outflow.

60.   **(c)**   The relationship between the NPV method and the IRR method can be summarized as follows:

NPV	IRR
NPV > 0	IRR > Discount rate
NPV = 0	IRR = Discount rate
NPV < 0	IRR < Discount rate

Since the problem states that Neu Co. has a positive net present value on the investment, then the internal rate of return would be > 12%.

61.   **(a)**   The requirement is to determine which mutually exclusive investment should be accepted. Answer (a) is correct because Project X has the higher net present value as calculated below.

Net present value of Project X= $6,800= ($40,000 × 3.170) – $120,000

Net present value of Project Y= $5,310= [($10,000 × 0.909) +($20,000 × 0.826) + ($60,000 × 0.751) + ($80,000 × 0.683)] – $120,000

62.   **(c)**   The requirement is to select the projects that should be undertaken assuming no budget constraints. Answer (c) is correct because the company should undertake all projects with a positive net present value. This would include Projects 2, 3, and 4. Answers (a), (b), and (d) are incorrect because Project 1 has a negative net present value and should not be undertaken.

63.   **(d)**   The requirement is to select the projects that should be undertaken assuming the company has only $600,000 available. Answer (d) is correct because Projects 3 and 4 have the highest NPV, profitability indexes, and IRRs, so they are the most profitable projects. Answer (a) is incorrect because Project 1 has a negative net present value. Answer (b) is incorrect because it violates the $600,000 restriction. Answer (c) is incorrect because the combined NPV of Projects 2 and 3 is less than the combined NPV of Projects 3 and 4.

64.   **(d)**   The requirement is to identify the project(s) that should be undertaken assuming the company has only $300,000 available. Answer (d) is correct; because Project 3 has the highest profitability index and a positive NPV, it should be undertaken. The profitability index provides a good measure for comparing investments of different amounts because it provides an indication of the NPV per dollar invested. Answer (a) is incorrect because it has a negative NPV. Answers (b) and (c) are incorrect because they violate the $300,000 constraint.

Determining Future Cash Flows

65. **(b)** The requirement is to define the nature of a tax shield. Answer (b) is correct because the benefit of depreciation in cash flow analysis is the resulting tax savings (reduction in income taxes). Answers (a), (c), and (d) are incorrect because they do not describe the nature of the tax shield.

66. **(a)** The requirement is to identify the effects of income taxes on future cash flows. Answer (a) is correct because income taxes decrease both revenues and costs in projecting future cash flows. Answers (b), (c), and (d) are incorrect because income taxes decrease both benefits and costs.

67. **(b)** The requirement is to determine which costs are economically relevant to Buff Co.'s decision of whether to replace an old machine with a new machine. Costs that will not differ among alternatives are not relevant for decision-making purposes. Sunk costs are those that are not avoidable and are the result of a past decision. The original cost, accumulated depreciation, and therefore the carrying amount of Buff's old machine are not relevant to the decision because this is a past cost that cannot be changed. The costs associated with the new machine are avoidable. The disposal value of a new machine is relevant to Buff's decision because it represents a cash inflow that differs between the alternatives.

68. **(b)** The requirement is to calculate the after-tax cash flows in year 2. Answer (b) is correct. The after-tax cash flows are calculated by deducting tax expense from the before-tax cash flows. Since depreciation is deductible for tax purposes it provides a tax shield. Therefore, income taxes for year 2 are equal to $15,000 [($140,000 – 90,000) × 30%], and after-tax cash flows are $125,000 ($140,000 – 15,000). Answer (a) is incorrect because $140,000 is the before-tax cash flows. Answer (c) is incorrect because this solution fails to consider the deductibility of depreciation.

69. **(c)** The requirement is to calculate the net present value of the investment. Answer (c) is correct. The net present value is equal to the present value of the future after-tax cash flows minus the initial investment. The after-tax annual cash flows are calculated by taking the before-tax cash flows and deducting income taxes. Since depreciation is deductible for tax purposes, annual tax expense is equal to $15,000 [($140,000 – 90,000) × 30%]. Therefore, annual cash flows after taxes are $125,000 ($140,000 – 15,000). The present value of $125,000 received annually for 5 years discounted at 10% is $473,875 ($125,000 × 3.791). To properly evaluate the project, the investment in working capital ($10,000) must be considered a part of the initial investment, and its recovery at the end of year 5 must be discounted back to its present value, along with the terminal value of the investment of $50,000. The present value of $60,000 received at the end of 5 years is equal to $37,260 ($60,000 × .621). Therefore, the net present value is equal to $1,135 ($473,875 + 37,260 – 500,000 – 10,000). Answer (a) is incorrect because it is the result when amounts are not discounted. Answer (b) is incorrect because it is the result when taxes are not considered.

Considering Risk in Capital Budgeting

70. **(b)** The requirement is to calculate the expected contribution of a new product. Answer (b) is correct because the expected value of the contribution margin is equal to $110,000 [($700,000 × 30%) + ($200,000 × 30%) + (-$400,000 × 40%)].

71. **(d)** The requirement is to determine the expected value of cost of goods sold. Answer (d) is correct because the estimated cost of goods sold is calculated by multiplying the cost of goods sold percentage by the expected value of sales. The expected value of sales is $84,000 [($60,000 × 25%) + (85,000 × 40%) + ($100,000 × 35%). Therefore, cost of goods sold is estimated to be $67,200 ($84,000 × 80%).

72. **(a)** The requirement is to identify the technique that would allow management to justify an investment based on considerations other than expected cash flows. Answer (a) is correct because the real options technique views an investment as purchasing an option. This may allow management to justify investments that do not currently have positive cash flows. Answers (b), (c), and (d) are all techniques that require expected return to exceed the initial investment.

73. **(c)** The requirement is to calculate the expected return for the project. Answer (c) is correct because the expected return is calculated by summing the outcomes weighted by their probability of occurrence. Therefore, the expected return is equal to $470,000 [($200,000 × .4) + ($500,000 × .3) + ($800,000 × .3)]. Answer (a) is incorrect because it is the simple average of the three potential outcomes. Answer (b) is incorrect because it is the median return.

74. **(b)** The requirement is to compute the coefficient of variation of the project. Answer (b) is correct because the coefficient of variation is equal to the standard deviation of returns divided by the amount of the expected return. The coefficient of variation is equal to .3191 ($150,000 ÷ 470,000).

75. **(c)** The requirement is to identify the technique that recognizes the series of decisions involved in an investment. Answer (c) is correct because decision tree provides management with a technique for evaluating investments that involve a series of decisions. Answer (a) is incorrect because probability analysis involves assigning probabilities to various outcomes. Answer (b) is incorrect because the risk-adjusted discount rate technique involves assigning different discount rates based on the risk involved. Answer (d) is incorrect because sensitivity analysis involves examining the sensitivity of results to changes in significant assumptions.

76. **(d)** The requirement is to identify the technique that is not used to consider risk. Answer (d) is correct because the traditional internal rate of return method does not explicitly include consideration of risk. Answer (a) is incorrect because probability analysis involves assigning probabilities to various outcomes. Therefore, it considers risk. Answer (b) is incorrect because the risk-adjusted discount rate method adjusts discount rates for risk. Answer (c) is incorrect because simulation techniques allow management to simulate results based on expected values and levels of risk.

77. **(d)** The requirement is to identify the type of risk that concerns investors in a diversified company. Answer (d) is correct because a diversified company can be thought of as an investment portfolio. The relevant risk for both management and investors is the weighted average of project risk. Answer (a) is incorrect because the firm has a diversified set of projects and, therefore, a single project risk is not relevant. Answer (b) is incorrect because pure play risk relates to a single project. Answer (c) is incorrect because the standard deviation of project risk does not adequately measure the risk of the portfolio.

78.   (a)   The requirement is to identify the nature of the next investment in a portfolio. Answer (a) is correct because to reduce the risk of a portfolio, the investor should select investments with negatively correlated returns. In that way, when one investment decreases in value others will increase. Therefore, the company should select an investment that correlates negatively to current portfolio holdings. Answer (b) is incorrect because an investment that is uncorrelated to the current holdings does not reduce risk as much as one that is negatively correlated. Answer (c) is incorrect because an investment that is highly correlated to the current holdings increases the risk of the portfolio. Answer (d) is incorrect because an investment that is perfectly correlated to the current holdings increases the risk of the portfolio.

79.   (c)   The requirement is to calculate Deet's estimated savings for 2009 if it leases an auxiliary generator for use during power outages. In 2008 Deet incurred the following costs due to power outages:

Number of outages per month		Number of months		Number of outages
0	×	3	=	0
1	×	2	=	2
2	×	4	=	8
3	×	3	=	9
		12		19

19 outages × \$400/outage = $\underline{\$7,600}$

The cost of leasing an auxiliary generator is only \$6,000 (12 mos. × \$500/mo). Therefore, Deet would be expected to save \$1,600 (\$7,600 – \$6,000) in 2009 by leasing the generator.

80.   (d)   The internal rate of return method determines the rate of return at which the present value of the cash flows will exactly equal the investment outlay. It will indicate the rate of return earned over the life of the project. The net present value method determines the present value of all future cash flows at a selected discount rate. If the NPV of the cash flows is positive, the return earned by the project is higher than the selected rate. Both methods will provide the information needed to decide if a project's rate of return will meet Polo Co.'s requirement.

81.   (b)   The requirement is to determine what the probability of frost must be for Cal to be indifferent to spending \$10,000 for frost protection. In other words, you must find the point at which the cost of the frost protection equals the expected value of the loss from frost damage. The table below summarizes the possible outcomes.

	Frost	Frost-free
Protected	\$90,000 Market value	\$60,000 Market value
Unprotected	\$40,000 Market value	\$60,000 Market value

The difference between the market value of protected and unprotected strawberries if a frost were to occur is \$50,000.

Since we want to determine the probability of a frost when the expected value of the loss from frost damage is \$10,000, this probability can be calculated as follows:

Loss from damage	×	Probability of frost	=	Expected value of the loss
\$50,000	×	P	=	\$10,000
		P	=	$\dfrac{\$10,000}{\$50,000}$
		P	=	.200

82.   (c)   Expected values are calculated as the weighted-average of all possible outcomes using the probabilities of the outcomes as weights. The expected number of additional muffin sales is

Additional sales		Probability		Expected value
60	×	0.6	=	36
100	×	0.4	=	40
				76

Since Dough earns \$1 profit per box (\$3 sales price – \$2 cost), this represents \$76 (76 boxes × \$1 profit) of additional profit. However, the twenty-four unsold boxes would have to be sold at a \$1 loss per box (\$1 sales price – \$2 cost) through Dough's thrift store. Therefore, the expected value of the decision to purchase the additional muffins is \$52 net profit (\$76 profit – \$24 loss).

83.   (b)   Because it is not always possible to make decisions under conditions of total certainty, decision makers must have a method of determining the best estimate or course of action where uncertainty exists. One method is probability analysis. Probabilities are used to calculate the expected value of each action. The expected value of an action is the weighted-average of the payoffs for that action, where the weights are the probabilities of the various mutually exclusive events that may occur. Cost-volume-profit analysis is used to predict profits at all levels of production in the relevant range. Program evaluation and review technique (PERT) is used to estimate, schedule, and manage a network of interdependent project activities. It is useful for managing large-scale, complex projects. The scattergraph method is a graphical approach to computing the relationship between two variables.

84.   (c)   A probability distribution describes the possible outcomes relating to a single action and the likelihood of occurrence of each possible outcome. Gift Co. selected the most likely sales volume from several possible outcomes, which was simply the sales volume with the greatest probability of occurring. Gift Co. did not calculate the weighted-average of the outcomes (the sum of the probability of each outcome occurring times the sales volume of that outcome) to find the expected value.

85.   (c)   Probability analysis is an extension of sensitivity analysis. There is no specified limit on the number of possible outcomes. The summation of the probability weights should always equal one. Probability analysis and sensitivity analysis are not incompatible.

PERFORMANCE MEASURES

A. Organizational performance measures (including financial and nonfinancial measures) are used for a variety of purposes including: resource allocation, incentive compensation, divisional and business unit evaluation, budgeting and planning, and setting targets. Performance measures are used to manage and monitor performance in many areas of the organization including: financial, customer, internal processes, employees, and suppliers.

1. **What Is Strategy?**

    Organizational performance measures should be aligned to the strategy of the organization and useful in executing that strategy.

    Strategy is the creation of a unique and valuable position involving a different set of activities, requiring tradeoffs in competing, to choose what not to do and involving creating "fit" among that company's activities. (Porter, "What Is Strategy?" *Harvard Business Review*, November-December 1996).

    The execution of the strategic activities of an organization requires use of the right performance measures, including both financial and nonfinancial measures.

2. **Strategy, Execution and Performance Measures. Strategy** describes how an organization uses its activities and resources to achieve its objectives. For a business, the objective is to ethically maximize financial value. **Execution** includes the performance measures used (1) to ensure the strategy of the organization is being executed and (2) to monitor performance. To be successful, an organization must have an effective strategy and an effective execution system in place, including performance measures that closely link to the strategy. **Performance measures** are the specific ways an organization measures outcomes and activities related to achieving its strategy.

3. **Types of Performance Measures.** Performance measures (or performance metrics) can be classified into a number of categories. The measures can be financial or nonfinancial, and can include traditional performance measures found in financial statement and cost accounting systems, as well as performance measures on customer performance, supplier performance, environmental performance, etc.

4. **Performance Measurement Frameworks.** There are a number of different types of performance measurement systems and frameworks used in organizations. In the 1990's, two performance measurement frameworks evolved: the **balanced scorecard** and **value-based management**. Many organizations have adopted one or both of these frameworks into their performance measurement systems.

B. Financial and Nonfinancial Performance Measures

    Both financial and nonfinancial performance measures are needed to manage an organization. Financial measures gauge performance, profitability, or costs and are expressed as dollar amounts, ratios, or other forms. Nonfinancial performance measures are expressed in nonmonetary terms and include measures of customer satisfaction, customer retention, on-time delivery, quality, employee satisfaction, etc.

C. Balanced Scorecard and Performance Measures

    The balanced scorecard, a performance measurement system that includes financial and nonfinancial performance measures, was developed by Kaplan and Norton.

1. **What Is the Balanced Scorecard?**

    The **balanced scorecard** is a strategic performance measurement and management framework for implementing strategy by translating an organization's mission and strategy into a set of performance measures. These performance measures are generally in four primary perspectives: **financial, customer, internal business processes**, and **learning and growth**.

2. **Four Perspectives of the Balanced Scorecard**

    a. **Financial perspective.** This perspective focuses on return on investment and other supporting financial performance measures. Example performance measures include profitability, return on invested capital, and revenue growth.

    b. **Customer perspective.** This perspective focuses on performance in areas that are most critical to the customer. Example performance measures include customer satisfaction and customer retention.

c. **Internal business processes perspective.** This perspective focuses on operating effectively and efficiently and includes performance measures on cost, quality and time for processes that are critical to the customers. Example performance measures include number of defects and cycle time.

d. **Learning and growth perspective.** This perspective focuses on performance measures relating to employees, infrastructure, teaming and capabilities necessary for the internal processes to achieve customer and financial objectives. Example performance measures include employee satisfaction, hours of training per employee, and information technology expenditures per employee.

3. **Components of the Balanced Scorecard**

   a. **Strategic objectives.** A statement of what the strategy must achieve and what is critical to its success.

   b. **Performance measures.** Describe how success in achieving the strategy will be measured and tracked.

   c. **Baseline performance.** The current level of performance for the performance measure.

   d. **Targets.** The level of performance or rate of improvement needed in the performance measure.

   e. **Strategic initiatives.** Key action programs required to achieve strategic objectives.

   Strategic objectives focus on **what** is to be achieved. Strategic initiatives focus on **how** it will be achieved and performance measures, baseline performance and targets relate to how it will be **measured**.

   The **value chain** in the balanced scorecard framework is the sequence of business processes in which usefulness is added to the products or services of a company and includes the **innovation process**, **operations process**, and **post-sales process**. The value chain is one way to describe the internal process perspective in the balanced scorecard and its performance measures.

4. **Characteristics of the Balanced Scorecard**

   Characteristic of the balanced scorecard include the following:

   • **Strategy-focused.** Performance measures are driven by mission, vision and strategy. The balanced scorecard communicates the strategy to all members of the organization.

   • **Balanced.** Performance measures are "balanced" in terms of financial and nonfinancial measures, leading and lagging measures and internal (internal processes) and external (customer) measures. Accordingly, the scorecard highlights suboptimal tradeoffs that managers may make when they fail to consider operational and financial measures together.

   • **Includes both financial and nonfinancial measures.** Performance measures include traditional financial measures, as well as nonfinancial measures.

   • **Cause-and-effect linkages.** Performance measures are connected using cause-and-effect linkages. Performance measures include **performance drivers** (leading indicators) and **outcome performance measures** (lagging indicators). The focus on cause and effect linkages limits the number of measures used by identifying the most critical ones.

   • **Unique to the strategy.** Performance measures are unique and customized to an organization's strategy.

5. **Strategy Maps and Cause-and-Effect Linkages**

   Strategy maps are diagrams of the cause-and-effect relationships between strategic objectives. When looking at cause and effect linkages in the balanced scorecard framework, it is important to remember that the classification of performance measures as leading or lagging is not a dichotomy, but rather must be considered as a continuum. For example, customer satisfaction may be a leading indicator (performance driver) to return on investment (the lagging indicator or outcome measure). However, customer satisfaction may be a lagging indicator to on-time delivery (the leading indicator).

   EXAMPLE: Balanced scorecard
   The following is a simple example of a balanced scorecard. Within each of the four perspectives are key strategic objectives and related performance measures.

Financial Perspective

<u>Strategic objective</u>	<u>Performance measure</u>
Increase return on investment (ROI)	ROI
Revenue growth	Percent growth in revenue
Increase profitability	Net income as a percentage of sales

Customer Perspective

<u>Strategic objective</u>	<u>Performance measure</u>
Increase customer satisfaction	Customer satisfaction ratings
Increase customer share	Revenue per customer
Attract new customers	Number of new customers
	Revenue from new customers

Internal Business Processes Perspective

<u>Strategic objective</u>	<u>Performance measure</u>
Improve on-time delivery	Percentage of on-time deliveries
Improve quality performance	Number of rejects

Learning and Growth Perspective

<u>Strategic objective</u>	<u>Performance measure</u>
Train employees on quality tools	Hours of training on quality tools
Use information systems to manage on-time delivery status	Percent of employees using information system

In this example, we see possible cause and effect relationships. Increasing the training in the use of quality tools may improve on-time delivery performance which may improve customer satisfaction and therefore increase return on investment. The connection between customer satisfaction and return on investment at some companies is based on the following observation: more satisfied customers pay invoices faster, therefore accounts receivable turnover (a component of return on assets) increases and return on investment increases.

6. **Performance Measures in the Balanced Scorecard**

Here are examples of performance measures that are classified within the four perspectives of the balanced scorecard.

<u>Financial perspective</u>
Return on investment
Economic profit
Economic value added
Cash flow ROI
Free cash flow
Net income/sales ratio
Sales/asset ratio
Revenue growth
Revenue from new products (existing customers)
Revenue from new products (new customers)
Cost of sales %

<u>Customer perspective</u>
Customer satisfaction
Customer retention
Customer acquisition
Percentage of highly satisfied customers
Depth of relationship
Percentage of business from customer referrals
Customer satisfaction with new product/service offerings

<u>Internal process perspective</u>
On-time delivery
Cost per unit
Percentage of late orders
Total cost of quality
Cycle time
Process efficiency
Capacity utilization
Inventory turnover
Lead times (order to delivery)

Internal process perspective
Percentage of on-time deliveries
Time to resolve customer complaints
Inventory obsolescence
Order backlog
Number of leads/conversion rate
Hours with customers
Time spent with target accounts
Number of new projects based on client input
Number of joint projects
Number of technology and product partners
Number of patents
Total time from concept to market
Time from pilot to full production
Manufacturing-process yield
Number of failures, defects and customer returns
Warranty costs
Number of safety incidents

Learning and growth perspective
Employee satisfaction and engagement
Employee turnover
Employee objectives linked to the balanced scorecard
Employee awareness of the strategy
Percentage of employees trained in total quality management
Number of six-sigma black belts
Performance improvement from employees' suggestions
Percentage of ideas and best practices shared across organization
Percentage of R&D employees to total employees
R&D expenditure as a percent to sales revenue

D. Value-Based Management (VBM) and Financial Performance Measures

VBM involves the use of value-based metrics (performance measures) in a strategic management system and as such may be viewed as a financial scorecard. The spectrum of value-based metrics include performance measures such as: return on investment (ROI), economic profit, economic value added (EVA), cash flow ROI, and residual income.

When is it appropriate to use economic value added measures (EVA) (or other value-based metrics) as a performance measure? EVA is particularly useful for incentive compensation, resource allocation and investor relations. Executive compensation and incentive compensation firmwide have been the most popular target of EVA. The premise is "pay for performance" where performance is defined as creating financial value (earning a return above the cost of capital). Using EVA alone can have certain disadvantages by failing to reflect all the pathways to value creation. This limitation can be minimized by integrating EVA with a balanced scorecard framework which would avoid the temptation to focus only on low-hanging fruit (cost reduction and increased asset intensity) but miss the opportunity to create additional value through growth strategies.

1. **Return on Investment (ROI)**

Return on investment is the ratio of a measure of "return" divided by a measure of "investment." There are various ways to measure ROI including: return on assets (ROA), return on net assets (RONA) and return on equity (ROE). ROI is most often computed using net income (income after interest and taxes) but it also may be computed using operating income or operating income after taxes.

2. **DuPont ROI Analysis**

DuPont ROI analysis looks at ROI as driven by two factors: return on sales (net income/sales) and asset turnover (sales/total assets). The calculation of DuPont ROI is as follows:

$$
\begin{aligned}
\text{ROI} \;&=\; \text{Net income/total assets} \\
&=\; \text{Net income/sales} \times \text{Sales/average investment} \\
&=\; \text{Return on sales} \times \text{Asset turnover ratio}
\end{aligned}
$$

The DuPont method highlights the two basic ways to improve profits: (1) increasing income per dollar of sales, and (2) using assets to generate more sales.

EXAMPLE: The following selected data pertain to the Amy Division of Cara Products, Inc. for 2009:

Sales	$20,000,000
Average invested capital (total assets)	5,000,000
Net income	1,250,000
Cost of capital	10%

ROI (based on total assets) and DuPont ROI would be calculated as follows:

$$
\begin{aligned}
\text{DuPont ROI} \quad &= \quad 1{,}250{,}000/5{,}000{,}000 = 25\% \\
&= \quad 1{,}250{,}000/20{,}000{,}000 \times 20{,}000{,}000/5{,}000{,}000 \\
&= \quad 6.25\% \times 4.0 \\
&= \quad 25\%
\end{aligned}
$$

The return on sales of 6.25% times the asset turnover ratio of 4.0 equals the ROI of 25%.

3. Residual Income

Residual income is net income (or operating income after taxes) minus a cost of capital based on capital invested in a division or project.

$$
\begin{aligned}
\text{Residual income} \quad &= \quad \text{Net income} - \text{Interest on investment} \\
&= \quad \text{Net income} - (\text{Required rate of return} \times \text{Invested capital})
\end{aligned}
$$

EXAMPLE: Using the data from the previous example for Amy Division

Sales	$20,000,000
Average invested capital	5,000,000
Net income	1,250,000
Required rate of return	10%

$$
\begin{aligned}
\text{Residual income} \quad &= \quad \$1{,}250{,}000 - (10\% \times \$5{,}000{,}000) \\
&= \quad \$1{,}250{,}000 - 500{,}000 \\
&= \quad \$750{,}000
\end{aligned}
$$

Remember that the ROI was 25% for this company and the required interest rate is 10%. The difference between the ROI and the required interest rate (cost of capital) is sometimes called the **spread**. *In this case the spread can be computed as follows:*

$$
\begin{aligned}
\text{Spread} \quad &= \quad \text{ROI} - \text{Cost of capital} \\
&= \quad 25\% - 10\% \\
&= \quad 15\%
\end{aligned}
$$

Notice that the residual income of $750,000 divided by the invested capital of $5,000,000 equals the spread of 15%.

4. Residual Income Profile

The **residual income profile** is a graphical way to look at the relationship between residual income and ROI.

The residual income profile shows the interrelationship between residual income and ROI. The vertical axis shows residual income in dollars. The horizontal axis shows the implicit cost of capital and ROI.

The formula for the residual income profile is

$$\text{Residual income} = \text{Net income} - i \,(\text{invested capital})$$

Where: i = cost of capital or required rate of return for computing residual income

The formula for the residual income profile is the same as the formula for residual income with the required rate of return as the coefficient. As the required rate of return increases, residual income decreases. Where residual income is zero, the required rate of return equals the ROI.

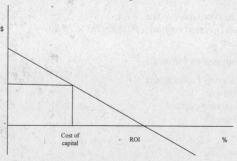

EXAMPLE: The following information is available for Iceman, Inc. for 2009:

Net income	$ 300,000
Average invested capital	$2,000,000
Cost of capital	12%

The ROI and residual income are computed below.

$$ROI \quad = \frac{\$300,000}{\$2,000,000} = 15\%$$

$$\begin{aligned} Residual\ income \quad &= \$300,000 - (12\% \times 2,000,000) \\ &= \$300,000 - 240,000 \\ &= \$60,000 \end{aligned}$$

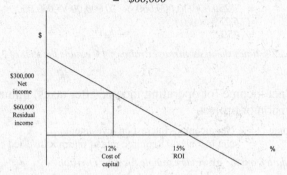

Notice that at an interest rate of 15%, the residual income is zero.

5. **Economic Profit and EVA**

Economic profit and economic value added measures stress the importance of making investments only when the return exceeds cost and, in the process, value to the stockholder is maximized. Economic profit is accounting profit minus the cost of capital. EVA is a variation of economic profit. Economic Value Added (EVA) is net operating profit (income) after taxes (NOPAT) minus the after-tax weighted-average cost of capital (WACC) multiplied by total assets (TA) minus current liabilities (CL) (net assets).

EVA = Net operating profit after taxes (NOPAT) − [(TA − CL) × WACC]

Market value added is the difference between the market value of a company (both equity and debt) and the capital that lenders and shareholders have entrusted to it over the years in the form of loans, retained earnings and paid-in capital. Market value added is a measure of the difference between "cash in" (what investors have contributed) and "cash out" (what they could get by selling at today's prices).

6. **Free Cash Flow**

Free cash flow can be computed as follows:

Free cash flow = Net operating profit after taxes (NOPAT) + Depreciation and amortization − Capital expenditures − The change in working capital requirements

EXAMPLES: The following information is available for Armstrong Enterprises:

Net operating profit (income) after taxes	$36,000,000
Depreciation expense	15,000,000
Change in net working capital	10,000,000
Capital expenditures	10,000,000
Invested capital (TA − CL)	90,000,000
Weighted-average cost of capital	10%

EVA would be computed as follows:

Net operating profit (income) after taxes	$36,000,000
Less: capital charge on invested capital (90,000,000 × 10%)	(9,000,000)
Economic value added	$27,000,000

Free cash flow would be computed as follows:

Net operating profit (income) after taxes	$ 36,000,000
Plus: Depreciation expense	+ 15,000,000
Less: Change in net working capital	(10,000,000)
Less: Capital expenditures	(10,000,000)
Free cash flow	$31,000,000

7. **Cash Flow ROI**

   Cash flow ROI represents the average real cash return of all existing projects as reflected in the financial statements. The cash flow ROI performance metric is an approximation of the average real internal rate of return earned by a firm on all its operating assets. As discussed in Module 42, the internal rate of return (IRR) is the discount rate that equates the present value of inflows with the present value of outflows.

8. **Determination of the Amount of Invested Capital**

   The amount of invested capital for computation of performance measures generally is determined in two ways: current cost or historical cost. Current cost is the current replacement cost of the existing investment and provides a better measure of the economic returns from the investment. The drawback to using current cost is that the estimates of current cost may be difficult and costly to obtain. When using historical cost the firm either uses the gross book value (original cost) or the net book value (original cost less accumulated depreciation). Advocates of gross book value indicate that it results in measures that are more comparable across business units. If net book value is used, ROI increases simply due to the effects of annual depreciation.

   Advocates of net book value indicate that it is consistent with the amount of assets shown on the balance sheet and with net income that is calculated after the depreciation deduction. Most firms use net book value to measure investment but may compensate by establishing target ROIs that adjust for the effects of the limitations of historical cost measures of investment.

E. Choosing among Different Performance Measures

1. Choosing among different performance measures involves understanding how the performance measure will be used. Is it being used for executive compensation, resource allocation or business unit performance evaluation? It also involves understanding how well the performance measure enables management to execute business strategy and monitor how well it is being executed. Here are some guidelines for choosing among different performance measures.

   a. **Strategy-focused.** How well does the performance measure reflect the strategy of the organization? This is where the balanced scorecard framework and the performance measures within the balanced scorecard framework can be useful. A well-designed balanced scorecard will include the right mix of performance measures to communicate and operationalize the strategy.

   b. **Economic reality and cash flow.** How well does the performance measure reflect the economic reality that a firm must earn a return on capital invested in excess of its cost of capital in order to create financial value? Here is where Value Based Management and its metrics (ROI, economic profit, free cash flow, and cash flow ROI) can be useful.

   c. **Quality of the performance measure.** The relevance and reliability of the performance measures also should be considered. For example, relevant and reliable manager performance measures are ones that are sensitive to factors within the control of the manager and not sensitive to factors beyond the manager's control.

2. The most common financial measures used for performance measurement include return on investment (ROI), residual income (RI), economic value added (EVA), and return on sales (ROS). It is important to distinguish between those measures that are used to evaluate the business unit and those that are used to evaluate a manager's performance.

3. Performance measures should not encourage decisions that maximize the measure in the short run but are in conflict with the long-term goals of the firm. For example, a manager could decide to postpone machine maintenance to make ROI for a particular year look better, but the decision may cause long-run profits to suffer. The focus on short-run performance may be mitigated by using measures with multiple-year time horizons or by using a combination of financial and nonfinancial measures. Compensation tied to changes in the value of the firm's stock also encourages managers to take a long-run perspective, because stock prices reflect the future value of current management decisions.

4. A focus on ROI as a performance measure may cause a lack of goal congruence. As an example, managers of very profitable business units may reject projects that from a firm-wide perspective should be accepted. In such situations, RI rather than ROI provides a performance measure that better aligns the goals of business unit managers with the goals of the overall organization.

   EXAMPLE: *Borke Company's cost of capital is 10%. One of Borke Company's division managers has the opportunity to invest in a project that will generate $45,000 of net income per year for eight years on an initial investment of*

$300,000. The division's current income is $250,000 from a total divisional asset base of $1,000,000. The manager should accept the project since it offers a 15% return and the company's cost of capital is 10%. Chances are the manager will reject the project since it will lower the division current ROI from

$$\frac{\$250,000}{\$1,000,000} \ = \ 25\% \quad to \quad \frac{\$250,000 + 45,000}{\$1,000,000 + 300,000} \ = \ 22.7\%$$

In this case the use of ROI has led to an incorrect decision.

F. Traditional Financial Statement Analysis

One type of commonly used set of financial measures is derived from traditional financial statement analysis. Financial statement analysis involves the calculation and comparison of financial statement ratios. Financial ratios used to evaluate the financial position and operations of firms typically are classified into the following five categories:

1. **Profitability ratios**
    • Gross margin
    • Operating profit margin
    • Return on assets
    • Return on equity
    • Dividend payout ratio

2. **Asset utilization ratios**
    • Receivable turnover
    • Average collection period
    • Inventory turnover
    • Fixed asset turnover
    • Total asset turnover

3. **Liquidity ratios**
    • Current ratio
    • Quick or acid ratio

4. **Debt utilization ratios**
    • Debt to total assets
    • Debt to equity
    • Times interest earned

5. **Market ratios**
    • Price/earnings ratio
    • Market/book ratio

The calculation of these ratios will be illustrated using the following financial statements from Home Depot.

The Home Depot, Inc. and Subsidiaries
CONSOLIDATED BALANCE SHEETS

Amounts in millions, except per share data	February 2, 2003	February 3, 2002
Assets		
Current assets:		
Cash and cash equivalents	$ 2,188	$ 2,477
Short-term investments, including current maturities of long-term		
investments	65	69
Receivables, net	1,072	920
Merchandise inventories	8,338	6,725
Other current assets	254	170
Total current assets	11,917	10,361
Property and equipment, at cost:		
Land	5,560	4,972
Buildings	9,197	7,698
Furniture, fixtures and equipment	4,074	3,403
Leasehold improvements	872	750
Construction in progress	724	1,049
Capital leases	306	257
	20,733	18,129

Amounts in millions, except per share data	February 2, 2003	February 3, 2002
Less accumulated depreciation and amortization	3,565	2,754
Net property and equipment	17,168	15,375
Notes receivable	107	83
Cost in excess of the fair value of net assets acquired, net of accumulated amortization of $50 at February 2, 2003, and $49 at February 3, 2002	575	419
Other assets	244	156
Total assets	$30,011	$26,394

Liabilities and Stockholders' Equity

Current liabilities:

Accounts payable	$ 4,560	$3,436
Accrued salaries and related expenses	809	717
Sales taxes payable	307	348
Deferred revenue	998	851
Income taxes payable	227	211
Other accrued expenses	1,134	938
Total current liabilities	8,035	6,501
Long-term debt, excluding current installments	1,321	1,250
Other long-term liabilities	491	372
Deferred income taxes	362	189
Total liabilities	$10,209	8,312

Stockholders' Equity

Common stock, par value $0.05; authorized: 10,000 shares, issued and outstanding 2,362 shares at February 2, 2003, and 2,346 shares at February 3, 2002	118	117
Paid-in capital	5,858	5,412
Retained earnings	15,971	12,799
Accumulated other comprehensive loss	(82)	(220)
Unearned compensation	(63)	(26)
Treasury stock, at cost, 69 shares at February 2, 2003	(2,000)	--
Total stockholders' equity	19,802	18,082
Total liabilities and stockholders' equity	$30,011	$26,394

The Home Depot, Inc. and Subsidiaries
CONSOLIDATED STATEMENTS OF EARNINGS

	Fiscal Year Ended		
Amounts in millions, except per share data	February 2, 2003	February 3, 2002	January 28, 2001
Net Sales	$58,247	$53,553	$45,738
Cost of merchandise sold	40,139	37,406	32,057
Gross profit	18,108	16,147	13,681
Operating expenses:			
Selling and store operating	11,180	10,163	8,513
Preopening	96	117	142
General and administrative	1,002	935	835
Total operating expenses	12,278	11,215	9,490
Operating income	5,830	4,932	4,191
Interest income (expense):			
Interest and investment income	79	53	47
Interest expense	(37)	(28)	(21)
Interest, net	42	25	26
Earnings before provision for income taxes	5,872	4,957	4,217
Provision for income taxes	2,208	1,913	1,636
Net earnings	$3,664	$3,044	$2,581
Weighted-average common shares	2,336	2,335	2,315
Basic earnings per share	$1.57	$1.30	$1.11
Diluted weighted-average common shares	2,344	2,353	2,352
Diluted earnings per share	$1.56	$1.29	$1.10

1. **Profitability Ratios**

   Profitability ratios measure how effective a firm is at generating profit from operations. They are some of the most closely watched and widely quoted financial ratios. Management attempts to maximize these ratios to maximize firm value.

   a. **Gross margin** measures the percentage of each sales dollar remaining after payment for the goods sold.

   $$\text{Gross margin} = \frac{\text{Gross profit}}{\text{Net sales}} = \frac{\$18,108}{\$58,247} = 31.09\%$$

   Remember that gross profit is equal to net sales minus cost of goods sold.

   b. To find the proportion of revenue that finds its way into profits, analysts look at profit margin. Profit margin is calculated as net income divided by net sales, as shown below.

   $$\text{Profit margin} = \frac{\text{Net income after interest and taxes}}{\text{Net sales}} = \frac{\$3,664}{\$58,247} = 6.29\%$$

   c. **Operating profit margin** measures the percentage of each sales dollar that remains after the payment of all costs and expenses except for interest and taxes. This ratio is followed closely by analysts because it focuses on operating results. Operating profit is often referred to as earnings before interest and taxes or EBIT.

   $$\text{Operating profit margin} = \frac{\text{Operating profit}}{\text{Net sales}} = \frac{\$5,830}{\$58,247} = 10.01\%$$

   d. **Return on assets (return on investment)** measures the percentage return generated on the assets available (investment). This ratio may be calculated as

   $$\text{Return on assets} = \frac{\text{Net income after interest and taxes}}{\text{Average total assets}} = \frac{\$3,664}{\$28,203} = 12.99\%$$

   $$
   \begin{aligned}
   \text{Average total assets} &= \text{(Ending total assets + Beginning total assets)/2} \\
   &= (\$30,011 + \$26,394)/2 \\
   &= \$28,203
   \end{aligned}
   $$

   As discussed previously, return on investment is calculated and dissected in a number of ways and is very important to value-based management.

   e. **Return on equity** measures the percentage return generated to common stockholders.

   $$\text{Return on equity} = \frac{\text{Net income after interest and taxes}}{\text{Average common stockholders' equity}} = \frac{\$3,664}{\$18,942} = 19.34\%$$

   $$
   \begin{aligned}
   \text{Average stockholders' equity (SE)} &= \text{(Ending SE + Beginning SE)/2} \\
   &= (\$19,802 + \$18,082)/2 \\
   &= \$18,942
   \end{aligned}
   $$

   f. **The dividend payout ratio** measures the dividend paid in relation to net earnings. If Home Depot's dividend for the year was $0.22, the dividend payout is calculated as

   $$
   \begin{aligned}
   \text{Dividend payout ratio} &= \frac{\text{Cash dividend per common share}}{\text{Earnings per common share}} \\
   &= \frac{\$0.22}{\$1.57} \\
   &= .14 \text{ or } 14\%
   \end{aligned}
   $$

2. **Asset Utilization (Activity) Ratios**

   Asset utilization ratios measure the time it takes to convert various assets to sales or cash. Asset utilization ratios are used to measure the efficiency with which assets are managed. For this reason, they are often called **asset management ratios**.

   a. **Receivables turnover** measures the number of times per year the balance of receivables is collected. This is a very important measure of the efficiency with which management is managing accounts receivable.

   $$\text{Receivables turnover} = \frac{\text{Net credit Sales}}{\text{Average accounts receivable}}$$

This ratio cannot be computed for Home Depot since the company does not break out the amount of credit sales.

b. The **average collection period** measures the average number of days it takes to collect an account receivable. This ratio is also referred to as **the number of days of receivable** and **the number of days' sales in receivables**.

$$\text{Average collection period} = \frac{\text{Average accounts receivable}}{\text{Average sales per day}}$$

Again, this ratio cannot be calculated for Home Depot because the company does not break out the amount of credit sales.

c. **Inventory turnover** measures the efficiency with which a firm utilizes (manages) its inventory.

$$\text{Inventory turnover} = \frac{\text{Cost of goods sold}}{\text{Average inventory}} = \frac{\$40,139}{\$7,532} = 5.33 \text{ times}$$

$$
\begin{aligned}
\text{Average inventory} &= (\text{Ending inventory} + \text{Beginning inventory})/2 \\
&= (\$8,338 + \$6,725)/2 \\
&= \$7,532
\end{aligned}
$$

d. A related measure is the number of days' sales in inventory.

$$\text{Number of days' sales in inventory} = \frac{\text{Average inventory}}{\text{Cost of goods sold} / 365}$$

$$= \frac{\$7,532}{\$40,139 / 365}$$

$$= 68.49 \text{ days}$$

e. **Fixed asset turnover** measures the efficiency with which the firm uses its fixed assets.

$$\text{Fixed asset turnover} = \frac{\text{Sales}}{\text{Average net fixed assets}} = \frac{\$58,247}{\$16,272} = 3.58 \text{ times}$$

$$
\begin{aligned}
\text{Average fixed assets} &= (\text{Ending fixed assets} + \text{Beginning fixed assets})/2 \\
&= (\$17,168 + \$15,375)/2 \\
&= \$16,272
\end{aligned}
$$

f. **Total asset turnover** measures the efficiency with which the firm uses its total assets.

$$\text{Total asset turnover} = \frac{\text{Sales}}{\text{Average total assets}} = \frac{\$58,247}{\$28,203} = 2.07 \text{ times}$$

3. **Liquidity Ratios**

Liquidity ratios measure the firm's ability to meet its short-term obligations as they come due.

a. The **current ratio** is the most common measure of short-term liquidity. It is sometimes referred to as the **working capital ratio** because net working capital is the difference between current assets and current liabilities.

$$\text{Current ratio} = \frac{\text{Current assets}}{\text{Current liabilities}} = \frac{\$11,917}{\$8,035} = 1.48$$

- **Current assets** include cash and cash equivalents, net accounts receivable, marketable securities classified as current, inventories and prepaid expenses.
- **Current liabilities** include accounts payable, short-term notes payable, current maturities of long-term debt, unearned revenue, and other accrued liabilities.

Changes in the current ratio can be misleading. As an example, if management simply borrows money from a bank and invests the funds in marketable securities, both current assets and current liabilities go up by an identical amount. Net working capital is unaffected but the current ratio changes. Thus the current ratio is subject to "window dressing" by management.

b. The **quick (acid) ratio** provides a more conservative measure of short-term liquidity. It takes out inventory because in times of financial difficulty inventory may be saleable only at liquidation value.

$$\text{Quick ratio} = \frac{\text{Current assets} - \text{Inventory}}{\text{Current liabilities}} = \frac{\$11,917 - 8,338}{\$8,035} = .45$$

4. **Debt Utilization Ratios**

   Debt utilization ratios measure the effectiveness with which management finances the assets of the firm. They are used to evaluate the financial leverage of the firm.

   a. The **debt to total assets** measures the proportion of total assets financed with debt and, therefore, the extent of financial leverage.

   $$\text{Debt to total assets} = \frac{\text{Total liabilities}}{\text{Total assets}} = \frac{\$10,209}{\$30,011} = 34.02\%$$

   b. The **debt to equity ratio** also measures the extent of the firm's financial leverage.

   $$\text{Debt to equity ratio} = \frac{\text{Total liabilities}}{\text{Total equity}} = \frac{\$10,209}{\$19,802} = 51.56\%$$

   c. The **times interest earned** measures the firm's ability to make contractual interest payments.

   $$\text{Times interest earned} = \frac{\text{Earnings before interest and taxes}}{\text{Interest expense}} = \frac{\$5,830}{\$37} = 157.57$$

5. **Market Ratios**

   Market ratios involve measures that consider the market value of the firm's common stock.

   a. The **price/earnings (PE) ratio** is the most commonly quoted market measure. Assuming that Home Depot's stock price is $34.00, the price/earnings ratio would be computed as follows:

   $$\text{Price/earnings} = \frac{\text{Stock price per share}}{\text{Earnings per share}} = \frac{\$34}{\$1.57} = 21.66$$

   b. The **market/book ratio** provides another evaluation of how investors view the firm's past and future performance. To calculate the ratio, the book value per share of the firm's stock must first be calculated.

   $$\text{Book value per share} = \frac{\text{Common stock equity}}{\text{Number of shares of common stock outstanding}}$$

   $$= \frac{\$19,802}{2,362} = \$8.38 \text{ per share}$$

   Again, assuming a $34 market price per share of common stock, the market/book ratio is calculated as follows:

   $$\text{Market/book ratio} = \frac{\text{Market value per share of common stock}}{\text{Book value per share of common stock}}$$

   $$= \frac{\$34.00}{\$8.38} = 4.06$$

6. **Interpreting Financial Ratios**

   How does one decide whether a particular ratio is good or bad? To get value from ratio analysis, the measures must be compared to benchmarks. There are two basic approaches to this analysis, horizontal analysis and cross-sectional analysis. While **horizontal analysis** involves an evaluation of the firm's ratios and trends over time, **cross-sectional analysis** involves benchmarking the ratios against ratios of similar firms at a point in time. Industry averages are often used for cross-sectional analysis. Averages for industries are published by the US Department of Commerce, Dun & Bradstreet, Robert Morris Associates, and others. Researching data on firms in the same industry is facilitated through the Standard Industrial Classification (SIC) system.

   The figure below illustrates horizontal (trend) and cross-sectional analysis of a firm's income statement. The figure also illustrates a **common-size** income statement, in which all revenues and expenses are presented as a percentage of net sales. A common-size balance sheet presents all assets, liabilities and stockholders' equity as a percentage of total assets. The development of common-size financial statements is also known as **vertical analysis**.

Carson Corporation

	Dollars (000s omitted)			Common-size statements		Industry averages
	20X6	20X7	Percent change	20X6	20X7	20X7
Gross sales	78,428	82,212	4.8	103%	105%	104%
Less: Returns and allowances	2,284	4,235	85.4	3%	5%	4%
Net sales	76,144	77,977	2.4	100%	100%	100%
Cost of goods sold	46,213	46,478	0.6	61%	60%	58%
Gross profit	29,931	31,499	5.2	39%	40%	42%
Selling & administrative expenses	20,105	22,487	11.8	26%	29%	28%
Income from operations	9,826	9,012	−8.3	13%	12%	14%
Interest expense	1,930	1,584	−17.9	3%	2%	3%
Net income before taxes	7,896	7,428	−5.9	10%	10%	11%
Income taxes	3,807	2,971	−22.0	5%	4%	4%
Net income	4,089	4,457	9.0	5%	6%	7%
EPS	0.78	0.84	10.5			
Ratios						
Current	1.7	1.9				2.1
Quick	1.0	1.1				1.3
Receivables turnover	5.3	5.6				5.1
Days' sales in ending receivables	68.1	64.3				65.6
Inventory turnover	4.7	3.2				3.5
Days' sales in ending inventory	76.0	75.0				74.4
Interest expense/ outstanding debt	0.11	0.08				0.09

Horizontal (Trend) analysis   Vertical Analysis   Cross-sectional analysis

To use ratio analysis effectively, analysts must be aware of the relationship between the items used in calculating the ratio. For example, in comparing the gross margin of a company over time, it should be remembered that this ratio may be affected by the fact that cost of goods sold is made up of fixed and variable costs or the fact that the sales mix has changed.

7. **Limitations of Financial Ratios**

While comparing the firm's ratios with those of similar firms in the same industry provides information about the performance of the firm, it does have limitations.

a. Other firms in the industry may not be comparable due to differences in size, diversification of operations, accounting principles used, different year-ends, etc.

b. Industry averages may not be reliable (e.g., based on too small a sample of firms).

c. There are variations in the way ratios are calculated.

d. Financial statements contain estimates that might distort results.

e. Ratios are only financial measures and do not provide a balanced view of performance.

G. Benchmarking and Best Practices

Benchmarking is the continuous process of comparing the levels of performance in producing products and services and executing activities against the best levels of performance. It is the search for and implementation of "best practices." There are different types of benchmarking including

- *Internal benchmarking* compares similar operations within different units of the same organization.
- *Competitive benchmarking* targets processes and methods used by an organization's direct competitors.
- *Functional or industry benchmarking* compares similar functions within the same broad industry.
- *Generic benchmarking* compares processes that are independent of industry.

Best practices are the best ways to perform a process. Best practices represent the means by which world-class organizations have achieved superior performance. However, no practice can be considered a "best practice" for all organizations or in all situations. The advice of Dr. W. Edwards Deming applies to benchmarking: "Adapt, don't adopt."

Benchmarks are the performance metrics used in benchmarking.

H. Quality Control Principles and Tools

1. **Total Quality Management (TQM** focuses on managing the organization to excel in quality in all dimensions of products and services for customers.

2. **Six-Sigma Quality**

     What is six-sigma?   A statistical measure expressing how close a product comes to its quality goal. One-sigma means 68% of products are acceptable; three-sigma means 99.7%. Six-sigma is 99.999997% perfect: 3.4 defects per million parts.

     Six-sigma black belts must attend a minimum of four months of training in statistical and other quality improvement methods. Six-sigma black belts are experts in the six-sigma methodology. They learn and demonstrate proficiency in the DMAIC methodology and statistical process control (SPC) techniques within that methodology. DMAIC is the structured methodology for process improvement within the six-sigma framework. It stands for define, measure, analyze, improve, and control.

3. **Quality Award Programs**

     There are a number of quality award programs. Here is a summary of some of the major programs.

     • **Malcolm Baldrige National Quality Award** is an award that was established in 1987 to recognize total quality management in American industry. The Baldrige award is given to businesses—manufacturing and service, small and large—and to education and health care organizations that apply and are judged to be outstanding in seven areas: leadership, strategic planning, customer and market focus, information and analysis, human resource focus, process management, and business results. Congress established the award program in 1987 to recognize US organizations for their achievements in quality and performance and to raise awareness about the importance of quality and performance excellence as a competitive edge. The award is not given for specific products or services. Three awards may be given annually in each of these categories: manufacturing, service, small business, education, and health care.

     • **The Deming Prize** is named after American statistician Dr. W. Edwards Deming, who developed the quality concepts for Japanese industry after World War II.

     • **European Quality Award.** The European Quality Award is Europe's most prestigious award for organizational excellence. It is open to every high-performing organization in Europe and focuses on recognizing excellence and providing detailed, independent feedback to all applicants to help them on their continuing journey to excellence.

4. **ISO Quality Standards**

     ISO 9000 Series is a series of standards agreed upon by the International Organization for Standardization (ISO) and adopted in 1987. ISO 9000 evolved in Europe. The ISO Series consists of five parts numbered 9000 through 9004.

     ISO 14000 series was developed to control the impact of an organization's activities on the environment and focuses on reducing the cost of waste management, conserving energy and materials, and lowering distribution costs.

5. **Quality Tools and Methods**

     a. **Total quality control (TQC).** The application of quality principles to all company activities. Also known as total quality management (TQM).

     b. **Continuous improvement and Kaizen**

          Continuous improvement (CI) seeks continual improvement of machinery, materials, labor, and production methods, through various means including suggestions and ideas from employees and customers.

          Kaizen is the Japanese art of continuous improvement. A philosophy of continuous improvement of working practices that underlies total quality management and just-in-time business techniques.

          PDCA (Plan-Do-Check-Act) Also called the Deming Wheel, focuses on the sequential and continual nature of the CI process.

     c. **Cause-and-effect analysis**

          Cause-and-effect (fishbone or Ishikawa) diagrams identify the potential causes of defects. Four categories of potential causes of failure are: human factors, methods and design factors, machine-related factors, and materials and components factors. Cause-and-effect diagrams are used to systematically list the different causes that can be attributed to a problem (or an effect). A cause-and-effect diagram can aid in identifying the reasons why a process goes out of control.

A **Pareto chart** is a bar graph that ranks causes of process variations by the degree of impact on quality. The Pareto chart is a specialized version of a histogram that ranks the categories in the chart from most frequent to least frequent. A related concept, the "Pareto Principle" states that 80% of the problems come from 20% of the causes. The Pareto Principle states that: "Not all of the causes of a particular phenomenon occur with the same frequency or with the same impact."

d. **Lean manufacturing philosophy.** Lean manufacturing is an operational strategy focused on achieving the shortest possible cycle time by eliminating waste. It is based on increasing the value-added work by eliminating waste and reducing incidental work. The technique often decreases the time between a customer order and shipment, and it is designed to improve profitability, customer satisfaction, throughput time, and employee morale.

e. **Control charts and robust design**

Control charts are statistical plots derived from measuring factory processes; they help detect "process drift," or deviation, before it generates defects. Control charts also help spot inherent variations in manufacturing processes that designers must account for to achieve "robust design."

Robust design is a discipline for making designs "production-proof" by building in tolerances for manufacturing variables that are known to be unavoidable.

f. **Poka-yoke (mistake-proofing).** Poka-yoke involves making the workplace mistake-proof. For example, a machine fitted with guide rails permits a part to be worked on in just one way.

g. **Theory of constraints (TOC)** refers to methods to maximize operating income when faced with some bottleneck operations. **Bottleneck resources** are any resource or operation where the capacity is less than the demand placed upon it. **Nonbottleneck resources** have capacity greater than demand. The objective of TOC is to increase *throughput contribution* while decreasing *investment* and *operating costs*. **Throughput contribution** is revenues minus the direct materials cost of goods sold. **Investment** is the sum of materials, cost in direct materials, work in process and finished goods inventories; research and development costs; and the costs of equipment and buildings. **Operating costs** include the salaries and wages, rental expense, utilities, and depreciation.

h. **Reengineering (business process reengineering)** is the fundamental rethinking and redesign of business processes to achieve improvements in critical measures of performance such as cost, quality, service speed and customer satisfaction. The scope of reengineering can affect operations and manufacturing processes, as well as financial and administrative processes such as accounts payables and procurement and can impact internal controls.

I. Cost of Quality

Cost of quality is based on the philosophy that failures have an underlying cause, prevention is cheaper than failures, and cost of quality performance can be measured. Cost of quality consists of four components.

- **Prevention cost**
- **Appraisal cost**
- **Internal failure cost**
- **External failure cost**

1. **Prevention cost.** The cost of prevention is the cost of any quality activity designed to help do the job right the first time. Examples of prevention cost include

- Quality engineering
- Quality training
- Quality circles
- Statistical process control activities
- Supervision of prevention activities
- Quality data gathering, analysis, and reporting
- Quality improvement projects
- Technical support provided to suppliers
- Audits of the effectiveness of the quality system

2. **Appraisal cost.** The cost of quality control including testing and inspection. It involves any activity designed to appraise, test, or check for defective products. Examples of appraisal costs include

- Test and inspection of incoming materials
- Test and inspection of in-process goods
- Final product testing and inspection
- Supplies used in testing and inspection
- Supervision of testing and inspection activities
- Depreciation of test equipment
- Maintenance of test equipment
- Plant utilities in the inspection area
- Field testing and appraisal at customer site

3. **Internal failure cost.** The costs incurred when substandard products are produced but discovered before shipment to the customer. Examples of internal failure costs include

- Scrap
- Spoilage
- Rework
- Rework labor and overhead
- Reinspection of reworked products
- Retesting of reworked products
- Downtime caused by quality problems
- Disposal of defective products
- Analysis of the cause of defects in production
- Reentering data because of keying errors
- Debugging software errors

4. **External failure cost.** The cost incurred for products that do not meet requirements of the customer and have reached the customer. Examples of external failure costs include

- Cost of field servicing and handling complaints
- Warranty repairs and replacements
- Product recalls
- Liability arising from defective products
- Returns and allowances arising from quality problems
- Lost sales arising from reputation for poor quality

MULTIPLE-CHOICE QUESTIONS (1-68)

1.   What is the most important purpose of a balanced scorecard?
   a.   Develop strategy.
   b.   Measure performance.
   c.   Develop cause-and-effect linkages.
   d.   Set priorities.

2.   Which of the following is not one of the four perspectives of the balanced scorecard?
   a.   Investment in resources perspective.
   b.   Customer perspective.
   c.   Learning and growth perspective.
   d.   Financial perspective.

3.   The balanced scorecard generally uses performance measures with four different perspectives. Which of the following performance measures would be part of those used for the internal business processes perspective?
   a.   Cycle time.
   b.   Employee satisfaction.
   c.   Hours of training per employee.
   d.   Customer retention.

4.   The balanced scorecard has been adopted by many corporations. Which of the following best describes the balanced scorecard?
   a.   A strategy that meets management's objectives.
   b.   A diagram illustrating cause and effect relationships.
   c.   A table of key actions to achieve strategic objectives.
   d.   A strategic performance measurement and management framework.

5.   The balanced scorecard and value-based management are techniques that are being used by a number of corporations. In comparison to the balanced scorecard, value-based management focuses on
   a.   Nonfinancial measures.
   b.   Financial measures.
   c.   Both financial and nonfinancial measures.
   d.   Quality measures.

6.   Management has identified a relationship between customer satisfaction and return on investment. This relationship could be depicted in a
   a.   Strategy map.
   b.   Value chain.
   c.   Customer perspectives chart.
   d.   Strategic initiatives list.

7.   Which of the following is not a component of the balanced scorecard?
   a.   Strategic objectives.
   b.   Targets.
   c.   Strategy initiatives.
   d.   Assessment of human resources.

8.   Which of the following best describes a value chain in the balanced scorecard framework?
   a.   The cause-and-effect linkages.
   b.   The baseline level of performance.
   c.   The sequence of business processes in which usefulness is added to products or services.
   d.   The chain of financial and nonfinancial measures.

9.   Which of the following is not a characteristic of the balanced scorecard?
   a.   Both financial and nonfinancial performance measures are included.
   b.   Cause-and-effect linkages between strategic objectives.
   c.   Customer performance measures are excluded.
   d.   Internal process performance measures are included.

10.   In the balanced scorecard framework, a survey of employee satisfaction is a potential measure in which of the four perspectives?
   a.   Financial.
   b.   Customer.
   c.   Internal business processes.
   d.   Learning and growth.

*11.   Which of the following is an example of an efficiency measure?
   a.   The rate of absenteeism.
   b.   The goal of becoming a leading manufacturer.
   c.   The number of insurance claims processed per day.
   d.   The rate of customer complaints.

12.   A strategy objective in the balanced scorecard framework is
   a.   A statement of what the strategy must achieve and what is critical to its success.
   b.   Key action programs required to achieve strategic objectives.
   c.   Diagrams of the cause-and-effect relationships between strategic objectives.
   d.   The level of performance or rate of improvement needed in the performance measure.

13.   A target in the balanced scorecard framework is
   a.   A statement of what the strategy must achieve and what is critical to its success.
   b.   A key action program required to achieve strategic objectives.
   c.   A diagram of the cause-and-effect relationships between strategic objectives.
   d.   The level of performance or rate of improvement needed in the performance measure.

Items 14 through 18 are based on the following information:

The following is selected data for the Consumer Products division of Arron Corporations for 200X:

Sales	$50,000,000
Average invested capital (assets)	20,000,000
Net income	2,000,000
Cost of capital	8%

14.   What is the return on sales (ROS) for the division?
   a.   8%
   b.   4%
   c.   10%
   d.   20%

---

15. What is the asset turnover ratio for the division?
    a.   .25
    b.   10
    c.   2.5
    d.   8

16. What is the return on investment (ROI) for the division?
    a.   10%
    b.   8%
    c.   4%
    d.   2%

17. What is the amount of residual income (RI) for the division?
    a. $2,000,000
    b. $1,600,000
    c. $1,000,000
    d. $ 400,000

18. What is the amount of interest rate spread for the division?
    a.   8%
    b.   10%
    c.   2%
    d.   20%

Items 19 and 20 are based on the following information:

The following is available for Cara Corp. for 2007:

Sales	$2,000,000
Average invested capital	500,000
Net income	300,000
Required rate of return	18%

19. What is the return on investment at Cara Corp.?
    a.   60%
    b.   33%
    c.   18%
    d.   15%

20. What is the residual income for Cara Corp.?
    a. $0
    b. $200,000
    c. $210,000
    d. $246,000

Items 21 and 22 are based on the following information:

On the graph below, the line (A-B-C) illustrates residual income (measured on the vertical axis in dollars) at various interest rates. Point D is the cost of capital or the required rate of return. Point E is the residual income at the cost of capital.

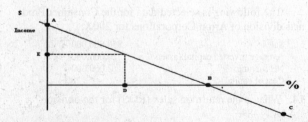

21. What does point B represent?
    a.   Return on sales.
    b.   Return on investment.
    c.   Asset turnover.
    d.   Operating income.

22. What does point A represent?
    a.   Return on sales.
    b.   Return on investment.
    c.   Asset turnover.
    d.   Net income.

23. On the graph below, lines A-B-C and D-E-F illustrates residual income (measured on the vertical axis in dollars) at various interest rates. Point G is the firm's cost of capital. Line ABC represents the residual income of Division X at various interest rates. Line DEF represents the residual income of Division Y at various interest rates.

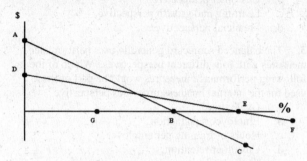

Based on the graph above, for Division X versus Division Y, is the residual income and ROI for Division X greater than or less than that of Division Y?

	Residual income of Division X is greater than the residual income for Division Y	Return on investment of Division X is greater than the ROI for Division Y
a.	Yes	Yes
b.	Yes	No
c.	No	Yes
d.	No	No

24. A company's rate of return on investment (ROI) is equal to the
    a.   Percentage of profit on sales divided by the capital employed turnover rate.
    b.   Percentage of profit on sales multiplied by the capital employed turnover rate.
    c.   Investment capital divided by the capital employed turnover rate.
    d.   Investment capital multiplied by the capital employed turnover rate.

25. Return on investment can be increased by
    a.   Increasing operating assets.
    b.   Decreasing operating assets.
    c.   Decreasing revenues.
    d.   Both b. and c.

26. The following information pertains to Bala Co. for the year ended December 31, 2008:

Sales	$600,000
Net income	100,000
Capital investment	400,000

Which of the following equations should be used to compute Bala's return on investment?
    a. $(4/6) \times (6/1) = \text{ROI}$
    b. $(6/4) \times (1/6) = \text{ROI}$
    c. $(4/6) \times (1/6) = \text{ROI}$
    d. $(6/4) \times (6/1) = \text{ROI}$

27. Select Co. had the following 2008 financial statement relationships:

Asset turnover	5
Profit margin on sales	0.02

What was Select's 2008 percentage return on assets?

- a.   0.1%
- b.   0.4%
- c.   2.5%
- d.   10.0%

28. The following selected data pertain to the Darwin Division of Beagle Co. for 2008:

Sales	$400,000
Net income	40,000
Capital turnover	4
Imputed interest rate	10%

What was Darwin's 2008 residual income?

- a. $0
- b. $ 4,000
- c. $10,000
- d. $30,000

29. Division A is considering a project that will earn a rate of return which is greater than the imputed interest charge for invested capital, but less than the division's historical return on invested capital. Division B is considering a project that will earn a rate of return that is greater than the division's historical return on invested capital, but less than the imputed interest charge for invested capital. If the objective is to maximize residual income, should these divisions accept or reject their projects?

	A	*B*
a.	Accept	Accept
b.	Reject	Accept
c.	Reject	Reject
d.	Accept	Reject

30. Which combination of changes in asset turnover and income as a percentage of sales will maximize the return on investment?

	Asset turnover	*Income as a percentage of sales*
a.	Increase	Decrease
b.	Increase	Increase
c.	Decrease	Increase
d.	Decrease	Decrease

*31. Residual income is often preferred over return on investment (ROI) as a performance evaluation because

- a.   Residual income is a measure over time while ROI represents the results for a single time period.
- b.   Residual income concentrates on maximizing absolute dollars of income rather than a percentage return as with ROI.
- c.   The imputed interest rate used in calculating residual income is more easily derived than the target rate that is compared to the calculated ROI.
- d.   Average investment is employed with residual income while year-end investment is employed with ROI.

32. What is a major disadvantage of using economic value added (EVA) alone as a performance measure?

- a.   It fails to focus on creating shareholder value.

- b.   It promotes the acceptance of unprofitable projects.
- c.   It fails to reflect all of the ways that value may be created.
- d.   It discourages cost cutting.

Items 33 and 34 are based on the following information:

The following are selected data for Walkin Corporation for the year ended 20X1:

Net operating profit before taxes	$31,250,000
Inventory	5,000,000
Long-term debt	40,000,000
Depreciation expense	9,000,000
Change in net working capital	5,000,000
Capital expenditures	8,000,000
Invested capital (net assets)	80,000,000
Weighted average cost of capital	10%
Tax rate	20%

33. Which of the following measures economic value added for Walkin Corporation for the year?

- a. $ 3,000,000
- b. $ 7,000,000
- c. $15,000,000
- d. $17,000,000

34. Which of the following measures the amount of free cash flow for Walkin Corporation for the year?

- a. $ 7,000,000
- b. $ 8,000,000
- c. $21,000,000
- d. $25,000,000

35. The following information is available for the wholesale products division of Watco:

Net operating profit before interest and taxes	$30,000,000
Depreciation expense	10,000,000
Change in net working capital	5,000,000
Capital expenditures	4,000,000
Invested capital (total assets – current liabilities)	50,000,000
Weighted average cost of capital	10%
Tax rate	40%

What is the amount of economic value added (EVA) for the division?

- a. $30,000,000
- b. $13,000,000
- c. $25,000,000
- d. $ 5,000,000

Items 36 and 37 are based on the following information:

The following information is available for Armstrong Enterprises for 2008:

Net operating profit (income) after taxes	$36,000,000
Depreciation expense	15,000,000
Change in net working capital	10,000,000
Capital expenditures	12,000,000
Invested capital (total assets – current liabilities)	100,000,000
Weighted average cost of capital	10%

36. What is the amount of the economic value added (EVA)?

- a. $20,000,000
- b. $26,000,000
- c. $15,000,000
- d. $36,000,000

37. What is the free cash flow for 2008?
  a. $36,000,000
  b. $30,000,000
  c. $29,000,000
  d. $26,000,000

38. Which of the following is not a measure of asset utilization?
  a. Inventory turnover.
  b. Average accounts receivable collection period.
  c. Fixed asset turnover.
  d. Debt to total assets.

39. What financial analysis technique would imply benchmarking with other firms?
  a. Horizontal analysis.
  b. Vertical analysis.
  c. Cross-sectional analysis.
  d. Ratio analysis.

Items 40 and 41 are based on the following information:

The Dawson Corporation projects the following for the year 2008:

Earnings before interest and taxes	$35 million
Interest expense	5 million
Preferred stock dividends	4 million
Common stock dividend payout ratio	30%
Common shares outstanding	2 million
Effective corporate income tax rate	40%

**40. The expected common stock dividend per share for Dawson Corporation for 2008 is
  a. $2.34
  b. $2.70
  c. $3.90
  d. $2.10

**41. If Dawson Corporation's common stock is expected to trade at a price/earnings ratio of eight, the market price per share (to the nearest dollar) would be
  a. $125
  b. $ 56
  c. $ 72
  d. $ 68

Items 42 through 46 are based on the following information:

The data presented below show actual figures for selected accounts of McKeon Company for the fiscal year ended December 31, 2008. McKeon's controller is in the process of reviewing the 2008 results. McKeon Company monitors yield or return ratios using the average financial position of the company. (Round all calculations to three decimal places if necessary.)

	12/31/08	12/31/07
Current assets	$210,000	$180,000
Noncurrent assets	275,000	255,000
Current liabilities	78,000	85,000
Long-term debt	75,000	30,000
Common stock ($30 par value)	300,000	300,000
Retained earnings	32,000	20,000

2008 Operations	
Sales*	$350,000
Cost of goods sold	160,000
Interest expense	3,000
Income taxes (40% rate)	48,000
Dividends declared and paid in 2008	60,000
Administrative expense	67,000

* All sales are credit sales.

	Current Assets	
	12/31/08	12/31/07
Cash	$ 20,000	$10,000
Accounts receivable	100,000	70,000
Inventory	70,000	80,000
Other	20,000	20,000

**42. McKeon Company's debt-to-total-asset ratio at 5/31/08 is
  a. 0.352
  b. 0.315
  c. 0.264
  d. 0.237

**43. The 2008 accounts receivable turnover for McKeon company is
  a. 1.882
  b. 3.500
  c. 5.000
  d. 4.118

**44. Using a 365-day year, McKeon's inventory turnover is
  a. 2.133
  b. 2.281
  c. 1.995
  d. 4.615

**45. McKeon Company's total asset turnover for 2008 is
  a. 0.805
  b. 0.761
  c. 0.722
  d. 0.348

**46. The 2008 return on assets for McKeon Company is
  a. 0.261
  b. 0.148
  c. 0.157
  d. 0.166

Items 47 through 53 are based on the following information:

Depoole Company is a manufacturer of industrial products and employs a calendar year for financial reporting purposes. These questions present several of Depoole's transactions during the year. Assume that total quick assets exceeded total current liabilities both before and after each transaction described. Further assume that Depoole has positive profits during the year and a credit balance throughout the year in its retained earnings account.

**47. Payment of a trade account payable of $64,500 would
  a. Increase the current ratio but the quick ratio would not be affected.
  b. Increase the quick ratio but the current ratio would not be affected.
  c. Increase both the current and quick ratios.
  d. Decrease both the current and quick ratios.

**   *CMA adapted*

**48. The purchase of raw materials for $85,000 on open account would
- a. Increase the current ratio.
- b. Decrease the current ratio.
- c. Increase net working capital.
- d. Decrease net working capital.

**49. The collection of a current accounts receivable of $29,000 would
- a. Increase the current ratio.
- b. Decrease the current ratio and the quick ratio.
- c. Increase the quick ratio.
- d. Not affect the current or quick ratios.

**50. Obsolete inventory of $125,000 was written off during the year. This transaction
- a. Decreased the quick ratio.
- b. Increased the quick ratio.
- c. Increased net working capital.
- d. Decreased the current ratio.

**51. The issuance of new shares in a five-for-one split of common stock
- a. Decreases the book value per share of common stock.
- b. Increases the book value per share of common stock.
- c. Increases total shareholders' equity.
- d. Decreases total shareholders' equity.

**52. The issuance of serial bonds in exchange for an office building, with the first installment of the bonds due late this year,
- a. Decreases net working capital.
- b. Decreases the current ratio.
- c. Decreases the quick ratio.
- d. Affects all of the answers as indicated.

**53. The early liquidation of a long-term note with cash affects the
- a. Current ratio to a greater degree than the quick ratio.
- b. Quick ratio to a greater degree than the current ratio.
- c. Current and quick ratio to the same degree.
- d. Current ratio but not the quick ratio.

54. Southwest Airlines benchmarked the process of turning around an airplane with the pit stop process for formula racecars. This is an example of
- a. Internal benchmarking.
- b. Generic benchmarking.
- c. Competitor benchmarking.
- d. Functional benchmarking.

55. Which measures would be useful in evaluating the performance of a manufacturing system?

  I. Throughput time.
  II. Total setup time for machines/Total production time.
  III. Number of rework units/Total number of units completed.

- a. I and II only.
- b. II and III only.
- c. I and III only.
- d. I, II, and III.

56. A tool which indicates how frequently each type of defect occurs is a
- a. Control chart.
- b. Pareto diagram.
- c. Cause-and-effect diagram.
- d. Fishbone diagram.

57. A tool which identifies potential causes for failures or defects is
- a. Control chart.
- b. Pareto diagram.
- c. Cause-and-effect diagram.
- d. Strategy map.

58. Which of the statements best describes the concept of six-sigma quality?
- a. 10 defects per million.
- b. 3.4 defects per million.
- c. 6.0 defects per million.
- d. 100 defects per million.

59. Which of the following quality tools is another term for continuous improvement?
- a. Theory of constraints.
- b. Kaizen.
- c. Six-sigma.
- d. Lean manufacturing.

60. In the theory of constraints, an operation or resource where the work performed approaches or exceeds the availability is referred to as
- a. A bottleneck.
- b. A time driver.
- c. Customer-response time.
- d. Manufacturing lead time.

**61. Antlers, Inc. produces a single product that sells for $150 per unit. The product is processed through the Cutting and Finishing departments. Additional data for these departments are as follows:

	Cutting	Finishing
Annual capacity (36,000 direct labor hours available in each department)	180,000 units	135,000 units
Current production rate (annualized)	108,000 units	108,000 units
Fixed manufacturing overhead	$1,296,000	$1,944,000
Fixed selling and administrative expense	$ 864,000	$1,296,000
Direct materials cost per unit	$ 45	$ 15

The current production rate is the budgeted rate for the entire year. Direct labor employees earn $20 per hour and the company has a "no layoff" policy in effect. What is the amount of the throughput contribution per unit as computed using the theory of constraints?
- a. $90.00
- b. $76.67
- c. $46.67
- d. $26.67

**62. Three of the basic measurements used by the Theory of Constraints (TOC) are
- a. Gross margin (or gross profit), return on assets, and total sales.
- b. Number of constraints (or subordinates), number of nonconstraints, and operating leverage.

---

    c.   Throughput (or throughput contribution), inventory (or investments), and operational expense.

    d.   Fixed manufacturing overhead per unit, fixed general overhead per unit, and unit gross margin (or gross profit).

63. Which statement best describes the objective of the theory of constraints?

	Throughput contribution	Investment	Operating costs
a.	Increase	Decrease	Decrease
b.	Increase	Increase	Increase
c.	Decrease	Increase	Decrease
d.	Increase	Increase	Decrease

64. In considering cost of quality methodology, quality circles are associated with

    a.   Prevention.
    b.   Appraisal.
    c.   Internal failure.
    d.   External failure.

65. In the cost of quality, which of the following is an example of an "internal failure"?

    a.   Cost of inspecting products on the production line by quality inspectors.
    b.   Labor cost of product designers whose task is to design components that will not break under extreme temperature conditions.
    c.   Cost of reworking defective parts detected by the quality assurance group.
    d.   Cost of parts returned by customers.

66. In the cost of quality, which of the following is an example of a "prevention cost"?

    a.   Cost of inspecting products on the production line by quality inspectors.
    b.   Labor cost of product designers whose task is to design components that will not break under extreme temperature conditions.
    c.   Cost of reworking defective parts detected by the quality assurance group.
    d.   Cost of parts returned by customers.

67. Delta Manufacturing Co. has had a problem with its product quality. The company has had a large amount of costs related to product recalls. In considering cost of quality methodology, if the company wants to reduce these costs, the most likely place to incur costs would be for

    a.   Prevention.
    b.   Appraisal.
    c.   Internal failure.
    d.   External failure.

68. In the cost of quality, costs incurred in detecting individual units of product that do not conform to specifications are

    a.   Prevention costs.
    b.   Appraisal costs.
    c.   Internal failure costs.
    d.   External failure costs.

MULTIPLE-CHOICE ANSWERS

1. b	__ __	16. a	__ __	31. b	__ __	46. c	__ __	61. a	__ __
2. a	__ __	17. d	__ __	32. c	__ __	47. c	__ __	62. c	__ __
3. a	__ __	18. c	__ __	33. d	__ __	48. b	__ __	63. a	__ __
4. d	__ __	19. a	__ __	34. c	__ __	49. d	__ __	64. a	__ __
5. b	__ __	20. c	__ __	35. b	__ __	50. d	__ __	65. c	__ __
6. a	__ __	21. b	__ __	36. b	__ __	51. a	__ __	66. b	__ __
7. d	__ __	22. d	__ __	37. c	__ __	52. d	__ __	67. a	__ __
8. c	__ __	23. b	__ __	38. d	__ __	53. b	__ __	68. b	__ __
9. c	__ __	24. b	__ __	39. c	__ __	54. b	__ __		
10. d	__ __	25. b	__ __	40. d	__ __	55. d	__ __		
11. c	__ __	26. b	__ __	41. b	__ __	56. b	__ __		
12. a	__ __	27. d	__ __	42. b	__ __	57. c	__ __		
13. d	__ __	28. d	__ __	43. d	__ __	58. b	__ __		
14. b	__ __	29. d	__ __	44. a	__ __	59. b	__ __	1st: __/68 = __%
15. c	__ __	30. b	__ __	45. b	__ __	60. a	__ __	2nd: __/68 = __%

MULTIPLE-CHOICE ANSWER EXPLANATIONS

Balanced Scorecard and Performance Measures

1.   (b)   The requirement is to identify the purpose of a balanced scorecard. Answer (b) is correct because the balanced scorecard uses financial and nonfinancial measures to measure performance. Answer (a) is incorrect because strategic planning is designed to develop strategy. Answer (c) is incorrect because developing cause-and-effect linkages is an important part of developing a balanced scorecard. Answer (d) is incorrect because setting priorities is a part of strategic planning.

2.   (a)   The requirement is to identify the item that is not one of the four perspectives of the balanced scorecard. Answer (a) is correct because investment in resources is not a perspective of the balanced scorecard. The balanced scorecard deals with performance measurement. Answer (b) is incorrect because customer perspective is used in the balanced scorecard. Answer (c) is incorrect because learning and growth perspective is used in the balanced scorecard. Answer (d) is incorrect because financial perspective is used in the balanced scorecard.

3.   (a)   The requirement is to identify the measure that is related to internal business processes. Answer (a) is correct because cycle time is the time it takes to manufacture a product and, therefore, is an important part of the business processes perspective. Answers (b) and (c) are incorrect because they are part of the learning and growth perspective. Answer (d) is incorrect because it is part of the customer perspective.

4.   (d)   The requirement is to define the balanced scorecard. Answer (d) is correct because the balanced scorecard is a strategic performance measurement and management framework. Answer (b) is incorrect because it is the definition of a strategy map. Answer (c) is incorrect because it is the definition of a list of strategic initiatives.

5.   (b)   The requirement is to identify the focus of value-based management. Answer (b) is correct because value-based management focuses on financial measures to measure performance. The balanced scorecard uses both financial and nonfinancial measures to measure performance.

6.   (a)   The requirement is to identify what illustrates cause-and-effect relationships. Answer (a) is correct because a strategy map displays cause-and-effect relationships within the balanced scorecard framework. Answer (b) is incorrect because the value chain is the sequence of business processes that add value to a good or service.

7.   (d)   The requirement is to identify the item that is not a component of the balanced scorecard. Answer (d) is correct because an assessment of human resources is not a component of a balanced scorecard. Answer (a) is incorrect because a statement of strategic objectives is a component of a balanced scorecard. Answer (b) is incorrect because targets for performance are part of a balanced scorecard. Answer (c) is incorrect because strategy initiatives are part of a balanced scorecard.

8.   (c)   The requirement is to identify the description of the value chain. Answer (c) is correct because the value chain is the sequence of business processes in which usefulness is added to the product or service. Answer (a) is incorrect because cause-and-effect linkages are used to develop the balanced scorecard. Answer (b) is incorrect because the baseline level of performance is the current level of performance. Answer (d) is incorrect because there is no chain of financial and nonfinancial measures.

9.   (c)   The requirement is to identify which item is not a characteristic of the balanced scorecard. Answer (c) is correct because customer performance is one of the four primary components of the balanced scorecard framework; therefore, it is not excluded. Answers (a), (b), and (d) are incorrect because they are all characteristics of the balanced scorecard.

10.   (d)   The requirement is to identify where in the balanced scorecard framework surveys of employee satisfaction should appear. Answer (d) is correct because surveys of employee satisfaction would appear in the learning and growth perspective which includes various employee measures including employee turnover. Answer (a) is incorrect because the financial perspective includes measures such as profitability and return on investment. Answer (b) is incorrect because the customer perspective includes measures like customer satisfaction. Answer (c) is incorrect because the internal business processes perspective includes measures related to cost, quality, and time.

11.   (c)   The requirement is to identify the efficiency measure. Answer (c) is correct because an efficiency measure relates output to a measure of input. Answer (a) is incorrect because it does not relate output to input. Answer (b) is incorrect because it is an effectiveness measure. Answer (d) is incorrect because it does not relate output to input.

12. (a) The requirement is to identify the definition of a strategy objective. Answer (a) is correct because it is the definition of a strategy objective in the balanced scorecard framework. Answer (b) is incorrect because it describes a strategic initiative. Answer (c) is incorrect because it is the definition of a strategy map. Answer (d) is incorrect because it is the definition of a target.

13. (d) The requirement is to identify the definition of a target. Answer (d) is correct because it is the definition of a target in the balanced scorecard framework. Answer (a) is incorrect because it is the definition of a strategic objective. Answer (b) is incorrect because it is the definition of strategy initiatives. Answer (c) is incorrect because it is the definition of a strategy map.

Value-Based Management: ROI and Residual Income

14. (b) The requirement is to calculate the return on sales for the division. Answer (b) is correct because return on sales is calculated as net income/sales which is equal to 4% ($2,000,000/$50,000,000).

15. (c) The requirement is to calculate the asset turnover ratio for the division. Answer (c) is correct because the asset turnover ratio is calculated by dividing sales by the average investment amount. Therefore, it is equal to 2.5 ($50,000,000/$20,000,000).

16. (a) The requirement is to calculate ROI for the division. Answer (a) is correct because ROI is calculated by dividing net income by the amount of the average investment. Therefore, ROI is equal to 10% ($2,000,000/$20,000,000).

17. (d) The requirement is to calculate RI for the division. Answer (d) is correct because RI is equal to net income minus interest on the investment. Therefore, RI is equal to $400,000 [$2,000,000 – ($20,000,000 × 8%)].

18. (c) The requirement is to calculate the interest rate spread for the division. Answer (c) is correct because the interest rate spread is the difference between the return on investment and the required rate of return (cost of capital). In this case, the spread is equal to 2% [($2,000,000/$20,000,000) – 8%].

19. (a) The requirement is to calculate the return on investment. Answer (a) is correct because the return on investment would be computed by dividing net income by average invested capital ($300,000/$500,000 = 60%).

20. (c) The requirement is to calculate the residual income. Answer (c) is correct because the residual income would be computed as follows: Net income ($300,000) minus the interest on invested capital $90,000 (18% × $500,000) is equal to $210,000.

21. (b) The requirement is to identify the graphical representation of ROI. Answer (b) is correct because point B is equal to ROI. Answer (a) is incorrect because return on sales (net income/sales) is not represented on this graph. Answer (c) is incorrect because asset turnover (sales/total assets) is not represented on this graph. Answer (d) is incorrect because operating income is located at point A.

22. (d) The requirement is to identify the graphical representation of net income. Answer (d) is correct because point A is equal to net income. Answer (a) is incorrect because return on sales (net income/sales) is not represented on this graph. Answer (b) is incorrect because ROI is represented at point B. Answer (c) is incorrect because asset turnover (sales/total assets) is not represented on the graph.

23. (b) The requirement is to identify the graphical representation of the relationship between residual income and ROI. Division X's residual income is located at point A and Division Y's residual income is located at point D. Division X has a larger residual income. Division X's ROI is located at point B and Division Y's ROI is located at point E. Thus Division Y's ROI is greater than Division X's ROI.

24. (b) The requirement is to identify the formula for ROI. Answer (b) is correct because it describes the DuPont ROI analysis: ROI = Return on sales multiplied by the capital employed turnover rate (which can be measured as total asset turnover).

25. (b) The requirement is to identify how ROI might be increased. One way of measuring ROI is return on assets (ROA). The formula is net income/total assets. Answer (b) is correct since if operating assets decrease (the denominator in ROI), then ROI would decrease. Answer (a) is incorrect because increasing operating assets would cause ROI to decrease. Answer (c) is incorrect because decreasing revenue would cause net income (the numerator) to decrease. A reduction in operating income would cause ROA to decrease.

26. (b) Return on investment (ROI) may be calculated using the following equation:

$$\frac{\text{Sales}}{\text{Investment}} \times \frac{\text{Net income}}{\text{Sales}} = \text{ROI}$$

Thus, the equation that should be used to compute Bala's return on investment is $(6/4) \times (1/6) = \text{ROI}$.

27. (d) Return on assets, also referred to as return on investment (ROI), is calculated as follows:

ROI	=	Profit margin	×	Asset turnover
ROI	=	0.02	×	5
ROI	=	0.10, or 10%		

28. (d) Residual income equals the net income of a division minus imputed interest on the division's assets. In this question, we are given Darwin's operating income and imputed interest rate, but Darwin's assets must be derived using sales and capital turnover, as shown below.

$$\text{Capital turnover} = \frac{\text{Sales of division}}{\text{Invested capital of division}}$$

$$4 = \frac{\$400,000}{x}$$

$$x = \frac{\$400,000}{4} = \$100,000$$

Since Darwin's invested capital is $100,000, its operating income is $40,000, and interest is imputed at 10%, residual income is calculated as follows:

$$\text{RI} = \frac{\text{Division}}{\text{net income}} - \frac{\text{Imputed interest on}}{\text{investment}}$$

RI = $40,000 – ($100,000 × 10%)
RI = $30,000

29. (d) Residual income is income minus an imputed interest charge for invested capital. Residual income will be maximized as long as the division earns a rate of return that exceeds the imputed charge. Division A's project will earn a rate of return **greater** than the imputed interest charge, so this project should be accepted. Division B's project will earn a rate of return **less** than the imputed interest charge, so this project should not be accepted.

30. (b) The DuPont formula is used to calculate return on investment.

$$\begin{array}{ccc} \text{Asset} \\ \text{turnover} \end{array} \times \begin{array}{ccc} \text{Income as a} \\ \text{percentage of} = \\ \text{sales} \end{array} \begin{array}{ccc} \text{Return on} \\ \text{investment} \\ \text{(ROI)} \end{array}$$

$$\frac{\text{Revenue}}{\text{Invested capital}} \times \frac{\text{Income}}{\text{Revenue}} = \frac{\text{Income}}{\text{Invested capital}}$$

The combination of changes which will maximize return on investment are to increase both asset turnover and income as a percentage of sales, since multiplying two larger numbers will result in a larger product.

31. (b) The requirement is to identify why residual income is preferred over return on investment as a performance evaluation technique. Answer (b) is correct because the focus on return on investment can cause high-performing divisions not to invest in projects that are in the best interest of the overall organization. Answer (a) is incorrect because both techniques can measure results for a single period. Answer (c) is incorrect because the imputed interest rate and the target rate should be the same. Answer (d) is incorrect because the investment level should be computed on the same basis.

Value-Based Management: EVA

32. (c) The requirement is to identify the major disadvantage of using EVA alone. Answer (c) is correct because many times value creation activities do not immediately increase return, and EVA (in the short run) does not reflect the value of these activities. Answer (a) is incorrect because a major advantage of EVA is its focus on creating shareholder value. Answer (b) is incorrect because EVA does not promote the acceptance of unprofitable projects. Answer (d) is incorrect because EVA encourages cost cutting activities.

33. (d) The requirement is to calculate EVA. Answer (d) is correct because EVA is equal to Operating profit after taxes – Cost of invested capital. Net operating profit after taxes is equal to Net operating profit before taxes multiplied by one minus the tax rate, or $25,000,000 [$31,250,000 × (1 – .20)]. Accordingly, EVA is equal to $17,000,000 [$25,000,000 – ($80,000,000 × 10%)].

34. (c) The requirement is to calculate free cash flow. Answer (c) is correct because free cash flow is equal to Net operating profit after taxes + Depreciation expense – Change in net working capital – Capital expenditures. Therefore, free cash flow is equal to $21,000,000 ($25,000,000 + $9,000,000 – $5,000,000 – $8,000,000).

35. (b) The requirement is to calculate EVA for the division. Answer (b) is correct because EVA is calculated as net operating profit after taxes (NOPAT) minus the capital charge on invested capital. In this case, NOPAT is equal to net operating profit before interest and taxes ($30,000,000) minus taxes ($30,000,000 × 40%), which is

equal to $18,000,000. EVA is then equal to $13,000,000 [$18,000,000 – ($50,000,000 × 10%)].

36. (b) The requirement is to calculate economic value added. The formula for EVA is Net operating profit after taxes – Cost of invested capital.

EVA would be computed as follows:

Net operating profit after taxes	$36,000,000
– Capital charge on invested capital ($100,000,000 × 10%)	(10,000,000)
= Economic value added	$26,000,000

37. (c) The requirement is to calculate free cash flow. Free cash flow would be computed as follows:

Net operating profit after taxes	$36,000,000
+ Depreciation expense	15,000,000
– Change in net working capital	(10,000,000)
– Capital expenditures	(12,000,000)
Free cash flow	$29,000,000

Traditional Financial Statement Analysis

38. (d) The requirement is to identify the ratio that does not measure asset utilization. Answer (d) is correct because the debt to total assets ratio is a debt utilization (financial leverage) ratio. Answers (a), (b), and (c) are incorrect because they are asset utilization ratios.

39. (c) The requirement is to identify the nature of benchmarking with other firms. Answer (c) is correct because cross-sectional analysis involves comparing results and ratios to those of other firms in the same industry. Answer (a) is incorrect because horizontal analysis involves comparisons of results and ratios for the same firm over time. Answer (b) is incorrect because vertical analysis involves comparisons of relationships in a firm's financial statements for a single year. Answer (d) is incorrect because ratio analysis does not imply any particular comparison.

40. (d) The requirement is to calculate the expected dividend per share. Earnings after interest is equal to $30 million ($35 million – $5 million). Net earnings after taxes is equal to $18 million [$30 million × 1 – Tax rate (40%)]. The net earnings after dividends to preferred shareholders is equal to $14 million ($18 million – $4 million), and the dividend for common stockholders is equal to $4,200,000 ($14 million × 30%). The dividend per share is equal to $4,200,000/$2 million shares = $2.10. Therefore, the correct answer is (d).

41. (b) The requirement is to calculate the market price from the earnings per share and price/earnings ratio. Net earnings is equal to $18 million ($35 million – $5 million) × (1 – 40%). Net earnings available to common stockholders is equal to $14 million ($18 million – $4 million). Earnings per share is equal to $14 million/2 million shares, or $7.00. Therefore, the estimated market price would be $7.00 × 8 = $56, or answer (b).

42. (b) The requirement is to calculate the debt-to-total-asset ratio. Answer (b) is correct. The debt-to-total-asset ratio is calculated by dividing total debt by total assets. Therefore, the debt-to-total-asset ratio is equal to 0.315 ($78,000 current liabilities + $75,000 long-term debt) ÷ ($210,000 current assets + $275,000 noncurrent assets). Answers (a), (c), and (d) are incorrect because the computations are not correct.

43. (d) The requirement is to calculate accounts receivable turnover. Answer (d) is correct. Accounts receivable turnover is calculated by dividing total credit sales by the average balance of accounts receivable. The average balance of accounts receivable is $85,000 [($100,000 + $70,000) ÷ 2]. Therefore, accounts receivable turnover is equal to 4.118 ($350,000 credit sales ÷ $85,000 average accounts receivable).

44. (a) The requirement is to calculate inventory turnover. Answer (d) is correct. Inventory turnover is calculated by dividing cost of goods sold by average inventory. Average inventory is equal to $75,000 [($70,000 + $80,0000) ÷ 2]. Therefore, inventory turnover is equal to 2.133 ($160,000 ÷ $75,000).

45. (b) The requirement is to calculate total asset turnover. Answer (b) is correct. Total asset turnover is calculated by dividing sales by average total assets. Average total assets is equal to $460,000 = [($210,000 + $275,000) + ($180,000 + $255,000)] ÷ 2. Therefore, total asset turnover is equal to 0.761 ($350,000 ÷ $460,000).

46. (c) The requirement is to calculate return on total assets. Answer (c) is correct. Return on assets is calculated by dividing net income by average total assets. As determined in the previous question, average total assets is equal to $460,000. Net income is equal to $72,000 ($350,000 sales – $160,000 cost of goods sold – $3,000 interest expense – $48,000 income taxes – $67,000 administrative expense). Therefore, return on assets is equal to 0.157 ($72,000 ÷ $460,000), or 15.7%.

47. (c) The requirement is to determine the effect of payment of an account payable. Answer (c) is correct. The quick ratio is equal to quick assets divided by current liabilities and the current ratio is equal to current assets divided by current liabilities. Since we are told that quick assets exceed current liabilities, both ratios are greater than one. With a ratio greater than one if you reduce the numerator and denominator by an equal amount, the ratio will increase.

48. (b) The requirement is to determine the effect of a purchase of raw materials on account. The correct answer is (b). Since we know that the current ratio is greater than one, an increase in the numerator and the denominator by an equal amount will decrease the ratio. Answers (c) and (d) are incorrect because working capital will not change.

49. (d) The requirement is to determine the effect of the collection of accounts receivable. Answer (d) is correct. Collection of accounts receivable has no effect on the quick or current ratio because both cash and accounts receivable are part of the numerator of both ratios.

50. (d) The requirement is to determine the effect of writing off inventory. Answer (d) is correct because a write-off of inventory will decrease the current ratio. Answers (a) and (b) are incorrect because inventory is not used in computing the quick ratio. Answer (c) is incorrect because working capital will be decreased.

51. (a) The requirement is to determine the effect of a five-for-one stock split. Answer (a) is correct because a stock split increases the number of shares outstanding and, therefore, reduces the book value per share. Answers (c) and (d) are incorrect because the transaction does not affect total stockholders' equity.

52. (d) The requirement is to determine the effect of issuing serial bonds in exchange for an office building. An-

swer (d) is correct because the first installment is a current liability which affects the quick ratio, the current ratio, and working capital.

53. (b) The requirement is to determine the effect of liquidating a long-term note with cash. Answer (b) is correct. Cash is included in the numerator of both the quick and current ratios. However, a reduction in cash affects the quick ratio more than the current ratio because it is smaller.

Benchmarking and Best Practices

54. (b) The requirement is to identify the definition of benchmarking outside of the firm's industry. Answer (b) is correct because generic benchmarking involves benchmarking to the best practices regardless of the industry. Answer (a) is incorrect because internal benchmarking involves benchmarking within the firm. Answer (c) is incorrect because competitor benchmarking involves benchmarking against direct competitors. Answer (d) is incorrect because functional benchmarking involves benchmarking within the same broad industry.

55. (d) All of these nonfinancial measures would be useful in evaluating the performance of a manufacturing system. Throughput (cycle) time measures the total amount of production time required per unit. This measure is important to assess the timeliness of the production process, which is required for on-time delivery of goods. The proportion of total production time consumed by setup activities reflects one aspect of production efficiency. Setup time represents money spent on a non-value-adding activity, and thus should be minimized as much as possible. The proportion of total units completed which require rework is a useful measure of product quality. An excessive rate of rework alerts management that it needs to examine its quality control procedures.

Quality Control Principles

56. (b) The requirement is to identify which tool is used to identify frequency of defects. Answer (b) is correct because a Pareto chart ranks the causes of process variations by the degree of impact on quality. Answer (a) is incorrect because a control chart is a statistical plot that helps to detect deviations before they generate defects. Answer (c) is incorrect because a cause-and-effect diagram is used to identify the potential causes of defects. Answer (d) is incorrect because a fishbone diagram is an alternative name for cause-and-effect diagrams.

57. (c) The requirement is to select which tool identifies causes of failures or defects. Answer (c) is correct because cause-and-effect diagrams identify causes of failures/defects and can be used to identify the reasons why a process goes out of control. Answer (a) is incorrect because a control chart is a statistical plot that helps to detect deviations before they generate defects. Answer (b) is incorrect because a Pareto diagram indicates how frequently a type of defect may occur. Answer (d) is incorrect because a strategy map is a statement of what the strategy must achieve and what is critical to its success.

58. (b) The requirement is to identify the concept of six-sigma quality. Answer (b) is correct because six-sigma is a statistical measure expressing how close a product comes to its quality goal. Six-sigma is 99.999997% perfect with 3.4 defects per million parts.

59. (b)   The requirement is to identify the terms used to identify continuous improvement. Answer (b), Kaizen, is correct because it is the Japanese art of continuous improvement. It underlies the total quality management and JIT business techniques. Answer (a) is incorrect because the theory of constraints is a method to maximize operating income when faced with some bottleneck operations. Answer (c) is incorrect because six-sigma is a statistical measure expressing how close a product comes to its quality goal. Six-sigma is 3.4 defects per million parts. Answer (d) is incorrect because lean manufacturing is an operational strategy focused on achieving the shortest possible cycle time by eliminating waste.

60. (a)   The requirement is to identify a component of the theory of constraints. Answer (a) is correct because a bottleneck is any resource or operation where the capacity is less than the demand placed upon it. Answers (b), (c), and (d) are incorrect because they are not components of the theory of constraints.

61. (a)   The requirement is to compute throughput contribution per unit. Answer (a) is correct because throughput contribution per unit is equal to revenue minus direct materials. Thus, throughput contribution per unit is equal to $150 (revenue per unit) – $45 (Cutting direct materials) – $15 (Finishing direct materials) = $90. Answers (b), (c), and (d) are incorrect because they represent incorrect computations of throughput contribution per unit.

62. (c)   The requirement is to identify the three basic measurements used by the Theory of Constraints. Answer (c) is correct because the Theory of Constraints focuses on throughput contribution, investment (or inventory), and operational expense (operating costs). Answers (a), (b), and (d) are incorrect because they represent other types of performance measures.

63. (a)   The requirement is to describe the objectives of the theory of constraints (TOC). The objective of TOC is to increase *throughput contribution* while decreasing *investment* and *operating costs*. **Throughput contribution** is revenues minus the direct materials cost of goods sold. **Investment** is the sum of materials cost in direct materials; work in process and finished goods inventories; research and development costs; and the costs of equipment and buildings. **Operating costs** include salaries and wages, rental expense, utilities, and depreciation.

Cost of Quality

64. (a)   The requirement is to identify the nature of quality circles. Answer (a) is correct because quality circles are designed to develop ways to prevent defects. Answer (b) is incorrect because appraisal costs are related to inspecting and testing to ensure product acceptability. Answer (c) is incorrect because internal failure involves the costs of finding defective units before they are shipped to customers. Answer (d) is incorrect because external failure is the cost of defects that reach the customer.

65. (c)   The requirement is to identify the item which reflects the internal failure component. An internal failure cost is a cost incurred when substandard products are produced but discovered before shipment to the customer. Reworking defective parts is an example of an internal failure. Answer (a) is incorrect because it is an example of an appraisal cost. Answer (b) is incorrect because it is an exam-

ple of a prevention cost. Answer (d) is incorrect because it is an example of an external failure cost.

66. (b)   The requirement is to identify the item which reflects the prevention cost component. A prevention cost is a cost incurred to prevent defects. These costs include the cost to identify the cause of the defect, take corrective action to eliminate the cause, train people, and redesign the product or the production process. Answer (b) is correct because it is an example of a quality activity designed to do the job right the first time. Answer (a) is incorrect because it is an example of an appraisal cost. Answer (c) is incorrect because it is an example of an internal failure cost. Answer (d) is incorrect because it is an example of an external failure cost.

67. (a)   The requirement is to identify where to incur costs to prevent product recalls. Answer (a) is correct because spending funds to prevent defects is generally most cost effective.

68. (b)   The requirement is to identify how costs incurred to detect nonconforming units are classified. Answer (b) is correct because appraisal costs are costs associated with quality control and include testing and inspection. Answer (a) is incorrect because prevention costs involve any quality activity designed to do the job right the first time. Answer (c) is incorrect because internal failures occur when substandard products are produced but discovered before shipment to the customer. Answer (d) is incorrect because external failure costs are incurred for products that do not meet requirements of the customer and have been shipped to the customer.

COST MEASUREMENT

A primary purpose of cost measurement is to allocate the costs of production (direct materials, direct manufacturing labor, and manufacturing overhead) to the units produced. It also provides important information for management decisions, such as product pricing decisions. Cost measurement is achieved through a costing system (job-order, process, activity-based) as described in this module. Before you begin the module, you should review the following key cost measurement terms.

BASIC COST MEASUREMENT TERMINOLOGY

Costing Systems

1. **Job order costing** is a system for allocating costs to groups of unique products made to customer specifications.
2. **Process costing** is a system for allocating costs to homogeneous units of a mass-produced product.
3. **Hybrid-costing** is a system that blends the characteristics of both the job order and process costing systems. Firms using this system typically produce large numbers of closely related products.
4. **Activity-based costing (ABC)** is a cost system that focuses on activities, determines their costs, and then uses appropriate cost drivers to trace costs to the products based on the activities. The following terminology is encountered in ABC:

    a. A **cost driver** is a factor that causes a cost to be incurred. Cost drivers may be volume-related (e.g., repair costs may depend on the volume of machine hours) and transaction-related (purchasing costs may depend on the number of purchase transactions).
    b. **Cost pools** are groupings of related costs accumulated together to be allocated to a product or some other cost object.
    c. **Non-value-added costs** are the cost of activities that can be eliminated without the customer perceiving a decline in product quality or performance.
    d. A **value-added cost** is the cost of activities that **cannot** be eliminated without the customer perceiving a decline in product quality or performance.
    e. A **value chain** is the sequence of business functions in which value is added to a firm's products or services. This sequence includes research and development, product design, manufacturing, marketing, distribution, and customer service.
    f. **Engineered costs** are determined from industrial engineering studies that examine how activities are performed and if/how performance can be improved.

5. **Activity-based management (ABM)** integrates ABC with other concepts such as Total Quality Management (TQM) and target costing to produce a management system that strives for excellence through cost reduction, continuous process improvement, and productivity gains.
6. **Backflush costing** is a costing system that omits recording some or all of the journal entries to track the purchase and production of goods. Goods are costed after they have been completed.
7. A **cost management system (CMS)** is a planning and control system that measures the cost of significant activities, identifies non-value-added costs, and identifies activities that will improve organizational performance.

Cost of Goods Manufactured and Cost Flows

8. **Product costs** are costs that can be associated with the production of specific goods. Product costs attach to a physical unit and become an expense in the period in which the unit to which they attach is sold. Product costs normally include direct manufacturing labor, direct materials, and factory overhead. **Period costs** cannot be associated (or matched) with manufactured goods (e.g., advertising expenditures). Period costs become expenses when incurred.
9. **Prime costs** are easily traceable to specific units of production and include direct manufacturing labor and direct materials. **Direct costs** are those easily traced to a specific business segment (e.g., product, division, department). **Indirect costs** are not easily traceable to specific segments and include factory overhead.
10. **Direct materials** is the cost of materials directly and conveniently traceable to a product. Minor material items (nails, glue) are not deemed conveniently traceable. These items are treated as **indirect materials** along with production supplies.

11. **Direct manufacturing labor** is the cost of labor directly transforming a product. This theoretically should include fringe benefits, but frequently does not. This is contrasted with **indirect manufacturing labor,** which is the cost of supporting labor (e.g., material handling labor, factory supervisors).

12. **Factory (manufacturing) overhead** normally includes indirect manufacturing labor costs, supplies cost, and other production facility costs such as plant depreciation, taxes, etc. It is comprised of all manufacturing costs that are not direct materials or direct manufacturing labor.

13. **Conversion costs** include direct manufacturing labor and manufacturing overhead. They're the costs of converting direct materials into finished products.

14. **Cost assignment** encompasses both **cost tracing** (assignment of direct costs to a cost object) and **cost allocation** (assignment of indirect costs to the cost object). A **cost object** is the item (product, department, process, etc.) for which cost is being determined.

15. **Direct materials inventory** includes the cost of materials awaiting entry into the production system. **Work in process inventory** includes the cost of units being produced but not yet completed. **Finished goods inventory** includes the cost of units completed but unsold.

16. **Actual activity level** is the level of production actually occurring for the period.

17. **Normal activity level** is the production level expected to be achieved over a number of periods or seasons under normal circumstances.

18. **Cycle time** (or **throughput time**) is the time required to complete a good from the start of the production process until the product is finished.

19. **Product life-cycle costing** tracks the accumulation of costs that occur starting with the research and development for a product and ending with the time at which sales and customer support are withdrawn.

20. **Computer-integrated manufacturing (CIM)** is a highly automated and integrated production process that is controlled by computers.

    a. A **flexible manufacturing system (FMS)** is a series of computer controlled manufacturing processes that can be **easily** changed to make a variety of products.

Joint and By-Products

21. **Joint costs** are costs common to multiple products that emerge at a split-off point. **Joint costing** is a system of assigning joint costs to **joint products** whose overall sales values are relatively significant. When a product has insignificant sales value relative to the other products, it is called a **by-product**.

Cost Behavior

22. **Cost estimation** is the examination of past relationships of costs and level of activity to develop predictions of future costs.

23. **Fixed costs** do not vary with the level of activity within the relevant range for a given period of time (usually one year), for example, plant depreciation.

24. **Variable costs** vary proportionately **in total** with the activity level throughout the relevant range (e.g., direct materials).

25. **Stepped costs (or semifixed costs)** are fixed over relatively short ranges of production levels (e.g., supervisors' salaries). Fixed, variable, and semifixed costs are diagrammed below.

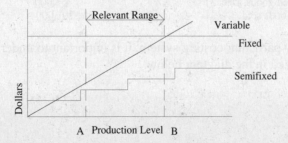

26. **Mixed costs (semivariable)** are costs that have a fixed component and a variable component. These components are separated by using the scattergraph, high-low, or linear regression methods.

27. **Relevant range** is the operating range of activity in which cost behavior patterns are valid (A to B in the preceding illustration). Thus, it is the production range for which fixed costs remain constant (e.g., if production doubles, an additional shift of salaried foremen would be added and fixed costs would increase).

28. **Nonlinear cost function** is a cost function that is not described by a straight line over the relevant range.

29. A **learning curve** is a function that demonstrates how productivity improves as workers become more proficient at producing the product.

A. Cost of Goods Manufactured

Regardless of which costing system is used, a cost of goods manufactured (CGM) statement is prepared to summarize the manufacturing activity of the period. CGM for a manufacturing firm is equivalent to purchases for a merchandising firm. Although it may take different forms, essentially the CGM statement is a summary of the direct materials and work in process (WIP) accounts.

$$BWIP + DM + DML + MOH - EWIP = CGM$$

A typical CGM statement is presented below.

Uddin Company
COST OF GOODS MANUFACTURED
Year Ended December 31, 2007

Direct materials		
Inventory, Jan. 1	$ 23,000	
Purchases	98,000	
Materials available for use	121,000	
Inventory, Dec. 31	16,000	
Direct materials used		$105,000
Direct manufacturing labor		72,000
Factory overhead		
Indirect labor	$ 14,000	
Supplies	4,000	
Utilities	8,000	
Depreciation	13,000	
Other	3,000	42,000
Manufacturing costs incurred, 2007		219,000
Add work in process inventory, Jan. 1		25,000
Manufacturing costs to account for		244,000
Deduct work in process inventory, Dec. 31		30,000
Cost of goods manufactured (completed)		$214,000

The result of the CGM statement is used in the cost of goods sold (CGS) statement or cost of goods sold section of the income statement, as indicated below.

Uddin Company
COST OF GOODS SOLD
Year Ended December 31, 2007

Finished goods, Jan. 1	$ 40,000
Add cost of goods manufactured (completed) per statement above	214,000
Cost of goods available for sale	254,000
Deduct finished goods, Dec. 31	53,000
Cost of goods sold	$201,000

B. Cost Flows

Before discussing any particular costing system, it is important to understand the flow of costs through the accounts, as summarized in the diagram below.

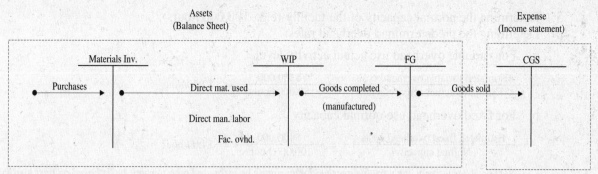

Analyze the diagram carefully before proceeding. The details will be explained further in the next few pages.

C. Job-Order Costing

Job-order costing is a system for allocating costs to groups of unique products. It is applicable to the production of customer-specified products such as the manufacture of special machines and even to cost a particular service (e.g., providing legal services for the client of a law firm). Each job becomes a cost center for which costs are accumulated. A subsidiary record (job-order cost sheet) is needed to keep track of all unfinished jobs (work in process) and finished jobs (finished goods). Note that the total of unfinished job cost sheets will equal the work in process balance.

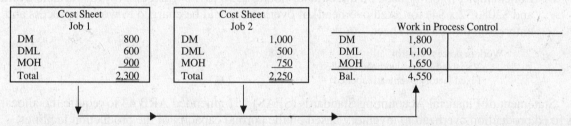

Note that whenever work in process is debited or credited in the above entries, the amount of the entry is the sum of the postings on the job-order cost sheets. The balances on the job-order cost sheets are also the basis for the entries transferring completed goods to finished goods inventory and transferring the cost of goods shipped to customers to cost of goods sold. The work in process account is analyzed below.

Work in Process Control	
1. Beginning balance	
2. Direct materials used	
3. Direct labor used	
4. Overhead applied	5. Cost of goods manufactured (CGM)
6. Ending balance	

A similar analysis can be performed on the finished goods account.

Finished Goods Control	
1. Beginning balance	
2. Cost of goods manufactured	3. Cost of goods sold (CGS)
4. Ending balance	

D. Accounting for Overhead

Accounting for manufacturing overhead is an important part of job-order costing and any other costing system. Overhead consists of all manufacturing costs other than direct materials and direct manufacturing labor. The distinguishing feature of manufacturing overhead is that while it must be incurred in order to produce goods, **it cannot be directly traced to the final product** as can direct materials and direct manufacturing labor. Therefore, overhead must be **applied,** rather than directly charged, to goods produced. The overhead application process is described below.

1. Overhead items are grouped by cost behavior (e.g., fixed and variable).
2. The fixed and variable overhead costs are estimated for the forthcoming period (e.g., $200,000 for variable overhead and $400,000 for fixed overhead).
3. A denominator (activity) base is chosen (see discussion below). A common choice is direct labor hours or machine hours.
4. The actual activity level is estimated for the forthcoming year (e.g., 80,000 hours).

5. Determine the normal capacity of the facility (e.g., 100,000 hours).
6. Determine the predetermined overhead rates:

a. For variable overhead use actual activity level

$$\frac{\text{Estimated variable overhead costs}}{\text{Estimated actual activity level}} = \frac{\$200,000}{80,000 \text{ hours}} = \$2.50/\text{hour}$$

b. For fixed overhead use normal capacity

$$\frac{\text{Estimated fixed overhead costs}}{\text{Normal capacity}} = \frac{\$400,000}{100,000 \text{ hours}} = \$4.00/\text{hour}$$

NOTE: *Alternatively, the variable overhead may simply be estimated on a per unit basis based on past history (e.g., $2.50 per unit).*

7. As actual overhead costs are incurred, they are debited to the factory overhead accounts.

Variable factory overhead (actual)	900	
Various accounts		900
Fixed factory overhead (actual)	1,000	
Various accounts		1,000

8. As jobs are completed, the predetermined overhead rate(s) is used to apply overhead to these jobs. For example, if job 17 used 52 direct labor hours, $338 [$130 (52 x $2.50)] for variable overhead and $208 (52 x $4) for fixed overhead] of overhead would be charged to work in process and entered on the job cost sheet.

Work in process control	338	
Variable factory overhead (applied)		130
Fixed factory overhead (applied)		208

Statement of Financial Accounting Standards (SFAS) 151 amended ARB 43 to require the allocation of fixed production overhead to inventory based on the normal capacity of the production facilities. Normal capacity is the production expected to be achieved over a number of periods or seasons under normal circumstances. The actual level of production may be used if it approximates normal capacity. Therefore, for financial reporting purposes companies must use normal capacity to allocate fixed overhead but the actual activity level is used to allocate variable overhead.

To allocate the costs of overhead to units produced, an **activity base** must be chosen for use in the computation of a predetermined overhead rate. This activity base should bear a causal relationship to the incurrence of overhead costs. Examples of activity bases are

1. Direct manufacturing labor hours
2. Direct manufacturing labor cost
3. Machine hours

For example, overhead may result from (be a function of) hours worked regardless of who works, which would mean that direct manufacturing labor hours should be the activity base. If, on the other hand, more overhead costs were incurred because of heavily automated operations, machine hours might be a more appropriate activity base.

However, for internal purposes, management may use a number of approaches to determine the activity level, as shown below.

Approach	*Definition*
Theoretical capacity	Output is produced efficiently 100% of the time. ↓
Practical capacity	ADJUSTED FOR: factors such as days off, downtime, etc. Output is produced maximum percentage of time practical (75-85%). ↓
Normal capacity	ADJUSTED FOR: long-run product demand. Average annual output necessary to meet sales and inventory fluctuations over 4-5-year period. ↓
Expected annual capacity	ADJUSTED FOR: current year fluctuations. Expected output for current year.

Note that theoretical capacity is larger than practical capacity, which is larger than normal volume. Expected annual capacity fluctuates above and below normal volume.

At year-end fixed overhead may be

1. **Overapplied**—More is applied than incurred because

    a. Overhead costs were overestimated,
    b. Actual activity was greater than normal capacity, and/or
    c. Actual overhead costs were less than expected.

2. **Underapplied**—Less overhead is applied than incurred because

    a. Overhead costs were underestimated,
    b. Actual activity was less than normal capacity, and/or
    c. Actual overhead costs were more than expected.

E. Disposition of Under- and Overapplied Overhead

1. If the under- or overapplied overhead is immaterial, it is frequently written off to cost of goods sold on grounds of expediency.

Cost of goods sold (debit or credit)	xx	
Factory overhead (debit or credit)		xx

2. If the amount of under- or overapplied variable overhead is significant, then an adjustment must be made to all goods which were costed at the erroneous application rate during the current period. The goods with the incorrect costs will be in three accounts: Work in Process Control, Finished Goods Control, and Cost of Goods Sold.

    Proration may be made based upon total ending balance (before proration) of the three accounts or on some other equitable basis. The exam will normally give specific directions on what allocation base should be used.

    The amount of under- or overapplied fixed overhead should always be charged to cost of goods sold.

F. Service Department Cost Allocation

A large firm will have several production departments, each of which may compute a separate predetermined overhead rate. A problem arises when a **service** (support) department (maintenance, receiving, etc.) incurs costs and benefits multiple production departments.

Costs of these service departments must be allocated to production departments because all manufacturing costs must ultimately be traced to products. For example, the costs of the materials-handling cost center may need to be allocated to the production departments (and possibly other service departments). Apportionment of service department costs should be based on meaningful criteria such as

1. Services provided
2. Services available
3. Benefits received
4. Equity

Examples of apportionment bases are

1. Square feet for building costs
2. Usage for electricity
3. Employees for cafeteria, personnel, and first aid
4. Usage for materials handling, maintenance, etc.

Service department costs can be allocated by

1. Direct method
2. Step method
3. Reciprocal method

1. Direct Method

The direct method simply allocates the costs of each service department to each of the producing departments based on a relative level of the apportionment base. For example, if a service department had costs of $140,000, and producing departments X and Y used 80% and 20% of the apportionment base, X and Y would be assigned $112,000 and $28,000 respectively. Note that the direct method ignores use of services by other service departments. For example, the direct method would ignore the fact that service department A uses the services of service department B. The essence of the direct method is shown in the following diagram.

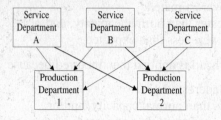

2. **Step Method**

    The step method allocates service department costs to other service departments as well as production departments. The allocation process is

    a. Select the service department serving the most other service departments

        (1) When more than one service department services an equal number of service departments, select the department with the highest costs

    b. Allocate the costs of the service department selected in step a. to the production departments and other service departments based on a relative level of the apportionment base as in the direct method.

    c. Allocate the costs of each remaining service department selected in the same manner as described in step a.

    d. Costs of service departments are never allocated back to departments whose costs have already been allocated.

Note that the step method ignores the fact that reciprocal services are used between some service departments.

EXAMPLE:

DEPARTMENTS

| | *Service* | | *Production* | | |
	A	*B*	*1*	*2*	*Totals*
Costs	$4,000	$6,000	$38,000	$42,000	$90,000
Use of A		10%	40%	50%	100%
Use of B	30%		40%	30%	100%

Direct Method—*Allocate A's and B's costs directly to production departments 1 and 2.*

	A	*B*	*1*	*2*
Costs prior to allocation	4,000	6,000	38,000	42,000
Allocation of A's costs*	(4,000)		1,778	2,222
Allocation of B's costs**		(6,000)	3,429	2,571
	0	0	43,207	46,793

    * 4/9 and 5/9

    ** 4/7 and 3/7 $90,000

Step Method—*Allocate B's costs (B has more costs than A) to departments A, 1, and 2. Next allocate A's costs to departments 1 and 2; you cannot allocate A's costs back to B, as B's costs have already been allocated.*

	A	*B*	*1*	*2*
Costs prior to allocation	4,000	6,000	38,000	42,000
Allocation of B's costs*	1,800	(6,000)	2,400	1,800
Allocation of A's costs				
($4,000 + $1,800)**	(5,800)		2,578	3,222
	0	0	42,978	47,022

    * 3/10, 4/10, and 3/10

    ** 4/9 and 5/9 $90,000

3. **Reciprocal Method**

   The reciprocal method provides a way to adjust for the reciprocal services provided among the service departments. Using this method, service department costs and service department reciprocal service relationships are described by a linear equation. Then, the equations are solved simultaneously providing a more precise allocation of costs to production departments because it considers the mutual services provided among the service departments.

G. Process Costing

Process costing, in contrast to job-order costing, is applicable to a continuous process of production of the same or similar goods, for example, oil refining and chemical production. Since the product is uniform, there is no need to determine the costs of different groups of products and each processing department becomes a cost center.

Process costing computations can be broken down into the 5 steps listed below.

1. Visualize the **physical flow of units**
2. Compute the **equivalent units of production**
3. Determine **costs to allocate**
4. Compute **unit costs**
5. **Allocate total costs** to

   a. Goods completed
   b. Ending work in process

Note that the five steps above can be memorized using the acronym: PECUA (**P**hysical Flow, **E**quivalent Units of Production, **C**osts to Allocate, **U**nit Costs, **A**llocate Costs).

1. **Flow of Units**

   The cost flow diagram shown under Section B in this module is the same for process costing except there will typically be several WIP accounts (i.e., one for every department). When solving a process costing problem, it is helpful to visualize the physical flow of units, as illustrated in the diagram below.

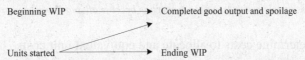

The units in BWIP are either completed or become spoiled. Units started during the period but not completed become EWIP.

2. **Equivalent Units of Production (EUP)**

   An EUP is the amount of work equivalent to completing one unit from start to finish. In a process costing system, products are assigned costs periodically (usually monthly). At any one moment some units are incomplete which makes the EUP calculations necessary to allocate manufacturing costs between

   1. Goods finished during the period (cost of goods manufactured)
   2. Ending work in process

   The two primary EUP methods used for process costing are first-in, first-out (FIFO) and weighted-average (WA). Past questions on the exam have emphasized the weighted-average method. Under the weighted-average approach, current costs are combined with prior period costs, and all units are carried at an average cost of production. Importantly, the method assumes that all units completed during a period are started and completed during that period. As a result, the **percentage** of work done last period on the beginning work in process inventory is ignored.

3. **Simple Process Costing Example**

   The BW Toy Company uses a weighted-average process cost system to collect costs. Data relevant to 2007 production is given below. Assume we begin with 800 units 25% complete for labor and overhead (conversion costs), and 100% complete for materials because they are introduced at the start of the process. We start 4,200 units. 4,000 units are completed, while 1,000 remain in EWIP (20%

complete for labor and overhead and 100% complete for materials). No spoilage exists. The costs are summarized in the following T-account:

Work in Process Control

BWIP				
materials	900			
labor + OH	532	1,432	???	Goods finished
Current				
materials	4,200			
labor + OH	14,000	18,200		
EWIP		???		

Step 1: The physical flow of units is accounted for.

BWIP	800
Started	4,200
To account for	5,000
Units completed	4,000
EWIP	1,000
Accounted for	5,000

Step 2: The units completed and ending work in process are converted to equivalent units.

		Equivalent units	
Description	*Total*	*Direct mtls.*	*Conv.*
Physical units to account for			
Beginning inventory	800		
Units started	4,200		
Units to be accounted for	5,000		
Equivalent units of production			
Good units completed and transferred out	4,000	4,000*	4,000**
Ending WIP	1,000	1,000*	200
Units accounted for	5,000	5,000	4,200

* *These units are 100% complete with respect to materials because materials are introduced at the start of the process.*

** *These units are 100% complete with respect to conversion because all units completed are **assumed** to be started and completed during the period.*

Steps 3 and 4: Determine costs to allocate and equivalent unit costs.

Manufacturing costs			
Beginning inventory	$ 1,432	$ 900	$ 532
Current costs	18,200	4,200	14,000
Total costs to account for	$19,632	$ 5,100	$14,532
Cost per equivalent unit		$ 1.02*	$ 3.46**

* *Notice the resulting costs are averages: $5,100 ÷ 5,000 equivalent units = $1.02.*

** *$14,532 ÷ 4,200 equivalent units = $3.46.*

Step 5: Allocate total costs to goods completed and ending work in process.

Units completed [4,000 x ($1.02 + $3.46)]		$17,920
Ending WIP:		
Mat. (1,000 x $1.02)	$1,020	
Conv. (200 x $3.46)	692	1,712
Total costs accounted for		$19,632

The allocation is accomplished by multiplying the individual equivalent unit figures by the unit costs.

4. **EUP for Material**

   In the above example, material was assumed to be added at the beginning of the production process. Material can also be added at different points in the process (e.g., 10%, 70%) or gradually during the process.

5. **FIFO Work in Process Assumption**

   The FIFO approach is not as popular as the weighted-average approach on the exam. Thus, we will focus solely on the calculation of equivalent units. With FIFO, the first batch into production (i.e., the beginning work in process inventory) is assumed to be the first batch completed. This batch is treated as a separate, distinct layer—separate from goods that are started and completed during the period.

The weighted-average assumption (all goods are assumed to be started and completed during the period) no longer holds for FIFO. Thus, any work done last period on the beginning work in process inventory must be taken into consideration. After all is said and done, the equivalent unit figures reflect the work done during the current accounting period. Also, the only difference between the two methods is the treatment of the beginning work in process inventory.

The equivalent-unit calculations for BW Toy follow.

Description	Total	Direct mtls.	Conv.
Physical units to account for			
Beginning inventory	800		
Units started	4,200		
Units to be accounted for	5,000		
Equivalent units of production			
Good units completed and transferred out:			
From beg. WIP	800	-0-*	600**
Started and completed	3,200	3,200***	3,200***
Ending WIP	1,000	1,000	200
Units accounted for	5,000	4,200	4,000

* All material was introduced last period.
** 75% of the work was necessary this period to complete the units.
*** 100% of the materials and conversions were introduced this period.

6. **Spoilage (Scrap) in Process Costing**

   The following terms are commonly used:

   - **Spoilage (scrap)**—Inferior goods either discarded or sold for disposal value
   - **Defective units**—Inferior goods reworked and sold as normal product

   A major distinction is made between normal and abnormal spoilage.

   a. Normal spoilage is the cost of spoiled units caused by the nature of the manufacturing process (i.e., which occur under efficient operating conditions).

      (1) Normal spoilage is a necessary cost in the production process and is, therefore, a **product cost**.

   b. Abnormal spoilage is the cost of spoiled units which were spoiled through some unnecessary act, event, or condition.

      (1) Abnormal spoilage is a **period cost** (e.g., "loss on abnormal spoilage").
      (2) Abnormal spoilage costs should not be included in cost of goods sold.

   Spoilage must be considered in EUP calculations. For example, if spoilage is discovered at the 60% point in processing and 100 units of abnormal spoilage are discovered, 60 EUP have occurred. The amount of abnormal loss would be the cost of 60 EUP (processing) plus the materials added to 100 units of production up to the 60% point. In contrast, if the spoilage was considered normal in nature, the spoilage cost would be treated as a product cost and simply added to the cost of the good units completed.

7. **Spoilage in Job Costing**

   In a job-order costing system, the costs of normal spoilage and defective units can be handled in two different ways. When spoilage is attributable to general factory conditions, net spoilage costs are allocated to all jobs through overhead application (i.e., estimated spoilage costs are included with other overhead in the computation of the overhead application rate). Alternatively, when spoilage is attributable to exacting job specifications, net spoilage costs are charged to specific jobs. With this approach, spoilage is **not** reflected in the predetermined overhead rate. Under both methods, the proceeds from the sale of spoiled goods should be offset against the cost of spoiled goods produced. Net spoilage cost would be charged to factory overhead in the first case and left in work in process in the second case.

   Costs of abnormal spoilage should **not** be charged to jobs but should be written off as a loss of the period.

H. **Hybrid-Costing System**

   Because of the nature of their operations certain manufacturers use costing systems that blend characteristics of both the job-order and process costing systems. Such so-called hybrid-costing systems are often used by firms that manufacture a relatively large number of closely related standardized parts (e.g., automobile manufacturers and clothing manufacturers). An example of a hybrid-costing system is the **operation-costing system** that applies costs to batches of similar, but not identical, products. Direct materials are traced directly to each batch, similar to job costing. Conversion costs are traced to each operation and allocated to products that pass through the operation.

I.   Backflush Costing

When a firm uses a **just-in-time (JIT)** production system, as described in Module 40, management may decide to use backflush costing for their products. Instead of using accounting records to track costs of goods as they are purchased and go through the production process, backflush costing uses normal or standard costs to work backward to "flush out" the costs of the goods finished or sold. Backflush costing does not strictly adhere to generally accepted accounting principles. However, because of the negligible amount of inventories that is characteristic of JIT production systems, the difference is often not material.

J.   Activity-Based Costing

Activity-based costing (ABC) is based upon two principles. First, activities consume resources. Second, these resources are consumed by products, services, or other cost objectives (output). ABC allocates overhead costs to products on the basis of the resources consumed by each activity involved in the design, production, and distribution of a particular good. This is accomplished through the assignment of costs to homogeneous cost pools that represent specific activities and then the allocation of these costs, using appropriate cost drivers, to the product. ABC may be used in conjunction with either job order or process costing systems.

Central to ABC are the activities performed to fulfill organizational objectives (producing products or services for customers). Activities may be value-added or non-value-added. **Value-added activities** are those which customers perceive as increasing the worth of a product or service and for which customers are willing to pay. They include only production activities. **Non-value-added activities** increase the cost of a product but do not increase its value to customers. Examples include materials handling and rework. Packaging is required for some products such as milk or potting soil, but it may be non-value-added for other products such as books (it is also costly and takes up huge amounts of landfill space). Thus, these activities may be eliminated and/or restructured without customers perceiving a decline in the value of the product/service. An activity (process) map is a flowchart which indicates all activities involved in the production process and identifies both value-added and non-value-added activities.

Cost drivers are those activities which have a direct cause and effect relationship to the incurrence of a particular cost. Traditional costing uses only variable and fixed or total overhead cost pools and views cost drivers at the output unit level, wherein costs are allocated based on labor hours, machine hours, etc. Some costs though, such as setup costs, vary at the batch level (batch-level costs) and should be spread over the units in the batch to which they relate (**not** machine hours). Product-sustaining (process-level) costs such as engineering change orders should be assigned to the products for which the orders were issued. Facility-sustaining costs incurred at the organizational level support operations and can only be arbitrarily assigned to products. As shown by the following table, ABC uses both transaction-related (e.g., purchase orders) and volume-related (e.g., machine hours) cost drivers. Traditional product costing tends to use only volume-related cost drivers.

Activity	*Cost driver*
Purchase of materials	Number of purchase transactions
Receiving	Number of shipments received
Disbursing	Number of checks issued
Setup costs	Number of setups or setup hours
Machining	Number of machine hours
Repair costs	Number of machine hours
Engineering changes to products	Number of engineering change notices

The activities listed above are all examples of direct activities which can be traced to an output or service. In contrast, indirect activities such as human resources are not directly attributable to output. The cost of indirect activities may be allocated or simply labeled as nontraceable.

To illustrate, ABC traces the costs of setup activities to the production batch that caused the setup costs to be incurred. The cost of each setup is then spread over the units in that batch. On the other hand, a traditional costing system would typically allocate setup costs as overhead on the basis of a volume-related cost driver such as direct manufacturing labor hours. Assume that product A and product B incur setup costs as follows:

	A	B	Total
Production volume	7,500	10,000	
Batch size	250	1,000	
Number of setups	30	10	
Total setup costs incurred	$60,000	$20,000	$80,000
Total cost per setup	$2,000	$2,000	
Direct manuf. labor hours/unit	3	3	
Total direct manuf. labor hours	22,500	30,000	52,500
Setup cost per DMLH ($80,000 ÷ 52,500)			$1.52
Traditional setup cost/unit			
A ($1.52 x 3 DMLH required)	$ 4.56		
B ($1.52 x 3 DMLH required)		$ 4.56	
ABC setup cost/unit			
A ($2,000/setup ÷ 250 units/batch)	$ 8.00		
B ($2,000/setup ÷ 1,000 units/batch)		$ 2.00	

In this case, products A and B are assigned different total setup costs. However, because they require the same number of direct manufacturing labor hours per unit, traditional costing allocates equal setup costs per unit to both products. In effect, one product picks up cost that was caused by another product (cross-subsidization), which distorts product costing information. ABC assigns different setup costs per unit to each product because **each unit** of product A demands more resources for setup activity than does **each unit** of product B. Note that the **total** setup cost remains the same under either method.

Activity-based management (ABM) integrates ABC with other concepts such as Total Quality Management (TQM) and target costing to produce a management system that strives for excellence through cost reduction, continuous process improvement, and productivity gains.

K. Joint Products

Joint products are two or more products produced together up to a split-off point where they become separately identifiable. They cannot be produced by themselves. For example, a steak cannot be produced without also producing roasts, ribs, liver, hamburger, etc. Other industries which produce joint products include

1. Chemicals   3. Mining
2. Lumber   4. Petroleum

Joint products incur common, or joint costs, before the split-off point. The split-off point is the point of production at which the joint products can be individually identified and removed from the joint, or common, process. The joint products can then be sold or processed further. Costs incurred after the split-off point for any one of the joint products are called separable costs.

Common costs are allocated to the joint products at the split-off point, usually on the basis of sales value at the split-off point, estimated net realizable value (NRV) at split-off point, or some physical measure. The estimated net realizable value method allocates joint costs using the estimated sales values of the joint products after further processing less the separable processing costs. Of the first two methods listed, the sales value at split-off method **must** be used if a sales value at split-off point exists. The following example illustrates the sales value at split-off and estimated net realizable value methods.

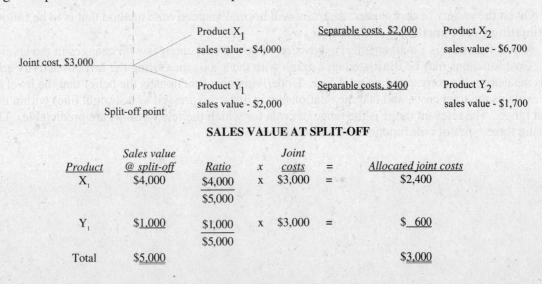

Product	Sales value @ split-off	Ratio	x	Joint costs	=	Allocated joint costs
X₁	$4,000	$4,000 / $5,000	x	$3,000	=	$2,400
Y₁	$1,000	$1,000 / $5,000	x	$3,000	=	$ 600
Total	$5,000					$3,000

If the sales value at split-off is not available or one did not exist, we would use the estimated net realizable value method (NRV).

ESTIMATED NET REALIZABLE VALUE METHOD (NRV)

Product	Final sales value	–	Separable costs	=	Estimated net realizable value	Ratio	x	Joint costs	=	Allocated joint costs
X_2	$6,700	–	$2,000	=	$4,700	$\frac{\$4,700}{\$6,000}$	x	$3,000	=	$2,350
Y_2	$1,700	–	$ 400	=	$1,300	$\frac{\$1,300}{\$6,000}$	x	$3,000	=	$ 650
Total					$6,000					$3,000

Physical measures (units, pounds, etc.) generally are not used because of the misleading income statement effect. With an allocation based on pounds, steak would show a big profit while ground beef would be a consistent loser; each pound would carry the same cost although steak sells for much more per pound.

Joint cost allocation is performed for the purpose of inventory valuation and income determination. However, joint costs should be **ignored** for any internal decisions including the decision on whether to process a joint product beyond the split-off point. Such costs are not relevant to the sell or process further decision. The **sell or process further** decision should be based on incremental revenues and costs beyond the split-off point. If incremental revenue from further processing exceeds incremental costs, then process further. If incremental costs exceed incremental revenues, then sell at the split-off point. In the previous example in which we assumed a sales value at the split-off point, both X_1 and Y_1 should be further processed.

	Incremental revenue		Incremental cost		Advantage of further processing
X_1:	$6,700 – $4,000 = $2,700	–	$2,000	=	$700
Y_1:	$1,700 – $1,000 = $ 700	–	$ 400	=	$300

If X_1 could have sold for only $5,500 after further processing, the incremental revenue ($1,500) would not cover the incremental cost ($2,000), and X_1 should not be further processed.

L. By-Products

By-products, in contrast to joint products, have little market value relative to the overall value of the product(s) being produced. Joint (common) costs are usually not allocated to a by-product. Instead, by-products are frequently valued at market or net realizable value (NRV) and accounted for as a contra production cost, that is, a reduction in the joint costs that will be allocated to the joint products.

Rather than recognizing by-product market value as a reduction of production cost, it is sometimes recognized when sold and disclosed as

1. Ordinary sales
2. Other income
3. Contra to cost of sales

Given the variety of approaches, the exam will normally specify the method that is to be followed.

M. Estimating Cost Functions

A **cost function** is a mathematical expression of how a cost changes with changes in the level of activity. Cost functions may be illustrated on a graph with the x-axis measuring the level of activity and the y-axis measuring the corresponding total cost. Underlying cost functions is the belief that the level of activity explains the total costs, and that the relationship is linear (expressed as a straight line) within the relevant range. The relevant range is the range of costs for which the relationships are predictable. The following three types of cost functions may be observed:

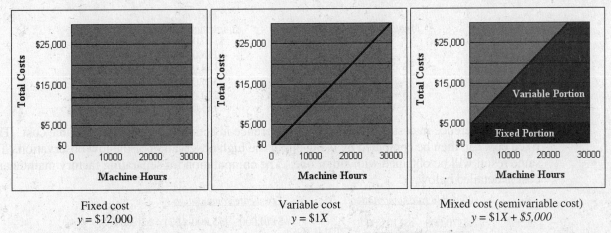

| Fixed cost | Variable cost | Mixed cost (semivariable cost) |
| $y = \$12,000$ | $y = \$1X$ | $y = \$1X + \$5,000$ |

As illustrated, the fixed cost is a constant amount of $12,000 over the relevant range, and the variable cost is equal to $1 per machine hour over the relevant range. The mixed cost is made up of $5,000 in fixed cost and $1 per unit of variable cost.

As indicated previously, one of the most important aspects of estimating a cost function is determining whether there is a causal relationship between the level of activity (the cost driver) and the cost. A causal relationship is necessary to developing reliable cost predictions.

There are four different basic approaches to cost estimation.

1. **Industrial engineering (work-measurement) method**—Estimates of cost functions are derived from analyzing the physical relationships between inputs (e.g., direct labor hours) and outputs. As an example, a time and motion study might be used to determine how many hours it takes to assemble a table. This method of developing cost functions is time-consuming and costly.

2. **Conference method**—Estimates of cost functions are derived from analysis and opinions about cost relationships by individuals from various departments. This method can be done quickly but may not be as reliable as those that are based on quantitative methods.

3. **Account analysis method**—Estimates of cost functions are derived by analyzing ledger accounts and designating them as containing fixed costs, variable costs, or mixed costs. This is a widely used method but to be reliable it must be performed by individuals who understand operations.

4. **Quantitative methods**—Estimates of cost functions are derived using formal mathematical models. Using quantitative methods, management identifies a cost and one or more cost drivers to be used to predict the cost. Then they collect historical data to estimate the cost function. A number of quantitative methods are used, including

   a. **Scattergraph method.** The scattergraph method is a graphical approach to computing the relationship between two variables. The dependent variable is plotted on the vertical axis and the independent variable on the horizontal axis. A straight line is then drawn through the observation points which best describes the relationship between the two variables. In the graph below, the broken line illustrates the relationship. This method lacks precision, because by freely drawing the line through the points, it is possible to obtain a line that does not minimize the deviations of the points from the line.

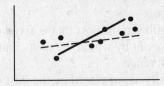

   b. **High-Low method.** The high-low method computes the slope for the variable rate based on the highest and lowest observations.

$$\text{Slope} = \frac{\text{Change in cost between high and low points}}{\text{Change in activity between high and low points}}$$

This method is illustrated using the following observations for factory maintenance costs (DMLH = Direct manufacturing labor hours).

Month	DMLH	Factory maintenance cost
1	45,000 (low)	$110,000
2	50,000	115,000
3	70,000	158,000
4	60,000	135,000
5	75,000 (high)	170,000
6	65,000	145,000

The difference in cost is divided by the difference in activity to obtain the variable cost. The fixed cost can then be computed by using either the high observation or the low observation. The same result will be obtained with either one. The computation for separating factory maintenance cost is detailed below.

Variable rate computation

$$\frac{\$170,000 - \$110,000}{75,000 - 45,000} = \$2/\text{DMLH}$$

Fixed rate computation

$$\$170,000 - (75,000 \times \$2) = \$20,000$$
or
$$\$110,000 - (45,000 \times \$2) = \$20,000$$

The high-low method is a rather crude technique compared to regression analysis. For example, this method may be inaccurate if the high and low points are not representative (i.e., are outliers) as illustrated by the solid line in the chart included with the discussion of the scattergraph method.

c. **Regression analysis.** Regression (least squares) analysis determines the functional relationship between variables with a measure of probable error. For example, you may wish to determine the relationship of electricity cost to level of activity. Based on activity levels and electricity charges of past months, the following chart (scattergraph) might be prepared.

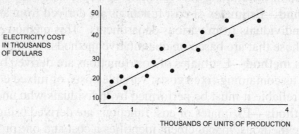

As production increases, electric costs increase. The relationship appears linear. Linearity is an assumption underlying regression. If the power costs begin to fall after 3,000 units of production, the relationship between electricity and production would not be linear, and linear regression would not be appropriate.

The method of least squares fits a regression line between the observation points such that the sum of the squared vertical differences between the regression line and the individual observations is minimized. The simple regression equation for a linear cost function is

$$y = a + bx$$

Where

y = estimated total cost
a = constant, the portion of the cost that is fixed over the relevant range
b = the slope, the amount by which the cost changes based on changes in the level of activity over the relevant range
x = the level of activity as measured by the cost driver

The goodness of the least squares fit (i.e., how well the regression line fits the observed data) is measured by the coefficient of determination (R^2). The better the line fits the observed data points (i.e., the closer the observed data points are to the line), the closer R^2 will be to 1.00 — R^2s of 90–99% are considered very good. However, you must remember that a high R^2 does not prove that there is a cause and effect relationship between the two variables.

If only one independent variable exists, the analysis is known as simple regression (as in the above example). **Multiple regression** consists of a functional relationship with multiple independent variables (e.g., cost may be a function of several cost drivers). Multiple regression is described in detail in the next module.

d. **Correlation analysis.** Correlation is the relationship between variables. If the variables move with each other, they have a direct relationship (positive correlation) as in A. If the variables move in opposite directions, they have an inverse relationship (negative correlation) as in B.

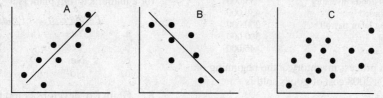

The degree and direction of correlation is measured from –1 to 1. The sign (negative or positive) describes whether the relationship is inverse or direct. The coefficient of correlation is measured by

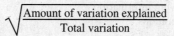

$$\sqrt{\frac{\text{Amount of variation explained}}{\text{Total variation}}}$$

If all of the observations were in a straight line, all of the variation would be explained and the coefficient of correlation would be 1 or –1 depending upon whether the relationship is positive or negative. If there is no correlation, as in C above, the coefficient of correlation is 0.

Note that the coefficient of correlation is similar in concept to the coefficient of determination discussed above in "method of least squares." The coefficient of determination cannot have a negative value, as can the coefficient of correlation, because the coefficient of determination is based on squared deviations (i.e., if you square a negative number, the result is positive).

Management often has a choice of cost drivers to use in estimating a particular cost. In evaluating the best driver to use, management should consider

- Economic plausibility—does the relationship between the cost and the cost driver make intuitive economic sense?
- Goodness of fit—historically how well do changes in the cost driver explain total costs?
- Slope of the regression line—a steep regression line indicates a stronger relationship than a flatter line.

Cost functions may also be nonlinear. For example, **step functions** are often encountered in which the cost increases in discrete amounts periodically as the level of activity increases. Nonlinear functions also occur due to **learning curves**. As an example, labor hours per unit to assemble a new product may decline as production increases due to workers getting better at doing their jobs. Two models that attempt to capture the effect of learning are

- **Cumulative average-time model**—The cumulative average time per unit declines by a constant percentage each time the quantity of units produced doubles.
- **Incremental unit-time learning model**—The incremental unit time needed to produce the last unit declines by a constant percentage each time the cumulative quantity of units produced doubles.

MULTIPLE-CHOICE QUESTIONS (1-57)

1. The following information was taken from Kay Company's accounting records for the year ended December 31, 2008:

Increase in raw materials inventory	$ 15,000
Decrease in finished goods inventory	35,000
Raw materials purchased	430,000
Direct manufacturing labor payroll	200,000
Factory overhead	300,000
Freight-out	45,000

There was no work in process inventory at the beginning or end of the year. Kay's 2008 cost of goods sold is

- a. $950,000
- b. $965,000
- c. $975,000
- d. $995,000

Items 2 through 4 are based on the following information pertaining to Arp Co.'s manufacturing operations:

Inventories	3/1/08	3/31/08
Direct materials	$36,000	$30,000
Work in process	18,000	12,000
Finished goods	54,000	72,000

Additional information for the month of March 2008:

Direct materials purchased	$84,000
Direct manufacturing labor payroll	60,000
Direct manufacturing labor rate per hour	7.50
Factory overhead rate per direct labor hour	10.00

2. For the month of March 2008, prime cost was

- a. $ 90,000
- b. $120,000
- c. $144,000
- d. $150,000

3. For the month of March 2008, conversion cost was

- a. $ 90,000
- b. $140,000
- c. $144,000
- d. $170,000

4. For the month of March 2008, cost of goods manufactured was

- a. $218,000
- b. $224,000
- c. $230,000
- d. $236,000

5. During the month of March 2008, Nale Co. used $300,000 of direct material. At March 31, 2008, Nale's direct materials inventory was $50,000 more than it was at March 1, 2008. Direct material purchases during the month of March 2008 amounted to

- a. $0
- b. $250,000
- c. $300,000
- d. $350,000

6. Fab Co. manufactures textiles. Among Fab's 2008 manufacturing costs were the following salaries and wages:

Loom operators	$120,000
Factory foreman	45,000
Machine mechanics	30,000

What was the amount of Fab's 2008 direct manufacturing labor?

- a. $195,000
- b. $165,000
- c. $150,000
- d. $120,000

7. The fixed portion of the semivariable cost of electricity for a manufacturing plant is a

	Period cost	Product cost
a.	Yes	No
b.	Yes	Yes
c.	No	Yes
d.	No	No

8. Gram Co. develops computer programs to meet customers' special requirements. How should Gram categorize payments to employees who develop these programs?

	Direct costs	Value-added costs
a.	Yes	Yes
b.	Yes	No
c.	No	No
d.	No	Yes

9. In a job-costing system, issuing indirect materials to production increases which account?

- a. Materials control.
- b. Work in process control.
- c. Manufacturing overhead control.
- d. Manufacturing overhead allocated.

10. Costs are accumulated by responsibility center for control purposes when using

	Job order costing	Process costing
a.	Yes	Yes
b.	Yes	No
c.	No	No
d.	No	Yes

11. Birk Co. uses a job order cost system. The following debits (credit) appeared in Birk's work in process account for the month of April 2008:

April	Description	Amount
1	Balance	$ 4,000
30	Direct materials	24,000
30	Direct manufacturing labor	16,000
30	Factory overhead	12,800
30	To finished goods	(48,000)

Birk applies overhead to production at a predetermined rate of 80% of direct manufacturing labor costs. Job No. 5, the only job still in process on April 30, 2008, has been charged with direct manufacturing labor of $2,000. What was the amount of direct materials charged to Job No. 5?

- a. $ 3,000
- b. $ 5,200
- c. $ 8,800
- d. $24,000

12. In a job cost system, manufacturing overhead is

	An indirect cost of jobs	A necessary element in production
a.	No	Yes
b.	No	No
c.	Yes	Yes
d.	Yes	No

13. Under Pick Co.'s job order costing system manufacturing overhead is applied to work in process using a predetermined annual overhead rate. During January 2008, Pick's transactions included the following:

Direct materials issued to production	$ 90,000
Indirect materials issued to production	8,000
Manufacturing overhead incurred	125,000
Manufacturing overhead applied	113,000
Direct labor costs	107,000

Pick had neither beginning nor ending work in process inventory. What was the cost of jobs completed in January 2008?

a. $302,000
b. $310,000
c. $322,000
d. $330,000

14. A direct manufacturing labor overtime premium should be charged to a specific job when the overtime is caused by the

a. Increased overall level of activity.
b. Customer's requirement for early completion of job.
c. Management's failure to include the job in the production schedule.
d. Management's requirement that the job be completed before the annual factory vacation closure.

*15. A company services office equipment. Some customers bring their equipment to the company's service shop; other customers prefer to have the company's service personnel come to their offices to repair their equipment. The most appropriate costing method for the company is

a. A job order costing system.
b. An activity-based costing system.
c. A process costing system.
d. An operations costing system.

16. In developing a predetermined variable factory overhead application rate for use in a process costing system, which of the following could be used in the numerator and denominator?

	Numerator	*Denominator*
a.	Actual variable factory overhead	Actual machine hours
b.	Actual variable factory overhead	Estimated machine hours
c.	Estimated variable factory overhead	Actual machine hours
d.	Estimated variable factory overhead	Estimated machine hours

17. A job order cost system uses a predetermined fixed factory overhead rate based on normal activity and expected fixed cost. At the end of the year, underapplied fixed overhead might be explained by which of the following situations?

	Actual volume	*Actual fixed costs*
a.	Greater than normal	Greater than expected
b.	Greater than normal	Less than expected
c.	Less than normal	Greater than expected
d.	Less than normal	Less than expected

18. Worley Company has underapplied variable overhead of $45,000 for the year ended December 31, 2008. Before disposition of the underapplied overhead, selected December 31, 2008, balances from Worley's accounting records are as follows:

Sales	$1,200,000
Cost of goods sold	720,000
Inventories:	
Direct materials	36,000
Work in process	54,000
Finished goods	90,000

Under Worley's cost accounting system, over- or underapplied variable overhead is allocated to appropriate inventories and cost of goods sold based on year-end balances. There are no amounts of under or overapplied fixed overhead. In its 2008 income statement, Worley should report cost of goods sold of

a. $682,500
b. $684,000
c. $756,000
d. $757,500

19. Parat College allocates support department costs to its individual schools using the step method. Information for May 2008 is as follows:

	Support departments	
	Maintenance	*Power*
Costs incurred	$99,000	$54,000
Service percentages provided to:		
Maintenance	--	10%
Power	20%	--
School of Education	30%	20%
School of Technology	50%	70%
	100%	100%

What is the amount of May 2008 support department costs allocated to the School of Education?

a. $40,500
b. $42,120
c. $46,100
d. $49,125

20. Kerner Manufacturing uses a process cost system to manufacture laptop computers. The following information summarizes operations relating to laptop computer model #KJK20 during the quarter ending March 31:

	Units	*Direct Materials*
Work in process inventory, January 1	100	$70,000
Started during the quarter	500	
Completed during the quarter	400	
Work-in-process inventory, March 31	200	
Costs added during the quarter		$750,000

Beginning work in process inventory was 50% complete for direct materials. Ending work in process inventory was 75% complete for direct materials. What were the equivalent units of production with regard to materials for March?

a. 450
b. 500
c. 550
d. 600

21. Kerner Manufacturing uses a process cost system to manufacture laptop computers. The following information summarizes operations relating to laptop computer model #KJK20 during the quarter ending March 31:

	Units	Direct Materials
Work in process inventory, January 1	100	$50,000
Started during the quarter	500	
Completed during the quarter	400	
Work in process inventory, March 31	200	
Costs added during the quarter		$720,000

Beginning work in process inventory was 50% complete for direct materials. Ending work in process inventory was 75% complete for direct materials. What is the total value of material costs in ending work in process inventory using the FIFO unit cost, inventory valuation method?

    a. $183,000
    b. $194,000
    c. $210,000
    d. $216,000

22. In a process cost system, the application of factory overhead usually would be recorded as an increase in

    a.   Finished goods inventory control.
    b.   Factory overhead control.
    c.   Cost of goods sold.
    d.   Work in process inventory control.

23. The following information pertains to Lap Co.'s Palo Division for the month of April:

	Number of units	Cost of materials
Beginning work in process	15,000	$ 5,500
Started in April	40,000	18,000
Units completed	42,500	
Ending work in process	12,500	

All materials are added at the beginning of the process. Using the weighted-average method, the cost per equivalent unit for materials is

    a. $0.59
    b. $0.55
    c. $0.45
    d. $0.43

24. The Forming Department is the first of a two-stage production process. Spoilage is identified when the units have completed the Forming process. Costs of spoiled units are assigned to units completed and transferred to the second department in the period spoilage is identified. The following information concerns Forming's conversion costs in May 2008:

	Units	Conversion costs
Beginning work in process (50% complete)	2,000	$10,000
Units started during May	8,000	75,500
Spoilage—normal	500	
Units completed and transferred	7,000	
Ending work in process (80% complete)	2,500	

Using the weighted-average method, what was Forming's conversion cost transferred to the second production department?

    a. $59,850
    b. $64,125
    c. $67,500
    d. $71,250

25. In computing the current period's manufacturing cost per equivalent unit, the FIFO method of process costing considers current period costs

    a.   Only.
    b.   Plus cost of beginning work in process inventory.

    c.   Less cost of beginning work in process inventory.
    d.   Plus cost of ending work in process inventory.

26. In process 2, material G is added when a batch is 60% complete. Ending work in process units, which are 50% complete, would be included in the computation of equivalent units for

	Conversion costs	Material G
a.	Yes	No
b.	No	Yes
c.	No	No
d.	Yes	Yes

27. A process costing system was used for a department that began operations in January 2008. Approximately the same number of physical units, at the same degree of completion, were in work in process at the end of both January and February. Monthly conversion costs are allocated between ending work in process and units completed. Compared to the FIFO method, would the weighted-average method use the same or a greater number of equivalent units to calculate the monthly allocations?

	Equivalent units for weighted-average compared to FIFO	
	January	February
a.	Same	Same
b.	Greater number	Greater number
c.	Greater number	Same
d.	Same	Greater number

28. A department adds material at the beginning of a process and identifies defective units when the process is 40% complete. At the beginning of the period, there was no work in process. At the end of the period, the number of work in process units equaled the number of units transferred to finished goods. If all units in ending work in process were 66 2/3% complete, then ending work in process should be allocated

    a.   50% of all normal defective unit costs.
    b.   40% of all normal defective unit costs.
    c.   50% of the material costs and 40% of the conversion costs of all normal defective unit costs.
    d.   None of the normal defective unit costs.

29. In its April 2008 production, Hern Corp., which does not use a standard cost system, incurred total production costs of $900,000, of which Hern attributed $60,000 to normal spoilage and $30,000 to abnormal spoilage. Hern should account for this spoilage as

    a.   Period cost of $90,000.
    b.   Inventoriable cost of $90,000.
    c.   Period cost of $60,000 and inventoriable cost of $30,000.
    d.   Inventoriable cost of $60,000 and period cost of $30,000.

Items 30 through 37 are based on the following:

Kimbeth Manufacturing uses a process cost system to manufacture Dust Density Sensors for the mining industry. The following information pertains to operations for the month of May 2008:

	Units
Beginning work in process inventory, May 1	16,000
Started in production during May	100,000
Completed production during May	92,000
Ending work in process inventory, May 31	24,000

The beginning inventory was 60% complete for materials and 20% complete for conversion costs. The ending inventory was 90% complete for materials and 40% complete for conversion costs.

Costs pertaining to the month of May are as follows:

- The beginning inventory costs are: materials, $54,560; direct labor, $20,320; and factory overhead, $15,240.
- Costs incurred during May are: materials used, $468,000; direct labor, $182,880; and factory overhead, $391,160.

**30. Using the first-in, first-out (FIFO) method, the equivalent units of production for materials are
   a. 97,600 units.
   b. 104,000 units.
   c. 107,200 units.
   d. 108,000 units.

**31. Using the FIFO method, the equivalent units of production for conversion costs are
   a. 85,600 units.
   b. 88,800 units.
   c. 95,200 units.
   d. 98,400 units.

**32. Using the FIFO method, the equivalent unit cost of materials for May is
   a. $4.12
   b. $4.50
   c. $4.60
   d. $4.80

**33. Using the FIFO method, the equivalent unit conversion cost for May is
   a. $5.65
   b. $5.83
   c. $6.00
   d. $6.20

**34. Using the FIFO method, the total cost of units in the ending work in process inventory at May 31 is
   a. $153,168
   b. $145,800
   c. $155,328
   d. $156,960

**35. Using the weighted-average method, the equivalent unit cost of materials for May is
   a. $4.12
   b. $4.50
   c. $4.60
   d. $5.03

**36. Using the weighted-average method, the equivalent unit conversion cost for May is
   a. $5.65
   b. $5.83
   c. $6.00
   d. $6.41

**37. Using the weighted-average method, the total cost of the units in the ending work in process inventory at May 31 is
   a. $ 86,400
   b. $154,800

---

* CIA adapted
** CMA adapted

   c. $155,328
   d. $156,960

*38. Which of the following would be a reasonable basis for allocating the material handling costs to the units produced in an activity-based costing system?
   a. Number of production runs per year.
   b. Number of components per completed unit.
   c. Amount of time required to produce one unit.
   d. Amount of overhead applied to each completed unit.

*39. An assembly plant accumulates its variable and fixed manufacturing overhead costs in a single cost pool which are then applied to work in process using a single application base. The assembly plant management wants to estimate the magnitude of the total manufacturing overhead costs for different volume levels of the application activity base using a flexible budget formula. If there is an increase in the application activity base that is within the relevant range of activity for the assembly plant, which one of the following relationships regarding variable and fixed costs is correct?
   a. The variable cost per unit is constant, and the total fixed costs decrease.
   b. The variable cost per unit is constant, and the total fixed costs increase.
   c. The variable cost per unit and the total fixed costs remain constant.
   d. The variable cost per unit increases, and the total fixed costs remain constant.

*40. In Belk Co.'s just-in-time production system, costs per setup were reduced from $28 to $2. In the process of reducing inventory levels, Belk found that there were fixed facility and administrative costs that previously had not been included in the carrying cost calculation. The result was an increase from $8 to $32 per unit per year. What were the effects of these changes on Belk's economic lot size and relevant costs?

	Lot size	Relevant costs
a.	Decrease	Increase
b.	Increase	Decrease
c.	Increase	Increase
d.	Decrease	Decrease

41. What is the normal effect on the numbers of cost pools and allocation bases when an activity-based cost (ABC) system replaces a traditional cost system?

	Cost pools	Allocation bases
a.	No effect	No effect
b.	Increase	No effect
c.	No effect	Increase
d.	Increase	Increase

42. Which of the following is true about activity-based costing?
   a. It should not be used with process or job costing.
   b. It can be used only with process costing.
   c. It can be used only with job costing.
   d. It can be used with either process or job costing.

43. In an activity-based costing system, what should be used to assign a department's manufacturing overhead costs to products produced in varying lot sizes?
   a. A single cause-and-effect relationship.
   b. Multiple cause-and-effect relationships.

c.   Relative net sales values of the products.
d.   A product's ability to bear cost allocations.

44. In an activity-based costing system, cost reduction is accomplished by identifying and eliminating

	All cost drivers	*Non-value-adding activities*
a.	No	No
b.	Yes	Yes
c.	No	Yes
d.	Yes	No

45. Nile Co.'s cost allocation and product costing procedures follow activity-based costing principles. Activities have been identified and classified as being either value-adding or non-value-adding as to each product. Which of the following activities, used in Nile production process, is non-value-adding?

a.   Design engineering activity.
b.   Heat treatment activity.
c.   Drill press activity.
d.   Raw materials storage activity.

46. Hoger Corporation accumulated the following cost information for its two products, A and B:

	A	*B*	*Total*
Production volume	2,000	1,000	
Total direct man. labor hrs.	5,000	20,000	25,000
Setup cost per batch	$ 1,000	$2,000	
Batch size	100	50	
Total setup costs incurred	$20,000	$40,000	$60,000
DMLH per unit	2	1	

A traditional costing system would allocate setup costs on the basis of DMLH. An ABC system would trace costs by spreading the costs per batch over the units in a batch. What is the setup cost per unit of product A under each costing system?

	Traditional	*ABC*
a.	$4.80	$10.00
b.	$2.40	$10.00
c.	$40.00	$200.00
d.	$4.80	$20.00

47. Lane Co. produces main products Kul and Wu. The process also yields by-product Zef. Net realizable value of by-product Zef is subtracted from joint production cost of Kul and Wu. The following information pertains to production in July 2008 at a joint cost of $54,000:

Product	*Units produced*	*Market value*	*Additional cost after split-off*
Kul	1,000	$40,000	$ 0
Wu	1,500	35,000	0
Zef	500	7,000	3,000

If Lane uses the net realizable value method for allocating joint cost, how much of the joint cost should be allocated to product Kul?

a. $18,800
b. $20,000
c. $26,667
d. $27,342

48. The diagram below represents the production and sales relationships of joint products P and Q. Joint costs are incurred until split-off, then separable costs are incurred in refining each product. Market values of P and Q at split-off are used to allocate joint costs.

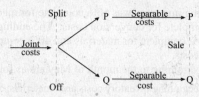

If the market value of P at split-off increases and all other costs and selling prices remain unchanged, then the gross margin of

	P	*Q*
a.	Increases	Decreases
b.	Increases	Increases
c.	Decreases	Decreases
d.	Decreases	Increases

49. For purposes of allocating joint costs to joint products, the sales price at point of sale, reduced by cost to complete after split-off, is assumed to be equal to the

a.   Joint costs.
b.   Total costs.
c.   Net sales value at split-off.
d.   Sales price less a normal profit margin at point of sale.

50. Mig Co., which began operations in 2008, produces gasoline and a gasoline by-product. The following information is available pertaining to 2008 sales and production:

Total production costs to split-off point	$120,000
Gasoline sales	270,000
By-product sales	30,000
Gasoline inventory, 12/31/08	15,000
Additional by-product costs:	
Marketing	10,000
Production	15,000

Mig accounts for the by-product at the time of production. What are Mig's 2008 cost of sales for gasoline and the by-product?

	Gasoline	*By-product*
a.	$105,000	$25,000
b.	$115,000	$0
c.	$108,000	$37,000
d.	$100,000	$0

51. The following information pertains to a by-product called Moy:

Sales in 2008	5,000 units
Selling price per unit	$6
Selling costs per unit	2
Processing costs	0

Inventory of Moy was recorded at net realizable value when produced in 2007. No units of Moy were produced in 2008. What amount should be recognized as profit on Moy's 2008 sales?

a. $0
b. $10,000
c. $20,000
d. $30,000

52. Kode Co. manufactures a major product that gives rise to a by-product called May. May's only separable cost is a $1 selling cost when a unit is sold for $4. Kode accounts for May's sales by deducting the $3 net amount from the cost of goods sold of the major product. There are no inventories. If Kode were to change its method of accounting for May from a by-product to a joint product, what would be the effect on Kode's overall gross margin?

   a. No effect.

   b. Gross margin increases by $1 for each unit of May sold.

   c. Gross margin increases by $3 for each unit of May sold.

   d. Gross margin increases by $4 for each unit of May sold.

53. In accounting for by-products, the value of the by-product may be recognized at the time of

	Production	Sale
a.	Yes	Yes
b.	Yes	No
c.	No	No
d.	No	Yes

54. Day Mail Order Co. applied the high-low method of cost estimation to customer order data for the first four months of 2008. What is the estimated variable order filling cost component per order?

Month	Orders	Cost
January	1,200	$ 3,120
February	1,300	3,185
March	1,800	4,320
April	1,700	3,895
	6,000	$14,520

   a. $2.00

   b. $2.42

   c. $2.48

   d. $2.50

55. Sender, Inc. estimates parcel mailing costs using data shown on the chart below.

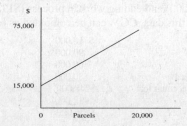

What is Sender's estimated cost for mailing 12,000 parcels?

   a. $36,000

   b. $45,000

   c. $51,000

   d. $60,000

56. Which of the following may be used to estimate how inventory warehouse costs are affected by both the number of shipments and the weight of materials handled?

   a. Economic order quantity analysis.

   b. Probability analysis.

   c. Correlation analysis.

   d. Multiple regression analysis.

57. Sago Co. uses regression analysis to develop a model for predicting overhead costs. Two different cost drivers (machine hours and direct materials weight) are under consideration as the independent variable. Relevant data were run on a computer using one of the standard regression programs, with the following results:

	Coefficient
Machine hours	
Y Intercept	2,500
B	5.0
$R^2 = .70$	
Direct materials weight	
Y Intercept	4,600
B	2.6
$R^2 = .50$	

What regression equation should be used?

   a. $Y = 2{,}500 + 5.0X$

   b. $Y = 2{,}500 + 3.5X$

   c. $Y = 4{,}600 + 2.6X$

   d. $Y = 4{,}600 + 1.3X$

MULTIPLE-CHOICE ANSWERS

1. a __ __	13. b __ __	25. a __ __	37. d __ __	49. c __ __
2. d __ __	14. b __ __	26. a __ __	38. b __ __	50. d __ __
3. b __ __	15 a __ __	27. d __ __	39. c __ __	51. a __ __
4. d __ __	16. d __ __	28. a __ __	40. d __ __	52. b __ __
5. d __ __	17. c __ __	29. d __ __	41. d __ __	53. a __ __
6. d __ __	18. d __ __	30. b __ __	42. d __ __	54. a __ __
7. c __ __	19. c __ __	31. d __ __	43. b __ __	55. c __ __
8. a __ __	20. b __ __	32. b __ __	44. c __ __	56. d __ __
9. c __ __	21. d __ __	33. b __ __	45. d __ __	57. a __ __
10. a __ __	22. d __ __	34. a __ __	46. a __ __	
11. b __ __	23. d __ __	35. c __ __	47. c __ __	1st: __/57 = __%
12. c __ __	24. c __ __	36. c __ __	48. d __ __	2nd: __/57 = __%

MULTIPLE-CHOICE ANSWER EXPLANATIONS

A. Cost of Goods Manufactured

1.   (a)   Three computations must be performed: raw materials used, cost of goods manufactured, and cost of goods sold.

(1)	Raw materials purchased	$430,000
	Less: Increase in raw materials inventory	15,000
	Raw materials used	$415,000

(2)	Beginning WIP	--
	Raw materials used (from above)	415,000
	Direct manufacturing labor	200,000
	Factory overhead	300,000
	Cost to account for	$915,000
	Less: Ending WIP	--
	Cost of goods manufactured	$915,000

(3)	Cost of goods manufactured	$915,000
	Add: Decrease in finished goods inventory	35,000
	Cost of goods sold	$950,000

The increase in raw materials inventory represents the amount of inventory that was purchased but was not used. Therefore, this increase must be subtracted from raw materials purchased to determine the amount of raw materials used. Work in process inventory is an adjustment in arriving at cost of goods manufactured (as shown above). For this question no adjustment is necessary because Kay has no work in process inventory. The decrease in finished goods inventory represents the amount of inventory that was sold in excess of the inventory manufactured during the current period. Therefore, this amount must be added to cost of goods manufactured to determine cost of goods sold. The freight-out of $45,000 is irrelevant for this question because freight-out is a selling expense and thus, would not be used in computing cost of goods sold.

2.   (d)   Prime cost is the sum of direct materials and direct manufacturing labor. Direct manufacturing labor is $60,000. Direct materials used must be computed. The solutions approach is to enter the information given into the materials T-account and solve for the unknown:

Direct Materials Control		
3/1/08 bal.	36,000	
Purchases	84,000	? Materials used
3/30/08	30,000	

Using the T-account above, direct materials used are easily computed as $90,000. Thus, prime cost incurred was $150,000 ($90,000 + $60,000).

3.   (b)   Conversion cost is the sum of direct manufacturing labor ($60,000, as given) and applied factory overhead.

The factory overhead rate per direct manufacturing labor hour is $10.00. To compute the number of direct manufacturing labor hours worked, the direct manufacturing labor payroll ($60,000) is divided by the direct manufacturing labor rate per hour ($7.50), resulting in 8,000 direct manufacturing labor hours. Factory overhead applied is 8,000 hours at $10 per hour, or $80,000. Thus, conversion cost incurred was $140,000 ($60,000 of direct manufacturing labor plus $80,000 of applied factory overhead).

4.   (d)   Cost of goods manufactured (CGM) is the cost of goods completed **and** transferred to finished goods. It is the sum of direct materials used, direct manufacturing labor used, applied factory overhead, and any adjustment for work in process inventories. Direct manufacturing labor used ($60,000) is given. Direct materials used ($90,000) and applied factory overhead ($80,000) were computed in the answers to the two previous questions. Beginning work in process ($18,000) and ending work in process ($12,000) are given. Using this data, CGM can be computed as follows:

BWIP	$ 18,000
DM used	90,000
DML	60,000
OH applied	80,000
Costs to account for	$248,000
EWIP	(12,000)
CGM	$236,000

5.   (d)   To determine Nale's direct materials purchases for the month of March, trace the flow of costs through the direct materials account.

Direct materials		
Beg. bal.	x	
Purchased		$300,000 Used
End. bal.	x + $50,000	

The beginning balance was not given, but the problem states that the ending balance was $50,000 greater. Thus, we can label the beginning balance X and the ending balance X + $50,000. Purchases may be determined as follows:

$$(x + \$50,000) + \$300,000 - x = \$350,000$$

6.   (d)   Direct manufacturing labor costs include all labor costs which can be directly traced to the product in an economically feasible way. All other factory labor is considered indirect manufacturing labor. For Fab Co., the wages of loom operators can be directly traced to the textiles produced. However, the labor cost of factory foremen and machine mechanics are **not** direct manufacturing labor since these workers do not work directly on the product. Thus, answer (d) is correct because the amount of Fab's direct manufacturing labor is the loom operator cost of $120,000.

7.   (c)   Product costs are costs that can be associated with the production of specific revenues. These costs attach to a physical unit and become expenses in the period in which the unit to which they attach is sold. Product costs include direct labor, direct material, and factory overhead. Period costs, on the other hand, cannot be associated with specific revenues and, therefore, become expenses as time passes. Answer (c) is correct because the cost of electricity for a manufacturing plant, whether fixed or variable, is included in factory overhead and, therefore, is a product cost.

8.   (a)   The labor cost incurred to develop computer programs for sale to customers represents both a direct cost and a value-adding cost. The software is the cost object, and direct costs include any costs that are both related to it and which are easily traceable to specific units of production. Value-adding costs are those that cannot be eliminated without the customer perceiving a decline in product quality or performance. Obviously, the computer programmers cannot be eliminated from the software development process, so these payroll costs add value to the product.

9.   (c)   The requirement is to identify the account that is increased when indirect materials are issued to production. Answer (c) is correct because the cost of indirect materials used increases the Manufacturing Overhead Control account and decreases Materials Control. Answer (a) is incorrect because Materials Control is decreased with the transfer. Answer (b) is incorrect because Work in Process Control is increased by costs of direct materials and direct labor and the allocation of manufacturing overhead. Manufacturing Overhead Allocated is credited when overhead is allocated to work in process and debited when it is closed out at the end of the period.

B.   Cost Flows

10.   (a)   A responsibility center is any point within an organization where control exists over cost incurrence, revenue generation, and/or the use of investment funds. A responsibility center can be an operation, a department, a division, or even an individual. The key point to note for this question is that no matter what product costing method is used, the responsibility center is always used for control purposes. In job order costing, costs are accumulated by responsibility center and then assigned to specific jobs or orders through the use of a job cost sheet. Even though the job cost sheet will usually reflect the efforts of a number of responsibility centers, it will not be used for control purposes. Any needed cost control will be handled on the responsibility center level. In process costing, costs are accumulated by the responsibility center and recorded on a production cost report that will be used to develop a product's cost. Since the production cost report shows the efforts of only one responsibility center, it is used for both product costing and control purposes. Thus, for control purposes, costs are accumulated by responsibility center for both job-order and process costing.

C.   Job-Order Costing

11.   (b)   The requirement is to determine the amount of direct materials charged to Job No. 5. The problem states that Job 5 is the only job still in process on April 30, so the total costs charged to this job must equal the ending balance in work in process.

Work in Process Control			
Beg. bal.	4,000		
DM	24,000		
DML	16,000		
O/H	12,800	48,000	To FG
End. bal.	8,800		

The total costs charged to Job 5 are $8,800. Direct manufacturing labor accounts for $2,000 of this figure and overhead accounts for $1,600 ($2,000 DL × 80% O/H rate).

Direct manufacturing labor	$2,000
Factory overhead	1,600
Direct materials	--
Total cost of Job 5	$8,800

The remaining cost of $5,200 [$8,800 − ($2,000 + $1,600)] must be the amount of direct materials.

12.   (c)   Manufacturing overhead is considered an indirect cost because it is not directly traceable to specific jobs, although overhead is a necessary (inevitable) cost of production.

13.   (b)   The requirement is to determine the cost of jobs completed in January 2008. In a job order costing system, manufacturing overhead cannot be traced to specific jobs. Instead, overhead is accumulated in an overhead control account and applied to work performed based on some predetermined overhead rate. The difference between actual and applied overhead is normally either allocated to work in process, finished goods, and cost of goods sold or written off to cost of goods sold. In this case the cost of jobs completed is being determined for January only. Under- or overapplied overhead is not usually considered on a monthly basis. Therefore, the cost of jobs completed should include allocated overhead only. The amount of indirect materials issued to production has already been included in overhead applied. These costs do not need to be considered again in determining the cost of jobs completed. The cost of jobs completed can be computed as follows:

Direct materials issued to production	$ 90,000
Manufacturing overhead applied	113,000
Direct labor costs	107,000
Cost of jobs completed	$310,000

14.   (b)   The requirement is to determine which situation would cause a direct manufacturing labor overtime premium to be charged directly to a specific job. Answer (b) is correct because overtime resulting from a customer's requirement of early completion of a job would result in overtime directly traceable to that job. Answer (a) is incorrect because overtime incurred due to an overall high level of activity should be prorated over all jobs. Since production scheduling is generally at random, a specific job should not be penalized simply because it happened to be scheduled during overtime hours. Answers (c) and (d) are incorrect because the overtime is a result of management inefficiency.

15.   (a)   The requirement is to identify the appropriate type of costing system. Answer (a) is correct because job-order costing systems are designed to accumulate costs for tasks or projects that are unique and nonrepetitive. Service organizations are interested in identifying the costs applicable to each customer and/or each service call. Answer (b) is incorrect because the primary purpose of activity-based costing systems focuses on generating more accurate cost information by costing activities using cost drivers. Answer (c) is incorrect because process costing systems are designed for homogeneous products that are mass produced in continuous production runs. Answer (d) is incorrect because operations costing systems are designed for batches of homogeneous products; operations costing is a hybrid costing method between job-order and process costing.

D.   Accounting for Overhead

16.   (d)   A variable overhead application rate is commonly called a predetermined variable overhead rate and is computed as follows:

$$\frac{\text{Estimated variable overhead costs}}{\text{Estimated activity level}} = \text{Predetermined variable rate}$$

Estimated figures are used because actual figures are not known at the beginning of a period. Estimated variable overhead (the numerator) is estimated variable overhead costs, and estimated machine hours (the denominator) is an estimated activity level. Actual figures (either overhead costs or activity levels) are not known until the end of the period.

17.   (c)   A predetermined factory overhead rate is developed by dividing estimated fixed overhead costs by the normal capacity based on a selected cost driver (DML, cost, machine hours, etc.). Overhead costs are then applied by multiplying the predetermined rate by the actual volume of the cost driver during the period. Overhead costs will be underapplied if (1) overhead costs are underestimated, making the application rate too small (actual costs are larger than expected), or (2) normal capacity is greater than actual activity, making the application rate too small (actual volume is less than normal).

E.   Disposition of Under- and Overapplied Overhead

18.   (d)   The requirement is to determine the amount of costs of goods sold to be reported on the 2008 income statement. The balance in the cost of goods sold account is $720,000. This amount must be increased by the portion of underapplied variable overhead allocated to cost of goods sold. The underapplied overhead is appropriately allocated to work in process, finished goods, and cost of goods sold. No overhead is allocated to direct materials inventory, since this account contains only the cost of unused materials. The other three accounts contain the cost of materials, labor, and overhead. The amounts to be allocated to work in process, finished goods, and cost of goods sold are determined by each account's relative balance as compared to the total balance in the accounts. The total balance of the three accounts is $864,000 ($720,000 + $54,000 + $90,000). Therefore, the amount allocable to cost of goods sold is [$720,000/$864,000 × ($45,000)] or $37,500. Since variable overhead was underapplied, not enough costs were applied to production during the year. Thus, cost of goods sold is increased to $757,500 ($720,000 + $37,500).

F.   Service Department Cost Allocation

19.   (c)   The step method of allocating support department costs uses a sequence of allocations which result in partial recognition of services rendered by one support department to another. Total costs of the support department that provides the greatest proportion of its services to other support departments are allocated first, followed by the department with the next highest proportion, and so forth. As

each "step" is allocated, each succeeding step involves one less department. Parat College's support department cost allocation is

	Support Departments		Operating Departments	
	Maintenance	Power	School of Education	School of Technology
Costs before allocation	$99,000	$54,000		
Allocation of maintenance $(\frac{2}{10},\frac{3}{10},\frac{5}{10})$	(99,000) $\underline{0}$	19,800	$29,700	$49,500
Allocation of power $(\frac{2}{9},\frac{7}{9})$		(73,800) $\underline{0}$	16,400 $\underline{\$46,100}$	57,400 $\underline{\$106,900}$

Therefore, $46,100 of May 2008 support department costs are allocated to the School of Education.

G.   Process Costing

20.   (b)   Equivalent units of production are calculated as follows:

Completed units	400
Plus: Equivalent units in ending inventory (200 × 75%)	150
Less: Equivalent units in beginning inventory (100 × 50%)	(50)
Equivalent units of production	500

21.   (d)   Material costs in ending work in process inventory is calculated as $216,000 = 150 (equivalent units in ending inventory) × $1,440 ($720,000/500) per equivalent unit. Equivalent units of production are calculated as: 500 = 400 completed units + 150 (200 × 75%) equivalent units in ending inventory – 50 (100 × 50%) equivalent units in beginning inventory.

22.   (d)   The application of factory overhead would increase the work in process inventory control account. In addition, the work in process account would be increased for other product costs (direct manufacturing labor and direct material). Only costs of completed products increase finished goods inventory control. Factory overhead control is increased by actual factory overhead costs incurred. Cost of goods sold is increased by the product costs of the finished units sold.

23.   (d)   The requirement is to determine the cost per equivalent unit for materials using the weighted-average method. Under the weighted-average method, equivalent units of production and cost per unit are based on **all** work (this period's and last period's) done on units completed plus all work done to date on the units in ending work in process. Since materials are added at the beginning of the production process, both the units completed and the ending work in process are 100% complete with respect to materials. The cost per equivalent unit can be computed as follows:

Units completed	42,500
Ending WIP	12,500
Total equivalent units	55,000
Cost of materials:	
Beginning WIP	$ 5,500
Units started	18,000
Total costs incurred	$23,500
Divide by EUP	÷ 55,000
Cost per equivalent unit	$ .43

24. **(c)** The requirement is to calculate the amount of conversion cost transferred by Forming to the next production department. First, the physical flow of units must be determined.

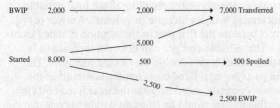

Next, equivalent units of production (EUP) must be calculated, in this case using the weighted-average (WA) method. The WA computations of EUP and cost per equivalent unit include both work done **last** period on the current period's BWIP and all work done in the current period on units completed and on EWIP. Forming's EWIP is 80% complete.

Spoiled units must be accounted for separately because Forming adds their cost only to the cost of units transferred. To ignore spoiled units would result in the same total cost being allocated to 500 fewer units, thus spreading spoilage costs over all work done during the period, including EWIP.

	Total units	Equivalent units
Started and completed	7,000	7,000
Spoilage—normal	500	500
EWIP (80% complete)	2,500	2,000*
	10,000	9,500

*2,500 units x 80% completion

Since conversion costs total $85,500 for the period ($10,000 for BWIP + $75,500 for units started), Forming's conversion cost per equivalent unit is $9.00 ($85,500 ÷ 9,500 EUP). These costs are assigned as follows:

Good units completed (7,000 × $9)	$63,000
Spoiled units (500 × $9)	4,500
Conversion cost transferred	$67,500
EWIP (2,000 × $9)	18,000
Total costs accounted for	$85,500

Therefore, $67,500 was transferred to the second department.

25. **(a)** The FIFO method determines equivalent units of production (EUP) based on the work done in the current period only. The work done in the current period can be dichotomized as: (1) the work necessary to complete beginning work in process (BWIP), and (2) the work performed on the units started in the current period.

26. **(a)** Conversion costs consist of direct manufacturing labor and factory overhead. Because the EWIP units are 50% in process 2, some conversion costs have been incurred. These units would be included in the computation of equivalent units for conversion costs. However, because material G is added only when a batch is 60% complete, this material has not yet been added to this batch. These units would not be included in the computation of equivalent units for material G.

27. **(d)** The requirement is to compare the number of equivalent units of production (EUP) computed using the weighted-average method to the EUP computed using the FIFO method for two months. The weighted-average method determines EUP based on the work done on the units in all periods, while the FIFO method uses only the work done in the current period. Because the system began in January, there was no beginning inventory for the first

month of the comparison. Both methods would compute the same number of EUP for January because the only work done on these units was done in the period under consideration. Because there was ending inventory in January, however, February would have a beginning inventory. The weighted-average method would therefore compute a greater number of EUP than FIFO for February because it would include the work done in January while FIFO would not.

28. **(a)** The requirement is to determine the proper allocation of **normal** defective unit costs to the ending work in process. **Normal** defective unit costs are spread over the units of **good** output because the attaining of good units necessitates the appearance of normal spoiled units. The cost of the normal defective units is included in the total costs of the **good** equivalent units of output. Ending inventory comprised one-half of the total units of good output produced during the year; therefore, it will bear 50% of the normal defective unit costs incurred during the year.

29. **(d)** Normal spoilage is the cost of spoiled units which results due to the nature of the manufacturing process. Normal spoilage may be unavoidable under efficient operating conditions and is thus a necessary cost in the production process. Since it is treated as a product cost, the $60,000 normal spoilage should be inventoried. Conversely, units become abnormally spoiled as a result of some unnecessary act, event, or condition. Therefore, the $30,000 abnormal spoilage is treated as a period cost.

30. **(b)** The requirement is to calculate the equivalent units of production for materials using the FIFO method. Equivalent units of production are calculated as follows:

Completed units	92,000
Plus: Equivalent units in ending inventory	
(24,000 × 90%)	21,600
Less: Equivalent units in beginning inventory	
(16,000 × 60%)	(9,600)
Equivalent units of production	104,000

31. **(d)** The requirement is to calculate the equivalent units of production for conversion costs using the FIFO method. Equivalent units of production are calculated as follows:

Completed units	92,000
Plus: Equivalent units in ending inventory	
(24,000 × 40%)	9,600
Less: Equivalent units in beginning inventory	
(16,000 × 20%)	(3,200)
Equivalent units of production	98,400

32. **(b)** The requirement is to calculate the equivalent unit cost of materials using the FIFO method. The amount is determined by dividing the cost of materials used during the month by the number of equivalent units of production, which is equal to $4.50 ($468,000 ÷ 104,000).

33. **(b)** The requirement is to calculate the equivalent unit cost of conversion using the FIFO method. The amount is determined by dividing the conversion costs incurred during the month by the number of equivalent units of production, which is equal to $5.83 [($182,880 + $391,160) ÷ 98,400].

34. **(a)** The requirement is to calculate the cost of units in ending work in process inventory using the FIFO method. The amount is determined as follows:

Ending WIP:

Material costs (24,000 units × 90%) × $4.50	$ 97,200
Conversion costs (24,000 units × 40%) × $5.83	55,968
Total	$153,168

35. (c)   The requirement is to calculate the equivalent unit cost of materials for the month using the weighted-average method. This amount is calculated as follows:

Units completed	92,000
Ending WIP (24,000 × 90%)	21,600
Total equivalent units	113,600
Cost of materials:	
Beginning WIP	$ 54,560
Units started	468,000
Total costs incurred	$522,560
Divide by EUP	÷ 113,600
Costs per equivalent unit	$4.60

36. (c)   The requirement is to calculate the equivalent unit conversion cost for the month using the weighted-average method. This amount is calculated as follows:

Units completed	92,000
Ending WIP (24,000 × 40%)	9,600
Total equivalent units	101,600
Conversion costs:	
Beginning WIP	$ 35,560
Units started	574,040
Total costs incurred	$609,600
Divide by EUP	÷ 101,600
Costs per equivalent unit	$6.00

37. (d)   The requirement is to calculate the total cost of the units in the ending work in process inventory using the weighted-average method. The amount is calculated as follows:

Ending WIP

Material costs (24,000 units × 90%) × $4.60	$ 99,360
Conversion costs (24,000 units × 40%) × $6.00	57,600
Total	$156,960

J. Activity-Based Costing

38. (b)   The requirement is to indicate the reasonable basis for allocating costs. Answer (b) is correct because there is a direct causal relationship between the number of components in a finished product and the amount of material handling costs incurred. Answer (a) is incorrect because this allocation basis is related to "batch" costs and not to individual unit costs. Answer (c) is incorrect because this allocation basis is the traditional basis for allocating overhead costs to the units produced when the production process is labor-intensive. Answer (d) is incorrect because this is not an allocation basis but rather the result of the allocation process when determining production costs.

39. (c)   The requirement is to identify the valid cost relationship. Answer (c) is correct because both parts of the solution are stated correctly. Within the relevant range for the application activity base, the variable cost per unit and the total fixed cost would be constant. Answer (a) is incorrect because the second part of the solution is stated incorrectly. The fixed cost per unit of activity would decrease (cost is spread over more units), but total fixed cost in the flexible budget would be constant within the relevant range for the application activity base. The first part of the solution (variable cost per unit is constant) is correctly stated resulting in the total variable cost increasing with an increase in volume. Answer (b) is incorrect because the second part of the solution is stated incorrectly. The fixed cost

per unit of activity would decrease (cost is spread over more units), but total fixed costs in the flexible budget would be constant within the relevant range for the application activity base. The first part of the solution (variable cost per unit is constant) is correctly stated resulting in the total variable cost increasing with an increase in volume. Answer (d) is incorrect because the first part of the solution is stated incorrectly. The variable cost per unit does not increase (it is constant); rather, total variable cost would increase. The second part (the total fixed costs remain constant) of the solution is correctly stated because the total fixed costs in the flexible budget would be constant within the relevant range for the application activity base.

40. (d)   The purpose of the just-in-time (JIT) production system is to decrease the size of production runs (and therefore inventory levels) by decreasing setup costs. Lot **sizes** would decrease as the **number** of lots processed during the year increases. Since inventory levels would decrease with JIT, relevant costs would also drop (i.e., capital invested in inventory could be invested in other assets—a cost savings). The **fixed** facility and administrative costs are irrelevant as fixed costs would remain the same regardless of changes for JIT. The unit costs will increase because fixed costs will be spread over fewer inventory units produced from JIT's eliminating effect on excess inventory production.

41. (d)   An activity-based costing system allocates costs to products by determining which activities being performed by the entity are driving the costs. An activity-based costing approach differs from traditional costing methods that accumulate costs by department or function. Activity-based costing accumulates and allocates costs by the specific activities being performed. Since most entities perform a variety of activities, the number of cost pools and allocation bases greatly increases under activity-based costing.

42. (d)   Activity-based costing can be used in conjunction with either process or job costing. Answer (a) is incorrect because activity-based costing can be used in conjunction with either process or job costing. Answer (b) is incorrect because activity-based costing can be used in conjunction with job costing. Answer (c) is incorrect because activity-based costing can be used in conjunction with process costing.

43. (b)   In an activity-based costing (ABC) system, the activities which drive the manufacturing department's overhead costs would be analyzed. Overhead would then be allocated to products based on the resources consumed in their production. The effect of producing different products in different lot sizes is that some products incur more setup costs than others; products produced in small batches must be produced more often, and thus require more setups to achieve a given level of output. Therefore, setup costs bear a cause and effect relationship with and should be assigned to each production **batch** (and then spread over the units in the batch). However, setups are not the only activities driving overhead costs. Other overhead cost drivers identifiable in production systems may include materials handling, engineering changes to products, and rework costs. Therefore, manufacturing overhead should be assigned to products based on **multiple** cause and effect relationships [answer (b) is correct and answer (a) is incorrect]. Answers (c) and (d) are incorrect because allocation via these methods would wholly defeat the purpose of ABC, which is founded upon cause and effect allocation of costs to products.

44. (c) Activity-based costing (ABC) involves the allocation of overhead costs to products based on the cost driver that actually **caused** those costs to be incurred. In contrast to traditional costing methods which accumulate costs by department or function, ABC accumulates costs by the specific activity being performed. For example, costs related to the purchase of materials may be allocated according to the number of purchase transactions which occurred. Therefore, cost drivers comprise a necessary part of any ABC system. On the other hand, non-value-added activities represent expenditures for which no value is added to the product. Hence, costs can be reduced by eliminating non-value-added activities without affecting the salability of the product.

45. (d) Activity-based costing focuses on incorporating into product costs only those activities that provide value to the product. Design engineering is a fundamental activity needed to design a good product. Heat treatment activities would strengthen and protect the product being produced. A drill press activity alters the physical product as it moves on toward becoming a finished good. Raw materials storage activity does nothing to alter or improve the value of a product. It is a non-value-adding activity.

46. (a) Under a traditional costing system, setup costs are allocated using a cost driver, in this case, direct manufacturing labor hours. The first step is to calculate the setup costs per direct manufacturing labor hour ($60,000 incurred ÷ 25,000 total DMLH) of $2.40. Since two DMLH are needed to produce one unit of product A, the total setup cost per unit of A is ($2.40 × 2 DMLH) $4.80. Under ABC, one **batch** of product A creates the demand for setup activities that produce value. The setup cost per unit of A under ABC is calculated as the setup cost **per batch** of A ($1,000) divided by the number of units per batch (100), or, $10.00.

K. Joint Products

47. (c) The requirement is to determine how to allocate joint cost using the net realizable value (NRV) method when a by-product is involved. NRV is the predicted selling price in the ordinary course of business less reasonably predictable costs of completion and disposal. The joint cost of $54,000 is reduced by the NRV of the by-product ($4,000) to get the allocable joint cost ($50,000). The computation is

	Sales value at split-off	Weighting	Joint costs allocated
Kul	$40,000	40,000/75,000 × 50,000	$26,667
Wu	35,000	35,000/75,000 × 50,000	23,333
	$75,000		$50,000

Therefore, $26,667 of the joint cost should be allocated to product Kul.

48. (d) When using the relative sales value at split-off method for joint products, joint costs are allocated based on the ratio of each product's sales value at split-off to total sales value at split-off for all joint products. If the market value at split-off (sales value) of joint product P increases, then a larger proportion of the total joint costs will be allocated to that product. Because all other costs and selling prices remain unchanged, the gross margin of product P will, therefore, decrease. Product Q's gross margin will, however, increase because a smaller proportion of the total joint costs will be allocated to it.

49. (c) Joint costs may be allocated to joint products based on either sales price or some physical measure. Methods which use estimated sales price include relative sales value at split-off, estimated net realizable value (NRV), and constant gross margin percentage NRV. Under the sales value at split-off method, joint costs are allocated based on the ratio of each product's sales value at split-off to total sales value at split-off for all joint products. The estimated NRV method allocates joint costs at the split-off point based on net sales value (Estimated sales value of the joint products – Separable processing costs). Under the constant gross margin percentage NRV method, the overall gross margin (GM) percentage for all joint products combined (after deducting both joint and separable costs) is used to determine the GM for each joint product. This GM is deducted from the sales price of each joint product to determine total costs, and separable costs are then deducted from total costs to determine the joint cost allocation. However, this is not the same as answer (d), which uses a predetermined profit margin and ignores actual costs. The constant GM percentage NRV method does not use a preset GM, it uses the actual overall GM and spreads it uniformly among products so that all joint products yield the same GM percentage. The sales price cannot be based solely on costs. Conversely, costs must be based on sales price (or some physical measure) because joint costs can only be allocated arbitrarily.

L. By-Products

50. (d) The requirement is to find the cost of sales for both gasoline and the gasoline by-product. The value of the by-products may be recognized at two points in time: (1) at the time of production, or (2) at the time of sale. Under the production method (as given in the problem), the net realizable value of the by-products **produced** is deducted from the cost of the major products **produced**. The net realizable value of the by-product is as follows:

Sales value of by-product	$30,000	
Less: separable costs	25,000	(10,000 + 15,000)
	$ 5,000	

Therefore, cost of sales for gasoline is calculated as follows:

Total production (joint) costs	$120,000
Less: net realizable value of by-product	5,000
Net Production Cost	115,000
Less: costs in 12/31/08 inventory	15,000
	$100,000

Therefore, total cost of gasoline sales is $100,000, and no cost of sales is reported for the by-product.

51. (a) Because the inventory of by-product Moy was recorded at its net realizable value of $20,000 [($6 – $2) × 5,000] when produced in 2007, no profit will be recognized in 2008. When the units of Moy were sold in 2008, the proceeds equaled the inventory cost plus disposal costs, resulting in $0 profit for 2008. The following journal entries help to illustrate the situation:

2007	Main product(s) inventory	xxxx	
	By-product inventory	20,000	
	Work in process control		xxxx
2008	Cash or accounts receivable	30,000	
	Inventory		20,000
	Selling expenses		10,000

52.　(b)　The difference between treating the product named "May" as a joint product versus a by-product would be that under by-product treatment, the selling cost is netted against May's selling price thus reducing gross margin whereas under joint-product accounting, the selling cost would be deducting below the gross margin line as a selling expense. Thus, if the change to joint-product accounting were made, gross margin would increase.

53.　(a)　The value of the by-products may be recognized at two points in time: (1) at the time of production, or (2) at the time of sale. Under the production method, the net realizable value of the by-products **produced** is deducted from the cost of the major products **produced**. Under the sale method, net revenue from by-products **sold** (gross revenue from by-product sales minus separable costs incurred) is deducted from the cost of the major products **sold**.

M. Estimating Cost Functions

54.　(a)　The requirement is to determine the variable component of order filling cost per order. The high-low method of analysis should be used to separate the mixed cost into its fixed and variable components. The formula used in developing the variable rate is

$$\frac{\text{Cost at high point} - \text{Cost at low point}}{\text{High activity point} - \text{Low activity point}} = \text{Variable rate}$$

In this problem, order filling costs are given at four levels of activity because the number of orders was different in each month. Substituting the highest and lowest cost ($4,320 and $3,120) and activity (1,800 and 1,200) figures into the formula yields the variable cost of order filling per order.

$$\frac{\$4,320 - \$3,120}{1,800 - 1,200} = \$2.00/\text{order}$$

55.　(c)　The graph depicts Sender's fixed and variable parcel mailing costs. Fixed costs total $15,000, since this amount of cost is incurred even when zero parcels are mailed. Variable costs at a mailing volume of 20,000 parcels is $60,000 ($75,000 total cost – $15,000 fixed cost), resulting in a per unit variable cost of $3.00 ($60,000 VC / 20,000 units). Therefore, Sender's estimated cost of mailing 12,000 parcels is $51,000 [$15,000 FC + ($3 VC × 12,000 units)].

56.　(d)　Regression analysis determines the functional relationship between variables and provides a measure of probable error. Multiple regression analysis involves the use of two or more independent variables (such as the number of shipments and the weight of materials handled) to predict one dependent variable (inventory warehouse costs). Economic order quantity analysis determines the amount to be ordered while minimizing the sum of ordering and carrying costs. Probability analysis is an application of statistical decision theory that, under conditions of uncertainty, leads to more reliable decisions. Correlation analysis determines the relationship between only two variables.

57.　(a)　The determination that needs to be made is which of the cost drivers would be the best predictor of overhead costs (machine hours or direct materials weight). The information given regarding the coefficient of determination (R^2) measures the correlation between the cost driver and overhead costs. The higher the R^2, the better the correlation. Therefore, machine hours would be the more accurate cost driver.

PLANNING, CONTROL, AND ANALYSIS

This module discusses a number of tools used internally for financial planning, control, and analysis. Before beginning the module you should review the following key terms.

Cost-Volume-Profit Analysis

1. **Cost-volume-profit (CVP) analysis** is a planning tool used to analyze the effects of changes in volume, sales mix, selling price, variable expense, fixed expense, and profit.
2. **Fixed costs** do not vary with the level of activity within the relevant range for a given period of time (usually one year), for example, plant depreciation.
3. **Variable costs** vary proportionately **in total** with the activity level throughout the relevant range (e.g., direct materials).
4. **Mixed costs (semivariable)** are costs that have a fixed component and a variable component. These components are separated by using the scattergraph, high-low, or linear regression methods.
5. **Relevant range** is the operating range of activity in which cost behavior patterns are valid (A to B in the preceding illustration). Thus, it is the production range for which fixed costs remain constant (e.g., if production doubles, and additional shift of salaried foremen would be added and fixed costs would increase).

Variable (Direct) vs. Absorption Costing

6. **Variable (direct) costing** considers all fixed manufacturing overhead as a period cost rather than as a product cost. Conversely, **absorption (full) costing** considers fixed manufacturing overhead to be product cost. The treatment of fixed manufacturing cost as a period cost rather than as a product cost is the only difference between variable costing and absorption costing. All other costs (i.e., variable manufacturing, fixed selling, and variable selling) are treated the same under both systems. Variable costing is not acceptable for external reporting per GAAP.

Financial Planning and Forecasting

7. **Planning** is selecting goals and choosing methods to attain those goals. **Control** is the implementation of the plans and evaluation of their effectiveness in attaining goals.
8. **Financial planning models** support the financial planning process by making it easier to construct projected financial scenarios. These models incorporate the interrelationships among operating activities, financial activities, and other factors that affect the business, and range from simple models to those that incorporate hundreds of equations.
9. **Tactical profit plan** is a defined short-term financial plan that includes assigned responsibilities at all levels.
10. **Cost management** refers to the approaches and activities used by management to make planning and control decisions for the firm.
11. **Multiple regression** is a model that estimates the relationship between a dependent variable and two or more independent variables. It is used to develop sales forecasts.

Budgeting and Responsibility Accounting

12. A **budget** is a quantification of the plan for operations. A **flexible budget** is a budget that is adjusted for changes in volume. **Performance reports** compare budgeted and actual performance.
13. A **master budget** is a comprehensive expression of management's operating and financial plans for a future period that is summarized as budgeted financial statements. It consists of the operating and financial budgets.
14. An **operating budget** is the budgeted income statement and related schedules.
15. A **financial budget** is the cash budget, the capital budget, the budgeted balance sheet, and the budgeted statement of cash flows.
16. **Life-cycle budgeting** involves estimating the revenues and costs attributable to each product from initial R&D to its final customer and support.
17. **Budgetary slack** is the practice of underestimating revenues and overestimating expenses to make budgeted targets more easily achievable.

18. **Activity-based budgeting** is a budgeting approach that focuses on the cost of activities required to produce and sell products. It is an extension of activity-based costing.

19. **Zero-based budgeting** involves developing budgets from the ground up by requiring each program or department to justify its level of funding. It is an alternative to **incremental budgeting** which requires only justification for increases in the funding over the prior period.

20. **Responsibility accounting** measures subunit performance based on the costs and/or revenues assigned to responsibility centers.

21. **Controllable costs** can be affected by a manager during the current period (e.g., amount of direct manufacturing labor per unit of production is usually under the control of a production supervisor). Uncontrollable costs are those that cannot be affected by the individual in question (e.g., depreciation is not usually controllable by the production supervisor).

22. **Contribution margin** equals revenue less **all** variable costs.

Product and Service Pricing and Transfer Pricing

23. **Target costing** identifies the estimated cost of a new product that must be achieved for that product to be priced competitively and still produce an acceptable profit. Often the product is redesigned and the production process simplified several times before the target cost can be met.

24. **Transfer pricing** is the determination of the price at which goods and services will be "sold" to profit or investment centers via internal company transfers.

Standards and Variances

25. **Standard costs** are predetermined target costs. **Variances** are differences between standards and actual results.

26. **Benchmarking** requires that products, services, and activities be continually measured against the best levels of performance either inside or outside the organization.

27. **Management by exception** focuses attention on material deviations from plans (e.g., variances in a performance report) while allowing areas operating as expected to continue to operate without interference.

Short-Term Differential Cost Analysis

28. **Sunk, past, or unavoidable costs** are committed costs which are not avoidable and are therefore irrelevant to the decision process.

29. **Avoidable costs** are costs that will **not** continue to be incurred if a department or product is terminated.

30. **Committed costs** arise from a company's basic commitment to open its doors and engage in business (depreciation, property taxes, management salaries).

31. **Discretionary costs** are fixed costs whose level is set by current management decisions (e.g., advertising, research, and development).

32. **Relevant costs** are future costs that will change as a result of a specific decision.

33. **Differential (incremental) cost** is the difference in cost between two alternatives.

34. **Opportunity cost** is the maximum income or savings (benefit) foregone by rejecting an alternative.

35. **Outlay (out-of-pocket) costs** is the cash disbursement associated with a specific project.

A. Cost-Volume-Profit (CVP) Analysis

1. Overview

Cost-volume-profit (CVP) analysis provides management with profitability estimates at all levels of production in the relevant range (the normal operating range). CVP (or breakeven) analysis is based on the firm's profit function. Profit is a function of sales, variable costs, and fixed costs.

$$\text{Profit (NI)} = \text{Sales (S)} - \text{Fixed Costs (FC)} - \text{Variable Costs (VC)}$$
$$\text{When profit is zero} \quad 0 = S - FC - VC$$
$$S = FC + VC$$

Fixed costs are constant in the relevant range, but both sales and variable costs are a function of the level of activity, and vary with respect to a single, output-related driver (e.g., units manufactured or sold). For example, if widgets are sold at $2.00/unit, variable costs are $.40/unit, and fixed costs are $20,000, breakeven is 12,500 units.

$$X = \text{Units of production and sales to breakeven}$$
$$\$2.00X = \$.40X + \$20,000$$
$$\$1.60X = \$20,000$$
$$X = 12,500 \text{ units (breakeven point)}$$

The cost-volume-profit relationship is diagrammed below.

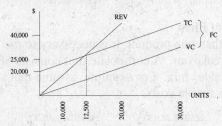

The breakeven point can be thought of as the amount of contribution margin (sales minus variable costs) required to cover the fixed costs, or the point of zero profit. In the previous example, the unit contribution margin (CM) is $1.60 ($2.00 – $.40). Thus, sales of 12,500 units are required to cover the $20,000 of fixed costs. This illustrates the possibility of two shortcut approaches.

Shortcut 1

$$\text{Units to break even} = \frac{\text{Fixed costs}}{\text{Unit CM}} = \frac{\$20,000}{\$1.60} = 12,500 \text{ units}$$

Shortcut 2

$$\begin{array}{c}\text{Dollars to}\\\text{break even}\end{array} = \frac{\text{Fixed costs}}{\begin{array}{c}\text{CM percentage}\\\text{(ratio)}\end{array}} = \frac{\text{Fixed costs}}{\dfrac{\text{CM per unit}}{\begin{array}{c}\text{Selling price}\\\text{per unit}\end{array}}} = \frac{\$20,000}{\dfrac{\$1.60}{\$2.00}} = \frac{\$20,000}{80\%} = \$25,000 \text{ sales dollars}$$

A number of variations on the basic CVP calculation are found on the CPA exam. These are illustrated in the following paragraphs:

a. **Target net income.** Selling price is $2, variable cost per unit is $.40, fixed costs are $20,000, and desired net income is $5,000. What is the level of sales in units?

| Equation $\longrightarrow$ | Sales = VC + FC + NI |
| | $2X = $.4X + $20,000 + $5,000 |

Shortcut $\longrightarrow$ $\dfrac{FC + NI}{CM} = \dfrac{\$20,000 + \$5,000}{\$1.60}$

Solution $\longrightarrow$ 15,625 units

b. **Target net income-percentage of sales.** Same facts, except desired net income is 30% of sales. What is the level of sales in units?

Equation $\longrightarrow$ Sales = VC + FC + NI
$2X = $.4X + $20,000 + .30($2X)

Solution $\longrightarrow$ 20,000 units

c. **No per-unit information given.** Fixed costs are $20,000, and variable expenses are 20% of sales. What is the breakeven level of sales in dollars?

Equation $\longrightarrow$ Sales = VC + FC
S = .2(S) + $20,000

Shortcut $\longrightarrow$ $\dfrac{FC}{CM\%} = \dfrac{20,000}{80\%}$

Solution $\longrightarrow$ $25,000 sales dollars

d. **Decision making.** Selling price is $2, variable cost per unit is $.40, and fixed costs are $20,000. Purchasing a new machine will increase fixed costs by $5,000, but variable costs will be cut by 20%. If the selling price is cut by 10%, what is the breakeven point in units?

Equation ⟶   Sales = VC + FC
                   $1.8X = $.32X + $25,000

Shortcut ⟶ $\dfrac{FC}{CM} = \dfrac{\$25,000}{\$1.48}$

Solution ⟶   16,892 units

2. Breakeven: Multiproduct Firm

If a firm makes more than one product, it is necessary to use composite units to find the number of units of each product to breakeven. A composite unit consists of the proportionate number of units which make up the firm's sales mix. For example, assume that a firm has two products with the following selling prices and variable costs.

Product	Selling price	Variable costs	Contribution margin
A	$.60	$.20	$.40
B	$.40	$.15	$.25

Also assume that the sales mix consists of 3 units of A for every 2 units of B (3:2) and fixed costs are $34,000.

The **first** step is to find the composite contribution margin.

Composite contribution margin = 3($.40) + 2($.25) = $1.70

Next compute the number of composite units to breakeven.

$$\dfrac{\$34,000 \text{ fixed costs}}{\$1.70 \text{ composite contribution margin}} = 20,000 \text{ composite units}$$

Finally, determine the number of units of A and B at the breakeven point by multiplying the composite units by the number of units of A (i.e., 3) and the number of units of B (i.e., 2) in the mix.

A: 20,000 × 3 = 60,000 units
B: 20,000 × 2 = 40,000 units

3. Assumptions of CVP Analysis

When applying CVP to a specific case and in interpreting the results therefrom, it is important to keep in mind the assumptions underlying CVP which are listed below.

a. Selling price does not change with the activity level
b. The sales mix remains constant
c. Costs can be separated into fixed and variable elements
d. Variable costs per unit are constant
e. Total fixed costs are constant over the relevant range
f. Productivity and efficiency are constant
g. Units produced = Units sold

B. Variable (Direct) and Absorption (Full) Costing

Variable (direct) costing is a form of inventory costing. Variable costing considers fixed manufacturing costs as period rather than product costs. It is advocated because, for internal reporting, it presents a clear picture of performance when there is a significant change in inventory. However, remember that variable costing is not acceptable as GAAP for external reporting.

Variable and absorption costing methods of accounting for fixed manufacturing overhead differ: under variable costing, fixed manufacturing overhead is expensed whereas under absorption costing, such amounts are treated as a product cost and inventoried. The treatment of fixed manufacturing overhead often results in different levels of net income between the absorption and variable costing methods. The differences are timing differences, which result from recognizing the fixed manufacturing overhead as an expense.

1. In the period incurred—variable costing
2. In the period in which the units to which fixed overhead has been applied are sold—absorption costing

The relationship between variable costing (VC) income and absorption costing (AC) income follows:

Sales = Production (no change in inventory)   No difference in income
Sales > Production (inventory decreases)   VC income greater than AC income
Sales < Production (inventory increases)   VC income less than AC income

EXAMPLE: Production begins in period A with 5,000 units. Fixed manufacturing costs equal $5,000 and variable manufacturing costs are $1/unit. Sales were 4,000 units at $3/unit. In period B, units produced and production costs were the same as in period A. Sales were 6,000 units at $3/unit.

	Variable costing		Absorption costing	
	Period A	Period B	Period A	Period B
Sales	$12,000	$18,000	$12,000	$18,000
Less costs	9,000	11,000	8,000	12,000
Profit	$ 3,000	$ 7,000	$ 4,000	$ 6,000

*With absorption costing, $1 of fixed manufacturing overhead is attached to each unit produced ($5,000 ÷ 5,000 units). Notice that both variable and absorption costing recognized $10,000 profit in periods A + B. Variable costing income in period A was less than absorption income, because production exceeded sales which resulted in $1,000 of fixed costs being **inventoried** under AC that were **expensed** under VC.*

	Fixed costs expensed		Variable costs expensed		Total costs expensed	
	Period A	Period B	Period A	Period B	Period A	Period B
Variable	$5,000*	$5,000*	$4,000	$6,000	$9,000	$11,000
Absorption	4,000**	6,000**	4,000	6,000	8,000	12,000

* The same every period.
** $1 per unit x number of units sold.

The yearly income difference between the two methods can normally be reconciled as follows:

Change in inventory units × Fixed overhead per unit (e.g., 1,000 units × $1)

If the example above included either variable or fixed selling costs, they would be handled the same under either method—deducted in total on the income statement in the period in which they were incurred.

Note that the format of the income statement changes under variable costing to reflect the alternate treatment given to the fixed manufacturing costs and to emphasize the contribution margin. The recommended format under variable costing follows:

    Sales
    –   <u>Variable manufacturing costs</u>
    =   Manufacturing contribution margin
    –   <u>Variable selling and administrative expenses</u>
    =   Contribution margin
    –   <u>Fixed manufacturing, selling, and administrative expenses</u>
    =   <u>Net income</u>

C. Financial Planning

1. Financial planning is the process of

   a. Analyzing the investment and financing alternatives available to a firm
   b. Forecasting the future consequences of the alternatives
   c. Deciding which alternatives to undertake
   d. Measuring subsequent performance against established goals

2. Financial planning must be tied to the strategic plans of top management. Good financial planning can help managers ensure that their financing strategies are consistent with their capital budgets. It also highlights the investing and financing decisions necessary to support management's strategic plans.

3. Management often uses a **financial planning model** to help assess the consequences of alternative operating and financial strategies. Such models range from those that are fairly simple to those that incorporate hundreds of variables and equations, using specialized software. The input to the models generally consists of current financial statements and expectations about future conditions.

4. In developing the financial plan, management generally will prepare a series of pro forma financial statements, one of which will represent the forecast. The forecast depicts the firm's most-likely future financial results. However, effective financial planning generally requires the development of a series of possible scenarios to allow management to plan for various contingencies. Sensitivity analysis may be used with the model to explore the effects of changes in significant variables on the firm's performance. In addition, financial planning can be used to explore the implications of the various decision alternatives.

Financial Planning Model

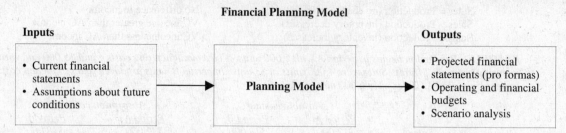

As shown in the exhibit above, the outputs of the financial planning process are pro forma financial statements, operating and financial budgets for the firm, and scenario analysis that explores other possible outcomes.

D. Budgeting

1. To be most effective, the firm's budget should be an integral part of the strategic plan. It must reflect management's objectives and plans. A **master budget** summarizes the results of all of the firm's individual budgets into a set of projected financial statements and schedules. Specifically the master budget summarizes the results of the following two major budgets:

   a. **The operating budget**—The budgeted income statement and supporting schedules.
   b. **The financial budget**—The capital budget, cash budget, and the budgeted balance sheet and statement of cash flows.

2. Budgets are prepared for some set period of time, usually one year. However, some budgets must be broken down into shorter time frames. For example, a cash budget is usually prepared monthly to allow management to plan for the firm's cash needs. Many firms use **rolling budgets** which are continually updated as time passes. As an example, a 12-month rolling budget adds a future month and drops the current month as it ends.

3. Budgets may be constructed in a number of ways.

   a. Top-down mandated approach—Upper-level management establishes the budget parameters and it is passed down through the organization to each operating unit.

      (1) Advantages include quick preparation time and clear communication of management's objectives.
      (2) Disadvantage is that lower-level management and employees may view it to be dictatorial and not fully embrace and accept the budget.

   b. Participative (bottom-up) is driven by involving lower-level management and employees.

      (1) Advantages are that employees may more readily accept the budget, morale may be improved, and budget input is provided by a larger number of individuals.
      (2) Disadvantages are that the process is time-consuming, and managers may try to pad their budgets.

   c. Many budgets are prepared using a blended approach that combines aspects of the top-down and bottom-up methods.

4. A budget displays a plan of action for future operations. The most important functions of a budget are to coordinate the various functional activities of the firm and to provide a basis for control of the activities. Budgets may be prepared for all elements of the value chain, which includes R&D, design, production, marketing, distribution, customer service, and administration. The budgets process begins with an estimate of sales and then proceeds systematically as outlined below.

   a. Develop a sales forecast
   b. Develop a production schedule to calculate production costs and costs of goods sold
   c. Estimate other expenses and revenues
   d. Complete the pro forma financial statements and budgets

   Pictorially, this process is shown below.

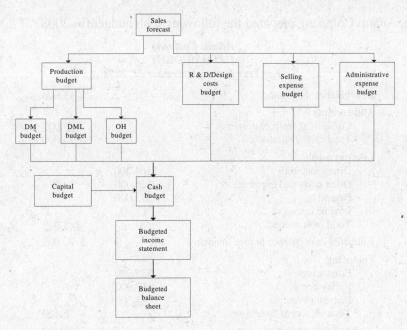

5. The basic formats of some of the key budgets are presented below.

Production budget		*DM budget*
Budgeted sales		Production needs
+ Desired end. FG inventory	× DM	+ Desired end. DM inventory
Total needs	per	Total needs
− Beg. FG inventory	unit	− Beg. DM inventory
Units to be produced		DM to be purchased (units)
		× Price per unit
		DM purchases in dollars

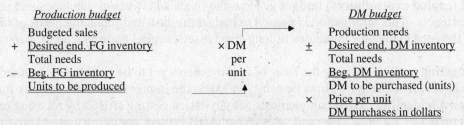

Note that before proceeding to the cash budget, DM purchases would have to be converted to **payments** for DM purchases, based on some payment schedule (e.g., 70% in month of purchase, 30% in month following). On the CPA exam you may be given questions that require you to calculate cash inflows from sales or cash outflows for expenses.

> *EXAMPLE: Assume that a firm sells all of its products on credit and collects 40% of the receivables in the month of sale, 50% in the following month, and 9% in the month after that. If the firm had the following monthly sales, how much is the estimated collections in June?*
>
> | *January* | *February* | *March* | *April* | *May* | *June* |
> |---|---|---|---|---|---|
> | *$20,000* | *$25,000* | *$30,000* | *$10,000* | *$20,000* | *$30,000* |
>
> *June's collections would consist of 40% of June's sales, 50% of May's sales, and 9% of April's sales. Therefore, June's collections would be estimated to be $22,900 [($30,000 × 40%) + ($20,000 × 50%) + ($10,000 × 9%)].*

6. Remember it is cash collections and cash payments that go into the cash budget, as shown below. Also remember that depreciation is not a cash expense.

> *Cash budget*
> Beginning cash balance
> + Receipts (collections from customers, etc.)
> Cash available
> − Payments (materials, expenses, payroll, etc.)
> Estimated cash balance before financing
> +/− Financing (planned borrowing or short-term investing to bring cash to desired balance)
> = Ending cash balance

To illustrate, Adams Company prepared the following cash budget for 2008.

Adams Company
CASH BUDGET
For Year Ending December 31, 2008

Cash balance, beginning		$ 15,000
Add receipts		
Collections from customers		723,000
Total cash available		$738,000
Less payments		
Direct materials	$184,000	
Other costs and expenses	126,000	
Payroll	395,000	
Income taxes	13,000	
Total cash needed		718,000
Estimated cash balance before financing		$ 20,000
Financing		
Borrowings	$25,000	
Repayments	(17,000)	
Interest payments	(1,600)	
Total effects of financing		6,400
Cash balance, ending		$ 26,400

7. The **capital (capital expenditures) budget** displays the financial effects of purchases and retirements of long-lived assets. This information is needed to budget the cash and financing needs of the firm. Because of the need to plan for purchases of long-lived assets, capital budgets tend to span several years.

8. **Kaizen budgeting** projects costs on the basis of improvements yet to be implemented rather than upon current conditions. The budget will not be achieved unless the improvements are actually made.

9. **Activity-based budgeting (ABB)** complements activity-based costing (ABC) by focusing on the costs of activities necessary for production and sales. When ABB is used, operating budgets are formulated for each activity in the activity management system. An activity-based budget is developed by multiplying the budgeted level of the cost driver for each activity by the budgeted cost rate and summing the costs by functional or spending categories. ABB budgeting estimates the costs of performing various activities, in contrast to traditional budgeting which directly budgets costs for functional or spending categories. Management is provided with more insight into what causes costs and is in a much better position to control them.

10. **Developing an Operating Budget—An Example**

    This example is designed to provide an overview of the process of developing an operating budget. On the CPA exam, you can expect multiple-choice questions that will deal with particular aspects of the process. As an example, you might be given manufacturing costs and inventory levels and be asked to compute cost of goods manufactured.

    In our example, Snyder Corporation is developing a financial plan for the year ending December 31, 2008. The company has two primary products, Product A and Product B. Based on an assessment of the projected economic conditions, management has developed forecasted sales of Product A of 25,000 units at a sales price of $100, and forecasted sales of Product B of 30,000 units at a sales price of $120. Therefore, total forecasted sales is $6,100,000.

    Assume that management wants an inventory of 1,200 units of Product A and 1,000 units of Product B at year-end. The beginning inventory is shown in the following schedule.

Schedule 1—Beginning Finished Goods Inventory

	Product A	Product B	Total
Units	1,200	1,200	
Cost per unit	$ 70	$ 80	
Total cost	$84,000	$96,000	$180,000

There was no work-in-process beginning inventory and none is anticipated at the end of the year. This information can then be used to prepare the production schedule shown below.

Schedule 2—Production Schedule

	Product A	Product B
Projected unit sales	25,000	30,000
Desired ending inventory	1,200	1,000
Beginning inventory	(1,200)	(1,200)
Units to be produced	25,000	29,800

Once the production schedule is developed, management can develop the raw materials usage budget and budgets for labor and overhead. Information to develop these schedules can be obtained from the following product specifications schedule.

Schedule 3—Product Specifications

	Product A	Product B	Estimated Cost
Materials			
Silver	7 oz.	6 oz.	$5.15 per oz.
Red Oak	1 b.f.		$3.95 per b.f.
Teak		1 b.f.	$6.10 per b.f.
Direct Labor	½ hour	¾ hour	$40 per hour

Schedule 4—Direct Materials Usage Budget

Physical Units	Silver oz.	Red Oak b.f.	Teak b.f.	Total
Product A				
Silver	175,000			
Red Oak		25,000		
Product B				
Silver	178,800			
Teak			29,800	
To be used in production	353,800	25,000	29,800	
Cost Budget				
Available from beginning inventory				
Silver 4,000 oz. @ $5.00 per oz.	$ 20,000			
Red Oak 1,000 b.f. @ $4.00 per b.f.		$ 4,000		
Teak 1,000 b.f. @ $6.00 per b.f.			$ 6,000	
From purchases				
Silver $5.15 × (353,800 – 4,000)	1,801,470			
Red Oak $3.95 × (25,000 – 1,000)		94,800		
Teak $6.10 × (29,800 – 1,000)			175,680	
Cost of direct materials to be used	$1,821,470	$98,800	$181,680	$2,101,950

Schedule 5—Direct Manufacturing Labor Budget

Product A	
(25,000 × ½ hour × $40 per hour)	$ 500,000
Product B	
(29,800 × ¾ hour × $40 per hour)	894,000
	$1,394,000

Schedule 6—Manufacturing Overhead Budget (at 34,850 budgeted direct labor hours)

Variable overhead costs:	
Supplies	$ 60,000
Indirect labor	135,000
Maintenance	50,000
Electricity	100,000
Miscellaneous	30,000
Fixed overhead costs:	
Depreciation	$306,400
Insurance	40,000
Plant supervision	90,000
Miscellaneous	25,000
Total manufacturing overhead	$836,400
Overhead application rate:	
Direct labor hours	
Product A (25,000 × ½ hour)	12,500
Product B (29,800 × ¾ hour)	22,350
Total direct labor hours	34,850
Application rate ($836,400 / 34,850)	$ 24 per hour

Based on the budgeted amounts of materials, labor, and overhead, management can now determine the unit production cots, and the ending inventories and costs of goods sold budgets as shown below.

Schedule 7—Unit Production Costs

	Product A	Product B
Materials	$40	$37
Direct labor	20	30
Manufacturing overhead ($24 per DLH)	12	18
	$72	$85

Schedule 8—Cost of Goods Sold Budget

	Schedule		
Beginning finished goods inventory	1		$ 180,000
Direct materials used	4	$2,101,950	
Direct labor	5	1,394,000	
Manufacturing overhead	6	836,400	
Cost of goods manufactured			4,332,350
Cost of goods available for sale			4,512,350
Deduct ending finished goods inventory			171,400
Cost of goods sold			$4,340,950

With estimates of sales and general and administrative expenses and the tax rate, management can now prepare the pro forma income statement for next period as shown below.

Snyder Corporation
PRO FORMA INCOME STATEMENT
For the Year Ending December 31, 2008

Sales	$6,100,000
Cost of goods sold	4,340,950
Gross profit	1,759,050
General & administrative expenses	1,020,000
Operating income (EBIT)	739,050
Interest expense	260,000
Earnings before taxes	479,050
Taxes (30%)	143,715
Net income	$ 335,335

E. Forecasting Methods

1. Management may choose from a number of methods for forecasting the firm's sales. Such methods are generally classified as qualitative or quantitative techniques. Qualitative approaches base the forecast on management judgment. Examples of qualitative techniques include

    a. Executive opinions
    b. Sales-force polling
    c. Customer surveys

2. Structured approaches, such as the **Delphi technique,** may be used to assist in developing qualitative forecasts. This technique develops consensus among a group about the future through a series of structured questionnaires and an iterative process. The results of prior questionnaires are used to develop subsequent questionnaires until consensus is achieved.

3. Quantitative approaches to the development of forecasts may be broken down into three major types: (1) approaches based on historical data, (2) approaches based on observed associations, (3) approaches based on forecasts of consumer behavior. Examples include the following:

    a. Approaches based on historical data

    (1) **Naive models**—These models are based exclusively on historical observation of sales or other variables. As an example, management might examine historical data on sales by product line and make a subjective estimate of the next period's sales.

    (2) **Moving average**—This technique simply uses the average of sales for the most recent periods to predict the next period's sales.

(3) **Exponential smoothing**—This technique is similar to moving average but the more recent sales data are weighted more heavily than older data in computing the forecast. Underlying the technique is the belief that more recent data are more relevant to predictions of future sales.

(4) **Decomposition of time series**—This technique is especially appropriate when sales are seasonal or cyclical in nature. The technique examines prior sales data and estimates seasonal and cyclical effects. When these effects are extracted from the prior data, historical trends may be observed and projected into the future. Once the trends are used to develop initial forecasts, seasonal and cyclical effects are reintroduced to develop the final forecast.

b. Approaches based on observed associations

(1) **Regression analysis**—This technique estimates sales based on an observed relationship between sales (the dependent variable) and one or more predictors of sales (independent variables).

(2) **Econometric models**—Involve the use of regression analysis to model the firm's sales based on economic data. For example, forecasts of personal disposable income, interest rates, etc. might be used to develop an estimate of future sales.

c. Approaches based on forecasts of consumer behavior

(1) **Markov techniques**—These techniques attempt to forecast consumer purchasing by considering factors such as brand loyalty and brand switching behavior. These data are used to predict changes in the firm's market share, which is then used to develop the sales forecast.

4. **Regression Analysis**

As described in Module 44, regression is a technique for estimating mathematically the average relationship between a dependent variable (y) and one or more independent variables (x). Simple regression involves only one independent variable and the estimation equation is shown below.

$$y = a + bx + e$$

Where:

    y = the dependent variable
    x = the independent variable
    a = the y-intercept or constant value
    b = the slope of the regression line
    e = an error term that is assumed to be normally distributed with a mean of 0

Since the random error term (e) is assumed to have a zero mean, it is ignored and the equation becomes simply

$$y = a + bx$$

a. Major assumptions underlying regression analysis include

(1) The relationship is linear within the relevant range.
(2) The variance of the error (residual) term is constant. A violation of this assumption is referred to as **heteroscedasticity**. While it does not affect the accuracy of the regression estimates (a and b), heteroscedasticity does reduce the reliability of the estimates of standard errors and therefore affects the precision of any estimates developed from the equation.
(3) The error (residual) values are independent.
(4) The error values are normally distributed around the regression line.

b. **Trend Analysis**

Regression might be used as a tool in performing **trend analysis**. In this case regression analysis is used to fit a trend line to a time series of data. As an example, assume that management believes that sales for the next period might be estimated based on the trend of prior sales. The following data have been collected:

Period	Sales	Period	Sales
1	$60,000	6	$67,500
2	$62,000	7	$69,000
3	$62,500	8	$71,000
4	$65,000	9	$71,500
5	$66,500	10	$72,500

The output of regression analysis of this data using a spreadsheet program is illustrated below.

Summary Output

Regression Statistics

Multiple R	0.994088
R Square	0.988211
Adjusted R Square	0.986738
Standard Error	498.4825
Observations	10

	Df	SS	MS	F	Significance F
Regression	1	1.67E+08	1.67E+08	670.6128	5.31E–09
Residual	8	1987879	248484.8		
Total	9	1.69E+08			

	Coefficients	Standard error	t-Stat	P-value	Lower 95%	Upper 95%
Intercept	58933.33	340.5284	173.0644	1.39E–15	58148.07	59718.59
Period	1421.212	54.88112	25.89619	5.31E–09	1294.656	1547.768

c. **Goodness of fit** measures how well the predicted values of the dependent variable match the actual amounts. Regression analysis computes a measure of goodness of fit, the **coefficient of determination**. The coefficient of determination (adjusted R Squared) in this case indicates that 98.6738% of the variance in sales is explained by the time series (period).

d. The significance of the relationship is measured by the t-Statistic. In this case, the t-Statistic for Period is 25.89619 which is very significant. The P-value of 5.31E–09 (0.00000000531) indicates that there is an extremely low probability (0.000000531%) that this relationship occurred by chance.

e. From the coefficients section we see that the equation to predict sales is as follows:

$$\text{Sales} = 58933.33 + (1421.212 \times \text{Period})$$

If we wanted to predict sales for period 11, we would simply substitute 11 for the period and calculate the estimate as shown below

$$\text{Sales} = 58933.33 + (1421.212 \times 11)$$
$$= \$74,566.66$$

5. **Multiple Regression**

Multiple regression is used when management wishes to forecast sales using two or more associated variables. As an example, assume that management of a growing toy manufacturer believes that an accurate estimate of sales can be obtained with two variables—expenditures for advertising and the number of newly introduced toys. Management has collected the following data:

Period	Sales	Advertising expenditures	Number of new toys	Period	Sales	Advertising expenditures	Number of new toys
1	$40,000,000	$1,000,000	5	6	$49,000,000	$1,000,000	12
2	$45,000,000	$1,250,000	7	7	$54,000,000	$1,600,000	12
3	$44,000,000	$ 900,000	9	8	$52,000,000	$1,500,000	4
4	$48,000,000	$1,500,000	9	9	$55,000,000	$1,500,000	13
5	$50,000,000	$1,200,000	14	10	$57,000,000	$1,500,000	15

a. The output of regression analysis of this data using a spreadsheet program is illustrated below.

Summary Output

Regression Statistics

Multiple R	0.910234
R Square	0.828526
Adjusted R Square	0.779534
Standard Error	2506160
Observations	10

	Df	SS	MS	F	Significance F
Regression	2	2.12E+14	1.06E+14	16.91129	0.002088
Residual	7	4.4E+13	6.28E+12		
Total	9	2.56E+14			

	Coefficients	Standard error	t-Stat	P-value	Lower 95%	Upper 95%
Intercept	24678459	4466529	5.525199	0.000883	14116805	35240114
Advertising	13.63897	3.302376	4.130049	0.004404	5.830102	21.44785
New Toys	705906.9	224772.5	3.140539	0.016367	174404.7	1237409

b. The **coefficient of determination** (Adjusted R Squared) is .779534. As discussed above, this is a measure of goodness of fit. In this case 77.9534% of the variation in sales is explained by advertising expenditures and the number of new toys introduced.

c. The equation for predicting sales is shown below.

> Estimated sales = $24,678,459 + (13.63897 × Ad. Exp.) + (705,906.9 × No. New Toys)

d. For the next period, assume that management estimates that $1,600,000 will be spent on advertising and 10 new toys will be introduced. The estimated sales for the period would be calculated as follows:

> Estimated sales = $24,678,459 + (13.63897 × $1,600,000) + (705,906.9 × 10)
> Estimated sales = $53,559,880

e. Other important regression statistics to consider include

(1) **The Standard Error of the Estimate and Confidence Level**—The standard error of the estimate, in this case 2,506,160, is the standard deviation of the regression. This number can be used to establish confidence intervals around the estimate of sales. If the manager wants a prediction to be 95% confident, the confidence interval would be the estimated value from the equation ± $2,506,160 × 2.3436. The 2.3436 is derived from a normal curve area table that shows the relative area under a normal curve from one standard deviation to another. For a normal distribution, 95% of the values fall within 2.3436 standard deviations from the mean. Using the estimated sales number calculated above, $53,559,880, management can be 95% confident that sales for the next period will fall within the range calculated below.

> 95% Confidence Interval = $53,559,880 ± $2,506,160 × 2.3436
> = $47,686,443 to $59,433,317

(2) **The *F*-Statistic**—This statistic provides an overall measure of the significance of the regression equation. In the above case the *F*-Statistic is 16.91129 and is significant at the .002088 level. This means that there is only about a two-tenths of one percent chance (0.2088%) that the relationship occurred by chance.

(3) **The *t*-Statistics**—Each independent variable will have a *t*-Statistic which indicates its significance. In the above case, the *t*-Statistics are 4.130049 and 3.140539 with P-values of .004404 and .016367, respectively. The P-values measure the level of significance of each variable to the equation. In this case both are significant at less than the .05 (5%) level, which means that there is less than a 5% probability that the relationship occurred by chance.

f. Previously, we described the assumptions underlying regression. In evaluating the results, consideration should be given to two related issues.

(1) **Multicollinearity**—When using more than one independent variable there may be a high correlation between the independent variables. This will cause the equation to be in error and may produce spurious forecasts. Indicators of multicollinearity include low *t*-Statistics for

variables that should be important, or variables with coefficients with illogical signs (e.g., a negative relationship between advertising and sales).

(2) **Autocorrelation**—Remember from the discussion above regression analysis assumes that the error term is randomly distributed and independent. If the errors are serially correlated this can again distort the results. Autocorrelation may indicate that a major independent variable is not included in the model. The Durbin-Watson statistic provides a test for autocorrelation.

F. Flexible Budgets

A flexible budget is a budget adjusted for changes in volume. In the planning phase, a flexible budget is used to compare the effects of various activity levels on costs and revenues. In the controlling phase, the flexible budget is used to help analyze actual results by comparing actual results with a flexible budget for the level of activity achieved in the period. Standard costing naturally complements flexible budgeting. However, even without standard costing, flexible budgeting can be used based upon actual costs and quantities of outputs (although lack of input data precludes computation of price and efficiency variances).

Presented below is a sample flexible budget for overhead costs.

FACTORY OVERHEAD
FLEXIBLE BUDGET

Direct manufacturing labor hours	18,000	20,000	22,000
Variable factory overhead			
Supplies	$ 18,000	$ 20,000	$ 22,000
Power	99,000	110,000	121,000
Idle time	3,600	4,000	4,400
Overtime premium	1,800	2,000	2,200
Total ($6.80 per DMLH)	$122,400	$136,000	$149,600
Fixed factory overhead			
Supervision	$ 15,000	$ 15,000	$ 15,000
Depreciation	32,000	32,000	32,000
Power	8,000	8,000	8,000
Property taxes	5,000	5,000	5,000
Insurance	1,500	1,500	1,500
Total	$ 61,500	$ 61,500	$ 61,500
Total overhead	$183,900	$197,500	$211,100

G. Responsibility Accounting

Responsibility accounting allocates those revenues and/or assets which a manager can control to that manager's responsibility center and holds the manager accountable for operating results. If a manager is only responsible for costs, his/her area of responsibility is called a **cost center**. Cost centers represent the most basic activities or responsibilities. Nonrevenue generating departments (purchasing and billing, for example) are usually organized as cost centers.

If the manager is responsible for both revenues and costs, his/her area of responsibility is called a **profit center**. A contribution income statement similar to the one shown below would be prepared for each profit center. Finally, if the manager is responsible for revenues, costs, and asset investment, his/her area of responsibility is called an **investment center**.

H. Segmented Reporting and Controllability

Variable (Direct) and Absorption (Full) Costing reports (as described in Section B) can be broken into further detail to emphasize controllability.

1. Variable manufacturing costs are deducted from sales to obtain **manufacturing contribution margin**.
2. Variable selling and administrative expenses are deducted from manufacturing contribution margin to obtain **contribution margin**.
3. Fixed costs controllable by segment managers at various levels (e.g., division, department) are deducted from contribution margin to obtain the **controllable contribution** at that level.
4. Fixed costs controllable by others at various levels are deducted from controllable contribution to obtain the **segment contribution** at that level.
5. Costs common to all operations are finally deducted to obtain **income before taxes**.

EXAMPLE CONTRIBUTION APPROACH INCOME STATEMENT

		Total	*Segment 1*	*Segment 2*
Sales		$600	$350	$250
	–Variable manufacturing costs	220	115	105
Manufacturing contribution margin		380	235	145
	–Variable selling and admin. exp.	100	70	30
Contribution margin		280	165	115
	–Controllable, traceable fixed costs	80	35	45
Controllable contribution		200	130	70
	–Uncontrollable, traceable fixed costs	90	60	30
Segment contribution		$110	$ 70	$ 40
	–Unallocable common costs	60*		
Income before taxes		$ 50		

* *Not allocated to any segment of the firm. Examples include corporate office salaries and advertising for firm name.*

Costs not controllable by a subdivision (cost or profit center) of a firm should not be allocated to the subdivision for evaluation or decision making purposes (see Section G. Responsibility Accounting).

Contribution margin data can be used in a variety of situations, including planning (CVP analysis) and decision making (which products to emphasize, which products should be retained and which should be eliminated, and so forth).

I. Standards and Variances

Standard costs are predetermined target costs which should be attainable under efficient conditions. The tightness, or attainment difficulty, of standard costs should be determined by the principles of motivation (e.g., excessively tight standards may result in employees feeling that the standards are impossible to achieve; consequently, they may ignore them). Standard costs are used to aid in the budget process, pinpoint trouble areas, and evaluate performance.

The tightness of standards is generally described by one of two terms. **Ideal** standards reflect the absolute minimum costs which could be achieved under perfect operating conditions. **Currently attainable** standards should be achieved under efficient operating conditions. Generally, currently attainable standards are set so they will be difficult, but not impossible, to achieve. Currently attainable standards are most often used since they are more realistic for budgeting purposes and are a better motivational tool than ideal standards.

Variances are differences between actual and standard costs. The total variance is generally broken down into subvariances to further pinpoint the causes of the variance.

1. Variance Analysis

In calculating the variances for direct material and direct manufacturing labor the following symbols will be employed as defined:

AP: Actual price paid per unit of input (e.g., price per foot of lumber, per hour of labor, per ton of steel, etc.)

SP: Standard price per unit of input

AQ: The actual quantity of input (feet, hours, tons, etc.) used in production

SQ: The standard quantity of input that should have been used for the good units produced

Variances can be computed using the diagram approach that follows.

2. Material Variances

The diagram for computing material variances is

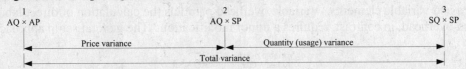

The price variance is unfavorable if AP > SP; the quantity variance is unfavorable if AQ > SQ. Favorable variances arise when actual amounts are less than standard amounts.

The only alternative allowed on the variances above concerns the material price variance. The price variance can be recognized when material is placed in production (as assumed in the previous discussion) or when material is purchased (which is desirable for early identification and control). If the price variance is to be recognized at the time of purchase, AQ (for the price variance **only**) becomes quantity **purchased** rather than quantity **used**.

The materials price variance is generally considered to be the responsibility of the purchasing department, while the materials quantity variance is the responsibility of the production department or production design engineers.

EXAMPLE: The following data relate to DFW Manufacturing, which produced 5,000 units of product during the period:

Direct materials standard per finished unit: 2 lbs. @ $1.60 per lb.
Actual: 10,100 lbs purchased @ $1.65 per lb., 9,500 lbs. used in production

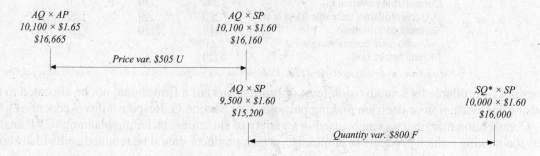

	AQ × AP		AQ × SP			SQ* × SP
	10,100 × $1.65		10,100 × $1.60			10,000 × $1.60
	$16,665		$16,160			$16,000

Price var. $505 U

		AQ × SP		SQ* × SP
		9,500 × $1.60		10,000 × $1.60
		$15,200		$16,000

Quantity var. $800 F

* SQ = 5,000 units × 2 lbs. per unit = 10,000 lbs.*

3. **Labor Variances**

The computational form of the labor variances is similar to the calculation of material variances—except that the price being used changes from price per pound of material to price (rate) per hour of labor, and the quantity changes from pounds, yards, etc., to hours. Therefore, the diagrams are the same, although the terminology differs.

Material variance		*Labor variance*
Price	⟶	Rate
Quantity	⟶	Efficiency

Both labor variances are usually considered to be the responsibility of the production department or production design engineers.

EXAMPLE:

The following data relate to DFW Manufacturing. Recall that the company produced 5,000 units of product during the period:

Direct labor standard per finished unit: 3 hours @ $2.50 per hour
Actual: 15,400 hours worked @ $2.60 per hour

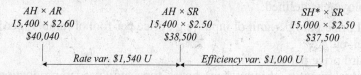

AH × AR		AH × SR		SH* × SR
15,400 × $2.60		15,400 × $2.50		15,000 × $2.50
$40,040		$38,500		$37,500

Rate var. $1,540 U   Efficiency var. $1,000 U

* SH = 5,000 units × 3 hours = 15,000 hours*

4. **Overhead Variances**

Overhead variances tend to be more complicated than those computed for direct materials and direct labor, primarily because of the different computation methods that are available. The easier approach to master is a parallel of the variance grids shown earlier, with overhead being subdivided into fixed and variable elements. Variable overhead parallels the calculation of direct labor variances; fixed overhead, in contrast, requires a minor modification. The general setup approach follows:

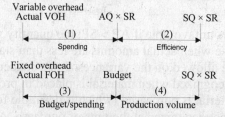

Variable overhead
Actual VOH   AQ × SR   SQ × SR
        (1)   (2)
       Spending   Efficiency

Fixed overhead
Actual FOH   Budget   SQ × SR
        (3)   (4)
    Budget/spending   Production volume

Notice the use of AQ and SQ. On virtually all CPA exams, direct labor hours is the base used to apply overhead to production.

EXAMPLE: To illustrate the proper approach, we will continue to focus on DFW Manufacturing, which applies overhead to production on the basis of hours. Recall from the earlier calculations that 5,000 units were manufactured. 15,400 hours were worked, and each unit is supposed to take 3 hours of labor time. Additional data follow.

Estimated (standard) factory overhead based on a "normal capacity" of 16,000 labor hours:

Variable	3 hours @ $1.50
Fixed	3 hours @ $0.50*

Actual overhead cost for the period

Variable	$22,800
Fixed	$ 8,100

* *$8,000 budgeted fixed overhead costs ÷ 16,000 direct labor hours*

Variable Overhead

	$AQ \times SR$	$SQ \times SR$
Actual	$15,400 \times \$1.50$	$15,000 \times \$1.50$
$22,800	$23,100	$22,500

| Spending var. $300 F | Efficiency var. $600 U |

Fixed Overhead

		$SQ \times SR$
Actual	Budget	$15,000 \times \$1.50$
$18,100	$8,000	$22,500

| Spending/budget var. $100 U | Production volume var. $500 U |

This example illustrates several key points.

According to the information presented, DFW has a capacity to work 16,000 hours, which is the equivalent of 5,334 units (16,000 ÷ 3 hours per unit). Since the firm produced only 5,000 units, the production volume variance is unfavorable.

Overhead in the SQ × SR column ($22,000 + $7,500 = $30,000) is the amount applied to production. Since actual overhead was $30,900 ($22,800 + $8,100), overhead is $900 underapplied. This latter amount will always coincide with the combination of all four variances ($300F − $600U − $100U − $500U = $900U).

The 3-variance approach. The 3-variance method results in the calculation of three variances rather than the four just illustrated. The **only** difference between these two approaches is in the calculation of the spending variance, which is a combination of (1) and (3) to create a total spending variance as shown below.

(1) + (3)	(2)	(4)
Total spending	Efficiency	Production volume

For DFW, the total spending variance is $200F ($300F − $100U).

The 2-variance approach. The 2-variance approach results in the calculation of only two variances: the production volume variance shown earlier and a combined spending/efficiency variance (see the following diagram).

(1) + (2) + (3)	(4)
Budget	Production volume
(Controllable)	

This latter variance for DFW is $400U ($300F − $100U − $600U).

Some computational hints. These variance approaches are fairly straightforward if you start with the 4-variance method and then work backwards to arrive at the 3-variance approach and then work that backwards to arrive at the last method. Occasionally, the exam may not give you enough data to perform all calculations to do this. The following hints have proven to be extremely helpful:

- The production volume variance is the same no matter what approach is used.
- The efficiency variance is the same for the 3- and 4-variance approach.
- When in doubt, you can calculate the total variance (the difference between actual total overhead and applied overhead [SQ × SR]), subtract the variances that you can compute, and the result, a forced figure, will often be the variance that is requested by the examiners.

Miscellaneous. The budget variance (also called the controllable variance) arises when the amount spent on both fixed and variable overhead differs from the amount budgeted for the actual hours worked.

The production volume variance is solely a **fixed** overhead variance. It is caused by under- or overutilization of capacity. If actual output is less than (more than) capacity activity, an unfavorable (favorable) output level variance results. The capacity volume is the activity level used to set the predetermined fixed overhead rate for product costing purposes (see Module 43).

5. **Disposition of Variances**

If insignificant, variances are frequently written off to cost of goods sold on the grounds of expediency. (ARB 43 states that you may report inventories using standard costs if they are based on currently attainable standards.) If significant, the variances must be allocated among the inventories and cost of goods sold, usually in proportion to the ending balances. Remember, SFAS 151 requires that fixed overhead costs be allocated based on normal capacity and variances related to fixed overhead volume should be allocated only to cost of goods sold (treated as a period cost).

J. Product and Service Pricing

Product pricing requires the use of judgment by the cost accountant and management to maximize the entity's profits and to increase shareholder wealth. To find the combination of sales price and volume yielding the greatest profits, management must make many assumptions regarding customer preferences, competitors' reactions, economic conditions, cost structures, etc. In maximizing shareholders' wealth, management must consider not only product costs but must also react to external changes, for example, a competitor's price on a relatively undifferentiated product. Additionally, management must consider the company's cost of capital in determining a desired **rate of return**. This rate of return represents the desired minimum markup on the cost of goods.

Costs are usually the starting point in determining prices. In the long run, all costs, including fixed costs, must be considered. However, decisions involving short-range pricing, such as a special order, may be evaluated on the basis of contribution margin. The **contribution margin approach** considers all relevant variable costs plus any additional fixed costs needed to sustain the new production level. Which costs are relevant is determined by analyzing how total costs of each component of the value chain will change if the order is accepted.

Cost-plus pricing is one model for the pricing decision; prices are set at variable costs plus a percentage markup, at full manufacturing or service cost plus a percentage markup, or at target ROI per unit. The percentage markup must cover fixed costs and profit (variable approach), operating expenses and a profit (full cost approach), or invested capital (target ROI approach). Consider the following example:

Annual sales—10,000 units		Invested capital—$100,000		Target ROI—15%
Manufacturing costs:		Operating costs:		
Fixed	$20,000	Fixed	$10,000	
Variable	$3/unit	Variable	$2.50/unit	

If price is set at total variable cost plus 60% ($5.50 × 160%), or full manufacturing cost plus 76% ($5.00 × 176%), the selling price would be $8.80. The selling price under the target ROI approach is calculated as follows:

Invested capital		$100,000
× Target ROI	×	15%
Total target ROI		15,000
÷ Annual sales	÷	10,000
Target oper. inc. per unit		1.50
+ Cost base (total cost)	+	8.50
Selling price		$ 10.00

Note that the rate of markup ($1.50/$8.50 = 17.65%) has nothing to do with target ROI (15%), which expresses operating income as a percentage of **investment**.

Another alternative is **target pricing,** which sets prices at the amount that consumers are willing to pay based on their perceived value of the product or service. Based on targeted prices and income, a target cost is determined; the targeted cost is the estimated cost of the product or service that yields the targeted income at the target price. To meet target costs, a company must often improve its products or increase efficiency. **Value engineering** examines all components of the value chain to find opportunities for improvements and cost reduction. Activity-based costing helps to identify opportunities for cost reduction by improving specific activities.

Finally, the use of **standard costs** that are attainable eliminates the effect of unusual efficiency/inefficiency on price.

K. Transfer Pricing

Decentralization of profit or investment centers requires pricing policies for optional internal transfers of intermediate goods or services between those centers. The transfer price represents revenue to the selling subunit and cost to the purchasing subunit, which are included in the operating income of the divisions. The goal of transfer pricing is to provide autonomous segment managers with incentive to maximize profits of the company as a whole, not just the performance of their own divisions.

In theory, outlay cost plus opportunity cost should determine the transfer price. However, opportunity cost may be difficult or impossible to measure. Therefore, three transfer pricing alternatives exist: cost-based price, market price, and negotiated price. Transfer prices based on cost may consider variable manufacturing costs, total manufacturing (absorption) costs, or full product costs. Actual costs are unstable (vary seasonally, etc.) and allow the producing division to pass its inefficiencies to the buyer; thus, standard costs should be used. Any variances from standard affect the operating income of the selling division (cannot be passed on).

A transfer price based on **full cost** includes the transferring division's fixed costs (absorption costing). A problem with full cost transfer pricing is that special orders at below full cost but above variable cost may be rejected because they result in losses for the selling division even though the contribution to fixed costs benefits the company as a whole (suboptimization). Thus, the use of full cost for transfer pricing could lead to poor motivation and dysfunctional decision making.

A **full product cost** transfer price includes absorption manufacturing cost plus a share of other costs of the value chain, such as R&D or other administrative, selling, or general expenses.

A transfer price based on the **market price** of similar products or services is justified if a competitive market exists for the product/service. A market transfer price may also be based on the transferring division's price to outside customers. However, if any costs can be avoided by selling internally rather than externally (e.g., commissions, advertising) then the market price should be reduced by these cost savings. Market transfer prices are useful because they are objective, they avoid the need to define cost, and because they show each division's contribution to company profit.

Alternatively, two divisions may establish a **negotiated transfer price**. Cost and market price information may be useful in the bargaining process, but it is not required that the transfer price be specifically related to either. However the resulting transfer price should fall within a range limited by a ceiling and a floor. The ceiling, which is the lowest external market price, helps the purchasing subunit keep costs down. The floor equals the transferring division's outlay plus opportunity costs, so the seller can cover costs. The transfer price serves to divide this amount between the divisions involved, which affects divisional operating income and thus performance measurement and responsibility accounting.

To enhance cooperation between divisions, prevent suboptimization by managers, encourage the transferring division to maximize income, and provide the purchasing division with cost information relevant for short-term decision making, a **dual transfer pricing** system may be established. Here, transfers are recorded by the selling subunit at one price while the purchaser records the transfer at a different transfer price.

L. Short-Term Differential Cost Analysis

Differential cost decisions include

1. Sell or process further (see also Section I., Module 43)
2. Special order
3. Outsourcing (make or buy)
4. Closing a department or segment
5. Sale of obsolete inventory
6. Scarce resources

These decisions would better be described as differential cost and **revenue** decisions, since basically the decision maker must consider differences in costs and revenues over various alternatives. All other things being equal, the alternative providing the greatest profit (or cost savings) should be chosen.

Three concepts relate to most differential cost decisions.

1. **The only relevant costs or revenues are those expected future costs and revenues that differ across alternatives.** If an alternative leads to increased revenues (costs) as compared to the present method used or other alternative considered, then these revenues (costs) are **relevant** (i.e., a differential cash flow).
2. **All costs incurred in the past (sunk costs) are irrelevant, unless they have future tax ramifications.** Past costs include joint costs, the cost of obsolete inventory, and fixed costs (in the short run).
3. **Opportunity cost, the income obtainable from an alternative use of a resource, must be considered.** If an alternative is profitable and that alternative is rejected in favor of others, the benefits foregone become a "cost" to be evaluated in the decision-making process.

To work a relevant cost problem, you must first identify the type of decision that is involved. Once you have identified the decision, you can determine which costs and revenues are relevant for accepting or rejecting an alternative and in reaching a decision. For example, in a decision to sell at split-off or process further, joint costs are irrelevant and a decision to process further is made if incremental revenue exceeds incremental cost. Finally, a decision is made based on the benefit or loss that would be derived from each alternative.

The table presented below summarizes various differential cost decisions and includes only **quantitative** factors.

Decision	*Description*	*Decision guideline*
1. Sell or process further	Should joint products be sold at split-off or processed further?	Ignore joint costs. Process further if incremental revenue exceeds incremental cost.
2. Special order	Should a discount-priced order be accepted when there is idle capacity?	If regular sales are not affected, accept order when the revenue from the order exceeds the incremental cost. Fixed production costs are usually irrelevant—they remain the same no matter what the company does.
3. Outsourcing (make or buy)	Should a part be manufactured or bought from a supplier?	Choose lower cost option. Fixed costs usually are irrelevant. Often opportunity costs are present.
4. Closing a department or segment	Should a segment of the company, such as a product line, be terminated?	Compare existing contribution margin with alternative. Consider any changes in future fixed costs.
5. Sale of obsolete inventory	Should obsolete inventory be reworked or junked?	Cost of inventory is sunk and ignored. Choose alternative with greatest excess of future revenue over future cost.
6. Scarce resources	Which products should be emphasized when capacity is limited?	Determine scarce resource (e.g., machine hours). Emphasize products with greatest contribution margin per unit of scarce resource.

Qualitative factors may be equally important in nonroutine decisions. For example, in the outsourcing decision, qualitative factors include

1. Quality of purchased part compared to manufactured part
2. Relationships with suppliers
3. Quickness in obtaining needed parts

Uncertainty also affects decision making. See the probability section at the end of this module for further discussion.

An example of a differential cost decision (special order) is presented below, comparing the simpler, more efficient **incremental** approach with the equally effective but more cumbersome **total** approach. Unless a problem requires the total approach, use of the incremental approach will save valuable exam time.

> EXAMPLE: *Potts Co. manufactures cookware. Expected annual volume of 100,000 sets per year is well below full capacity of 150,000. Normal selling price is $40/set. Manufacturing cost is $30/set ($20 variable and $10 fixed). Total fixed manufacturing cost is $1,000,000. Selling and administrative expenses are expected to be $500,000 ($300,000 fixed and $200,000 variable). A catalog company offers to buy 25,000 sets for $27/set. No extra selling and administrative costs would be caused by the order, and acceptance will not affect regular sales. Should the offer be accepted?*

INCREMENTAL APPROACH

Incremental revenue (25,000 × $27)	$ 675,000
Incremental cost (25,000 × $20)	(500,000)
Benefit of accepting order (contribution margin)	$ 175,000

TOTAL APPROACH

		Without order		*With order*
Sales (100,000 × $40) less Variable costs:		$4,000,000	[+(25,000 × $27)]	$4,675,000
Manufacturing	(100,000 × $20)	(2,000,000)	[+(25,000 × $20)]	(2,500,000)
Sell. and admin.	(100,000 × $2)	(200,000)		(200,000)
		1,800,000		1,975,000
Contribution margin less Fixed costs:				
Manufacturing		(1,000,000)		(1,000,000)
Sell. and admin.		(300,000)		(300,000)
Operating income		$ 500,000		$ 675,000

At first glance, it may appear that the order should not be accepted because the selling price of $27 is less than the $30 manufacturing cost per set. However, fixed costs do not increase if the order is accepted and are therefore irrelevant to this decision. The result is that, with either the incremental or the total approach, operating income is increased by $175,000. Therefore, Potts Company should accept the order.

MULTIPLE-CHOICE QUESTIONS (1-83)

1. At the breakeven point, the contribution margin equals total
- a. Variable costs.
- b. Sales revenues.
- c. Selling and administrative costs.
- d. Fixed costs.

2. The most likely strategy to reduce the breakeven point, would be to
- a. Increase both the fixed costs and the contribution margin.
- b. Decrease both the fixed costs and the contribution margin.
- c. Decrease the fixed costs and increase the contribution margin.
- d. Increase the fixed costs and decrease the contribution margin.

3. Del Co. has fixed costs of $100,000 and breakeven sales of $800,000. What is its projected profit at $1,200,000 sales?
- a. $ 50,000
- b. $150,000
- c. $200,000
- d. $400,000

**4. Associated Supply, Inc. is considering introducing a new product that will require a $250,000 investment of capital. The necessary funds would be raised through a bank loan at an interest rate of 8%. The fixed operating costs associated with the product would be $122,500 while the contribution margin percentage would be 42%. Assuming a selling price of $15 per unit, determine the number of units (rounded to the nearest whole unit) Associated would have to sell to generate earnings before interest and taxes (EBIT) of 32% of the amount of capital invested in the new product.
- a. 35,318 units.
- b. 32,143 units.
- c. 25,575 units.
- d. 23,276 units.

5. During 2007, Thor Lab supplied hospitals with a comprehensive diagnostic kit for $120. At a volume of 80,000 kits, Thor had fixed costs of $1,000,000 and a profit before income taxes of $200,000. Due to an adverse legal decision, Thor's 2008 liability insurance increased by $1,200,000 over 2007. Assuming the volume and other costs are unchanged, what should the 2008 price be if Thor is to make the same $200,000 profit before income taxes?
- a. $120.00
- b. $135.00
- c. $150.00
- d. $240.00

6. Breakeven analysis assumes that over the relevant range
- a. Unit revenues are nonlinear.
- b. Unit variable costs are unchanged.
- c. Total costs are unchanged.
- d. Total fixed costs are nonlinear.

7. Product Cott has sales of $200,000, a contribution margin of 20%, and a margin of safety of $80,000. What is Cott's fixed cost?

- a. $16,000
- b. $24,000
- c. $80,000
- d. $96,000

8. On January 1, 2008, Lake Co. increased its direct manufacturing labor wage rates. All other budgeted costs and revenues were unchanged. How did this increase affect Lake's budgeted breakeven point and budgeted margin of safety?

	Budgeted Breakeven point	Budgeted margin of safety
a.	Increase	Increase
b.	Increase	Decrease
c.	Decrease	Decrease
d.	Decrease	Increase

Items 9 and 10 are based on the following:

The diagram below is a cost-volume-profit chart.

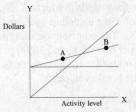

9. At point A compared to point B, as a percentage of sales revenues

	Variable costs are	Fixed costs are
a.	Greater	Greater
b.	Greater	The same
c.	The same	The same
d.	The same	Greater

10. If sales dollars are used to measure activity levels, total costs and total revenues may be read from the X and Y axis as follows:

	Total costs	Total revenues
a.	X or Y	X or Y
b.	X or Y	X only
c.	Y only	X or Y
d.	Y only	X only

**11. Which one of the following is and advantage of using variable costing?
- a. Variable costing complies with the US Internal Revenue Code.
- b. Variable costing complies with generally accepted accounting principles.
- c. Variable costing makes cost-volume relationships more easily apparent.
- d. Variable costing is most relevant to long-run pricing strategies.

12. In the profit-volume chart below, EF and GH represent the profit-volume graphs of a single-product company for 2007 and 2008, respectively.

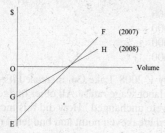

If 2007 and 2008 unit sales prices are identical, how did total fixed costs and unit variable costs of 2008 change compared to 2007?

	2008 total fixed costs	2008 unit variable costs
a.	Decreased	Increased
b.	Decreased	Decreased
c.	Increased	Increased
d.	Increased	Decreased

13. Thomas Company sells products X, Y, and Z. Thomas sells three units of X for each unit of Z, and two units of Y for each unit of X. The contribution margins are $1.00 per unit of X, $1.50 per unit of Y, and $3.00 per unit of Z. Fixed costs are $600,000. How many units of X would Thomas sell at the breakeven point?
- a. 40,000
- b. 120,000
- c. 360,000
- d. 400,000

14. In calculating the breakeven point for a multi-product company, which of the following assumptions are commonly made when variable costing is used?

I. Sales volume equals production volume.
II. Variable costs are constant per unit.
III. A given sales mix is maintained for all volume changes.

- a. I and II.
- b. I and III.
- c. II and III.
- d. I, II, and III.

15. In the budgeted profit/volume chart below, EG represents a two-product company's profit path. EH and HG represent the profit paths of products #1 and #2, respectively.

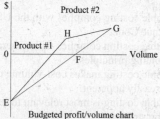

Budgeted profit/volume chart

Sales prices and cost behavior were as budgeted, actual total sales equaled budgeted sales, and there were no inventories. Actual profit was greater than budgeted profit. Which product had actual sales in excess of budget, and what margin does OE divided by OF represent?

	Product with excess sales	OE/OF
a.	#1	Contribution margin
b.	#1	Gross margin
c.	#2	Contribution margin
d.	#2	Gross margin

16. In its first year of operations, Magna Manufacturers had the following costs when it produced 100,000 and sold 80,000 units of its only product:

Manufacturing costs	Fixed	$180,000
	Variable	160,000
Selling and admin. costs	Fixed	90,000
	Variable	40,000

How much lower would Magna's net income be if it used variable costing instead of full absorption costing?
- a. $36,000
- b. $54,000
- c. $68,000
- d. $94,000

17. Using the variable costing method, which of the following costs are assigned to inventory?

	Variable selling and administrative costs	Variable factory overhead costs
a.	Yes	Yes
b.	Yes	No
c.	No	No
d.	No	Yes

18. At the end of Killo Co.'s first year of operations, 1,000 units of inventory remained on hand. Variable and fixed manufacturing costs per unit were $90 and $20, respectively. If Killo uses absorption costing rather than variable (direct) costing, the result would be a higher pretax income of
- a. $0
- b. $20,000
- c. $70,000
- d. $90,000

19. A manufacturing company prepares income statements using both absorption and variable costing methods. At the end of a period actual sales revenues, total gross profit, and total contribution margin approximated budgeted figures, whereas net income was substantially greater than the budgeted amount. There were no beginning or ending inventories. The most likely explanation of the net income increase is that, compared to budget, actual
- a. Manufacturing fixed costs had increased.
- b. Selling and administrative fixed expenses had decreased.
- c. Sales prices and variable costs had increased proportionately.
- d. Sales prices had declined proportionately less than variable costs.

20. A single-product company prepares income statements using both absorption and variable costing methods. Manufacturing overhead cost applied per unit produced in 2008 was the same as in 2007. The 2008 variable costing statement reported a profit whereas the 2008 absorption costing statement reported a loss. The difference in reported income could be explained by units produced in 2008 being
- a. Less than units sold in 2008.
- b. Less than the activity level used for allocating overhead to the product.
- c. In excess of the activity level used for allocating overhead to the product.
- d. In excess of units sold in 2008.

21. Which of the following is an output of a financial planning model?
- a. Strategic plan.

b.   Actual financial results.
c.   Projected financial statements.
d.   Variance analysis.

22. Mien Co. is budgeting sales of 53,000 units of product Nous for October 2008. The manufacture of one unit of Nous requires four kilos of chemical Loire. During October 2008, Mien plans to reduce the inventory of Loire by 50,000 kilos and increase the finished goods inventory of Nous by 6,000 units. There is no Nous work in process inventory. How many kilos of Loire is Mien budgeting to purchase in October 2008?

a.   138,000
b.   162,000
c.   186,000
d.   238,000

23. The master budget
a.   Shows forecasted and actual results.
b.   Reflects controllable costs only.
c.   Can be used to determine manufacturing cost variances.
d.   Contains the operating budget.

Items 24 and 25 are based on the following information:

Operational budgets are used by a retail company for planning and controlling its business activities. Data regarding the company's monthly sales for the last 6 months of the year and its projected collection patterns are shown below.

The cost of merchandise averages 40% of its selling price. The company's policy is to maintain an inventory equal to 25% of the next month's forecasted sales. The inventory balance at cost is $80,000 as of June 30.

Forecasted Sales

July	$775,000
August	750,000
September	825,000
October	800,000
November	850,000
December	900,000

Types of Sales

Cash sales	20%
Credit sales	80%

Collection Pattern for Credit Sales

In the month of sale	40%
In the first month following the sale	57%
Uncollectible	3%

*24. The budgeted cost of the company's purchases for the month of August would be
a. $302,500
b. $305,000
c. $307,500
d. $318,750

*25. The company's total cash receipts from sales and collections on account that would be budgeted for the month of September would be
a. $757,500
b. $771,000
c. $793,800
d. $856,500

26. Which of the following **best describes tactical profit plans?
a.   Detailed, short-term, broad responsibilities, qualitative.
b.   Broad, short-term, responsibilites at all levels, quantitative.
c.   Detailed, short-term, responsibilities at all levels, quantitative.
d.   Broad, long-term, broad responsibilities, qualitative.

27. Which of the following budgeting systems focuses on improving operations?
a.   Responsibility budgeting.
b.   Activity-based budgeting.
c.   Operational budgeting.
d.   Kaizen budgeting.

28. Which of the following is included in a firm's financial budget?
a.   Budgeted income statement.
b.   Capital budget.
c.   Production schedule.
d.   Cost of goods sold budget.

29. Rolling Wheels purchases bicycle components in the month prior to assembling them into bicycles. Assembly is scheduled one month prior to budgeted sales. Rolling pays 75% of component costs in the month of purchase and 25% of the costs in the following month. Component cost included in budgeted cost of sales are

April	*May*	*June*	*July*	*August*
$5,000	$6,000	$7,000	$8,000	$8,000

What is Rolling's budgeted cash payment for components in May?
a. $5,750
b. $6,750
c. $7,750
d. $8,000

30. A 2008 cash budget is being prepared for the purchase of Toyi, a merchandise item. Budgeted data are

Cost of goods sold for 2008	$300,000
Accounts payable 1/1/08	20,000
Inventory—1/1/08	30,000
12/31/08	42,000

Purchases will be made in twelve equal monthly amounts and paid for in the following month. What is the 2008 budgeted cash payment for purchases of Toyi?
a. $295,000
b. $300,000
c. $306,000
d. $312,000

**31. Trumbull Company budgeted sales on account of $120,000 for July, $211,000 for August, and $198,000 for September. Collection experience indicates that 60% of the budgeted sales will be collected the month after the sale, 36% the second month, and 4% will be uncollectible. The cash from accounts receivable that should be budgeted for September would be
a. $169,800
b. $194,760
c. $197,880
d. $198,600

---

*   *CIA adapted*
**   *CMA adapted*

32. Cook Co.'s total costs of operating five sales offices last year were $500,000, of which $70,000 represented fixed costs. Cook has determined that total costs are significantly influenced by the number of sales offices operated. Last year's costs and number of sales offices can be used as the bases for predicting annual costs. What would be the budgeted costs for the coming year if Cook were to operate seven sales offices?

    a. $700,000
    b. $672,000
    c. $614,000
    d. $586,000

*33. In regression analysis, which of the following correlation coefficients represents the strongest relationship between the independent and dependent variables?

    a.   1.03
    b.   −.02
    c.   −.89
    d.   .75

*34. The internal auditor of a bank has developed a multiple regression model which has been used for a number of years to estimate the amount of interest income from commercial loans. During the current year, the auditor applies the model and discovers that the r^2 value has decreased dramatically, but the model otherwise seems to be working okay. Which of the following conclusions are justified by the change?

    a.   Changing to a cross-sectional regression analysis should cause r^2 to increase.
    b.   Regression analysis is no longer an appropriate technique to estimate interest income.
    c.   Some new factors, not included in the model, are causing interest income to change.
    d.   A linear regression analysis would increase the model's reliability.

*35. All of the following are useful for forecasting the needed level of inventory except:

    a.   Knowledge of the behavior of business cycles.
    b.   Internal accounting allocations of costs to different segments of the company.
    c.   Information about seasonal variations in demand.
    d.   Econometric modeling.

Items 36 thru 38 are based on the following information:

In preparing the annual profit plan for the coming year, Wilkens Company wants to determine the cost behavior pattern of the maintenance costs. Wilkens has decided to use linear regression by employing the equation $y = a + bx$ for maintenance costs. The prior year's data regarding maintenance hours and costs, and the result of the regression analysis are given below.

Average cost per hour	$9.00
a	684.65
b	7.2884
Standard error of a	49.515
Standard error of b	.12126
Standard error of the estimate	34.469
R^2	.99724

	Hours of activity	Maintenance costs
January	480	$ 4,200
February	320	3,000
March	400	3,600
April	300	2,820
May	500	4,350
June	310	2,960
July	320	3,030
August	520	4,470
September	490	4,260
October	470	4,050
November	350	3,300
December	340	3,160
Sum	4,800	$43,200
Average	400	$ 3,600

*36. In the standard regression equation $y = a + bx$, the letter b is best described as a(n)

    a.   Independent variable.
    b.   Dependent variable.
    c.   Constant coefficient.
    d.   Variable coefficient.

*37. The letter x in the standard regression equation is best described as a(n).

    a.   Independent variable.
    b.   Dependent variable.
    c.   Constant coefficient.
    d.   Coefficient of determination.

*38. Based upon the data derived from the regression analysis, 420 maintenance hours in a month would mean the maintenance costs (rounded to the nearest dollar) would be budgeted at

    a. $3,780
    b. $3,600
    c. $3,790
    d. $3,746

Items 39 thru 42 are based on the following information:

Lackland Ski Resort uses multiple regression to predict ski lift revenue for the next week based on the forecasted number of dates with temperatures above 10 degrees and predicted number of inches of snow. The following function has been developed:

Sales = 10,902 + (255 × no. of days predicted above 10 degrees) + (300 × no. of inches of snow predicted)

Other information generated from the analysis include

Coefficient of determination (Adjusted r squared)	.6789
Standard error	1,879
F-Statistic	6.279 with a significance of .049

39. Which variables(s) in this function is(are) the dependent variable(s)?

    a.   Predicted number of days above 10 degrees.
    b.   Predicted number of inches of snow.
    c.   Revenue.
    d.   Predicted number of days above 10 degrees and predicted number of inches of snow.

40. Assume that management predicts the number of days above 10 degrees for the next week to be 6 and the number of inches of snow to be 12. Calculate the predicted amount of revenue for the next week.

    a. $10,902
    b. $11,362

---

* *CIA adapted*

c. $16,032
d. $20,547

41. Which of the following represents an accurate interpretation of the results of Lackland's regression analysis?

    a. 6.279% of the variation in revenue is explained by the predicted number of days above 10 degrees and the number of inches of snow.

    b. The relationships are not significant.

    c. Predicted number of days above 10 degrees is a more significant variable than number of inches of snow.

    d. 67.89% of the variation in revenue is explained by the predicted number of days above 10 degrees and the number of inches of snow.

42. Assume that Lackland's model predicts revenue for a week to be $13,400. Calculate the 95% confidence interval for the amount of revenue for the week. (The 95% confidence interval corresponds to the area representing 2.3436 deviations from the mean.)

    a. $13,400 ± 6,279

    b. $13,400 ± 4,404

    c. $13,400 ± 6,786

    d. $13,400 ± 8,564

43. Which of the following is a quantitative approach used to develop sales forecasts based on analysis of consumer behavior?

    a. Markov techniques.

    b. Regression analysis.

    c. Econometric models.

    d. Exponential smoothing.

44. Which of the following is a quantitative approach to developing a sales forecast?

    a. Delphi technique.

    b. Customer surveys.

    c. Moving average.

    d. Executive opinions.

**45. A forecasting technique that is a combination of the last forecast and the last observed value is called

    a. Delphi.

    b. Least squares.

    c. Regression.

    d. Exponential smoothing.

46. Using regression analysis, Fairfield Co. graphed the following relationship of its cheapest product line's sales with its customers' income levels:

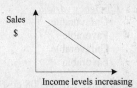

If there is a strong statistical relationship between the sales and customers' income levels, which of the following numbers best represents the correlation coefficient for this relationship?

    a. -9.00

    b. -0.93

    c. +0.93

    d. +9.00

47. The basic difference between a master budget and a flexible budget is that a master budget is

    a. Only used before and during the budget period and a flexible budget is only used after the budget period.

    b. For an entire production facility and a flexible budget is applicable to single departments only.

    c. Based on one specific level of production and a flexible budget can be prepared for any production level within a relevant range.

    d. Based on a fixed standard and a flexible budget allows management latitude in meeting goals.

48. A flexible budget is appropriate for a

	Marketing budget	Direct material usage budget
a.	No	No
b.	No	Yes
c.	Yes	Yes
d.	Yes	No

49. When production levels are expected to increase within a relevant range, and a flexible budget is used, what effect would be anticipated with respect to each of the following costs?

	Fixed costs per unit	Variable costs per unit
a.	Decrease	Decrease
b.	No change	No change
c.	No change	Decrease
d.	Decrease	No change

50. Controllable revenue would be included in a performance report for a

	Profit center	Cost center
a.	No	No
b.	No	Yes
c.	Yes	No
d.	Yes	Yes

51. The following is a summarized income statement of Carr Co.'s profit center No. 43 for March 2008:

Contribution margin		$70,000
Period expenses:		
Manager's salary	$20,000	
Facility depreciation	8,000	
Corporate expense allocation	5,000	33,000
Profit center income		$37,000

Which of the following amounts would most likely be subject to the control of the profit center's manager?

    a. $70,000

    b. $50,000

    c. $37,000

    d. $33,000

52. Wages earned by machine operators in producing the firm's product should be categorized as

	Direct labor	Controllable by the machine operators' foreman
a.	Yes	Yes
b.	Yes	No
c.	No	Yes
d.	No	No

53. Companies in what type of industry may use a standard cost system for cost control?

	Mass production industry	Service industry
a.	Yes	Yes
b.	Yes	No
c.	No	No
d.	No	Yes

54. In connection with a standard cost system being developed by Flint Co., the following information is being considered with regard to standard hours allowed for output of one unit of product:

	Hours
Average historical performance for the past three years	1.85
Production level to satisfy average consumer demand over a seasonal time span	1.60
Engineering estimates based on attainable performance	1.50
Engineering estimates based on ideal performance	1.25

To measure controllable production inefficiencies, what is the best basis for Flint to use in establishing standard hours allowed?

    a. 1.25
    b. 1.50
    c. 1.60
    d. 1.85

55. Which of the following standard costing variances would be **least** controllable by a production supervisor?
    a. Overhead volume.
    b. Overhead efficiency.
    c. Labor efficiency.
    d. Material usage.

56. The standard direct material cost to produce a unit of Lem is four meters of material at $2.50 per meter. During May 2008, 4,200 meters of material costing $10,080 were purchased and used to produce 1,000 units of Lem. What was the material price variance for May 2008?
    a. $400 favorable.
    b. $420 favorable.
    c. $ 80 unfavorable.
    d. $480 unfavorable.

57. Dahl Co. uses a standard costing system in connection with the manufacture of a "one size fits all" article of clothing. Each unit of finished product contains two yards of direct material. However, a 20% direct material spoilage calculated on input quantities occurs during the manufacturing process. The cost of the direct material is $3 per yard. The standard direct material cost per unit of finished product is
    a. $4.80
    b. $6.00
    c. $7.20
    d. $7.50

58. Carr Co. had an unfavorable materials usage variance of $900. What amounts of this variance should be charged to each department?

	Purchasing	Warehousing	Manufacturing
a.	$0	$0	$900
b.	$0	$900	$0
c.	$300	$300	$300
d.	$900	$0	$0

59. Yola Co. manufactures one product with a standard direct manufacturing labor cost of four hours at $12.00 per hour. During June, 1,000 units were produced using 4,100 hours at $12.20 per hour. The unfavorable direct labor efficiency variance was
    a. $1,220
    b. $1,200
    c. $ 820
    d. $ 400

60. The following direct manufacturing labor information pertains to the manufacture of product Glu:

Time required to make one unit	2 direct labor hours
Number of direct workers	50
Number of productive hours per week, per worker	40
Weekly wages per worker	$500
Workers' benefits treated as direct manufacturing labor costs	20% of wages

What is the standard direct manufacturing labor cost per unit of product Glu?
    a. $30
    b. $24
    c. $15
    d. $12

61. On the diagram below, the line OW represents the standard labor cost at any output volume expressed in direct labor hours. Point S indicates the actual output at standard cost, and Point A indicates the actual hours and actual cost required to produce S.

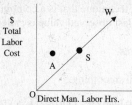

Which of the following variances are favorable or unfavorable?

	Rate variance	Efficiency variance
a.	Favorable	Unfavorable
b.	Favorable	Favorable
c.	Unfavorable	Unfavorable
d.	Unfavorable	Favorable

62. The following were among Gage Co.'s 2008 costs:

Normal spoilage	$ 5,000
Freight out	10,000
Excess of actual manufacturing costs over standard costs	20,000
Standard manufacturing costs	100,000
Actual prime manufacturing costs	80,000

Gage's 2008 actual manufacturing overhead was
    a. $ 40,000
    b. $ 45,000

c. $ 55,000
d. $120,000

63. Baby Frames, Inc. evaluates manufacturing overhead in its factory by using variance analysis. The following information applies to the month of May:

	Actual	Budgeted
Number of frames manufactured	19,000	20,000
Variable overhead costs	$4,100	$2 per direct labor hour
Fixed overhead costs	$22,000	$20,000
Direct labor hours	2,100	0.1 hour per frame

What is the fixed overhead spending variance?
a. $1,000 favorable.
b. $1,000 unfavorable.
c. $2,000 favorable.
d. $2,000 unfavorable.

64. Under the 2-variance method for analyzing overhead, which of the following variances consists of both variable and fixed overhead elements?

	Controllable (budget) variance	Volume variance
a.	Yes	Yes
b.	Yes	No
c.	No	No
d.	No	Yes

65. During 2008, a department's 3-variance overhead standard costing system reported unfavorable spending and volume variances. The activity level selected for allocating overhead to the product was based on 80% of practical capacity. If 100% of practical capacity had been selected instead, how would the reported unfavorable spending and volume variances be affected?

	Spending variance	Volume variance
a.	Increased	Unchanged
b.	Increased	Increased
c.	Unchanged	Increased
d.	Unchanged	Unchanged

66. The following information pertains to Roe Co.'s 2008 manufacturing operations:

Standard direct manufacturing labor hours per unit	2
Actual direct manufacturing labor hours	10,500
Number of units produced	5,000
Standard variable overhead per standard direct manufacturing labor hour	$3
Actual variable overhead	$28,000

Roe's 2008 unfavorable variable overhead efficiency variance was
a. $0
b. $1,500
c. $2,000
d. $3,500

67. Which of the following variances would be useful in calling attention to a possible short-term problem in the control of overhead costs?

	Spending variance	Volume variance
a.	No	No
b.	No	Yes
c.	Yes	No
d.	Yes	Yes

Items 68 and 69 are based on the following:

The diagram below depicts a factory overhead flexible budget line DB and standard overhead application line OA. Activity is expressed in machine hours with Point V indicating the standard hours required for the actual output in September 2008. Point S indicates the actual machine hours (inputs) and actual costs in September 2008.

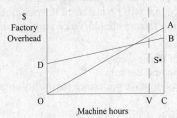

68. Are the following overhead variances favorable or unfavorable?

	Volume (capacity) variance	Efficiency variance
a.	Favorable	Favorable
b.	Favorable	Unfavorable
c.	Unfavorable	Favorable
d.	Unfavorable	Unfavorable

69. The budgeted total variable overhead cost for C machine hours is
a. AB
b. BC
c. AC minus DO
d. BC minus DO

70. Lanta Restaurant compares monthly operating results with a static budget. When actual sales are less than budget, would Lanta usually report favorable variances on variable food costs and fixed supervisory salaries?

	Variable food costs	Fixed supervisory salaries
a.	Yes	Yes
b.	Yes	No
c.	No	Yes
d.	No	No

71. Cuff Caterers quotes a price of $60 per person for a dinner party. This price includes the 6% sales tax and the 15% service charge. Sales tax is computed on the food plus the service charge. The service charge is computed on the food only. At what amount does Cuff price the food?
a. $56.40
b. $51.00
c. $49.22
d. $47.40

72. Based on potential sales of 500 units per year, a new product has estimated traceable costs of $990,000. What is the target price to obtain a 15% profit margin on sales?
a. $2,329
b. $2,277
c. $1,980
d. $1,935

73. Briar Co. signed a government construction contract providing for a formula price of actual cost plus 10%. In addition, Briar was to receive one-half of any savings resulting from the formula price being less than the target price of $2,200,000. Briar's actual costs incurred were

$1,920,000. How much should Briar receive from the contract?

- a. $2,060,000
- b. $2,112,000
- c. $2,156,000
- d. $2,200,000

74. Vince, Inc. has developed and patented a new laser disc reading device that will be marketed internationally. Which of the following factors should Vince consider in pricing the device?

- I. Quality of the new device.
- II. Life of the new device.
- III. Customers' relative preference for quality compared to price.

- a. I and II only.
- b. I and III only.
- c. II and III only.
- d. I, II, and III.

75. The budget for Klunker Auto Repair Shop for the year is as follows:

Direct labor per hour	$ 30
Total labor hours	10,000
Overhead costs:	
Materials handling and storage	$ 10,000
Other (rent, utilities, depreciation, insurance)	$120,000
Direct materials cost	$500,000

Klunker allocates materials handling and storage costs per dollar of direct materials cost. Other overhead is allocated based on total labor hours. In addition, Klunker adds a charge of $8 per labor hour to cover profit margin. Tardy Trucking Co. has brought one of its trucks to Klunker for an engine overhaul. If the overhaul requires twelve labor hours and $800 parts, what price should Klunker charge Tardy for these repair services?

- a. $1,160
- b. $1,256
- c. $1,416
- d. $1,472

76. Ajax Division of Carlyle Corporation produces electric motors, 20% of which are sold to Bradley Division of Carlyle and the remainder to outside customers. Carlyle treats its divisions as profit centers and allows division managers to choose their sources of sale and supply. Corporate policy requires that all interdivisional sales and purchases be recorded at variable cost as a transfer price. Ajax Division's estimated sales and standard cost data for the year ending December 31, 2008, based on the full capacity of 100,000 units, are as follows:

	Bradley	Outsiders
Sales	$ 900,000	$ 8,000,000
Variable costs	(900,000)	(3,600,000)
Fixed costs	(300,000)	(1,200,000)
Gross margin	$(300,000)	$ 3,200,000
Unit sales	20,000	80,000

Ajax has an opportunity to sell the above 20,000 units to an outside customer at a price of $75 per unit during 2008 on a continuing basis. Bradley can purchase its requirements from an outside supplier at a price of $85 per unit.

Assuming that Ajax Division desires to maximize its gross margin, should Ajax take on the new customer and drop its sales to Bradley for 2008, and why?

- a. No, because the gross margin of the corporation as a whole would decrease by $200,000.
- b. Yes, because Ajax Division's gross margin would increase by $300,000.
- c. Yes, because Ajax Division's gross margin would increase by $600,000.
- d. No, because Bradley Division's gross margin would decrease by $800,000.

77. The management of James Corporation has decided to implement a transfer pricing system. James' MIS department is currently negotiating a transfer price for its services with the four producing divisions of the company as well as the marketing department. Charges will be assessed based on number of reports (assume that all reports require the same amount of time and resources to produce). The cost to operate the MIS department at its full capacity of 1,000 reports per year is budgeted at $45,000. The user subunits expect to request 250 reports each this year. The cost of temporary labor and additional facilities used to produce reports beyond capacity is budgeted at $48.00 per report. James could purchase the same services from an external Information Services firm for $70,000. What amounts should be used as the ceiling and the floor in determining the negotiated transfer price?

- a. Floor, $36.00; Ceiling $56.00.
- b. Floor, $45.60; Ceiling $56.00.
- c. Floor, $48.00; Ceiling $70.00.
- d. Floor, $57.00; Ceiling $82.00.

**78. Systematic evaluation of the trade-offs between product functionality and product cost while still satisfying customer needs is the definition of

- a. Activity-based management.
- b. Theory of constraints.
- c. Total quality management.
- d. Value engineering.

79. Which of the following statements regarding transfer pricing is false?

- a. When idle capacity exists, there is no opportunity cost to producing intermediate products for another division.
- b. Market-based transfer prices should be reduced by any costs avoided by selling internally rather than externally.
- c. No contribution margin is generated by the transferring division when variable cost-based transfer prices are used.
- d. The goal of transfer pricing is to provide segment managers with incentive to maximize the profits of their divisions.

80. Clay Co. has considerable excess manufacturing capacity. A special job order's cost sheet includes the following applied manufacturing overhead costs:

Fixed costs	$21,000
Variable costs	33,000

The fixed costs include a normal $3,700 allocation for in-house design costs, although no in-house design will be done. Instead the job will require the use of external designers costing $7,750. What is the total amount to be included in the calculation to determine the minimum acceptable price for the job?

- a. $36,700
- b. $40,750

    c. $54,000
    d. $58,050

81. For the year ended December 31, 2008, Abel Co. incurred direct costs of $500,000 based on a particular course of action during the year. If a different course of action had been taken, direct costs would have been $400,000. In addition, Abel's 2008 fixed costs were $90,000. The incremental cost was

    a. $ 10,000
    b. $ 90,000
    c. $100,000
    d. $190,000

82. Mili Co. plans to discontinue a division with a $20,000 contribution margin. Overhead allocated to the division is $50,000, of which $5,000 cannot be eliminated. The effect of this discontinuance on Mili's pretax income would be an increase of

    a. $ 5,000
    b. $20,000
    c. $25,000
    d. $30,000

**83. Following are the operating results of the two segments of Parklin Corporation

	Segment A	Segment B	Total
Sales	$10,000	$15,000	$25,000
Variable cost of goods sold	4,000	8,500	12,500
Fixed cost of goods sold	1,500	2,500	4,000
Gross margin	4,500	4,000	8,500
Variable selling and administrative	2,000	3,000	5,000
Fixed selling and administrative	1,500	1,500	3,000
Operating income (loss)	$ 1,000	$ (500)	$ 500

Fixed costs of goods sold are allocated to each segment based on the number of employees. Fixed selling and administrative expenses are allocated equally. If Segment B is eliminated, $1,500 of fixed costs of goods sold would be eliminated. Assuming Segment B is closed, the effect on operating income would be

    a.   An increase of $500.
    b.   An increase of $2,000.
    c.   A decrease of $2,000.
    d.   A decrease of $2,500.

**   *CMA adapted*

MULTIPLE-CHOICE ANSWERS

1. d		19. b		37. a		55. a		73. c	
2. c		20. a		38. d		56. b		74. d	
3. a		21. c		39. c		57. d		75. c	
4. b		22. c		40. c		58. a		76. c	
5. b		23. d		41. d		59. b		77. b	
6. b		24. c		42. b		60. a		78. d	
7. b		25. b		43. a		61. d		79. d	
8. b		26. c		44. c		62. a		80. b	
9. d		27. d		45. d		63. d		81. c	
10. c		28. b		46. b		64. b		82. c	
11. c		29. c		47. c		65. c		83. c	
12. a		30. c		48. c		66. b			
13. b		31. a		49. d		67. c			
14. c		32. b		50. c		68. b			
15. a		33. c		51. a		69. d			
16. a		34. c		52. a		70. b			
17. d		35. b		53. a		71. c		1st: __/83 = __%	
18. b		36. d		54. b		72. a		2nd: __/83 = __%	

MULTIPLE-CHOICE ANSWER EXPLANATIONS

A. Cost-Volume-Profit (CVP) Analysis

1. (d) Any income statement can be expressed as

Sales – Variable costs – Fixed costs = Operating income

At the breakeven point, operating income = $0. In addition, the Contribution margin = Sales – Variable costs. Therefore, the above equation may be restated as

Sales – Variable costs – Fixed costs = 0
Sales – Variable costs = Fixed costs
Contribution margin = Fixed costs

This makes sense because, by definition, the breakeven point is the point at which revenues equal expenses; after variable costs are subtracted from sales, the contribution margin remaining will be just enough to cover fixed costs.

2. (c) The short-cut breakeven point formula is calculated as follows:

$$\text{Breakeven (units)} = \frac{\text{Fixed costs}}{\text{Contribution margin}}$$

Thus, by decreasing the numerator (fixed costs) and increasing the denominator (contribution margin), the breakeven point will be reduced.

3. (a) The solutions approach is to work backward from breakeven sales to determine the contribution margin (CM) ratio. The CM ratio can then be used to determine Del's projected profit at $1,200,000 sales. This is accomplished by plugging fixed costs and breakeven sales into the breakeven equation.

$$\text{Breakeven sales} = \frac{\text{Fixed costs}}{\text{CM ratio}}$$

$$\$800,000 = \frac{\$100,000}{\text{CM ratio}}$$

CM ratio = 0.125, or 12.5%

Therefore, projected total contribution margin from $1,200,000 sales is $150,000 ($1,200,000 × 12.5%), and projected profit is $50,000 ($150,000 CM – $100,000 fixed costs).

4. (b) The requirement is to calculate the number of units that must be sold to generate earnings before interest

and taxes (EBIT) in an amount equal to 32% of the amount of capital invested. Answer (b) is correct because the number of units is 32,143 as calculated below.

Desired return (EBIT) = 32% × $250,000 (investment = $80,000

Required number of units = (Fixed costs + desired EBIT)/Contribution margin
= ($122,500 + $80,000)/($15 × 42%) = 32,143

5. (b) The requirement is to determine the price that Thor Lab should charge to make the same profit with increased fixed costs. The first step in solving this problem is to calculate the variable cost per unit. The variable cost component is determined as follows:

Sales	–	VC	–	FC	=	Profit
(80,000 × $120)	–	(80,000x)	–	$1,000,000	=	$200,000
$9,600,000	–	80,000x	–	$1,000,000	=	$200,000
				$8,400,000	=	80,000x
				$105	=	x

The next step is to substitute the variable cost component and the increased fixed cost amount into the above equation to determine the necessary price. The price can be computed as follows:

80,000x – (80,000 × $105) – $2,200,000 = $200,000
80,000x = $10,800,000
x = $135

6. (b) Breakeven analysis is based on several simplified assumptions. One assumption is that, over the relevant range, variable costs **per unit** remain unchanged. It is assumed that over the relevant range, selling price per unit remains constant. Thus, unit revenues are linear. Total variable costs increase with increases in production; therefore, total costs also increase. Over the relevant range, total fixed costs are always linear since they do not change.

7. (b) The requirement is to determine Cott's fixed cost using only sales, contribution margin, and margin of safety. First, Cott's breakeven sales should be determined. Since the margin of safety defines how far revenues can fall before the breakeven point is reached, breakeven sales equal $120,000 ($200,000 sales – $80,000 margin of safety). We also know that Cott's contribution margin is 20% of sales.

Contribution margin (CM) equals sales minus all related variable costs (VC), and the contribution margin percentage is calculated as

$$CM\% = \frac{Total\ CM}{Revenues}$$

Or, in this case,

$$20\% = \frac{Total\ CM}{\$120,000}$$

Total CM at breakeven = ($120,000) (20%) = $24,000

At the breakeven point, no profit exists and Sales – VC = FC. Therefore, the CM at the breakeven point equals fixed costs, and Cott's fixed costs total $24,000.

8.   (b)   The budgeted breakeven point is the volume at which total revenues equal total expenses. An increase in direct manufacturing labor wage rates would result in higher variable expenses and a lower contribution per unit. Accordingly, this **increases** the volume of sales necessary to breakeven. The budgeted margin of safety is the excess of budgeted total revenues minus total revenues at the breakeven point. As discussed above, the increase in direct manufacturing labor wages increased the breakeven point. This higher breakeven point **decreases** the budgeted margin of safety.

9.   (d)   To answer this question, an understanding of cost behavior patterns and CVP charts is needed. The CVP chart presented in the problem can be interpreted as follows:

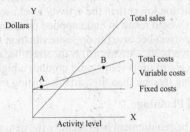

Within a relevant range, **total** variable costs vary directly with the number of units produced and sold. Because these costs remain constant per unit, the variable costs associated with point A and point B will be the same percentage of total sales associated with each point. Total fixed costs remain constant in total at any activity level. Because these costs are allocated evenly to units produced and sold, they represent a higher percentage of lower sales than of higher sales. Point A is to the left of point B, indicating a lower sales level for point A. The fixed costs will, therefore, be a greater percentage of sales at point A than at point B.

10.   (c)   If sales dollars are used to measure activity levels, the various activity levels on the X axis would be expressed in terms of sales. Total costs could be read by comparing a point on the total cost line to the Y axis only, because total costs are a dependent variable, which are measured on the Y axis. Total revenues could be read by comparing a point on the total sales line to either the Y axis or the X axis.

11.   (c)   The requirement is to identify an advantage of using variable costing. Answer (c) is correct because a major advantage of the use of variable costing is that it makes cost-volume relationships more apparent. Answer (a) is incorrect because variable costing does not comply with the US Internal Revenue Code. Answer (b) is incorrect because

variable costing does not comply with generally accepted accounting principles. Answer (d) is incorrect because variable costing is not most relevant to long-run pricing strategies. In the long run all costs must be recovered.

12.   (a)   The profit-volume (P/V) chart provides a quick condensed comparison of how alternatives for pricing, variable costs, and/or fixed costs may affect net income as volume levels change. In this problem, sales prices remain constant and, therefore, are not relevant. In a P/V chart, the vertical (Y) axis represents net income/loss in dollars. The horizontal (X) axis represents volume in units or dollars. Points on the Y axis above the intersection with the X axis represent profits while points below the intersection represent losses. Total fixed costs are represented by the point at which a specific P/V line intersects the Y axis. This point is always below zero on the Y axis. Because point G (where the P/V line for 2008 intersects the Y axis) is closer to zero than point E (where the P/V line for 2007 intersects the Y axis), point G is less negative; therefore, total fixed costs decreased from 2007 levels. The effect of total variable costs on net income is represented by the positive slope of a P/V line. Variable costs stay the same per unit but change in total as volume levels change. Therefore, a higher per unit amount of variable costs causes a lower per unit amount of net income across various volume levels. Because the graph represents changes in levels of totals, a steeper P/V line slope indicates more profit per unit. Because the slope of line GH (the P/V line for 2008) is **less** steep than the slope of line EF (the P/V line for 2007), net income per unit is less in 2008 than in 2007. Variable costs, therefore, rose between 2007 and 2008.

A.2. Breakeven: Multiproduct Firm

13.   (b)   The requirement is to determine how many units of product X (one of three products) Thomas would sell at the breakeven point. The solutions approach is first to find the number of composite units to breakeven; a composite unit consists of the number of units of each of the three products in the mix. Since Thomas sells three units of X for each unit of Z and two units of Y for each unit of X, they are selling six units of Y for each unit of Z; therefore, a composite unit consists of 3X, 6Y, and 1Z. The total contribution margin for one composite unit is

X (3) ($1.00)	=	$ 3
Y (6) ($1.50)	=	$ 9
Z (1) ($3.00)	=	$ 3
		$15

The breakeven point in terms of units of the product mix group is

$600,000 ÷ $15 = 40,000 composite units

Since there are three units of X in each composite unit, (40,000) (3) or 120,000 units of X are sold at breakeven.

14.   (c)   Breakeven analysis is based upon several simplified assumptions. Included in these assumptions is that variable costs are constant per unit and, for a multiproduct company, that a given sales mix is maintained for all volume changes. When absorption costing is used, operating income is a function of **both** production volume and sales volume. This is because an increase in inventory levels causes fixed costs to be held in inventory while a decrease in inventory levels causes fixed costs to be charged to cost of goods sold. These fluctuations can dramatically affect income and the breakeven point. On the other hand, when variable costing is used the same amount of fixed costs will be deducted from income whether or not inventory levels fluctuate. As a result, the breakeven point will be the same even if production does not equal sales. Hence, operating income under variable costing is a function **only** of sales, and assumption I. is incorrect.

15. (a) If sales prices, cost behavior, and actual **total** sales were as budgeted, then the excess profit must have resulted from a departure from budget by the **individual** products. Since the slope of line EH is greater than that of line HG (the slope representing profit per unit), Product 1 had the excess sales. Line OE represents fixed costs and line OF represents quantity sold up to the breakeven point. OE/OF is the contribution margin that may offset fixed costs until the breakeven point, F, is reached.

B. Variable (Direct) and Absorption (Full) Costing

16. (a) The difference between net income under variable costing and net income under full absorption costing is $36,000, which is equal to 20,000 × $180,000/100,000. The difference between the two methods is the fixed cost of manufacturing in the ending inventory that would be capitalized under the full absorption costing method and expensed under the variable costing method. Answer (b) is incorrect because the fixed selling and administration costs would be expensed under either method.

17. (d) Under variable costing, both variable direct and variable indirect manufacturing costs are assigned to inventory. All fixed costs are considered sunk costs and thus are written off as an expense of the period. Additionally, variable selling and administrative costs are also treated as period costs and thus not assigned to inventory.

18. (b) The requirement is to determine the different results obtained using absorption and variable costing. Under absorption costing, fixed costs are applied to units produced and are inventoried as product costs. Variable costing considers fixed costs to be period rather than product costs. Killo Co.'s inventoried costs under both methods are as follows:

	Absorption		*Variable*	
Variable costs	1,000 × $90	= $90,000	1,000 × $90	= $90,000
Fixed costs	1,000 × $20	= 20,000		
Total cost of inventory		$110,000		$90,000

Under the variable method, the $20,000 of fixed cost was charged to income, whereas with absorption costing the fixed costs were absorbed into inventory. Therefore, absorption costing results in a pretax income that is higher by $20,000.

19. (b) The solutions approach is to visualize each income statement as shown below.

Absorption costing IS

      Sales
− Cost of goods sold
      Gross profit (margin)
− Selling & Admin. Expenses
      Operating income

Variable costing IS

      Sales
− Variable expenses
      Contribution margin
− Fixed expenses
      Operating income

Because the question states that actual sales revenue, total gross profit, and total contribution margin approximated budgeted figures, CGS and variable expenses must have also approximated budgeted figures. Net income is substantially greater, therefore, because selling and administrative fixed expenses had decreased. If manufacturing fixed costs had increased, gross margin would have decreased. If sales prices and variable costs had increased proportionately, the contribution margin would have increased by the same percentage. If sales prices had declined proportionately less than variable costs, the contribution margin would have again increased.

20. (a) The requirement is to determine what situation would cause variable costing net income to be higher than absorption costing net income. Answer (a) is correct because this difference in reported income is explained if units produced in 2008 are less than units sold in 2008. This is true because under variable costing, the amount of overhead included in cost of goods sold is the amount applied in 2008 (since all units produced were sold), whereas under absorption costing the overhead released to cost of goods sold includes that applied in 2008 as well as overhead included in the 2007 year-end inventory. Answer (b) is incorrect since a level of production lower than the activity level used to allocate overhead would result in underapplied overhead. Answer (c) is incorrect because the opposite situation results in overapplied overhead. Answer (d) is incorrect because production in excess of units sold would produce a higher absorption costing income than the variable costing income.

C. Financial Planning

21. (c) The requirement is to identify the item that is an output from a strategic plan. Answer (c) is correct. A financial planning model is a mathematical model that attempts to forecast future financial results. Sets of projected financial statements are a major output from the model. Answer (a) is incorrect because strategic plans drive the financial planning process and must be developed before employing the financial planning model. Answers (b) and (d) are incorrect because the planning model does not provide outputs related to actual results.

D. Budgeting

22. (c) The requirement is to determine the number of kilos of chemical Loire that Mien is planning to purchase in October. The first step is to prepare a production budget for product Nous.

Sales	53,000
Increase in ending inventory	6,000
Total units needed	59,000

Next, a purchases budget for raw material Loire should be prepared.

Production needs (59,000 × 4)	236,000
Decrease in ending inventory	(50,000)
Total kilos needed	186,000

Note that the production needs for Loire equal the number of units of Nous to be produced times the number of kilos of Loire needed per unit (4).

23. (d) The requirement is to identify a characteristic of the master budget. Answer (d) is correct because the master budget is a comprehensive budget that includes both the operating and financial budgets. Answer (a) is incorrect because the master budget does not show actual results. Answer (b) is incorrect because the master budget shows all costs, controllable and uncontrollable. Answer (c) is incorrect because the master budget is not structured for the computation of variances.

24. (c) The requirement is to calculate the budgeted cost of purchases for the month of August. The cost of inventory needed to meet August forecasted sales is equal to $300,000 ($750,000 × 40%). The required ending inventory for August is equal to $82,500 ($825,000 September sales × 40% × 25%). The ending inventory for July is equal to $75,000 ($750,000 August sales × 40% × 25%). Budgeted cost of purchases for August would equal to $307,500 ($300,000 cost of goods sold + $82,500 required ending inventory − $75,000 beginning inventory). Therefore, answer (c) is correct. Answer (a) is incorrect because the June 30 inventory is deducted. Answer (b) is incorrect because it deducts what should be the ending inventory for June. Answer (d) is incorrect because it results from using sales prices for the beginning and ending inventories.

25. (b) The requirement is to calculate the budgeted amount of cash receipts from sales and collection for September. Forecasted sales for September are $825,000 of which $165,000 (20%) are cash sales. In addition, 40% of credit sales are collected in the month of sale, which is equal to $264,000 ($825,000) × 80% × 40%). Collections of August sales in September are equal to $342,000 ($750,000 × 80% × 57%). Accordingly, the projected collections for September are $771,000 ($165,00 + $264,000 + $342,000), and answer (b) is correct. Answer (a) is incorrect because $757,000 ignores cash sales. Answer (c) is incorrect because $793,800 assumes 57% of October sales are collected in September. Answer (d) is incorrect because $856,500 assumes the collections in September for August sales are 57% of total sales.

26. (c) The requirement is to define a tactical profit plan. Answer (c) is correct because tactical profit plans have the characteristics of being quantified, detailed and short-term, and assigning responsibilities at all levels. Answer (a) is incorrect because tactical profit plans are quantitative with detailed assigned responsibilities. Answer (b) is incorrect because tactical profit plans are detailed. Answer (d) is incorrect because tactical profit plans are detailed, short-term, quantitative, and include assigned responsibilities at all levels.

27. (d) The requirement is to identify the budgeting technique that focuses on improving operations. Answer (d) is correct because Kaizen budgeting projects costs on the basis of improvements to be implemented. Answer (a) is incorrect because responsibility budgeting focuses on the ability of the manager to control the cost. Answer (b) is incorrect because activity-based budgeting uses cost drivers to determine budgeted costs. Answer (c) is incorrect because operational budgeting focuses on budgeting operating costs.

28. (b) The requirement is to identify the item that is part of a financial budget. Answer (b) is correct. The financial budget includes the capital budget, cash budget, and the budgeted statement of cash flows. The operating budget includes the budgeted income statement and supporting budgets. Answers (a), (c), and (d) are incorrect because they are part of the operating budget.

29. (c) Calculation of the cash payments for components in May is shown below.

Payments for June sales	$1,750 ($7,000 × 25%)
Payment for July sales	$6,000 ($8,000 × 75%)
Total cash payments	$7,750

Answer (a) is incorrect because parts are ordered two months prior to sales. Therefore, costs of components for sales of June and July should be considered. Answer (b) is incorrect because parts are ordered two months prior to sales. Therefore, costs of components for sales of June and July should be considered. Answer (d) is incorrect because parts are ordered two months prior to sales. Therefore, costs of components for sales of June and July should be considered.

30. (c) The requirement is to determine budgeted cash disbursements for purchases for 2008. The solutions approach is to use T-accounts to trace the flow of budgeted costs through the accounts.

	Inventory		
Bal. 1/1/08	30,000		
Purchases	?	300,000	CGS
Bal. 12/31/08	42,000		

T-account analysis reveals that total purchases of inventory for the year must be $312,000.

Goods sold or on hand at 12/31	−	Beginning inventory	=	Purchases
($300,000 + $42,000)	−	$30,000	=	$312,000

Payments for purchases are made in the month following purchase. Thus, accounts payable at 1/1/08 will be paid in January 2008 and 1/12 of 2008 purchases (since Toyi is purchased in equal amounts each month) will be paid for in January 2009.

Accounts payable is depicted as follows:

	Accounts Payable		
Cash disbursements	306,000*	20,000	Bal. 1/1/08
		312,000	Purchases
		26,000**	Bal. 12/31/08

* ($312,000 purchases x 11/12) + $20,000 beg. AP
** $312,000 purchases x 1/12

Therefore, budgeted cash payments for Toyi for 2008 is $306,000.

31. (a) The requirement is to calculate the budgeted cash from collection of accounts receivable. Answer (a) is correct because the amount is equal to July's collections in September plus August's collections in September. This amount is $169,800 (36% × $120,000 + 60% × $211,000).

32. (b) The requirement is to find the total budgeted costs for the seven stores in the coming year. Fixed costs last year were $70,000, and therefore variable costs totaled $430,000. The key is to find the variable costs per store. This is calculated by dividing variable costs ($430,000) by the number of stores last year (five), or, $86,000. Therefore, total costs budgeted in the new year is calculated as follows:

Variable cost per store	$86,000
Number of stores	× 7
Total budgeted variable costs	602,000
Add: fixed costs	70,000
Total budgeted costs	$672,000

E. Forecasting Methods

33. (c) The requirement is to identify the correlation coefficient that represents the strongest relationship between the independent and dependent variables. Regression coefficients can range from -1.00 (perfect negative correlation to 1.00 (perfect positive correlation, and the closer to -1.00 or 1.00 the stronger the relationship. Answer (c) is correct because it is the coefficient closest to -1.00 or 1.00. Answer (a) is incorrect because it is not possible to have a correlation coefficient greater than 1.00. Answers (b) and (d) are incorrect because they are both further from -1.00 or 1.00.

34. (c) The requirement is to provide an explanation for a drop in r^2. The coefficient of determination (r^2) provides a measure of amount of variation in the dependent variable (interest income) explained by the independent variables. If there is a dramatic decrease in the coefficient of determination, the implication is that there are some new factors that are causing interest income to change. Therefore, answer (c) is correct. Answer (a) is incorrect because cross-sectional regression is not appropriate. Management is attempting to estimate interest income over time. Answer (b) is incorrect because regression analysis may still be appropriate. Answer (d) is incorrect because multiple regression is a linear model. Management may want to try other models such as nonlinear multiple regression.

35. (b) The requirement is to identify the factor that is not relevant to forecasting the needed level of inventory. Answer (b) is correct because knowledge of the internal accounting allocations is not relevant to determining the demand for the product. Answers (a), (c), and (d) are incorrect because they are all relevant to determining demand for the product and, therefore, the needed level of inventory.

36. (d) The requirement is to identify the meaning the of the letter *b* in the regression equation. Answer (d) is correct because *b* is the coefficient for the independent variable. The variable coefficient that describes the slope of the regression function. Answer (a) is incorrect because *x* is the independent variable. Answer (b) is incorrect because *y* is the dependent variable. Answer (c) is incorrect because *a* is the constant coefficient.

37. (a) The requirement is to identify the meaning of the letter *x* in the regression equation. Answer (a) is correct because *x* is the independent variable, the variable that is being used to predict the dependent variable. Answer (b) is incorrect because *y* is the dependent variable. Answer (c) is incorrect because *a* is the constant variable. Answer (d) is incorrect because r^2 is the coefficient of determination.

38. (d) The requirement is to use the regression equation to determine the amount of predicted maintenance costs. Substituting 420 maintenance hours into the equation results in a budgeted cost of $3,746.

$$y = a + bx$$
$$y = 684.65 + 7.2884 (420)$$
$$y = \$3,746$$

Therefore, (d) is the correct answer.

39. (c) The requirement is to identify the dependent variable. Answer (c) is correct because the dependent variable is the one being predicted, in this case revenue. Answers (a), (b), and (d) are incorrect because predicted number of days above 10 degrees and predicted number of inches of snow are both independent variables.

40. (c) The requirement is to calculate the predicted revenue for the next week. Answer (c) is correct because revenue is equal to $10,902 + (255 × 6) + (300 × 12) = 16,032. Answers (a), (b), and (d) are all incorrect computations of the prediction.

41. (d) The requirement is to identify the appropriate conclusion. Answer (d) is correct because the coefficient of determination indicates that 67.89% of revenue is explained by the predicted number of days above 10 degrees and the number of inches of snow. Answer (a) is incorrect because the *F*-Statistic measures the significance of the relationship. Answer (b) is incorrect because the *F*-Statistic indicates that the regression is significant. Answer (c) is incorrect because there is no information provided to make this determination.

42. (b) The requirement is to calculate the 95% confidence interval for the prediction of revenue. Answer (b) is correct because the 95% confidence interval is calculated by multiplying the standard error of the regression by 2.3436. Therefore, it is equal to 4,404 (1,879 × 2.3436).

43. (a) The requirement is to identify the sales forecasting technique that involves estimating sales based on analysis of consumer behavior. Answer (a) is correct because Markov techniques attempt to forecast consumer purchasing by considering factors such as brand loyalty and brand switching behavior. Answer (b) is incorrect because regression analysis forecasts sales based on the relationship between sales and one or more predictors. Answer (c) is incorrect because econometric models forecast sales based on the relationship between sales and economic data. Answer (d) is incorrect because exponential smoothing is used to forecast sales based on historical data.

44. (c) The requirement is to identify the quantitative technique to developing a sales forecast. Answer (c) is correct because the moving average technique uses the average of sales for the most recent periods to predict next period's sales. Answer (a) is incorrect because the Delphi technique is simply a structured approach to developing a subjective estimate from a group of people. Answers (b) and (d) are incorrect because they involve qualitative approaches to developing a sales forecast.

45. (d) The requirement is to identify the forecasting technique that is determined by a combination of the last forecast and the last observed value. Answer (d) is correct because exponential smoothing is a quantitative technique that forecasts sales based on prior data with the most recent observation being weighted more heavily. Answer (a) is incorrect because the Delphi technique forecasts with a consensus of opinion. Answers (b) and (d) are incorrect because least squares and regression forecast sales based on the correlation of sales with one or more independent variables.

46. (b) The correlation coefficient is a relative measure of the relationship between two variables. The range of the correlation coefficient is from -1 (perfect negative correlation) to +1 (perfect positive correlation). A correlation coefficient of zero means that there is **no** correlation between the two variables. Since the level of sales **increases** as the level of income **decreases,** this relationship represents a strong **negative** correlation. Answer (c) is incorrect because it represents a **positive** correlation. Answers (a) and (d) are incorrect because they lie outside of the range for correlation coefficients.

F. Flexible Budgets

47. (c) A flexible budget is simply a static budget adjusted for various possible volume levels within the relevant range. A master budget or a flexible budget may be used during both the planning phase, when the budget is prepared, and the controlling phase, when actual results are compared to the budget. A flexible budget may be prepared for any unit for which costs vary with changes in activity level. Flexible budgets provide as much cost control as do master budgets because they are based on costs **allowable** at different activity levels. In fact, flexible budgets may offer an even greater degree of control because valid guidelines are available to managers even if output deviates from expectations, whereas static budgets supply information regarding only the planned volume.

48. (c) The requirement is to determine whether a flexible budget is appropriate for a marketing and/or a direct material usage budget. Flexible budgets are used to analyze changes in costs and revenues as changes in activity levels take place. If no changes are expected to occur and thus all amounts in the flexible budget remain constant throughout the relevant range (i.e., all costs are fixed), there is no need for a flexible budget. A marketing budget includes expenses incurred for promotion and sales. Some of these items, such as sales commissions or sample promotional products change with activity level. Direct material usage is directly dependent on activity level. Since a flexible budget would be appropriate for both a marketing and a direct materials usage budget, answer (c) is correct.

49. (d) Within the relevant range, **total** fixed costs remain constant. As production levels increase, the same amount of fixed cost is spread over a greater number of units, and fixed costs **per unit** decrease. In contrast, variable costs **per unit** do not change within the relevant range.

G. Responsibility Accounting

50. (c) Responsibility accounting allocates to responsibility centers those costs, revenues, and/or assets which a manager can control. If a manager is only responsible for costs, the area of responsibility under his/her control is called a cost center. If the manager is responsible for both revenues and costs, his/her area of control is called a profit center. Thus, controllable revenue pertains to the profit center but not the cost center.

51. (a) A manager of a profit center is responsible for both the revenues and the costs of that center. Costs charged directly to a profit center, excluding fixed costs, are subject to the control of the profit center manager. As a result, the profit center's contribution margin (Sales – All variable costs) is controllable by the center manager. In this case, the manager of Carr Co.'s center No. 43 would be most likely to control the center's contribution margin of $70,000. The period expenses shown in the problem would not be subject to the manager's control and thus are irrelevant items.

52. (a) Direct manufacturing labor costs are labor costs that can be easily traced to the manufacture of a product. Wages earned by machine operators producing a firm's product are, therefore, direct manufacturing labor costs. Controllable costs are those which can be directly influenced by a given manager within a given time span. Wages earned by machine operators are controllable by the machine operators' foreman.

H. Standards and Variances

53. (a) Many service firms, nonprofit organizations, and governmental units, in addition to manufacturing firms, use standard cost systems. For example, a trucking company may set standards for fuel costs.

54. (b) Standard costs are predetermined target costs which should be attainable under **efficient** conditions. Currently attainable standards should be achieved under efficient operating conditions. Therefore, engineering estimates based on attainable performance would provide the best basis for Flint in establishing standard hours allowed.

55. (a) The requirement is to determine the standard costing variance which would be **least** controllable by a production supervisor. The overhead output level (volume) variance arises because the **actual** production volume level achieved usually does not coincide with the production level used as a denominator volume for calculating a budgeted overhead **application** rate. The overhead output level variance results from treating a **fixed cost** as if it were a **variable cost**. Answers (b), (c), and (d) are incorrect because all of these variances arise when the quantity of actual inputs used differs from the quantity of inputs that should have been used. A production manager would have more control over inputs to production than over the determination of the denominator volume.

56. (b) The requirement is to determine Lem's material price variance for May. The direct materials price variance is the difference between actual unit prices and standard unit prices multiplied by the actual quantity, as shown below.

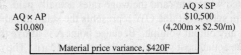

The $420 price variance is favorable because the actual purchase price of the material was lower than the standard price. Since the material was purchased for only $2.40 per meter ($10,080 cost ÷ 4,200m), Lem saved $.10 per meter compared to the standard price, for a total price savings of $420 (4,200m × $.10/m). Note that the standard quantity of materials is ignored in order to isolate these price differences; differences in quantity are addressed by the materials usage variance.

57. (d) Each unit of finished product contains two yards of direct material. However, the problem states that the 20% direct material spoilage is calculated on the quantity of direct material **input**. Although not mentioned, the facts in this question infer that the spoilage is normal and should be part of the product's standard cost. The solutions approach would be to set up the following formula:

Input quantity	–	Spoilage	=	Output amount
X	–	.2X	=	2 yds.
		.8X	=	2 yds.
		X	=	2.5 yds.

Thus, the standard direct material cost per unit of finished product is $7.50 (2.5 yds. × $3).

58.   **(a)**   The materials usage variance measures the **actual** amount of materials **used** versus the standard amount that should have been used given the level of output. Normally the only department with controls over usage of materials is the manufacturing department. The purchasing department normally controls the cost of materials **purchased,** and not the amounts used (materials price variance). The warehouse department has little or no control over the materials used.

59.   **(b)**   The solutions approach to compute the direct manufacturing labor efficiency variance is to set up a diagram as follows:

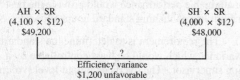

AH × SR	SH × SR
(4,100 × $12)	(4,000 × $12)
$49,200	$48,000

Efficiency variance
$1,200 unfavorable

NOTE: To compute the Standard Hours (SH), multiply the Standard Hours allowed per unit produced (4) by the number of units produced (1,000).

60.   **(a)**   Standard costs are predetermined target costs which should be attainable under efficient conditions. The standard direct manufacturing labor cost per unit of product Glu is calculated as follows:

Weekly wages per worker	$500
Benefits treated as DML cost	100
Total DML per week per worker	$600
Hours per week	÷40
DML cost per hour	$ 15
Hours required for each unit	× 2
Standard DML cost per unit	$ 30

61.   **(d)**   A labor rate variance is the difference between budgeted wage rates and the wage rates actually paid. The problem states that line OW represents the standard labor cost at any output volume. Because point A is **above** the line, the actual cost was higher than the standard. The rate variance is, therefore, unfavorable. A labor efficiency variance is the difference between actual hours worked and standard hours allowed for output. On the diagram, point S is further on the X axis (Direct manufacturing labor hours) than point A indicating that the standard hours allowed are higher than the actual hours worked. Because actual hours are less than standard hours, this variance would be favorable.

62.   **(a)**   To determine Gage's actual manufacturing overhead from the information given, total actual manufacturing costs must first be computed.

Standard manufacturing cost	$100,000
Excess of actual manufacturing cost over standard costs	20,000
Total actual costs	$120,000

Since prime costs consist of direct materials and direct manufacturing labor, these costs are deducted from total actual costs to derive the portion that are overhead costs. Ordinarily, normal spoilage is not added to actual manufac-

turing overhead. The cost of normal spoilage should be added to the cost of good units produced. Freight out is also excluded because it is a selling expense.

Total actual costs	$120,000
Prime costs	(80,000)
Actual manufacturing overhead	$ 40,000

63.   **(d)**   The fixed overhead spending variance is calculated as follows:

Budgeted fixed overhead	$20,000
Actual fixed overhead	22,000
Unfavorable fixed overhead spending variance	$ 2,000

64.   **(b)**   The requirement is to determine which of the variances given consist of both variable and fixed overhead elements under a two-variance method. As shown in the diagram below, the controllable or budget variance includes both variable and fixed overhead elements, because the actual overhead amount, the first vertical line, includes both elements as does the budgeted overhead amount, the middle vertical line.

Actual	Budget for outputs achieved FOH + (SQ × SVR)	Applied SQ × STR*
	Budget var.	Volume var.

*   *STR = Standard variable rate (SVR) + Standard fixed rate (SFR)*

The output level (volume) variance includes only the variance of fixed overhead, because the SQ × SVR is common to both amounts (i.e., it is included in the STR) used to determine the output level variance. The difference in the two amounts is the output level variance. It arises because the middle vertical line includes the total amount of budgeted fixed overhead, whereas the third vertical line includes the amount of fixed overhead applied using a per unit amount based on normal volume or level of activity. Whenever the standard activity level based on good output (SQ) is different than the normal activity level, a volume variance will arise. Therefore, both variable and fixed overhead elements are included in the controllable variance but not in the output level variance.

65.   **(c)**   The requirement is to determine how unfavorable spending and output level (volume) variances computed using the three-variance method would be affected if the estimated activity level were increased. An increase in the activity level used to allocate overhead to the product will lower the standard fixed application rate (SFR). The formula for computing the SFR is

$$\text{Predetermined overhead rate} = \frac{\text{Estimated fixed overhead cost}}{\text{Estimated activity level}}$$

If the denominator in this formula is raised, the SFR is lowered. However, an increase in activity level used to allocate overhead will not affect the standard variable application rate (SVR). This rate is computed using the high-low method or regression analysis. The diagram for the 3-variance method is

Actual	Budget for actual inputs FOH + (AQ × SVR)	Budget for outputs achieved FOH + (SQ × SVR)	Applied (SQ × STR)*
	Spending var.	Efficiency var.	Output level var.

Net (overall) overhead variance

*STR = Standard variable rate (SVR) + Standard fixed rate (SFR)

When computing the standard variance, the SVR is used but the SFR is not. Therefore, this variance will not change with a change in activity level. The output level variance is computed by comparing the budgeted amount of total overhead costs for outputs achieved with the total amount of overhead applied. Both computations use SVR, but only the applied figure uses the SFR. In this problem, the output level variance is unfavorable indicating that the budgeted amount is more than the applied amount. When the SFR is lowered with the increase in activity level, less cost will be applied for every unit produced. The output level variance will therefore be increased and become more unfavorable.

66. (b)   The solutions approach to compute the variable overhead efficiency variance is to set up a diagram as follows:

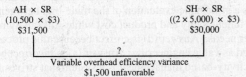

AH × SR   SH × SR
(10,500 × $3)   ((2 × 5,000) × $3)
$31,500 $30,000

?
Variable overhead efficiency variance
$1,500 unfavorable

67. (c)   A spending variance is caused by differences between the actual amount spent on fixed and variable overhead items and the amounts budgeted based on actual inputs. An output level variance is the difference between budgeted fixed overhead and applied fixed overhead. It is caused by under- or overutilization of plant capacity. Differences between actual and budgeted amounts (spending variances) occur often and can be corrected by changing the accounting estimates used in the budgeting process or the purchasing policies used. A difference in under- or over-utilization of plant capacity is a complex problem not easily corrected. Spending variances indicate short-term problems dealing with amounts spent on overhead while output level variances indicate long-term problems dealing with plant capacity.

68. (b)   The output level variance is solely a **fixed** overhead variance and is caused by under-/overutilization of capacity. This variance is computed by comparing the amount of fixed overhead budgeted with the amount of fixed overhead applied.

On the graph, line DB represents the flexible budget line for various outputs achieved and line OA represents the standard application line for various outputs achieved. Point V represents the standard quantity allowed for the output achieved. The dashed line extended vertically from V indicates the amount of overhead applied (where dashed line crosses OA) and the flexible budget amount (where dashed line crosses DB). Because the point on DB is below the point on OA, a larger amount was applied than the flexible budget amount. The output level variance is, therefore, favorable.

An overhead efficiency variance is solely a **variable** overhead variance and is caused by more (less) variable overhead being incurred due to inefficient (efficient) use of inputs. This variance is computed by comparing the flexible budget amount for actual inputs (Actual quantity of inputs × Standard variable application rate) with the amount applied (Standard quantity allowed for achieved output × Standard variable application rate). On the graph, Point S indicates the actual hours (inputs) used. Point V indicates the standard quantity allowed for the achieved outputs. Point S falls on the X axis further from zero than does Point V. Therefore, more hours were actually used than budgeted for the output achieved. The efficiency variance is unfavorable.

69. (d)   On the graph, line DB represents the total factory overhead flexible budget line for various outputs achieved. Point D (the Y intercept) indicates the amount of fixed overhead included in the flexible budget. Line BC represents the total flexible budget amount estimated for the level of inputs used at Point C. Budgeted total variable overhead cost for C machine hours is total overhead budget (BC) less fixed overhead budgeted (DO).

70. (b)   The requirement is to determine if favorable variances for variable food costs and fixed supervisory salaries would be reported by comparing actual results to amounts in a static budget. A static budget has only one planned volume level. The budget is not adjusted or altered to reflect changes in volume or other conditions during the budget period. In this problem, the actual level of sales was lower than the level used to make the static budget. Because variable costs remain the same per unit but change with levels of activity within the relevant range, actual variable costs would be lower than those in the budget. The variance reported for these costs would therefore be favorable. Fixed costs, however, are assumed to remain the same in total at all activity levels within the relevant range unless a change is specifically indicated. Because no such change is indicated in this problem concerning the fixed supervisory salaries, the actual amount for this cost would be the same as the amount in the static budget. There would be no variance reported for this fixed cost.

I. Product and Service Pricing

71. (c)   The solutions approach is to algebraically reconstruct how Cuff Caterers determined the total price per person. Three components comprise the total price: the cost of the food, the service charge, and the sales tax. The 15% service charge is computed on the food (F) only. The 6% sales tax is computed on the food plus the service charge. The following equation is used to compute the price:

$$F + .15F + .06(F + .15F) = \$60.00$$

Where

F	=	the cost of the food alone
.15F	=	the service charge
.06 (F + .15F)	=	the sales tax

Solving algebraically

1.219F	=	$60.00
F	=	$49.22

72. (a)   The target price is to be set at a budgeted ratio of operating income to revenue, or a profit margin on sales of 15%. This problem may be solved using the following equation:

Let x	=	Target price
Revenue – Cost	=	Profit
500x – $990,000	=	.15(500x)
.85(500x)	=	$990,000
425x	=	$990,000
x	=	$2,329

73. (c)   The requirement is to determine the amount that Briar should receive from the contract. This amount can be computed as follows:

Actual costs incurred	$1,920,000
Multiply by 110% (cost + 10%)	× 1.10
Formula price	$2,112,000

The target price of $2,200,000 exceeds the formula price of $2,112,000 by $88,000. Briar is to receive 50% of this amount, or $44,000, in addition to the formula price. Therefore, Briar is to receive a total of $2,156,000 ($2,112,000 + $44,000).

74. (d) To determine the price at which expected product sales will yield the greatest profits, many factors such as customer preferences, competitors' reactions, cost structures, etc. must be considered. A customer's perception of the quality and durability (life) of a product affects how much s/he is willing to pay for that product. However, in some cases a customer may prefer to pay less money and receive a product of lesser quality. Therefore, Vince should consider the quality and life of the new device as well as customers' relative preference for quality compared to price.

75. (c) Klunker is using a "time and material" pricing approach. The charges for each are calculated below.

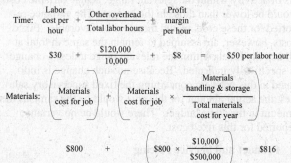

The total price for the overhaul should therefore be $1,416 [($50/hr. × 12 hrs) + $816)]. Note that materials handling and storage costs are allocated at $0.02 per dollar of materials, and other overhead is allocated at $12 per labor hour.

J.   Transfer Pricing

76. (c) The requirement is to determine whether Ajax should take on a new customer and end its sales to the Bradley division and why. As a profit center, Ajax will make the decision independent of the effects on the corporation as a whole. If Ajax sells to the new customer, its revenues will increase to $1,500,000 ($75 × 20,000), but its costs will remain the same at $1,200,000 ($900,000 + $300,000). This results in a positive gross margin of $300,000 ($1,500,000 – $1,200,000). The new gross margin is $600,000 [$300,000 – (–$300,000)] greater than the original gross margin. The shortcut (incremental) approach is to multiply 20,000 units times the $30 increase ($75 – $45) in Ajax's unit selling (transfer) price.

77. (b) Negotiated transfer prices should fall within a range limited by a ceiling and a floor. The ceiling is the lowest market price that could be obtained from an external supplier, and the floor equals the outlay costs plus opportunity cost of the transferring division. Since James' MIS department does not have to option to sell services to external customers, its opportunity cost is $0. Since all costs of service departments must be covered by the revenue-producing departments, the MIS department's outlay cost equals its total costs. The department's full capacity level is 1,000 reports per year. However, the user departments will be requesting 1,250 reports (5 user subunits × 250 reports each). Thus, the MIS department will incur costs of $12,000 [$48 × (1,250 – 1,000)] for the 250 reports above capacity,

in addition to the $45,000 budgeted costs for full capacity. The total cost of $57,000 ($45,000 + $12,000) is used to calculate the floor. The ceiling is based on the $70,000 that would be incurred to purchase MIS services externally. Since the MIS department will be producing 1,250 reports, the floor is $45.60 ($57,000 ÷ 1,250), and the ceiling is $56.00 ($70,000 ÷ 1,250). At full capacity, any differential costs of additional production are added to the floor. $48.00 represents only the differential cost of producing each report above full capacity, not cost per report for total production. Budgeted costs are based on production of 1,250 reports, not 1,000.

78. (d) The requirement is to identify the process that involves a systematic evaluation of the trade-offs between product functionality and product cost while still satisfying customer needs. Answer (d) is correct because this process is defined as value engineering. Answer (a) is incorrect because activity-based management is a system that strives for excellence through cost reduction, process improvement, and productivity gains. Answer (b) is incorrect because the Theory of Constraints refers to methods to maximize operating income when faced with some bottleneck operations. Answer (c) is incorrect because total quality management involves the application of quality principles to all company activities.

79. (d) The goal of transfer pricing is to encourage managers to make transfer decisions which maximize profits of the company as a **whole**. Some transfers may not be profitable to a particular division, but would effect a cost savings to the company by avoiding costs of purchasing externally. For example, when a division is already operating at full capacity and uses variable cost transfer prices, additional production for internal transfer would result in a loss for the transferring division because no contribution margin is earned to cover the differential fixed costs incurred. Conversely, internal production may be cheaper to the corporate entity than purchasing the product, in which case the division should accept the order. However, the division manager is likely to engage in suboptimization by rejecting the order to enhance the division's performance, while adversely affecting overall company performance.

K.   Short-Term Differential Cost Analysis

80. (b) When determining a price for a special order when there is idle capacity, only the differential manufacturing costs are considered. The underlying assumption is that acceptance of the order will not affect regular sales. In the short run, fixed costs are sunk costs and are irrelevant. Since regular sales will not be affected by the special order, fixed and variable costs incurred during normal operations are not considered. Clay Company should consider only the variable costs associated with the order and the differential cost of using the external designers. The costs to be considered total $40,750 ($33,000 + $7,750). The order is accepted if revenue from the order exceeds the differential costs.

81. (c) When deciding between alternatives, the only relevant costs or revenues are those expected future costs and revenues that differ across alternatives. In the short run, fixed costs are sunk costs and are irrelevant. Thus, Abel's 2008 fixed costs are ignored for purposes of short-term differential cost analysis. The incremental cost was $100,000 ($500,000 – $400,000).

82. (c) The requirement is to evaluate the effect on pretax profit if a department is discontinued. The solutions approach is to isolate those revenues and costs that would differ if the department is discontinued. If the department is discontinued, $20,000 of contribution margin would be lost. The $5,000 of allocated overhead will continue regardless of the decision made. Thus, $45,000 ($50,000 – $5,000) of allocated overhead cost would be eliminated or avoided. The net effect on pretax profit would be an increase of $25,000 ($45,000 of cost avoided less $20,000 of contribution margin lost).

83. (c) The requirement is to determine the effect on operating income of closing Segment B. Answer (c) is correct because if Segment B is closed overall sales will be reduced by $15,000, variable costs of goods sold will be reduced by $8,500, fixed costs of goods sold will be reduced by $1,500, and variable selling and administrative expenses will be reduced by $3,000, resulting in a $2,000 ($15,000 – 8,500 – 1,500 – 3,000) decrease in operating income.

BUSINESS ENVIRONMENT AND CONCEPTS

TESTLET 1

1. Under the Revised Uniform Limited Partnership Act which of the following is required in the certificate of limited partnership filed with the Secretary of State?
   a. The names of all of the limited partners.
   b. The names of all of the general partners.
   c. The names of all of the partners.
   d. None of the above.

2. Which of the following is **not** considered to be an advantage of organizing a business as a sole proprietorship?
   a. Easy and inexpensive to organize.
   b. Allows freedom of action for the entrepreneur.
   c. Provides strong incentives to manage the business efficiently.
   d. Allows the proprietor to carry out all basic management functions.

3. Able, Bray, and Carry form a general partnership to produce and sell widgets. Able is a CPA, Bray has an MBA, and Carry has few skills. In their partnership agreement, they decide to split any profits they have in the following respective proportions: 45%, 45%, and 10%. They fail to agree on how they will share any losses. At the end of the first year of operations they have a large loss. Assuming each of the partners has sufficient assets to cover the loss of their partnership, how will they split the losses between Able, Bray, and Carry, respectively?
   a. 45%, 45%, and 10%.
   b. Equally.
   c. It cannot be determined yet until they agree upon a loss-sharing plan.
   d. A court of law will have to decide upon the way they will each share the loss.

4. Several individuals form a Limited Liability Company (LLC) under an LLC state statute that is like the statutes that the majority of states have passed. Which of the following characteristics will this LLC have?
   I. All of the owners have limited liability.
   II. Owners designated as limited partners have limited liability.
   III. The LLC is a separate legal entity.

   a. I only.
   b. II only.
   c. I and III.
   d. II and III only.

5. Which of the following is not a fundamental characteristic of a Subchapter C corporation?
   a. The shareholders have limited liability.
   b. Those that manage the corporation must be shareholders.
   c. The shareholders generally elect the board of directors.
   d. The corporation is a legal entity in itself.

6. Which of the following is a part of the central processing unit?
   a. Analog translator converter.
   b. Arithmetic/logic unit.
   c. Optical disk.
   d. Printer unit.

7. A data model developed specifically for use in designing accounting information databases is
   a. REA data model.
   b. Data definition language.
   c. Entity-relationship model.
   d. Networked model.

8. The type of system most likely to be used to initially record the daily processing of transactions
   a. Transaction processing system.
   b. Management information system.
   c. Decision support system.
   d. Executive information system.

9. Which of the following is correct concerning the Internet?
   a. All communications are processed using URL—Uniform Resource Language.
   b. It is composed of an international collection of networks of independently owned computers.
   c. It requires the use of viruses, which invariably escape their proper primary use and infect user computers.
   d. The operating center of the Internet is headquartered in the New York World Wide Web Center.

10. A method to originally capture data to multiple magnetic disks is referred to as
    a. Analog approach.
    b. Parallel magnetic drums.
    c. RAID.
    d. Zip drive approach.

11. A system that stores transactions in a single database, but process them at various sites is referred to as
    a. Centralized system.
    b. Database management normalization system.
    c. Decentralized system.
    d. Distributed system.

Items 12 and 13 are based on the following information:

Total production costs of prior periods for a company are listed below. Assume that the same cost behavior patterns can be extended linearly over the range of 3,000 to 35,000 units and that the cost driver for each cost is the number of units produced.

Production in units per month	3,000	9,000	16,000	35,000
Cost X	$23,700	$52,680	$86,490	$178,260
Cost Y	47,280	141,840	252,160	551,600

12. What is the average cost per unit at a production level of 8,000 units for cost X?
    a. $5.98
    b. $5.85
    c. $7.90
    d. $4.83

13. Identify the cost curve for the average cost per unit for cost Y.

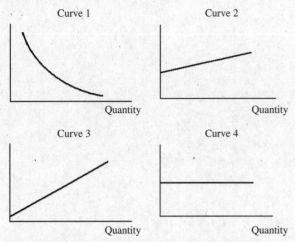

Curve 1   Curve 2

Quantity   Quantity

Curve 3   Curve 4

Quantity   Quantity

    a.   Curve 1.
    b.   Curve 2.
    c.   Curve 3.
    d.   Curve 4.

14. Layton Co. has an average accounts payable balance of $850,000 and its cost of goods sold for the year is $8,750,000. Using a 365-day year, calculate the firm's payables deferral period.
    a.   25.50 days.
    b.   30.50 days.
    c.   35.46 days.
    d.   42.33 days.

15. A strategy map in the balanced scorecard framework is
    a.   A statement of what the strategy must achieve and what is critical to its success.
    b.   Key action programs required to achieve strategic objectives.
    c.   Diagrams of the cause-and-effect relationships between strategic objectives.
    d.   The level of performance or rate of improvement needed in the performance measure.

Items 16 and 17 are based on the following information:

The following are selected data for Lenley Manufacturing Company for the year ended 20X1.

Sales	$30,000,000
Average invested capital (total assets)	10,000,000
Total fixed assets	6,000,000
Net income	3,000,000
Net cash flow	5,000,000
Imputed interest rate	10%

16. Which of the following measures the return on investments for Lenley Manufacturing Company for the year?
    a.   2%
    b.   8%
    c.   10%
    d.   30%

17. Which of the following measures residual income for Lenley Manufacturing Company for the year?
    a. $1,000,000
    b. $2,000,000
    c. $3,000,000
    d. $6,000,000

18. Which type of economic market structure is characterized by many firms selling a differentiated product with no significant barriers to entry?
    a.   Monopoly.
    b.   Oligopoly.
    c.   Perfect competition.
    d.   Monopolistic competition.

Items 19 and 20 are based on the following information:

The operating results in summarized form for a retail computer store for 2007 are

Revenue:	
Hardware sales	$4,800,000
Software sales	2,000,000
Maintenance contracts	1,200.00
Total revenue	$8,000,000
Costs and expenses	
Cost of hardware sales	$3,360,000
Cost of software sales	1,200,000
Marketing expenses	600,000
Customer maintenance costs	640,000
Administrative expenses	1,120,000
Total costs and expenses	$6,920,000
Operating income	$1,080,000

The computer store is in the process of formulating its operating budget for 2008 and has made the following assumptions:

- The selling prices of hardware are expected to increase 10% but there will be no selling price increases for software and maintenance contracts.
- Hardware unit sales are expected to increase 5% with a corresponding 5% growth in the number of maintenance contracts; growth in unit software sales is estimated at 8%.
- The cost of hardware and software is expected to increase 4%.
- Marketing expenses will be increased 5% in the coming year.
- Three technicians will be added to the customer maintenance operations in the coming year, increasing the customer maintenance costs by $120,000.
- Administrative costs will be held at the same level.

19. The retail computer store's budgeted total revenue for 2007 would be
    a. $8,804,000
    b. $8,460,000
    c. $8,904,000
    d. $8,964,000

20. The retail computer store's budgeted total costs and expenses for the coming year would be
    a. $7,252,400
    b. $7,526,960
    c. $7,558,960
    d. $7,893,872

21. The marginal cost of capital (MCC) curve for a company rises twice, first when the company has raised $75 million and again when $175 million of new funds have been raised. These increases in the MCC are caused by
    a.   Increases in the returns on the additional investments undertaken.
    b.   Decreases in the returns on the additional investments undertaken.

    c.   Decreases in the cost of at least one of the financ-
ing sources.

    d.   Increases in the cost of at least one of the financing
sources.

22. Inventory turnover is calculated as follows:

    a. $\dfrac{\text{Net sales}}{\text{Year-end inventory}}$

    b. $\dfrac{\text{Year-end inventory}}{\text{Net sales}}$

    c. $\dfrac{\text{Cost of goods sold}}{\text{Average inventory}}$

    d. $\dfrac{\text{Net sales}}{\text{Average inventory}}$

23. Which one of the following is **not** a determinant in valuing a call option?

    a.   Exercise price.

    b.   Expiration date.

    c.   Forward contract price.

    d.   Interest rate.

24. A company obtaining short-term financing with trade credit will pay a higher percentage financing cost, everything else being equal, when

    a.   The discount percentage is lower.

    b.   The items purchased have a higher price.

    c.   The items purchased have a lower price.

    d.   The supplier offers a longer discount period.

25. An analyst covering Guilderland Mining Co. common stock estimates the following information for the next year.

Expected return on the market portfolio	12%
Expected return on Treasury securities	5%
Expected beta of Guilderland	2.2

Using the CAPM, the analyst's estimate of next year's risk premium for Guilderland's stock is closest to

    a.   7.0%

    b.   10.4%

    c.   15.4%

    d.   21.4%

BUSINESS ENVIRONMENT AND CONCEPTS
ANSWERS TO TESTLET 1

1. b	5. b	9. b	13. d	17. b	21. d	25. c
2. d	6. b	10. c	14. c	18. d	22. c	
3. a	7. a	11. d	15. c	19. d	23. c	
4. c	8. a	12. a	16. d	20. b	24. d	

Business Environment and Concepts Hints

1. Only general partners must be listed.

2. Professional management is desirable.

3. Losses are essentially negative profits.

4. All of the owners have no personal liability.

5. Ownership and management of the corporation can be kept separate.

6. Think of the type of processing the computer itself often performs.

7. One of these is less familiar terminology in general IT, but more familiar in the area of accounting information systems.

8. Nothing difficult here, "transactions" is the key.

9. Most of these replies are nonsense.

10. RAID means redundant array of independent (previously, inexpensive) disks.

11. Two of the replies would suggest various sites. One of those ordinarily includes a single database.

12. Cost X is a mixed cost.

13. Use the high-low method.

14. Deferral period is equal to payables divided by cost of goods sold per day.

15. Strategy maps associate strategies with measures.

16. ROI is equal to operating income divided by total fixed assets.

17. RI is equal to operating income minus a charge for the cost of capital.

18. No tricks here.

19. Be sure to consider all the changes in the variables.

20. Be sure to consider all the changes in the variables.

21. The marginal cost of capital is the weighted-average of the costs of different financing sources.

22. Inventory turnover is equal to CGS divided by average inventory.

23. Value is based on price, time, and interest rate.

24. Recall the formula for trade credit interest rate.

25. CAPM = Beta × (Expected return of portfolio – Risk-free rate)

BUSINESS ENVIRONMENT AND CONCEPTS

TESTLET 2

1.   Apex, Bail, and Call formed a general partnership recently. Which of the following is not true concerning this partnership or these partners under the Revised Uniform Partnership Act?

   a.   The partners each have limited liability similar to the liability of shareholders of a typical corporation.

   b.   The partners have joint and several liability for any breaches of contract of their partnership.

   c.   The partners have joint and several liability for any lawsuits against their partnership based on tort law.

   d.   The partnership may legally own property in its own name.

2.   Three partners have formed a general partnership that they desire to last for several years. They have not agreed to any specified time period. Which of the following is true under the Revised Uniform Partnership Act?

   a.   The partnership agreement is required to be in writing.

   b.   All three partners are required to share profits or losses equally.

   c.   Each of the three partners has an equal right to participate in the management of the partnership.

   d.   A partner may assign his or her interest in the partnership only if the other two agree.

3.   Which of the following statements concerning the effect of an assignment of a general partnership interest is(are) true?

   I.   The assignment gives the assigner's interest in the partnership profits to the assignee.

   II.   The assignee becomes a partner in place of the assignor.

   a.   I only.

   b.   II only.

   c.   Both I and II.

   d.   Neither I nor II.

4.   Which of the following is true concerning the rights of shareholders?

   a.   Shareholders have the right to receive dividends when the corporation makes a profit.

   b.   Shareholders have the right to manage the corporation.

   c.   Shareholders have no right to inspect the books and records of the corporation.

   d.   Shareholders can vote by proxy when they have voting rights.

5.   A common input device is a(n)

   a.   Compiler.

   b.   Printer.

   c.   Expert system.

   d.   Point-of-sale recorder.

6.   Which of the following is most likely to be considered an advantage of a sophisticated multiuser database?

   a.   It may be operated and maintained without particular computer expertise.

   b.   Information may be retrieved quickly.

   c.   Conversion of traditional files to such a format is ordinarily extremely simple.

   d.   It is easy to distribute information to every possible user.

7.   Which of the following is not a widely used disaster recovery approach?

   a.   Hot site.

   b.   Firewall.

   c.   Regular backups.

   d.   Cold site.

8.   Using sophisticated techniques from statistics, artificial intelligence, and computer graphics to explain, confirm, or explore relationships among data is referred to as

   a.   Data mining.

   b.   Data warehousing.

   c.   Decision support.

   d.   Distributed analysis.

9.   The network most frequently used for private operations designed to link computers within a building in a research park is referred to as a(n)

   a.   Bulletin board service.

   b.   Local area network.

   c.   Wide area network.

   d.   Zero base network.

10.   As used in information technology, a protocol is a set of rules for

   a.   Exchanging data between two computers.

   b.   Operating an operating system.

   c.   Identifying proper computer technology needs.

   d.   Measuring IT transmission speed.

Items 11 and 12 are based on the following information:

The power and maintenance departments of a manufacturing company are service departments that provide support to each other as well as to the organization's two production departments, plating and assembly. The manufacturing company employs separate departmental manufacturing overhead rates for the two production departments requiring the allocation of the service department costs to the two manufacturing departments. Square footage of area served is used to allocate the maintenance department costs while percentage of power usage is used to allocate the power department costs. Department costs and operation data are as follows:

	Service Departments		Production Departments	
Costs:	Power	Maintenance	Plating	Assembly
Labor	$60,000	$180,000		
Overhead	1,440,000	540,000		
Total costs	$1,500,000	$720,000		
Operating Data:				
Square feet	6,000	1,500	6,000	24,000
Percent of Usage:				
Long-run capacity	--	5%	60%	35%
Expected actual use	--	4%	70%	26%

11.   The allocation method that would provide this manufacturer with the theoretically best allocation of service department costs would be

   a.   A dual-rate allocation method allocating variable cost on expected actual usage and fixed costs on long-run capacity usage.

   b. The step-down allocation method.
   c. The direct allocation method.
   d. The reciprocal (or linear algebra) allocation method.

12. Without prejudice to your answer in 11, assume that the manufacturing company employs the step-down allocation method to allocate service department costs. If it allocates the cost of the maintenance department first, then the amount of the maintenance department's costs that are directly allocated to the plating department would be
   a. $144,000
   b. $120,000
   c. $115,200
   d. $ 90,000

13. Economists generally agree that business cycles are caused by changes in
   a. Aggregate expenditures resulting from technological changes, political events, or government monetary policy.
   b. Stock prices resulting from the need for market corrections, inflation, or government intervention.
   c. Public expectations about the future direction of prices resulting from government policies.
   d. Federal government fiscal policy, particularly changes in effective income tax rates.

14. In the cost of quality, liability claims are examples of
   a. Prevention costs.
   b. Appraisal costs.
   c. Internal failure costs.
   d. External failure costs.

15. If the economy is facing demand-pull inflation, which of the following would be a logical action by the government?
   a. Decrease income taxes.
   b. Sell government securities.
   c. Lower the discount rate.
   d. Increase government spending.

Items 16 and 17 are based on the following information:

The following information is available for Lopinsky, Inc.:

Balance Sheet

Current assets	$ 500,000
Property, plant, & equipment	4,000,000
Total assets	$4,500,000
Current liabilities	$ 30,000
Long-term debt	2,500,000
Common stock	200,000
Retained earnings	1,770,000
Total liabilities and stockholders' equity	$4,500,000

Cost of debt before tax	7%
Cost of equity	12%
Tax rate	25%

16. What is Lopinsky's weighted-average cost of capital?
   a. 9.50%
   b. 8.75%
   c. 8.22%
   d. 6.10%

17. What is Lopinsky's debt-to-equity ratio?
   a. 1.28
   b. 0.56
   c. 1.20
   d. 2.10

18. What is the best measure of risk for a well-diversified portfolio?
   a. Beta.
   b. Standard deviation.
   c. Variance.
   d. Expected value.

19. An organization has an opportunity to establish a zero balance account system using four different regional banks. The total amount of the maintenance and transfer fees is estimated to be $8,000 per annum. The organization believes that it will increase the float on its operating disbursements by an average of two days, and its cost of short-term funds is 4%. Assuming the organization estimates its average daily operating disbursements to be $80,000, what decision should the organization make regarding this opportunity?
   a. Do not open the zero balance accounts due to the additional cost of $8,000.
   b. Do not open the zero balance accounts due to an excess of costs over benefits of $1,600.
   c. Open the zero balance accounts due to an estimated savings of $1,200.
   d. Open the zero balance accounts due to an estimated savings of $6,200.

20. The formula for calculating the times-interest-earned ratio is
   a. $\dfrac{\text{Earnings before interest and taxes}}{\text{Interest expense}}$
   b. $\dfrac{\text{Earnings before taxes}}{\text{Interest expense}}$
   c. $\dfrac{\text{Interest expense}}{\text{Earnings before interest and taxes}}$
   d. $\dfrac{\text{Interest expense}}{\text{Earnings before taxes}}$

21. A company expects to produce 100,000 units of a product at a total cost of $500,000. The selling price of the product that will provide the company with a 15% before-tax return, to the nearest cent, is
   a. $0.75
   b. $1.15
   c. $5.75
   d. $7.67

22. The economic order quantity for inventory is higher for an organization that has
   a. Lower annual unit sales.
   b. Higher fixed inventory ordering costs.
   c. Higher annual carrying costs as a percentage of inventory value.
   d. A higher purchase price per unit of inventory.

23. X and Y are complementary products. If the price of product Y increases, the immediate impact on product X is that its
   a. Price will decrease.
   b. Quantity demanded will decrease.

c. Quantity supplied will decrease.
d. Price, quantity demanded, and supplies will remain unchanged.

24. A consultant recommends that a company hold funds for the following two reasons.

Reason 1: Cash needs can fluctuate substantially throughout the year.

Reason 2: Opportunities for buying at a discount may appear during the year.

The cash balances used to address the reasons given above are correctly classified as

	Reason 1	*Reason 2*
a.	Speculative balances	Speculative balances
b.	Speculative balances	Precautionary balances
c.	Precautionary balances	Speculative balances
d.	Precautionary balances	Precautionary balances

25. Gild Company has been offered credit terms of 3/10, net 30. Using a 365-day year, what is the nominal cost of not taking advantage of the discount if the firm pays on the 35th day after the purchase?

a. 14.2%
b. 32.2%
c. 37.6%
d. 45.2%

BUSINESS ENVIRONMENT AND CONCEPTS

ANSWERS TO TESTLET 2

1. a	5. d	9. b	13. a	17. a	21. c	25. d
2. c	6. b	10. a	14. d	18. a	22. b	
3. a	7. b	11. d	15. b	19. b	23. b	
4. d	8. a	12. b	16. c	20. a	24. c	

Business Environment and Concepts Hints

1. Partners of a general partnership have unlimited liability.

2. Partners have many rights in a partnership unless they give up those rights.

3. The assignment transfers the right to receive the profits, but not the right to be a partner.

4. Shareholders may assign their voting rights.

5. Think carefully about ways you know that data may be input into a computer.

6. This is a "sophisticated, multiuser database"—not a database ordinarily used by one or two individuals.

7. One reply involves attempting to avoid a disaster, rather than help in the event of a disaster.

8. Exploring is the key.

9. This is within one building.

10. IT protocols ordinarily involve multiple computers.

11. Which method theoretically results in the best answer?

12. Plating has 6,000 square feet of the total allocation base of 36,000 square feet.

13. Business cycles are caused by changes in aggregate demand.

14. Liability claims result from defective products that are distributed to customers.

15. What action decreases demand?

16. Remember cost of debt is after tax.

17. Debt-to-equity is equal to total debt divided by total equity.

18. It is the covariance that is important.

19. Compare cost to interest savings.

20. No trick here.

21. Sales must equal 115% of cost.

22. EOQ balances order costs against holding costs.

23. Complementary products are used together.

24. Speculative balances are for investing.

25. Rate = [Discount percent/(100% – Discount)] × [365 days/(Total pay period – Discount period)].

BUSINESS ENVIRONMENT AND CONCEPTS
TESTLET 3

1. Which of the following is(are) true concerning the duty of due care by members and managers of a limited liability company?
   a. They owe a duty not to be grossly negligent so that the LLC is not injured.
   b. The duty of due care does not include negligence.
   c. Both of the above are true.
   d. None of the above are true.

2. Which of the following is(are) included in the Articles of Incorporation when a corporation is formed?
   a. The number of authorized shares of stock.
   b. The name of the registered agent of the corporation.
   c. The names and addresses of the incorporators.
   d. All of the above.

3. Which of the following actions of a corporation generally require the approval of its shareholders?
   a. Giving loans to its own employees when they benefit the corporation.
   b. Giving loans to its own directors.
   c. Making charitable contributions.
   d. Acquiring its own shares of stock.

4. Connect Corporation is going to sell additional shares of its stock. Which of the following would constitute valid consideration for the purchase of those additional shares?
   a. Services already performed.
   b. Services that are agreed to be performed later.
   c. Both of the above.
   d. None of the above.

5. Which of the following is **not** a control for limiting access to particular electronic information within the IT system?
   a. Database replication.
   b. Views.
   c. Passwords.
   d. Restricting privileges.

6. A combination of hardware and software that links to different types of networks is referred to as a
   a. Bridge.
   b. Gateway.
   c. Switch.
   d. Router.

7. In encryption, a value that must be placed into the algorithm to decode an encrypted message is referred to as a(n)
   a. Key.
   b. Algoret.
   c. Router.
   d. Alphanumeric.

8. One would most frequently expect a "help desk" to be a responsibility of
   a. Applications programming.
   b. Data library.
   c. Operations.
   d. Systems programming.

9. When using a "join" operation with SQL, one would most likely be

   a. Adding a new computed column to a table.
   b. Combining some or all of the information in two tables.
   c. Extending computer memory capability by combining two or more CPUs.
   d. Encrypting data.

10. A commercial disaster recovery service that allows a business to continue computer operations in the event of a computer disaster is a
   a. Hot site.
   b. Checkpoint.
   c. Rollback.
   d. DOS (Disaster Operating System).

11. In forecasting purchases of inventory for a firm, all of the following are useful **except**:
   a. Knowledge of the behavior of business cycles.
   b. Internal allocations of costs to different segments of the firm.
   c. Information on the seasonal variations in demand.
   d. Econometric modeling.

Items 12 and 13 are based on the following information:

	Total Cost	Unit Cost
Sales (40,000 units)	$1,000,000	$25
Raw materials	160,000	4
Direct labor	280,000	7
Factory overhead:		
Variable	80,000	2
Fixed	360,000	
Selling and general expenses:		
Variable	120,000	3
Fixed	225,000	

12. How many units does the company need to produce and sell to make a before-tax profit of 10% of sales?
   a. 65,000 units.
   b. 36,562 units.
   c. 90,000 units.
   d. 29,250 units.

13. Assuming that the company sells 80,000 units, what is the maximum that can be paid for an advertising campaign while still breaking even?
   a. $ 135,000
   b. $1,015,000
   c. $ 535,000
   d. $ 695,000

14. A reduction in economic activity will be displayed by all of the following except:
   a. Decreased housing starts.
   b. Increase in the quantity of unemployment claims.
   c. Reduction in the amount of luxury purchases.
   d. Increase in personal travel.

15. The primary reason for adopting TQM is to achieve
   a. Greater customer satisfaction.
   b. Reduced delivery time.
   c. Reduced delivery charges.
   d. Greater employee participation.

16. Deming Corporation utilizes the capital asset pricing model (CAPM) to estimate the cost of its common stockholder equity. Calculate CAPM given the following: the

risk-free rate of return is 5%, the expected rate of return is 10%, and firm's beta is 1.
  a. 11%
  b. 10%
  c. 5%
  d. 15%

17. The best reason corporations issue Eurobonds rather than domestic bonds is that
  a. These bonds are denominated in the currency of the country in which they are issued.
  b. These bonds are normally a less expensive form of financing because of the absence of government regulation.
  c. Foreign buyers more readily accept the issue of both large and small US corporations than do domestic investors.
  d. Eurobonds carry no foreign exchange risk.

18. From an investor's viewpoint, the **least** risky type of bond in which to invest is a(n)
  a. Debenture bond.
  b. Deep discount bond.
  c. Income bond.
  d. Secured bond.

19. If a movie theater increases ticket prices for the matinee shows by 10% and the quantity of tickets demanded decreases by 5% then the demand for matinee movie tickets is
  a. Inelastic.
  b. Elastic.
  c. Unitary.
  d. Not related to the change in price.

Items 20 and 21 are based on the following information:

The standard direct labor cost to produce one pound of output for a company is presented below. Related data regarding the planned and actual production activities for the current month for the company are also given below.

NOTE: DLH = Direct Labor Hours.

Direct Labor Standard:
   .4 DLH @ $12.00 per DLH = $4.80

Planned production	15,000 pounds
Actual production	15,500 pounds
Actual direct labor costs (6,250 DLH)	$75,250

20. The company's direct labor rate variance for the current month would be
  a. $10 unfavorable.
  b. $240 unfavorable.
  c. $248 unfavorable.
  d. $250 unfavorable.

21. The company's direct labor efficiency variance for the current month would be
  a. $600 unfavorable.
  b. $602 unfavorable.
  c. $2,400 unfavorable.
  d. $3,000 unfavorable.

22. Davis Corp. is considering establishing a lockbox system. The bank will charge $30,000 annually for the service, which will save the firm approximately $15,000 in processing costs. The lockbox system will reduce the float for cash receipts by 2 days. Assuming that the average daily cash receipts are equal to $400,000, and short-term interest costs

are 4%, calculate the benefit or loss from adopting the lockbox system.
  a. $30,000 loss.
  b. $15,000 loss.
  c. $12,000 benefit.
  d. $17,000 benefit.

23. A call option on a share of common stock is more valuable when there is lower
  a. Market value of the underlying share.
  b. Exercise price on the option.
  c. Time to maturity on the option.
  d. Variability of market price on the underlying share.

Items 24 and 25 are based on the following information:

The financial management team of a company is assessing an investment proposal involving a $100,000 outlay today. Manager number one expects the project to provide cash inflows of $20,000 at the end of each year for six years. She considers the project to be of low risk, requiring only a 10% rate of return. Manager number two expects the project to provide cash inflows of $5,000 at the end of the first year, followed by $23,000 at the end of each year in years two through six. He considers the project to be of medium risk, requiring a 14% rate of return. Manager number three expects the project to be of high risk, providing one large cash inflow of $135,000 at the end of the sixth year. She proposes a 15% rate of return for the project.

Additional information

Number of years	Discount rate (percent)	Present value of $1 due at the end of n periods (PVIF)	Present value of an annuity of $1 per period for n periods (PVIFA)
1	10	.9091	.9091
1	14	.8772	.8772
1	15	.8696	.8696
5	10	.6209	3.7908
5	14	.5194	3.4331
5	15	.4972	3.3522
6	10	.5645	4.3553
6	14	.4556	3.8887
6	15	.4323	3.7845

24. According to the net present value criterion, which of the following is true?
  a. Manager one will recommend that the project be accepted.
  b. Manger two will recommend that the project be accepted.
  c. All three managers will recommend acceptance of the project.
  d. All three managers will recommend rejection of the project.

25. Which manager will assess the project as having the shortest payback period?
  a. Manager one.
  b. Manager two.
  c. Manager three.
  d. All three managers will agree on the payback period.

BUSINESS ENVIRONMENT AND CONCEPTS

ANSWERS TO TESTLET 3

1. c	**5.** a	**9.** b	**13.** a	**17.** b	**21.** a	**25.** a
2. d	**6.** b	**10.** a	**14.** d	**18.** d	**22.** d	
3. b	**7.** a	**11.** b	**15.** a	**19.** a	**23.** b	
4. c	**8.** c	**12.** c	**16.** b	**20.** d	**24.** d	

Business Environment and Concepts Hints

1. This duty of due care is more limited.

2. The Articles of Incorporation contain much important information.

3. Directors have a lot of power in a corporation.

4. Consideration for stock includes both services already performed as well as services contracted for the future.

5. One of these replies suggests "more," rather than less.

6. This one you need to understand the computer term.

7. To decode is similar to "unlocking" the code.

8. Which department deals with keeping the system functional on an hour-to-hour basis?

9. Which is most similar to joining a group?

10. Recovery operations often take place at another location.

11. Which item is arbitrary?

12. Calculate the contribution margin.

13. Calculate profit at 80,000 units.

14. Which item indicates improving conditions?

15. What is the ultimate value proposition for high-quality products?

16. CAPM = Risk-free rate + (Market rate – Risk-free rate) × Beta.

17. Eurobonds are denominated in US dollars.

18. What makes a bond less risky?

19. Elasticity of demand is equal to percentage of change in quantity divided by the percentage change in price.

20. DLRV is equal to direct labor hours times the difference between the standard rate and the actual rate.

21. DLEV is equal to the standard direct labor rate times the difference between the direct labor hours allowed and the actual hours worked.

22. The additional processing costs versus the interest savings.

23. An option value depends on option price, stock price, stock price variability, and maturity.

24. Calculate the NPV for each manager.

25. Payback period is equal to the number of years to recover initial investment.

BUSINESS ENVIRONMENT AND CONCEPTS TESTLETS RELEASED BY AICPA

1. Which of the following statements concerning the similarities between a general partnership and a corporation are correct?

    a. Corporate stockholders and general partners have limited personal liability.

    b. Corporations and general partnerships have perpetual existence.

    c. Corporations and general partnerships can declare bankruptcy.

    d. Corporations and general partnerships are recognized as taxpayers for federal income tax purposes.

2. Furl Corp., a corporation organized under the laws of Sate X, sued Row, a customer residing in State Y, for nonpayment for goods sold. Row attempted to dismiss the suit brought by Furl in State Y on the grounds that Furl was conducting business in State Y but had not obtained a certificate of authority from State Y to transact business therein. Which of the following actions by Furl would generally result in the court ruling that Furl was conducting business in State Y?

    a. Maintaining bank accounts in State Y.

    b. Shipping goods across state lines into State Y.

    c. Owning and operating a small manufacturing plant in State Y.

    d. Holding board of directors meetings in State Y.

3. In which of the following situations would there be inelastic demand?

    a. A 5% price increase results in a 3% decrease in the quantity demanded.

    b. A 4% price increase results in a 6% decrease in the quantity demanded.

    c. A 4% price increase results in a 4% decrease in the quantity demanded.

    d. A 3% decrease results in a 5% increase in the quantity demanded.

4. A project should be accepted if the present value of cash flows from the project is

    a. Equal to the initial investment.

    b. Less than the initial investment.

    c. Greater than the initial investment.

    d. Equal to zero.

1. **(c)** The requirement is to identify the similarity between a general partnership and a corporation. Answer (c) is correct because under the federal securities laws both a corporation and a general partnership may file for bankruptcy. Answer (a) is incorrect because general partners do not have limited liability for partnership debts. Answer (b) is incorrect because while corporations have perpetual existence general partnerships do not. Answer (d) is incorrect because while a corporation is a taxpaying entity, a partnership is a flow-through entity. The partners of the partnership pay the taxes.

2. **(c)** The requirement is to identify the actions that would result in Furl Corp. legally conducting business in a state. Furl Corp. is a domestic corporation in State X because Furl incorporated there. Furl is a foreign corporation in State Y because it was not incorporated in that state. When Furl is conducting business in State Y, Furl may be denied access to the courts to sue persons residing in State Y unless it qualified to do business in State Y by obtaining a certificate of authority from that state. Therefore, an important issue that the court examines is whether Furl was conducting business in State Y since Furl sued Row, a customer residing in this state. Generally a foreign corporation is ruled as conducting business in a state if the corporation's transactions are continuous rather than isolated. Owning and operating even a small manufacturing plant in the state would generally result in a ruling that Furl is conducting business in that state. Answer (a) is incorrect because merely maintaining a bank account in the state does not meet the definition of conducting business in that state. Answer (b) is incorrect because solely shipping goods across state lines into State Y does not meet the definition of conducting business in that state. Answer (d) is incorrect because Furl Corp. may hold its meetings for the board of directors in a state without meeting the definition of conducting business in that state.

3. **(a)** The requirement is to identify the situation in which there is inelastic demand. Demand elasticity is measured by the change in the quantity demanded divided by the change in the price. If the ratio is greater than one, demand is said to be elastic. If the ratio is less than one, demand is inelastic, and if the ratio is equal to one, demand is unitary. Accordingly, answer (a) is correct because it is the only situation that results in a ratio less than one, $3/5 = 0.60$. Answer (b) is incorrect because it indicates elastic demand, $6/4 = 1.5$. Answer (c) is incorrect because it indicates unitary demand, $4/4 = 1$. Answer (d) is incorrect because it indicates elastic demand, $5/3 = 1.67$.

4. **(c)** The requirement is to identify the decision rule for acceptance of a project. Answer (c) is correct because if a project's present value of cash flows is greater than the initial investment, the investment is expected to cover the cost of capital plus provide some additional return. Answer (a) is incorrect because it is not as desirable as answer (c). Answer (b) is incorrect because if management invests using this rule it will not cover the firm's cost of capital. Answer (d) is incorrect because acceptance of this project would result in losses.

5. Which of the following cash management techniques focuses on cash disbursements?
   a. Lockbox system.
   b. Zero-balance account.
   c. Preauthorized checks.
   d. Depository transfer checks.

5. (b) The requirement is to identify the cash management technique that focuses on cash disbursements. Answer (b) is correct because the zero-balance account technique involves establishing regional bank accounts to which just enough funds are transferred daily to pay the checks presented. It is a cash management technique for cash disbursements. Answer (a) is incorrect because a lockbox system is one in which customer payments are sent to a post office box that is maintained by the bank. Therefore, it involves cash receipts. Answer (c) is incorrect because use of preauthorized checks is not a cash management technique. Answer (d) is incorrect because depository transfer checks are used in conjunction with concentration banking which is a cash receipts management technique.

6. A customer intended to order 100 units of product Z96014, but incorrectly ordered nonexistent product Z96015. Which of the following controls would detect this error?
   a. Check digit verification.
   b. Record count.
   c. Hash total.
   d. Redundant data check.

6. (a) The requirement is to identify the control that would detect the error. Answer (a) is correct because check digit verification involves use of an extra (redundant) digit added to an identification number to detect errors in inputting or processing a transaction. The check digit allows the computer to detect and reject items that are not valid. Answer (b) is incorrect because a record count is simply a control total of the number of records processed. It would not detect an invalid part number. Answer (c) is incorrect because a hash total is a control total with a total that is meaningless. It would not detect an invalid part number. Answer (d) is incorrect because a redundant data check uses two identifiers in each transaction record (e.g., customer account number and the first five letters of the customer's name). While this control might be established to detect the error, it would not be as effective as a check digit.

7. The greatest financial threat to an organization that implemented the financial accounting module of an enterprise resource planning (ERP) system from a major vendor exists from errors detected during which of the following times?
   a. Project initiation.
   b. Requirements determination.
   c. Table configuration.
   d. Implementation.

7. (d) The requirement is to identify the phase in which there is the greatest financial threat to an organization that implemented an ERP system. Answer (d) is correct because in the implementation phase the system is operating with real data that could be corrupted by operation of the new system. Answers (a), (b), and (c) are incorrect because they all involve development phases where real data is not being used.

8. Which of the following procedures would an entity **most** likely include in its disaster recovery plan?
   a. Convert all data from EDI format to an internal company format.
   b. Maintain a Trojan horse program to prevent illicit activity.
   c. Develop an auxiliary power supply to provide uninterrupted electricity.
   d. Store duplicate copies of files in a location away from the computer center.

8. (d) The requirement is to identify the item most likely included in a disaster recovery plan. A disaster recovery plan should include priorities, insurance, backup approaches, specific assignments, periodic testing and updating, and documentation. As a part of backup approaches the plan would include procedures for storing backup files. Therefore, answer (d) is correct. Answer (a) is incorrect because conversion of data is not a part of disaster recovery. Answer (b) is incorrect because Trojan horses are not part of disaster recovery. Answer (c) is incorrect because developing an auxiliary power supply is not part of disaster recovery. Normal power interruption is not considered a disaster.

9. Which of the following definitions best characterizes benchmarking?
   a. A technique that examines product and process attributes to identify areas for improvements.
   b. The comparison of existing activities with the best levels of performance in other, similar organizations.
   c. The development of the most effective methods of completing tasks in a particular industry.
   d. The complete redesign of a process within an organization.

9. (b) The requirement is to identify the best characterization of benchmarking. Answer (b) is correct because benchmarking involves comparison of existing activities with the best levels of performance in other or similar organizations. Answer (a) is incorrect because it describes continuous improvement. Answer (c) is incorrect because it describes best practices. Answer (d) is incorrect because it describes process reengineering.

10. Which of the following is true about activity-based costing?

    a.   It should not be used with process or job costing.

    b.   It can be used only with process costing.

    c.   It can be used only with job costing.

    d.   It can be used with either process or job costing.

10. **(d)** The requirement is to identify the true statement about activity-based costing. Activity-based costing involves assigning costs to products or cost centers based on activities and cost drivers. Answer (d) is correct because it can be used in conjunction with either process or job order costing. Answer (a), (b), and (c) are incorrect because it can be used in conjunction with either process or job order costing.

BUSINESS ENVIRONMENT AND CONCEPTS

1. Which of the following statement(s) is(are) true regarding the relationship between absorption costing net income and variable costing income?

I. When production exceeds sales, variable costing income exceeds absorption costing net income.

II. When sales exceeds production, absorption costing income exceeds variable costing net income.

    a.   I only.
    b.   II only.
    c.   Both I and II.
    d.   Neither I nor II.

1. **(d)** The requirement is to identify the true statement or statements about the relationship between absorption costing and variable costing. Under variable costing only variable production costs are capitalized as a cost of the product. Fixed costs are expensed in the period in which they are incurred. Under absorption costing variable and fixed costs are capitalized as a cost of the product. When production exceeds sales, variable and fixed costs are capitalized as a cost of the product. When production exceeds sales, variable costing income will be less than absorption costing because under absorption costing some fixed costs will be capitalized as a part of the cost of the added inventory. Under variable costing all of the fixed costs will be expensed. In addition, when sales exceeds production, variable costing income will exceed absorption costing income because under absorption costing, fixed costs capitalized as a part of the cost of beginning inventory will be expensed in the current year. Therefore, neither of the statements is true and answer (d) is the correct answer.

2. Which of the following statements is (are) correct regarding corporate debt and equity securities?

I. Both debt and equity security holders have an ownership interest in the corporation.

II. Both debt and equity securities have an obligation to pay income.

    a.   I only.
    b.   II only.
    c.   Both I and II.
    d.   Neither I nor II.

2. **(d)** The requirement is to indicate which of the statements are true regarding debt and equity securities. Answer (d) is correct because neither statement is true. Debt security holders generally do not have an ownership interest in a corporation and debt security holders are not generally paid from net income of the corporation.

3. Selected information concerning the operations of a company for the year ended December 31 is as follows:

Units produced	20,000
Units sold	18,000
Direct materials used	$80,000
Direct labor incurred	$40,000
Fixed factory overhead	$50,00
Variable factory overhead	$24,000
Fixed selling and administrative expenses	$60,000
Variable selling and administrative expenses	$9,000

    a. $23,900
    b. $19,400
    c. $17,000
    d. $14,400

3. **(d)** The requirement is to calculate the finished goods inventory cost under the variable (direct) costing method. Under variable costing, inventory cost would consist of only the variable production costs, including direct materials, direct labor, and variable overhead. The variable production costs for the period are equal to $144,000 ($80,000 + $40,000 + $24,000), and the variable cost per unit would be equal to $7.20 ($144,000/20,000 units produced). Since there were no beginning or ending inventories of work in process, the cost of the ending inventory is equal to $14,400, which is equal to the 2,000 (20,000 – 18,000) unsold units multiplied by the cost per unit. Therefore, answer (d) is the correct answer.

4. Which of the following circumstances may permit the piercing of the corporate veil of a closely held corporation and thus may cause its shareholders to be held personally liable?

I. The corporation is thinly capitalized.

II. The corporation borrows money from a shareholder without giving the shareholder a security interest in corporate assets.

    a.   I only.
    b.   II only.
    c.   Both I and II.
    d.   Neither I nor II.

4. **(a)** The requirement is to identify the circumstances that would permit piercing of the corporate veil. Piercing the corporate veil may occur when the corporation is used to perpetrate fraud (e.g., forming an undercapitalized corporation), the owners and officers do not treat the corporation as a separate entity, shareholders commingle assets, or corporate formalities are not followed. The concept of piercing the corporate veil is designed to protect creditors. Therefore, answer (a) is correct because only statement I, "the corporation is thinly capitalized," is true.

5. The principle that protects corporate directors from personal liability for acts performed in good faith on behalf of the corporation is known as
   a.   The clean hands doctrine.
   b.   The full disclosure rule.
   c.   The responsible person doctrine.
   d.   The business judgment rule.

6. What type of business organization may generally be formed without filing an organizational document or certificate with a state government agency or office?
   a.   A corporation.
   b.   A limited liability company.
   c.   A general partnership.
   d.   A limited partnership.

7. Which of the following is usually a benefit of using electronic funds transfer for international cash transactions?
   a.   Creation of multilingual disaster recovery plans.
   b.   Reduction in the frequency of data entry errors.
   c.   Off-site storage of foreign source documents.
   d.   Improvement in the audit trail for cash transactions.

8. Which of the following acts is most likely to cause a court to pierce the corporate veil?
   a.   Failure to designate a registered agent in the articles of incorporation (Charter).
   b.   Retention of excess capital.
   c.   Failure to conduct a significant portion of business in the chartering state.
   d.   Using corporate assets for the owner's personal purposes.

9. What business entity can be voluntarily dissolved and terminated without filing a dissolution document with the state of organization?
   a.   A corporation.
   b.   A general partnership.
   c.   A limited liability limited partnership.
   d.   A limited partnership.

10. JacKue Co. plans to produce 200,000 pairs of roller skates during January of next year. Planned production for February is 250,000 pairs. Sales are forecasted at 180,000 pairs for January and 240,000 pairs for February. Each pair of roller skates has eight wheels. JacKue's policy is to maintain 10% of the next month's production in inventory at the end of a month. How many wheels should JacKue purchase during January?
   a.   195,000
   b.   205,000
   c.   1,560,000
   d.   1,640,000

5. **(d)** The requirement is to identify the principle that protects corporate directors from personal liability for acts performed in good faith on behalf of the corporation. Answer (d) is correct because the "business judgment rule" relieves the director from liability providing that he or she acted in good faith. Answers (a), (b) and (c) are not correct because they are not terms used in conjunction with director conduct.

6. **(c)** The requirement is to identify the type of business organization that may generally be formed without filing an organizational document or certificate with a state government, agency or office. Answer (c) is correct because a joint venture is an association of two or more entities organized to carry out a single business undertaking (or a series of related undertakings). There generally are no requirements for filing documents with a state. Answers (a), (b) and (d) are incorrect because these entities are generally required to file formation documents with a state.

7. **(b)** The requirement is to identify the benefit of using electronic funds transfer for international cash transactions. Answer (b) is correct because electronic funds transfer systems minimize the need for entry of information and, therefore, reduce the chance of entry errors. Answers (a), (c) and (d) are incorrect because they do not describe characteristics of electronic funds transfer.

8. **(d)** The requirement is to identify the circumstances that would most likely cause the court to pierce the corporate veil. Piercing the corporate veil may occur when the corporation is used to perpetrate fraud (e.g., forming an undercapitalized corporation), the owners and officers do not treat the corporation as a separate entity, shareholders commingle assets, or corporate formalities are not followed. The concept of piercing the corporate veil is designed to protect creditors. Therefore, answer (d) is correct because using corporate assets for owner's personal purposes involves commingling of assets.

9. **(b)** The requirement is to identify the business entity that can be voluntarily dissolved and terminated without filing a dissolution document with the state of organization. Answer (b) is the correct answer because a general partnership is the only one of the listed entities that does not require the filing of a dissolution document with the state.

10. **(d)** The requirement is to calculate the number of wheels that should be purchased. Assuming that JacKue is planning to produce 200,000 pairs in January and 250,000 pairs in February, and maintains 10% of next month's production in inventory, the beginning inventory of wheels for January would be expected to be 160,000 wheels (10% × 200,000 pairs × 8 wheels per pair) and the needed inventory at the end of January would be 200,000 wheels (10% × 250,000 × 8 wheels per pair). Production of 200,000 pairs in January would require 1,600,000 wheels (200,000 pairs × 8 wheels per pair). Therefore, the needed purchases would be 1,640,000 (1,600,000 – 160,000 expected beginning inventory + 200,000 required ending inventory). Therefore, answer (d) is correct.

11. The following information is available on Crain Co.'s two product lines:

	Chairs	Tables
Sales	$180,000	$48,000
Variable costs	(96,000)	(30,000)
Contribution margin	84,000	18,000
Fixed costs:		
Avoidable	(36,000)	(12,000)
Unavoidable	(18,000)	(10,800)
Operating income (loss)	$ 30,000	($4,800)

Assuming the tables line is discontinued, and the factory space previously used to make tables is rented for $24,000 per year, operating income will increase by what amount?
    a. $13,200
    b. $18,000
    c. $24,000
    d. $28,800

12. Which of the following decision-making models equates the initial investment with the present value of the future cash inflows?
    a. Accounting rate of return.
    b. Payback period.
    c. Internal rate of return.
    d. Cost-benefit ratio.

13. Hughes and Brody start a business as a closely-held corporation. Hughes owns 51 of the 100 shares of stock issued by the firm and Brody owns 49. One year later, the corporation decides to sell another 200 shares. Which of the following types of rights would give Hughes and Brody a preference over other purchasers to buy shares to maintain control of the firm?
    a. Shareholder derivative rights.
    b. Preemptive rights.
    c. Cumulative voting rights.
    d. Inspection rights.

14. Which of the following listings correctly describes the order in which the four types of budgets must be prepared?
    a. Production, direct materials purchases, sales, cash disbursements.
    b. Sales, production, direct materials purchases, cash disbursements.
    c. Cash disbursements, direct materials purchases, production, sales.
    d. Sales, direct materials purchases, production, cash disbursements.

15. Which of the following statements is correct regarding financial decision making?
    a. Opportunity cost is recorded as a normal business expense.
    b. The accounting rate of return considers the time value of money.
    c. A strength of the payback method is that it is based on profitability.
    d. Capital budgeting is based on predictions of an uncertain future.

11. (**b**)   The requirement is to calculate the amount by which income will increase if the Tables line is discontinued. To make the determination you would compare the amount of revenue from renting the factory space to the contribution margin less the avoidable costs from producing tables. The unavoidable costs allocated to the Tables line would be incurred regardless of the decision and, therefore is irrelevant. Answer (b) is correct because income would increase by $18,000 [$24,000 rent – ($18,000 contribution margin – $12,000 avoidable costs].

12. (**c**)   The requirement is to identify the decision-making model that equates the initial investment with the present value of the future cash inflows. Answer (c) is correct because the internal rate of return determines the interest rate that equates the initial investment with the present value of the future cash inflows. Answer (a) is incorrect because the accounting rate of return method computes an approximate rate of return ignoring the time value of money. Answer (b) is incorrect because the payback period method equates investments on the length of time until recapture of investment. Answer (d) is incorrect because the cost-benefit ratio method computes a ratio of all costs and benefits of a project or investment.

13. (**b**)   The requirement is to identify the term used to refer to the rights giving owners preference regarding the issuance of new corporate shares. Answer (b) is correct because the term "preemptive rights" refers to the preference that existing owners have when new shares of stock are issued by a corporation. Answers (a), (c) and (d) are incorrect because they are not terms that are used in relation to shareholders' rights to acquire stock.

14. (**b**)   The requirement is to identify the listing that correctly describes the sequence of budget preparation. Answer (b) is correct because the sequence of budget preparation is sales budget, production budget, budget of other expenses and revenues, complete pro forma financial statements. Answers (a), (c) and (d) are incorrect because they do not specify the appropriate sequence of budgeting.

15. (**d**)   The requirement is to identify the correct statement regarding financial decision making. Answer (d) is correct because all capital budgeting methods are based on predictions of future income or cash flows. Answer (a) is incorrect because opportunity cost is a hypothetical cost. Answer (b) is incorrect because the accounting rate of return ignores the time value of money. Answer (c) is incorrect because the payback method ignores profitability. It simply determines how many periods it will take to recover the initial investment.

16. A company purchases an item for $43,000. The salvage value of the item is $3,000. The cost of capital is 8%. Pertinent information related to this purchase is as follows:

	Net cash flows	Present value factor at 8%
Year 1	$10,000	0.926
Year 2	15,000	0.857
Year 3	20,000	0.794
Year 4	27,000	0.735

What is the discounted payback period in years?
a. 3.10
b. 3.25
c. 2.90
d. 3.14

16. (b) The requirement is to compute the discounted payback periods in years. The discounted payback is the number of periods it takes to recover the initial investment in discounted dollars. To compute the payback period, you first must compute the discounted future cash flows as shown below.

			Cumulative
Year 1	($10,000 × 0.926)	$9,260.00	$9,260.00
Year 2	($15,000 × 0.857)	$12,850.50	$22,110.50
Year 3	($20,000 × 0.794)	$15,880.00	$37,990.50
Year 4	($27,000 × 0.735)	$19,845.00	$57,835.50

Answer (b) is correct because the company gets back its initial investment of $43,000 in about 3 years ($37,990.50) plus 25% of the 4th year ($4,961.25 = $19,845 × .25). Note that the salvage value is ignored because it represents cash flow at the end of year 4.

17. What is an internal rate of return?
a. A net present value.
b. An accounting rate of return.
c. A payback period expected from an investment.
d. A time-adjusted rate of return from an investment.

17. (d) The requirement is to identify the description of the internal rate of return. Answer (d) is correct because the internal rate of return is the time-adjusted rate of return from an investment. Answer (a) is incorrect because the net present value is present value of the future cash flows from the investment reduced by the amount of the initial investment. Answer (b) is incorrect because the accounting rate of return is the return on the initial investment not adjusted for the time value of money. Answer (c) is incorrect because the payback period is the number of periods required to recoup the initial investment.

18. For the current period production levels, Woodwork Co. budgeted 11,000 board feet of production and purchased 15,000 board feet. The material cost was budgeted at $7 per foot. The actual cost for the period was $8.50 per foot. What was Woodwork's material price variance for the period?
a. $6,000 unfavorable.
b. $16,500 unfavorable.
c. $19,500 unfavorable.
d. $22,500 unfavorable.

18. (d) The requirement is to calculate the material price variance for the period. Answer (d) is correct because the material price variance is calculated by multiplying the actual price ($8.50) minus the standard price ($7.00) by the actual quantity used (15,000). Therefore, the material price variance is equal to $22,500 unfavorable [($8.50 – $7.00) × 15,000].

19. Snyder Co. manufactures fans with direct material costs of $10 per unit and direct labor of $7 per unit. A local carrier charges Snyder $5 per unit to make deliveries. Sales commissions are paid at 10% of the selling price. Fans are sold for $100 each. Indirect factory costs and administrative costs are $6,800 and $37,200 per month, respectively. How many fans must Snyder produce to break even?
a. 1,375
b. 648
c. 564
d. 530

19. (b) The requirement is to compute how many fans must be produced to break even. The breakeven point is determined by dividing the product's contribution margin by the amount of fixed cost. The contribution margin for each fan is equal to $68 ($100 sales price – $10 commission – $10 direct materials – $7 direct labor – $5 delivery charge). Therefore, answer (b) is correct because breakeven in units is equal to 648 ($44,000 indirect costs ÷ $68 per unit).

20. The difference between standard hours at standard wage rates and actual hours at standard wage rates is referred to as which of the following types of variances?
a. Labor rate.
b. Labor usage.
c. Direct labor spending.
d. Indirect labor spending.

20. (b) The requirement is to identify the variance that is calculated as the difference between standard hours at standard wage rates and actual hours at standard wage rates. Answer (b) is correct because the description is of the labor usage variance. Answer (a) is incorrect because the labor variance is calculated by taking the difference between the actual and standard labor rate times the actual hours. Answers (c) and (d) are incorrect because the direct labor spending and the indirect labor spending variance are not commonly used terms.

21. Which of the following events would decrease the internal rate of return of a proposed asset purchase?
a. Decrease tax credits on the asset.
b. Decrease related working capital requirements.
c. Shorten the payback period.
d. Use accelerated, instead of straight-line depreciation.

21. (a) The requirement is to identify the event that would decrease the internal rate of return of a proposed asset purchase. An event that would decrease the internal rate of return would have to either decrease or extend the cash flows from, or increase the initial cost of, the investment. Answer (a) is correct because a decrease in tax credits would increase the initial cost of the investment. Answer (b) is incorrect because a decrease in related working capital requirements would increase the cash flow from the investment. Answer (c) is incorrect because shortening the payback period would increase the rate of return of the investment. Answer (d) is incorrect because using accelerated depreciation would result in less tax expense in the earlier years and, therefore, increase the rate of return.

22. Which of the following changes would result in the highest present value?
a. A $100 decrease in taxes each year for four years.
b. A $100 decrease in the cash outflow each year for three years.
c. A $100 increase in disposal value at the end of four years.
d. A $100 increase in cash inflow each year for three years.

22. (a) The requirement is to identify the changes that would result in the highest present value. Answer (a) is correct because a decrease in taxes by $100 each year for four years would result in the highest present value. Answer (b) is incorrect because a decrease in cash outflow of $100 for three years would not increase the present value by as much as (a). Answer (c) is incorrect because a $100 increase in disposal value would not increase present value by as much as (a). Answer (d) is incorrect because a $100 increase in cash inflow each year for three years would not increase present value by as much as (a).

23. Which of the following internal control procedures would prevent an employee from being paid an inappropriate hourly wage?
a. Having the supervisor of the data entry clerk verify that each employee's hours worked are correctly entered into the system.
b. Using real-time posting of payroll so there can be **no** after-the-fact data manipulation of the payroll register.
c. Giving payroll data entry clerks the ability to change any suspicious hourly pay rates to a reasonable rate.
d. Limited access to employee master files to authorized employees in the personnel department.

23. (d) The requirement is to identify the internal control procedure that would prevent an employee from being paid an inappropriate hourly wage. Answer (d) is correct because limiting access to employee master files to authorized employees would help prevent unauthorized changes in the wage rates in the master files. Answer (a) is incorrect because it would only affect the accuracy of the hours worked. Answer (b) is incorrect because using real-time posting of payroll would not improve the accuracy of wage rates. Answer (c) is incorrect because data entry clerks should not be authorized to change wage rates.

24. ABC, Inc. assessed overall risks of MIS systems projects on two standard criteria: technology used and design structure. The following systems projects have been assessed on these risk criteria. Which of the following projects holds the highest risk to ABC?

	Technology	Structure
a.	Current	Sketchy
b.	New	Sketchy
c.	Current	Well defined
d.	New	Well defined

24. (b) The requirement is to identify the project with the highest risk. Answer (b) is correct because the project involves both new (more risky than current) technology and sketchy (more risky than well-defined) structure. Answers (a), (c) and (d) are incorrect because they all have at least one less risky component.

25. A lender and a borrower signed a contract for a $1,000 loan for one year. The lender asked the borrower to pay 3% interest. Inflation occurred and prices rose by 2% over the next year. The borrower repaid $1,030. What is the amount worth in real terms, after inflation?
a. $1,060.90
b. $1,050.60
c. $1,019.80
d. $1,009.80

25. (d) The requirement is to calculate the amount of the repayment in real (after inflation) terms. Answer (d) is correct because the real value is equal to $1,009.80 ($1,030.00 ÷ 1.02%).

26. Which of the following is an advantage of net present value modeling?

    a.   It is measured in time, **not** dollars.

    b.   It uses accrual basis, **not** cash basis accounting for a project.

    c.   It uses the accounting rate of return.

    d.   It accounts for compounding of returns.

27. Which of the following individuals would be most hurt by an unanticipated increase in inflation?

    a.   A retiree living on a fixed income.

    b.   A borrower whose debt has a fixed interest rate.

    c.   A union worker whose contract includes a provision for regular cost-of-living adjustments.

    d.   A saver whose savings was placed in a variable-rate savings account.

28. An accounts payable clerk is accused of making unauthorized changes to previous payments to a vendor. Proof could be uncovered in which of the following places?

    a.   Transaction logs.

    b.   Error reports.

    c.   Error files.

    d.   Validated date file.

29. A client wants to know how many years it will take before the accumulated cash flows from an investment exceed the initial investment, without taking the time value of money into account. Which of the following financial models should be used?

    a.   Payback period.

    b.   Discounted payback period.

    c.   Internal rate of return.

    d.   Net present value.

30. If the dollar price of the euro rises, which of the following will occur?

    a.   The dollar depreciates against the euro.

    b.   The euro depreciates against the dollar.

    c.   The euro will buy fewer European goods.

    d.   The euro will buy fewer US goods.

26.   **(d)**   The requirement is to describe the advantage of net present value modeling. Answer (d) is correct because net present value modeling takes into account the compounding of returns (the time value of money). Answer (a) is incorrect because net present value is measured in dollars. Answer (b) is incorrect because net present value uses cash flows, not accrual basis income. Answer (d) is incorrect because new present value does not use the accounting rate of return.

27.   **(a)**   The requirement is to identify the individual that would be most hurt by an unanticipated increase in inflation. Answer (a) is correct because a retiree living on a fixed income would see his or her purchasing power decrease with inflation. Answer (b) is incorrect because a borrower with a fixed-interest debt would pay the debt with dollars with less purchasing power. Answer (c) is incorrect because the contract would allow the worker to maintain the purchasing power of his or her wages. Answer (d) is incorrect because with a variable rate account the savings rate would be adjusted for inflation.

28.   **(a)**   The requirement is to identify the best source of information about an unauthorized change to previous payments to vendors. Answer (a) is correct because transaction logs maintain records of any changes in data. Answer (b) is incorrect because error reports contain information about transactions that do not meet certain criteria. Answer (c) is incorrect because error files would contain details of how errors were resolved. Answer (d) is incorrect because a validated data file is not a typical control term.

29.   **(a)**   The requirement is to identify the term that describes a method that measures the number of years it takes to recoup an initial investment without considering the time value of money. Answer (a) is correct because the definition describes the payback period. Answer (b) is incorrect because the discounted payback period takes into account the time value of money. Answer (c) is incorrect because the internal rate of return measures the rate of return generated from the investment. Answer (d) is incorrect because the net present value compares the time adjusted future cash flows from the investment with the amount of the initial investment.

30.   **(a)**   The requirement is to identify the consequence of an increase in the dollar value of the euro. Answer (a) is correct because if the euro increases in value in terms of dollars, the dollar depreciates. Answer (b) is incorrect because the euro is appreciating, not depreciating. Answer (c) is incorrect because how many European goods the euro will buy by depends on inflation. Answer (d) is incorrect because the euro is likely to buy more US goods.

31. The calculation of depreciation is used in the determination of the net present value of an investment for which of the following reasons?
   a. The decline in the value of the investment should be reflected in the determination of net present value.
   b. Depreciation adjusts the book value of the investment.
   c. Depreciation represents cash outflow that must be added back to net income.
   d. Depreciation increases cash flow by reducing income taxes.

32. Which of the following is a characteristic of a flexible budget?
   a. Provides budgeted numbers for various activity levels.
   b. Allows for modification during the budgeted period.
   c. Isolates the impact of variable costs on the overall budget.
   d. Can be utilized by several product divisions.

33. Wilson and Thomas are partners. Wilson contributed $150,000 to the partnership, and Thomas contributed $50,000. Wilson does 40% of the work, and Thomas does 60%. They do not have a partnership agreement that addresses the sharing of profits and losses. By the end of the year , the partnership has earned a profit of $200,000. What is Wilson's share of the profit under the Revised Uniform Partnership Act?
   a. $ 80,000
   b. $100,000
   c. $115,000
   d. $150,000

34. A fast-growing service company is developing its information technology internally. What is the first step in the company's systems development life cycle?
   a. Analysis.
   b. Implementation.
   c. Testing.
   d. Design.

35. Which of the following best describes a hot site?
   a. Location within the company that is most vulnerable to a disaster.
   b. Location where a company can install data processing equipment on short notice.
   c. Location that is equipped with a redundant hardware and software configuration.
   d. Location that is considered too close to a potential disaster area.

36. Which of the following attributes of a management report has the greatest impact on management's ability to make effective decisions?
   a. Summarization.
   b. Exception orientation.
   c. Relevance.
   d. Conciseness.

31. (d) The requirement is to identify the reason depreciation is considered in the determination of the net present value of an investment. Answer (d) is correct because depreciation is a noncash expense that affects future cash flows through its effect on income taxes. Answer (a) is incorrect because net present value measures the value of an investment based on the amount of future cash flows. Answer (b) is incorrect because the book value of the investment has no impact on its net present value. Answer (c) is incorrect because depreciation does not represent a cash outflow.

32. (a) The requirement is to identify the characteristic of a flexible budget. Answer (a) is correct because it describes the distinguishing characteristic of a flexible budget. Answer (b) is incorrect because all budgets allow for modification during the budgeted period. Answer (c) is incorrect because a flexible budget may or may not isolate the impact of variable costs on the overall budget. Answer (d) is incorrect because it does not describe the distinguishing characteristic of a flexible budget.

33. (b) The requirement is the determine Wilson's share of the profit under the Revised Uniform Partnership Act (RUPA). Answer (b) is correct because RUPA provides that in the absence of a profit-sharing agreement, profits are shared equally by the partners. Answer (a) is incorrect because it reflects profit sharing based on the proportion of services provided. Answer (c) is incorrect because it reflects profit sharing based on the proportion of services and the proportion of investments. Answer (d) is incorrect because it reflects profit sharing based on the proportion of investments.

34. (a) The requirement is to identify the first step in the systems development life cycle. Answer (a) is correct because the steps in the systems development life cycle are analysis, design, build, test, and implement. Answers (b), (c), and (d) are incorrect because they all represent later steps in the process.

35. (c) The requirement is to identify the description of a hot site. Answer (c) is correct because a hot site is one that is equipped with redundant hardware and software that may be used quickly when the primary site goes down. Answers (a) and (d) are incorrect because a hot site is a redundant site that should not be located near a potential disaster area. Answer (b) is incorrect because a hot site should be able to assume operations on short notice.

36. (c) The requirement is to identify the attribute of a management report that has the greatest impact on management's ability to make effective decisions. Answer (c) is correct because relevance means that the report provides information that bears on a decision. Answer (a) is incorrect because summarization does not ensure the information in the report bears on a decision. Answer (b) is incorrect because exception orientation simply means that the report illustrates exceptions, not that the exceptions bear on a decision. Answer (d) is incorrect because conciseness simply means the report is short.

37. A company's controller is adjusting next year's budget to reflect the impact of an expected 5% inflation rate. Listed below are selected items from next year's budget before the adjustment:

Total salaries expense	$250,000
Health costs	100,000
Depreciation expense	65,000
Interest expense on 10-year fixed-rate notes	37,750

After adjusting for the 5% inflation rate, what is the company's total budget for the selected items before taxes for next year?

    a. $470,250
    b. $472,138
    c. $473,500
    d. $475,388

37. (a) The requirement is to determine the total budget for the selected items assuming a 5% inflation rate. Answer (a) is correct because only the total salaries expense and health costs are adjusted for inflation. Depreciation and interest expense are fixed. Therefore, the adjusted budget is equal to $470,250 [($250,000 × 105%) + ($100,000 × 105%) + $65,000 + $37,750].

38. Compared to online real-time processing, batch processing has which of the following disadvantages?

    a.   A greater level of control is necessary.
    b.   Additional computing resources are required.
    c.   Additional personnel are required.
    d.   Stored data are current only after the update process.

38. (d) The requirement is to identify the disadvantage of batch processing as compared to online real-time processing. Answer (d) is correct because batch-processed data is not updated until the batch is processed. Answer (a) is incorrect because a greater level of control is necessary in an online real-time system. Answer (b) is incorrect because a batch system often takes less computing resources than an online real-time system. Answer (c) is incorrect because a batch system often requires less personnel.

39. An economy is at the peak of the business cycle. Which of the following policy packages is the most effective way to dampen the economy and prevent inflation?

    a.   Increase government spending, reduce taxes, increase money supply, and reduce interest rates.
    b.   Reduce government spending, increase taxes, increase money supply, and increase interest rates.
    c.   Reduce government spending, increase taxes, reduce money supply and increase interest rates.
    d.   Reduce government spending, reduce taxes, reduce money supply, and reduce interest rates.

39. (c) The requirement is to identify the policy package that would be most effective at dampening the economy and preventing inflation. Answer (c) is correct because reducing government spending, increasing taxes, reducing the money supply, and increasing interest rates all have the effect of dampening the economy and preventing inflation. Answer (a) is incorrect because all of these items have the effect of expanding the economy and causing inflation. Answer (b) is incorrect because increasing the money supply has the effect of expanding the economy and causing inflation. Answer (d) is incorrect because increasing taxes and interest rates have the effect of expanding the economy and causing inflation.

40. Which of the following strategies would the Federal Reserve most likely pursue under an expansionary policy?

    a.   Purchase federal securities and lower the discount rate.
    b.   Reduce the reserve requirement while raising the discount rate.
    c.   Raise the reserve requirement and lower the discount rate.
    d.   Raise the reserve requirement and raise the discount rate.

40. (a) The requirement is to identify the strategy the Federal Reserve would most likely pursue under an expansion policy. Answer (a) is correct because purchasing federal securities and lowering the discount rate would increase the supply of money and lower its cost. This would encourage investment. Answer (b) is incorrect because raising the discount rate would increase the cost of investment. Answer (c) is incorrect because raising the reserve requirement would reduce the supply of money for investment. Answer (d) is incorrect because raising the reserve requirement and raising the discount rate would reduce the supply of money and increase its cost.

41. Which of the following represents the procedure managers use to identify whether the company has information that unauthorized individuals want, how these individuals could obtain the information, the value of the information, and the probability of unauthorized access occurring?

    a.   Disaster recovery plan assessment.
    b.   Systems assessment.
    c.   Risk assessment.
    d.   Test of controls.

41. (c) The requirement is to identify the process that involves identifying whether the company has information unauthorized individuals want, how the individuals could obtain the information, the value of the information, and the probability of unauthorized access. Answer (c) is correct because the process of risk assessment is described. Answer (a) is incorrect because disaster recovery plan assessment is an evaluation of the plan for recovery when the information system fails. Answer (b) is incorrect because a systems assessment is an evaluation of the adequacy of a system in providing required enformation. Answer (d) is incorrect because tests of controls test the operating effectiveness of the controls.

42. A value-added network (VAN) is a privately owned network that performs which of the following functions?
- a. Route data transactions between trading partners.
- b. Route data within a company's multiple networks.
- c. Provide additional accuracy for data transmissions.
- d. Provide services to send marketing data to customers.

42. (a) The requirement is to identify the function of a value-added network. Answer (a) is correct because a value-added network is a system that routes data transactions between trading partners. Answers (b), (c) and (d) are incorrect because they do not describe functions of a value-added network.

43. The business judgment rule is a rule that immunizes corporate
- a. Management from liability for actions that result in corporation losses or damages if the actions are undertaken in good faith but are **not** within the power of the corporation or the authority of management to make.
- b. Management from liability for actions that result in corporate losses or damages if the actions are undertaken in good faith and are within both the power of the corporation and the authority of management to make.
- c. Shareholders from liability for actions that result in corporate losses or damages if the actions are undertaken in good faith and are within both the power of the corporation and the authority of shareholders to make.
- d. Shareholders from liability for actions that result in corporate losses or damages if the actions are undertaken in good faith but are **not** within the power of the corporation or the authority of shareholders to make.

43. (b) The requirement is to identify the protection provided by the business judgment rule. Answer (b) is correct because the business judgment rule protects management and directors from liability for business judgments made in good faith and within the power of the corporation or authority of management. Answer (a) is incorrect because the business judgment rule does protect management when management acts outside of its authority. Answers (c) and (d) are incorrect because the business judgment rules does not apply to shareholders.

44. A company uses a standard costing system. At the end of the current year, the company provides the following overhead information:

Actual overhead incurred	
Variable	$90,000
Fixed	$62,000
Budgeted fixed overhead	$65,000
Variable overhead rate (per direct labor hour)	$8
Standard hours allowed for actual production	12,000
Actual labor hours used	11,000

What amount is variable overhead efficiency variance?
- a. $8,000 favorable.
- b. $8,000 unfavorable.
- c. $6,000 favorable.
- d. $2,000 unfavorable.

44. (a) The requirement is to calculate the variable overhead efficiency variance. Answer (a) is correct because the variable overhead efficiency variance is calculated by deducting the standard labor hours from the actual labor hours and multiplying by the standard variable overhead rate. In this case the variable overhead efficiency variance is equal to $8,000 favorable [(11,000 – 12,000) × $8.00].

45. DJ Co. has a job-order cost system. The following debits (credits) appeared in the Work in Process account for the month of March:

March 1, balance	$12,000
March 31, direct materials	40,000
March 31, direct labor	30,000
March 31, manufacturing overhead applied	27,000
March 31, to finished goods	(100,000)

DJ Co. applies overhead at a predetermined rate of 90% of direct labor cost. Job No. 101, the only job still in process at the end of March, has been charged with manufacturing overhead of $2,250. What was the amount of direct materials charged to Job No. 101?
- a. $2,250
- b. $2,500
- c. $4,250
- d. $4,725

45. (c) The requirement is to calculate the amount of direct materials charged to Job No. 101. To calculate the direct materials, you must first calculate the total costs charged to Job No. 101. Since it is the only job in process at the end of the month, its cost is equal to the amount of cost left in work in process (WIP) at year-end, or $9,000 ($12,000 beginning WIP + $40,000 direct materials + $30,000 direct labor + $27,000 overhead applied – $100,000 transferred out). If the amount of overhead applied to the job is $2,250 and overhead is applied at a rate of 90% of direct labor, direct labor charged to the job should be $2,500 ($2,250 ÷ 90%). Therefore, the direct materials charged to Job No. 101 must be $4,250 ($9,000 – $2,250 – $2,500).

46. The owners of a limited liability company are known as which of the following?
- a. Partners.
- b. Members.
- c. Stockholders.
- d. Shareholders.

47. ABC Co. had debt with a market value of $1 million and an after-tax cost of financing of 8%. ABC also had equity with a market value of $2 million and a cost of equity capital of 9%. ABC's weighted-average cost of capital would be
- a. 8.0%
- b. 8.5%
- c. 8.7%
- d. 9.0%

48. Which of the following is a key difference in controls when changing from a manual system to a computer system?
- a. Internal control principles change.
- b. Internal control objectives differ.
- c. Control objectives are more difficult to achieve.
- d. Methodologies for implementing controls change.

49. Relevant information for material A follows:

Quantity purchased	6,500 lbs.
Standard quantity allowed	6,000 lbs.
Actual price	$3.80
Standard price	$4.00

What was the direct material price variance for material A?
- a. $1,300 favorable.
- b. $1,200 favorable.
- c. $1,200 unfavorable.
- d. $1,300 unfavorable.

50. Relevant information for product A follows:

Actual variable overhead cost per hour	$8.00
Standard variable overhead cost per hour	$7.50
Actual hours	4,500
Standards hours	5,000

What was the variable overhead spending variance for product A?
- a. $2,250 favorable.
- b. $4,000 favorable.
- c. $2,250 unfavorable.
- d. $4,000 unfavorable.

46. (b) The requirement is to identify the owners of a limited liability company. Answer (b) is correct because owners of a limited liability company are known as members. Answer (a) is incorrect because owners of a partnership are known as partners. Answer (c) and (d) are incorrect because stockholders and shareholders are owners of a corporation.

47. (c) The requirement is to compute the weighted-average cost of capital. Answer (c) is correct as calculated below:

	Cost of Capital	Weight	Weighted average
Debt	8%	33 1/3%	2.667%
Equity	9%	66 2/3%	6.000%
			8.667%

48. (d) The requirement is to identify the key differences in controls when changing from a manual system to a computer system. Answer (d) is correct because the methods of achieving control are different for a computer system. Answer (a) is incorrect because the control principles do not change. Answer (b) is incorrect because the control objectives do not change. Answer (c) is incorrect because control objectives are not more difficult to achieve.

49. (a) The requirement is to calculate the material price variance for material A. Answer (a) is correct because the material price variance is calculated by multiplying the difference between the actual price and the standard price by the actual equity. In this case, the material price variance is equal to $1,300 favorable [($3.80 – $4.00) × 6500 lbs].

50. (c) The requirement is to calculate the variable overhead spending variance for product A. Answer (c) is correct because the variable overhead spending variance is calculated by multiplying the difference between the actual overhead rate and the standard overhead rate by the actual hours. In this case, the variable overhead spending variance is equal to $2,250 unfavorable [($8.00 – $7.50) × 4,500 hours].